CONSTITUTION

The metaphor of 'dialogue' has been used to describe and evaluate institutional interactions and constitutional arrangements involving many of the most fundamental questions concerning democracy and rights. It has been put to a variety of descriptive and evaluative uses by constitutional and political theorists concerned with understanding interactions between democratic institutions, particularly interactions concerning rights. But it has also featured prominently in the opinions of courts, and even the rhetoric and deliberations of legislators. This volume brings together many of the world's leading constitutional and political theorists – both proponents and critics of dialogue theory. Together, they debate the nature and merits of constitutional dialogues between the judicial, legislative, and executive branches, explore dialogue's democratic and republican significance, examine its relevance to the functioning and design of different constitutional institutions, examine rights dialogues in specific constitutional contexts and cases of dialogue concerning certain rights, and explore constitutional dialogues from both international and transnational perspectives.

GEOFFREY SIGALET is a postdoctoral fellow in the Faculty of Law at Queen's University and a fellow at Stanford Law School's Constitutional Law Center. He completed his PhD in political theory and public law at Princeton University, where his dissertation developed a neo-republican political theory of 'dialogical' judicial review and constitutional interpretation. Dr Sigalet earned an MA in political theory and public law from Princeton in 2014 and completed an MA in political theory at McGill University, where he was a member of the McGill Research Group on Constitutional Studies. He earned his BA (Hons.) in political science and philosophy at the University of Alberta.

GRÉGOIRE WEBBER holds the Canada Research Chair in Public Law and Philosophy of Law at Queen's University and is a visiting fellow at the London School of Economics and Political Science. He clerked for the Quebec Court of Appeal and the Supreme Court of Canada, and served in the Government of Canada as senior policy advisor with the Privy Council Office and as legal affairs advisor to the Minister of Justice and Attorney General of Canada. He is the author of *The Negotiable Constitution*, joint editor of *Proportionality and the Rule of Law*, and joint author of *Legislated Rights*, all published by Cambridge University Press.

ROSALIND DIXON is a professor of law at UNSW Sydney, and co-president of the International Society of Public Law. Her work focuses on comparative constitutional law and constitutional design, constitutional democracy, theories of constitutional dialogue and amendment, and socio-economic rights and constitutional law and gender, and has been published in leading journals in the United States, Canada, the United Kingdom, and Australia. She previously served as an assistant professor at the University of Chicago Law School, and has been a visiting professor at the University of Chicago, Columbia Law School, Harvard Law School, and the National University of Singapore.

CAMBRIDGE STUDIES IN CONSTITUTIONAL LAW

The aim of this series is to produce leading monographs in constitutional law. All areas of constitutional law and public law fall within the ambit of the series, including human rights and civil liberties law, administrative law, as well as constitutional theory and the history of constitutional law. A wide variety of scholarly approaches is encouraged, with the governing criterion being simply that the work is of interest to an international audience. Thus, works concerned with only one jurisdiction will be included in the series as appropriate, while, at the same time, the series will include works which are explicitly comparative or theoretical – or both. The series editor likewise welcomes proposals that work at the intersection of constitutional and international law, or that seek to bridge the gaps between civil law systems, the US, and the common law jurisdictions of the Commonwealth.

Series Editors

David Dyzenhaus
Professor of Law and Philosophy, University of Toronto, Canada
Thomas Poole
Professor of Law, London School of Economics and Political Science, United Kingdom

Editorial Advisory Board

T. R. S. Allan, Cambridge, UK
Damian Chalmers, LSE, UK
Sujit Choudhry, Berkeley, USA
Monica Claes, Maastricht, Netherlands
David Cole, Georgetown, USA
K. D. Ewing, King's College London, UK
David Feldman, Cambridge, UK
Cora Hoexter, Witwatersrand, South Africa
Christoph Moellers, Humboldt, Germany
Adrienne Stone, Melbourne, Australia
Adam Tomkins, Glasgow, UK
Adrian Vermeule, Harvard, USA

CONSTITUTIONAL DIALOGUE

Rights, Democracy, Institutions

Edited by

GEOFFREY SIGALET

Stanford University

GRÉGOIRE WEBBER

Queen's University

ROSALIND DIXON

University of New South Wales

CAMBRIDGE
UNIVERSITY PRESS

CAMBRIDGE
UNIVERSITY PRESS

University Printing House, Cambridge CB2 8BS, United Kingdom

One Liberty Plaza, 20th Floor, New York, NY 10006, USA

477 Williamstown Road, Port Melbourne, VIC 3207, Australia

314-321, 3rd Floor, Plot 3, Splendor Forum, Jasola District Centre, New Delhi - 110025, India

79 Anson Road, #06-04/06, Singapore 079906

Cambridge University Press is part of the University of Cambridge.

It furthers the University's mission by disseminating knowledge in the pursuit of
education, learning and research at the highest international levels of excellence.

www.cambridge.org
Information on this title: www.cambridge.org/9781108405485
DOI: 10.1017/9781108277938

First published 2019
First paperback edition 2020

A catalogue record for this publication is available from the British Library

Library of Congress Cataloging in Publication data
Names: Sigalet, Geoffrey, 1987– editor. | Webber, Grégoire C. N. (Grégoire Charles N.), editor. |
Dixon, Rosalind, editor.
Title: Constitutional dialogue : rights, democracy, institutions / edited by Geoffrey Sigalet,
Grégoire Webber, Rosalind Dixon.
Description: Cambridge [UK] ; New York, NY : Cambridge University Press, 2019. |
Series: Cambridge studies in constitutional law ; 21
Identifiers: LCCN 2018046211 | ISBN 9781108417587 (hardback) |
ISBN 9781108405485 (paperback)
Subjects: LCSH: Constitutional law. | Constitutional law–Philosophy. | Civil rights. | Democracy.
Classification: LCC K3165 .C5883 2019 | DDC 342.001–dc23
LC record available at https://lccn.loc.gov/2018046211

ISBN 978-1-108-41758-7 Hardback
ISBN 978-1-108-40548-5 Paperback

CONTENTS

CONTRIBUTORS

DENNIS BAKER
Associate Professor of Political Science *University of Guelph*

ROSALIND DIXON
Professor of Law *University of New South Wales*

RICHARD EKINS
Tutorial Fellow in Law at *St. John's College* and Associate Professor of Law *University of Oxford*

JOHN FINNIS
Emeritus Professor of Law and Legal Philosophy *University of Oxford* and Biolchini Family Professor of Law *University of Notre Dame*

JANET L. HIEBERT
Professor in Political Studies *Queen's University*

JAMES B. KELLY
Professor in Political Science *Concordia University*

JEFF KING
Professor of Law *University College London*

JACOB T. LEVY
Tomlinson Professor of Political Theory *McGill University*

STEPHEN MACEDO
Laurance S. Rockefeller Professor of Politics *Princeton University*

DWIGHT NEWMAN
Canada Research Chair in Indigenous Rights in Constitutional and International Law *University of Saskatchewan*

KENT ROACH
Prichard Wilson Chair in Law and Public Policy *University of Toronto*

FREDERICK SCHAUER
David and Mary Harrison Distinguished Professor of Law *University of Virginia*

GEOFFREY SIGALET
Post-Doctoral Fellow *Queen's University* and Research Fellow *Stanford Law School*

GRÉGOIRE WEBBER
Canada Research Chair in Public Law and Philosophy of Law *Queen's University*

RIVKA WEILL
Professor of Law Radzyner School of Law

ALISON L. YOUNG
Professorial Fellow of Robinson College and Sir David Williams Professor of Public Law *University of Cambridge*

PREFACE AND ACKNOWLEDGEMENTS

This volume originates from a conference on 'constitutional dialogue' held at Princeton University in April 2016. The conference was sponsored by the Princeton's University Center for Human Values, the James Madison Program, the Law and Public Affairs Program, and the Bouton Law Lecture Fund, as well as by the Canada Research Chair in Public Law and Philosophy of Law. The scholars who participated in the conference were drawn from different legal jurisdictions in order to reflect the international influence and importance of theorising interactions between constitutional institutions as a matter of 'dialogue'.

We are grateful to the variety of centres and programs that sponsored the conference, to all conference participants, and to all of the contributors, some of whom joined the volume after the conference. We also thank the faculty and staff of Princeton's Department of Politics for providing academic support and logistical assistance for the conference. Thanks for research support in developing the volume are due to the University of New South Wales Faculty of Law and the University's HSF Law and Economics Initiative. University of New South Wales Law School student Nathan Leivesley provided excellent research and editorial assistance in completing the volume. We also thank Melissa Voigt and Queen's Law student Daniel Broadus for editorial assistance.

The note accompanying the cover image's *Serment du Jeu de Paume* ('Tennis Court Oath') by Jacques-Louis David was expertly drafted by Christopher T. Green of The Graduate Center, The City University of New York.

This is the first edited volume to be included in the *Cambridge Studies in Constitutional Law* series and we thank the series' founding editor, David Dyzenhaus, for this welcome opportunity.

NOTE ON THE COVER IMAGE

Serment du Jeu de Paume ('Tennis Court Oath'); oil on canvas by

Jacques-Louis David (1792)

The painting illustrating the cover of this volume is a reproduction of the unfinished *Le Serment du Jeu de Paume* by Jacques-Louis David, begun in 1790 and abandoned four years later. The revolutionary government commissioned the famed neoclassical painter to capture in the grandeur of history painting the Tennis Court Oath at Versailles, where representatives of the Third Estate signed an oath dedicating themselves to a government of the people and set into motion the French Revolution. In the painting, David – whose work typically drew on classical subjects of ancient Greece and Rome to represent themes of civic virtue – represents the moment that Jean-Sylvain Bailly, president of the Third Estate, read the oath aloud to the gathered deputies, whose uproarious accord is depicted in a thrust of hands reaching toward Bailly, standing at the peak of a pyramid of outstretched arms and gazes. David inserted a cast of recognizable characters amidst the crowd, including political theorist Abbé Emmanuel Joseph Sieyès, seated at centre, and Maximilien Robespierre, who rises from the crowd to the left of Bailly. In the middle foreground, Catholic and Protestant clergymen clasp hands with a patriot to symbolize the solidarity of the church and the people, personified by the families and commoners cheering on the proceedings from the upper corners.

Winds blowing through the curtained windows of the Tennis Court portend revolutionary change. But the lightning and clouds seen outside also suggest the incoming storm of political turbulence; many of the depicted figures – including Bailly – would later be imprisoned and executed as counter-revolutionaries and enemies of the republic during Robespierre's Reign of Terror. Likewise, Honoré-Gabriel Riqueti, comte de Mirabeau, a principal constitutional figure whom David prominently featured in the right foreground looking heavenward, was discovered to have been a secret advisor to the monarchy and posthumously deemed a traitor. David, himself savvy to the political tidings, and deeply tied to reactionary movements, left the monumental work unfinished, unable to finance it and unwilling to complete the painting, given the unstable status of many of the revolutionary heroes in the eyes of the rotating regimes of Revolutionary France. He would go on to paint some of the best-known portraits of Napoléon Bonaparte, demonstrating the flexibility of the neoclassical style to accommodate both revolutionary ideals and imperial power.

Introduction

The 'What' and 'Why' of Constitutional Dialogue

GEOFFREY SIGALET, GRÉGOIRE WEBBER, AND
ROSALIND DIXON[*]

What is 'constitutional dialogue' and why should it interest constitutional and political scholars and actors? The metaphor of dialogue has been appealed to in describing various aspects of constitutional interactions between the judicial and legislative (and, to a lesser extent, executive) branches in a wide range of constitutional democracies. In addition to its appeal for describing institutional practices of constitutional interaction, the metaphor of dialogue has also been used to evaluate, justify, and criticise interactions or their absence. The metaphor's appeal has not been limited to scholars. Constitutional actors – judges, legislators, and members of the executive branch – have employed the metaphor to describe and to justify their constitutional acts and reactions. This raises the stakes for understanding whether the 'what' and 'why' of constitutional dialogue help illuminate constitutional debates or whether, as the Canadian scholars largely responsible for popularising the idea of 'dialogue' once put it, all of this talk is 'much ado about metaphors'.[1]

Since the question of 'what' constitutional dialogue is involves understanding the content of a metaphorical concept, answering the question invites an analysis of the uses of the metaphor. Metaphors transfer a name or descriptive word to objects or actions distinct from, but also in some way related to, 'that which it is literally applicable'.[2] A metaphor is always like *and unlike* what it is used to describe. From the Greek *metapherein*, meaning 'to transfer', a metaphor is a comparison

---

[*] We thank Claudia Geiringer and Rivka Weill for assistance in relation to the parts of this Introduction dealing with New Zealand and Israel.

[1] Peter W. Hogg, Allison A. Bushell Thornton, and Wade K. Wright, 'Charter dialogue revisited: or "much ado about metaphors"' (2007) 45 *Osgoode Hall Law Journal* 1.

[2] *Oxford English Dictionary* (Oxford: Oxford University Press, 2017), 'metaphor'.

by analogy. The analogy is imperfect; dialogue between institutions is both like and unlike dialogue between persons. The transfer of meaning is incomplete, but sufficient to capture some truth to make it apposite. In this way, understanding *what* the uses of a metaphor mean will always involve asking *why* a word has been transferred to an object or act that is both like and unlike, related and unrelated, to its comparator. Objections to dialogue as being *literally untrue* of the relationship between constitutional institutions miss their mark; metaphors are symbolic, not literal. More promising have been scholarly inquiries into the different ways in which inter-institutional dialogue is like and unlike interpersonal dialogue, evaluating the ways in which constitutional dialogue is akin to dialogue as 'conversation' or 'deliberation' or 'a dialectic'.[3] These investigations seek to explore the ways in which the metaphor can illuminate or dim our constitutional understandings.

I   Westminster and Washington

Answering the question 'what is constitutional dialogue?' invites one of two inquires: how and why it has been used in particular contexts (for example, 'what is constitutional dialogue *in Canada today*?') or, more generally, how and why it warrants a place, if any, in constitutional and political theory.[4] These inquiries, though separable, inform each other insofar as a survey of the reasons for the metaphor's particular uses helps situate the theoretical debate regarding the general reasons for and against applying the metaphor to the idea of a constitution.

We begin, in this section, with a survey of the metaphor's uses in select constitutional systems, notably those of the United States, Canada, the United Kingdom, Australia, and New Zealand. Is the same metaphor in play in each of these jurisdictions or is the extension of the metaphor to a variety of institutional contexts and interactions itself an exercise in analogy, such that different metaphorical appeals to 'dialogue' are in play from one context and interaction to the next? As we will review, the appeal to the metaphor can be said to channel some of the underlying

---

[3] See Luc B. Tremblay, 'The legitimacy of judicial review: the limits of dialogue between courts and legislatures' (2005) 3 *International Journal of Constitutional Law* 617 and Grégoire Webber, 'The unfulfilled potential of the court and legislature dialogue' (2009) 42 *Canadian Journal of Political Science* 452.

[4] See Grégoire Webber, 'Asking why in the study of human affairs' (2015) 60 *American Journal of Jurisprudence* 51.

constitutional debates alive in each of these constitutional systems, such that the singular word 'dialogue' may capture a plurality of *different* metaphors across institutional contexts and interactions. In addition, whereas the term 'dialogue' emerged to describe and evaluate patterns of institutional organisation and interaction between the branches of *domestic* constitutions, it has also, over time, become an increasingly popular term to describe and evaluate the interactions between federal, transnational, international, and even extra-institutional popular layers of constitutional government. What about the metaphor lends its use to these different constitutional contexts?

At a sufficient level of abstraction, it may be said that one general feature is a constant across almost all appeals to 'dialogue': the simple idea that the institutions interact. Yet this common feature does little to distinguish the notion of dialogue from other accounts of constitutionalism, or the constitutional separation of powers, and fails to track differences between the uses of the metaphor. As Aileen Kavanagh among others has recently noted, institutions interact in a myriad of ways and lest 'dialogue' be no more than a synonym for terms already available to the constitutional and political theorist and actor, its special contribution should be discerned by interrogating the reasons why institutions interact and by identifying which of those reasons warrant the introduction of a new concept in constitutional and political thought.[5]

One prominent, albeit controverted, use of the dialogue metaphor, then, involves debating whether judicial conclusions on the constitutionality of legislative or executive action are *the final word* on these matters. In Peter W. Hogg and Allison A. Bushell's classical formulation, 'dialogue . . . consists of those cases in which a judicial decision striking down a law on *Charter* grounds is followed by some action by the competent legislative body'.[6] That 'action' could include, on their account, both legislative action that 'chang[es] the outcome in a substantive way' or action that simply 'repeal[s] or amend[s] an unconstitutional law'.[7] On this view, the court does not have the final

---

[5] Aileen Kavanagh, 'The lure and the limits of dialogue' (2016) 66 *University of Toronto Law Journal* 83. See also Swati Jhaveri and Anne Scully-Hill, 'Executive and legislative reactions to judicial declarations of constitutional invalidity in Hong Kong: engagement, acceptance or avoidance?' (2015) 13 *International Journal of Constitutional Law* 507.

[6] Peter W. Hogg and Allison A. Bushell, 'The Charter dialogue between courts and legislatures (or perhaps the Charter of Rights isn't such a bad thing after all)' (1997) 35 *Osgoode Hall Law Journal* 75, 82.

[7] Hogg and Bushell, 'The Charter dialogue', 98.

word if the legislature replies, even if the legislative reply is to repeal the unconstitutional statute or statutory provisions. As the subtitle of the Hogg and Bushell's article made clear – 'Perhaps the Charter of Rights Isn't Such a Bad Thing after All' – their claim that, in Canada, 'Charter decisions usually leave room for, and usually receive, a legislative response' was intended to push back against claims of the anti-democratic nature of judicial review under the Canadian Charter of Rights and Freedoms. Even in those cases where the legislature merely implemented a court's ruling, that legislative action could be read as substantive agreement with, rather than acquiescence in, judicial reasoning if it was open to the legislature to legislate differently.[8] And, as Hogg and Bushell were right to emphasise, the Charter affords legislatures with opportunities to dissent from judicial conclusions regarding rights.

Those opportunities draw primarily on two textual references in the Canadian Charter: first, the 'limitations clause' in s. 1, which provides that 'reasonable limits' may be 'prescribed by law' subject to being 'demonstrably justified in a free and democratic society'; and second, the 'notwithstanding clause' in s. 33, which provides that the legislature 'may expressly declare in an Act . . . that the Act or a provision thereof shall operate notwithstanding' select guarantees in the Charter.[9] These textual references empower a legislature to challenge a constitutional conclusion by a court without the need to have recourse to the constitution's amendment formula and, so, without changing the text of the constitution.

Although the Canadian debate over 'dialogue' began with Hogg and Bushell's avowedly *descriptive* appeal to the idea of dialogue, the Canadian debate now involves the explicit development of 'dialogue theory', which is rooted in a deeper set of normative concerns for the democratic legitimacy of judicial decisions striking down or

---

[8] Hogg and Bushell, 'The Charter dialogue', 98: 'After all, it is always possible that the outcome of a dialogue will be an agreement between the participants! And even if we did exclude those cases [of repeal or amendment in line with judicial rulings], there would still be a significant majority of cases in which the competent legislative body has responded to a Charter decision by changing the outcome in a substantive way.'

[9] Hogg and Bushell added the 'internal qualification' of some rights (e.g., *unreasonable* search and seizure; *arbitrary* arrest and detention) and the equality provision, although these aspects of their analysis have not generally been taken up by others working on constitutional dialogue.

altering political decisions made by elected legislatures.[10] Many advocates of dialogue theory endorse some version of the claim that the existence of legislative sequels responding to judicial decisions qualifies, even if it does not wholly answer, the democratic objection to judicial review. Some dialogue theorists claim that the possibility of ordinary statutes setting 'reasonable limits' to judicial interpretations of Charter rights or invoking s. 33 to override such interpretations creates a more democratically legitimate, conversational relationship between the judiciary and the other branches – one distinct from a model of judicial interpretive supremacy where the constitution is what the courts say it is.[11] Some critics of dialogue theory have expressed the worry that, at least with any legislative recourse to s. 33, the legislature's price of admission to inter-institutional dialogue is to express *misgivings* about rights.[12] Such critics of dialogue theory have often taken the view that the Charter's legislative override is not an effective tool for legislatures engaging in dialogue with courts, and that true dialogue should proceed via a judicial appreciation that the legislature, no less than the court, takes rights seriously and that, in evaluating legislation against the requirements of the Charter, the court should recall that

---

[10] See Christopher P. Manfredi and James B. Kelly, 'Six degrees of dialogue: a response to Hogg and Bushell' (1999) 37 *Osgoode Hall Law Journal* 513; Tremblay, 'The legitimacy of judicial review'; Grant Huscroft, 'Rationalizing judicial power: the mischief of dialogue theory', in James B. Kelly and Christopher P. Manfredi (eds.), *Contested Constitutionalism: Reflections on the Charter of Rights and Freedoms* (Vancouver: UBC Press, 2009), p. 50; Dennis Baker, *Not Quite Supreme: The Courts and Coordinate Constitutional Interpretation* (Montreal: McGill-Queen's University Press, 2010).

[11] One of the most prominent and articulate defenders of this dialogue theory is Kent Roach. See Kent Roach, 'Dialogue or defiance: legislative reversals of Supreme Court decisions in Canada and the United States' (2006) 4 *International Journal of Constitutional Law* 347; Kent Roach, *The Supreme Court on Trial: Judicial Activism or Democratic Dialogue* (Toronto: Irwin Law, 2001); Kent Roach, 'Dialogue in Canada and the Dangers of Simplified Law and Populism' in this volume. Some authors maintain the distinctiveness of the Canadian model of judicial review from judicial supremacy while rejecting dialogue theory: Stephen Gardbaum, *The New Commonwealth Model of Constitutionalism: Theory and Practice* (Cambridge: Cambridge University Press, 2013), pp. 15–16.

[12] F. L. Morton, 'Dialogue or monologue?', in Paul Howe and Peter Russell (eds.), *Judicial Power and Canadian Democracy* (Montreal: McGill-Queens University Press, 2001), p. 111; Andrew Petter, *The Politics of the Charter* (Toronto: University of Toronto Press, 2010).

reasonable institutions may reasonably disagree on the scope, content, and requirements of constitutional rights.[13]

The Supreme Court of Canada has on occasion recognised that the legislature has authority to develop an alternative interpretation of constitutional rights. The high-water mark of its endorsement of dialogue came in *R v. Mills* (1999), in which the Court confronted the Parliament of Canada's legislative reply to *R v. O'Connor* (1995), a split Supreme Court decision on access to the private records of complainants and witnesses in sexual assault trials. In upholding the legislative reply, the majority of the Supreme Court wrote that:

> ... this Court has previously addressed the issue of disclosure of third party records in sexual assault proceedings: see *O'Connor, supra*. However, it is important to keep in mind that the decision in *O'Connor* is not necessarily the last word on the subject. The law develops through dialogue between courts and legislatures ... Against the backdrop of *O'Connor*, Parliament was free to craft its own solution to the problem consistent with the *Charter*.[14]

On this view, the relevant standard for assessing the constitutionality of legislation is the Charter, not the Court's interpretation of the Charter.

This high-water mark of judicial endorsement of dialogue and the promise of coordinate constitutional interpretation was short lived. A few years later, a majority of the Supreme Court dismissed the idea that a court and legislature dialogue allows for legislative dissent from judicial constitutional rulings: 'The healthy and important promotion of a dialogue between the legislature and the courts should not be debased to a rule of "if at first you don't succeed, try, try again".'[15] This quip prompted one scholar to describe the judgment as 'the day dialogue died'.[16]

In the United States, the metaphor of dialogue has been used in the context of debates between, on the one hand, defenders of 'departmentalist' and 'co-ordinate construction' accounts of constitutional meaning, who deny that any single institutional interpreter is supreme and final, and, on the other hand, proponents of the view that the judiciary is the

---

[13] Rosalind Dixon, 'The Supreme Court of Canada, Charter dialogue, and deference' (2009) 47 *Osgoode Hall Law Journal* 235; Jeremy Waldron, 'Some models of dialogue between judges and legislators' (2004) 23 *The Supreme Court Law Review* 7.

[14] *R v. Mills* [1999] 3 S.C.R. 668, para. 20.

[15] *Sauvé v. Canada (no. 2)* [2002] 3 SCR 519, para. 17.

[16] Christopher P. Manfredi, 'The day the dialogue died: a comment on *Sauvé v. Canada*' (2007) 45 *Osgoode Hall Law Journal* 105.

only or the supreme constitutional interpreter.[17] In this context, the metaphor has thus been used in a debate regarding constitutional authority. Departmentalists see a wider set of circumstances for extra-judicial institutions to co-ordinate their interpretative activities to respond to, and even to resist, the presumed finality of judicial interpretations. In turn, judicial supremacists contend that the set of circumstances in which a judicial determination of constitutional meaning could be contested by another constitutional actor is highly limited at best and, in most cases, would constitute interpretive insubordination.[18]

These more or less explicit uses of the metaphor in the United States touch not only on potentially confrontational constitutional exchanges between the main branches of the federal government, but also on intra-branch dialogues between different courts, and extra-institutional dialogues where the citizenry itself complements interpretive conflicts between the branches with their own expressions of popular constitutional reasoning and contestation.[19] This expansive, extra-institutional use of the

---

[17] Departmentalism is also variously referred to as 'co-ordinate construction', 'co-ordinate interpretation', and 'constitutional supremacy'. For a modern classic articulation see Walter Murphy, 'Who shall interpret? The quest for the ultimate constitutional interpreter' (1986) 48 *The Review of Politics* 401.

[18] The view of legislative or executive supremacy has not been prominent in recent debates involving dialogue, nor has the Calhounian view that the US states are the supreme interpreters (a view that has become unpopular since the Civil War): see Keith Whittington, 'Extrajudicial constitutional interpretation: three objections and replies' (2002) 80 *North Carolina Law Review* 773; Ming-Sung Kuo, 'In the shadow of judicial supremacy: putting the idea of judicial dialogue in its place' (2016) 29 *Ratio Juris* 90; Louise Fisher, *Constitutional Dialogues: Interpretation as Political Process* (Princeton: Princeton University Press, 2014); Barry Friedman, *The Will of the People: How Public Opinion Has Influenced the Supreme Court and Shaped the Meaning of the Constitution* (New York: Farrar, Strauss and Giroux, 2009); Christine Bateup, 'The dialogic promise: assessing the normative potential of theories of constitutional dialogue' (2006) 71 *Brooklyn Law Review* 1109; Neal Devins and Louis Fisher, 'Judicial exclusivity and political instability' (1998) 84 *Virginia Law Review* 83.

[19] See Robert Post and Reva Siegel, 'Popular constitutionalism, departmentalism, and judicial supremacy' (2004) 92 *California Law Review* 1027; Larry Kramer, *The People Themselves: Popular Constitutionalism and Judicial Review* (Oxford: Oxford University Press, 2004), pp. 106–27; Keith Whittington, *Constitutional Interpretation: Textual Meaning, Original Intent, and Judicial Review* (Lawrence: University of Kansas Press, 1999), pp. 110–52. Discussions of the relationship between popular sovereignty and US constitutionalism often focus on the ninth and tenth amendments of the US Constitution. The ninth amendment explicitly maintains that the rights entrenched do not 'deny or disparage' other rights of 'the people'. The tenth amendment guarantees that all non-enumerated powers of government are *denied* to the federal government, and left to the states and 'the people'.

metaphor often implies a more abstract sense of dialogue. This is disclosed by the use of synonyms such as Alexander Bickel's description of the 'continuing colloquy' between courts, political institutions, and the wider society they serve, in which constitutional principle is 'evolved conversationally not perfected unilaterally'.[20] The expansive American use of the metaphor can perhaps be traced to the influence of the idea of the sovereignty of the extra-institutional 'people' over their constitutional institutions. The more implicit and abstract use of *dia-logue* – which can be traced to the Greek *dia-logoi*: 'through voices/reasoning speeches' – may reflect the fact that the debate between departmentalists and judicial supremacists is about the shape institutional exchanges should take between the US Constitution's greater separation of the executive and legislative branches, such that their voices are more distinguishable in interactions between the three branches of government. The American reasons for appealing to the metaphor in this institutionally expansive fashion may be related to underlying normative concerns animating strands of popular constitutionalist thought, whereby popular sovereignty is challenged by judicial control over constitutional interpretation.

In Canada and the United States, the appeal to dialogue has been especially related to the question of which branch's interpretation of the constitution has authority (final or otherwise) and in which circumstances. But what of the place of dialogue in jurisdictions without an entrenched bill of rights?

The United Kingdom, some Australian jurisdictions and New Zealand have all adopted some form of *statutory* bill of rights over the last three decades. In the United Kingdom, the Human Rights Act 1998 gives legal effect in British law to 'Convention rights', defined as select rights from the European Convention on Human Rights and its Protocols. The Human Rights Act remains the locus of the debate about dialogue in Britain in large part because it adopts a novel set of remedies: it tasks courts with interpreting legislation, 'so far as it is possible to do so', in a manner that is compatible with Convention rights (s. 3) and empowers courts to declare statutes incompatible with Convention rights, but specifies that such declarations do not affect the validity of the impugned statutes (s. 4). Interestingly, the fact that Parliament retains the authority

---

[20] Alexander M. Bickel, *The Least Dangerous Branch: The Supreme Court at the Bar of Politics* (Indianapolis: Bobbs-Merrill Company, 1962), p. 70.

to amend or repeal the Act has not been an area of focus for dialogue scholars.[21]

Numerous scholars have also suggested that the Human Rights Act's distinctive remedial architecture creates important opportunities for 'dialogue' between British courts and Parliament: by limiting the immediate *domestic* effect of a declaration of incompatibility, s. 4 of the Act gives Parliament an opportunity to amend relevant legislation to make it more consistent with judicial understandings of Convention rights.[22] Parliament may, in this context, face practical pressures to respond to a declaration, due to public opinion in favour of the court's ruling or to the prospect of a further challenge to the law before the European Court. But Parliament is under no legal duty to do so and has the option of engaging in a kind of dialogue simply via inaction. This, as one of us has suggested previously, can also be important: legislative 'burdens of inertia' can mean that it is much easier for legislators to engage in dialogue through inaction rather than action.[23]

Constitutional scholars in the United Kingdom, as in Canada, disagree as to the scope for and desirability of dialogue of this kind.[24] In general, approval for rights dialogues involving the Human Rights Act has come from British proponents of 'legal constitutionalism', who take the constitution to feature a more prominent role for courts in holding political power to account and reject the traditional conception of parliamentary sovereignty in favour of 'shared sovereignty' between the judiciary and Parliament.[25] In turn, disapproval of the idea of rights dialogues has been

---

[21] See T. R. S. Allan, 'Constitutional dialogue and the justification of judicial review' (2003) 23 *Oxford Journal of Legal Studies* 563. See also Rosalind Dixon, 'A minimalist charter of rights for Australia: the UK or Canada as a model?' (2009) 37 *Federal Law Review* 335. But see Rivka Weill, 'The new commonwealth model of constitutionalism notwithstanding: on judicial review and constitution-making' (2014) 62 *American Journal of Comparative Law* 127.

[22] See Tom R. Hickman, 'Constitutional dialogue, constitutional theories and the Human Rights Act 1998' [2002] *Public Law* 306 and *Public Law after the Human Rights Act* (Oxford: Hart Publishing, 2010), pp. 57–97.

[23] See Dixon, 'The Supreme Court of Canada'; Rosalind Dixon, 'The core case for weak-form judicial review' (2017) 38 *Cardozo Law Review* 2193; Manfredi and Kelly, 'Six degrees of dialogue'; Morton, 'Dialogue or monologue'.

[24] See e.g., Kavanagh, 'The lure and limits'; James Allan, 'Statutory bills of rights: you read words in, you read words out, you take Parliament's clear intention and you shake it all about – doin' the Sankey hanky panky", in Tom Campbell, K. D. Ewing, and Adam Tompkins (eds.), *The Legal Protection of Human Rights: Sceptical Essays* (New York: Oxford University Press, 2011).

[25] See Allan, 'Constitutional dialogue and the justification'.

voiced by scholars favouring 'political constitutionalism', who emphasise and approve of the way the constitution holds political power to account through political processes and institutions, and who usually defend the Westminster tradition of parliamentary sovereignty.[26] Alternatively, some authors have sought to justify dialogues between courts and legislatures by arguing for a 'third way' or dynamic model of constitutional dialogue drawing on the values of political and legal constitutionalism.[27]

But the empirical assessment of the reality of dialogue between courts and legislatures sometimes cuts across these normative commitments. For example, at least one legal constitutionalist proponent of the judicial invigilation of political power has argued that the introduction of the judicial power of declaring statutory rights violations and 'reading in' clearly unintended legislative intentions, and the fact of parliamentary acquiescence to most examples of such judicial declarations and interpretations, has de facto created a form of judicial supremacy and control over rights questions which cannot be characterised as democratically legitimate dialogue.[28]

The metaphor has been put to similar uses and criticisms in recent constitutional debates in New Zealand and Australia. In New Zealand, the concept of dialogue has primarily been used in similar ways to that in the United Kingdom, i.e., to analyse rather than to motivate the relationship between courts and legislators under the Bill of Rights Act 1990. Like the United Kingdom's Human Rights Act, the New Zealand Bill of Rights Act lacks any formal degree of entrenchment, and judicial decisions giving effect to it are thus formally subject to broad legislative override.[29]

---

[26] See James Allan, 'Portia, Bassano or Dick the Butcher? Constraining judges in the twenty-first century' (2006) 17 *King's College Law Journal* 1. For discussion of political constitutionalism, see Graham Gee and Grégoire Webber, 'What is a political constitution?' (2010) 30 *Oxford Journal of Legal Studies* 273.

[27] See Gardbaum, *The New Commonwealth Model of Constitutionalism*, pp. 156–203 (although Gardbaum used the metaphor in his earlier work, he rejected its usefulness in his exploration of the kinds of interactions and dynamics created by reforms to many of the commonwealth constitutions); Alison L. Young, *Democratic Dialogue and the Constitution* (Oxford: Oxford University Press, 2017), pp. 173–254.

[28] See Aileen Kavanagh, 'What's so weak about "weak-form review"? The case of the UK Human Rights Act 1998' (2015) 13 *International Journal of Constitutional Law* 1008; for criticism of this view, which rejects the metaphor but argues against characterising the United Kingdom as having rejected the form of political constitution, see Stephen Gardbaum, 'What's so weak about "weak-form review"? A reply to Aileen Kavanagh' (2015) 13 *International Journal of Constitutional Law* 1008.

[29] See Dixon, 'A minimalist charter'; Petra Butler, '15 years of the NZ Bill of Rights: time to celebrate, time to reflect, time to work harder?' (2006) 4 *Human Rights Research Journal* 1;

The Act also explicitly prevents courts from *invalidating* legislation for inconsistency with the Act (s. 4).[30] The Supreme Court has held that this does not prevent New Zealand courts from making a declaration of 'inconsistent interpretation' similar in effect to a declaration of incompatibility under the United Kingdom's Human Rights Act.[31] Earlier, the Court of Appeal also held that it was open to courts to make 'indications' of inconsistency in the course of their reasoning.[32] In February 2018, the New Zealand Cabinet approved in principle a commitment to amend the Bill of Rights Act 1990 to provide a statutory power for senior courts to make declarations of inconsistency under the Act, and to require Parliament to respond to such declarations.[33]

Declarations of 'inconsistent interpretation' do not affect the validity or the operation of legislation, and so a number of New Zealand scholars have suggested that the Act creates the same kind of potential for judicial–legislative dialogue as in the United Kingdom: it ultimately gives broad scope to Parliament to determine whether and how to respond to a range of judicial decisions on the scope and meaning of rights.[34] As elsewhere, there is of course debate in New Zealand as to how broad that scope is in real terms.[35] New Zealand courts have recently begun to refer to the idea of dialogue in the making of declarations.[36] In addition, there

---

Andrew Geddis, 'Inter-institutional "rights dialogue" under the New Zealand Bill of Rights Act', in Campbell, Ewing, and Tomkins (eds.), *The Legal Protection of Human Rights*; Claudia Geiringer, 'On a road to nowhere: implied declarations of inconsistency and the New Zealand Bill of Rights Act' (2009) 40 *Virginia University of Wellington Law Review* 613.

[30] Butler, '15 years of the NZ Bill'.

[31] *Attorney General v Taylor* [2018] NZSC 104. See Butler, '15 years of the NZ Bill', pp. 9–10; Geiringer, 'On a road to nowhere'.

[32] *Moonen v. Film and Literature Board of Review* [2000] 2 NZLR 9 (CA).

[33] See Andrew Little, 'Government to provide greater protection of rights under the NZ Bill of Rights Act 1990', *Labour* (26 February 2018) (available at www.labour.org.nz/government_to_provide_greater_protection_of_rights_under_the_nz_bill_of_rights_act_1990).

[34] See Butler, '15 years of the NZ Bill', pp. 21–23. See Paul Rishworth, 'The inevitability of judicial review under "interpretive" bills of rights' (2004) 23 *Supreme Court Law Review* 233; Philip Joseph, 'Constitutional review now' (1998) *New Zealand Law Review* 85; Stephen Gardbaum, 'The new Commonwealth model of constitutionalism' (2001) 49 *American Journal of Comparative Law* 707.

[35] One difference between the UK and New Zealand in this context, which arguably increases the practical scope for the New Zealand Parliament not to respond to the making of such a declaration, is the broader transnational context. See e.g., Rosalind Dixon, *Designing Constitutional Dialogue* (Harvard SJD Thesis, 2008).

[36] See *AG v. Taylor* [2017] NZCA 215, para. 149: the expressive use of a declaration of inconsistency is 'part of a dialogue' with 'the political branches of government'.

is ongoing debate among New Zealand scholars about the proper scope of judicial review under the statutory bill of rights, and this debate often recalls debates about constitutional dialogue. Some scholars criticise the courts for taking too limited or deferential a role in the interpretation and enforcement of the statutory rights, while others, such as James Allan, criticise the courts for taking an overly expansive approach – especially in cases such as *Baigent's Case* and *Moonen*.[37] In turn, Peta Butler, Paul Rishworth, and Philip Joseph, among others, broadly defend the courts' approach on dialogic grounds, suggesting that the courts have played a valuable 'interstitial' role in implementing the Act.[38]

New Zealand scholars and lawyers have used the concept of dialogue to draw attention to broader aspects of the New Zealand constitutional system, which involve ongoing interaction between various constitutional actors. Judge Mathew Palmer, for example, suggests that the notion of constitutional dialogue should be understood to encompass not just Bill of Rights Act cases and debates about the availability of damages under its provisions,[39] but also the interpretation and enforcement of the Treaty of Waitangi. This also involves close attention to the contribution to constitutional dialogue made by the Waitangi Tribunal, the Maori Land Court, and the executive, as well as the Supreme Court, the Court of Appeal, and the New Zealand Parliament. Palmer also draws attention to the ongoing dialogue between *lower* courts and the Parliament in New Zealand over a range of other 'constitutional' or quasi-constitutional questions unassociated with the Bill of Rights Act, such as parliamentary privilege, the legal position of public servants, and the extent of police surveillance powers.[40]

In Australia, the dialogue metaphor has been used in three distinct contexts: first, to analyse the pattern of institutional interaction between the High Court of Australia and the Commonwealth Parliament in the

---

[37] See James Allan, 'Speaking with the tongues of angels: the Bill of Rights, Simpson and the Court of Appeal' (1994) *Bill of Rights Bulletin* 2 (issue no. 1, September).

[38] Butler, '15 years of the NZ Bill'; Rishworth, 'The inevitability of judicial review'; Joseph, 'Constitutional review now'. Compare Leonid Sirota, 'Constitutional dialogue: the New Zealand Bill of Rights Act and the noble dream' (2017) 27 *New Zealand Universities Law Review* 897.

[39] The Hon. Justice Matthew Palmer, 'Constitutional Dialogue and the Rule of Law' (Keynote Address to Constitutional Dialogue Conference, Faculty of Law, Hong Kong University, 9 December 2016) emphasising the damages question as part of the distinctive NZ debate about rights dialogue.

[40] Ibid. at 10–12. These cases could, of course, also be said to involve Bill of Rights Act issues, but were primarily analysed on common law terms.

'implementation' of Australia's written, formally entrenched constitutional provisions; second, to frame proposals for the broadening of judicial rights protection, both at a national and subnational level; and third, to inform debates over the interpretation of the Australian Capital Territory's and Victoria's statutory rights charters.

As Hogg and Bushell defined it, the Canadian notion of dialogue depends heavily on the way in which courts approach the reasonableness of legislative limitations on rights. On this basis, Leighton McDonald has argued there are also potentially interesting parallels between the dialogue that exists in Canada under s. 1 of the Charter and the interaction between the Australian High Court and Commonwealth Parliament over the scope and limits of the implied freedom of political communication, which the High Court has identified as implicit in the constitutionally prescribed (and entrenched) system of representative and responsible government in Australia.[41] Like dialogue critics in Canada, however, McDonald raises express doubts as to whether this interaction is in fact adequate to answer democratic objections to the practice of strong-form judicial review of the kind exercised by the High Court under the Australian Constitution. He further notes the important contextual differences between Canada and Australia in this context, which would tend in any event to give decisions of the High Court a stronger degree of de facto finality: unlike the Canadian Senate, which is an appointed and relatively deferential house of review, the Australian Senate is an elected and politically powerful second house, which often makes it difficult to enact legislative sequels.

The notion of dialogue has also been invoked at various times in Australia to support arguments for the adoption of a national bill of rights, and state statutory rights charters. In Victoria, in particular, both the government and committee that drafted the Victorian Charter of Right and Responsibilities explicitly emphasised the capacity of the Charter to 'promote dialogue, education, discussion and good practice' in relation to human rights.[42] As Scott Stephenson notes, the notion of dialogue has also arguably been partially transformed – or

---

[41] See Leighton McDonald, 'Rights "dialogue" and democratic objections to judicial review' (2004) *Federal Law Review* 1. For this formulation of the implied freedom, and variants on it, see *Lange v. Australian Broadcasting Corporation* (1997) 189 CLR 520; *Coleman v. Power* (2004) 220 CLR 1; *McCloy v. NSW* [2015] HCA 34.

[42] Department of Justice (Vic.), *Human Rights in Victoria: Statement of Intent* (2005). See Julie Debeljak, 'Parliamentary sovereignty and dialogue under the Victorian Charter of Human Rights and responsibilities: drawing the line between judicial interpretation and

're-engineered' – in this context compared to earlier Canadian versions.[43] First, it has come to connote the idea of legislative pre-scrutiny of legislation, as well as the potential for legislative responses to court decisions. And second, it has encompassed broad notions of community dialogue, input and consultation. In Canada, in contrast, these broader aspects of legislative and popular constitutional debate have played a less central role in notions of dialogue: while Canadian constitutional practice clearly involves a significant degree of 'first look' review of legislation for compliance with the Charter, both the text of the Charter and Charter defenders place less emphasis on legislative pre-scrutiny and broader consultation mechanisms than their Australian counterparts.[44]

Finally, the dialogue metaphor has been debated in Australia as part of controversies surrounding the interpretation and enforcement of the Australian Capital Territory Human Rights Act and Victorian Charter. Some scholars, such as Julie Dbeljak, have defended a quite broad, strong form of judicial review under these rights instruments. Dbeljak points in this context both to the relatively familiar normative arguments in favour of such an approach and, in Victoria in particular, to the legislative history that supports this approach.[45] Scholars have also raised concerns about the potential for the idea of dialogue to dilute or undermine a robust approach of this kind – or imply the need for an overly deferential approach by Australian courts to the interpretation and enforcement of rights.[46]

The metaphor has also been criticised by the High Court in cases involving the interpretation of the Victorian Charter, and its relationship

---

judicial law-making' (2007) 33 *Monash University Law Review* 9, 10 (discussing the statement and the relationship between the government committee in this context).

[43] Scott Stephenson, 'Constitutional reengineering: dialogue's migration from Canada to Australia' (2013) 11 *International Journal of Constitutional Law* 870. For an illuminating discussion of the metaphor more generally in Australia, see also Scott Stephenson, *From Dialogue to Disagreement in Comparative Rights Constitutionalism* (Leichardt, New South Wales: Federation Press, 2016).

[44] Pre-enactment legislative rights review is set to become more robust with amendments to the *Department of Justice Act* that require the Minister of Justice to table "Charter Statements" explaining the compatibility of government bills with the *Charter*. See Bill C-51, *An Act to Amend the Criminal Code and the Department of Justice Act*, cl. 73 (42nd Parliament, 1st session). See now *Department of Justice Act*, s. 4.2.

[45] See Debeljak, 'Parliamentary sovereignty and dialogue'; Julie Debeljak, 'Proportionality, rights-consistent interpretation and declarations under the Victorian Charter of Human Rights and Responsibilities: the *Momcilovic* litigation and beyond' (2014) 40 *Monash University Law Review* 340.

[46] Debeljak, 'Parliamentary sovereignty and dialogue', 25, 58,

to constitutionally entrenched notions of the separation of judicial and nonjudicial power. The metaphor, various members of the High Court suggested in *Momcilovic*, is 'inapposite', 'apt to mislead', or 'an inappropriate description of the relations between the Parliament and the courts' in this context.[47] The key reason for this, one can infer from the Court's reasoning, is that the metaphor suggests a relatively 'conversational',[48] fluid relationship between courts and legislators under the Charter, when in fact – unlike in the United Kingdom – the Commonwealth Constitution contains a range of *entrenched limits* on the scope of, and relationship between, judicial and nonjudicial power in Australia.

First, it prevents federal courts from exercising nonjudicial power, other than as a necessary incident of the exercise of the judicial power of the Commonwealth.[49] The High Court was also unanimous in *Momcilovic* in finding that the making of a UK-style 'declaration of incompatibility' under s. 36 of the Charter did not involve the exercise of Commonwealth judicial power.[50] Second, the Constitution limits federal courts to hearing 'matters' (s. 75), and the High Court to hearing appeals from 'judgments, orders or decrees' (s. 73). A majority of the Court held that the making, or non-making, of a declaration of incompatibility did not involve a matter, or a judgment from which an appeal could be brought to the High Court.[51] Third, the Constitution, and the integrated system of constitutional justice it contemplates, prevents state legislatures from conferring powers on state courts that impair their institutional integrity and independence as courts capable of exercising federal jurisdiction, within the meaning of Chapter III of the Constitution.[52]

---

[47] *Momcilovic* v. *The Queen* [2011] HCA, paras. 95 (French CJ), 146 (Gummow J), 534 (Crennan and Kiefel JJ).

[48] See Rosalind Dixon's chapter in this volume and sources cited therein.

[49] This is the so-called *Boilermakers* principle.

[50] Only two justices (Crennan and Kiefel JJ) also found it a necessary incident thereto: see Rosalind Dixon and Melissa Vogt, 'Comparative constitutional law and the *Kable* doctrine', in Rebecca Ananian-Welsh and Jonathan Crowe (eds.), *Judicial Independence in Australia: Contemporary Challenges, Future Directions* (Leichardt, New South Wales: Federation Press, 2016).

[51] *Momcilovic* v. *The Queen* [2011] HCA; Dixon and Vogt, 'Comparative constitutional law'.

[52] This is known as the '*Kable* principle'. For subsequent restatements and refinements of its language and textual and structural basis, see Dixon and Vogt, 'Comparative constitutional law'; Jeffrey Goldsworthy, '*Kable, Kirk* and judicial statesmanship' (2014) 40 *Monash University Law Review* 75; Gabrielle Appleby, 'The High Court and *Kable*: a study in federalism and rights protection' (2014) 40 *Monash University Law Review* 673; James Stellios, '*Kable*, preventative detention and the dilemmas of Chapter III' (2014) 88

Only four justices were also willing to hold that if state courts were exercising state jurisdiction (which was not the case on the specific facts of *Momcilovic*), they could issue s. 36 declarations consistent with this principle.

II   Beyond Westminster and Washington

The notion of dialogue has also been used to analyse the pattern of judicial–legislative interaction in other parts of the common law world – most notably, in common law Asia. Po Jen Yap, for instance, has suggested that the idea of dialogue usefully captures the general pattern of interaction between courts and legislators in Hong Kong, Singapore, and Malaysia. Unlike in Canada (or at least the version of the Canadian experience depicted by Hogg and Bushell[53]), he suggests that dialogue of this kind has depended on a range of judicial doctrinal choices or devices, i.e., (1) provisional or advisory determinations in constitutional matters, (2) a preference for administrative over constitutional review, (3) reliance on common law liberties or statutory rights that are reversible by the ordinary legislative process, (4) judicial reliance on procedural constitutional rules, (5) rational basis review by courts of legislative actions, and (6) delayed declarations of invalidity by courts.[54] Yap has further defended this kind of dialogue as an attractive compromise between the extremes of purely strong- and weak-form judicial review.[55]

In recent years, the metaphor of dialogue has also been increasingly used outside of the American and Commonwealth common law contexts. One of us suggested in 2007 that it provided a useful way of understanding debates about strong versus weak judicial review in the interpretation and enforcement of social rights guarantees in a range of

---

Australian Law Journal 52; Scott Guy, 'The constitutionality of the Queensland Criminal Organisation Act: *Kable*, procedural due process and state constitutionalism' (2013) 32 *University of Queensland Law Journal* 265; Tarsha Gavin, 'Extending the reach of *Kable*: *Wanotu v. New South Wales*' (2012) 34 *Sydney Law Review* 395.

[53] Cf. Roach, 'Dialogue or defiance' (emphasising common law-style decision making and delayed remedies as key to dialogue); Dixon, 'The Supreme Court of Canada',

[54] Po Jen Yap, *Constitutional Dialogue in Common Law Asia* (Oxford: Oxford University Press, 2015), pp. 4, 79–105.

[55] Ibid. at 7–27.

contexts, including South Africa.[56] Constitutional scholarship on social rights over the last decade has also quite frequently invoked the notion of dialogue. This includes India, Brazil, and Colombia.[57] The term has also gained broader currency in South Africa.[58] Latin American scholars, such as Roberto Gargarella, have likewise begun to use the term 'dialogue' to connote broader ideas about deliberative, participatory forms of constitutionalism.[59] The term has also been used to describe the interactions between courts in the region.[60]

In Israel, a number of scholars have analysed debates over the interpretation of the Basic Laws on Liberty and Dignity and Occupational Freedom through the lens of dialogue. Adam Shinar and Rivka Weill have both separately connected notions of dialogue to debates over strong versus weak judicial review under the Basic Laws.[61] Aharon Barak, in turn, has linked the notion of dialogue to purposive and deliberative approaches to interpretation of the Basic Law.[62] This analysis is also continued in this volume, and remains highly relevant in light of repeated interaction – and tension – between the Supreme Court of Israel, the Knesset and the government in the last few years in a range

---

[56] Rosalind Dixon, 'Creating dialogue about socioeconomic rights: strong-form versus weak-form judicial review revisited' (2007) 5 *International Journal of Constitutional Law* 391.

[57] See e.g., Vanice Regina Lirio do Valle, 'Dialogic constitutionalism manifestations in the Brazilian judicial review' (2014) 1 *Revista De Investigacoes Constitucionais* 59; Madhav Khosla, 'Making social rights conditional: lessons from India' (2010) 8 *International Journal of Constitutional Law* 739.

[58] Chief Justice Sandile Ngcobo, 'Constitutional dialogue: a framework for understanding co-operative governance' (Address at University of Cape Town, Democratic Governance and Rights Unit's Constitution Week, 2011).

[59] Roberto Gargarella, "We the People" outside of the Constitution: the dialogic model of constitutionalism and the system of checks and balances' (2014) 67(1) *Current Legal Problems* 1; Roberto Gargarella, 'Interpretation and democratic dialogue' (2015) 60(2) *Revista da Faculdade de Direito Universidade Federal Do Paraná* 41.

[60] See Michael Mohallem, 'Horizontal judicial dialogue in South America', in A. Müller and H. E. Kjos (eds.), *Judicial Dialogue and Human Rights* (Cambridge: Cambridge University Press, 2017), p. 67.

[61] Adam Shinar, 'Idealism and realism in Israeli constitutional law', in E. H. Ballin, M. Adams and A. Meuwese (eds.), *Constitutionalism and the Rule of Law: Bringing Idealism and Realism* (Cambridge: Cambridge University Press, 2017); Rivka Weill, 'Reconciling parliamentary sovereignty and judicial review: on the theoretical and historical origins of the Israeli legislative override power' (2011) 39 *Hastings Constitutional Law Quarterly* 451; Rivka Weill, 'Hybrid constitutionalism: the Israeli case for judicial review and why we should care' (2012) 30 *Berkeley Journal of International Law* 349.

[62] Aharon Barak, 'Foreword: A judge on judging: the role of a Supreme Court in a democracy' (2002) 116 *Harvard Law Review* 19.

of cases, especially cases involving the detention of asylum-seekers.[63] This interaction has been direct, heated and conflictual, and thus one that has pressed Israeli scholars to consider the outer bounds of productive versus destructive forms of constitutional 'dialogue'.

Increasingly, the term dialogue has also been used to describe a variety of transnational interactions. When domestic and international courts look beyond their jurisdictions to borrow legal doctrines or concepts from foreign courts, some speak of a 'transnational dialogue' between courts.[64] The paradigm cases of this phenomenon involve domestic or international courts borrowing doctrines, principles, modes of reasoning, and arguments from the opinions of foreign and international courts and the texts of foreign constitutions and international treaties. As is the case with dialogues between constitutional institutions in domestic contexts, the controversies surrounding the idea of transnational dialogue between courts is related to some underlying normative commitments. Some scholars and judges have argued that transnationally borrowing good constitutional ideas and rejecting bad ones will lead to a kind of marketplace of ideas for recognising and spreading better (more sound, more meritorious) constitutional concepts, doctrines, principles, and methods of interpretation.[65] Some appeal to the universality of human rights as justification for looking beyond the immediate confines of *this* community's laws and precedents. Other scholars and judges, in turn, have objected to the idea of transnational dialogue on the grounds that it will erode, distort, or even warp the laws of the domestic constitution or statutory bill of rights.[66] The task of the judge, some will argue, is to resolve disputes according to *law*, meaning the law of the domestic community. To look too far beyond the confines of the community's law is to invite the judge to undertake a different task.

Some scholars even use the word 'dialogue' to describe more formal interactions between international and domestic actors under international law. They suggest in particular that dialogue is an apt way to understand the relationship between different legal traditions and

---

[63] See Ilan Lior, 'Israel's High Court rejects part of third anti-infiltration law', *Haaretz*, 11 August 2015, www.haaretz.com/israel-news/.premium-1.670645.

[64] See A. Müller and H. E. Kjos 'Introduction' in A. Müller and H. E. Kjos (eds.), *Judicial Dialogue and Human Rights* (Cambridge: Cambridge University Press, 2017), pp. 1–24.

[65] See Vicki Jackson, 'Constitutional comparisons: convergence, resistance, engagement' (2005) 119 *Harvard Law Review* 109.

[66] See Robert J. Delahunty and John Yoo, 'Against foreign law' (2005) 29 *Harvard Journal of Law and Public Policy* 291.

systems, and different states, in the interpretation and development of international law, including the treaty-based law of the European Union. The EU is a developing case of such international appeals to the metaphor. The EU Court of Justice is the apex court in deciding matters of law established by the EU Treaties, and it has led the EU judicial system in enforcing EU law by invalidating measures of national member states and EU institutions. Some scholars have suggested that the diversity of legal traditions and systems of judicial review in the member states, the political and legal disagreements that exist between member states concerning matters related to EU law, and the increasing need for the adjudication of conflicting values within the EU Treaty's values, all point to the normative attractiveness of dialogue. Insofar as dialogue allows the question of who has the final word to be pushed off, it allows for a *détente* between judicial institutions competing for supremacy.

*

* *

The foregoing review suggests that there is a wide range of evaluative and descriptive reasons for appealing to the metaphor of dialogue in the context of institutional interactions and constitutional design across the range of national, federal, transnational, international, and even extra-institutional layers of constitutional government. Surveying the favourable appeals to the metaphor allows one to note a variety of reasons for using the metaphor of dialogue. Allowing for a simplification of the rich texture of the debates alive in the jurisdictions just surveyed, we note some of the different motivations for appealing to the metaphor of dialogue. In the US context, the metaphor is primarily used for describing and evaluating the relationship between popular sovereignty and interactions between the three branches of the federal government. In Canada, dialogue is discussed and theorised in order to understand the significance of the Charter and its limitation and notwithstanding clauses. In the British, Australian, and New Zealand contexts, the metaphor is used to frame the relationship between parliamentary bills of rights and Westminster traditions of parliamentary sovereignty. In each of these contexts, the descriptive reasons for using the metaphor relate to the ways in which different interactions between constitutional decision-making institutions can alter the legal distribution of decision-making power.

Thinking through the metaphor of dialogue beyond the confines of a given time and place requires interrogating the reasons why constitutional actors should understand their interactions as less than confrontation and more than conformity. It requires thinking through institutional roles and responsibilities, the separation of powers, constitutional supremacy and interpretation, and – in the rights context – assumptions surrounding principle and policy, rights and their limitations, and their institutional forums. The essays in this collection think through these deep questions of constitutional and political thought. Most do so from the perspective of one of the three main themes signalled by our subtitle: rights, democracy, and institutions. Others do so by examining specific case studies of constitutional dialogue. Still others do so by tracing dialogue's reach into the international and transnational space. Together, they capture the debates that make constitutional dialogue such a rich and elusive idea.

III   Dialogue and Democracy

Part I of this collection begins by exploring the relationship between constitutional dialogue and democracy.

In the collection's opening contribution (Chapter 2), Alison L. Young argues that accounts of democratic dialogue get a bad press due to misconceptions of its nature and scope. She claims that while they appear to promise a strong protection of rights which counteracts accusations of democratic deficit, legal systems which adopt this approach demonstrate that dialogue is unstable, failing to fulfil its objective. However, she argues that these difficulties arise not because dialogue is wrong; but because it is misunderstood. Young proposes that democratic dialogue cannot provide a 'middle way' between legal and political protections of rights. Interactions between the legislature and the judiciary occur in most legal systems which provide for a legal protection of human rights. In addition, democratic dialogue is not unique to commonwealth models of rights protections. Dialogue can take place in a range of legal systems and those systems with a commonwealth model of rights protections may operate in a manner that does not facilitate dialogue. For Young, if we are to understand dialogue properly we need to recognise its role as a constitutional model, focusing on analysing interactions between institutions and identifying the values that may be promoted by such interactions. She concludes that the real value of commonwealth models is that they may ensure these values are more easily realised.

In his contribution to the collection, Jacob T. Levy (Chapter 3) begins by reference to the constitutional order of the French *ancien régime*, under which the *parlements* had authority to issue a formal remonstrance against royal edicts thus denying their registration as laws. The king was empowered to reply with an order for registration, which could in turn be subject to another remonstrance. The king could ultimately appear personally before the *parlement* and read his edict into the record, thus ending the dispute. Levy draws on this historical example to offer some lessons, among them that Canadian and Commonwealth constitutionalism may be less distinctively dialogic than is often thought. In this vein, Levy explores departmentalism in US constitutional thought, according to which the separate branches of government each have an independent duty to obey and uphold the Constitution, which means that each has a duty to interpret it. Though there is overlap between dialogue and departmentalism, they diverge when the branches disagree and reach an impasse. On the departmentalist view, the standoff may be settled in the long run by public opinion and events, such as new Supreme Court appointments and elections. Departmentalist settlements will often result from contestatory politics. On the dialogic view, however, the impasse in rights cases is framed around the question of 'reasonable limits', as in s. 1 of the Canadian Charter. Dialogic settlements, on this ideal theory of dialogue, will result from deliberative reason-giving. Levy appeals to political realism and contestatory democracy to argue that we should deflate our expectations for constitutional dialogue. While he does not deny that deliberation plays a role in democratic forms of dialogue, he argues that the departmentalist emphasis on disagreement and contestation offers a clearer and more ubiquitous notion of constitutional dialogue. Sometimes the resolution of an impasse will not be the result of persuasion or the culmination of democratic legitimacy. Sometimes it will be a reminder that politics is not only about persuasion; it is also about coercion. The chapter notes that this departmentalist conception of dialogue indicates why dialogue is not a democratic panacea, but also how its remonstrations and contestations could help render power less arbitrary, even in the context of the French *ancien régime*.

In Chapter 4, Geoffrey Sigalet distinguishes between different forms of rights dialogue in relation to the different normative purposes dialogues can serve. He evaluates what he calls the 'interrogative', 'interruptive', and 'constructive' reasons for favouring dialogue between courts and legislatures in light of contemporary republican political theory. He argues that dialogue might be valued as a means by which courts

interrogatively distinguish justifiable reasons for legislatures to limit
rights from unjustified infringements made in pursuit of certain objectives. A second reason he thinks dialogue could be valued is as a means of
providing both a counter-majoritarian chance for courts to interrupt
legislative processes or statutory schemes concerning rights, and a democratic chance for legislatures to deliberatively respond to such interruptions. He contends that a third reason for valuing dialogue is as a means
by which courts and legislatures coordinately construct the legally indeterminate meaning of rights in a way that protects both rights and the
democratic legitimacy of political decisions implicating rights.

Sigalet argues that the republican conception of freedom from
domination justifies constitutional construction as the ideal republican
norm of dialogue between courts and legislatures concerning most rights.
In contrast with this norm, he makes the case that interrogative dialogue
increases the risk of domination by exhorting courts to engage in a form
of political contestation better suited to ancient courts than to the independence and professionalism of modern judiciaries. In his view such
interrogative interactions also delegitimise legislative responsibility for
rights. On Sigalet's republican argument, interruptive dialogue isn't
much better insofar as it solicits aggressive judicial review in 'first look'
cases that minimises the probability of legislative responses to unjust
forms of adjudication, and thereby stifles the very dialogues it is supposed to provoke. In contrast, he favours the norm of constructive
dialogue as a means of encouraging courts to minimise the risk judicial
review poses to political justice by using their institutional independence
and professionalism to primarily enforce the determinate meaning of
rights, while recognising and respecting prospective legislative rights
constructions. He claims that this norm of dialogue will also promote
the legislative duty to correct unjust adjudicative constructions.

IV   Dialogue and Institutions

The chapters in Part II explore dialogue from the perspective of the great
institutions of government.

In his contribution to the volume (Chapter 5), Grégoire Webber makes
the case that reflecting on the foundations of legislative and adjudicative
responsibility helps articulate the responsibility of the legislative body for
the community's *future*, a future to be directed by the law as it is now to
be. By contrast, the power to adjudicate conclusively on the breach of a
law discloses a responsibility of a different orientation, a responsibility to

relate to the *present* dispute the law as it was at that time *past* when the violation of the law allegedly occurred. For Webber, this basic division of responsibility – for the community's future; for relating the community's past acts to present disputes – is a division informed by the need to address different needs in human communities. Among those needs will be the requirement to realise justice and rights. He argues that where a community decides to qualify the legal jurisdiction to change the law in the name of justice and rights, it may do so in the manner of open-ended qualifications, as are common in bills of rights. The conferral of a power on courts to determine whether legislation runs afoul these open-ended commitments to justice and rights requires the exercise of judicial responsibility partially unmoored from the past and open to the future. In such circumstances, adjudicative authority is being exercised, not with a view to the past, but to the future. Webber holds that it is here that the institution designed to take responsibility for the future may understand itself to be empowered to reply to the exercise of judicial responsibility by engaging in a dialogue on the community's future.

In Chapter 6, Rosalind Dixon argues that the idea of a constitutional 'dialogue' between courts and legislatures is at once potentially both useful and misleading: it is useful, in that it helps draw attention to the possibility that judicial review may be de facto 'weak' or non-final in nature. But it is also dangerous if understood to suggest that judicial review is always, inevitably, de facto weak or non-final. The true finality of judicial review, Dixon suggests, ultimately depends on the willingness of courts to defer to certain kinds of legislative constitutional judgments in 'second look' cases. Deference of this kind is also inherently contro-versial both among judges and scholars, including many dialogue theor-ists. At least some uses of the dialogue metaphor, therefore, may downplay legitimate concerns in many constitutional systems about the 'counter-majoritarian difficulty' associated with strong forms of judicial review. Whether or not this is sufficient to point to a move away from the metaphor depends in part on volumes such as this, and whether they can encourage a more contingent, qualified view of the idea of dialogue – and one more closely connected to ideas about (certain kinds of limited) constitutional deference by courts.

In Chapter 7, Jeff King sets out two tasks for himself. The first is to clarify different senses of the term 'dialogue'. It explores whether dialogue implies an egalitarian relationship between institutions, whether it justi-fies judicial review, who has the last word under the metaphor, and how, importantly, it relates to the 'passive virtues' tradition of judicial restraint

associated with Alexander Bickel, John Hart Ely, and Cass Sunstein. The
second task is to point out certain problems with the dialogue metaphor,
and in particular those relating to recent reformulations of the idea. King
argues that the equivocation over who has the last word in rights disputes
puts rights at substantial risk, that the dialogue metaphor pays insufficient attention to the need for finality and authoritative resolutions of
law, and that the separation of powers is put in doubt where legislatures
are invited to reject the constitutional interpretations of the judicial
branch. Agreeing with these criticisms does not commit one to a robust
view of judicial supremacy, one that makes no room for judicial
restraint. To the contrary, the passive virtues tradition that dialogue
theory seeks to replace or compete with has fewer of these problems.

V   Rights Dialogues

Part III focuses on the relationship between constitutional dialogue and
rights in specific constitutional contexts. Whereas the essays of Parts I
and II of the volume considered the general relationship between dialogue and democracy and institutions, often using examples of real-life
dialogues to demonstrate the role of dialogue in constitutional and
political theory, the essays in Part III investigate the question of how
and why dialogue has been and should be used in the context of specific
systems and constitutional instruments. These inquiries primarily concern aspects of constitutional contexts thought to prove salutary or
inimical to rights dialogues, such as the Canadian Charter's 'notwithstanding' and 'limitations' clauses, the pre-enactment rights review
requirements attending the New Zealand and UK statutory bills of rights,
and 'savings clauses' that shield statutes enacted before a bill of rights
from judicial review.

Dwight Newman opens Part III by focusing on dialogues in the
Canadian context, and in particular their relationship to the 'notwithstanding clause' (Chapter 8). He seeks to re-engage with the underlying
philosophy of the notwithstanding clause in Canada's Charter of Rights
and Freedoms, and argues that the clause actually enacts a relatively
unique model of constitutionalism attentive to traditions of parliamentary democracy and to respect for distinct national identities within
Canada, thus responding to the distinctive historical forerunners. To
make this argument, he first draws on the history of the clause and the
thought of the premiers who particularly advocated for the clause,
notably Allan Blakeney and Peter Lougheed, linking their thought on

the clause to their broader theories of constitutionalism and identity. Second, he argues that returning to their conception of the clause allows for a different reading of the text than has been supposed by those who read the clause narrowly, notably such authors as Jeffrey Goldsworthy and Jeremy Waldron, whose considerations of the clause relate to relatively abstract, decontextualised aspects of interpretation. In doing so, he shows that their approach has focused on narrow aspects of the clause and missed a wider potential within Canada's constitution for more coordinate approaches to rights interpretation. Third, he explains the clause's fit with the distinctive circumstances of Canada in the context of issues about how to apply the clause, showing how it opens possibilities going beyond dialogue on rights interpretation to the implementation of principled coordinate approaches to rights interpretation and the colocation of rights with other aspects of national identity. Throughout his contribution, Newman argues that these distinctive features of Canadian constitutionalism need to shape interpretation of the clause's contribution to dialogue theory.

In Chapter 9, Janet L. Hiebert and James B. Kelly examine the promise the rights dialogues in the New Zealand and UK Parliaments. The New Zealand Bill of Rights Act 1990 and the United Kingdom's Human Rights Act 1998 are examples of 'third wave' bills of rights that attempt to combine the virtues of judicial review in a manner that respects the principles of parliamentary democracy. In this spirit, the model is premised on a human rights 'inter-institutional dialogue' that is suggested to emerge at critical points in the development and passage of a draft bill. In this chapter, Hiebert and Kelly survey the experiences of New Zealand and the United Kingdom and consider whether inter-institutional dialogue has emerged in these 'parliamentary' bills of rights. Their empirical findings suggest that the theory of the new model does not match the reality of the parliamentary experience of rights-based dialogue. They contend that rights-based dialogue is significantly compromised by the durable characteristics of parliamentary democracy, which are majoritarianism, executive dominance, and the careerism of elected officials. They demonstrate their claims by analysing several bills introduced with reports of inconsistency, and their passage –without amendments – by parliamentary committees and processes that operate in an environment of executive dominance and control.

Kent Roach was one of earliest and most articulate proponents of 'dialogue theory' in the Canadian context, and in Chapter 10 of this volume he continues to elaborate on his defence of dialogue. The first part of his argument seeks to demonstrate that reports of the 'death' of dialogue in Canada have been greatly exaggerated. Dialogue offers a good explanation of proportionality analysis under ss. 1 and 7 of the Canadian Charter of Rights and Freedoms and the remedy of suspended declarations of invalidity. Legislative replies to recent Charter decisions on labour relations, supervised injection sites, sex work, and assisted dying affirm the reality of dialogue. The second part argues that binary models that contrast weak-form or Commonwealth review to strong-form judicial review simplify and distort comparative law. The drafting of the Charter, parliamentary government, tight party discipline, weak pre-enactment review, and other contextual factors help make Canada's form of judicial review distinct. The third part argues that Jeremy Waldron's defence of majoritarian democracy downplays the problem of persistent minorities fuelled by the growing reality of penal and anti-migrant populism. Dialogue can be rescued from criticisms that it undermines the judicial role, but this requires courts to reject symbolic and populist legislative objectives and automatic deference to legislative replies. It also requires courts to pay attention to the need for effective remedies.

In Chapter 11, Rivka Weill examines how some constitutions use "savings clauses" to shield from judicial review laws that have been in force prior to their adoption, thereby fostering a unique type of dialogue between the representative bodies and the courts. Such savings clauses state that existing laws shall remain valid even if they are inconsistent with the constitution. Many scholars view this phenomenon as esoteric, appearing in African or Caribbean countries alone. But according to Weill, this phenomenon is widespread, occurring in many civil law and common law countries. Over the years, countries have used such provisions to shield discriminatory religious and gender practices, the death penalty, and even slavery. This puzzling phenomenon should have spurred discussion, yet there is no literature offering a comprehensive theoretical and comparative framework. When the rationale for adopting a savings clause is that existing law is good, this might lead to an originalist interpretation of the constitution. Past laws may affect the interpretation of the constitution rather than the opposite. In contrast, when savings clauses are adopted to stabilise the system or shield discriminatory practices, courts may try to read them narrowly to minimise their effects. For Weill, savings clauses suggest that constitutional development is more evolutionary than typically suggested. But she also claims that these clauses might postpone rather than resolve the conflict over the most sensitive social issues, and that in some cases no less than a revolution will be needed to restart the constitutional system free of the burden of savings clauses.

VI Case Studies of Dialogue

The chapters in Part IV of the collection are case studies of constitutional dialogue at work. The essays focus not only on specific constitutional contexts, but on cases of dialogue regarding certain specific rights. The chapters included here survey and evaluate dialogues regarding prisoner voting rights in the Commonwealth and Europe, same-sex marriage rights in the United States, and the right to medical assistance in dying in Canada. Together they illustrate many kinds of rights dialogues between constitutional institutions.

In Chapter 12, John Finnis opens this part of the collection with a case study of prisoner voting cases before the European Court of Human Rights and the final courts of appeal in Australia, Canada, New Zealand, and South Africa. His analysis subjects the judicial reasoning in these cases to the sort of close examining courts are said to subject legislation and attorneys general to when assessing the constitutionality of legislative measures for compliance with human rights. Finnis concludes that the Strasborg Court's reasoning from *Hirst* v. *UK (no. 2)* (2005) to *Scoppola* v. *Italy* (2012) discloses no thread of integrity in legal reasoning, thus frustrating any attempt by legislatures to dialogue with the Court in designing prisoner voting restrictions. His review of these European cases, as well as of the Supreme Court of Canada's decision in *Sauvé (no. 2)* (2002) highlights how courts are liable to pay only lip service to the Attorney General's formulation of the legislature's aims and ends, freely substituting the legislative objective under its proportionality assessment of the measures. The lack of care and competence in judicial reasoning across jurisdictions is reviewed in light of the ready abandonment of judicial method with the substitution of interpretation via original public meaning with 'living instrument' or 'living tree' interpretation, according to which a bill of rights should be interpreted and applied not only in the light of present-day conditions but also according to judicial opinions about better political or social arrangements, even when doing so is contrary to the instrument's original public meaning. Finnis's essay concludes with an invitation to legislatures, when confronted with judicial precedents founded upon such 'interpretations', to rectify the law.

Shifting to the case of the right to same-sex marriage, Stephen Macedo (Chapter 13) traces how constitutional dialogue among the judicial, legislative, and executive branches, and local, state, and federal officials, and citizens organised at every level of government, has played out in the case of gay rights, especially in the United States. Macedo argues that the sustained and decades-long dialogue about same-sex marriage across each of the branches of government and engaging citizens at all levels helps make the case that a 'strong form' of judicial review is not inconsistent with wide democratic involvement and inclusive deliberation over constitutional questions. At a more abstract level, he makes the case that counter-majoritarian judicial review can *in principle* serve as a means of protecting basic rights, especially minority rights that may be given short shrift among elected officials. This understanding of democracy rejects majoritarianism in favour of substantive protections for the equal status of citizens and the special protection of minority interests. Macedo concludes that rights cannot be secured by courts alone, and that the right to same-sex marriage in the United States was achieved through an astonishingly nuanced array of interactions between legislative, executive, popular, and judicial actors at both the state and federal levels of government. The American dialogue about same-sex marriage is analysed from the Vermont legislature's creation of same-sex civil unions in response to the state Supreme Court's incrementalist decision in *Baker* v. *State*, to the federal Supreme Court's recognition of the constitutional right to same-sex marriage in *Obergefell* v. *Hodges*. The chapter concludes by comparing the US Supreme Court's constructive participation in the dialogue about same-sex marriage with its more pre-emptive intervention in the case of abortion. It also comments on how dialogues about same-sex marriage have involved courts in other constitutional contexts featuring 'weaker' forms of judicial review.

Turning back to the Canadian context in Chapter 14, Dennis Baker argues that a recent interaction between Canada's national Parliament and judiciary regarding the right to assisted suicide provides insight into how the formal separation of powers informally impacts dialogues in this system. He begins his chapter by noting that the 'Canadian case' often sits awkwardly in theories of comparative judicial power. For Baker, this is in part because of a failure to appreciate the complexities of Canada's constitutional order, which allows for considerable informal flexibility within formal boundaries. From the perspective of constitutional dialogue, the typical Canadian case might lead observers to find its system indistinguishable from judicial supremacy. Such an approach would miss, however, the infrequent but real opportunities for nonjudicial actors to play a role in the development of its constitutional principles. In other words, it is the formal separation of powers – deeply engrained in Canada's constitutional design – that ultimately determines the course of any constitutional dialogue. One such formal 'coordinate moment' recently occurred in Canada with Parliament's response to the Supreme Court's ruling in the assisted suicide case of *Carter* v. *Canada*. In Baker's view, this case – and the response it generated – demonstrates one feature of how Canadian constitutional supremacy is reconciled with an interinstitutional approach that does not privilege the judiciary. As such, and understood in this way, Baker claims that the Canadian case has lessons to offer other Westminster systems that may be struggling with the role Parliament might play when a written and entrenched constitution is supreme.

VII   International and Transnational Dialogues

The chapters in Part V of the collection explore dialogue from an international and transnational perspective.

Frederick Schauer's contribution (Chapter 15) begins by reviewing the idea of dialogue beyond the domestic context, where it is often used to refer to the idea that the decisions of courts are subject to further modification, override, or even nullification by the legislature. In the international and transnational context, the language and idea of dialogue is employed to refer to the process in which constitutional courts take account of the constitutional provisions and decisions in other countries. Schauer reviews two different arguments often made in defence of dialogue in this context. The first argument tracks the marketplace of ideas justification often associated with freedom of expression, according to which sound constitutional ideas will prevail over unsound ones, at least in the long run, when both the sound and the unsound ideas are offered and become the subject of discussion and criticism. The second argument treats transnational dialogue as facilitative or constitutive of transnational cooperation, such that transnational constitutional dialogue is the vehicle for increased transnational cooperation, and that such cooperation is a good in itself, irrespective of the soundness of the ideas that emerge. Schauer's critical review of the first argument suggests that there may be little basis for very much confidence that a process of transnational constitutional dialogue will systematically incline towards soundness. In turn, Schauer's critical review of the second argument invites us to question just what the idea of dialogue is contributing to what we otherwise might know and think about the advantages and disadvantages of international cooperation.

In the concluding chapter (Chapter 16), Richard Ekins argues against the usefulness of the metaphor of dialogue for describing interactions between the UK Parliament, its courts, and European courts. Ekins begins by noting that in the Westminster tradition, Parliament stands at the centre of a public conversation about what is to be done. The courts have not been parties to this conversation, but have upheld settled law, which forms part of the framework within which deliberation takes place and is itself the object of public deliberation and decision. He argues that this arrangement has been unbalanced by a changing under-standing of the judicial role and by the reach of international obligations that subject the United Kingdom to the jurisdiction of international courts. In this way, he notes that new conversations have been intro-duced to the British constitution, including exchanges between domestic and European courts, the main significance of which has been to com-promise parliamentary democracy. He argues that the UK's decision to leave the EU follows in part from the alienation of citizens from Euro-pean lawmaking and action and from a corresponding concern to restore self-government. In reaching and implementing that decision to leave, Ekins sees the capacity of parliamentary democracy to enable the political community to reason and act together, but also the risks posed by wayward domestic judicial action.

*

*   *

It has been two decades since Hogg and Bushell published their survey of instances of dialogue between the Supreme Court of Canada and legisla-tures on the requirements of the Canadian Charter. The idea of dialogue has captured the imagination of many constitutional and political actors and scholars, even if only some of them adhere to the specific account of dialogue promoted by Hogg and Bushell. As we have aimed to demon-strate in this Introduction, the appeal to the metaphor can be said to channel some of the underlying constitutional debates alive in different constitutional systems and in the scholarship, such that the singular word 'dialogue' may capture a plurality of different metaphors across insti-tutional contexts and interactions. It does so both by describing and by evaluating patterns of institutional organisation and interaction between the branches of domestic constitutions and, increasingly, international and transnational legal orders.

As our survey of jurisdictions in this Introduction illustrated, the answer to what constitutional dialogue is turns in greater measure on the reasons why the metaphor is appealed to. We hope that the essays in this collection help identify a range of reasons and, in turn, help account for why the same metaphor can be used to describe and to evaluate such a diverse range of institutional interactions over some of the more fundamental questions alive in political and constitutional thought.

PART I

Dialogue and Democracy

2

Dialogue and Its Myths

'Whatever People Say I Am, That's What I'm Not'

ALISON L. YOUNG*

Constitutional or democratic dialogue has become almost ubiquitous in current constitutional discourse. It is most commonly found in debates surrounding how constitutions should protect human rights, touted as the panacea to the great debate as to whether courts or legislatures are the best-placed institution to provide the more legitimate protection of human rights, with better decisions as to the content of human rights. Dialogue appears to allow constitutional theorists to 'have their cake and eat it' – to borrow a metaphor that appears to be rising in popularity[1] – advocating a combination of legal and political protections of rights. It is often linked with the commonwealth model, a model of constitutional design that aims to facilitate dialogue by providing legal and political means through which the legislature can respond to judicial determinations of human rights.[2] However, the utility of dialogue does not end here. It has also been used to describe relationships between courts, both when referring to interactions between courts in a hierarchical structure and between those in a non-hierarchical relationship.[3]

---

* With apologies to the Arctic Monkeys for borrowing one of their song titles as an homage to my home city. The argument presented in this paper draws on my book *Democratic Dialogue and the Constitution* (Oxford: Oxford University Press, 2017). Earlier versions of this paper were presented at the University of Edinburgh and the University of Durham, and I am grateful to all who attended those seminars for helping me to refine my ideas.

[1] This metaphor was seen on a notepad of a government aide and described by the media as the UK's strategy in the Brexit negotiations, only for this to be played down by the government: www.theguardian.com/politics/2016/nov/29/greg-clark-minister-dismisses-having-cake-and-eating-it-brexit-notes.

[2] See S. Gardbaum, *The New Commonwealth Model of Constitutionalism: Theory and Practice* (Cambridge: Cambridge University Press, 2012).

[3] See, for example, A.-M. Slaughter, 'A Typology of Transjudicial Communication' (1994) 29 *University of Richmond Law Review* 99; L. Helfer and A.-M. Slaughter, 'Towards a Theory of Effective Supranational Adjudication' (1997) 107 *Yale Law Journal* 273; and M. A. Waters, 'Meeting Norms and Identity: The Role of Transnational Judicial Dialogue in Creating and Enforcing International Law' (2005) 93 *Georgetown Law Journal* 487.

In particular, it has been used to describe the relationship between the European Court of Human Rights and UK courts,[4] as well as illustrating constitutional and legal pluralism in the interactions between the Court of Justice of the European Union and domestic courts.[5]

However, despite having been the darling of constitutional law, dialogue appears to have fallen out of favour – described in a powerful critique by Aileen Kavanagh as a 'misleading metaphor' that 'distorts' rather than informs constitutional theory.[6] It is easy to understand why this is the case. First difficulties arise as to the scope of 'democratic dialogue'. Does it apply only to those legal systems that have adopted a commonwealth model of rights protections, or does it also apply in legal systems that have adopted a different model of rights protections? Second, the use of the term 'dialogue' appears to do little more than conjure up an idea of a conversation between institutions of the constitution, it provides little account of the nature of these conversations. As such, there is a broad range of accounts of the nature of the relationship between, for example, the legislature and the courts that can fall within the sphere of 'dialogue'. Third, it can be hard to distinguish 'dialogue' from other accounts of protections of human rights, particularly when arguments used to justify granting either the courts or the legislature the final say over human rights are also used to explain the type of dialogue that should take place between these institutions. All of these weaknesses suggest that 'dialogue' is so hard to pin down and define because every attempt to provide a definition appears to lead to the conclusion that there either is no distinct conception of 'dialogue', or that 'dialogue' is ubiquitous.

Given these difficulties, most theorists shy away from providing a definition of democratic dialogue. This chapter, by contrast, aims to provide a workable definition. In doing so, it is arguably playing the role of a foolish angel, to borrow yet another metaphor; rushing in where

---

[4] C. McCrudden, 'A Common Law of Human Rights? Transnational Conversations on Constitutional Rights' (2000) 20 *Oxford Journal of Legal Studies* 499; and M. Amos, 'The Dialogue between the United Kingdom Courts and the European Court of Human Rights (2010) 61 *International and Comparative Law Quarterly* 557.

[5] M. Paoires Maduro, 'Contrapunctual Law: Europe's Constitutional Pluralism in Action' in N Walker (ed) *Sovereignty in Transition* (Oxford: Oxford University Press, 2003), 501; and M. Kumm, 'The Jurisprudence of Constitutional Conflict: Constitutional Supremacy in Europe before and after the Constitutional Treaty' (2005) 11 *European Law Journal* 262.

[6] A. Kavanagh, 'The Lure and Limits of Dialogue' (2016) 66 *University of Toronto Law Journal* 83, 85.

many others have feared to tread. It will propose the following account of democratic dialogue:

> Democratic dialogue is a constitutional model which focuses on inter-institutional interactions to both describe and evaluate how legal systems protect rights. It explains how inter-institutional interactions can serve two aims, constitutional collaboration and constitutional counterbalancing. It explains how inter-institutional interactions may facilitate the values underpinning democratic dialogue – a better protection of human rights, the facilitation of deliberative and participatory democracy, as well as how interactions may act as a means of checks and balances between institutions and of avoiding and resolving constitutional crises. The way in which these aims interact, and the mechanisms through which these aims can be facilitated, depends upon and draws upon the different constitutional powers and institutional features of the legislature and judiciary in a particular legal system, applying differently to distinct types of human rights and applying in a manner which is sensitive to path-dependent behavioural choices.

The long-winded nature of this definition draws attention to the most important lesson any theorist can learn about democratic dialogue: it is a complex theory that applies differently in a range of constitutions. If the search for an account of democratic dialogue has been difficult, it is not because the theory is worthless. Rather, it is to recognise that all theories of constitutionalism are complex and schools of thought are often broad churches.

To fully defend this account, we need first to focus on what dialogue is not; to debunk the myths surrounding accounts of dialogue in order to propose a new definition. First, we will explore the scope of democratic dialogue by examining the myth that democratic dialogue is a specific model of rights protections and its related myth, that it is an account of constitutional behaviour. This exploration will lead to the first aspect of our definition – that democratic dialogue is neither an account of a specific protection of rights nor a mere explanation of behaviour. Rather, it is a constitutional model that focuses on providing an account of aspects of the constitution through focusing on how institutions of the constitution interact with one another.

Second, we will examine the myths surrounding the definition of dialogue. Two aspects of an understanding of 'dialogue' appear to provide a better account of democratic dialogue: that democratic dialogue requires a form of equality between the parties participating in the dialogue and that accounts of dialogue are dynamic, focusing on events that happen over time. However, the requirement for equality appears to undermine other aspects of democratic dialogue, specifically as regards the ability of democratic dialogue to provide for a better protection of rights that maximises the advantages and minimises the disadvantages of legal and political protections of rights. It will be argued here that democratic dialogue requires interactions that aim to achieve two distinct aims – constitutional collaboration and constitutional counterbalancing.

Third, we will focus on the myth that democratic dialogue is able to provide a 'middle ground' between predominantly legal and predominantly political protections of human rights. Democratic dialogue has been criticised for inevitably collapsing into a strong or a weak protection of human rights in practice. This instability is also argued to occur at a deeper level. The arguments for democratic dialogue appear to be parasitic upon accounts advocating a predominantly political or a predominantly legal protection of rights. The chapter will argue that dialogue can be used to provide a better protection of rights, but that its ability to do so relies upon an assessment of the institutional characteristics of legislatures and courts in different legal systems, focusing in particular upon their relative ability to reason about rights. It will also argue that democratic dialogue can promote other values; its merit does not lie solely in whether it can provide for a better protection of human rights. An exploration of these myths will be used to explain and defend the proposed definition of democratic dialogue.

I   From Constitutional Design to Constitutional Model

Dialogue is often seen as synonymous with the commonwealth model of rights protections. However, it is hard to separate out democratic dialogue from the commonwealth model. The two appear to be synonymous, particularly as commonwealth models are advocated because they provide for a blending of legal and political mechanisms of protecting human rights, the aim being to maximise the advantages and minimise the disadvantages of both forms of rights protection. However, dialogue can occur in legal systems that have not adopted a commonwealth model.[7]

---

[7] See, for example, the accounts of dialogue in the United States in L. Fisher, *Constitutional Dialogues: Interpretation as a Political Process* (Princeton: Princeton University Press, 1998); B. Friedman, 'A Different Dialogue: The Supreme Court, Congress and Federal Jurisdiction' (1990) 85 *Northwestern University Law Review* 1; B. Friedman 'Dialogue and Judicial Review' (1993) 91 *Michigan Law Review* 557. See also the classifications of dialogue in different legal systems in C. Bateup, 'The Dialogic Promise: Assessing the Normative Potential of Theories of Constitutional Dialogue (2006) 71 *Brooklyn Law*

Moreover, systems that have adopted a commonwealth model of rights find themselves criticised for collapsing into systems with a constitutional protection of rights in all but name,[8] or systems that appear to provide little more protection of rights than would be found in purely parliamentary models of rights.[9] Is dialogue a model of rights protection that is doomed to failure, or are these failures in the model occurring because the theory provides little guidance as to how institutions should exercise their powers? Either way, it would appear hard to argue with Mark Tushnet's seminal article, which argues that dialogue models will inevitably collapse,[10] or with Christopher P. Manfredi's conclusion that dialogue is both empirically problematic and normatively flawed.[11]

When providing his account of the commonwealth model, Gardbaum is careful to distinguish his commonwealth model from an account of dialogue. He considers dialogue to be 'somewhat vague and over-inclusive',

---

Review 1109; and M. Cohn, 'Sovereignty, Constitutional Dialogues and Political Networks: A Comparative and Conceptual Study' in R. Rawlings, P. Leyland and A. L. Young (eds), *Sovereignty and the Law: Domestic, European and International Perspectives* (Oxford: Oxford University Press, 2013). Fredman also argues that dialogue occurs in the South African Constitution; see S. Fredman, 'From Dialogue to Deliberation: Human Rights Adjudication and Prisoners' Right to Vote' [2013] *Public Law* 292.

[8] This criticism is levelled in particular at the Canadian model found in the Canadian Charter, see, inter alia, G. Huscroft, 'Constitutionalism from the Top Down' (2007) 45 *Osgoode Hall Law Review* 91; A Vermeule, 'The Atrophy of Constitutional Powers' (2012) 32 *Oxford Journal of Legal Studies* 421, 425; and Gardbaum, above n 2, pp. 102–128; C. P. Manfredi, 'The Day the Dialogue Died: A Comment on *Sauvé v Canada*' (2007) 45 *Osgoode Hall Law Review* 106; D. Stuart, 'Zigzags No Rights of Accuse: Brittle Majorities, Manipulative Weasel Words of Dialogue, Deference and Charter Values' (2003) 20 *Supreme Court Law Review* 267; D. M. Brown, '*Sauvé* and Prisoners' Voting Rights: The Death of the Good Citizen?' (2003) 20 *Supreme Court Law Review* 12; and R. Dixon, 'The Supreme Court of Canada, Charter Dialogue and Deference' (2009) 47 *Osgoode Hall Law Journal* 235.

[9] See, for example, the criticisms of the New Zealand Bill of Rights Act 1990, in particular, A. Geddis, 'The Comparative Irrelevance of the NZBORA to Legislative Practice' (2009) 23 *New Zealand Universities Law Review* 465; and A. Geddis, 'Prisoner Voting and Rights Deliberation: How New Zealand's Parliament Failed' (2011) *New Zealand Law Review* 443; G. Huscroft, 'The Attorney-General's Reporting Duty' in P. Rishworth, G. Huscroft, S. Optician and R. Mahoney (eds), *The New Zealand Bill of Rights Act* (Oxford: Oxford University Press, 2013), p. 196; J. L. Hiebert, 'Rights-Vetting in New Zealand and Canada: Similar Idea, Different Outcomes' (2005) 3 *New Zealand Journal of Public and International Law* 63; and J. L. Hiebert and J. B. Kelly, *Parliamentary Bills of Rights: The Experience of New Zealand and the United Kingdom* (Cambridge: Cambridge University Press, 2015).

[10] M. Tushnet, 'New Forms of Judicial Review and the Persistence of Rights and Democracy-Based Worries' (2003) 38 *Wake Forest Law Review* 813.

[11] C. P. Manfredi, 'The Day the Dialogue Died: A Comment on Sauve v. Canada' (2007) 45 *Osgoode Hall Law Journal* 106.

drawing on some of the issues adumbrated in the Introduction.[12] First, he recognises that to focus on dialogue as a middle ground between 'strong constitutional' and 'weak parliamentary' protections of rights appears to give the misleading impression that commonwealth models provide a weaker protection of rights than that found in legal systems where courts are given the power to strike down legislation that breaches constitutionally protected rights, given that commonwealth models appear to provide a 'midway' protection of rights. However, this search is misleading, as it fails to take account of factors that may influence how legal systems exercise their powers. Even legal systems with a strong constitutional protection of rights may provide a weaker protection of rights than that found in legal systems that adopt the commonwealth model. If, for example, courts have the power to strike down legislation that breaches human rights, but courts routinely refrain from striking down legislation unless legislation demonstrates a blatant or manifest breach of constitutionally protected human rights, then human rights may be protected to a lesser extent than they would be protected in a system that had adopted a commonwealth model. Moreover, Gardbaum argues that dialogue is overinclusive if we regard dialogue as including any protection of rights where there is the possibility of legislative response to judicial determinations of human rights. If this is the case, then, Gardbaum argues, dialogue occurs in every legal system as it is nearly always possible for the legislature to respond, in some manner or other, to a judicial determination of a human right.[13]

Gardbaum's response to the vague and potentially ubiquitous nature of dialogue is to focus on the commonwealth model as a new form of constitutional design, providing a novel means of protecting human rights. When we focus on constitutional design, legal systems appear to bifurcate into those that provide a constitutional protection of rights, where courts can strike down legislation that breaches human rights, and those that provide for a purely parliamentary protection of rights, where courts can interpret legislation according to the will of the legislature, but can go no further. The commonwealth model has four distinct features. First, rights are protected through a codified charter of rights. This codified charter goes beyond the sporadic protection of rights in a series of statutes, or the use of principles of the common law to protect rights. Second, this codified charter of rights is found not in a constitutional

---

[12] Gardbaum, above n 2, p. 15.
[13] Gardbaum, above n 2, pp. 111–121.

document, but in legislation. Courts do not have the ability to strike down legislation that contravenes this statutory Bill of Rights. Third, courts can go beyond their normal powers of interpretation of legislation in order to protect human rights. Courts do not merely ensure that their legislative interpretations comply with the will of the legislature. Rather, they can interpret legislation so as to protect human rights in a manner that, whilst respecting linguistic limits, goes beyond a mere clarification of legislative intent. Fourth, despite the powers of the courts to perform constitutional review, the final, formal power to definitively determine the content of legislation, including the content of legislation that harms or promotes human rights, must rest with the legislature. Moreover, the legislature must be able to determine this content through the ordinary lawmaking procedure. Gardbaum argues that these four features distinguish the commonwealth model from other models of constitutional design, combining legal and political controls over rights, aiming to maximise the benefits and minimise the weaknesses of both parliamentary and constitutional protections of human rights.

Gardbaum avoids the problem of the vague nature of the definition of dialogue by embracing its vagueness and proposing, instead, an account of a separate model of rights protections. However, whilst this may help to provide an account of a new model of constitutional design, similar difficulties arise when we evaluate the extent to which the commonwealth model is able to maximise the benefits and minimise the weaknesses of judicial and parliamentary protections of rights. First, in the same manner that systems with a constitutional protection of rights can provide weaker or stronger protections of rights depending on how the judiciary and the legislature exercise their relative powers in the constitution, the same is true of commonwealth models. The extent to which commonwealth models provide for a better protection of human rights depends on how the institutions of the constitution exercise their powers. As Gardbaum's own analysis of the commonwealth models of rights protections found in Canada, the United Kingdom, Australia and New Zealand demonstrates, the commonwealth model itself has a range of varieties providing a range of experiences of balancing legal and political protections of rights.[14]

Second, inter-institutional interactions may occur in a variety of means in any one legal system. This can be exemplified by the protection

---

[14] Gardbaum, above n 2, chapters 5–8.

of rights found in the United Kingdom's Human Rights Act 1998. There are arguments that dialogue is only promoted through section 4 of the Act, which empowers courts of the level of the high court or above to issue a declaration of incompatibility.[15] A declaration of incompatibility does not affect the validity, force or legal effect of the legislation declared incompatible with Convention rights – i.e., the rights found in Schedule 1 to the Human Rights Act 1998, which incorporates provisions of the European Convention on Human Rights into the United Kingdom.[16] As such it does not directly protect human rights. Any protection of human rights requires either legislative intervention, or the enactment of a remedial order by the government, to modify legislation and protect Convention rights.[17] This provides a clear example of a weaker judicial protection of rights, combined with legislative intervention in response to judicial determinations of rights.

However, dialogue may also arise through section 3 of the Human Rights Act, the provision that obliges courts to read and give effect to legislation in a manner compatible with Convention rights, so far as it is possible to do so. Tom Hickman argues that dialogue may arise through section 3 as there are limits to the extent to which courts can read legislation to ensure its compatibility with Convention rights. If there are some legislative provisions that it is not possible to interpret in a manner compatible with Convention rights, then this inevitably means that it is possible to enact legislation that is not compatibly with Convention rights. This is reinforced by section 19(1)(b) of the Human Rights Act, which enables a minister to make a statement as to the intention of the government to enact legislation, even in circumstances when the minister is not able to state that the proposed legislation will be compatible with Convention rights.[18] Moreover, it gives rise to the possibility of legislative response to Convention-compatible interpretations of legislation. Legislatures can respond by enacting new provisions that provide a clear account of the legislature's definition of a right that the courts cannot possibly reinterpret, given the limitations of section 3. Commentators on

---

[15] See, for example, F. Klug 'Judicial Deference under the Human Rights Act 1998' (2003) *European Human Rights Law Review* 126; and D. Nicol, 'Law and Politics after the Human Rights Act 1998' [2006] *Public Law* 722.

[16] Human Rights Act 1998, section 4.

[17] Ibid. section 10.

[18] This was the case as regards section 321(2) Communications Act 2003, as discussed in *R (Animal Defenders International)* v. *Secretary of State for Culture, Media and Sport* [2008] UKHL 15, [2008] 1 AC 1312.

the Human Rights Act 1998 provide differing accounts of when courts should deploy section 3 or section 4, giving rise to diverse accounts of how the Human Rights Act maximises the benefits and minimises the disadvantages of legal and political protections of rights.[19]

Third, the way in which courts and legislatures exercise their powers under the commonwealth model is affected by the way in which each institution perceives its role. Empirical research on the effectiveness of parliamentary protections of rights demonstrates that problems arise when parliamentarians perceive the definition of rights as a legal issue, with courts providing the definitive definition of a right, to which parliamentarians must adhere.[20] This may explain, for example, why most declarations of incompatibility issued in the United Kingdom are complied with.[21] The judiciary may also continue to exercise powers in a manner that corresponds with their understanding of their traditional role, rather than through exercising their powers under the new commonwealth model in a manner that facilitates dialogue. To return to the experiences of the United Kingdom, courts may exercise deference, either through applying proportionality less stringently, or through defining rights in a more or less precise manner, providing legislatures with a greater or lesser range of legislative choices that are compatible with judicial interpretations of human rights.[22] Courts may also use deference by deciding to exercise their discretion not to issue a declaration of incompatibility, even when legislation is potentially incompatible with Convention rights.[23]

---

[19] T. Hickman, *Public Law after the Human Rights Act* (Hart Publishing, 2010), chapter 3.

[20] J. L. Hiebert and J. B. Kelly, *Parliamentary Bills of Rights: The Experiences of New Zealand and the United Kingdom* (Cambridge: Cambridge University Press, 2015).

[21] According to the latest figures, from the commencement of the Act until the end of July 2016, thirty-four declarations of incompatibility had been issued, of which twenty-two were final, four were subject to appeal and eight were overturned. Of those twenty-two, all have been remedied save one, on prisoner voting, which is still under consideration. See Ministry of Justice, 'Responding to Human Rights judgments' Report to the Joint Committee on Human Rights on the Government's response to Human Rights judgments 2014–16, November 2016, Cm 9360. Since then, the Supreme Court has issued one further declaration of incompatibility. See J. King, 'Parliament's Role following Declarations of Incompatibility under the Human Rights Act' in M. Hunt, H. Hooper and P. Yowell (eds), *Parliaments and Human Rights: Redressing the Democratic Deficits* (Hart Publishing, 2015).

[22] A. L. Young, 'The Practicalities of Dialogue: Is Dialogue working under the Human Rights Act 1998?' [2011] *Public Law* 773.

[23] See, for example, the judgment of Lord Neuberger in *R (Nicklinson)* v. *Ministry of Justice* [2014] UKSC 38, [2015] AC 657.

Our exploration of Gardbaum's account demonstrates the difficulties of determining the scope of democratic dialogue. Vagueness appears to plague both an assessment of dialogue independent from a commonwealth model of rights protections and an account of commonwealth models of rights protections distinct from a theory of dialogue. If there is a myth surrounding our exploration of dialogue, it would appear to be that of its existence as an independent account of protections of rights. That said, Gardbaum's focus on issues of constitutional design, and references to models of rights protection, helps to provide one means of refining the definition of democratic dialogue. As discussed in the introduction: *Democratic dialogue is a constitutional model that focuses on inter-institutional interactions to both describe and evaluate how legal systems protect rights.* Democratic dialogue is best understood as a constitutional model.[24] By this I mean an account of how to understand one aspect of how constitutions can operate in practice, as well as an account of normative values that may be achieved by the model. With regard to democratic dialogue, the model is designed to provide an account of how institutions interact with one another. The constitutional model of democratic dialogue aims to provide a more accurate account of how constitutions operate in practice by focusing not just on the powers granted to institutions of the constitution, and how the actors in the constitution use these powers, but also by focusing on how the actions of one institution can cause reactions in the other, as well as how an institution may exercise its powers differently due to the anticipated reaction of another.

We can understand this further by returning to our discussion of the Human Rights Act 1998. As discussed previously, we can provide an account of this Act through explaining how far its provisions exemplify a commonwealth model of rights protections. We can also examine the Act in practice, assessing whether the Act produces legislative responses to judicial decisions on human rights. If we adopt an approach that looks at democratic dialogue as a constitutional model, we would go further than merely describing the relative powers of the legislature and the judiciary under sections 3 and 4 of the Act. Moreover, we would not merely focus on how the judiciary and the legislature exercise their

---

[24] For a discussion of what is meant by a 'model' see G. Gee and G. Webber, 'What Is a Political Constitution?' (2010) 30 *Oxford Journal of Legal Studies* 273, 291; and A. L. Young, *Democratic Dialogue and the Constitution* (Oxford: Oxford University Press, 2017), 173–175.

powers under the Act. Rather, we would look at how each institution responded to the actions of the other, or modified the way in which they exercised their powers in anticipation of an expected reaction of the other, both as regards the use of section 3 and of section 4. An approach that focused on democratic dialogue as a constitutional model would also examine how legislatures used section 19 of the Act – which requires a minister to make a statement before Parliament when introducing legislation as to the compatibility of the proposed legislation with Convention rights – and the response of the courts to these statements, which may be evidenced, inter alia, in their judgments generally and the extent to which the courts choose to refer to parliamentary debate or to reports of the Joint Committee on Human Rights to determine the scope of Convention rights.[25]

In addition to this descriptive aspect, constitutional models also have a normative dimension. A model of democratic dialogue evaluates inter-institutional interactions, determining when these interactions may provide for a better protection of rights, both in terms of legitimacy and outcome. A model of democratic dialogue also explains how inter-institutional interactions can achieve other values – for example, when interactions can facilitate deliberation, encourage participation and act as a safety valve to relieve tension between institutions whilst facilitating change in the relative roles of the legislature and the judiciary. These values can be achieved to a greater or lesser extent. The achievement of these values rests, in part, on whether the assumptions on which an account of democratic dialogue is based are found in the legal system where a model of democratic dialogue is applied.[26]

Understanding democratic dialogue in this manner helps to explain some of the weaknesses of current accounts of dialogue. It explains how dialogue can occur in legal systems that have not adopted a commonwealth model of rights protections, in addition to explaining why a system that has adopted a commonwealth model may, or may not, provide a stable theory of dialogue or provide for a better protection of

---

[25] M. Hunt, H. Hooper and P. Yowell, 'Parliaments and Human Rights: Redressing the Democratic Deficit' AHRC Public Policy Series, 5, www.ahrc.ac.uk/documents/project-reports-and-reviews/ahrc-public-policy-series/parliaments-and-human-rights-redressing-the-democratic-deficit/; 'Introduction' in *Parliaments and Human Rights: Redressing the Democratic Deficit*, above n 21; and A. Kavanagh, 'Proportionality and Parliamentary Debate: Exploring Some Forbidden Territory' (2014) 34 *Oxford Journal of Legal Studies* 44.

[26] For a discussion of the assumptions on which a model of democratic dialogue rests, see Young, above n 24, chapter 6.

rights, maximising the advantages and minimising the disadvantages of legal and political protections of rights. It can, therefore, help to refine our definition of democratic dialogue. However, at this stage, our definition is too abstract. It merely sees democratic dialogue as a model used to describe and evaluate constitutions, without saying anything further about the distinctive nature of the model of democratic dialogue. To refine the definition further, we need to investigate more myths about dialogue.

II From Dialogue to Constitutional Counterbalancing and Constitutional Collaboration

The search for a meaningful account of democratic or constitutional dialogue does not appear to be helped by the adoption of the word 'dialogue'. Theories that focus on analysing the meaning of dialogue point to the need for interactions between institutions, or a dynamic approach to understanding how the scope of a human right is determined. Much has also been made of the fact that dialogue needs to be between equal parties.[27] However, this has done little to clarify accounts of dialogue. A plethora of theories abound, with Tom Hickman, for example, drawing further delineations between strong-form and weak-form dialogue,[28] and Kent Roach providing accounts of dialogue where courts and legislatures play distinct and complementary roles, or where each institution decides on human rights issues for itself, or where legislatures hold courts to account for their determinations of rights.[29] There are also delineations between theories that advocate complementary roles for courts and legislatures, ranging from those that advocate that each institution reasons independently, exercising comity as regards to each institution's relative constitutional functions,[30] and those that focus on providing complex accounts of each institution giving weight to the determinations of the other, depending on the nature of the rights-issue, the relative constitutional powers of the legislature and the courts and institutional

[27] L. Tremblay, 'The Legitimacy of Judicial Review: The Limits of Dialogue between Courts and Legislatures' (2005) 3 *International Journal of Constitutional Law* 617; and G. Phillipson, 'The Human Rights Act, Dialogue and Constitutional Principles' (2013) *Proceedings of the British Academy* 25.

[28] Hickman, above n 19, pp. 58–61.

[29] K. Roach, *The Supreme Court on Trial* (Irwin Press, 2001), pp. 241–243.

[30] See, for example, the account of J. L. Hiebert, *Charter Conflicts: What Is Parliament's Role?* (McGill-Queen's University Press, 2002), chapter 3.

issues that relate to each institution's relative ability to better determine rights issues.[31] Accounts of a deeper understanding of dialogue are incapable of evaluating the relative merits of these accounts of democratic or constitutional dialogue.

Although understanding the meaning of 'dialogue' may not provide a full account of democratic dialogue theories, it nevertheless provides two further characteristics of dialogue. First, dialogue can only occur between equal parties, where both have an equal say and both find their views equally respected. Second, dialogue is dynamic, focusing on interactions in a manner that is not found in other accounts of constitutionalism. However, both ultimately prove to be unfruitful avenues of exploration in our search for an understanding of dialogue; they merely serve to provide two further myths. Nevertheless, by challenging these myths, we can suggest a further refinement of democratic dialogue, as referred to in our initial definition, which states that a model of democratic dialogue *explains how inter-institutional interactions can serve two aims: constitutional collaboration and constitutional counterbalancing.* As will be explained in more detail later in this chapter, constitutional counterbalancing is required to ensure the element of equality needed for dialogue to be effective. Constitutional collaboration, however, recognises and reflects the way in which the legislature and the courts have different constitutional roles and different institutional features that influence both how these institutions reason about rights and also their legitimate role in determining human rights. Constitutional collaboration is designed to ensure that institutions work together to provide a better protection of human rights.

The requirement for equality in democratic dialogue stems from the work of Luc Tremblay.[32] Tremblay argues that there are two types of dialogue – dialogue as conversation and dialogue as deliberation. Whilst dialogue as conversation is spontaneous and informal, with no precise or specific purpose, dialogue as deliberation is designed for a specific mutual purpose. Accounts of democratic dialogue, therefore, are best understood as examples of dialogue as deliberation, with the legislature and the judiciary working together for a common purpose; to determine the scope and application of human rights, furnishing normative legitimacy

---

[31] See A. L. Young, *Democratic Dialogue and the Constitution* (Oxford: Oxford University Press, 2017), chapter 7.

[32] L. Tremblay, 'The Legitimacy of Judicial Review: The Limits of Dialogue between Courts and Legislatures' (2005) 3(4) *International Journal of Constitutional Law* 617.

for that determination.[33] Dialogue as deliberation requires interaction
between equal partners, exchanging information in a shared space of
meaning. If there is no element of equality, then problems may arise as
one institution may dominate the other, limiting both the extent to which
dialogue is a distinct account from legal systems with a constitutional
protection of rights, or a purely parliamentary protection of rights, in
addition to making it difficult to support the claim that democratic
dialogue is able to maximise the benefits and minimise the disadvantages
of political and legal protections of rights. However, difficulties can also
arise when trying to achieve this requisite equality. If equality is needed,
what does this mean? How can institutions be treated equally and yet
play a distinct role in order to provide a better means of protecting
human rights? Moreover, how can equality be squared with the need
for finality?

Equality between the legislature and the judiciary can be maintained in
a variety of ways. Janet L. Hiebert, for example, advocates that both the
legislature and the judiciary should ensure that they act in a manner that
complies with the values and rights found in the Canadian Charter of
Rights and Freedoms. She also advocates comity. As such, both the
legislature and the judiciary should respect their relative roles. This
element of respect does not stem from a recognition that one institution
or the other may be better able to reason about specific aspects of rights.
Rather, it stems from an understanding and a recognition of the different
roles the Charter and the provisions of the Canadian constitution give to
the legislature and the judiciary.[34] Similarly, Danny Nicol, when examining the provisions of the Human Rights Act 1998, argues that courts
should predominantly use section 4 as opposed to section 3. He advocates what Hickman classifies as 'principle-posing' dialogue, a form of
dialogue that occurs when the courts provide their account of a Convention right, but where this account is neither binding on the legislature,
nor to be given any specific weight as stemming from the courts. Rather,
the legislature is to regard the court's account as precisely that – an
account of the scope of a right that stands or falls on the basis of its
merits alone. Equality is maintained as both the legislature and the
judiciary should not hold back when determining rights-issues. Courts
should present their account of rights in a forthright manner, providing a
clear account of what the judiciary believe to be the correct scope and

---

[33] Ibid. pp. 631–634.
[34] Hiebert, above n 30, chapter 3.

application of a human right. The legislature should pay attention to this account, but it too should be willing to respond in an equally forthright manner, providing a clear account of its understanding of rights.[35] Neither account requires the legislature or the judiciary to give weight to the opinion of the other. If there is respect, it merely appears to require paying attention to opinions and taking them seriously, in the sense of not ignoring the opinion of the other institution or dismissing this opinion out of hand.

Understood in this manner, it is easy to see why dialogue is criticised. First, issues may arise regarding finality – which institution, if any, has the final say, or are determinations as to the scope and application of a particular right meant to be left unresolved? One answer to this conundrum is to refer to the experience of the application of dialogue in legal systems. Hiebert's account focuses on the commonwealth model of rights protections adopted by Canada. Here, the Canadian Supreme Court has the power to strike down legislation that contravenes the Charter. This is counterbalanced by the power of the legislature to enact legislation notwithstanding select provisions of the Charter. This may appear to grant equal power to the legislature and the judiciary. However, given the lack of use of the 'notwithstanding' clause, there is frequent and sustained academic criticism that the final word rests effectively with the judiciary – such that, in practice, the Charter provides a protection of rights that is little different from that found in a legal system that empowers the judiciary to strike down legislation that contravenes human rights.[36] Before reaching this conclusion, it is important to recognise that the notwithstanding clause is not the only mechanism in the Charter that can be used to facilitate dialogue. Section 1 of the Charter provides an ability for some rights to be restricted, provided these restrictions are reasonable limits that can be justified in a 'free and democratic society'.[37] When determining whether restrictions are reasonable, the Canadian courts apply a proportionality test. Proportionality can be applied more or less stringently. The more stringently the test is applied, the smaller the range

---

[35] Nicol, above n 15.

[36] G. Huscroft, 'Constitutionalism from the Top Down' (2007) 45 *Osgoode Hall Law Journal* 91; C. P. Manfredi, 'The Day the Dialogue Died: A Comment on *Sauvé v Canada*' (2007) 45 *Osgoode Hall Law Journal* 106; Gardbaum, above n 2, pp. 102–128. See also D. Newman's contribution to this volume.

[37] Canadian Charter of Rights and Freedoms, section 1. See G. Webber, 'The Unfulfilled Potential of the Court and Legislature Dialogue' (2009) 42(2) *Canadian Journal of Political Science* 443.

of policy choices left to the legislature when legislating in a manner that may restrict Charter rights – and vice versa. The ability to apply proportionality more or less stringently means that it may not be accurate to describe the judiciary as always having the final say on rights determinations. However, this can be countered by the argument that it is the courts who determine the test of proportionality, as well as determining how stringently the test should be applied in particular situations.

The opposite conclusion appears to be reached when we examine the Human Rights Act 1998. If, as Nicol advocates, courts should predominantly deploy section 4 as opposed to section 3 of the Act, then it appears easy to argue that legislatures have the final say in the United Kingdom. Under section 4, courts are unable to provide individuals with an effective remedy, given that the declaration of incompatibility does not have an impact on the legal effect of the legislation declared incompatible with Convention rights. However, it is arguable that this does not match the reality of the application of the Human Rights Act 1998 in practice, given that nearly all declarations of incompatibility lead to amendments that bring the legislation into line with the Convention right, as defined by the court. However, as with our assessment of the Canadian Charter, because UK courts apply a test of proportionality when applying Articles 8 to 11 of the European Convention on Human Rights, the judiciary may use deference when applying proportionality, applying the test less stringently and thereby leaving more discretion to the legislature when selecting between policy-choices that are compatible with Convention rights.

The more we focus on ensuring that the legislature and the judiciary play equal roles, the more problems appear to arise with regard to delineating those roles. Do the legislature and judiciary really play equal roles, or does the need for finality demonstrate that, eventually, either the legislature or the judiciary have the final say when determining rights? As well as raising issues for finality in rights-determinations, the search for equality between the legislature and the judiciary gives rise to further problems. First, there may be issues for the separation of powers.[38] We can see these issues when we revisit Nicol's account of dialogue under the Human Rights Act 1998. Nicol encourages courts to speak out, being bold and giving their own interpretation of the scope and application of a Convention right. Does this transgress the separation of powers, by

---

[38] K. Roach, *The Supreme Court on Trial* (Irwin Law Press, 2001), pp. 243–246.

requiring courts to focus less on precedent, paying close attention to past case law, and to focus instead on reaching their own personal opinion on the scope of Convention rights? If so, this may transgress the separation of powers, in addition to potentially undermining the independence of the judiciary. Similar concerns about the separation of powers and the constitutionally acceptable roles of the legislature and the judiciary may also explain why the UK Parliament tends to respond to declarations of incompatibility by enacting legislation that complies with the judiciary's determination of a Convention right and why Canadian legislatures are reluctant to use the notwithstanding clause. As Hiebert and Kelly's work illustrates, many politicians perceive their role as being to determine policies and perceive the constitutional role of the courts as being that of determining rights.[39] Dialogue appears to require legislatures and courts to act differently from their constitutional roles, which may provide an explanation for why commonwealth models of rights protections may not succeed in achieving their objective of providing an alternative means of protecting rights. Adopting a new model of protecting rights may not change behaviours, meaning that both the courts and the legislature may continue to act in the manner that preceded the change to a new model of rights protections.

Similar problems arise when we investigate the second myth which draws on an understanding of dialogue – that dialogue requires dynamic interactions. Can this element of dynamic interaction provide a means through which to distinguish democratic dialogue from other accounts of constitutionalism? It is not hard to find examples of dialogue theories that focus on dynamic interactions. The seminal work of Hogg and Bushell defined dialogue as occurring '[w]here a judicial decision is open to legislative reversal, modification or avoidance'.[40] This clearly contemplates interaction. Dialogue occurs when the legislature reacts in some way to judicial determinations of rights. It is hard to find any account of dialogue that does not draw on interactions between legislatures and courts, particularly those accounts of dialogue that focus on commonwealth models of rights protection. Gardbaum's account of the key features of the commonwealth model of rights protection focuses on

---

[39] J. L. Hiebert and J. B. Kelly, *Parliamentary Bills of Rights: The Experience of New Zealand and the United Kingdom* (Cambridge: Cambridge University Press, 2015).

[40] P. W. Hogg and A. A. Bushell, 'The Charter Dialogue between the Courts and Legislatures (Or Perhaps the Charter of Rights Isn't Such a Bad Thing After All)' (1997) 35 *Osgoode Hall Law Journal* 75, 97–98.

the extent to which these models facilitate interactions between legislatures and courts by enabling legislatures to respond to judicial determinations of rights. The component of dynamic interaction is also present in those accounts of dialogue that are based neither on the commonwealth model of rights protection, nor necessarily on the extent to which interactions occur between institutions of the constitution. Friedman, for example, provides an account of dialogue in the US Constitution, arguing that the interpretation of the US Constitution is best understood as an 'elaborate discussion between judges and the body politic' – the 'body politic' extending to include citizens and not just institutions.[41]

Although dynamic interactions between the institutions of the constitution, including those that occur through political means and that engage the public more generally in addition to the legislature and the judiciary, are a necessary component of accounts of democratic dialogue, they are not sufficient to provide a definitive account. This is because we can find accounts of dynamic interactions in other accounts of constitutionalism, including in accounts we would regard as prime examples of legal constitutionalism, which argues for predominantly judicial protections of rights, and political constitutionalism, which in turn advocates that legislatures should have the main role in protecting rights. Trevor Allan's account of common-law constitutionalism, for example, includes a dynamic element. Allan's theory, although founded on the importance of the rule of law, does not provide a detailed and precise account of the content of the rule of law. Rather, his theory recognises that the content of the rule of law modifies over time, through the evolution of the common law. However, courts are not the only institution with a role to play in the development of the precise content of the rule of law. Parliament too should act according to the rule of law, and it plays a specific role in the determination of how general principles that derive from principles of equal citizenship should apply in particular circumstances, determining general rules. When courts interpret legislation applying these general principles, they are capable of determining when these general rules breach the rule of law in their specific application. In doing so, courts refine the content of the rule of law. There is a role for both the legislature and the courts in developing the content of the rule of law through general measures and the interpretation and the application of these general measures to specific situations.

---

[41] B. Friedman, 'Dialogue and Judicial Review' (1993) 91 *Michigan Law Review* 577, 653. See also, L. Fisher, *Constitutional Dialogues: Interpretation as Political Process* (Princeton: Princeton University Press, 1988), pp. 201–228.

Moreover, the determination of the content of the rule of law is dynamic, evolving at least in part through the relative roles and interaction between the legislature and the judiciary.[42]

On the opposite end of the spectrum, examples can also be found of dynamic accounts of political constitutionalism. The clearest example can be found in the work of J. A. G. Griffith. Griffith also provides an account of how rights, which Griffith conceptualises as political claims, evolve over time, depending upon the extent to which these political claims are accepted as worthy of protection following political debate. In addition, the rules that constitute the institutions of government, and the relationship between the governed and the governors, are dynamic in nature. Interactions occur between the institutions of the constitution, including between the legislature and the judiciary. For Griffith, the constitution takes shape as a result of political upheavals and the battle between rival solutions to contentious issues, in a similar manner to the way in which legal 'rights' are recognised and protected following disputes between competing political claims.[43]

Accounts of dialogue, therefore, would appear to be unable to provide a stable theory of democratic dialogue. A requirement of dynamic interaction may be a necessary component of democratic dialogue, but it is not sufficient to distinguish democratic dialogue from other accounts of constitutionalism. Although a need for equality may be required for dialogue to work effectively and to produce legitimate outcomes, the potential confusion over how equality is meant to operate and concerns for the need for finality may exacerbate the inherent instability in accounts of democratic dialogue. In addition, it is hard to see how dialogue can combine the advantages and minimise the disadvantages of political and legal controls over human rights if both institutions merely talk past one another, or contribute to debate without taking account of the views of the other beyond respecting that these views come from a different institution of the constitution. However, as with our discussion of the connection between dialogue and the commonwealth model, debunking the myth of dialogue helps to provide a further means of refining our definition of democratic dialogue.

---

[42] See, in particular, T. R. S. Allan, *The Sovereignty of Law: Freedom, Constitution and the Common Law* (Oxford: Oxford University Press, 2013), chapter 3.

[43] See J. A. G. Griffith, 'The Political Constitution' (1979) 42 *Modern Law Review* 1; 'The Brave New World of Sir John Laws' (2000) 63 *The Modern Law Review* 159; and 'The Common Law and the Political Constitution' (2001) 117 *Law Quarterly Review* 42.

It is not the case that both the legislature and the judiciary need to play an equal role in dialogue about human rights. However, it is the case that no one institution should always be able to impose its solution on the other in all situations. In addition, although there needs to be this minimal element of equality, if dialogue is to combine the advantages and minimise the disadvantages of legal and political protections of rights, then the balance between the institutions, and the extent to which each may have the final word, will depend upon their relative ability to reach better or more legitimate conclusions as to the scope and application of human rights. This will depend upon the constitutional and institutional features of the legislature and the judiciary. From this, we can understand that democratic dialogue can serve two purposes: constitutional counterbalancing and constitutional collaboration. Constitutional counterbalancing is the means through which each institution is able to protect its constitutional role from erosion by the other institution. It aims to ensure that neither institution can always impose its definition of a right on the other. Constitutional collaboration aims to facilitate co-operation between the legislature and the judiciary. Rather than merely listening to the views of the other, constitutional collaboration occurs when each institution gives weight to the views of the other, given the relative ability of each to reason about rights.[44]

Further insight into constitutional counterbalancing and constitutional collaboration can be gleaned from the discussion of how dynamic interactions can occur in accounts of legal and political constitutionalism. Allan provides an account of interaction that focuses on values and the rule of law. Both the judiciary and the legislature aim to further the rule of law, but do so by drawing on their different constitutional roles and institutional features – hence legislatures are more able to facilitate social equality, and courts are better able to recognise when general rules, when applied in specific cases, fail to protect the values of the rule of law. Griffith, on the other hand, focuses more on conflict. Interest groups aim to promote their own interests and tensions between these interests eventually lead to resolution. Allan's account of dynamic interactions focuses on the aim of constitutional collaboration. Griffith's account of conflict and tension is more in line with the aim of constitutional counterbalancing. However, it is important to recognise the limits of this comparison. Constitutional counterbalancing is not designed to reach a

---

[44] For a more detailed discussion, see Young, above n 24, chapters 4 and 5.

particular outcome as to the scope of application of a human right. Rather, constitutional counterbalancing occurs to ensure that each institution has the ability to challenge instances where the other is trying to act in a manner beyond its proper constitutional role. In addition, the mechanisms can be used to prevent one institution from always ensuring its will prevails when determining the scope and application of a human right. In this sense, the aim of constitutional counterbalancing resembles what Nick Barber and I have referred to in the past as constitutional self-defence mechanisms.[45]

Our definition has moved from recognising that dialogue is a constitutional model, where dialogue can occur in legal systems that do and do not adopt a commonwealth model of rights protections, to explaining how inter-institutional interactions have two aims – constitutional collaboration and constitutional counterbalancing. However, if we are to provide a more complete account of democratic dialogue, we need to focus on one further myth; namely that democratic dialogue provides the best of both worlds, maximising the advantages and minimising the disadvantages of both legal and political protections of rights.

III From the Best of Both to a Plethora of Values and Mechanisms

It is not hard to find arguments in favour of the claim that democratic dialogue, or the commonwealth model of rights protection, provides a better protection of rights through combining the strengths and minimising the weaknesses of other models of rights protection. Hogg and Bushell explained how the ability of the legislature to respond to judicial determinations of rights casts doubt on the counter-majoritarian criticism of strong, constitutional protections of rights.[46] How can it be undemocratic to allow the courts to strike down legislation if the legislature has a chance to respond to these judgments? Gardbaum's argument in favour of the commonwealth model of rights protections focuses on its ability to provide a better protection of rights through combining the

---

[45] N. W. Barber and A. L. Young, 'The Rise of Prospective Henry VIII Clauses and Their Implications for Sovereignty' [2003] *Public Law* 112. See also, N. W. Barber, 'Self-Defence for Institutions' (2013) 72 *Cambridge Law Journal* 558, 559–564; P. Joseph, 'Parliament, the Courts, and the Collaborative Enterprise' (2004) 15(2) *King's College Law Journal* 321.

[46] P. W. Hogg, A. A. Bushell Thornton and W. K. Wright, 'Charter Dialogue Revisited: Or Much Ado about Metaphors' (2007) 45 *Osgoode Hall Law Journal* 75, 76, 102–103, and 105.

advantages and minimising the disadvantages of legal and political protections of rights.[47] A similar defence of democratic dialogue in the
UK constitution is found in the work of Tom Hickman, which draws
on the work of Bickel and Dicey to show how dialogue is designed not
just to provide for a stronger protection of human rights, but also to
reconcile the tension between rights and democracy.[48] Other accounts
focus on how proportionality review can be regarded as facilitating
dialogue, promoting Socratic dialogue,[49] or how aspects of commonwealth models may provide a means through which to protect dignatar-
ian conceptions of procedural fairness,[50] or to correct legislative blind
spots in the protection of rights.[51]

Our previous discussion has already suggested that the myth that
democratic dialogue or the commonwealth model of rights can provide
for a better protection of rights appears to collapse in practice. We
discussed examples of criticisms of how the commonwealth model of
rights protections in Canada and the United Kingdom appear, in practice, to provide the same protection as that found in a system with a
constitutional protection of rights, with no possibility of legislative
response or for the legislation to act notwithstanding human rights. This
already casts doubt on the extent to which dialogue can provide for a
better protection of rights. Further problems arise when we examine
these arguments in more detail. There is a commonality between theories
as to the relative institutional strength and constitutional merits of the
legislature and the judiciary when reasoning about human rights. In
particular, legislatures are regarded as better institutions to weigh up
competing interests, and as more legitimate institutions to evaluate these
competing interests. Courts, on the other hand, are regarded as better
institutions to determine rights and values, given their independence and
the way in which they reach conclusions through judicial reasoning.
Differences between theories of legal constitutionalism, which focus on

---

[47] Gardbaum, above n 2, pp. 51–61. See also the chapter by K. Roach in this volume.

[48] Hickman, above n 19, pp. 71–81.

[49] M. Kumm, 'Institutionalizing Socratic Contestation: The Rationalist Human Rights
Paradigm, Legitimate Authority and the Point of Judicial Review' (2007) 1 *European
Journal of Legal Studies* 153. See also, R. Fallon, 'The Core of an Uneasy Case for Judicial
Review' (2008) 121 *Harvard Law Review* 1693.

[50] A. Harel and A. Shinar, 'Between Judicial and Legislative Supremacy: A Cautious Defense
of Constrained Judicial Review' (2012) 10 *International Journal of Constitutional Law* 950.

[51] R. Dixon, 'The Core Case for Weak-Form Judicial Review' (2017) 38 *Cardozo Law
Review*, 2193.

providing courts with the ability to protect rights, and political constitutionalism, with a preference for a political protection of rights, tend to be more ones of degree or focus than examples of theories providing polar opposites. This makes it a hard job to find a clear middle ground for accounts of democratic dialogue to occupy.[52]

However, the problem of instability runs deeper. Some accounts of dialogue that do provide an account of the relative roles of the legislature and the courts in the protection of rights draw on arguments that have been used to advocate providing courts or legislatures with the last word in the protection of rights. Arguments focus on both constitutional legitimacy and the relative institutional competences of the legislature and the courts to reason about rights. Whilst an independent judiciary is deemed the legitimate institution to determine values, democratically composed and democratically accountable legislatures provide a more legitimate means through which to weigh competing interests and policies. This tends to suggest that the greater the contestable nature of the right, the greater the role of the legislature should be. Courts are regarded as a means through which to correct legislative pathologies, where majorities fail to pay sufficient attention to minority interests. Legislatures are the more legitimate means through which to develop policies, their role being to correct or prevent situations where courts inadvertently interfere with policy choices when performing their legitimate function of protecting legal rights.

In terms of relative institutional competence, legislatures are frequently regarded as better able to reason about rights more broadly as opposed to deciding the specific case before them. They are able to hear a wide variety of views, balancing a wide range of interests represented indirectly in the legislative body. The opposite is argued to be the case for courts, which are perceived as better able to determine when broad statutory provisions harm rights in their specific application, given their focus on the particular arguments of the parties before the court. Legislatures are regarded as better able to provide mechanisms to positively protect rights, for example, by establishing legislative or administrative mechanisms to ensure rights are protected, or to prevent discrimination. Courts, however, can only declare action unlawful. In addition, legislatures are better able to ensure rights are better protected in the future, being able to initiate legislation to protect rights. Courts look to past

---

[52] See Young, above n 24, chapter 1.

actions, correcting actions that breached rights. However, in doing so, courts may be better placed to ensure that legislation does not inadvertently override long-standing legal principles or long-standing human rights.[53] All of these arguments, however, resemble those used to argue for providing courts or legislatures with the final say in the protection of rights. There is no wonder, therefore, that accounts of dialogue appear to collapse in theory and in practice.

Gardbaum provides one of the clearest accounts of the relative strengths and weaknesses of legislatures and courts when reasoning about rights, which he then applies to his account of the components of the commonwealth model of rights protection. Legislatures can provide a better outcome because they can balance interests without the confines of legal doctrine and precedent and can take account of a broader range of interests than courts. In terms of their legitimacy, the democratic composition and accountability of legislatures means that they are a more legitimate means of evaluating competing rights and interests. However, legislatures are not as good as courts when it comes to protecting minority interests, which may get lost in the evaluation of competing mainstream interests. Also, when looking forward and providing broader protections of rights, legislatures may override long-standing principles, or may enact legislation that upholds rights when applied generally, but that nevertheless overrides rights in its specific application. These conclusions are reversed when we analyse the relative strengths and weaknesses of courts.[54]

These relative strengths and weaknesses of the legislature and courts when reasoning about rights are also found in other accounts. Hickman's work, for example, illustrates how similar concerns influenced Bickel's account of judicial minimalism, designed to respond to the counter-majoritarian criticism of strong constitutional protections of rights.[55] They also constitute a common theme found in accounts of legal constitutionalism, or arguments for a constitutional protection of rights, and in political constitutionalism, or arguments for a parliamentary protection of rights. Where disagreement arises, it can be found either in terms of the extent to which these arguments are reflected in reality; or as to the assumptions on

---

[53] Hickman, above n 19, chapter 3; and Gardbaum, above n 2, chapter 2.

[54] Gardbaum, above n 2, pp. 51–61.

[55] See Hickman, above n 19, drawing on A. M. Bickel, *The Least Dangerous Branch: the Supreme Court at the Bar of Politics* (Bobbs-Merrill, 1962), pp. 25–26; and A. M. Bickel, *The Supreme Court and the Idea of Progress* (Harper and Row, 1970), pp. 82, 177.

which arguments for a legal or a political protection of rights are based; or concerning mechanisms that are used to minimise the relative weaknesses of both legal and political protections of rights. Jeremy Waldron, for example, questions the extent to which courts focus on legal reasoning and the extent to which they are able to spot and correct problems that arise when legislation that complies with human rights in general nevertheless harms human rights in its specific application.[56] Richard Bellamy, who also advocates a political protection of rights, questions the extent to which legislatures override minority interests, arguing that any majority found in a legislature is often composed of an amalgamation of minority interests.[57] Both are questioning the evidence on which arguments in favour of legal or political protections of rights are based. The answer to these criticisms does not lie in making broad generalisations. Rather, it requires us to focus much more specifically on the institutional features of legislatures and courts in any particular legal system.

Waldron's defence of a predominantly political as opposed to legal protection of rights is also based on the adoption of different assumptions. Waldron famously bases his argument against a constitutional protection of rights, where courts can strike down legislation that contravenes human rights, on a series of four assumptions. First, he assumes that a particular legal society has democratic institutions that operate in a reasonably good manner, facilitating representative democracy with a sufficient protection of political equality and a suitably broadly composed electorate, and democratic institutions with a good standard of deliberation. Second, he assumes the same of the judiciary, with this entailing a sufficiently strong protection of the independence of the judiciary, where the judiciary settles disputes through the application of legal principles. Third, Waldron assumes that there is a broad commitment to the protection of human rights amongst officials in the legal system. Fourth, Waldron assumes that there is persistent and substantial good-faith agreement about the scope and application of human rights.[58]

Richard Fallon's justification of a constitutional protection of rights is also based on the same four assumptions used by Waldron. However, he adds in a further assumption: that it is better for rights to be

---

[56] J. Waldron, 'The Core of the Case against Judicial Review' (2006) 115 *Yale Law Journal* 1346, 1360, 1382–1386.

[57] R. Bellamy, *Political Constitutionalism: A Republican Defence of the Constitutionality of Democracy* (Cambridge: Cambridge University Press, 2007).

[58] Waldron, above n 56, 1360–1367.

overprotected as opposed to under-protected. To this he adds the assumption that courts are better able to determine some errors that may be made by legislatures – focusing specifically on how courts can determine when legislation that generally protects human rights nevertheless fails to protect human rights in its specific application. It may be the case that to provide courts with the power to strike down legislation that breaches human rights may lead to an overprotection of rights. However, if we believe that this is a price worth paying, because it is better than the situation that arises when rights are under-protected, then there is a justification for adopting a legal system that empowers courts to have the final say in the protection of human rights.[59]

In reaching this conclusion, Fallon recognises that there may be situations in which his argument would not justify empowering the courts to have the final say when determining human rights. First, he recognises that legal systems may adopt different hierarchies of rights. In legal systems where the right to vote is seen as more important than any other right, for example, there would be a justification for providing legislatures with the final say in rights determinations.[60] Second, Fallon also argues that his assumption that it is better to overprotect rather than under-protect human rights does not apply to 'zero-sum controversies' – i.e., those situations in which human rights are balanced against each other, such that providing a stronger protection of one right results in a weaker protection of the other right.[61] This is the case, for example, when determining the extent to which newspapers can report on the lives of celebrities, where a stronger protection of the right to privacy would lead to a weaker protection of the right to freedom of expression and vice versa. When we apply this reflection to Waldron's argument in favour of a political protection of rights, it seems easy to conclude that these differences explain why Waldron and Fallon reach opposite conclusions. Is Waldron merely recognising that the right to vote is more fundamental and that, in his experience, there are more zero-sum controversies?

Another way of accounting for this disagreement is to recognise that Waldron's and Fallon's arguments are distinguished from one another merely in terms of their perspective. Mark Tushnet reaches this conclusion.[62]

---

[59] Fallon, above n 49.
[60] Ibid. 1712.
[61] Ibid. 1712–1713.
[62] M. Tushnet, 'How Different Are Waldron's and Fallon's Core Cases For and against Judicial Review?' (2010) 30 *Oxford Journal of Legal Studies* 49.

He argues that theorists from a background of legal constitutionalism, with a constitutional protection of rights, start with the presumption that this protection of rights is justified, but recognise the need for this to be modified due to the counter-majoritarian nature of allowing the non-democratically composed and non-democratically accountable judiciary to strike down legislation. Theorists from a background of political constitutionalism, or systems with a more political protection of rights, reason from a different starting point. They assume that a political protection of rights is justified, but that this may need to be defended from criticisms that this form of protection of rights fails to protect minority interests, or may undermine long-standing constitutional principles.

This leads to the suspicion that normative accounts of legal and political constitutionalism blur into one another. They may reach similar conclusions from different starting points, thereby leaving no clear middle ground for an account of democratic dialogue to occupy. It is no surprise, therefore, if accounts of dialogue or commonwealth models of rights protections appear to collapse in practice. This suspicion is furthered when we look at accounts of legal and political constitutionalism. There is no pure theory of legal or political constitutionalism. Rather, as illustrated by our discussion of the dynamic accounts of legal and political constitutionalism illustrated by Allan and Griffith, both recognise that the legislature and judiciary play a role in protecting rights, although the roles are different.

What our analysis of those accounts of legal and political constitutionalism also demonstrates is that the way in which interactions between the legislature and the judiciary occur is different. Griffith, for example, focuses on interactions where both institutions protect rights through a strong assertion of interests, in a manner similar to the account of dialogue favoured by Nicol.[63] Allan, however, focuses on how courts define rights in a manner that, albeit focusing on the nature of the right, nevertheless recognises that some rights can be facilitated through a range of policy choices, whereas other rights place more restrictions on legitimate policy choices. Both Allan and Griffith recognise that different

---

[63] As discussed earlier in the chapter, Griffith regarded 'rights' as political claims. I am referring to 'rights' here for ease of reference. This is not to argue that Griffith believed in rights. Rather, it is to recognised that the 'rights' that may have been protected as 'legal human rights' would have been determined through political means, a choice between different claims from different groups arguing for the protection of their interests as legally recognised and legally enforced rights.

institutional features of the legislature and the courts may make them more suited to different forms of decision-making, and may interact in the protection of rights. However, how these interactions occur differs. Whilst Allan does not advocate deference, he does recognise that rights can be defined with greater or lesser precision, depending on the nature of the right. The more precise the determination of the right, the smaller the range of legitimate policy choices that can be made by the legislature without contravening this right. The less precise the definition, the greater the role of the legislature in choosing between policy determinations that do not breach the human right as defined by the courts, providing the legislature with the opportunity of further refining the definition of the right.[64] Griffith, on the other hand, argues that both legislatures and courts should define rights as strongly as possible, seeing these rights as merely assertions of different interests.[65] Both institutions play a role in determining rights – but a different role from that advocated by Allan.

Having questioned the myth that democratic dialogue can occupy a middle ground between legal and political constitutionalism, or gain its unique nature through advocating that both legislatures and the courts play a role in the protection of human rights, we need to use these criticisms to reinvent our conception of dialogue. This is achieved in three ways. First, accounts of democratic dialogue have a different focus than, or starting point from, accounts of legal or political constitutionalism. Theories of democratic dialogue focus on interactions between the institutions rather than focusing predominantly on either the role of the legislature or of the judiciary. Second, accounts of democratic dialogue look to when interactions can facilitate the promotion of values in the constitution. Third, accounts of democratic dialogue focus on mechanisms of inter-institutional interactions, examining which mechanisms are more or less suited to achieving these normative objectives in different constitutions. It is these aspects that give rise to the final section of our definition of democratic dialogue:

> It explains how inter-institutional interactions may facilitate the values underpinning democratic dialogue – a better protection of human rights, the facilitation of deliberative and participatory democracy, as well as how interactions may act as a means of checks and balance between institutions and of avoiding and resolving constitutional crises. The way in

[64] Allan, above n 42, particularly chapters 1 and 3.
[65] Griffith, 'The Political Constitution', above n 43.

which these aims interact, and the mechanisms through which these aims can be facilitated, depends upon and draws upon the different constitutional powers and institutional features of the legislature and judiciary in a particular legal system, applying differently to distinct types of human rights and applying in a manner that is sensitive to path-dependent behavioural choices.

The main objective of democratic dialogue is to promote a better protection of rights, with 'better' being understood both in terms of reaching better outcomes and in terms of providing a more legitimate protection of rights. However, democratic dialogue may also facilitate the achievement of other values. For example, interactions between the legislature and the judiciary may facilitate deliberation. This may occur both through the way in which the judiciary can facilitate deliberation through its own reasoning, and in prompting legislatures to engage with values and evaluating evidence when responding to judicial determinations.[66] Moreover, these deliberations can facilitate participatory democracy in society more broadly, as the general public discusses legal decisions, legislation, and legislative responses to judicial determinations of rights.[67] In addition, inter-institutional interactions can provide a more legitimate means of avoiding conflict or resolving potential constitutional crises. Each institution can exercise the powers it has been given in a particular constitutional settlement. When doing so, it is aware that the other institution has a means of responding to its determinations, both in order to aid the other institution to work together to provide a better protection of rights, and also to defend its own area of decision-making, should this be intruded upon by the other institution. This anticipation of possible reaction by the other institution may mean that each institution is inclined to respect its proper constitutional role, acting in a manner to avoid conflicts between institutions. These interactions may also allow for checks and balances between the powers of the legislature and the court to evolve over time.

The mechanisms used to facilitate dialogue may depend upon the way in which different legal systems protect rights. In the United Kingdom, for example, theorists focus on when courts should use section 3 or

---

[66] Fredman, above n 7; and C. Sunstein, 'If People Would Be Outraged by Their Rulings, Should Judges Care?' (2007) 60 *Stanford Law Review* 155.

[67] See, for example, L. Fisher, *Constitutional Dialogues: Interpretation as a Political Process* (Princeton: Princeton University Press, 1988); and L. Fisher and N. Devins *The Democratic Constitution* (Oxford: Oxford University Press, 2004).

section 4 of the Human Rights Act 1998. However, accounts of democratic dialogue can also provide generalisations as to the type of mechanism that is more or less likely to facilitate democratic dialogue in a range of legal systems. For example, constitutional collaboration is more likely to be facilitated when courts and legislatures provide transparent and reasoned justifications for their conclusions as to the scope and application of a particular right. In addition, constitutional collaboration is more likely to be facilitated when both institutions are able to give weight to the conclusions of the other, the weight to be given depending on their relative ability to reason about rights and on evidence of each institution having reasoned about rights in a manner suited to their relative constitutional powers and institutional features. Constitutional counterbalancing, however, is different in nature. This should only be used in those situations in which one institution believes that the other has transgressed the proper sphere of its constitutional powers.[68]

IV   Conclusion

This chapter has aimed to redefine democratic dialogue in the light of recent criticisms. Rather than undermine the criticisms, the chapter challenges some of the myths of dialogue, using these to build a clearer, if more complex, account of democratic dialogue. The work in this chapter provides an account of democratic dialogue at an abstract level. This is deliberate. If democratic dialogue is to work effectively, its precise application needs to be refined in the light of the legal system in which it is applied. Two general factors influence its application. First, any account of democratic dialogue must relate to the particular constitutional division of power between the legislature and the judiciary and their institutional features. This is not only to ensure that applications of democratic dialogue do not contradict the separation of powers, as understood in a particular legal system, but also to recognise that officials in the legal-system work within path-dependent parameters. An account of dialogue that only achieves its objectives through requiring legislatures and courts to act differently from their usual patterns of behaviour may not succeed unless an incentive can be provided for inducing changes in behaviour. Second, democratic dialogue applies differently depending on the extent to which there exist genuine disagreements about rights in

[68] Young, above n 24, chapters 4 and 5.

different societies, in addition to the nature of the right to which an account of dialogue is being applied.

Nevertheless, despite the abstract nature of this account, it may still provide some insight into some of the criticisms made of the application of commonwealth models of rights protection. First, an understanding of the difference between constitutional collaboration and constitutional counterbalancing can help to explain some of the criticisms of the commonwealth model. The application of the Charter in Canada, for example, has been criticised because there is little use of the notwithstanding clause. However, the lack of use of the notwithstanding clause is understandable when we recognise that this mechanism of inter-institutional interaction is more likely to facilitate constitutional counterbalancing than it is to facilitate constitutional collaboration. The aim of the clause is to empower legislatures to act in a manner that exempts legislation from the Charter.[69] It is, understandably, regarded as hard to use in a legitimate manner, exacerbated by the example of some of its earlier applications by legislatures in Québec and Alberta. However, when we view this clause as predominantly designed to facilitate constitutional counterbalancing, we can see that the clause is legitimately used only in circumstances where the legislature strongly believes that the judiciary has overstepped the proper constitutional limits of its powers. In a legal system with a written constitution setting out the limits of the power of the judiciary and the legislature, this is unlikely to occur frequently.[70] Moreover, it is harder to justify claims that an institution has overstepped the proper limits of its constitutional power when there is a constitutional text that can provide legitimacy, as opposed to the UK constitution, where such assertions have fewer legal texts on which to base themselves. To recognise that the notwithstanding clause is used infrequently, therefore, is not conclusive proof that dialogue is not working. Rather, it is to recognise that the notwithstanding clause is not the main engine that produces dialogue in the Charter – this being found through applications of proportionality instead. Moreover, the inter-institutional interactions that occur through modifications in the

---

[69] For another understanding of the notwithstanding clause, See D. Newman's chapter in this volume.

[70] See A. L. Young, 'Exporting Dialogue: Critical Reflections on Canada's Commonwealth Model of Human Rights Protections' in R. Albert and D. Cameron (eds) *Canada in the World: Comparative Perspectives on the Canadian Constitution* (Cambridge: Cambridge University Press, 2017), p. 305.

stringency with which the test of proportionality is applied are more likely to facilitate constitutional collaboration, focusing more on combining the relative strengths and weaknesses of the legislature and the courts to provide a better protection of rights.

Second, our new definition of democratic dialogue recognises the need for sensitivity to the nature of the right to which an account of dialogue is applied. This sensitivity can help us to understand some of the criticisms of the application of dialogue in Canada, New Zealand and the United Kingdom in the area of prisoner voting rights.[71] Criticisms are made of Canada's decisions on prisoner voting in *Sauvé I*[72] and *Sauvé II*.[73] The Supreme Court concluded that the legislation allowing only those prisoners serving sentences of less than two years to vote breached the right to vote in the Canadian Charter. Should the courts have been more lenient, recognising that the legislature had taken account of its concerns in the *Sauvé I* decision and had reached a determination that balanced competing social interests and policies? Or was the court right to focus on the key importance of the right to vote, underpinning a democratic society? Rather than seeing these cases as an example where dialogue breaks down, the cases can also be regarded as an example of the court ensuring that fundamentally important rights are protected, the right to vote having more importance in a legal system that adopts a commonwealth model of rights, given that the adoption of this model is designed to ensure that democracy – which requires a strong protection of the right to vote – is not undermined by judicial determinations of rights. In addition, the protection of the right to vote may be more fundamental, as the commonwealth model of rights protections, like Waldron's argument against the constitutional protection of rights, rests on the assumption that the society in which it is applied has a legislature working in a reasonably good order, including one that has a broad franchise.

This may also explain the particularly strong criticism of the UK's lack of modification of its general ban on prisoner voting, in the face of judicial determinations of both UK courts and the European Court of Human Rights. This is particularly so, given that the defence of refusing prisoners the right to vote appears to be based more on arguments of

---

[71] For an overview of the significant cases on prisoner voting rights, see J. Finnis's chapter in this volume. For a comparative analysis, and an evaluation of its application to dialogue, see Young, above n 24, chapter 1.

[72] *Sauvé v. Canada (Attorney General) (Sauvé I)* [1993] 2 SCR 438.

[73] *Sauvé v. the Attorney General of Canada (Sauvé II)* [2002] 3 SCR 519.

populism than reasoned debate. In addition, we can begin to understand the problems faced in New Zealand, where the Supreme Court developed the declaration of inconsistency in the light of legislation removing all prisoners from the franchise.[74] Given the lack of such power in the New Zealand Bill of Rights Act 1990, the development of the declaration of inconsistency may be regarded as beyond the constitutional powers of the court. On the other hand, the court may have regarded the legislation as transgressing the powers of the legislature, given its contravention of the rights protected in the 1990 Act, justifying a strong reaction given the importance of the right to vote.[75]

This chapter does not in and of itself provide a particular justification for the previous examples. However, it aims to cast light on how we evaluate these examples and myths. If we are to move on, we need to recognise that democratic dialogue is complex and that the reliance on overly simplistic myths – either to support or destroy dialogue – will not suffice. We should not abandon democratic dialogue as fruitless. Rather, we need to recognise that it is complex, but may nevertheless offer a new lens through which to evaluate constitutional protections of rights, as well as constitutions more generally.

---

[74] *Attorney General v Taylor* [2018] NZSC 104.

[75] See A. Geddis 'Prisoner Voting and Consistency with the New Zealand Bill of Rights Act' [2016] *Public Law* 352.

3

Departmentalism and Dialogue

JACOB T. LEVY

Under the constitutional order of the French *ancien régime*, the thirteen *parlements* – aristocratic courts of appeals in twelve provinces and in Paris – served as what the eighteenth-century theorist the Baron de Montesquieu described as the "depository of the laws." In order to fulfill their judicial functions, they held records of the laws applicable within their jurisdictions – no simple task given the patchwork of customary law, Roman civil law, canon law, municipal law, manorial law, mercantile law, and so on that made up late medieval and early modern French law. New sources of law, including royal edicts, accordingly also needed to be deposited with the *parlements* and recorded into the body of the law.

The *parlements,* particularly the Parisian court, gradually successfully asserted the authority to issue a formal remonstrance against royal edicts that could not be made to fit with the overall legal order. Under a presumption that monarchs guarded the traditional laws and liberties of their subjects, official legal innovation was suspect. This much was not unique to France; an early modern canon of construction in England held that statutes in derogation of the common law were to be strictly construed, as though the monarch-in-Parliament could not *really* intend to change the common law, even when doing so was evidently the purpose of legislation. The French case differed from the English in several ways, though. One was the formal character of the court's action: not a narrowing of the new law by interpretation or construction, but a rejection. Judicial interpretation in the common law sense lay outside the *parlements'* authority, but they had the power to refuse to enter new law onto the law books at all. The second was the political and constitutional weight of the cases in which remonstrances were applied. The common law rule affected Parliament's ability to reform the private law, but the *parlements* often (and especially in the eighteenth century) remonstrated against changes in the public law over such fundamental matters as taxation and public finance. This was especially true during the century and a half just before the French Revolution when the Estates-General were in abeyance. The *parlements* repeatedly claimed that certain kinds of fundamental change in the basic law of the kingdom could only be made by legislation of the Estates, not by simple royal edict.

And the third difference was the remarkable procedure that followed a remonstrance. The king might first reply with a *lettre de jussion,* perhaps modifying the edict, perhaps not, but in any event ordering its registration; the courts could reply with successive remonstrances. The monarch's final tool was the *lit de justice:* a personal appearance in the *parlement* during which he would read the edict into the record, brooking no disagreement. Whether matters de facto remained settled once the king left the chamber varied over the decades, as the balance of power between throne and nobility shifted. But typically the *lit de justice* would end the legal dispute over at least the particular edict at issue.

There is good reason to think of the *parlements* and their remonstrances as part of the ancestry of the modern institution of judicial review. Montesquieu served on the *parlement* of Bordeaux early in his career, and while he seems not to have enjoyed the work, the institution left its mark on his thinking. In *The Spirit of the Laws* decades later he accorded the *parlements* special importance: the site in which aristocratic vanity and attachment to privilege was channeled into the rule of law and constitutional checks on would-be absolute kings.[1] This seemed to inform his strange reconstruction of the English constitution as one that observed a separation among three fundamental powers: executive, legislative, and judicial. This vision of the English constitution's separation of powers and its tight association with liberty as a fundamental value in turn deeply affected American thought of the revolutionary and founding eras. At a time when both de facto and (in William Blackstone's hands) doctrinal British constitutionalism was shifting in the direction of Parliamentary absolutism, American thought remained committed to a judicial role in ensuring the conformity of new laws to fundamental law.

It is not novel – somewhat controversial, yes, but not novel – to identify this much long-term legacy of the *parlementaires* and their struggles against the crown in the seventeenth and eighteenth centuries. I will not defend this historical narrative here.[2] But I do not think the

---

[1] Charles de Secondat Baron de Montesquieu, *The Spirit of the Laws* (Cambridge: Cambridge University Press, 1989).

[2] I have said somewhat more in its defense in 'Montesquieu's Constitutional Legacies' in Rebecca E. Kingston, (ed.), *Montesquieu and His Legacy* (Albany: State University of New York Press, 2010).

relevance of this history has been noted for the debates in Canadian and Commonwealth constitutionalism over the last few decades. If the *parlements* exercised a power of judicial review, it was not what we have come to think of as the "strong form" of judicial review *cum* judicial supremacy associated with the US system. They argued; the king argued back; they argued some more; sometimes the king would appear in person to insist that his edict be made law notwithstanding the court's objection. This looks less like the American model than like the iterative Canadian process that has served as the paradigmatic case in our modern metaphor of constitutional dialogue.

The kind of dialogue that is foregrounded in contemporary constitutional theory is more metaphorical and less literal than that suggested by the *lit de justice*. As Hogg famously described it, "Where a judicial decision is open to legislative reversal, modification, or avoidance, then it is meaningful to regard the relationship between the Court and the competent legislative body as a dialogue. In that case, the judicial decision causes a public debate in which Charter values play a more prominent role than they would if there had been no judicial decision."[3] Different branches lay out arguments in public; legislators and prime ministers do not appear in person in court to make their replies to charges of unconstitutional action. On the other hand, the *lit de justice* involved no conversational give-and-take, even though it took place in person. So, like the modern processes, French ancient constitutional dialogue (if we are to think of it that way) really depended on iterative, asynchronous actions and statements by official actors occupying different institutional roles. They might learn from each other's public statements about each other's demands, limits, and boundaries of tolerance. And the argument might not only be *in* public, that is, in the open, but also *before* the public, that is, aiming to sway the inchoate but powerful constitutional judge that is public opinion. Neither then nor now do we find much possibility for the kind of direct speaking and listening that characterizes dialogue in normal settings.

I take this history, and the connection to constitutional dialogue, to be suggestive of at least three possible lessons.

First, a constitutional dialogue or an iterative process of judicial review does not *necessarily* make the system as a whole more democratic. At best,

---

[3] Peter W. Hogg and Allison A. Bushell, 'The Charter Dialogue between Courts and Legislatures (Or Perhaps the Charter of Rights Isn't Such a Bad Thing After All)' (1997) 35 *Osgoode Hall Law Journal* 75.

its democratic character rises or falls with the democratic credentials of the relevant non-judicial branches, and so is a matter of degree. The idea of a public exchange of reasons has gradually come to be treated as tightly connected with democracy – especially but not only among so-called deliberative democrats – and as connected with republican freedom by contemporary neo-republicans such as Philip Pettit, Richard Bellamy, and (in this volume, with some qualifications) Geoffrey Sigalet. But kings and aristocrats can just as easily exchange reasons and arguments as elected officials. When we take seriously the elite character of all branches of government in a large modern state and the general incoherence or unavailability of anything like a unified popular will on most subjects, the counter-pluralitarian dilemma – the potential threat to democracy posed by non-electorally accountable institutions overturning decisions made by institutions representing political pluralities and coalitions of minorities – will loom less large, but metaphorical interbranch dialogues will also seem less like a decisive, transformative solution to it.[4]

Second, the iterative process of public argument could be interesting and consequential, even though one of the actors appears to have a way to assert finality. Only Louis XIV ever really succeeded in closing off the right of remonstrance, and it was quickly reasserted upon his death. The availability of the *lit de justice* did not ultimately suffice to allow Louis XV or XVI to impose financial reforms over *parlementaire* opposition. Through iterative remonstrances, the *parlements* were sometimes able to swing public opinion to their side even though they were widely seen as bastions of both religious intolerance and aristocratic privilege. This matters in light of the influential charge that constitutional dialogue in Canada has been shown to be a sham, a thin veil over the reality of judicial supremacy – or, on the other hand, the charge that the notwith-standing clause effectively destroys the substance of judicial review.[5]

And finally, features of Canadian or Commonwealth constitutionalism that have been taken to be characteristically dialogic might not be as unusual or distinctive as is often thought. They might be typical, which could either lead us to dethrone strong-form judicial review as the

---

[4] I will explain this choice of terminology in greater depth later in the chapter.
[5] See, perhaps most famously, Christopher P. Manfredi, 'The Day the Dialogue Died? A Comment on *Sauvé* v. *Canada*' (2007) 45 *Osgoode Hall Law Journal* 105. See also Emmett Macfarlane, 'Dialogue or Compliance? Measuring Legislatures' Policy Responses to Court Rulings on Rights' (2012) 34(1) *International Political Science Review* 39; and Christopher P. Manfredi and James B. Kelley, 'Six Degrees of Dialogue: A Response to Hogg and Bushell' (1999) 37(3) *Osgoode Hall Law Journal* 513.

presumed default or baseline, or could lead us to look more closely at whether systems that we think of as strong-form actually share these features.

If all of this is right, then it suggests that constitutional interpretation through interbranch dialogue is somewhat broader than the literature about that metaphor has often taken it to be. To see this, consider the relationship between dialogue and the tradition in American constitutional thought referred to as "departmentalism."

I Departmentalism

Departmentalism at its basic level refers to the idea that the coordinate branches in the American constitutional order – executive, legislative, and judicial – each have an independent duty to obey and uphold the Constitution, which means that each has its own duty to interpret it. That is, it denies judicial uniqueness or supremacy in the task of constitutional interpretation, in favor of the idea that, at least sometimes, the executive and the legislature must work out their own understanding of what is constitutionally forbidden, permitted, or required. The president who has sworn his own oath to the Constitution bears his own responsibility to fulfill that oath according to his own best understanding and conscience, not merely to obey the understandings and consciences of five out of nine justices. A legislature enacting a law based on its own understanding of the rights that are implicated and the values that are at stake confronts a judiciary that weighs them differently, and does not give way.

Departmentalism, like dialogue, is something less determinate than a doctrine or even a fully developed theory. Both were developed by commentators and scholarly observers as a way to draw out, tie together, and emphasize some practices of constitutional interpretation, construction, and politics. The ideas are simultaneously descriptive and prescriptive, aiming to make sense of things that official actors have already said and done, and to show that they can be understood as part of an attractive ongoing model of constitutional engagement. Departmentalists and dialogists both insist that the judiciary is not the sole proprietor, guardian, or interpreter of the constitution. The legislature also has its responsibilities to discharge on questions of constitutional principle. The emphasis is different, because the two traditions seek to overcome different initial presumptions. Departmentalism is a response to strong-form American judicial review or judicial supremacy, and so it stresses the independent responsibility of legislatures and (especially) executives. The dialogue metaphor developed as a way to think about judicial review in a political culture that was still not quite used to it, to legitimize it against Westminsterian worries about the counter-pluralitarian difficulty.

I think that, as traditionally construed, departmentalist and dialogic understandings of interbranch constitutional engagement diverge when we consider *impasses:* what ultimately happens when the branches disagree?

Weak departmentalism, which simply calls on legislators and executives to exercise their own constitutional judgment in *refraining from* the use of their power, perhaps engenders no stand-offs: the Court interprets a grant of congressional power broadly, but members of Congress in their independent judgment disagree, and so refrain from passing a law they think useful but outside their authority. A president vetoes a law he thinks unconstitutional; a governor grants clemency on the grounds that a punishment has been excessive, even though a competent court did not find an Eighth Amendment violation. This much departmentalism should be uncontroversial, though disappointingly and perhaps surprisingly it is not.

But invocations of departmentalism normally suggest something stronger and more controversial than that: an authority to *affirmatively* act in the face of judicial opposition, a refusal by legislatures or (again, especially) executives to accept judicial constitutional judgments as final. In some of the strongest assertions of departmentalism, we have found American executives arguing that Supreme Court interpretations of the Constitution not only did not bind the president but indeed could be limited to the case immediately at hand, and need not bind lower courts in other cases with other parties.[6]

And this means at least the possibility of an impasse of legitimacy, settled in the long run by some combination of events and opinion: election returns, new Supreme Court appointments, or a civil war. An impasse is not the only available result, of course. As Mariah Zeisberg has shown,[7] the possibility of constitutionally informed antagonism between branches is complemented by the possibility of constitutionally informed

---

[6] This is aptly named 'Lincoln–Meese departmentalism' for its two most famous exponents, in Kevin C. Walsh, 'Judicial Departmentalism: An Introduction' (2016) 58 *William & Mary Law Review* 1713.

[7] Mariah Zeisberg, *War Powers: The Politics of Constitutional Authority* (Princeton: Princeton University Press, 2013) – one of the finest elaborations of what departmentalism can mean as a sustained practice.

cooperation. Similarly, Keith Whittington has argued that presidential departmentalist challenges to the Supreme Court have been more constructive and specific than one might think, aiming to argue against particular judicial doctrines rather than to assert general and arbitrary presidential power.[8]

But the possible standoff is, I think, a precondition of the possible productive cooperation. Congress's ability to sometimes *refuse* to legitimize executive-driven foreign policy decisions means that the president must engage with Congress rather than ignore it. And the looming threat of an Andrew-Jackson-style executive action in the face of judicial prohibition, or an Abraham-Lincoln-style marginalization of the judiciary, is what gives a president leverage when he confronts a court.

II   Dialogue and Impasses

The dialogical model of judicial review as it has generally been understood seems quite different. In the paradigmatic Canadian case, the judiciary strikes down a piece of legislation as violating Charter rights. The legislature is then faced with choices: (1) let the ruling stand and the legislation fall; (2) pass new legislation within the prescribed timeframe that repairs the constitutional faults as the court has identified them; (3) pass legislation "notwithstanding" the conflict under section 33; or (4) pass new legislation that does not meet the court's standard, arguing under section 1 that it is reasonable and demonstrably justified. For the most part, (1) or (2) is chosen, with (3) being famously rare outside Quebec, and since 1987 even within that province. (1) and (2) are legislative *compliance*: the court speaks, and the legislature listens. Some prominent critics[9] have argued that the word "dialogue" is out of place there. Choice (3) does not offer much dialogue either, any more than the similarly unused power of jurisdiction-stripping in the US Constitution does: the judiciary speaks, and the legislature shuts it up.

Those three options all offer clear resolutions without any need for long public debate, and they involve no real pushing and pulling back-and-forth between branches. The very messiness of a departmentalist standoff, so departmentalists hope, calls forth a public argument on the question at hand. This seems to be what Abraham Lincoln called for in

---

[8] Keith E. Whittington, 'Presidential Challenges to Judicial Supremacy and the Politics of Constitutional Meaning' (2001) 33(3) *Polity* 365.

[9] See Manfredi and Kelley, above n 5; Macfarlane, above n 5.

his famous appeals to departmentalism: let us not give the *Dred Scott* court the last word on slavery, let us not yet treat that question as settled, let us keep debating and contesting and voting on it as a matter of principle. But (1), (2), and (3) *all* effectively grant the Court the last word on the meaning of the Charter. The notwithstanding clause's authorization of legislation is *not* "notwithstanding a judgment of the court" but *notwithstanding a conflict with the Charter.*[10] Invoking the clause means *conceding* the existence of the conflict. And in all three cases, the path to settlement is clear, and does not run through any election or any more public debate than accompanies any other piece of legislation.

None of this is a reason to prefer one model to the other; clear rules of settlement are an advantage for some purposes and perhaps a disadvantage for others. But it is a reason not to assimilate the dialogue model as it has generally been understood, and its normative reconstruction of the post-1982 Canadian constitutional order, with the departmentalist critique of American judicial supremacy.

The fourth possibility – a section 1 rather than a section 33 response, in terms of the Canadian Charter – is the one that leaves open the possibility of constitutional dialogue. The question is whether this possibility for the most part collapses into one of the other three. If the legislature genuinely has a different account or weighing of the section 1 values at stake, what does it mean for the legislature to listen and respond to the judiciary's account? If it passes new legislation that is incompatible with the court's ruling – as is arguably the case in the Canadian government's replacement of its struck-down prostitution legislation – then what? In the prostitution case, we don't yet know, but it seems likely enough that a court will strike the new legislation down, in which case we seem to be back at (1) or (2), in which the judiciary's monologue is all that matters. If the revised legislation stands in the face of the conflict with the court's ruling, the difficulty is to distinguish the outcome from a section 33 "notwithstanding" override and legislative supremacy. The dialogic needle to thread is to show that the legislation is a) meaningfully different from the legislature's initial preferences, in ways that are responsive to the reasons offered by the court and b) supported by section 1 reasons that the court learns about in light of the legislature's debates and justifications, to which the court is

---

[10] But see Dwight Newman, 'Canada's Notwithstanding Clause, Dialogue, and Constitutional Identifies' in this volume.

responsive in turn. Critics have offered empirical reason to doubt that the needle is threaded in this way relevantly frequently, though others of course disagree.

III   Do Impasses Matter?

Part of what I mean to suggest by calling attention to the *ancien régime* history of the *parlements* is that these problems of impasses and finality need not be fatal to the idea of constitutional dialogue. Relations between *parlement* and crown were indeed marked by impasses when it was not formally clear whose interpretation should carry the day, as when relatively strong *parlements* issued new remonstrances on the same topic after a *lit de justice*. And they were marked by episodes of finality that are incompatible with genuine conversation: not only a *lit de justice* itself, but sometimes a royal suspension or dismissal of a *parlement*. In these respects they call to mind either departmentalism or the failed dialogue identified in Canada by critics of the dialogue metaphor. And yet over the years, the exchanges between courts and crown unquestionably found an audience, and shaped opinion – learned opinion, jurists' opinion, and ultimately public opinion. And the opinions thus formed about constitutional legitimacy genuinely constrained political actors, up to and including forcing Louis XVI to summon the Estates-General.

Politics is persuasion as well as coercion, and even the most formally absolute political actors depend on other actors' perceptions about legitimacy. This was true even before the rise of mass literacy, newspapers, and "public opinion" as that came to be understood in the eighteenth century; it was true of powerful elite actors monitoring one another. But since the eighteenth century, even in undemocratic regimes, public opinion has always been one important audience for debates about legitimacy. Often, if at unpredictable moments, it has been the *most* important audience. This means that formal institutional finality is not always the end of the story, and apparent impasses between institutions, neither of which can decisively overrule the other, can still be in some sense resolved. And the exchanges of reasons and arguments between those institutions and actors can be part of that process of opinion formation, even if reasons are offered in bad faith and bad temper, even if they never genuinely respond to the reasons offered by the other side, and so on. There can still be something meaningfully like dialogue.

And this is something like what departmentalism has been in practice, most of the time. Andrew Jackson's message on the veto of the Second

Bank of the United States, and Abraham Lincoln's speech on *Dred Scott*, probably the two most important statements of departmentalism, were arguments presented to the public – arguments not only about the extent of judicial power, but also about the underlying constitutional question. We often describe departmentalism as the idea that the judiciary does not have the final word on the meaning of the US Constitution. That is partly a way of saying that it does not have unique and supreme *power* on constitutional questions, but it is also a way of saying something about *words,* about the ability of debate to carry on. Lincoln's speech in particular stands out as acknowledging a kind of long-run pride of place for settled judicial doctrines, while arguing that a fractured bare majority of the court in one case was not the same thing, and that it allowed for argument, contestation, and institutional pushback. This is a dialogue without the clear back-and-forth institutional tennis match Hogg idealized from the Canadian case – legislature, court, legislature, court – but by the same token it helps us see that constitutional dialogue before the public need not be so structured, and might continue even when the immediate case has been authoritatively settled.

Zeisberg's and Whittington's reconstructions of departmentalism help to mitigate a longstanding worry: that departmentalism in theory is untrammeled executive power in practice. Departmentalism in American constitutional history has most often been articulated by presidents, and indeed by particularly strong presidents with particularly expansive visions of their own power. This is grounds for serious worry. Whatever the merits of the Jeremy Waldron/Richard Bellamy-style defense of *legislative* authority against judicial supremacy, judicial review of *executive* action is a core feature of the rule of law, as we have known since Montesquieu if not Coke and the writ of *habeas corpus*. I am not sure that the worry should go away, and it has perhaps been aggravated in recent decades by the gradual transfer of rulemaking authority from legislatures to executives (in Westminster systems too, but especially in the United States). When American presidents are deciding on the constitutionality of their own authority to hold people indefinitely without trial or prisoner-of-war status, whether in Guantanamo or in border enforcement detention centers; when they are deciding on the constitutionality of their own authority to order torture or to commit assassinations by drone strikes or to pardon themselves, the challenge to the rule of law and constitutionalism is severe. And the fact that Lincoln's departmentalism extended to his own suspension of the writ of *habeas corpus* counts as a deep and dangerous precedent in American departmentalism. But such cases are not the whole of departmentalism, and one could imagine a judiciary refusing to allow them while still respecting the broader constitutional dialogue Lincoln endorsed.

If we were to expand the metaphor of dialogue in this way, we might also expand it beyond horizontal exchanges among officially coequal coordinate branches. An exchange of reasons by official actors defending their prerogatives before a long-term public audience could also take place vertically, among institutions that are not formally equal: provinces and federal governments, for example. Elsewhere[11] I have discussed the possibility of interpretive exchanges that go both ways between the US federal and state courts about the meaning of constitutional protections that appear in both state constitutions and the federal constitution. I suggest that there is reason not to treat state constitutional texts as interpretively completely independent from the federal – but also vice versa. While that argument is specific to judiciaries and to the specific case of rights that are protected, often using precisely the same words, in both levels of constitutional text, I think the idea could be extended both beyond the judiciary and beyond interpreting the boundaries of rights-protections.

But it is important to reiterate that this expanded sense of when the metaphor of dialogue might be useful, a sense that might survive the challenge of Canadian skeptics of it, comes at a price. This is a more diffuse understanding of how the exchange of reasons and arguments about constitutional meaning works. It will take place at different times among actors and institutions of different levels of power and authority. It will be a part of the fabric of contestatory and competitive political life, not a calm deliberation. It will be better by far from the standpoint of public legitimacy than mere raw exercises of power, but it will not be nearly as normatively attractive as some romanticizers of "constitutional dialogue" have sometimes thought. And, for those who are exercised about the democratic credentials of entrenched constitutionalism and judicial review, it will not provide a decisive normative response to the counter-pluralitarian difficulty.

IV   Dialogue and Democracy

I have already introduced the ugly neologism "counter-pluralitarian" and will continue to use it. "Countermajoritarian" is of course conventional,

---

[11] Jacob T. Levy, 'States of the Same Nature: Bounded Variation in Subnational Constitutionalism' in James A. Gardner and Jim Rossi, (eds.), *New Frontiers in State Constitutional Law* (Oxford: Oxford University Press, 2011).

but it is tendentious, claiming for the parties in control of legislatures more support than they almost ever have in Canada in particular. No federal Canadian government has been elected with a majority of the popular vote since 1984. No British government has been elected with a majority of the popular vote since 1931. In the United States, four out of the last seven presidential elections have been won on the basis of less than a majority of the popular votes cast (whether a plurality or, as in 2000 and 2016, not even a plurality), and the same applies to four of the last nine majorities in the House of Representatives.

Why do I insist on this? It's well-known how pluralities of votes convert into majorities of seats in first-part-the-post systems, or sometimes into minority governments – pluralities of seats that can command the confidence of a parliament. And of course in multiparty proportional representation systems, popular majorities are even rarer and coalition governments are common. It's all institutionally legitimate and I do not mean to cast doubt on that. But the intuition that underlies the counter-majoritarian difficulty is that the elected branches of government command something more than institutional legitimacy. They speak for the extra-institutional people in some way that gives them a strong presumption that they should get their way. It may be that the elected branches are entitled to such a presumption, for example on the basis of their accountability and removability. But representative government is not government by referendum or plebiscite, and elected governments often *do not* have the electoral support of a majority of the voters. Moreover, even governments that *do* represent a majority of voters do not represent a coherent already-existing majority opinion.[12] If none of that matters, if a plurality or a fractured majority is as good as a coherent majority for purposes of speaking on behalf of the people, then calling attention to it shouldn't matter.[13] But if it does matter – if legislatures, like courts, have a legitimacy that is primarily or exclusively institutional – then referring

---

[12] Christopher H. Achen and Larry M. Bartels, *Democracy for Realists* (Princeton: Princeton University Press, 2016).

[13] I think Richard Bellamy, *Political Constitutionalism: A Republican Defence of the Constitutionality of Democracy* (Cambridge: Cambridge University Press, 2007); and Jeremy Waldron, *Political Political Theory* (Cambridge, MA: Harvard University Press, 2016) both offer accounts of the legitimacy of the elected legislature that do not depend on a coherent pre-institutional majority opinion or on the general idea of speaking for the people as a whole. I have them in mind with this sentence; calling it the counter-pluralitarian difficulty should not matter much if they are right, because they do not depend on that majoritarian image of the popular will.

to the "countermajoritarian difficulty" obscures something important. In the latter case, the legitimacy advantage that legislatures have over judiciaries is not so decisive as the traditional debate over the counter-majoritarian difficulty has assumed.

This discussion of the fractured character of public opinion introduces the idea of the permanence of conflict and disagreement in political life. This is a theme that has been central to the so-called realist turn in political theory.[14] Against the consensual idealizations of a variety of kinds of political theory, idealizations that treat reasoning together toward agreement as the normal and normative condition of political life, realism emphasizes the centrality to politics of coordination and cooperation in circumstances of deep disagreement.[15] The metaphor of constitutional dialogue shares obvious affinities with the deliberative democracy that has been one of realism's chief foils,[16] and I suspect has been a philosophical inspiration for dialogue theory's academic proponents. Theories of contestatory and partisan democracy[17] treat democracy more in line with realism's emphasis on managed disagreement. These literatures – the contestatory critique of deliberation, the realist critique of deliberation, and dialogue theory's tacit reliance on deliberation – have mostly proceeded without reference to each other. What could they learn from each other? In particular, if the realist and contestatory critiques of deliberation are correct, must dialogue theory be modified or abandoned?

Thinking in this way means approaching dialogue theory from a somewhat different angle from the criticism that post-1982 Canadian judicial review has shown very little dialogue in practice. That fact is compatible with some very different normative theories:

1) Dialogue theory correctly describes an ideal to which we should aspire. Practice often fails to live up to ideals, and that is unfortunate but to be expected; but that in itself is no criticism of the ideal. It may

---

[14] Bernard Williams, 'Realism and Moralism in Political Theory' in *In the Beginning Was the Deed* (Princeton: Princeton University Press, 2005); William Galston, 'Realism in Political Theory' (2010) 9(4) *European Journal of Political Theory* 385.

[15] Jeremy Waldron, *Law and Disagreement* (Oxford: Oxford University Press, 1999).

[16] Luc B. Tremblay, 'The Legitimacy of Judicial Review: The Limits of Dialogue between Courts and Legislatures' (2005) 3(4) *International Journal of Constitutional Law* 617.

[17] Bellamy, above n 13; Nancy L. Rosenblum, *On the Side of Angels* (Princeton: Princeton University Press, 2008).

well be that practice is morally improved by articulating the ideal, and encouraging political actors to live up to it.

2) Dialogue theory's purpose was as an apology for judicial review, to overcome its apparent democratic defects by linking it to a prestigious theory of the democratic ideal. When it is shown that practice does not match the theory, the apology has failed, and judicial review again stands exposed to the counter-pluralitarian difficulty, the distinction between the strong and weak forms exposed as more or less a sham.

3) Dialogue theory rests on a mistaken normative aspiration in the first place, and so the failure of the facts to support its minor premise does not do much damage to it, and indeed might suggest ways in which practice improves on the theory.

In order to bring realism and contestatory theory into engagement with dialogue theory, it is (3) I mean to explore.

It is at least apparently paradoxical that contestatory democrats such as Waldron and Bellamy, who have argued so strenuously against the holism of the popular democratic will are also among the leading critics within political theory of judicial review, while Habermas, Rawls, and many deliberative democrats have been strong supporters of it. At least the public debates about judicial review and the counter-pluralitarian difficulty suggest that the pairings should be otherwise: the counter-pluralitarian difficulty is a *difficulty* because pluralitarian decision-making is entitled to considerable presumptive moral weight. In popular discourse this presumption stands because the majority is the voice of *the people*. In American debates, the language of the disunited and factional-ized people is a traditional account of unusual and pathological condi-tions that might justify judicial correction; think of John Hart Ely and *Carolene Products'* "discrete and insular minorities."[18]

But the political theory debates have unfolded very differently. In different ways, both Habermas' and Rawls' neo-Kantian idealizations deny any real conflict between popular sovereignty and judicial protec-tion of (in particular) individual rights – "co-original" principles, in Habermas' phrasing.[19] Rawls' well-ordered society is characterized by a consensus around principles of justice.[20] In light of that, a court's ability

---

[18] John Hart Ely, *Democracy and Distrust* (Cambridge, MA: Harvard University Press, 1981).

[19] Jürgen Habermas, *Between Facts and Norms* (Oxford: John Wiley & Sons, 2015).

[20] John Rawls, *A Theory of Justice* (Cambridge, MA: Harvard University Press, 1971); John Rawls, *Political Liberalism* (New York: Columbia University Press, 2005).

to uphold basic liberties instantiates, not frustrates, the people's real moral will. More generally, the judicial practice of reason-giving and issuing opinions rather than only disposing of cases has seemingly made deliberative democrats strikingly comfortable with judicial review. The model of democratic decision-making that models it on mutual reason-giving and persuasion sometimes seems, if anything, *more* comfortable with judicial reason-giving than with majoritarian and partisan winning and losing.

It seems to me that there is some risk in allowing the metaphor of "dialogue" to borrow for inter-institutional conflicts the halo of legitimacy that attaches to variations on the idea of speaking together within a populace or within a single body like an assembly or a legislative chamber. I think that too much can be made of the Aristotelian idea of politics as a coming together to reason and speak about what justice demands, or the related Arendtian idea of politics as the special kind of action that consists in speech.[21] Politics is, again, always about both persuasion and coercion, and often it is also about convention and coordination besides. A speech-centric model of politics will, I think, always be distorting. But there's something enduringly attractive about the *part* of politics that consists in coming together as formal equals in a shared conversation, debating and then deciding what is to be done about matters of public concern. This is true even in nondemocratic settings: within the traditional House of Lords, or the assemblies of the First and Second Estates, or a king's cabinet, the deliberations within the chamber were distinguished from the business of extramural power politics through at least formal equality of the participants in the conversation and a norm of free and open debate.[22]

But since the late eighteenth century there has been an especially strong association between deliberative conversation and exchange of ideas, on one hand, and *democratic* legitimacy on the other. There is no school of political theory devoted to deliberative aristocracy or deliberative autocracy. Given the *very* strong halo effect that attaches to "democracy" in modern political conditions – think of the unwillingness of almost any political regime to *identify* as anything but democratic,

---

[21] See Waldron, above n 13.

[22] See Melissa Schwartzberg, *Counting the Many* (Cambridge, MA: Cambridge University Press, 2013) on the frankly aristocratic origins of counting votes; it was among elites that each person's view was considered worth recording, as distinct from democratic processes of acclamation.

even when a "people's democracy" in name is a totalitarian dictatorship in practice – that further magnifies the sense of goodness and niceness that an idea like "dialogue" can carry.

Just insofar as that's true, though, we ought to be careful about borrowing the attractiveness of that part of the concept of politics and applying it where it doesn't belong. Treating outcomes as if they were deliberative or dialogic when they were not is a way of pretending that parties were equal participants in a shared conversation when they were not. It is often a way of telling the losers in political confrontations (and there are always losers) that the decision was theirs too, as it arose out of a conversation they took part in. It tells them not to feel hard done by. On the one hand, their loss was their own fault since they failed to persuade their fellows, and on the other hand it wasn't really a loss at all since what happened was still *their decision*, in a manner of speaking. I think Bernard Williams was right about the disrespect this insistence on treating politics as if it were deliberation ultimately conveys:

> [W]e should not think that what we have to do is simply to argue with those who disagree: treating them as opponents can, oddly enough, show more respect for them as political actors than treating them simply as arguers – whether as arguers who are simply mistaken, or as fellow seekers after truth. A very important reason for thinking in terms of the political is that a political decision – the conclusion of a political deliber-ation which brings all sorts of considerations, considerations of principle along with others, to one focus of decision – is that such a decision does not in itself announce that the other party was morally wrong or, indeed, wrong at all. What it immediately announces is that *they have lost*.[23]

Rendering inter-institutional conflicts that reach some resolution or another as "dialogue" could well prove to be such an ideological obfus-cation, providing the outcome with more apparent legitimacy than the merits call for while treating the losers as if they failed rather than simply lacking decisive institutional power.

Returning again to the French *ancien régime*, the constitutional dia-logue (if such it was) took place between two unrepresentative insti-tutions that lacked democratic legitimacy. The merits of that dialogue, if there were any, were not that it bolstered the democratic credentials of the eventual outcome. What I am suggesting here is that we should similarly deflate expectations for constitutional dialogue in really existing

---

[23] Bernard Williams, *In the Beginning Was the Deed: Realism and Moralism in Political Argument* (Princeton: Princeton University Press, 2005), p. 13.

constitutional democracies. The exchange of arguments, reasons, institutional posturing, campaign platforms, and the rest takes place before a
public audience that is rarely attentive to or informed about constitutional questions, and that does not have a coherent majority opinion that
the legislature or elected government can purport to be the agent of.
There might be, as I think there is, a level of improvement and refinement in the exercise of political power that comes from the need to
articulate reasons and offer arguments in public. But it is not enough to
extend to the judiciary the level of democratic legitimacy that the legislature was thought to have by pre-realist democratic theory. The good
news is that legislatures do not have that either. A deflated and realistic
account of constitutional dialogue might not be able to solve the counter-
pluralitarian dilemma. But it might give us reason to doubt that the
dilemma is so serious in the first place.

4

On Dialogue and Domination

GEOFFREY SIGALET[*]

I Introduction

Metaphors can play many different roles in constitutional theories, especially theories that seek to evaluate how different constitutional arrangements and practices enable or restrict freedom. This chapter is concerned with the normative role played by the metaphor of dialogue in constitutional theory, that is, the reason *why* dialogue between courts and legislatures about rights, and the constitutional structures designed to promote it, might in truth be desirable. One of the most important dynamics that the metaphor of dialogue has been used to evaluate and describe is the inter-institutional relationship between courts and legislatures regarding the specification of rights. 'Dialogue' does not signify any one constitutional theory, nor one prescribed pattern of interaction between courts and legislatures concerning rights. Perhaps 'dialogue' rings in the ears of some political and legal theorists with the ideal of equality, but this is doubtlessly related to specific normative commitments contingently filtering what they hear. Metaphors are not theories, and they do not search for theories to explain their hidden import.[1] Instead, dialogue is a metaphor that has been given different normative meanings in different constitutional contexts and in distinctive theories of how the ideals of constitutionalism and freedom are related to interactions between courts and legislatures. When we sift particular uses of the metaphor concerning interactions between courts and

[*] For detailed comments on a draft of this essay, I thank my fellow editors Grégoire Webber and Rosalind Dixon. I am also grateful for comments and conversations on drafts by Jan-Werner Müller, Keith Whittington, Philip Pettit, Kim-Lane Scheppele, Cameron Cotton-O'Brien, Bradley Miller, Grant Huscroft, Stephen Gardbaum, Dwight Newman, Michael McConnell, William Baude, Mark Storslee, Lance Sorenson, Charles Tyler, Theodore Lechterman, Corey Brettschneider, Ben Ewing, Kent Roach, Cristoph Möllers, Rainer Knopff, Joanna Baron, Jason Iuliano, Briana McGinnis, and Sean Beienburg.
[1] A. Kavanagh, 'The Lure and the Limits of Dialogue' (2016) 66 *University of Toronto Law Journal* 120.

legislatures for a better sense of why dialogue between these institutions might be a good thing, three general reasons and corresponding norms of dialogue emerge.

The first reason for favouring dialogue is tied to the view that dialogue involves the principled judicial interrogation of legislative reasons for infringing rights. On this view, the reason for valuing dialogue is that it offers a chance for the judiciary to interrogatively distinguish justifiable reasons for legislatures to infringe rights from the unjustifiable legislative pursuit of objectives that are simply 'symbolic articulations of disgust, anxiety, national solidarity, animus, or other strong emotions'.[2] *Interrogative* dialogue, as I shall call it, does not involve much concern for legislative participation in determining the meaning of rights, as it presupposes that the exchange of reasons regarding rights will concentrate on whether different infringements might be reasonably justifiable under certain circumstances.

A second reason for valuing dialogue takes the commitment to both constitutional rights and democracy to justify the judicial interruption of democratic legislative processes implicating rights, provided that these interruptions are 'non-final' and can be overridden or ignored. Where courts interrupt legislative processes afflicted with 'burdens of inertia', i.e., where legislatures fail to pass or consider legislation in the face of political gridlock, or where courts simply interrupt the application of statutes that could be thought to threaten minority rights, they help protect against unjustifiable infringements of rights.[3] There are two prominent theories of *interruptive* dialogue, as I shall call this norm of dialogue, and both take the purpose of judicial interruptions to be the protection of rights and the provocation of legislative responses to judicial decisions that can help promote democratic responsibility and a measure of control over rights.

A third reason for encouraging dialogue is that it could allow courts and legislatures to co-ordinately construct the meaning of rights in a way

---

[2] Kent Roach, 'Dialogue in Canada and the Dangers of Simplified Comparative Law and Populism' in this volume.

[3] R. Dixon, 'Dialogue and Deference' in this volume; 'The Core Case for Weak-Form Judicial Review' (2017) *Cardozo Law Review* 38, 2193; 'The Supreme Court of Canada, Charter Dialogue, and Deference' (2009) 47(2) *Osgood Hall Law Journal* 235; the idea of 'burdens of inertia' was developed in an earlier article, see R. Dixon, 'Creating Dialogue About Socio-Economic Rights: Strong-Form vs. Weak-Form' (2005) 5(1) *International Journal of Constitutional Law* 391; S. Gardbaum, *The New Commonwealth Model of Constitutionalism* (Cambridge: Cambridge University Press, 2013) pp. 111–121.

that protects both rights and the democratic legitimacy of political decisions implicating rights. Like the interruptive reason for favouring dialogue, this constructive reason involves the possibility that legislatures can help specify the meaning of rights and what it means for them to be violated. Yet unlike the interruptive norm, *constructive* dialogue is incompatible with the idea that legislatures can justifiably infringe the rights of citizens. If the value of dialogue is the constructive specification of what rights mean, given certain conditions and circumstances, then it would seem that legislative replies to judicial decisions cannot be about their justified or unjustified violation. Evaluating the justified or unjustified infringement of rights involves, at least in the current practice of courts, assessing the ends and means of legislative schemes, according to which the specified meaning of rights falls from view. The constructive value of dialogue lies in the possibility that courts and legislatures can learn from one another in co-ordinately specifying the legal meaning of rights, and that such learning will protect the democratic legitimacy of decisions involving rights as much as rights themselves.[4]

Which of these reasons for valuing dialogue between courts and legislatures should guide constitutional design and practice? In this chapter I evaluate the interrogative, interruptive, and constructive reasons for favouring dialogue and their corresponding norms in light of the contemporary republican political theory of the relationship between freedom and constitutionalism. Republican freedom is best conceptualized as *non-domination*, or freedom from exposure to the arbitrary will of another. I argue that the conception of freedom as non-domination justifies constitutional construction as the ideal republican value of dialogue between courts and legislatures concerning rights. Freedom from domination requires that the law of the state is maximally open to the equal control of the citizenry, such that its pattern of interference or potential interference in their lives is politically just (section II). Different institutions and constitutional arrangements will promote and protect this conception of freedom from domination in distinctive ways depending on the norms of the institutional practices and the civic virtues they rely on to function. The institutional features and practices of modern courts and legislatures will secure citizens from domination in a fashion that is distinct from that of the institutions and practices of ancient courts and legislatures.

---

[4] G. Webber, 'The Unfulfilled Potential of the Court and Legislature Dialogue' (2009) 42(2) *Canadian Journal of Political Science* 443, 452–455.

While this conception of freedom can justify the judicial review of statutes for their compliance with rights by institutionally independent and professional modern courts, it is also threatened by the risk that courts will use this power to unjustly usurp rather than enforce the equal control of the citizenry over the law (section III). The risk is that modern courts will misuse their institutional independence and professional techniques of reasoning to enforce changes to legal rights in pursuit of the political purposes of ancient courts, thereby presenting the vice of misusing their unequal power to change the law under the guise of modern adjudicative virtue. On the conception of freedom from domination, the fact that judicial interference with the legislative function is often negative in character does not render the risk judicial review poses to political justice any less morally significant than the risk entailed by the more active form of interference attending legislative changes to the law. This suggests that insofar as the risks courts and legislatures pose to political justice are of equal moral significance, just forms of judicial review must mitigate the risk it poses to political justice by allowing legislatures to correct unjust exercises of adjudication.

Of the three reasons for favouring dialogue between courts and legislatures and their corresponding norms of inter-institutional interaction, interrogative and interruptive dialogues jar with the institutional features and practices of modern courts, and only the norm of coordinating rights constructions will animate politically just forms of interference between courts and legislatures (section IV). The interrogative norm of dialogue increases the risk of political injustice by exhorting courts to pursue the political purposes of ancient courts under the cover of modern judicial independence and professionalism, and by delegitimizing legislative responsibility for rights. Interrogations exclude legislatures from sharing in the interpretive role, treating them as suspects rather than equal partners in specifying the meaning of indeterminate rights. The interruptive norm of dialogue is more promising than the interrogative norm, and it comes in two influential varieties. But both versions of the interruptive norm of dialogue encourage aggressive judicial review on the 'first look' that minimizes the probability of legislative responses to unjust forms of adjudication. Interruptions stifle the very dialogues they are supposed to provoke. In contrast, the norm of constructive dialogue will encourage courts to minimize the risk judicial review poses to political justice by using their institutional independence and professionalism to enforce the determinate meaning of rights, while recognizing and respecting prospective legislative rights constructions, and promoting the legislative responsibility to correct unjust adjudicative constructions.

II   Republican Freedom

The republican conception of freedom from domination is primarily opposed to the understanding of freedom as non-interference, which was historically popularized in the works of writers such as Jeremy Bentham and William Paley, and in more recent intellectual history by Isaiah Berlin.[5] The ideal of non-domination is a conception of freedom as a status in which norms and laws secure citizens from arbitrary interference by other persons.[6] In contrast, the ideal of freedom as non-interference is a conception of freedom as a state of affairs in which there is an absence of interference with the choices of an agent. The ideal of freedom as non-interference includes the thesis that the interference of others in the choices of an agent is always a violation of their freedom.[7] It also entails the thesis that only the actual interference of others in the choices of an agent will violate their freedom.[8] The philosophical thrust of the republican theory of freedom from domination rests on the rejection of these theses. The thesis that freedom is only violated by actual inter-ference in the choices of an agent is compatible with the possibility of an alien will invigilating the choices of an agent without actively interfering in its choices. The paradigm case for demonstrating the distinction between freedom as non-domination and freedom as non-interference is the case of the master and the slave. If interference alone can violate freedom, then relations of ingratiation, intimidation, and beneficent invigilation are compatible with freedom. Thus the central reason repub-licans take non-domination to be a superior evaluative conception of freedom is that, unlike freedom as non-interference, non-domination is incompatible with the idea that ingratiating or placating the demands of an arbitrary power can provide a just state of freedom.

---

[5] It is also opposed to the Hobbesian concept of freedom as non-frustration, that is, freedom understood as the absence of invasive obstruction to the choices actually preferred by individuals; see P. Pettit, 'The Instability of Freedom as Non-Interference: The Case of Isaiah Berlin' (2011) 121(4) *Ethics* 693.

[6] P. Pettit, *On the People's Terms: A Republican Theory and Model of Democracy* (Cam-bridge: Cambridge University Press, 2012), pp. 64–67.

[7] P. Pettit, 'Law and Liberty' in S. Besson and J. Marti (eds.), *Legal Republicanism: National and International Perspectives* (Oxford: Oxford University Press, 2009), pp. 45–46.

[8] Ibid., p. 44.

The second reason republicans take non-domination to be a superior evaluative conception of freedom is that, insofar as freedom as non-interference entails the thesis that interference always violates the freedom of individuals, it opposes freedom to the exercise of all coercive political power. The problem with this is that political communities of every variety necessarily employ different forms of interference, and coercive interference in particular, to achieve the justifiable common aims of their community. Such political interference is exercised for the common good at the expense of individual discretion. Freedom as non-interference thereby opposes freedom to a defining element of all political life, politically expedient interference. The upshot of this opposition between freedom and political interference is the Benthamite thesis that *all* governmental interference in the lives of citizens threatens their freedom. The republican theory of freedom as non-domination rejects this thesis in favour of the view that government interference channelled by the democratic rule of law is legitimate. To use James Harrington's words, unlike the 'empire of men', a democratic 'empire of law' is not necessarily a dominating regime.[9] The central concept at work in the republican rejection of the interference-always thesis is that of control. Where an agent A's freedom to choose from choices x, y, and z is not subject to the alien control of another agent B, agent A can be said to be free. This formulation leaves room for the possibility that agent B might interfere with the choices of agent A, and yet this interference not be a case of domination if that interference is traceable to the control of agent A. On the view of freedom as non-domination, it is possible for laws subject to the control of agents to interfere with such controlling agents as free subjects of the law. To the extent that interference is subject to the robust control of the interferee, it will constitute a case of self-control and the exercise of freedom as non-domination.

Freedom from domination also better captures the evaluative allure of freedom than its rival because it provides a more plausible conceptual map of the connections between freedom and justice. Freedom as non-interference's connection to justice is always negative; that is, insofar as freedom is just, justice is the absence of some form of interference in the affairs of individuals, and it will have the same negative character regardless of whether unjust interference is carried out by individuals, gangs, or agents of the state. But the connection between justice and freedom

---

[9] Ibid., p. 45.

seems intuitively present in both the absence of unjust forms of interference, and just forms of interference protecting individuals from forms of interference that threaten choices they conclude to be just. Insofar as this is true, and state institutions are constituted by specialized groups of individuals who promulgate and enforce standards and rules regulating the behaviour of individuals in their community on behalf of that community, the interference and potential interference of such institutions will have a special effect on the freedom of individuals depending on whether or not the institutions are just. Freedom as non-domination can map this special effect because it is divisible into two kinds of relations of justice: the freedom of *politically just* relations of non-arbitrary interference between citizens and the state, and the freedom of *socially just* relations of non-arbitrary interference between citizens.[10] Although early modern republicanism was intertwined with the commonwealthmen natural rights tradition, a tradition which featured elements of deontological thinking, contemporary republican rights can be reconceptualized as the just political rights of citizens against arbitrary interference by the state and just social rights against the arbitrary interference of citizens against each other.[11]

While there are clashing theories of the patterns of interpersonal relationships that will characterize socially just freedom from domination, it seems clear that relations of politically just rule between a state and its citizenry demand robustly democratic institutions. The political justice of non-domination requires the kinds of institutions necessary to achieve a form of popular control over the state and its laws.[12] Such democratic institutions must operate according to norms and laws that all members of a community can affirm as treating their practical reasoning about the direction of the state's interference in their individual and collective choices on equal terms with the practical reasoning of their fellow citizens.[13] However just or unjust the order of social relations citizens develop between one another, the ideal of

---

[10] Pettit, above n 6, p. 76.

[11] The role of rights in modern republican political theory is somewhat undertheorized. The role of rights on the view of the connection between justice and freedom developed here is consistent with rights as absolute specifications of just constraints on state or individual actions to realize the goal of freedom insofar as they are necessary for this goal. P. Pettit, *Republicanism* (Oxford: Oxford University Press, 1997), pp. 102–103; P. Pettit, 'The Consequentialist Can Recognize Rights' (1988) 38 *The Philosophical Quarterly* 42, 49.

[12] Pettit, above n 6, p. 131.

[13] Ibid., pp. 254–259.

non-domination requires that any state imposing and promoting such patterns of social relations must do so according to public laws and norms that effectively open up state coercion to the equal and minimally conditioned control of the citizenry.[14] While there is an array of potential decision-making institutions to choose from, modern republicanism favours electorally responsive and representative legislatures as the primary type of institution for changing the law.[15] Republican representative legislatures will only allow for the equal control of citizens' practical reasoning if the equal votes of the assembly make decisions to change the law that are sufficiently deliberative and coherently responsive to the equal votes of citizens.[16] The modern republican approach to constitutional design has given rise to rival schools of thought on the potential for federal divisions of power and the judicial review of statutes for compliance with legal rights to protect citizens from domination.[17]

While modern republican constitutional theory offers an alternative to liberal approaches tied to the ideal of freedom as non-interference, it faces its own criticisms regarding the ideal of freedom from domination. For some critics, the modern republican adoption of this conception of freedom is philosophically mistaken because it requires a commitment either to the thesis that states alone must ensure the non-arbitrary equal control of citizens over their choices, or to the thesis that only coalitions of citizens can collectively ensure non-arbitrary equal control over the state by maintaining the power of individuals participating in a coalition

---

[14] Ibid., pp. 130–132.

[15] Ibid., pp. 201–205. Of course, there are contemporary republican theorists who dissent, reject electorally representative democracy and independent professional courts, and call for a return to the ancient contestatory, plebian-friendly, lottery based form of republicanism; see J. McCormick, *Machiavellian Democracy* (Cambridge: Cambridge University Press, 2011). I take it that the modern republican view must be willing to reject aspects of its heritage by directly arguing that this ancient form of government may have been more *directly* responsive, but was often incoherent in it interstitial decision-making such that its responsiveness was less *controlled*.

[16] Ibid., pp. 192–194; P. Pettit, 'Deliberative Democracy, the Discursive Dilemma, and Republican Theory' in J. Fishkin and P. Laslett (eds.), *Debating Deliberative Democracy* (Oxford: Blackwell Publishing, 2003), p. 138; P. Pettit and Christian List, *Group Agency* (Oxford: Oxford University Press, 2011); R. Ekins, *The Nature of Legislative Intent* (Oxford: Oxford University Press, 2012), ch. 6.

[17] For a republican justification of federalism see H. Kong, 'Republicanism and the Division of Powers in Canada' (2014) 64(3) *University of Toronto Law Journal* 359; for a republican theory opposed to federalism see R. Bellamy, *Political Constitutionalism* (Cambridge: Cambridge University Press, 2007).

to resist the unequally controlled interference of the state in their choices.[18] This philosophical critique holds that for citizens to be free from domination by one another, the state must be powerful enough to protect citizens from coalitions of their fellow citizens, but this will grant the officials of the state dominating powers of arbitrary interference in the lives of citizens. In turn, for citizens to be free from the domination of the state, extra-institutional coalitions of the citizenry must have the power to resist the state, and the problem arises that any such coalition might have the power to arbitrarily interfere in the choices of other coalitions and individual citizens in exactly the manner that republicans take to justify the state's power of interference. The dilemma is summarized pithily by Thomas Simpson: 'the citizens must be powerful, but they must also not be.'[19] The significance of this critique for republican constitutional theory is that it has been taken to signal that the ideal of non-domination entails the abandonment of the traditional republican emphasis on civic virtue, and the embrace of the Humean view that strong government institutions will provide the status of freedom, independently of the civic virtues of the citizenry.[20]

The republican response to these criticisms helps clarify the philosophical nature of freedom from domination and its relevance to constitutional theory. The philosophical critique misses the irreducibly political character of non-domination by presupposing that it is an 'on-or-off' binary state of affairs, that is either fully attained, or not at all. The philosophical critique presupposes that non-domination is a state of affairs where every citizen X is dominated or not dominated by either every other individual citizen Y (dyadic) or set of citizens $A, B, C \ldots$ (polyadic), and X might be dominated by any one individual citizen Y, but not another, or as a member of one set by another set, and yet not by others.[21] This is incompatible with the ideal of freedom from domination

---

[18] T. Simpson, 'The Impossibility of Republican Freedom' (2017) 45(1) *Philosophy and Public Affairs* 27; a related critique of non-domination focused on the thesis that only coalitions can provide non-domination from the state is found in K. Dowding 'Republican Freedom, Rights, and the Coalition Problem' (2011) 10(3) *Politics, Philosophy, and Economics* 301.

[19] Ibid., Simpson, at 27.

[20] David Hume took it as a 'political maxim' that 'every man must be supposed a knave' from 'Of the Independency of Parliament' (I.VI.1) in E. Miller (ed.), *Essays: Moral, Political, Literary* (Indianapolis: Liberty Fund, 1987).

[21] Polyadic domination is defined as 'the relation that holds between some group of people, G, and A, when, by acting in a co-ordinated way, the members of G have the uncontrolled power to interfere with A'. Ibid., p. 36.

as a set of political norms and laws reducing the arbitrariness of the state's interference in the lives of citizens as they come to inform the practical reasoning of citizens. Political norms are nothing less than regularities of behaviour that can be expected to inform the lives of citizens as a result of the judgement that they will draw approval of others in relation to some judgements they share with others.[22]

This can be demonstrated by using a hypothetical example. Imagine that an adult citizen X follows the laws specifying the proper exercise of the right of every adult citizen to vote, at least insofar other citizens A, B, C . . . also respect laws protecting this right, with the expectation that this behaviour will be met with the approval of most of her fellow citizens who share the judgement that protecting and exercising this right is essential to directing state interference in a less arbitrary fashion. Insofar as this norm of exercising and respecting the legal right to vote is widespread, and complemented by norms guiding free and fair elections for sufficiently deliberative representatives with equal votes, it should go some way towards reducing the domination of the *set of individuals* who share the expectations that make it a common norm. The imaginary citizen's expectation that any one citizen or group of citizens will dominate her will be reduced in proportion to the inclusion of that citizen or group in the *number* of individuals participating in these norms and the *depth* of their participation.[23] This does not resolve the problem of explaining what these norms and laws should be, nor which institutionally distinctive norms might help secure different state institutions from capture by a coalition, but it does explain the sense in which the citizenry secured from domination must at once be powerful and subject to state power. The citizenry must be powerful in the sense that they share norms ensuring the protection of their equal control over the state with their elected representatives, judges, and bureaucrats, and yet subject to the just interference of the state provided it follows such norms and laws.

---

[22] Pettit, above n 6, p. 128; Norms are not merely regularities of behaviour, like eating three times a day, but patterns of behaviour related to the expected approval or disapproval of a social group. They can be evil, as is the case with racist norms of discriminatory behaviour towards one group of people based on their skin colour, or obviously good, as is the case with the norm that one should apologize profusely when one has unintentionally run into an innocent person with a grocery cart.

[23] It's worth keeping in mind the concern that too many citizens, or too many representatives given the number of citizens in a polity, could lead to the frustration of legislative deliberation and responsiveness, which runs against norms of non-domination. See Ekins, *The Nature of Legislative Intent*, pp. 146–154.

Democracies are always vulnerable to the informal collapse of the shared norms animating the political justice of formal laws, and so the threat of domination cannot be eliminated, but must instead be securely minimized. Yet the more such republican norms and laws take root in the practical reasoning of ordinary citizens and their representatives, the less dominated they will be *as a political community.*[24]

The significance of the ideal for constitutional theory is not a commitment to the Humean view that institutions alone can secure the freedom of individuals independently of civic virtue. On the contrary, constitutional institutions cannot secure citizens against domination if specific republican norms are not engrained in the practical reasoning of citizens and public officials alike. The philosophically virtue-oriented dimension of freedom from domination signals that, in order to be effective and to minimally condition the reasoned choices of the citizenry, republican laws must inculcate norms of civility and participation that enable citizens to expect their fellow citizens and agents of the state to disapprove of vices that threaten the conditions commonly judged necessary to treat citizens' practical reasoning about the direction of state interference equally.[25] The freedom of modern citizens from domination thus crucially depends not only on specifics of constitutional design and widespread democratic norms among the citizenry, but also on the constitutional practices and virtues of state officials who are elected and appointed to office. This includes norms regarding interactions between courts and legislatures as they exercise their distinctively modern, but sometimes overlapping, legal functions.[26] There are specific institutional features and virtuous practices that distinguish modern republican courts and legislatures from their ancient predecessors in terms of the way in which they secure citizens from politically unjust domination. Outlining the reasons for the general differences in the design of modern and

---

[24] In other words, non-domination must be normatively transitive in relation to the *breadth* and *depth* of norms reinforcing laws protecting citizen's equal control over state interference. The virtuous republican citizen cannot be free without virtuous company. *Pace* Simpson, above n 18, p. 41.

[25] Republican constitutional theory thus has an 'aretaic' dimension; for a sense of what this means, see L. Solum, 'The Aretaic Turn in Constitutional Theory' (2004) 70(2) *Brooklyn Law Review* 475.

[26] Properly understood, the modern republican approach cannot be simply categorized as either a primarily 'principle-oriented' or 'virtue-oriented' theory, for it is necessarily concerned with both the principles and virtues of just institutions. C. Farrelly, 'Civic Liberalism and the "Dialogical Model" of Judicial Review' (2006) 25(5) *Law and Philosophy* 489.

ancient institutions as they relate to their distinctive functions will allow
us to discern the limitations such modern institutions and practices place
on the republican justification of judicial review and the kind of dialogue
between courts and legislatures that will prove virtuous in the circumstances of modern politics.

Modern courts exist primarily to remedy the inefficient lack of deter-
minacy and uncertain validity of the application of laws to particular
circumstances by adjudicating whether or not legal rules admitted in the
past have been violated in particular cases.[27] Courts may be institutionally granted a higher political profile by extending their power to allow
them to refuse to apply laws in relation to still more fundamental laws,
but they will remain institutionally wedded to the general legal purposes
of discovering what the law means and whether it has been violated, and
applying just remedies for violations according their legal system's
norms.[28] These legal purposes justify designing modern republican
courts such that they enjoy a measure of independence from legislative
institutions designed to change the law and are staffed by specialists
trained in the techniques of reasoning required to distinguish valid laws
from the conclusions of unrestricted moral reasoning or raw preferences.

This combination of institutional independence and legal professionalization can be achieved in a variety of ways. Both aims can be reinforced
by creating a political system for appointing judges that is insulated from
direct elections, entrenching difficult standards of impeachment,
granting judges immunity from legal actions related to their judgements,
providing judges with salaries adequate to render bribes ineffective, and
instituting procedures requiring parties to legal disputes (including the
representatives of state) to treat tribunals as independent arbiters of legal
questions.[29] Modern legal systems demand very different institutional
arrangements from the judicial arrangements that were characteristic of
the classical republics. Ancient courts were composed of hundreds of

---

[27] H. L. A. Hart, *The Concept of Law* (Oxford: Oxford University Press, 1994), pp. 96–99.

[28] F. Lovett, *A Republic of Law* (Cambridge: Cambridge University Press, 2016),
pp. 140–161.

[29] Other innovations serving this purpose include promulgating rules disallowing judges and
lawyers alike from participating in cases where they have a conflict of interest, creating
legal societies to enforce norms of behaviour reinforcing the special responsibilities of
judges and other roles in the legal system, limiting the number of judges on appellate
courts to maintain coherent decision-making outcomes, etc. For a helpful analysis of the
ways in which various elements in the institutional design and practices of modern courts
can contribute to the virtuous pursuit of the judicial function, see G. Webber, 'Past,
Present, and Justice in the Exercise of Judicial Responsibility' in this volume.

ordinary citizens selected by lot, and governed by procedural rules that often allowed for individuals to contest the legal validity or democratic purpose of laws, and to prosecute the citizens responsible for them, thereby encouraging the use of law as an alternative political channel for individuals or coalitions to challenge the lawmaking of legislative assemblies.[30] While modern courts can include elements of popular participation and accountability, such as publishing signed judicial opinions explaining a judge's reasons for supporting or dissenting from a legal holding, their institutional independence and professionalism are meant to constrain their decision-making in a way that stands starkly opposed to the political purpose of the Athenian practice of having trials judged by several hundred ordinary political citizens selected by lot.[31]

Modern legislatures exist as a matter of law to remedy the defect of static rules by deliberately changing and updating their meaning for shifting normative and empirical reasons related to the path a political community will take, both in the present and the future.[32] Modern democratic legislatures harness the legal purpose of remedying the defect of static rules to the political purpose of responsively representing and incorporating the reasoning of the citizenry in the deliberate changes it makes to the law as a result of its collective reasoning.[33] As

---

[30] M. Hansen, *The Athenian Democracy in the Age of Demosthenes* (Oxford: Basil Blackwell Ltd., 1991), pp. 178–180; For example, in ancient Athens it was assumed that most private legal quarrels would be dealt with by arbitration; yet the people's court (*dikasteron*) had the power to challenge the validity or democratic credentials of laws, conduct political trials, and make administrative decisions controlling the assembly (*ekklesia*), as well as other magistrates and political leaders. In fact, the ancient idea of the judicial function, in the modern sense of deciding particular legal disputes and remedies, was so explicitly bent to the political purpose of ensuring that the resolution of legal disputes was not controlled by the arbitrary will of one faction of society that judicial powers were sometimes distributed beyond institutional courts to roving elected magistrates with the ability to obstruct the application of valid legislation. For an interesting discussion of the democratic role of Roman tribunes see A. Lintott, *The Constitution of the Roman Republic* (Oxford: Oxford University Press, 1999), pp. 121–128.

[31] Ibid., p.180.

[32] Webber, above n 29; Hart, above n 27, pp. 95–96.

[33] R. Ekins, 'How to Be a Free People' (2013) 58(2) *The American Journal of Jurisprudence* 163, 174–179. Interesting disagreements exist between contemporary republican constitutional theorists regarding questions such as the advantages or pitfalls of federally dividing the representative power to change the law between multiple legislatures, or whether to internally divide decision-making into superior and inferior separate chambers with different forms of accountability, or whether to organize assemblies to be more responsive to the electorate as a whole or for individual legislators to be more responsive to their specific constituents.

with modern courts, modern republican legislatures differ significantly from their ancient predecessors. Their difference is primarily between their ways of representing citizens in the changes they make to the law. Ancient legislatures often incorporated the reasoning of citizens into different decision-making assemblies by using lotteries to directly select their members from pools of citizens with specific personal character-istics such as wealth, poverty, area of residence, military service, etc.[34] The idea was that with different segments of the population directly represented in distinct decision-making bodies, the character of the various legal functions allocated to the assemblies would reflect their distinctive interests and balance them against those reflected in other assemblies.[35] While modern republican legislatures are sometimes organized according to indicative modes of representation for special purposes, they are primarily structured to have their members selected by competitive elections, in which political parties link prospective members to programs of political action.[36] Their central legal function of allowing deliberative changes to be enacted into the law is usually governed by procedural rules, such as subjecting bills to multiple readings and allowing opportunities for private members to introduce bills, that are meant to guarantee that actual changes to the law are subject to deliberations reflecting actual disagreements among the citi-zenry, while remaining coherent.[37] The ancient legislature was more of an assembly offering a segment of a community the opportunity to influence the law; the modern legislature is primarily a means of equally incorporating the practical reasoning of every citizen into changes to the law. This sketch of how modern courts and legislatures relate to the ideal of freedom from domination will help inform the following section's explanation of the risk of political domination entailed by judicial review.

---

[34] M. Crawford, *The Roman Republic* (Cambridge: Cambridge University Press, 1978); B. Manin, *The Principles of Representative Government* (Cambridge: Cambridge University Press, 1997).

[35] For an illuminating contrast between this more ancient idea of 'balancing' power and the modern idea of 'separating' it, see Bellamy, *Political Constitutionalism*, pp. 195–208.

[36] Ekins, *The Nature of Legislative Intent*, pp. 146–154.

[37] The modern legislature remains distinct from its ancient relatives in that elected legisla-tors are, as individuals, members of a political party, members of a particular legislative chamber, and members of the legislature as a whole, causally responsive to the practical reasoning of citizens about how well they are serving the common good of the commu-nity in their contributions to reasoning and voting on changes to the law. Pettit, *On the People's Terms*, pp. 197–207.

III   Republican Judicial Review

This section provides both a principled justification for the judicial review of statutes for rights compliance and a principled limitation on the justifiable forms such judicial review can take. It draws both of these lessons from the manner in which distinctive legal and political functions inform the institutional designs and practices of modern republican legislatures and courts. These lessons will help guide the subsequent section's inquiry into the ideal republican reasons and forms of dialogue between courts and legislatures. On the one hand, judicial review is *prima facie* justifiable, though not strictly necessary, as a means of allowing the modern adjudicative function of courts to indirectly reinforce the modern legal and political functions of republican legislatures. This lesson does not constitute a systematic or conclusive republican justification of judicial review, but demonstrates how judicial review can theoretically help secure citizens from domination by addressing the legal defects of the uncertain validity and the inefficient resolution of indeterminacies afflicting legislative changes to the law that enable or restrict future changes to the law meant to protect citizens from domination. On the other hand, the ideal of non-domination is incompatible with norms of interaction between modern courts and legislatures that restrict the legislature's ability to respond to unjust judicial invalidations of statutes. This is because the theory of non-domination provides grounds for rejecting the liberal prejudice in favour of *negative* state action. If unjust legislative interference with the negative task of adjudication is *prima facie* as much a risk and threat to freedom as unjust judicial interference in the active task of legislation, then norms governing interactions between courts and legislatures must allow for courts to correct unjust legislation and for legislatures to rectify unjust adjudication.

Taken together, the distinctive legal and political republican purposes of modern courts and legislatures are compatible with many different constitutional arrangements. But the institutional independence and professionalism that allows modern courts to realize their adjudicative function can be used to indirectly reinforce the link between modern legislatures' legal and political functions. From this it can be inferred that allowing courts to review statutes for compliance with legally specified rights is one justifiable way of securing citizens from domination by reinforcing the ability of modern legislatures to enact deliberative changes to the law that equally incorporate the practical reasoning of citizens. The modern political function of republican legislatures is to equally incorporate the reasoning of every citizen into coherent and electorally responsive changes to the law. This political function is achieved by the procedures enabling the legal function of modern legislatures: deliberatively enacting changes into the law. Although some of the procedural rules enabling these legal and political functions will be customary political norms, many will themselves be legal rules of legislative process, and therefore prone to the same kinds of disputes and positive defects as other legal rules.[38] These defects include the same static quality of many legal rules that it is the legislature's legal function to address, but also the validity and indeterminacy of the application of laws to particular circumstances, which it is the role of adjudication to address by determining what the law means, whether it has been violated, and what remedies it demands in particular circumstances. Because legal rules of legislative process are themselves prey to the defect of stasis in the face of changing normative and empirical circumstances, it is possible for even more fundamental laws to be established governing such procedural rules. An example of such fundamental rules might be constitutionally entrenched rights restricting the kinds of changes ordinary legislative procedures can make to the law with the purpose of protecting the political community's future ability to equally influence changes to static rules in circumstances that threaten this possibility. But any set of such fundamental rules will themselves face the threat of stasis, especially if they are subject to a difficult amending formula. This does not eliminate such fundamental rules as a valid legislative choice for a political community, but it does raise the possibility that the stasis of rules restricting legislative changes may themselves require legislative changes or adjudicative determinations left legally unspecified by the community. The political community must accordingly enact such rules with great care, as they may prove to be a kind of beginning that can never begin in the very same fashion again.[39]

It seems plausible that both legislative changes to the laws of legislative process, and even legislative changes restricting the future changes the legislative process can enact, could coherently and equally reflect the practical reasoning of citizens about the need for basic liberties against the state, such that these changes could help secure citizens' freedom from domination.[40] Insofar as republican constitutional theorists

---

[38] Lovett, above n 28, p. 187.
[39] H. Arendt, *On Revolution* (New York: Penguin, 1973), p. 206.
[40] Pettit, above n 6, pp. 92–107.

recognize (as most do) that the modern legal function of legislation can politically help secure citizens from domination, the institutional independence and professional practices that help courts exercise their general adjudicative function well could also have the secondary effect of minimizing domination.[41] This secondary effect of protecting citizens from domination would result from the judicial resolution of disputes regarding the validity or indeterminate implications of legislative changes to the law as they relate to past changes specifying rules and rights of legislative process, or to restrictions on changes to the law meant to protect individual rights. The institutions and practices of modern courts can thus indirectly help secure citizens from domination by resolving the defects of uncertain validity and the inefficient resolution of indeterminacies of legal rules that can interfere with the legislature's legal capacity to change the law in a way that incorporates the citizenry's practical reasoning about the just direction of state interference. The judicial review of statutory changes to the law involving legal rights can have this indirect effect.

The lesson is *not* that the power of modern courts to conduct the judicial review of statutes for rights compliance is justified by the *direct* adjudicative pursuit of a 'system of individualized contestation', allowing 'openings for particular individuals and subgroups to test the laws or proposals for how far the process in which they are generated respects the value of equal access to influence and, more generally, the value of equal status'.[42] This was the political purpose that guided the institutional design and practices of ancient courts, and the independent institutional design and professional practices of modern courts are ill-suited to the direct judicial pursuit of this purpose. The institutional independence of modern courts is achieved by features of curial design, discussed previously, such as the political appointment rather than election of judges, high thresholds for the impeachment of judges, etc. This political independence will help reinforce the ability of judges to resolve legal disputes as disputes about legal rules rather than disputes about moral values such as 'equal access to influence' and 'equal status', because it will reduce any incentive to favour certain legal outcomes in order to avoid popular sanctions and maintain their office. While institutional independence promotes virtuous legal decision-making, it magnifies the adjudicative vice of resolving legal disputes as though they were open-textured

---

[41] I am grateful to Philip Pettit for helping me see this point.

[42] Pettit, above n 6, p. 213.

disputes about moral values because it will shield such moral decision-making from the equal contestatory control of the citizenry.

The legal professionalism of modern adjudicative institutions and practices is also inimical to the modern pursuit of ancient adjudicative purposes. Judicial professionalization can be reinforced by forms of institutional independence that reduce the extent to which a judge's knowledge of artificial forms of legal reasoning will be directly evaluated in terms of their moral or political significance, creating special codes of conduct to help ensure a commitment to judicially appropriate techniques of legal reasoning, etc. Moral reasoning might play some part in the legal direction of adjudication, but as a part of *virtuous* modern adjudicative reasoning it will always be restricted by considerations of 'fit', such as the constitutional text, inferences about constitutional structure, historical materials bearing on its meaning, and applicable precedents set in the past by courts or legislatures.[43] It may be that certain types of law, and rights in particular, invite adjudicative moral reasoning more than other legal concepts, but there is often the risk that such moral reasoning will become untethered from positive legal sources. This risk is underlined by the fact that Ronald Dworkin, the legal philosopher who advocated judges christening legal rules with the 'justification' of moral reasoning where the 'fit' of legal materials ran out, appeared to never find an actual litigated instance where legal 'fit' restrained moral 'justification'.[44] By pursuing the ancient political purpose of morally contesting the equality-protecting status of laws, even where the law itself appears to direct courts towards such moral reasoning, modern professionalized judges run the risk of disguising unconstrained moral reasoning as the kind of virtuous technical adjudication that has the potential to help secure citizens from domination.[45] To justify judicial review as a means for modern courts to directly pursue the more ancient purpose of courts is to invite the transformation of the modern institutions and practices that might guide the justifiable exercise of judicial review into instruments allowing courts to cloak the vice

---

[43] M. McConnell, 'Time, Institutions, Interpretation' (2015) 95 *Boston University Law Review* 1745, 1776.

[44] M. McConnell, 'The Importance of Humility in Judicial Review: A Comment on Ronald Dworkin's Moral Reading of the Constitution' (1997) 65(4) *Fordham Law Review* 1269.

[45] This has the added danger of polarizing and politicizing the legal profession such that it either becomes a political coalition in its own right or factionalized into coalitions aligned with other political actors.

of abusing their unequal power to interfere with legal changes to the law in the garb of adjudicative virtue.[46]

The second lesson that can be gleaned from the institutional features and functional practices of modern courts and legislatures is that recruiting the legal function of courts to the modern political purpose of republican legislatures carries the serious risk of political injustice. The moral seriousness of this risk is equal to that posed by the legislature. The threats these institutions pose to freedom from domination require institutional arrangements and practices allocating the capacity to contest unjust legislative interference to courts, and the ability to directly respond to and contest unjust judicial forms of interference with legislation. The reason why republicans should take the risk of political injustice posed by courts as morally equal to that posed by legislatures is implicit in their understanding of the connection between justice and freedom as non-domination. Constitutional theorists who understand political freedom as non-interference, and who take rights to stake out areas of freedom against interference by the state or other individuals, may have reason to favour adjudicative forms of state interference over legislative forms. Some constitutional theorists have argued that the negative character of adjudication as a form of state interference in the lives of citizens renders it a lesser threat to freedom than the ability of legislatures to change the law without the possibility of having their changes invalidated for violating rights.[47] This might make sense given a commitment to freedom as non-interference. But on the view that freedom should be conceived of as freedom from the domination or from subjection to the arbitrary will of another, and the auxiliary thesis that political justice is characterized by citizens' maximally equal control over state interference and

---

[46] Of course, this is not a systematic argument in favour of considering such judicial review a republican 'constitutional essential', and any such argument would be conditioned by the second lesson that can be drawn from the distinctive institutional features and functional practices of modern courts and legislatures. For the idea of a 'constitutional essential', see, J. Rawls, *Political Liberalism* (New York: Columbia University Press, 2005), p. 232.

[47] R. H. Fallon, Jr., 'The Core of an Uneasy Case for Judicial Review' (2008) 121(7) *Harvard Law Review* 1693; Mark Tushnet argues that Fallon's argument functions on the assumption of a 'libertarian presupposition', that it is worse for a statute to be enacted than not enacted or disapplied because only an enacted and applied statute can threaten to interfere with rights – a presupposition which appears to lean on the theory of freedom as non-interference, although perhaps not the interference-alone thesis. M. Tushnet, 'How Different Are Waldron's and Fallon's Core Cases for and against Judicial Review' (2010) 30(1) *Oxford Journal of Legal Studies* 49, 52.

non-interference alike, the negative character of a state action grants it no special advantage as a means of protecting freedom and justice.

If the negative character of a state action grants it no special philosophical advantage in protecting the justice of freedom from domination, then the fact that judicial invalidations of just statutes constitute a negative type of state action provides no reason to prefer the risk of the unjust exercise of judicial review over the enactment and application of unjust statutes. There may be nonideal, context specific reasons for republicans to subject legislatures or courts to varying levels of suspicion regarding their propensity for injustice, but there is no *prima facie* reason to vary such suspicion in an asymmetrical fashion. This implication of the republican critique of the concept of freedom as non-interference not only deflates one prominent justification for judicial review, but also inferentially restricts the forms of judicial review that can be justified as an ideal means of securing modern citizens from unjust domination. The inference is that because the risk of legislatures enacting politically unjust legislation is equal to the political risk of courts unjustly exercising their interpretive powers, republican constitutional norms must grant courts and legislatures equal powers of interference in their respective functions. Thus the principle implied by the republican critique of the conception of freedom as non-interference is that, absent certain nonideal political contexts, the equally significant (though not necessarily equally *probable*) threats that modern courts and legislatures pose to citizens' freedom requires that legislatures not be restricted from contesting politically unjust judicial interference in the task of making the law, nor courts from contesting politically unjust legislative interference in the adjudicative task of applying the law.

But what does it mean for courts to 'unjustly' or 'justly' interfere with legislation, or for legislatures to 'unjustly' or 'justly' interfere with judicial decisions? Modern courts can justly interfere with arbitrary exercises of the legislative function by carrying out their proper task of applying and determining the meaning of the law and refusing to apply laws that violate constitutional rights. Courts can unjustly interfere with the republican task of legislation by invalidating statutes that reflect valid changes to the law or applying statutes reflecting invalid changes, in either case enacting arbitrary changes to the law. This implies that just legislative corrections to adjudicative abuses will primarily be tied to the task of responding to the risk of unequal and technically camouflaged judicial changes to the law. Insofar as such just corrections respond to unjust judicial decision-making, they will often simply involve legislatures' reasserting their jurisdiction over judicial usurpations of the legislative function. However, where there is disagreement between the branches regarding what the determinate meaning of the law is, it may be unclear whether the law is in need of interpretive application or creative change. In such cases of reasonable disagreement, which institution has jurisdiction over a legal matter is up for debate and in these circumstances legislative corrections of adjudicative abuses may appear to take the form of legislative incursions on the judicial task of interpretation. Modern legislatures can interfere with the adjudicative function by fulfilling their legal-cum-political task of deliberately changing the law in a way that causes the judiciary to adapt its interpretive methods to determine the meaning of such changes. Legislatures can unjustly interfere with the task of adjudication by enacting changes that directly entail invalid applications and determinations of legal rules or standards. This suggests that the just judicial task of correcting invalid legislative exercises of the adjudicative power of interpretation will often straightforwardly involve asserting their interpretive task of applying the law in particular cases and circumstances. But where the law is indeterminate, and especially where there is inter-institutional disagreement about whether the law is indeterminate as a matter of its interpretive application or its openness to legislative change, judicial corrections of what courts take to be invalid legislation may well appear to take the shape of adjudicative lawmaking.

IV Republican Dialogue

Which of the reasons and corresponding senses of dialogue outlined in the introductory section of this chapter will prove virtuous as a norm for realizing politically just forms of legislation and adjudication? Which norm of dialogue will allow for legislatures and courts to correct the unjust incursions of one branch into the function of its counterpart, including in forms of redress that appear to take the shape of modern judicial lawmaking and legislative interpretation concerning legal rights? Recall that there are at least three basic normative reasons why dialogue between courts and legislatures regarding legal rights might be desirable, and each of these reasons is reliant on specific normative premises and corresponds to a particular norm of what dialogue entails. The first reason for valuing dialogue between courts and legislatures is that it will allow courts to interrogate legislatures for justifiable reasons for statutes to override rights. The second is that dialogue between courts and legislatures can allow courts to interrupt the legislature's exercise of its ongoing responsibility to protect rights without unjustly interfering with the legislative function. Such interruptions are valued for their potential to facilitate the legislature's task by means of judicial deference to any reasonable legislative responses they provoke in order to help prevent unjustifiable infringements of rights, primarily in cases where legislatures suffer from political gridlock or blind spots. The third reason is that dialogue between courts and legislatures can allow them to co-ordinate the construction of the indeterminate meaning of rights in a way that helps maintain the citizenry's control over rights.

In this section I shall argue that the third constructive reason for dialogue, and its corresponding conception of what dialogue entails, is the ideal republican norm for animating politically just forms of legislation and adjudication, including what might appear to be corrective forms of judicial lawmaking and legislative interpretation concerning legal rights. Constructive dialogue is a norm that can be equally avowed by modern republican judges, legislators, and citizens alike in a system featuring judicial review. This is because it mitigates the risks of politically unjust adjudication by providing citizens and officials alike with the expectation that legislatures not only can, but should actively contest abuses of adjudication by using their ability to change the law to correct what they take to be mistaken interpretations of or changes to legal rights. In contrast, interrogative and interruptive forms of dialogue threaten to turn modern courts toward the political injustice of directly pursuing the political purposes of ancient courts, thereby creating an unequal and deceitful parallel system of individualized control over changes to the law.

A   Interrogative Dialogue

Interrogative arguments in favour of dialogue advocate the most clearly anti-republican norm of dialogue. This view takes the value of dialogue to be the subjection of legislatures to a kind of Socratic interrogation by courts. The interrogative reason for favouring dialogue is rooted in the view that legislatures should be expected to regularly enact changes infringing legal rights, especially the rights of vulnerable minorities, and as result dialogue should be restricted to the ability of legislatures to justify infringing rights to courts. This ideal of dialogue fails to account for the threat to political justice posed by forms adjudicative reasoning that are unrestricted by legal sources, and unjustifiably excludes or minimizes the possibility that just forms of legislation can correct the injustice of unequal and technically camouflaged judicial changes to the law.

Socrates' favoured form of *elenchic* interrogation does not resemble the kind of technical legal reasoning that the modern institutional independence and professionalization of courts is designed to achieve. As such, it is quite likely that turning judicial reasoning about the violation of rights towards such a legally undirected form of reasoning will unacceptably increase the risk that this reasoning will promote the judicial pursuit of the ancient political purpose of courts, but with the unequal institutional platform and distortive technical jargon that characterizes modern courts. This Socratic ideal of dialogue is usually tied to a conception of rights as non-relationally defined and as normatively inconclusive interests. Proponents of the interrogative conception of dialogue explicitly favour dialogue as an opportunity for courts to engage in 'proportionality analysis', or the 'judicial testing of the arguments and evidence presented by the government to justify limits on rights rather than abstract and static questions of interpretation'.[48] This form of practical reasoning is favoured because it 'ensures that legislators and judges exercise the virtues of fair social cooperation'.[49] What this means is proportionality based dialogue will ensure that legislatures only override rights where they have good reason and that democracy will be strengthened by

> judicial reminders about the rights of unpopular minorities, and of fundamental values that both the legislature and the executive may cast overboard in response to real or perceived emergencies. Judicial mistakes can be corrected by legislation that broadens the policy debate, refines legislative objectives and educates the court about the practical trade-offs and difficulties in achieving legislative objectives.[50]

On the view of rights informing the proportionality approach, rights are taken to be interests or values defined independently of one another and legal rules.[51] They are also normatively inconclusive insofar as they can be justifiably infringed if they happen to have the optimized relationship to other interests in circumstances where the law infringed them for a good public purpose and does so as minimally as possible.[52] For purposes of this chapter, I will assume that even if this conception of rights is

---

[48] Roach, above n 2, p. 291.
[49] C. Farrelly, above n 26, p. 525.
[50] Roach, above n 2, p. 290.
[51] G. Webber, *The Negotiable Constitution* (Cambridge: Cambridge University Press, 2009), pp. 66–68.
[52] Ibid., pp. 68–80.

compatible with the unrestricted *moral* practical reasoning of republican citizens, it is not the kind of legally restricted reasoning that the institutions and practices of modern courts were designed to achieve.[53]

It will suffice to note that this conception of rights invites unelected judges to evaluate the 'reasonableness' or 'substantiality' of the legislative purpose for changes to the law under the hollow pretext of deploying a technical legal 'test' such as a 'rational basis test', 'proportionality test', 'balancing test', or 'endorsement test'.[54] It invites them to second-guess the judgement of the legislature about the purposes of statutes and the means they employ to achieve them. Judicially questioning the purposes and means of statutes as they relate to rights involves exercising what is 'the quintessence of a legislative decision' under the 'moderate guise' of false techniques of legal reasoning.[55] In ancient courts, citizen jurors could often seek to nullify and even punish legislators responsible for laws with unjustifiable purposes, but the justification of the judicially contested purposes and means of laws would be openly debated and then decided by hundreds of their fellow representative citizen-jurors.[56] On the interrogative view, unelected and institutionally independent judges should take on the role of citizen inquisitors using the 'technocratic camouflage (a multi-prong legal sounding test)' of proportionality analysis, and legislative replies to judicial decisions can seek to correct mistakes about the judicial deployment of this analysis, not mistakes about the interpretation of the content of rights.[57] The legislature is a suspect in an interrogation designed not to discover its guilt, but whether it had good reason to infringe legal rights, and the citizens' representative legislature is thereby presumed guilty until proved utilitarian. The interrogative norm of dialogue thus not only encourages courts to risk the political injustice of pursuing ancient political ends by abusing the unequal institutional platform and opaque techniques of modern courts, but also caricatures modern legislative changes to the law as decisions

---

[53] One interesting attempt to explore the relationship between this conception of rights and the republican conception of freedom is found in E. Daly, 'Freedom as Non-Domination in the Jurisprudence of Constitutional Rights' (2016) 28(2) *Canadian Journal of Law and Jurisprudence* 289.

[54] *United States v. Carolene Products Co.* 304 U.S. 144 (1938); *R. v. Oakes* [1986] 1 S.C.R. 103 at [71]; *Mathews v. Eldridge* 424 U.S. 319 (1976) at 319; *City of Allegheny v. ACLU* 492 U.S. 573 (1989).

[55] McConnell, above n 43, p. 1782.

[56] M. Hansen, above n 30, p. 175.

[57] M. Kumm, 'The Idea of Socratic Contestation and the Right to Justification' (2010) 4(2) *Law and Ethics of Human Rights* 142, 174.

that can 'educate the court about the practical trade-offs' involving policy objectives and rights, yet never as extra-judicial interpretations of law meant to correct abuses of adjudication. It thereby increases the risk of political injustice, and delegitimizes the primary way of mitigating it.

B   Interruptive Dialogue

As a reason for valuing dialogue between courts and legislatures, interruption is taken by many theorists to balance the interrogative concern for the unjustifiable legislative violation of rights, especially minority rights, with the constructive concern for the consistent specification and democratic legitimacy of rights. This reason justifies a norm of dialogue that is meant to allow the judiciary to interrupt the application of statutes that could reasonably be interpreted as violating legal rights, such as where laws are suspect directly on a court's view of their legal 'merits', or which suffer from either realist 'blind spots' (e.g., laws touching on the rights of underrepresented minorities) or the 'burdens of inertia' (e.g., where rights issues internally divide political parties, creating gridlock) while protecting the equal control of citizens over changes to the law. The citizenry's equal control is protected in spite of such interruptions, either by the judicial inability to subject legislative responses to interruptions to further review, or by ex post deferring to such responses.[58] The first prominent variation on the norm requires the formal ability of legislatures to disregard or insulate their replies to judicial decisions from further judicial review, provided they reconsider their prior political judgement.[59] The second maintains that the primary means of expressing such reconsideration should be by enacting an ordinary statutory reply.[60] The interruptive norm of dialogue is clearly

---

[58] Dixon, 'Dialogue and Deference' in this volume; Dixon, 'The Supreme Court of Canada, Charter Dialogue, and Deference', above n 3, pp. 257–266; Gardbaum, *The New Commonwealth Model*, above n 3, pp. 85–87.

[59] Stephen Gardbaum essentially argues in favour of an interruptive norm of dialogue featuring 'respectful but unapologetic' judicial review on the merits and the use of insulated (or ignoring declarations of rights incompatibility) statutory replies for legislative expressions of deliberatively reconsidered and reasonable rights disagreements with courts. In his more recent work, he does not use the term 'dialogue' and has explicitly commented on the infelicity of the metaphor. See Gardbaum, *The New Commonwealth Model*, above n 3, pp. 15–16.

[60] This variation of the theory roughly corresponds to at least part of Rosalind Dixon's intriguing 'new dialogue theory', which differs from Gardbaum primarily in its prescription for the use of ordinary statutes as expressions of reasonable legislative disagreement

more promising than the interrogative norm insofar as its proponents acknowledge the risk of political injustice inherent in the exercise of judicial review. In the ordinary circumstances of politics, however, the interruptive norm of dialogue increases the risk of political injustice.[61]

The first influential variation of the norm supports courts leveraging their 'virtues of skilled professionalism and judicial independence' to invalidate or declare rights-incompatible statutes that on their 'first look' they take to violate rights given 'the best legal view on the merits'.[62] This variation holds that the 'legal merits' of statutes are evaluated using the dominant proportionality approach to rights, and that legislative responses to such decisions should take a form that is immune to further judicial review.[63] It thereby recommends an interrogative variety of interruptive dialogue. That is, it risks the interrogative political injustice of having unelected modern courts pursue the political function of ancient courts using methods of unconstrained moral reasoning disguised as professional techniques of legally directed reasoning, but with the possibility of legislatures formally contesting conclusions. On the second influential variation of the interruptive norm, in their 'first look' analysis of whether statutes comply with rights, courts should use their institutional independence to abandon the professional techniques of legal reasoning that require them to treat the legislature as a formal entity. They should liberate themselves from this kind of formalism by

---

with 'first look' judicial decisions. See Dixon, 'The Supreme Court of Canada, Charter Dialogue, and Deference', above n 3, pp. 257–266. However, Dixon also favours constructive judicial decision-making, as evidenced in an aspect of her discussion of positive 'blind spots of application', where courts interpret indeterminate laws by drawing on their 'significant experience in *applying* laws to particular cases'; Dixon, 'The Core Case for Weak-Form Judicial Review', above n 3, pp. 2214–2216. But, like Gardbaum, Dixon also considered proportionality analysis to be a useful way of assessing the application of laws implicating rights in specific cases and circumstances, and on the argument offered here, proportionality analysis (at least in the interrogative sense advocated by Kent Roach and Mattias Kumm) is incompatible with the norm of legally constructing rights for particular cases and circumstances. Her view is thus partially interruptive (and interrogative in some cases), and partially constructive.

[61] The ordinary 'circumstances of politics' is 'the felt need among the members of a certain group for a common framework or decision or course of action on some matter, even in the face of disagreement about what that framework, decision or action should be', J. Waldron, *Law and Disagreement* (Oxford: Oxford University Press, 1999), p. 102; also see A. Weale, *Democracy* (Basingstoke: Macmillan, 1999), pp. 8–13.

[62] Gardbaum, *The New Commonwealth Model*, above n 3, pp. 84–86.

[63] See S. Gardbaum, 'Proportionality and Democratic Constitutionalism' in G. Huscroft, B. W. Miller, and G. Webber (eds.) *Proportionality and the Rule of Law: Rights, Justification, Reasoning* (Cambridge: Cambridge University Press, 2014), p. 270.

attending to realist concerns, such as the relation between the under-representation of minorities in the legislature to statutes implicating their rights, or blockages to legislative changes implicating rights caused by partisan gridlock that is the result of internal divisions in parties regarding rights issues, competing legislative priorities, bureaucratic delays, etc.[64] This version of the norm risks political injustice by guiding courts to the aggressive 'first look' interruption of statutes implicating rights because they fail to correct for the formal 'application of laws to particular cases in a way that limits rights' and a host of informal-realist concerns regarding the legislative process.[65]

Unlike the interrogative norm of dialogue, both of these versions of the interruptive norm attempt to mitigate the risk of political injustice by allowing legislatures to reply to unjust forms of adjudication. But in spite of the possibility of legislative replies to such aggressive 'first look' adjudication, both accounts of the interruptive norm of dialogue diminish the likelihood of such replies and thereby augment the risk of judicial domination. The first version of the norm encourages courts to strike down statutes on their 'first look' using proportionality analysis, and this diminishes the likelihood of legislative replies correcting unjust refusals to apply laws or misinterpretations of rights, because it casts such replies in the interrogative light of challenges to the judicial evaluation of the unjustified infringement of rights, not alternative legislative interpretations of rights. In some contexts, constitutional instruments of 'non-finality' could allow legislatures to ignore such decisions, or to immunize their statutory replies from further review in ways that clearly indicate that statutes can express 'rights-dissensus' to disagree with and displace such aggressive judicial decisions as they relate to particular interpretations of rights.[66] But even if these kinds of mechanisms filter interrogative dialogue featuring judicial interruptions of statutes implicating rights, the interrogative character of adjudication will influence judges, legislators, and even citizens to think of statutes implicating rights adjudication as expressions of 'rights-misgivings', or disagreements about whether taking rights 'to an extreme or applying [them] in cases where

---

[64] Dixon, 'The Supreme Court of Canada, Charter Dialogue, and Deference', above n 3, pp. 257–266.

[65] Ibid., 257–258.

[66] J. Waldron, 'Some Models of Dialogue Between Judges and Legislators' (2004) 23 *The Supreme Court Law Review*, 11–12, 38–39.

other important interests ... are much more urgently engaged'.[67] If the police continually treat a criminal suspect's alibi, documents, and other forms of exculpatory evidence as more or less satisfactory justifications for violating the law, then it seems likely that the suspect's defence lawyers, witnesses, and even an innocent suspect himself, will begin to play this game.

The second version of the interruptive norm also exacerbates the threat of judicial domination by diminishing the likelihood of just legislative replies. It does this by exhorting courts to interfere with statutes in 'first look' cases where the risk judicial review poses to political justice is heightened, and its rewards are negligible, and to defer to statutes in 'second look' cases where the risk of legislatively enacted injustice is greatest. The norm exhorts courts to interrupt statutes in circumstances where the exercise of judicial review poses the greatest risk of political injustice because it asks them to disapply the statutes that legislatures are either the least willing and the most incapable of replacing or, alternatively, the most likely to replace with unjust laws. Where courts use realist techniques of looking into the informal 'black box' of the legislative process to discover whether the legislature excluded or failed to consider the perspectives of minorities with rights implicated by a statute, they risk making mistaken political or social-scientific judgements.[68] If minority rights really are at stake, there is the risk that the court's realist analysis will prove inaccurate or even mistakenly land it on the side of the hostile majority or plurality.[69] Where such 'first look' judgements are used to invalidate a statute implicating such minority rights, they compound the risk of reasoning outside their professional area of competence with the risk of displacing a reasonable legislative interpretation of the rights at stake. Yet in cases featuring real majoritarian threats to indeterminate rights, the reward of taking such risks is likely to be offset by the interruptive norm's requirement that in 'second look' cases courts will defer to such socially unjust yet legally reasonable interpretations of rights. Where courts interrupt oppressive but legally indeterminate statutory rights schemes enacted by truly *tyrannical* majorities, their

---

[67] Ibid., 34–39; As Waldron makes clear, it is also possible for the design of such mechanisms to exacerbate this problem with the norm.

[68] For the idea of informal reasoning as looking into a 'black box', see R. Pildes, 'Institutional Formalism and Realism in Constitutional and Public Law' (2013) 1 *The Supreme Court Law Review* 1.

[69] K. Whittington, 'Extrajudicial Constitutional Interpretation: Three Objections and Responses' (2001) 80 *North Carolina Law Review* 773, 831–835.

interruption is likely to be reversed or even possibly to stir up much uglier statutes targeting minorities. The interruptive dialogue suggests that courts should take a *realist* look inside the informal 'black box' of the democratic process, opinion polls, etc. to aggressively invalidate statutes taken to threaten rights in light of such extralegal judgements. This first realist look is itself risky, but the potential reward of the risk is betrayed by the interruptive norm's recommendation that courts bracket their realist judgement and treat responses to their 'first look' judgement in a legally formal and deferential fashion.

On this theory of interruptive dialogue, courts can also aggressively invalidate statutes on their 'first look' and develop new legal rules or standards to directly address the inertia created by difficulties such as competing legislative priorities or cross-pressured coalitions of minorities. In many of these cases, judicial interruptions are unlikely to provoke 'dialogic' legislative replies, and therefore lack any superior respect for citizens' equal control over changes to the law. There is considerable evidence that the prospect of judicial interference in cases where changes to the law are already a low priority actually further *lowers* the priority of such changes and discourages legislation dealing with matters featuring high electoral risks.[70] The true effect of interruptions meant to address low priority legislation is to help minority factions within majority government coalitions achieve their aims without forging a consensus between minority factions. Such factions will be unaccountable to the electorate for the judicial decision that favours their preferences, even if they help provoke the judicial interruption by politically blocking or delaying legislation. It seems unlikely that courts following this norm with regard to low priority legislation should expect their interruptions to spark any kind of dialogue at all. Amending statutes that implicate rights that are subject to the reasonable disagreements of cross-pressuring coalitions of minorities is unlikely to be a priority for democratic leaders, and judicial interference with such statutes would also seem unlikely to provoke dialogues involving corrective legislative responses. Such hotly contested cross-partisan issues are often low in legislative priority due to their serious moral significance, and therefore it is all the more crucial that they be resolved in a fashion that respects citizens' equal right to control the content of the state's law. When courts interrupt statutory

---

[70] K. Whittington, '"Interpose Your Friendly Hand": Political Supports for the Exercise of Judicial Review by the United States Supreme Court' (2005) 99(4) *American Political Science* 583.

rights schemes in order to address the 'burdens of inertia', their interruptions can potentially *contribute* to these burdens by incentivizing
political actors to ignore or downplay their accountability for rights. In
both versions of the norm of interruptive dialogue, the regularities of
judicial and legislative behaviour solicited by the norm appear to minimize the probability of legislative responses correcting for the mistaken
adjudicative application or invalidation of laws, and the changes such
decisions can make to the law.[71] This might have been acceptable for
ancient courts, which counterbalanced the threat of domination from
one segment of the population in legislative a assembly by allowing
another indicatively represented segment of the population to interrupt
its legislative acts. But the institutional independence and professionalism of modern courts means that they risk unequally and unjustly
changing the law. As such, republican modern courts should adjudicate
statutes with indeterminate rights implications in ways that increase the
chances that their mistakes will be corrected. The interruptive norm
directly conflicts with this imperative by encouraging courts to risk the
political injustice of unequally changing the law to provoke 'dialogues'
they can safely bet they'll never face.

C   Constructive Dialogue

Constructing legal rights is a good republican reason for encouraging
dialogue between courts and legislatures because it is consistent with the

---

[71] A good example of why this norm of dialogue is misguided is how it would explain
Canada's *R. v. Morgentaler* [1993] 1 S.C.R. 30. (On the second version of the interruptive
dialogue theory, the Supreme Court of Canada faced a situation in which coalitional
inertia on both the left and right prevented the passage of a law liberalizing the Criminal
Code prohibition on abortion.). The Court then struck down the prohibition for violating
the Charter (section 7) right of Canadian women to 'security of person'. A pro-life bill
which would have overturned the decision, and a pro-choice bill that would have
affirmed it were both solidly defeated. The first compromise bill put forward by the
Mulroney government, which would have imposed legal restrictions on the right the
Court linked to the Charter, was then defeated by a 'paradoxical coalition of pro-life and
pro-choice MP's . . . by a vote of 147–76'. Mulroney then invoked party discipline to pass
the bill in the House of Commons by a vote of 140–131, but the bill was then defeated by
a tie vote (43–43) in the Senate. Canada remains one of the only modern jurisdictions
with no abortion laws, even though the Supreme Court decision clearly invited a legislative response to its interruption. F. L. Morton and R. Knopff, *The Charter Revolution and
the Court Party* (Peterborough: Broadview Press, 2001), pp. 162–163; The interruptive
dialogue theory thus appears to justify judicial domination over all issues subject to the
most politically cross-cutting kinds of reasonable disagreements about rights and should
therefore be rejected by republicans.

virtues of modern institutions and practices, and can serve as a norm for guiding dialogues involving rights in a way that helps maintain the citizenry's control over their legal rights. In practice, a republican norm of constructive dialogue will reduce the risk of political injustice inherent in the exercise of the judicial review of statutes by providing standards for guiding courts and legislatures towards just ways of correcting unjust forms of adjudication and legislation, corrections that may even appear to be forms of judicial lawmaking and legislative interpretation. In particular, the republican norm of constructive dialogue will reduce the threat of judicial domination in that the standards that judges, legislators, and citizens will share for distinguishing rights constructions from unjust forms of judicial lawmaking and legislative interpretation will include the expectation that legislators can and should use their power to change the law to reassert their jurisdiction over the ability to change the law against mistaken judicial interpretations usurping this function, and to enact constructions of indeterminate rights, especially to correct mistaken constructions of the judiciary. This norm of dialogue is crucial, absent special nonideal factors, to maintaining just forms of judicial review. And while it is compatible with many different constitutional systems, it is incompatible with systems that formally or informally exclude legislatures from engaging in legal constructions of rights.

But what exactly is legal construction? A legal construction is not the interpretively discovered meaning of a legal text, nor the kind of change in legal meaning that is the effect of the invention of a wholly new meaning in a legal act of creation, but rather a kind of in-between mode of elaborating legal meaning that 'is essentially creative, though the foundations for the ultimate structure are taken as given'.[72] Construction corresponds to James Madison's concept of 'liquidation', which he explained in his observation in Number 37 of *The Federalist* that:

> All new laws, though penned with the greatest technical skill, and passed on the fullest and most mature deliberation, are considered as more or less obscure and equivocal, until their meaning be liquidated and ascertained by a series of discussions and adjudications.[73]

---

[72] K. Whittington, *Constitutional Interpretation: Textual Meaning, Original Intent, and Judicial Review* (Lawrence: University Press of Kansas, 1999).

[73] J. Madison, 'No. 37' in G. Carey and J. McClellan (eds.), *The Federalist Papers* (Indianapolis: Liberty Fund, 2001), p. 183.

Madison's twofold point is that legal texts do not have a fully determined meaning and that these indeterminacies must be filled in with the
constructions or liquidations involving the contributions of political and
legal actors over time.[74] A legal construction or liquidation is a kind of
legal change that makes plain (*liquidus*: clear, evident) and determinate
what was legally indeterminate, either in the sense of suffering from
multiple ambiguous senses or the vagueness of borderline cases, through
a sufficient threshold of interaction between political and adjudicative
forms of practical reasoning.[75]

This chapter has so far referred to the possibility that judicial corrections to unjust legislation may appear as 'judicial lawmaking' and that
legislative corrections of unjust adjudication may appear to take the
shape of a kind of 'legislative interpretation'. Many such judicial corrections will appear as 'judicial lawmaking' to those who disagree with the
interpretation of the determinate meaning of the law informing the
correction, and many such legislative corrections will appear as a kind
of illicit 'legislative interpretation' to those who simply take their changes
to be mistaken. Yet in cases where legislation violates the determinate
meaning of the law, what some might take to be 'judicial lawmaking' will
simply turn out to be interpretive corrections of legislation, or judicial
assertions of the adjudicative power to interpret the law. Courts can
correct determinately unsound legislative changes to the law by holding
them invalid using their ordinary power of interpretation. Similarly, what
some improperly take to be exercises of 'legislative interpretation' will at
times turn out to be proper legislative changes to the law that reassert
legislative jurisdiction against mistaken judicial decisions. Legislatures
can sometimes correct judicial incursions into the legislative function
by simply exercising their proper function. Such ordinary corrective
exercises of the judicial and legislative functions are not a matter of
dialogue insofar as applying and changing the law according to the

---

[74] I owe my awareness of Madison's thoughts on this matter to conversations with William
Baude, and to his thoughtful paper on the same subject, see William Baude, 'Constitutional Liquidation': on file with the author. For another exposition of the idea of
'liquidation', see C. Nelson, 'Stare Decisis and Demonstrably Erroneous Precedents'
(2001) 87(1) *Virginia Law Review* 1, esp. 10–21; C. Nelson, 'Originalism and Interpretive
Conventions' (2003) 70(2) *The University of Chicago Law Review* 519, esp. 525–529; and
C. Nelson, 'The Constitutionality of Civil Forfeiture' (2016) 125 *Yale Law Journal* 2446,
esp. 2452–2453.

[75] For the distinctive use of the concepts of 'ambiguity' and 'vagueness', see L. Solum, 'The
Interpretation-Construction Distinction' (2010) 27 *Constitutional Commentary* 95.

determinate meaning of the law is not a politically unjust form of interference with the co-ordinate branch's function, at least not in the ordinary circumstances of politics.[76] But in other cases, judicial and legislative corrective interference with the alternate branch's function will appear to be incursions for want of an understanding of the concept of a legal construction. Where the law is relevant but indeterminate in relation to whether its indeterminacy should be resolved in its interpretive application, or through changes enacted for shifting reasons, courts and legislatures can both employ their legal functions to construct the underspecified meaning of the law, including correcting and contesting the alternate branch's contributions to such construction. Judicial decisions that appear to 'change' the law are often neither determinate interpretive applications of the law, nor fully indeterminate 'changes' to the law, but rather candidate constructions of the law's meaning left open by interpretation but structured by law. Legislative enactments that appear to 'interpret' the law's meaning can also turn out not to change nor interpretively apply the law, but rather to constitute potential constructions of legally indeterminate meaning.

But what is it that makes dialogues constructive rather than conflictive contests between the branches? There are two conditions for constructive dialogue. First, constructive dialogue will not take as its subject any determinate legal rule and, second, it will require a democratically justifiable form of interaction between courts and legislatures. The first condition ensures that constructive dialogues will be consistent with the institutional independence and professional techniques that minimize the republican risk of judicial review. Any constructive dialogue will be limited by the determinate meaning of legal texts themselves, insofar as these can be ascertained using different legal techniques of reasoning and methods of interpretation.[77] Of course, in the contexts of both written and unwritten constitutions, there is a great deal of first-order

---

[76] See Webber, above n 29.

[77] It even seems possible for constructive dialogue to take place regarding unwritten constitutional rules, such as the Westminster norm of parliamentary supremacy, provided a determinate core legal effect of the rule is not the subject of the dialogue. This could be one way (although it might be stretch) of describing the contestation of the consistency of a 'manner and form' restriction on the abolition of the Upper Chamber (legislative council) in the struggles between the alternating governments in the Lower House state legislature in New South Wales, the Australian and Commonwealth Courts, and the people of NSW; see *Attorney General* (New South Wales) v. *Trethowan* (1931) CLR 395 and *Clayton* v. *Heffron* (1960) 105 CLR 214.

disagreement about how to interpret constitutions.[78] This would seem to suggest that rights constructions require some first-order agreement on how to discern the determinate meaning of the text of the constitutional bill of rights or on how a legal system's unwritten hybrid rule of recognition and change restricts methods of statutory interpretation for discovering the determinate meaning of a statutory bill of rights.

Indeed, without *some* threshold of agreement on the rules for recognizing determinately valid laws, there can be no valid consensus between adjudicative and legislative constructions.[79] The professionalism of modern judges is tethered to the existence of some such threshold, however evolving or precarious it might be. The republican case for judicial review involving modern courts rests largely on the existence of some threshold of professional agreement, as the authors of the *The Federalist* recognized in their arguments for judicial independence.[80] This does not mean that constructions cannot exist in the face of interpretive disagreements within the legal profession, or between legislatures and courts. Provided that a threshold of similar considerations of legal 'fit' constrict the legal reasoning of legislators and judges, inevitable disagreements about the priority of these methods in different circumstances will leave room for political and adjudicative activity to resolve some vague or ambiguous legal rights.[81] Courts engaged in constructive dialogue will look for *positive* blind spots that legislatures might have regarding how the application of their laws to particular cases and circumstances implicate rights.[82] Unlike the interrogative and interruptive norms of dialogue,

---

[78] K. Whittington, 'On Pluralism within Originalism' in G. Huscroft and B. W. Miller (eds.), *The Challenge of Originalism* (Cambridge: Cambridge University Press, 2011), pp. 70–86.

[79] Baude, 'Constitutional Liquidation', p. 62.

[80] '... there is a still greater absurdity in subjecting the decisions of men selected for their knowledge of the laws, acquired by long and laborious study, to the revision and control of men who, for want of the same advantage, cannot but be deficient in that knowledge. The members of the legislature will rarely be chosen with a view to those qualifications which fit men for the stations of judges; and as, on this account, there will be great reason to apprehend all the ill consequences of defective information; so, on account of the natural propensity of such bodies to party divisions, there will be no less reason to fear, that the pestilence breath of faction may poison the fountains of justice.' A. Hamilton, 'No. 81' in G. Carey and J. McClellan (eds.), *The Federalist Papers* (Indianapolis: Liberty Fund, 2001), pp. 417–418.

[81] McConnell, above n 43, p. 1786.

[82] As mentioned previously, constructive dialogue at least partially overlaps with Rosalind Dixon's salutary recommendation that judges address 'blind spots of application' in dialogue with legislatures: Dixon, 'The Core Case for Weak-Form Judicial Review', above n 3, p. 2214.

this basic condition on constructive dialogue orients courts towards a legally constrained form of reasoning suited to their institutional independence and professional practices, and away from contemplating 'justified infringements' of rights that would fall outside the bounds of constructions of what rights *are*.[83] This alone renders the norm of constructive dialogue superior to its rivals.

The second condition differentiates republican constructions from politically unjust interpretations of legal rights that would otherwise appear to be 'permissible' candidates for construction as a matter of their legal indeterminacy.[84] Republican constructions can involve moral reasoning in the area of indeterminacy beyond the dimension of 'fit', and where the order or blend of techniques for distinguishing determinate from indeterminate legal rules is itself indeterminate, reasoning about legal meaning will be morally constrained by the requirement that its conclusions must be the result of co-ordinated interactions between courts and legislatures that are justifiable in relation to the risk of the political injustice of domination. This will require what Madison called a 'course of authoritative expositions sufficiently deliberate, uniform, and settled' in which each branch (which for him included the presidential executive, but need not in a parliamentary system) directly engages with both the indeterminate question of law and the other branch's engagement.[85] Madison vaguely indicated that this course of practice would have a moral dimension insofar as it would 'carry with it the public sanction'.[86] Now, how will a norm guiding dialogue between courts and legislatures towards the construction of rights ensure that they have the equal sanction of citizens? It will not prove satisfactory to say that, with alternating considerations of the opposite branch's prospective rights construction, the construction that de facto lasts or appears to

---

[83] This is why Webber contrasts rights constructions with the dominant proportionality approach to reasoning about rights as 'justified' or 'unjustified infringements' on rights, see Webber, above n 52, pp. 165–173.

[84] Caleb Nelson compares this space of 'permissible' legal constructions to the range of permissible interpretations of rules statutes grant administrative agencies under the doctrine of *Chevron* deference. Nelson, 'Stare Decisis and Demonstrably Erroneous Precedents', above n 74, pp. 5–8.

[85] Letter from James Madison 'To Charles E. Haynes, February 25th (1831)' in G. Hunt (ed.), *The Writings of James Madison, Volume IX* (New York/London: G. P. Putnam's Sons, 1900), pp. 442–443, cited in Baud, 'Constitutional Liquidation', p. 15.

[86] Letter from James Madison 'To M. L. Hurlbert, May— (1830)' in G. Hunt (ed.), *The Writings of James Madison, Volume IX* (New York/London: G. P. Putnam's Sons, 1900), p. 372, cited in Baud, 'Constitutional Liquidation', p. 18.

'synthesize' and track 'public opinion' is the de jure valid construction of legal meaning.[87] Popular opinion might favour interactions between courts and legislatures that undermine the determinate 'fit' of legal rules, or unequally subordinate the practical reasoning of citizens over changes to the law to unelected judges.[88] Nor will it suffice to say that just rights constructions require that legislatures and courts both exercise a 'partial-agency' over legal interpretation.[89] This fails to explain what would be wrong with legislatures ceding all but the most obliging and minimal exercise of their partial agency in response to aggressive judicial interrogations or interruptions.[90]

The norm of constructive dialogue will only justify constructions where courts recognize that the risks courts and legislatures pose to political justice requires that legislatures have a responsibility to construct rights that are equal to their own. The norm also entails that justifiable constructions will require legislatures to actively exercise this responsibility to correct judicial applications of invalid laws, invalidations of valid laws, and judicial interpretations of indeterminate legal rights they disagree with. In simpler words, it requires mutually reinforcing forms of judicial sharing and legislative caring. Judicial sharing of the constructive role cannot be a matter of mere verbiage. Professions of judicial deference, or declarations of the existence of dialogue between the branches, are insufficient to instantiate the norm of constructive dialogue. Constructive dialogue is not tantamount to judicial deference or opinions declaring courts committed to dialogue. Courts deferentially upholding invalid laws pose a risk to political justice, and declarations of dialogue can be used to mask dominating forms of judicial interrogation and interruption. Declarations of judicial supremacy, that is, assertions of the exclusive judicial authority to constructively interpret the indeterminate law, even if limited to legal rights, are themselves inimical to the

---

[87] B. Friedman, 'Dialogue and Judicial Review' (1993) 91 *Michigan Law Review* 577, esp. 668–671; also see B. Friedman, *The Will of the People: How Public Opinion Has Influenced the Supreme Court and Shaped the Meaning of the Constitution* (New York: Farrar, Strauss and Giroux, 2009).

[88] C. Brettschneider, 'Popular Constitutionalism and the Argument for Judicial Review' (2006) 34 *Political Theory* 516; J. Waldron, 'Judicial Review and Government' in C. Wolfe (ed.), *That Eminent Tribunal: Judicial Supremacy and the Constitution* (Princeton: Princeton University Press, 2004), pp. 164–166.

[89] D. Baker, *Not Quite Supreme: The Courts and Coordinate Constitutional Interpretation* (Montreal: McGill-Queen's University Press, 2010), pp. 150–152.

[90] G. Webber, above n 4, p. 457.

norm of constructive dialogue. This is because they actively discriminate against the equal responsibility of legislatures to construct the law in particular cases and contribute to broader norms of dialogue in which legislatures do not exercise, and are not expected to exercise, their responsibility to challenge prospective judicial constructions.[91]

Justly sharing the constructive aspect of the adjudicative role requires judicial recognition of the ability of legislatures to enact prospective constructions of rights at odds with prior judicial attempts to offer constructions of the same rights.[92] Courts declaring themselves committed to constructive dialogue must make good on their words by restricting the doctrine of *res judicata* ('the matter is judged') to discrete cases as they relate to particular controversies and parties, and relaxing the vertical and horizontal dimensions of the doctrine of *stare decisis* ('stand by prior decisions') to treat statutes elaborating prospective rights constructions, and especially those enacted in the wake of judicial decisions implicating the same indeterminate rights, as rival but equal candidates for precedents to relevant judicial holdings.[93]

---

[91] This is also why judicial supremacy cannot itself be a justifiable republican construction, as it would preclude the conditions necessary for its own just affirmation. Whittington, above n 70, p. 784; see also, S. Gardbaum, 'What Is Judicial Supremacy?' in G. Jacobsohn and M. Schor (eds.), *Comparative Constitutional Theory* (Cheltenham, Edward Elgar Publishing, 2018). For an explicit justification of judicial supremacy, see L. Alexander and F. Schauer, 'On Extrajudicial Constitutional Interpretation' (1997) 110(7) *Harvard Law Review* 1359.

[92] *R. v. Mills* [1999] 3 S.C.R. 668 at [55] genuine but, alas, not robust over time.

[93] If the common law doctrine of *res judicata* is taken to preclude the reconsideration of laws that a court (of any level) has refused to apply on the basis of reasoning involving a prospective rights construction, even in the face of new litigants and laws raising alternative constructions, then legislatures will be unable to contest or affirm such prospective constructions. Restricting *res judicata* to discrete cases and circumstances need not involve the relitigation of legal issues, as allowing the relitigation of indeterminate constructions will not prevent prior holdings from binding past litigants in the particular circumstances related to their case and future litigants, insofar as the issues they raise in their own circumstances touch on judicial constructions that have been affirmed by legislation. In fact, restricting *res judicata* in this way could return the doctrine to its Blackstonian roots. If the common law doctrine of *stare decisis* is taken to exclude consideration of legislation enacting what could be reasonably understood to be alternative rights constructions, either by lower courts bound to vertically obey the constructive holdings of higher courts, or higher courts bound to follow their past commitment to one reasonable rights construction, then legislatures will not be able to confine, contest, or affirm such constructions. Expanding *stare decisis* to allow courts to consider alternative rights constructions contradicting those of higher courts or past decisions need not free courts from treating past judicial constructions as binding when they have been affirmed by legislation, nor from treating the precedential judicial

Legitimate constructions also depend on a legislative duty of care. The robust instantiation of the norm of constructive dialogue demands that legislatures complement judicial commitments to sharing the interpretive role by exercising their responsibility to enact statutes pre-empting or responding to unjust exercises of judicial review, and by offering amendments and affirmations to prospective judicial rights constructions. If legislatures cannot be expected to enact statutes contradicting judicial decisions that invoke purported rights constructions to apply invalid laws or invalidate valid laws, then no amount of judicial willingness to share the interpretive role will instantiate the norm. On the other hand, legislative replies to judicial rights constructions will not contribute to the norm if they simply contradict or preclude the outcome of a particular judicial decision without at least deliberately considering the rights implications of the changes the statute will enact into law – even if the considered rights implications are quite distinct from those of the courts.[94] If co-ordinated with a judiciary that takes its duty to share the constructive role seriously, the legislative responsibility of care should come to inform its responsiveness to the practical reasoning of citizens concerning how legal rights relate to disagreements regarding different political issues.

While proponents of interrogative and interpretive dialogue claim legislative acquiescence to judicial lawmaking as a potential indicator of democratically accountable adjudication, these norms of dialogue make any legislative contestation of judicial lawmaking concerning rights almost impossible. It is hard to see how the failure of legislatures to respond to judicial interrogations or interruptions could be taken as an

---

enforcement of determinate rights as binding regardless of its legislative contestation. D. Baker, above n 89, pp. 92–106; Loosening the doctrine of *stare decisis* in this fashion is far more reasonable and democratic than what some common law courts have done with the doctrine, and could transform the binding force of holdings regarding indeterminate rights back into the form of 'persuasive reasoning' that it resembled at the time when constitutional judicial review was first introduced into the courts of the United States in its founding era. B. Meyler, 'Towards a Common Law Originalism' (2006) 59 *Stanford Law Review* 551, 579–580; For recent Canadian Supreme Court cases showing evidence of disdain for the doctrine of *stare decisis*, see *Saskatchewan Federation of Labour v. Saskatchewan* [2015] 1 S.C.R. 245 paras. 32 and 33, and *Canada v Bedford*, [2013] 3 S.C.R. 1101, para. 42.

[94] The view that legislatures are not concerned with rights or legal matters is often exaggerated, and would be counteracted by the existence of something like a norm of constructive dialogue. See Webber, above n 52, pp. 168–173.

indicator of the democratic credentials of such risky forms of adjudication.[95] The reality is that the lack of a particular legislative reply to a particular judicial decision implicating rights will increase in democratic significance the more citizens and legislators alike come to expect that, *in general*, legislatures should and will contest judicial decisions they disagree with. The more citizens and legislators themselves come to expect that legislatures should and will contest judicial decisions they disagree with, the more plausible it will be for courts to take legislative affirmations or amendments to adjudicative holdings as contributing to the justification of such constructions. Conversely, the more courts can be expected to share the constructive role, the more plausible it will be for judges, legislators, and citizens to take past judicial deference or forbearance from intervening in legal areas where political activity has carved out a 'longstanding consensus' as contributing to the justification of the rights constructions forming part of this consensus.[96] Extrajudicial rights constructions can emerge from such political consensus, not as a matter of one election or poll, but from 'the acquiescence of many different decision makers over a considerable period of time'.[97] Insofar as they require both legislatures' responsive deliberation and adjudicative consideration, legal constructions are inherently a matter of dialogue.

When a responsive line can be drawn between the equal practical reasoning of citizens, the legislative reasoning of equal democratic representatives, and judicial reasoning concerning indeterminate rights, dialogue about such rights will stand a better chance of concluding in politically just rights constructions. Tracing this line will depend on the particular arrangements of different kinds of modern courts and legislature in different constitutional and political contexts. But wherever courts and legislatures are characterized by the general modern features discussed earlier, the line will more equally incorporate the practical reasoning of citizens into changes to the law implicating indeterminate rights where courts share their interpretive role with legislatures and legislatures actively take their collective stake in such shared construction

---

[95] This view of acquiescence as dialogue is endorsed in one of the most seminal discussions of the metaphor: P. Hogg and A. Bushell, 'The Charter Dialogue between Courts and Legislatures (Or Perhaps the Charter of Rights Isn't Such a Bad Thing After All)' (1997) 35 *Osgoode Hall Law Journal* 75.

[96] M. McConnell, 'The Right to Die and the Jurisprudence of Tradition' (1997) 3 *Utah Law Review* 665, 682.

[97] Ibid.

as a variable they will be held accountable for.[98] Beyond the general need for constructions to be legally indeterminate and settled by deliberative political and adjudicative inter-institutional interactions, Madison himself was quite vague as to precisely when 'liquidations' of legal rights might become justifiably established. The norm of constructive dialogue improves on this vagueness by adding the expectation of active legislative contestations of adjudicative specifications of indeterminate rights as an evaluative condition of justified constructions. Even so, it shares the opacity of Madison's remarks with regard to the nature and order of the methods of interpretation used to circumscribe the limits of indeterminacy, and the precise number and character of legislative and judicial affirmations of indeterminate conceptions of rights necessary to establish justified rights constructions. In spite of this vagueness, the norm establishes that, if judicial review is part of a constitutional system, it is in the midst of constitutional dialogues featuring the shared responsibility of courts and legislatures for indeterminate legal rights that citizens themselves stand the best chance of looking both their modern representatives and judges in the eye as equals with different jobs.[99]

V   Conclusion

Which norms of dialogue inform contemporary interactions between courts and legislatures in actual constitutional systems? Are these norms encouraged or discouraged by particular ways of arranging courts and legislatures? What can be said on the theory offered thus far is that the interrogative and interruptive reasons for favouring dialogue between courts and legislatures jar with the basic institutional features and practical functions of modern republican institutions. As norms, they both twist modern judicial institutions and practices towards more ancient political purposes better suited to the representative judicial assemblies of the Roman and Athenian past. It may be that reforming modern courts to have more ancient institutional features, such as periodic elections by lot, could reduce the risk that the exercise of judicial review poses to political justice by refusing to apply valid statutes, upholding invalid laws,

---

[98] Both jointly, as an institution representing the people as a single whole and as members of the government responsible for setting and executing the legislative agenda, and singularly, as representative agents within that legislative institution and its dominant government remain individually subject to the demands of their own particular constituencies.

[99] Pettit, above n 6, pp. 177–179.

and unequally changing the law through the binding effect of adjudicative reasoning in such cases.[100] But such reforms are liable to feature their own risks, especially to the application of legal rules to particular circumstances, and even to the overall coherence of changes to the law as a political community reasons together about the direction of state interference. Unlike such risky norms of dialogue or institutional reforms, dialogues that limit and enable the state's interference in the lives of its citizens will prove more likely to secure them from the political injustice of domination where courts and legislatures are equally held to account for the construction of indeterminate rights. And with such equal responsibility, comes equal suspicion.

---

[100] Thanks to Ben Ewing for correctly insisting that I address this possibility. I do not directly address the peculiar mix of modern and ancient judicial institutions in modern contestatory judicial elections, but I take it that even the more modern mode of responsive representation has the liability of interfering with the point of judicial independence and professionalism. For an excellent discussion of this difficulty, see M. Zeisberg, 'Should We Elect the Supreme Court?' (2009) 7(4) *Perspectives on Politics* 785.

PART II

Dialogue and Institutions

5

Past, Present, and Justice in the Exercise of Judicial Responsibility

GRÉGOIRE WEBBER*

I   Change and Adjudication

Law aims to remedy certain defects in human communities. H. L. A. Hart's distinguished contribution to this thought was to draw attention to defects often left untouched by students of legal philosophy before him. Generally known to legal philosophy were the wrongs of violence, theft, and deception. Law seeks to facilitate life in common by restricting and punishing those wrongful acts that 'human beings are tempted [to perform] but which they must, in general, repress, if they are to coexist in close proximity to each other'.[1] Law's remedial role here is to suppress or to frustrate a negative state of affairs in human communities. In doing so, however, law's role is not unique; social rules may emerge to address these unwelcome 'truisms about human nature'.[2] Are there, in turn, good states of affairs in human communities that can be secured only through law?

To answer this question, we can begin, with Hart, by thinking through the possibility that some human communities can regulate their affairs by unofficial primary rules of obligation alone, rules that Hart would have called 'custom' but for the term's unwelcome connotations.[3]

---

* Email: gregoire.webber@queensu.ca. For comments on a previous draft, I thank Richard Ekins, Graham Gee, Dimitrios Kyritsis, Bradley Miller, Owen Rees, Jean Thomas, Leah Trueblood, Francisco Urbina, Mark Walters, Jacob Weinrib, Paul Yowell, and my joint editors. I also thank participants at the workshop 'Constitutional Dialogue: What's in the Metaphor?' (Princeton University, April 2016) and at a faculty work-in-progress seminar (Queen's University, March 2018). I am grateful to Mikolaj Barczentewicz for a fruitful exchange on the relationship between the rule of recognition and the rule of change in Hart's thought.

[1] H. L. A. Hart, *The Concept of Law* (3rd ed, Oxford: Oxford University Press, 2012), p. 91.
[2] Ibid.
[3] For Hart, the unwelcome connotations associated with the term 'custom' are the thoughts that the rules are 'very old' and supported by weak social pressure: Ibid.

Hart allowed for that possibility if three conditions were to hold: (a) a community's primary rules of obligation restrict basic wrongful acts; (b) those 'dissidents and malefactors' who 'reject the rules except where fear of social pressure induces them to conform' constitute no more than a minority; and (c) the community is small and 'closely knit by ties of kinship, common sentiment, and belief, and placed in a stable environment'.[4] Absent these conditions, however, there will emerge defects not open to remedy by the emergence of new, unofficial primary rules of obligation. For communities without these beneficial conditions, an order of complexity in the management of life in common will be needed to replace what a 'simple form of social life' and 'simple form of social control' cannot provide.[5] As Hart's account demonstrates, that complexity will emerge as remedies to defects, remedies that, absent law, would be unrealisable in human communities.

One such defect is *uncertainty* 'as to what the rules are or as to the precise scope of some given rule',[6] to which Hart identifies as a remedy a rule of recognition that will 'specify some feature or features possession of which by a suggested rule is taken as a conclusive affirmative indication that it is a rule of the group'.[7] Another defect is the more or less *static* character of unofficial primary rules, 'whereby courses of conduct once thought optional become first habitual or usual, and then obligatory' only then to be followed, perhaps, by 'the converse process of decay'.[8] To remedy this defect, Hart identifies a rule of change for 'deliberately adapting' the primary rules of obligation to 'changing circumstances'.[9] In relation to the defect of *inefficiency* in the imperfect enforcement of primary rules by the 'diffuse social pressure by which the rules are maintained', Hart identifies a rule of adjudication to empower some person or body to adjudicate conclusively on the disputed question whether a primary rule has been violated.[10] Together, these three remedial rules 'specify the ways in which the primary rules may be conclusively ascertained, introduced, eliminated, varied, and the fact of their violation conclusively determined'.[11] They constitute a step from 'the pre-legal

[4] Ibid. pp. 91–92.
[5] Ibid. pp. 93, 92.
[6] Ibid. p. 92.
[7] Ibid. pp. 92, 94.
[8] Ibid. pp. 92–93.
[9] Ibid. p. 92.
[10] Ibid. p. 93.
[11] Ibid. p. 94.

into the legal world', from a world without to a world with positive law and legal officials.[12]

My focus in this chapter will be on the rule of change and the rule of adjudication – rules that empower a person or body to perform the acts of legislating and adjudicating. Taking inspiration from Hart's insights into the reasons favouring the rules of change and of adjudication, I reflect on how institutions can be designed to exercise these powers *well*, that is, with the necessary capacities to fulfil their constitutional roles under the rules (section 2). These reflections point to the foundations of legislative and adjudicative responsibility and to a basic division in orientation. I argue that the responsibility of the person or body exercising the power to change the law is to care for the community's *future*, a future to be directed by guiding and coordinating human behaviour in community by setting out rights and responsibilities (section 3). By contrast, the power to adjudicate conclusively on the violation of a primary rule discloses a responsibility of a different orientation, a responsibly to relate to the *present* dispute the law as it was at that time *past* when the violation of the rule is alleged to have occurred (section 4). This basic division of responsibility – for the community's future; for relating the community's past acts to present disputes – is a division informed by the need to remedy different defects in human communities.[13] (I leave aside the responsibility of the executive to carry out the community's legal commitments by administering the law in the present.)

With this division in view, I turn to the idea that the legislature's jurisdiction may, in law, be circumscribed so as to deny as a matter of legal jurisdiction what is denied as a matter of moral jurisdiction: injustice in the law, including the injustice of violating human rights (section 5). Where the legislature's jurisdiction is circumscribed in an open-ended manner and subject to judicial review, the exercise of judicial responsibility is partially unmoored from the past and open to the future. My special focus will be on judicial review under charters of rights, many of which guarantee rights and freedoms in a manner that avoids answering many of the questions that arise in disputes about the requirements of rights and justice. In adjudicating whether a legislated change in the law

---

[12] Ibid.

[13] My thinking on these matters was greatly influenced by John Finnis's Gray's Inn Hall lecture, 'Judicial Power: Past, Present and Future' (20 October 2016), published under the same title at *Oxford Legal Studies Research Paper* no. 2/2016 and in John Finnis, *Judicial Power and the Balance of Our Constitution* (London: Policy Exchange, 2017).

complies with the open-ended requirements of a charter of rights, a court is invited to choose between different possible understandings of those requirements and, in so doing, is invited to chart a path for the community's future (section 6). It is a role for which the court is institutionally ill-designed, as revealed by a series of court-led reforms to the judicial forum. I explore the role for dialogue in this context, arguing that the institution designed to take responsibility for the community's future may understand itself to be empowered to do what it would otherwise be unreasonable for it to do: to challenge the exercise of judicial authority. This possibility for dialogue between court and legislature is open because adjudicative authority here is being exercised, not with a view to the past, but to the future (section 7).

II   From Rules to Institutions

Hart's account of secondary rules did not carry the burden of institutional design, but his explanatory method of identifying defects in need of remedy assists one in thinking through answers to the questions: 'What is a legislature?' and 'What is a court?'. By identifying the purpose (objective, goal, end) of the rule of change and the purpose of the rule of adjudication, Hart's methodology begins to chart a path for understanding the nature of the legislature and the nature of the court, even if it is a path he did not pursue.[14] It is a path charted before him by Aristotle and Aquinas that ties together the nature of something and its reasons for being: 'the *nature* of *X* is understood by understanding *X*'s *capacities* or capabilities, those capacities or capabilities are understood by understanding their activations or *acts*, and those activations or acts are understood by understanding their *objects*', their objectives, purposes, reasons.[15]

Following this methodological path, we may explore the nature of the legislature by understanding the capacity of the legislature, a capacity

---

[14] I do not claim that Hart charted this path or is best read as having done so. I argue only that it is a path invited by his method, even if it is a method that Hart distanced himself from in the 'Postscript' in *The Concept of Law*. On different readings of *The Concept of Law*'s celebrated ch. V, see John Gardner, 'Why Law Might Emerge: Hart's Problematic Fable' in Luís Duarte D'Almeida, James Edwards, and Andrea Dolcetti (eds), *Reading HLA Hart's The Concept of Law* (Oxford: Hart Publishing, 2013).

[15] The quotation is from John Finnis, *Aquinas: Moral, Political, and Legal Theory* (Oxford: Oxford University Press, 1998), p. 29, with cites to *De Anima* II, 4: 415a16–21 and *ST* I q 87, a 3c.

understood by reference to legislative action, an action itself understood by interrogating the reasons for legislating. Those reasons, in brief: to 'deliberately adapt' primary rules to 'changing circumstances, either by eliminating old rules or introducing new ones'.[16] So too with the nature of the court: it is explored by understanding the capacity of the court, a capacity understood by reference to judicial action, action itself understood by interrogating the reasons for adjudicating. Those reasons, in brief: to resolve disputes by 'determin[ing] authoritatively the fact of violation of the rules'.[17]

This strategy for understanding the nature of something affirms that, in the study of human affairs, to understand, describe, and explain *what* something brought about by human judgment and choice is (its nature) requires that one ask *why* that something was brought about (its point, purpose, end, reasons for).[18] When the 'something' that is the subject matter of one's inquiry is situated in time and place, such as the Conseil d'État at its 1799 founding by Napoléon Bonaparte or the Westminster Parliament today, one's inquiry is directed to the reasons (goals, purposes) of those situated persons responsible for instituting and for maintaining the institution. In turn, if one's inquiry is general and not situated in this or that time and place, then so too is one's inquiry general: it is not historical or anthropological or sociological, but philosophical. One seeks to inquire into the good reasons why anyone – any community of persons – should favour exercising human judgment and choice to bring about that something. One then begins, as did Hart, by identifying defects in need of remedy in any community deprived of certain beneficial conditions and, by thinking through the *acts* needed to remedy the defects, and so the *capacities* needed to act and act well, one arrives at an understanding of the *nature* of the remedies and the responsibilities of those charged with realising them.

The design of a good institution, with the necessary capacities to legislate well or to adjudicate well, will be explored in the following sections (3 and 4). For now, a preliminary question is considered: do philosophical reflections on the nature of the legislature and the nature of

---

[16] Hart, *The Concept of Law*, pp. 92–93.
[17] Ibid. pp. 93–94.
[18] See Grégoire Webber, 'Asking Why in the Study of Human Affairs' (2015) 60 *American Journal of Jurisprudence* 51; John Finnis, *Natural Law & Natural Rights* (2nd edn, Oxford: Oxford University Press, 2011), ch. 1; John Finnis, 'Law and What I Truly Should Decide' (2003) 48 *American Journal of Jurisprudence* 107; Finnis, *Aquinas*, ch. II.

the court counsel for or against dividing legislative and adjudicative responsibilities between different persons or bodies of persons? Perhaps the same person (the Queen) or body (the Queen's Privy Council) should be entrusted with the responsibilities to legislate *and* to adjudicate. The responsibilities of legislating and of adjudicating are different in kind, but, in principle, the same person could exercise different roles, mindful of the different norms that bear on the exercise of each. And yet it is telling that the political theorists of the constitution-making seventeenth and eighteenth centuries warned against the concentration of power in any one person or body. *The Federalist* captures the widely held political judgment that 'the accumulation of all powers, legislative, executive, and judiciary, in the same hands, whether of one, a few, or many' is the 'very definition of tyranny'.[19] This judgment, being more than a summary of political experience, is alive to the need to think through good constitutional design in the circumstances of human affairs and not in ideal worlds untroubled by human imperfection.

The political tradition of thought emerging from that constitution-making period offers important lessons in constitutional design, including the principle of checks and balances and the principle of the separation of powers, lessons that speak against the idea that a good constitution can be designed without awarding different powers to different institutions. In counselling the distribution of legislative and adjudicative responsibilities to different persons and institutions, the principles of checks and balances and of the separation of powers are said to serve as bulwarks against tyranny and to be in the service of liberty and the rule of law.[20] For the purposes of the present argument, however, the division of responsibilities between different persons and bodies can be arrived at by another path: one of aligning form to function.[21]

In thinking through the capacities that an institution will require in order to perform well its remedial function, one may query whether the capacities that are necessary in order to change the law well are the same as the capacities necessary in order to adjudicate well. If one concludes, as

---

[19] *The Federalist Papers*, No. 47 (1788), available at http://avalon.law.yale.edu/18th_century/fed47.asp.

[20] See Jeremy Waldron 'Separation of Powers and the Rule of Law' in *Political Political Theory: Essays on Institutions* (Cambridge, MA: Harvard University Press, 2016).

[21] For discussion of the relationship of form to function in the separation of powers, see N. W. Barber 'Prelude to the Separation of Powers' (2001) 60 *Cambridge Law Journal* 59.

do sections 3 and 4, that the capacities needed for good lawmaking differ in their fundamentals from the capacities needed for good adjudicating, then the division of legislative and adjudicative responsibilities can be justified on the grounds that law will serve better as a remedy to defects in human communities if the legislative and adjudicative powers are awarded to different institutions.

For the rule of change to serve its remedial purpose, it must empower a person or body not only to make changes, but to make *good* changes, changes that are soundly responsive to the defect of more or less static primary rules, changes that do not themselves beget yet more defects in need of remedy. As Hart's account shows in outline, the responsibility that accompanies the rule of change is not to change the law for the sake of change. It is to change the law to 'changing circumstances', that is: when there are reasons to favour a change in the law.[22] In turn, for the rule of adjudication to serve its remedial purpose, it must empower an adjudicator to rule not on the basis of the flip of a coin (which would be more efficient) or on the basis of what the primary rule should have been either in the past, when the alleged rule violation occurred, or today, when the matter is set for resolution; rather, the rule of adjudication must empower a person or body to settle disputes fairly on the basis that a primary rule has been violated.

How then to achieve good legislation and good adjudication? As the following sections aim to illustrate, the design of a good legislative institution and the design of a good adjudicative institution recommend different institutional features. And, as subsequent sections will aim to demonstrate, the features that award an institution the capacity to adjudicate well will frustrate that same institution's ability to legislate well. These considerations, I argue, invite reflections on the merits of and opportunities for dialogue between court and legislature.

III   Responsibility for the Future

To legislate – to change the law – is to take responsibility for the community's future by determining that the set of interpersonal relationships governed by the law should be this way rather than that. It is to determine what, as a matter of law, is to be prohibited, permitted, and required for the good and rights of the community's members. The

---

[22] See Richard Ekins, *The Nature of Legislative Intent* (Oxford: Oxford University Press, 2012), p. 127 and, generally, ch. 5.

power to make this determination and to act on it is in contrast with the defective state of affairs that lead Hart to identify the need for a rule of change: the 'slow process of growth' with unofficial primary rules, 'whereby courses of conduct once thought optional become first habitual or usual, and then obligatory' only then to be followed, perhaps, by 'the converse process of decay, when deviations, once severely dealt with, are first tolerated and then pass unnoticed'.[23] To remedy this defect of the more or less static character of primary rules, there is a need for a power to 'deliberately adapt' the primary rules of obligation to 'changing circumstances, either by eliminating old rules or introducing new ones'.[24]

Hart's rule of change is introduced to empower a person or body to change the law deliberately (consciously, with resolve, for reasons) in response to a change in circumstances. Though left underexplored by Hart, those circumstances are far-reaching and include changes both to *factual premises* (confirmation or contradiction of factual predictions, technological advances, changes in membership and environment, etc.) and to *normative premises* (evaluations of right and wrong, good and bad, benefits and burdens, fair distributions, etc.). Some premises will be informed by expertise on which there is broad consensus; others will be arrived at tentatively due to the burdens of judgment. Though identified by Rawls as sources of reasonable disagreement *between* persons, the burdens of judgment are here intended to encompass the difficulties each one of us will encounter in making sound judgments. Among those difficulties will be difficulties in assessing and evaluating conflicting and complex evidence, difficulties in identifying the relevant considerations and in determining their weight, difficulties in making overall assessments given incommensurabilities, and difficulties in ranking alternative courses of action.[25]

Factual and normative premises are *reasons* favouring (or not) a change in the law. Any change in relationships governed by law will be intended to achieve good ends and may have unintended, but accepted side effects, all held in view in choosing whether to change the law. That choice will be made by evaluating the fairness and justice of the status quo against this or that proposal for change, evaluations that deny easy answers and for which it is reasonable to anticipate that reasonable

---

[23] Hart, *The Concept of Law*, pp. 92–93.
[24] Ibid. p. 92.
[25] John Rawls, *Political Liberalism* (expanded edn, New York: Columbia University Press, 2005), pp. 54–58, esp. 56–57.

persons will disagree. The reasonableness of that disagreement turns not only on the burdens of judgment that surround the making of decisions where moral truth cannot be demonstrated without contest and where predictions of future behaviour will be imperfect, but turns also on the open-ended nature of choice when confronted with reasonable alternatives, alternatives each supported by reason but left unranked by it.

These realities speak to the design of a good lawmaking body and the institutional capacities that will facilitate the responsible exercise of its lawmaking power. Consider membership. Because the community's future concerns each one of its members and because those members will take a view regarding the status quo and alternatives to it, in principle every member should be invited to participate in the lawmaking activity: *quod omnes tangit ab omnibus decidentur* (what touches/affects all should be decided by all).[26] That principle may be qualified in keeping with the institution's responsibility, which is to act deliberately when there are reasons to change the law. Too large a membership will frustrate the ability of an institution to reason and to act well.[27] When the legislature's membership is qualified in number, as it will be in any community that does not satisfy Hart's conditions for a simple form of social life, the membership *within* the institution should be related to the membership *outside* the institution by a principle of representation, so that those who look upon the lawmaking institution can understand its activity as their activity, its members as their members, and its debates as their debates.[28] This principle of representation, which requires that the legislature's membership be selected by the community's members, promotes the accountability of the lawmakers to the community they serve. From time to time, the community ought to be afforded the opportunity to substitute the membership of the legislature with a new group of members who propose different commitments for the community's future, or who make claim to implement existing commitments with greater competence and resolve.

---

[26] I leave aside debates in political theory on the different principles of inclusion or participation suggested by the Latin *tangere* (touch). For discussion, see Robert E. Goodin 'Enfranchising All Affected Interests, and Its Alternatives' (2007) 35 *Philosophy & Public Affairs* 40; and Arash Abizadeh 'On the Demos and Its Kin: Nationalism, Democracy, and the Boundary Problem' (2012) 106 *American Political Science Review* 874.

[27] Ekins, *Nature of Legislative Intent*, p. 149.

[28] For further discussion, see Richard Ekins, 'Constitutional Conversations in Britain (in Europe)', section 2, in this volume.

So as to legislate well, the institution should have the capacity to inform itself of empirical premises by commissioning studies and receiving expert witnesses and their reports. So too should the institution have the capacity to ensure that it is well seized of the competing normative premises central to the exercise of its responsibility. To this end, its lawmaking process should be designed to emphasise deliberation, where the reasons for and against a proposal may be freely debated, with a view to identifying a full range of the normative premises bearing on the proposal's merits. Identifying a full range of reasons will be facilitated if the process invites the contributions of persons who are not members of the assembly, but who may make known their views, either directly as witnesses and by submitting briefs or indirectly by contributing to wider public debates known to members within the legislature.[29]

The good lawmaking institution will evaluate the ends of the proposal, the merits of the proposed and alternative measures to secure those ends, its anticipated impact on the overall scheme of benefits and burdens shared by members of the community, and the proposal's relationship to the rights of each member of the community. It will be mindful of the existing state of the law and the disruption caused by fundamental change. The resulting choice – to change the law this way or that or not at all – will, in many instances, be *free*, in the sense that reason, having eliminated countless options as unavailable because they are unreasonable or outranked in all respects by other superior options, will leave the lawmakers with a decision to make as between two or more reasonable alternatives, so that nothing but the choosing itself will determine what is to be done.[30] That resulting choice will be whether the community's future is to continue on its present path or to proceed on the new path charted in the law-making proposal.

Given the need to remedy the defect of *stasis* and to keep all primary rules under ready review, the good legislature requires the capacity to initiate, of its own motion, changes to the law. The importance of this capacity is affirmed by the need for self-correction, so that the lawmaker is empowered to reverse previous choices for the community's future when they prove to be misdirected, as some inevitably will be given the

---

[29] In Grégoire Webber, *The Negotiable Constitution: On the Limitation of Rights* (Cambridge: Cambridge University Press, 2009), pp. 150–155, I capture some of these thoughts by referring to the legislature as 'a forum of justification'.

[30] On free choice, see John Finnis, *Fundamentals of Ethics* (Washington, D.C.: Georgetown University Press, 1983), p. 137. See further, pp. 138–140.

many imperfections – both factual and normative – in predicting the course of human affairs.

These reflections on the good lawmaker's *capacities* to exercise lawmaking powers responsibly are all informed by the *reasons* favouring a power to legislate: a power to change the law in response to reasons, including a change in the factual or moral premises informing the community's current legal commitments. In turn, these reflections on capacity inform an understanding of the legislature's *acts*. The morally significant lawmaking choices for the community's future can be carried out responsibly by employing a sort of technique to guide human conduct. It is a technique that requires a firm, even if necessarily imperfect, demarcation between the open-ended deliberation on the merits of a change in the law that precedes a legislative enactment and deliberation according to the enacted law.[31]

For the law to be changed with a view to directing human conduct for the good and rights of the community's members, there is a need for 'the law's distinctive devices: defining terms, and specifying rules, with sufficient and necessary artificial clarity and definiteness to establish the "bright lines" which make so many real-life legal questions *easy questions*' under law, even as they remain otherwise *hard questions* in moral inquiry.[32] These technical devices aim to achieve what moral reasoning will often leave unsettled: unanimity on the law's settlement on the direction of the community's future, in the absence of unanimity on what that settlement should have been or should now be. This unanimity is made possible by the law's ability to settle patterns of rights, duties, liberties, powers, immunities, and so forth, such that even those who disagree on the merits of such patterns can agree on the fact that they are the community's selected patterns. This agreement aligns with a principle of continuity in the community's legal affairs: the legislature's *past* decision settled then and settles *now* how the community is to be governed into the *future* and will continue to do so until a new legislative decision is taken for a different future.

---

[31] See also Mark D. Walters, 'Deliberating about Constitutionalism' in Hoi Kong, Ron Levy, Graeme Orr, and Jeff King (eds), *The Cambridge Handbook of Deliberative Constitutionalism* (Cambridge: Cambridge University Press, 2018) pp. 167–180, at 171: 'Is there a difference between deliberating about what rules to adopt and deliberating about what rules mean?'. Walters's answer is yes.

[32] John Finnis, 'Legal Reasoning as Practical Reasoning' in *Reason in Action, Collected Essays I* (Oxford: Oxford University Press, 2011), p. 220. This is not to deny that there will be value in indeterminacy for some legislative enactments.

IV Continuity between Past and Present

As a remedy for the defect of interminable disputes over whether 'an admitted rule has or has not been violated',[33] the power conferred on an adjudicator is not simply the power to resolve disputes, but to do so according to – on the basis of – law, the admitted rules: 'to make authoritative determinations of the question whether, on a particular occasion, a primary rule has been broken'.[34] The power to make this determination and to act on it is in contrast with the defective state of affairs that lead Hart to identify the need for a rule of adjudication: disputes over whether a primary rule has been violated may 'continue interminably', in addition to which there will be 'waste of time involved in the group's unorganized efforts to catch and punish offenders', not to mention the standing risk of 'smouldering vendettas' that may result from 'self-help'.[35] To this defect labeled by Hart as *inefficiency* – but which his own brief account expands to include the defects of violence and injustice – is proposed a power to adjudicate conclusively on the disputed question whether a primary rule has been violated.[36]

The responsibility of the adjudicator to the parties in dispute, captured by our legal tradition's commitment to do 'justice according to law', participates in the principle of continuity of bringing the past (the law that predates and governs the dispute) to bear on the present dispute. In the special context of adjudication, that principle manifests itself as the distinctively judicial responsibility to adjudicate between parties in dispute over their legal rights and duties by applying to the facts of the dispute the law that defined those rights and duties at that time past when the matter in dispute arose.[37] This responsibility is to bring the past to bear on the present, such that the resolution of the dispute, though issued *now*, by *this judge*, is attributable to the *community's law, then* settled.

To design an institution that can adjudicate well is to recall how law and legal reasoning are, in important measures, technique and technical

---

[33] Hart, *The Concept of Law*, p. 93.

[34] Ibid. p. 96.

[35] Ibid. p. 93.

[36] Ibid. I interpret the defect of 'injustice' by reference to Hart's discussion of the 'standing danger' that the fair-minded community members who do their part will 'risk going to the wall' if there is no 'special organization for ... detection and punishment': pp. 197–198.

[37] Finnis, 'Judicial Power', p. 4.

reasoning. This appeal to law's imperfect demarcation of legal reasoning from more general, unconstrained moral reasoning is celebrated in *Prohibitions del Roy* (1607), in which Chief Justice Sir Edward Coke resisted the judicial intervention of James I by insisting that the resolution of disputes in English courts is 'not to be decided by natural reason but by the artificial reason and judgment of law'.[38] The King, though endowed by God with 'excellent science, and great endowments of nature', had not attained 'cognisance' of the art of law and reasoning according to it, an art and mode of reasoning that 'requires long study and experience'. Coke's appeal to the artificial (technical) reason of the law contains within it an appeal to a principle of fairness, a principle that is at the heart of a community's commitment to the rule of law: that one should be treated impartially by the law, in the sense that one is to be as nearly as possible 'treated by each judge as [one] would be treated by every other judge'.[39]

The technique that constrains the scope of natural reasoning when reasoning according to law is not an obstacle to realising justice or fairness, but is in their service. Contrary to the idea that there is an inevitable trade-off in judicial reasoning between legalistic rule of law values and substantive values of justice and fairness, the artificial reason and judgment of the law is in the service of law's pursuit of justice and fairness, including the justice and fairness of human self-direction. The alternative is to break the continuity between past legal decisions and present dispute resolution, substituting the law as it was and is now and which will have guided subjects in planning their affairs with what the adjudicator thinks should now be the case or should have been the case all along. But more than this, the technique that informs legal reasoning is necessary for sound adjudication. Adjudicating without legal direction confronts any number of outcome-related and intrinsic problems, problems that recall Lon Fuller's allegory of the well-intentioned but hapless law reformer King Rex.[40] None of this denies that, in determining what choice was made for the community in the lawmaking act, the good

---

[38] (1607) 12 Co, Rep. 63.

[39] Finnis, 'Legal Reasoning as Practical Reason' at 228–229. Cf. Jeremy Waldron, 'Lucky in Your Judge' (2008) 9 *Theoretical Inquiries in Law* 185.

[40] See Francisco J. Urbina, *A Critique of Proportionality and Balancing* (Cambridge: Cambridge University Press, 2017), ch. 7; and Lon L. Fuller, The Morality of Law (revised edn, New Haven: Yale University Press, 1969), ch. II. Urbina's discussion includes the parable of Judge Berta, a lay adjudicator unguided by the law in the resolution of disputes. The parable powerfully tracks the lessons of Fuller's parable of King Rex, albeit squarely in the

judge may need to retrace the legislature's chain of unconstrained moral reasoning so as properly to interpret the lawmaker's choice. That task is an exercise in unconstrained moral reasoning, but it is an exercise oriented to understanding the choices and decisions of the legislature, not an exercise oriented to making choices and decisions oneself.

All this informs the capacities necessary for adjudicating well. Given the ambitions of adjudication according to law, the institution responsible for resolving disputes should have a membership with expertise in the law and legal reasoning. The good court will have as members (judges) persons learned in the law, with demonstrated skill in legal reasoning. The capacity of the judge to understand the law and its relationship to the facts will be assisted by awarding those whose dispute is before the court the right to be heard, so that they – through counsel learned in law – may present to the judge their best understanding of the dispute's just resolution according to law.

The capacity of the judge to decide disputes according to law is promoted by removing fear and favour from the judicial office, so that nothing risks deflecting the judge's commitment to resolve the dispute according to the community's legal commitments. The judge participates in the community's legal order by affirming the parties' rights and entitlements and duties and debts as determined by the law properly applicable at the time of the matter in dispute. This end of doing justice according to law is promoted by granting judges security of tenure and a salary of sufficient value to render unattractive gifts from parties seeking to deflect the bearing of the law of their case. It is an end promoted by disallowing a judge from presiding over disputes in which the judge has (or reasonably appears to have) a connection to the parties or an interest in the dispute's resolution. And it is strengthened by granting judicial officeholders immunity from liability for their judgments and, more generally, by making them unanswerable for their decisions save through the legal reasons they give in support of them.

In speaking law to power, judges are to be lions,[41] fearless in resolving disputes according to law. The judge's independence – from litigants and others – is all in service of the judicial duty to resolve disputes according to law. By imputing their decisions to the law, judges are empowered to

---

context of adjudication. See also Paul Yowell 'Legislation, Common Law and the Virtue of Clarity' in Richard Ekins (ed), *Modern Challenges to the Rule of Law* (LexisNexis, 2011).

[41] The thought is Francis Bacon's from his essay, 'Of Judicature' (c. 1601): 'let them [judges] be lions, but yet lions under the throne'.

challenge those in authority or with high standing in the community. In the judicial act of rendering judgment, the court brings the community's past commitments to bear on the resolution of the dispute by concluding that the law, as it was *then* established, resolves *today's* dispute between the parties in this rather than that way. Although the minimal requirement for the rule of adjudication is the judge's conclusion itself – 'an admitted rule has or has not been violated' – the reason for the rule favours accompanying that conclusion with legal reasons that demonstrate how that conclusion was reached.

These reflections on the *capacity* of the court and its judicial *acts* all point to the *nature* of adjudication as bringing the past to bear on the present dispute. The rule of adjudication gives expression to a principle of continuity, whereby the law enacted by the legislature or incrementally developed by the common law legally directs what is to be done by the judge when tasked to resolve a dispute. This focus on the judicial disposition to look back to the law as it was at the time of the disputed action suggests that it is a violation of judicial office for a judge to depart from the law in resolving a dispute. The idea that judges 'make law', that they look not to the past but to the future, strains the judicial vocation. And yet it is known that, in the common law, judges do sometimes depart from the law as judicially approved in the past and on the basis of which a community's members will have acted. Is there no way to make sense of these judicial (common law) acts – even when explicitly said to be acts of overruling precedent – save by denying their judicial quality? There is, and it is a sense that maintains the judicial commitment to bring the past to bear on the present.

The idea of the law's integrity can be understood by situating a rule of law not only within 'particular doctrines here and there', but also within 'the whole structure of law'.[42] The choice of a judge to depart from *this* rule of law and thus to make this change in this law may be motivated by the evaluation that the rule now changed is 'out of line with principles, policies and standards acknowledged (now, and when the dispute arose) in comparable parts of our law', parts that are *already in existence* and *already* shape our community's future.[43] The common law rule now changed in the wake of adjudication is changed because it is concluded to have been a mistake, understood not only on its substantive merits, but principally on account of its fit with the other parts of the community's

---

[42] Ronald Dworkin, *Justice in Robes* (Cambridge, MA: Belknap Press, 2006), p. 250.
[43] Finnis, 'Judicial Power', p. 5.

law. The judicial development of the law differs from a true act of taking responsibility for the community's future precisely because the change in the law is brought about by *looking back* to the whole of the law as it stands.[44] That judicial act of change differs from legislating insofar as it is not taken by *looking forward* to what would be, all things considered, 'a better pattern of inter-relationships', even if unmoored from the past.[45]

In this way, some changes in the common law can be said to be true to the common law's claim to 'declare' and not 'make' the law, because 'though new in relation to the subject-matter and area of law directly in issue between the parties', the new changes are nevertheless '*not a novelty* or act of legislation (taking our law as a whole), and can fairly be applied to the parties and dispute before the court'.[46] Of course, in one sense, the thought that a new common law rule, like the rule it replaces, is 'declared' is falsified by the fact that it, like much of the history of the common law, is a change in the law. However, when evaluated in the light of the judicial responsibility to relate the past to the present, this change in the law can be said to be a declaration of the state of the law rather than a new legal proposition because of the method by which the change in the law is brought about, a method that speaks to 'the duty of judges to differentiate their authority and responsibility, and thus their practical reasoning, from that of legislatures'.[47] Indeed, common law courts – even at the apex of the judicial system – have sometimes lamented a long line of common law precedent as having 'taken a wrong turn' and being

---

[44] See Gerald J. Postema 'Classical Common Law Jurisprudence (Part I)' (2003) 2 *Oxford University Commonwealth Law Journal* 155, 178: 'In 17th century common law parlance, for a ... judgment to be "against reason" (or often "inconvenient") was for it to be inconsistent with the law as a whole, to fail to fit coherently into the common law. To understand law as rational (*summa ratio*, as Coke liked to say) was not to regard it as derivable from universal first principles, but rather to approach it on the assumption that it exists as a coherent whole.'

[45] Finnis, 'Judicial Power', pp. 5–6.

[46] Ibid p. 5 (emphasis added).

[47] John Finnis, 'The Fairy Tale's Moral' (1999) 115 *Law Quarterly Review* 170, 173, reprinted as 'Adjudication and Legal Change' in John Finnis, *Philosophy of Law: Collected Essays, Volume IV* (Oxford: Oxford University Press, 2011), pp. 397–403. It is a claim that, albeit with different motivations, is defended by Ronald Dworkin, *Taking Rights Seriously* (Cambridge, MA: Harvard University Press , 1997), p. 81: 'It remains the judge's duty, even in hard cases, to discover what the rights of the parties are, not to invent new rights retrospectively.' For a review of the evolution of Dworkin's thought on this matter, see Paul Yowell, 'Dworkin, Interpretation and Legal Change' in Simone Glanert and Fabien Girard (eds), *Law's Hermeneutics: Other Investigations* (Abingdon: Routledge, 2017).

worthy of change, but declined to make that change themselves. They have declined on the basis that some aspects of the common law are so established, and the line of precedents so deep, that 'until there is legislative change, the courts must live with them and any judicial developments must take them into account'.[48] The thought is that some changes to the law cannot be declared, but can only be made, and thus only be made by the legislature.

V Jurisdiction to Change the Law

The accounts of the good legislature and the good court outlined earlier track the design of the modern legislature and the modern common law court. They do so not because they take these modern institutions as their starting point, but rather because these institutions, like these accounts, track the reasons that favour empowering a person or body with the responsibility to change the law and the reasons that favour empowering a person or body to make conclusive determinations whether a rule of law has been violated. Those reasons point to the acts that the legislature and adjudicator need to perform (legislation; judgment), which in turn point to the design of the capacities that the legislature and court are to be equipped with, which in turn point to the nature of each institution. The nature of the legislature and of the court is thus informed by an investigation into the reasons favouring each institution in a community of persons.

We turn, now, to interrogate the relationship between these two institutions and their responsibilities. If the rule of change is simple and provides only that 'what the Queen in Parliament enacts is law', the relationship between the legislative and judicial responsibilities will be correspondingly simple: the court will adjudicate disputes according to the law enacted by the legislature. Not all complexity will be avoided, however, as there will be a need to resolve contradictions between imperfectly crafted positive laws and, more generally, to determine the 'precise scope of some given rule'[49] in the light of the existing corpus of law, including the common law. This complexity, however, will pale in

---

[48] *White and Others v. Chief Constable of South Yorkshire and Others* [1998] UKHL 45, [1999] 2 AC 455, 504 (Lord Hoffman).

[49] Hart, *The Concept of Law*, p. 92.

comparison to the complexity introduced if the legislature's legal jurisdiction is restricted.[50]

Some restrictions will be straightforward, and their transgressions easily identified (e.g., any Act of the US Congress providing that one may assume the office of the president at the age of majority would transgress the constitutional requirement that no 'Person [shall] be eligible to that Office who shall not have attained to the Age of thirty five Years'[51]). Some restrictions, in turn, may be complex and require very able legal learning to comprehend (e.g., determining the scope of the restriction on the Parliament of Canada's jurisdiction 'in relation to all Matters not coming within the Classes of Subjects by this Act assigned exclusively to the Legislatures of the Provinces', especially in light of the conferral of provincial jurisdiction over 'Generally all Matters of a merely local or private Nature in the Province').[52] In cases both straightforward and complex, a legislative enactment may give rise to a dispute over legal jurisdiction, a dispute that – lest the defect of *inefficiency* resurface – will fall to a court for authoritative settlement.[53]

The reasons why legislative jurisdiction may be qualified will be plural. They may include the distribution of legislative powers between provincial and central authorities, as in federal constitutions, or the formalisation of the rule of law's injunctions against *ex post facto* laws, as under the US Constitution.[54] The reasons of special interest for present purposes are related to the requirements of justice and rights. There is no doubt that the legislature is not empowered, as a moral matter, to act unjustly and in violation of rights. The question is how to deny as a matter of *legal* jurisdiction what is already denied as a matter of *moral* jurisdiction and to do so in a manner that does not frustrate the reasons favouring the rule of change and the legislature's responsibility to care for the community's future.[55]

---

[50] I leave to one side the question whether, on Hart's own account, such restrictions are best understood to be part of the rule of change or part of the rule of recognition. Different passages in Hart support different conclusions.

[51] US Constitution, Art. 2, sec. 1, cl. 5.

[52] Constitution Act, 1867, ss. 91 and 92(16).

[53] There may be other, non-legal restrictions on jurisdiction that would not fall to a court for determination (such as constitutional conventions) or legal restrictions that a court may decline to adjudicate on (such as under a 'political questions' doctrine).

[54] See US Constitution, Art. 1, sec. 9, cl. 3: 'No Bill of Attainder or ex post facto Law shall be passed.'

[55] See Ekins, *Nature of Legislative Intent*, p. 120: 'the common good will not be well served if the lawmaking body lacks sufficient freedom to change the law as reason demands'.

One manner of doing so is to specify precisely the requirements of justice and rights and so to specify precisely the limits on the legislature's legal jurisdiction. Where the requirements are precise, they will participate in the law's technique of specifying terms and applicable conditions so that those learned in the law can determine whether a legislative enactment is within the legislature's legal jurisdiction. The adjudication of disputes will not be especially controversial where the constitution's provisions are sufficiently determinate to settle, within the bounds of legal interpretation, which changes are authorised and not by the legislature's delimited jurisdiction. In such cases, where a court exercises its power of adjudication to deny validity to an Act of the legislature, it is performing its distinctive judicial responsibility to bring the past to bear on the present: to determine that this past superior *constitutional* rule continues to bear on this present inferior *legislative* rule and, by contradicting it, denies it today, as it would have yesterday and will tomorrow, recognition as a law in this community because of this community's past choices.[56]

In proceeding with specific constitutional rules, however, there is a risk that moral evaluations today will reveal themselves to be moral errors in time. What is more, predictions today about the possible risks of injustice and violations of rights in future will be imperfect. And so the good constitutional drafter will appreciate that some injustices and some violations of rights will escape reasonable attempts to settle, now, specific acts that must or must not be enacted or performed. The good constitutional drafter may thus decide that a responsible course of action is to avoid committing the community to a specific understanding of the requirements of justice and rights, all the while acknowledging the risks of doing so.[57] In the alternative, and the one that animates my argument here, the constitutional drafter may conclude it best to prohibit *not* (or *not only*) this or that instance of injustice or violation of rights, but rather to prohibit, more generally, *injustice* and *rights-violations* without much further specification. In many respects, this is the course of action favoured in charters of rights, many of which guarantee rights and

---

[56] See Richard Ekins, 'How To Be a Free People' (2013) 58 *American Journal of Jurisprudence* 163, 176.

[57] On the absence of any 'grand balance sheet to be drawn up' that would tally risks, see John Finnis, 'Human Rights and their Enforcement' in *Human Rights & Common Good: Collected Essays*, vol. III (Oxford: Oxford University Press, 2011), p. 44.

freedoms in a manner that avoids answering many of the questions that arise in disputes about the requirements of rights and justice.

What of adjudication on the validity of legislation against such open-ended standards of justice and rights? Is this at one with the judicial responsibility to bring the community's past legal settlements to answer disputes today? On its face, the exercise of judicial power under a charter of rights is at one with the judicial responsibility to relate past to present. Canadian courts review legislation further to the past decision to confer them this power under the Canadian Charter 1982; the Strasbourg Court reviews member state legislation further to the past decision to confer it this power under the European Convention on Human Rights; British courts review legislation further to the past decision to confer them this power under the Human Rights Act 1998. On its face: past to present. On further inspection, however, the analysis breaks down insofar as the decisions captured in the Charter, Convention, and like instruments are incomplete attempts to settle what is permitted, required, or forbidden in the name of justice and rights. Charters of rights standardly identify one class of persons ('Everyone', 'Every citizen', 'Every accused person') and one subject matter ('life', 'liberty', 'expression') and unite them by declaring that a class of persons has *a right to* a subject matter. But what is it for everyone to have a right *to life*, or *to liberty*, or *to expression*? The answers are not settled in the charters of rights themselves.[58] Those responsible for these instruments choose to leave it to others to determine how that *past* inchoate commitment to justice and rights will, henceforth and into the *future*, secure a pattern of interrelationships that will give to each his and her rights. The formulation of rights in charters of rights like the Convention and Charter is open-ended in the sense that the requirements of justice and rights are open to the future. The determination of what the guarantee of rights requires, prohibits, and allows is left 'to a later day'.[59]

How, then, should a court, institutionally designed to bring the community's past legal commitments to bear on present disputes, approach a

---

[58] For discussion, see Grégoire Webber, Paul Yowell, Richard Ekins, Maris Köpcke, Bradley Miller, and Francisco Urbina, *Legislated Rights: Securing Human Rights through Legislation* (Cambridge: Cambridge University Press, 2018), esp. ch. 2 ('Rights and persons').

[59] Webber, *The Negotiable Constitution*, p. 7 (emphasis in original). See also Rosalind Dixon and Tom Ginsburg 'Deciding Not To Decide: Deferral in Constitutional Design' (2011) 9 *International Journal of Constitutional Law* 636.

dispute concerning a legislative act and its conformity with the constitution's open-ended requirements to realise justice and secure rights?

VI Adjudicating for the Future

The open-ended formulation of many charters of rights stands in contrast to other parts of the law, where the formulation of rights and duties is of sufficient precision as to be legally directive in adjudication. On this basis, the invitation under charters of rights for the courts to take responsibility for the community's future has been declined by at least one judge as being inconsistent with the judicial office. Justice Heydon, dissenting in the first case under the Charter of Human Rights and Responsibilities (Victoria) to reach the High Court of Australia, concluded that the Charter 'contemplates the making of laws by the judiciary', a task inconsistent, on his view, with the judicial power under the Australian Constitution.[60] His reasons pay special attention to the Victorian Charter's general limitation clause, which provides that a 'human right may be subject under law only to such reasonable limits as can be demonstrably justified in a free and democratic society based on human dignity, equality and freedom'.[61] The determination of what constitutes a 'reasonable limit' based on the open-ended standards of dignity, equality, and freedom, themselves all evaluated against the open-ended standard of a 'free and democratic society', requires, in Justice Heydon's view, 'giving a meaning to a particular "human right"'.[62] That task is one 'which the legislature failed to carry out' insofar as the choices and decisions required in order to give that meaning to the right were not made by the legislature in the Charter itself. Making those choices and decisions *now* would require one to make choices and decisions respecting the community's future. The Charter's invitation to the courts to make these choices and decisions, on Justice Heydon's view, constitutes a delegation of lawmaking authority from a lawmaking institution to a lawapplying institution, a delegation said to be 'not possible under the

---

[60] *Momcilovic* v. *The Queen* [2011] HCA 34, para. 431.
[61] Charter of Human Rights and Responsibilities Act 2006 (Victoria), s. 7(2). The provision continues with 'and taking into account all relevant factors, including – ', followed by five factors inspired by the South African Bill of Rights, s. 36.
[62] *Momcilovic*, para. 434.

Australian Constitution', even if, as Justice Heydon recognised, it 'may be possible under some [other] constitutions'.[63]

And indeed it is possible under other constitutions. Under many constitutions, courts take responsibility for the future in the wake of adjudication under open-ended charters of rights. They do so by concluding that this or that legislative attempt to take responsibility for the future should be denied because it is contrary to the charter of rights. The charter of rights is incompletely formulated, such that it is open to the court to give meaning to the rights in a manner that charts the community on a course for the future, a future in which hate speech may (or may not) be criminalised; assisted suicide may (or may not) be prohibited; campaign financing may (or may not) be strictly regulated; religious accommodations may (or may not or must) be provided for; and so on. The open-ended language of constitutional rights guarantees is described by Dworkin as 'very broad and abstract' and as formulated with 'exceedingly abstract moral language', capturing a commitment by the constitutional drafters to a 'general principle'.[64] The interpretation of those principles should, even on Dworkin's account of a moral reading of the law, be true to 'language, precedent, and practice' – in short, it must *fit* 'the broad story of [the community's] historical record'.[65] Even with this discipline, however, '[v]ery different, even contrary, conceptions of a constitutional principle' will often be open to a judge, so that nothing but the judge's *choosing* from among different futures for the community will settle which future direction shall be pursued in the community.[66] History, practice, and integrity are the anchor for the judicial exercise of choice, but 'we must not exaggerate the drag of that anchor' when it comes to charters of rights deliberately left open to the future.[67] The judge has a choice to make and the community's future will be directed by it.

---

[63] *Momcilovic*, para. 434. For further insights into Justice Heydon's constitutional thought, see J. D. Heydon 'Are Bills of Rights Necessary in Common Law Systems?' (2014) 130 *Law Quarterly Review* 392. See also Richard Ekins 'Human Rights and the Separation of Powers' (2015) 34 *University of Queensland Law Journal* 217, esp. 224–228.

[64] Ronald Dworkin, *Freedom's Law: The Moral Reading of the American Constitution* (Cambridge, MA: Harvard University Press , 1996), pp. 2, 7, 9. Dworkin is here referring to the US Bill of Rights, but his evaluations are relevant more generally.

[65] Ibid. 11.

[66] Ibid.

[67] Ibid.

Many features of adjudication – features that allow a court to adjudicate well when looking to the past to resolve a present dispute between parties – may deflect a judge from a fair and sound evaluation of the just requirements of the community's future. An institution designed in order to *adjudicate well* will not be designed – will not have the capacities – to *legislate well*. A number of features of adjudication will deflect a court from making sound choices for the future, and I here review seven such features.[68] As we will see below (section 8), courts have been mindful to address the failings of these features for their new responsibilities under charters of rights.

First, the commitment to legal reasoning. As reviewed earlier in the chapter, legal reasoning is in the service of the judicial responsibility to resolve disputes according to law. By the standards not of legislative (normative and factual) inquiry but of legal adjudication, this commitment to legal reasoning is sound. It participates in the principle of fairness and facilitates good adjudication, all the while empowering judges to speak law to power. However, when the judicial task is repurposed to evaluate the overall justice or rights-compliance of legislation under charters of rights, legal reasoning may read as 'technical, at best, and flawed and heteronomous, at worst'.[69] It is a distraction to think that the answers to hard moral questions turn on answers to statutory interpretation, for example. As Jeremy Waldron has rightly argued, '[w]e may use the phrase "freedom of speech" to pick out the sort of concerns we have in mind in invoking a particular right; but that is not the same as saying that the *word* "speech" (as opposed to "expression" or "communication", etc.) is the key to our concerns in the area'.[70] And yet, the commitment to legal reasoning directs some to think that evaluations of constitutionality are to proceed by asking whether pornography is speech or flag burning is speech or racial abuse is speech, and so forth. The constraints of legal reasoning are not fit for purpose when the question is not one of determining which commitments *were* made, but rather of determining which commitments *should now* be made.

---

[68] The features that follow overlap in important respects with those outlined in Abram Chayes 'The Role of the Judge in Public Law Litigation' (1976) 89 *Harvard Law Review* 1281, 1282–1283. Chayes referred to the 'traditional conception of adjudication' as 'central to our understanding and our analysis of the legal system'.

[69] Jeremy Waldron, 'Judges as Moral Reasoners' (2009) 7 *International Journal of Constitutional Law* 2, 13.

[70] Jeremy Waldron, 'A Rights-Based Critique of Constitutional Rights' (1993) 13 *Oxford Journal of Legal Studies* 18, 26.

Second, the requirement that facts be established on a balance of probabilities. This requirement is sound in an *inter partes* adversarial setting when 'adjudicative facts' are in dispute, facts about 'what the parties did, what the circumstances were, what the background conditions were'.[71] It is well suited to the adversarial context of common law courts, where one or the other party will be held to be in the right and the other in the wrong as a matter of law. The evidentiary standard is too exacting, however, when the available empirical premises informing choices for the community's future are a contest between imperfect predictions affecting the whole community. The facts here are, as Kenneth Culp Davis aptly puts it, '*legislative* facts', facts about economic, social, political, and other matters that inform '*legislative* judgment'.[72] They are not about who did what, when, where, and why, but are rather concerned with conflicting and complex empirical and scientific evidence that will be imperfectly assessed and evaluated.

Third, the absence of capacity for commissioning research. The struggle with legislative facts is compounded by the absence of capacity for the court to seek the assistance of non-parties in being exposed to and understanding a range of legislative facts. The court is reliant on the parties to submit evidence in support of the positions they wish to advance. Evidence that may provide a more complete picture of legislation and its impact on the community's future is not otherwise available to the court.

Fourth, the adversarial contest between two parties, each with one position (I win, the other party loses). This feature of adjudication is justified in response to the resolution of disputes between two disputants on whether an admitted rule has been breached by one of them. When making decisions for the future of the community and *all* of its members, however, this feature denies a voice to those who want and in fairness are entitled to it.

Fifth, the insistence that a decision by a court may not, subject to appeal, be revisited by the parties (*res judicata*: the matter is judged) nor, subject to exceptional circumstances, questioned by a subsequent court in another dispute (*stare decisis et non quieta movere*: stand by things

---

[71] This is the account of 'adjudicative facts' provided by Kenneth Culp Davis in his classical essay introducing the key terms 'adjudicative facts' and 'legislative facts': 'An Approach to Problems of Evidence in the Administrative Process' (1942) 55 *Harvard Law Review* 364, 402.

[72] Ibid. (emphasis added).

decided and do not disturb what is settled). Both of these features of adjudication are justified for the purposes of providing authoritative rulings on whether an admitted rule has been violated at some time past, but they impede the ability of the community to revisit the court's direction for the community's future if that path proves unwelcome or if some of its premises – empirical or normative – prove defective after the passage of time.

Sixth and relatedly, a court may not initiate a dispute by its own motion. If, after ruling that the community's future is to be charted this rather than that way, the court concludes that the ruling was made in error, it must await another dispute before being afforded the opportunity to overturn or reorient its decision within the confines set by the fifth feature of adjudication, just reviewed. Given the reasons why the rule of adjudication is needed as a remedy for the resolution of disputes, the court's passive reception of disputes is sound. However, when the court's function shifts from bringing the past to bear on present disputes to making choices for the community's future, its inability to revisit those choices in the light of changes in factual premises and changes in evaluations of moral premises can frustrate a community's ability to chart a responsible future.

Seventh, concessions by counsel on a point of law or of fact. Such concessions are quite proper for narrowing the points in dispute in the normal course of adjudication between two parties, but in evaluations about the community's future concessions may close off from consideration matters that no responsible legislature would allow to be removed from view. Indeed, courts have sometimes openly criticised an attorney general for concessions that shield from view consideration of the issues. In a 1992 decision respecting the right to equality and its relationship to legislative measures providing different parental benefits to natural parents and adoptive parents, the Chief Justice of Canada 'register[ed] the Court's dissatisfaction with the state in which' the case came before the Court. The Attorney General of Canada had conceded that the equality right was violated, which precluded the Supreme Court from examining the equality issue 'on its merits' and left the Court without argument on 'the legislative objective' and in 'a factual vacuum with respect to the nature and extent of the [conceded] violation'.[73]

---

[73] *Schatcher* v. *Canada* [1992] 2 SCR 679, 695. For similar expressions of judicial frustration with concessions by counsel, see *Sauvé* v. *Canada* [2002] 3 SCR 519 para. 78 and *R* v. *Sharpe* [2001] 1 SCR 45 para. 151.

VII   Dialogue over the Future

Responsible courts have not been blind to these imperfections of the adjudicative process for taking responsibility for the community's future. Many courts have sought, within the confines of the judicial role, to effect changes to the adjudicative process so as to allow the judicial forum better to assume its responsibilities for the community's future.

In relation to the first feature of adjudication (legal reasoning), some courts have sought to relax the technical aspects of legal reasoning by recourse to the doctrines of proportionality and balancing. Evaluations of proportionality and overall balance invite open-ended moral reasoning unconstrained by the traditional confines of legal doctrine and precedent.[74] The doctrines invite courts to evaluate the importance of a legislative objective, the relationship between that objective and the means employed to pursue it, the availability and merits of alternative but unselected means to achieve the legislative objective with comparable success, and the all-things-considered overall balance of benefits and burdens realised by the legislative scheme. The scholarly consensus is that the open-ended structure of reasoning under proportionality and balancing calls upon court and counsel to engage in 'an exercise of general practical reasoning, without many of the constraining features that otherwise characterise legal reasoning'.[75] Legal learning and expertise in legal reasoning – the hallmarks of adjudicating *well* under the rule of adjudication – offer little assistance, given that 'arguments relating to legal authorities – text, history, precedence, etc. – have a relatively modest role to play'.[76]

In relation to the second feature of adjudication (standard of proof), some courts have relaxed or substituted the standard of proof in charters of rights cases, maintaining that 'reason, logic or simply common sense'

---

[74] For discussion and criticism, see Grégoire Webber 'Rights and the Rule of Law in the Balance' (2013) 129 *Law Quarterly Review* 399.

[75] Mattias Kumm, 'Political Liberalism and the Structure of Rights: On the Place and Limits of the Proportionality Requirement' in G. Pavlakos (ed), *Law, Rights and Discourse: The Legal Philosophy of Robert Alexy* (Oxford: Hart Publishing, 2007), pp. 131, 139. See also Kai Möller, *The Global Model of Constitutional Rights* (Oxford: Oxford University Press, 2012); Urbina, *A Critique of Proportionality and Balancing*, ch 6.

[76] Mattias Kumm 'The Idea of Socratic Contestation and the Right to Justification: The Point of Rights-Based Proportionality Review' (2010) 4 *Law & Ethics of Human Rights* 142, 144.

may be relied upon to make findings of legislative fact.[77] Where there is 'very little quantitative or empirical evidence either way' to assist the court in evaluating the justice and rights-compliance of legislation, some courts will look beyond the materials known to legal learning to 'the analysis of human motivation, the determination of values, and the understanding of underlying social or political philosophies'.[78] These standards for evaluating factual premises are better suited to receive legislative facts.

In relation to this and the third feature of adjudication (commissioning research), some courts will invite, and able counsel will know to prepare and submit, 'Brandeis briefs', in which social science and other evidence is compiled and presented on the justice and rights-compliance of the measure in dispute.[79] Good counsel will know that proportionality analysis invites evaluations of the necessity of measures and the comparable efficacy of alternative measures, as well as evaluations of benefits and burdens in determinations of overall balance. All of this speaks to the importance of presenting to the court social science and other evidence and for counsel to commission experts to prepare studies in support of argument and to seek out evidence from other jurisdictions.

In relation to the fourth feature of adjudication (two parties), some courts have relaxed the rules for intervention by persons and groups not party to the immediate dispute. Although this attempt falls short of the principle *quod omnes tangit ab omnibus decidentur* (what touches/affects all should be decided by all), it nonetheless recognises the importance of

---

[77] *RJR-Macdonald Inc* v. *Canada*, [1995] 3 SCR 199, para. 184; see also para. 137. But compare *Chaoulli* v. *Quebec (Attorney General)* [2005] 1 SCR 791, para. 150: 'The task of the courts . . . is to evaluate the issue in the light, not just of common sense or theory, but of the evidence'.

[78] *Sauvé* v. *Canada (Chief Electoral Officer)*, [2002] 3 SCR 519, para. 90.

[79] Such briefs are named after Louis Brandeis, who, before his appointment to the US Supreme Court, argued *Muller* v. *Oregon*, 208 U.S. 412 (1908) before that very court. His brief was submitted in defence of Oregon's labour law restrictions on the working hours of women, highlighting – as the Court's approving summary puts it – that a 'woman's physical structure and the performance of maternal functions place her at a disadvantage in the struggle for subsistence' and that, 'by abundant testimony of the medical fraternity continuance for a long time on her feet at work, repeating this from day to day, tends to injurious effects upon the [female] body' (ibid, 423, 421). On the strength of its reading of the social science evidence submitted, the Supreme Court upheld the labour law, notwithstanding that *Lochner* v. *New York*, 198 U.S. 45 (1905) had been decided only three years earlier. For discussion, see Paul Yowell 'Proportionality in United States Constitutional Law' in Liora Lazarus, Christopher McCrudden, and Nigel Bowles (eds), *Reasoning Rights: Comparative Judicial Engagement* (Oxford: Hart Publishing , 2014), pp. 110–111.

hearing voices beyond those of the parties to the dispute, the resolution of which will directly impact not only them but many others. Intervenors will be invited to speak on the application of law to facts, but they will be invited, too, to speak more generally about the requirements of justice and rights for the community's future.

In relation to the fifth feature of adjudication (*res judicata, stare decisis*), some courts have sought to relax the force of *stare decisis* where circumstances have changed, especially when social science evidence is in play. The Supreme Court of Canada has been especially transparent in this regard: the doctrine of precedent, so central to the artificial reason of the law and the relationship of past to present, provides no bar – not even against a trial court confronting 'settled rulings of higher courts' – if 'there is a change in the circumstances or evidence that "fundamentally shifts the parameters of the debate"'.[80] This is not a restriction that aligns with a view that the court 'declares' rather than 'makes' the law. The alternative, in the Court's view (with echoes of Hart's discussion on the need for a rule of change), would be to 'condemn the law to stasis'.[81] The case law of even an apex court under open-ended charters of rights is therefore less controlling under *stare decisis* than is the case law in other areas of law.

The changes courts have introduced to the adjudicative process are the result of evaluations that many features of adjudication are unsuited to taking responsibility for the community's future. Confronted with institutional features designed to relate the community's past commitments as embodied in law to present disputes, courts have fashioned changes in order to reorient the exercise of judicial power. My argument here reports these changes without a thoroughgoing evaluation of their merits. Such evaluation would note that not every problematic feature of adjudication has been modified and some important features persist – the sixth (passive jurisdiction) and seventh (concessions by counsel) have proved harder to reform. Yet, even if these features of adjudication could be addressed with more wholesale reforms, it remains that nothing can eliminate the risk that judges will make choices for the community's future that are misdirected and in need of correction. Part of that risk is the common standing risk of injustice that afflicts all exercises of public

---

[80] *Carter* v. *Canada (Attorney General)*, [2016] 1 SCR 13, para. 44; *Canada* v. *Bedford*, [2013] 3 S.C.R. 1101, para. 42.

[81] *Carter*, para. 44: '*stare decisis* is not a straitjacket that condemns the law to stasis'. See also *R* v. *Comeau*, 2018 SCC 15, paras. 26–43.

power. But the greater part of the risk is with the exercise of *judicial power* – a power distinguished in its capacity to *adjudicate well* – in determining the course of the community's future. The imperfect changes to the judicial process are like renovations made to repurpose an existing edifice – no matter the merits of the reforms, they remain reforms to an institution designed for another purpose, a purpose that it continues to serve on a very regular basis when not confronted with a case challenging legislation under a charter of rights.

Constitutional drafters who set out to design an institution to supervise the justice and rights-compliance of legislation would be unlikely to take the judicial forum – even as refashioned – as a model. The increased use of Brandeis briefs, for example, assists in putting more research before the court, but does not equip the court with the resources necessary for the sound interpretation and assessment of legislative facts nor does it address the dependence of the court on parties or intervenors for the presentation of such facts. A more wholesale reform would be to redesign the court so that it has a dedicated research service.[82] Similarly, the doctrines of proportionality and balancing allow judges to escape the confines of legal reasoning, but precisely because there is 'nothing particularly *legal*' about these doctrines, the professional qualifications of a lawyer do not make one 'more qualified to apply a balancing test' than someone without legal qualifications.[83] Judges have expertise in the law, but not necessarily in the great many other fields of factual and moral inquiry that will be required in order to arrive at sound evaluations of legislation's conformity with open-ended charters of rights. The changes to the judicial forum are the changes that, short of significant constitutional reform, are within the realm of the possible. A wholesale, *tabula rasa* design of an institution to supervise the justice and rights-compliance of legislation would likely include new capacities to commission studies, to consult experts, to initiate reviews of its own motion, to revisit previous decisions on its own motion, to have a diversified membership with expertise in a range of empirical and moral matters, etc. Such an institution would likely warrant the name 'Council of Revision'

---

[82] For discussion, see K. C. Davies 'Judicial, Legislative, and Administrative Lawmaking: A Proposed Research Service for the Supreme Court' (1986) 71 *Minnesota Law Review* 1.

[83] Paul Yowell, *Constitutional Rights and Constitutional Design* (Oxford: Hart Publishing, 2018), pp. 155–156.

rather than court. Indeed, a made-for-purpose institution would likely have the capacities and design of a legislature, not of a court.[84]

Given these realities, what is a legislature to do when it concludes that the court has erred in adjudicating for the future? May the legislature engage in an institutional dialogue with the court over the future direction of the community? The answers to these questions should begin by affirming that, when a court settles a dispute by bringing to bear on the *present* the *past* constitutional decision that the community's *future* be directed in law this way rather than that, there is (on the argument here developed[85]) no place for dialogue between court and legislature. The legislature is to respect the court's decision as a decision on the requirements of the law. But a court's decision under the open-ended requirements of a charter of rights is not a decision on the requirements of the law as it was; it is a decision on the requirements of the law as it should henceforth be. In challenging a court decision on the future direction of the community, the legislature is not challenging the court over what the law can reasonably be said to have been all along – *that* would be an affront to the rule of law. But *that* is not where dialogue finds its place. It finds its place in a dialogue *over the future*, that is, in specifying the open-ended commitments of the charter of rights that cannot be said to have settled what the community's view of a rights- and justice-respecting future will be.

A legislature whose act has been declared invalid by a court for being inconsistent with the constitution's open-ended guarantees of rights may choose to reply by re-enacting legislation of more or less substantially the same form, not because it seeks to promote injustice and the violation of rights, but rather because it takes a different view of the justice- and rights-compliant future of the community. That different view may be motivated by a better appreciation and assessment of the relevant factual premises, either because the factual record before the court was

---

[84] For discussion, see Yowell, *Constitutional Rights and Constitutional Design*, ch 7. Yowell's argument concludes (at 163): 'the argument for *judicial* review of legislation is better thought of as an argument for review by a quasi-legislative body that resembles a legislature in all important respects but one: crucially, it is not elected'.

[85] Other arguments extend dialogue's reach even to this scenario, including proponents of 'coordinate construction': see Mark Tushnet, *Taking the Constitution Away from the Courts* (Princeton: Princeton University Press, 1999); Larry Kramer, *The People Themselves* (Oxford: Oxford University Press, 2004); Dennis Baker, *Not Quite Supreme: The Courts and Coordinate Constitutional Interpretation* (Montreal: McGill-Queen's University Press, 2010).

imperfectly presented by parties and intervenors or because the court's interpretation and assessment was lacking in some or several respects.[86] A different view may be motivated by a better appreciation and evaluation of the myriad moral premises, which may have been deflected from full consideration in the judicial forum due to the manner in which the case was argued by counsel or otherwise framed by the court. It may, in turn, be motivated by a change in circumstances since the court's decision. The different legislative view need not turn on the conclusion that the court's decision is itself unjust and a violation of rights – in responsible communities, neither court nor legislature should arrive at obviously unjust or rights-violating conclusions. Rather, the legislative view that motivates a reply to a judicial decision may rest on different evaluations under the burdens of judgment in matters where both the moral and the factual premises are open to reasonable contest. The judicial exercise of a legislative power to care for the community's future is answerable under dialogue to all of the reasons favouring the rule of change and the empowerment of an institution designed to change the law and to do so well.

The responsible legislature will keep under ready review every legal determination of relationships between persons that seek to give effect to the rights of each and all. The need for this review recalls the reasons identifying the need for self-correction, so that when previous choices for the community's future prove to be misdirected, as some inevitably will be given the many imperfections in predicting the course of human affairs, the community's institutions are empowered to set out a new course for the community. When the previous choices for the community's future were made by the legislature, it is uncontroversial that the legislature should be empowered to right the wrong. However, when the previous choices for the community's future were made by the court, what should follow? On the argument here defended, the same conclusion is called for: the legislature should be empowered to right the wrong.

The burdens of judgment on legislatures and courts that afflict attempts to arrive at right decisions on the community's future make it reasonable to assume that a community will take many wrong turns in

---

[86] For an example of how complex social science evidence can be differently appreciated by sophisticated apex courts, consider the different conclusions of the Supreme Court of Canada and the UK Supreme Court on the question whether a regime for assisted dying can be designed in a manner that addresses the risks to vulnerable persons: cf. *Carter* and *Nicklinson* v. *Ministry of Justice* [2014] UKSC 38.

the course of its history. Many wrong turns will be at the legislature's direction; some will be at the judiciary's. One chief merit of dialogue for those communities that have made the choice to confer on their courts the power to evaluate legislation for compliance with open-ended charters of rights lies in the recognition that no institution has a monopoly on the risk of acting unjustly and in the violation of rights in the pursuit of good, well-intentioned actions, actions never intended to do wrong. The legislature and the court will encounter that risk for different reasons. Among those reasons will be the one explored here: that an institution designed to bring the past to bear on the present will be imperfectly equipped to take responsibility for the community's future.

VIII   Conclusion

The judicial role under open-ended charters of rights is not the judicial role contemplated by the institutional design of courts. The capacities of courts empower them to adjudicate well in the resolution of disputes according to law. Those same capacities, even when imperfectly refashioned, do not facilitate sound judicial decisions over the community's future. The idea of dialogue under charters of rights empowers the legislature to do what it would be unreasonable for the legislature to do in the normal course of adjudication: to challenge the exercise of judicial authority by determining that the community's just and rights-respecting future should proceed in a manner that differs from the way charted by the court. It is a conclusion arrived at by interrogating the nature of the court and the legislature, a nature informed by those two institutions' capacities, acts, and reasons for being introduced and maintained in communities of persons.

6

Constitutional 'Dialogue' and Deference

ROSALIND DIXON*

As many other contributors to this volume recognize, the idea of 'dialogue' is often understood by scholars in quite different ways. In Canada, the United Kingdom and United States, the term 'dialogue' is sometimes used to connote the idea of judicial review as quite literally a form of 'conversation' between courts, parliament and the executive.[1] In the United States, it is often used to describe departmentalist theories, or theories of 'coordinate construction', that emphasize the authority of both legislative and executive officials as well as courts to interpret the Constitution.[2] And in Canada, it is used to emphasize the non-final nature of judicial decision-making under the Canadian Charter of Rights and Freedoms.[3] Theorists in each country also frequently use the term quite differently.

* The author thanks Aileen Kavanagh, Stephen Gardbuam, Kent Roach and Grégoire Webber for helpful comments, and Melissa Vogt for outstanding research assistance.
[1] See e.g., T. R. S. Allan, 'Constitutional dialogue and the justification of judicial review' (2003) 23 *Oxford Journal of Legal Studies*, 563; Luc B. Tremblay, 'The legitimacy of judicial review: The limits of dialogue between courts and legislatures' (2005) 3 *International Journal of Constitutional Law*, 617; Christine Bateup, 'Extending the conversation: American and Canadian experiences of constitutional dialogue in comparative perspective' (2007) 21 *Temple International and Comparative Law Journal*, 1.
[2] See e.g., Louis Fisher, *Constitutional Dialogues: Interpretation as Political Process* (Princeton: Princeton University Press, 2014); Christine Bateup, 'The dialogic promise: Assessing the normative potential of theories of constitutional dialogue' (2006) 71 *Brooklyn Law Review*, 1109; Neal Devins and Louis Fisher, 'Judicial exclusivity and political instability' (1998) 84 *Virginia Law Review*, 83; Dan T. Coenen, 'A constitution of collaboration: Protecting fundamental values with second-look rules of interbranch dialogue' (2001) 41 *William and Mary Law Review*, 1575.
[3] See e.g., Peter W. Hogg and Allison A. Bushell, 'The Charter dialogue between courts and legislatures (or perhaps the Charter of Rights isn't such a bad thing after all)' (1997) 35 *Osgoode Hall Law Journal* 75; Kent Roach, 'Dialogue or defiance: Legislative reversals of Supreme Court decisions in Canada and the United States' (2006) 4 *International Journal of Constitutional Law*, 347; James B. Kelly and Matthew A. Hennigar, 'The Canadian Charter of Rights and the minister of justice: Weak-form review within a constitutional Charter of Rights' (2012) 10 *International Journal of Constitutional Law*, 35.

This chapter explores the usefulness of these different understandings of the dialogue metaphor: first, as a means of highlighting the communicative or persuasive dimension to judicial decision-making; and second, as highlighting the range of informal, as well as formal, ways in which legislatures may be able to narrow or modify the effect of court decisions with which they disagree. This second dimension to the dialogue metaphor, the chapter further suggests, is important to assessing potential democratic objections to judicial review: if judicial review does not take place in a vacuum, potential democratic concerns about the practice of judicial review must also be assessed against the backdrop of this broader institutional matrix.[4]

At the same time, the metaphor also carries with it certain dangers: it has the capacity to understate both the coercive *and* final nature of judicial review in certain contexts. It may therefore also understate concerns about the democratic legitimacy of judicial review.[5] In Canada in particular, dialogue scholars often suggest that judicial review under the Canadian Charter of Rights and Freedoms is inevitably revisable or non-final in nature. The chapter, however, argues that the actual finality of judicial review will often depend on the degree to which courts such as the Supreme Court of Canada (SCC) are willing to show deference to legislative constitutional judgments in 'second look' cases.[6] Deference of this kind is also inherently controversial: while courts have at times endorsed such an approach in Canada, in other cases they have explicitly rejected the idea of deference of this kind. Most proponents of the dialogue metaphor also expressly oppose the idea of additional judicial deference to dialogic legislative sequels.[7]

---

[4] See e.g., Kent Roach, *The Supreme Court on Trial: Judicial Activism or Democratic Dialogue* (Irwin Law Inc., 2001); Jamie Cameron, 'Collateral thoughts on "dialogue's" legacy as metaphor and theory: A favourite from Canada' (2016) 35 *University of Queensland Law Journal*, 157. Compare also Jeremy Waldron, 'The core of the case against judicial review' (2006) 115 *Yale Law Journal*, 1346; Rosalind Dixon, 'The core case for weak-form judicial review' (2017) 38(6) *Cardozo Law Review*, 2193; Mattias Kumm, 'Institutionalising Socratic contestation: The rationalist human rights paradigm, legitimate authority and the point of judicial review' (2007) 1 *European Journal of Legal Studies*, 153; Mark Tushnet, 'New forms of judicial review and the persistence of rights-and-democracy-based worries' (2003) 38 *Wake Forest Law Review*, 813.

[5] Compare Aileen Kavanagh, 'The lure and limits of dialogue' (2016) 66 *University of Toronto Law Journal*, 83.

[6] Rosalind Dixon, 'The Supreme Court of Canada, Charter dialogue, and deference' (2009) 47 *Osgoode Hall Law Journal*, 235.

[7] Ibid.

The chapter thus argues that dialogue is both a useful and somewhat misleading metaphor: it helps point to the possibility of a form of de facto 'weak' judicial review, which can substantially address democratic objections to the practice of judicial review. But at the same time, it suggests that the existence of de facto weak review of this kind is both more widespread and inevitable than is in fact the case; and therefore tends to downplay legitimate concerns about the 'counter-majoritarian difficulty' associated with judicial review in many constitutional systems.[8] Whether this is sufficient to warrant a move away from the term 'dialogue', toward a greater emphasis on other ways of describing or conceptualizing the judicial–legislative relationship is a question that is touched on by the conclusion, but largely left for another day.

The remainder of the chapter is divided into three sections following this introduction. Section I sets out existing understandings of constitutional 'dialogue' between courts and parliaments, and how proponents of the dialogue metaphor suggest that this relationship helps address democratic objections to the practice of judicial review. Section II highlights the extent to which this depends on a form of heightened judicial deference to reasonable legislative sequels.

I The Dialogue Metaphor and Its Value

The idea of constitutional 'dialogue' has been understood by different scholars in a wide variety of ways. In both Canada and the United Kingdom, the term 'dialogue' has been used to describe theories of judicial review that are 'conversational' rather than more metaphorically dialogic in nature.[9] Proponents of this view thus suggest that the role of

---

[8] See Alexander Bickel, *The Least Dangerous Branch: The Supreme Court at the Bar of Politics* (New Haven: Yale University Press, 1986). See also Barry Friedman, 'The counter-majoritarian problem and the pathology of constitutional scholarship' (2001) 96 *Northwestern University Law Review*, 933; Barry Friedman, 'The history of the countermajoritarian difficulty, part one: The road to judicial supremacy' (1998) 73 *New York University Law Review*, 333; Barry Friedman, 'The history of the countermajoritarian difficulty, part II: Reconstruction's political court' (2002) 91 *Georgetown Law Journal*, 1; Barry Friedman, 'The history of the countermajoritarian difficulty, part three: The lesson of Lochner' (2001) 76 *New York University Law Review*, 1383; Barry Friedman, 'The history of the countermajoritarian difficulty, part four: Law's politics' (2000) 148 *University of Pennsylvania Law Review*, 971; Barry Friedman, 'The birth of an academic obsession: The history of the countermajoritarian difficulty, part five' (2002) 112 *Yale Law Journal*, 153.

[9] See e.g., Francesca Klug, *Values for A Godless Age: The Story of the UK's New Bill of Rights* (Penguin Books, 2000). Conversational theories have also been advocated in the United

courts in this understanding that the role of courts is simply '*to deliberate and not to decide* ... *[i]t is conversation rather than the substance of decisions that is key to the conversational perspective*'.[10]

In the United States, a range of scholars have likewise linked the idea of dialogue to theories of shared constitutional interpretive authority such as 'departmentalism' or 'coordinate construction'. In a departmentalist approach, each branch of government is entitled to advance their own understanding of the constitution, unconstrained by the interpretations of other branches.[11] In moderate departmentalist accounts, *executive* officials may be bound by a court decision if they are party to the relevant proceedings; and legislators may be constrained in their ability to reverse the effect of court decisions in particular concrete cases.[12] However, executive officials and legislators will be entirely free to ignore courts' *reasoning* about constitutional rights when it comes to the making of future decisions about policy or legislation. As independent interpretive authorities, they will be free to form their own independent judgments about these questions without regard to anything courts may previously have said.

In Canada, in contrast, the most well-known theory of dialogue is a theory of de facto weak review.[13] The concept of weak-form review was first introduced by Mark Tushnet, as a way of describing systems of constitutional review in which courts do not enjoy true legal finality.[14] The distinction, however, can be understood in a variety of different ways: it can be used to track either the formal *or* substantive finality of judicial decisions in various constitutional systems, and to describe the

---

States: see Robert W. Bennett, 'Counter-conversationalism and the sense of difficulty' (2001) 95 *Northwestern University Law Review*, 845; and, in Canada, see Tsvi Kahana, 'Understanding the notwithstanding mechanism' (2002) 52 *University of Toronto Law Journal*, 221.

[10] Bennett, 'Counter-conversationalism', 891, emphasis added.

[11] See Larry D. Kramer, *The People Themselves: Popular Constitutionalism and Judicial Review* (Oxford: Oxford University Press), p. 249 (suggesting that in a departmentalist theory, '[j]ustices can be impeached, the Court's budget can be slashed, the President can ignore its mandates, Congress can strip it of jurisdiction or shrink its size or pack it with new members or give it burdensome new responsibilities or revise its procedures', and that these are all legitimate tools of legislative and executive disagreement).

[12] Mark Tushnet, 'Alternative forms of judicial review' (2003) 101 *Michigan Law Review*, 2781, 2782.

[13] Compare Cameron, 'Collateral thoughts on "dialogue's" legacy'.

[14] Tushnet, 'Alternative forms of judicial review', 2782.

finality of judicial decisions *or* the scope of judicial review *ex ante*.[15] Against this backdrop, it is also clear that the concepts of 'weak'- and 'strong'-form review are not true binary categories, but rather, concepts that describe a continuum of different models or patterns of judicial review, all of which involve some degree of judicial non-finality.[16] In Canada, the emphasis of dialogue theorists has also been on the idea of judicial review under the Canadian Charter of Rights and Freedoms as weak in this more 'continuuized', de facto sense.[17]

The most famous articulation of dialogue theory, in Canada, is found in the 1997 article by Peter W. Hogg and Allison A. Bushell in the *Osgoode Hall Law Journal*, 'The charter dialogue between courts and legislatures',[18] and the monograph by Kent Roach, *The Supreme Court on Trial*.[19] At the heart of the idea of constitutional dialogue, for these Canadian scholars, is also the idea that Parliament and provincial legislatures in Canada have scope to respond to court decisions under the Canadian Charter of Rights and Freedoms 1982, in ways that answer concerns about the democratic legitimacy of judicial review.

Hogg and Bushell, for example, argue that judicial review under the Charter is not in fact a true 'veto over the politics of the nation' but rather 'the beginning of dialogue as to how best to reconcile the individualistic values of the Charter with the accomplishment of social and economic policies for the benefit of the community as a whole'.[20] They identify all legislation passed in response to a court decision as a form of dialogue in this context, and suggest that on this definition, there is a near-perfect record of dialogue between courts and legislatures in Canada. And even on a narrower definition, which focuses on legislative sequels expressing

---

[15] Aileen Kavanagh, 'What's so weak about "weak-form review"? The case of the UK Human Rights Act 1998' (2015) 13 *International Journal of Constitutional Law*, 1008.

[16] Ibid.

[17] See e.g., Cameron, 'Collateral thoughts on "dialogue's" legacy'. For the concept of a continuuized understanding, see e.g., Mark Tushnet, 'Weak Form Review' (forthcoming 2019) 17 *International Journal of Constitutional Law*; Rosalind Dixon, 'Responsive Judicial Review' (working paper 2018), unpublished.

[18] Hogg and Bushell, 'The charter dialogue between courts and legislatures'.

[19] Roach, *The Supreme Court on Trial*. See also Kent Roach, 'Constitutional and common law dialogues between the Supreme Court and Canadian legislatures' (2001) 80 *Canadian Bar Review* 481; Roach, 'Dialogue or defiance'; Kent Roach, 'Remedial and international dialogues about rights: The Canadian experience' (2005) 40 *Texas Journal of International Law* 537; Kent Roach, 'A dialogue about principle and a principled dialogue: Justice Iacobucci's substantive approach to dialogue' (2007) 57 *University of Toronto Law Journal*, 449.

[20] Hogg and Bushell, 'The charter dialogue between courts and legislatures', 105.

some form of disagreement with a court decision, they suggest that 'dialogue [is] quite prevalent as between Canadian courts and legislatures'.[21] On this basis, they also suggest that 'the critique of the Charter based on democratic legitimacy [could not] be sustained'.[22]

Kent Roach, in *The Supreme Court on Trial*, likewise argued that 'the Charter broke new ground by avoiding the dangers of both judicial supremacy and legislative supremacy', by 'promot[ing] and structur[ing] democratic dialogue' among courts, legislatures and society about the way rights and freedoms will be treated. The key to this, he further suggested, was 'section 1 of the Charter which allows legislatures to justify reasonable limits on the rights that the Court finds in the Charter'. This provision, he argued, provided 'legislatures with a vehicle to respond to decisions and to justify contextual departures from the principle is that the court recognises'.[23]

The idea of constitutional dialogue has a number of advantages in this context. The emphasis in the United Kingdom and United States on dialogue as 'conversation' usefully draws attention to one important aspect of judicial review, and its relationship to democratic political processes – i.e., its capacity to have persuasive or communicative effects. Leading US scholars, such as Nate Persily, have shown clear evidence of the *limits* to courts' capacity for persuasion.[24] But courts in some cases may also have at least some indirect influence on public debate – by drawing media and public attention to certain issues, or by causing legislators to pay increased attention to certain arguments or legal options.[25]

This, I have argued, is one way in which courts can contribute to overcoming a range of blockages in democratic political processes, including 'blindspots' and 'burdens of inertia'.[26] By drawing attention to this potential role, the dialogue metaphor itself also contributes to our

---

[21] Ibid. 98.

[22] Ibid. 105.

[23] Roach, *The Supreme Court on Trial*, p. 7.

[24] Nathaniel Persily, 'Introduction', in Nathaniel Persily, Jack Citrin and Patrick J. Egan (eds.), *Public Opinion and Constitutional Controversy* (Oxford: Oxford University Press, 2008); Patrick J. Egan and Jack Citrin, 'The limits of judicial persuasion and the fragility of judicial legitimacy' (Working paper, July 2011).

[25] See Dixon, 'The core case for weak-form judicial review'.

[26] Ibid.; Rosalind Dixon, 'Creating dialogue about socioeconomic rights: Strong-form versus weak-form judicial review revisited' (2007) 5 *International Journal of Constitutional Law*, 391.

understanding of the argument in favour of certain forms of weak judicial review.[27]

Similarly, the emphasis of US departmentalists and Canadian dialogue theorists on the scope for legislative response to court decisions usefully highlights the range of ways in which judicial review may be de facto as well as formally 'weak', or non-final, in nature. This, in turn, helps contribute to debates about the democratic legitimacy of judicial review: Leading political constitutionalists, such as Jeremy Waldron, make powerful arguments against 'strong' or final forms of judicial review on democratic grounds. Strong forms of judicial review, they argue, 'privileg[e] majority voting among a small number of unelected and unaccountable judges', and thereby 'disenfranchise[e] ordinary citizens and brus[h] aside cherished principles of representation and political equality in the final resolution of issues about rights'.[28] At the same time, they generally concede that the same objections do not apply to judicial review that is 'weak' rather than strong in nature,[29] or does not involve the *final* resolution of issues about rights'.[30]

The actual strength or weakness of judicial review, however, is ultimately a question of degree, not kind.[31] It also depends on a range of legislative and judicial practices, as well as formal institutional design features of a system (such as a power of amendment or legislative override).[32] By drawing attention to this, the dialogue metaphor also has the capacity to contribute a more nuanced debate about the legitimacy of judicial review across different constitutional contexts and systems.

---

[27] See e.g., Dixon, 'The core case for weak-form judicial review'. Contrast Bateup, 'The dialogic promise' (suggesting dialogue does not provide any useful guidance in this context).

[28] Waldron, 'The core of the case against judicial review', 1353.

[29] See Hogg and Bushell, 'The Charter dialogue between courts and legislatures'; Hogg, Bushell and Wright, 'Charter dialogue revisited'; Tushnet, *Weak Courts, Strong Rights*.

[30] Waldron, 'The core of the case against judicial review', 1353, emphasis added. Compare also Stephen Gardbaum, *The New Commonwealth Model of Constitutionalism: Theory and Practice* (Cambridge: Cambridge University Press, 2013), p. 36.

[31] Kavanagh, 'What's so weak about "weak-form review"?'; Rosalind Dixon and Adrienne Stone, 'Constitutional Amendment and Political Constitutionalism: A Philosophical and Comparative Reflection', in David Dyzenhaus and Malcolm Thorburn (eds.), *Philosophical Foundations of Constitutional Law* (Oxford: Oxford University Press, 2016); Mark Tushnet and Rosalind Dixon, 'Weak-Form Review and Its Constitutional Relatives: An Asian Perspective', in Rosalind Dixon and Tom Ginsburg (eds.), *Comparative Constitutional Law in Asia* (Edward Elgar Publishers, 2014).

[32] Dixon, 'Responsive Judicial Review'.

II   Dialogue: Advantages and Disadvantages to the Metaphor

The idea of constitutional dialogue, however, also carries with it certain dangers: as currently understood, the metaphor has the capacity to understate both the coercive *and* final character to judicial review under a charter of rights. In this sense, it may also tend to overstate – or exaggerate – its claim to democratic legitimacy.

A   Judging and Coercion

Judging, as Robert Cover argued, is always a process that, in least in concrete cases, involves some form of coercion against the losing party.[33] Others have put the point even more strongly: Sandy Levinson argues that 'the massive disruption in lives that can be triggered by a legal case is not a conversation',[34] while Frank I. Michelman argues that '[j]udges produce socially potent arbitral decisions about specifically who must (or need not) do (or suffer) specifically what [and] [i]t is this arbitral use of power that demands justification.[35]

The only meaningful exception to this, under the new Commonwealth constitutional rights charters, is where courts issue declarations of incompatibility (i.e., Human Rights Act 1998 [UK] [HRA] s. 4 remedies, or equivalent remedies in New Zealand and Australia). Remedies of this kind constitute a statement by a court that they regard legislation as incompatible with human rights. But they have no immediate legal effect, at least as a matter of domestic law: instead their effectiveness as a remedy depends entirely on how parliament chooses to respond to the making of such a declaration.[36] They have thus been described as truly 'conversational' in nature: Conor Gearty, for example, has suggested that s. 4 remedies are best seen as 'courteous requests for a conversation, not pronouncements of truth from on high'.[37]

---

[33] Robert Cover, 'Violence and the word' (1986) 95 *Yale Law Journal*, 1601.

[34] Sanford Levinson, 'Law as literature' (1982) 60 *Texas Law Review*, 373, 386.

[35] Frank I. Michelman, 'Justification (and Justifiability) of Law in a Contradictory World', in J. Roland Pennock and John W. Chapman (eds.), *Nomos XXVIII: Justification* (New York University Press, 1986), p. 71.

[36] The only qualification to this is that, in some jurisdictions, the making of such a declaration enlivens a duty on the party of the attorney general to report such a declaration to parliament: see *Charter of Human Rights and Responsibilities Act 2006* (Vic) s. 36(7). The making of a declaration can also enliven certain powers of delegated lawmaking; see e.g., *Human Rights Act 1998* (UK) s. 10.

[37] Conor Gearty, *Can Human Rights Survive?* (Cambridge: Cambridge University Press, 2006), p. 96.

Even declarations of this kind, however, have a hidden coercive potential. While they do not purport to coerce *government* officials, they may contribute to serious forms of coercion against *individuals*. By upholding the legal effect of a law, even while noting its incompatibility with human rights, declarations of this kind can contribute to a decision by a court to impose a range of coercive sanctions, including imprisonment, fines or civil damages.[38] Sanctions of this kind are not only coercive. Their effects are also often extremely difficult to reverse: especially in civil and criminal cases, constitutional commitments to non-retrospectivity will often prevent parliament from alleviating the effects of any unjustified coercion by way of a legislative remedy.[39]

This, I have suggested elsewhere, is also one reason why both declarations of incompatibility – and the idea of judicial review as conversational in nature – seem so ill-suited to a criminal or civil, as opposed to pure public law, setting.[40] Take a case such as *Re McR*, [2002] NIQB 58, a case under the HRA concerning a Northern Irish law prohibiting 'buggery'. The court in this case effectively held that a provision of this kind imposed an unreasonably disproportionate limitation on the right to sexual privacy of the defendant under Article 8 of the European Convention. The law under challenge was itself clearly the product of legislative inertia, not any considered judgment on the part of the North Ireland legislature to maintain a criminal prohibition of this kind. Yet the language of the relevant statute made it extremely difficult for the court to rely on an interpretive reading down as a remedy: it was quite explicit in stating that buggery was *any 'sexual intercourse per anum by a man with a man or a woman'*.[41] The only real remedy available to the court, under the HRA, was thus a legally non-binding declaration of incompatibility under s. 4 of the HRA. The consequence of this, however, would have been to allow McR to be sentenced to a term of imprisonment – the ultimate form of state coercion, when the court itself had found any form of criminal punishment to be *unreasonable* and disproportionate in the circumstances. The only way to remove this coercion would also have

---

[38] Rosalind Dixon, 'A minimalist charter of rights for Australia: The UK or Canada as a model?' (2009) 37 *Federal Law Review*, 335; Kavanagh, 'What's so weak about "weak-form review"?'; Roach, 'Constitutional, remedial and international dialogues'; Fergal F. Davis and David Mead, 'Declarations of incompatibility, dialogue and the criminal law' (2014) 43 *Common Law World Review*, 62.

[39] Dixon, 'A minimalist charter'.

[40] Ibid.

[41] See discussion in *McR* [2002] NIQB 58, emphasis added.

been for the executive to pardon McR, or exercise another form of discretion to release him as a matter of discretion rather than right.[42]

This is also arguably one reason the court in *McR* ultimately chose to go beyond the limits on its remedial power under the HRA, and make an order (beyond its remedial powers) quashing the appellant's conviction.[43] The alternative would have been extremely difficult to justify in a free and democratic society: it would have implied an unjustified form of coercion by the state, in which the courts were integrally involved.

A similar analysis applies to the decision of the Victorian Court of Appeal in *Momcilovic*.[44] *Momcilovic* involved a challenge under the Victorian Charter of Rights and Responsibilities to provisions of a Victorian law that purported to adopt two sets of deeming provisions: first, a presumption that anyone in physical control of premises on which an illicit substance was found had effective possession of that substance; and second, that where the quantity of that substance exceeded a particular amount, it was possessed with the intention of supply. Together, the Court held, these provisions were also clearly an unjustifiable limitation on a defendant's right to a fair trial. Yet the Court held that the language of the statute prevented it from curing this breach via a process of interpretation, and it thus issued a declaration of incompatibility. This also left the defendant liable to a serious criminal conviction, and sentence of imprisonment, without any proof that she had even known about the existence of the relevant substance – let alone had an actual intention to supply it.

The High Court of Australian was highly critical of this result, and noted its capacity to undermine public confidence in the judiciary.[45] This was also one reason the Court overturned the decision of the Court of Appeal, and found that it was incompatible with the exercise of federal judicial power to make such a declaration, and that instead the lower court should have read down the relevant statute to create an ordinary

---

[42] Even stronger limits on legislative or executive reversal also arguably apply to private law cases involving the right to property, which impose barriers to the legislative and executive reversal of a prior court decision in a particular case. See Dixon, 'A minimalist charter'.

[43] See discussion in *McR* [2002] NIQB 58.

[44] *Momcilovic* v. *The Queen* (2011) 245 CLR 1. For an excellent discussion, see e.g., Davis and Mead, 'Declarations of incompatibility'.

[45] See especially *Momcilovic* v. *The Queen* (2011) 245 CLR 1, 93–97 (Gummow J). Justices Crennan and Kiefel JJ also noted and sought to respond to this in their dissenting judgment on the scope of Chapter III (at 226-29).

requirement of proof beyond a reasonable doubt, at least in respect of actual possession of the relevant substance.

B   Dialogue, Deference and De Facto Weak versus Strong Review

In many cases, the proponents of dialogue theory also often overstate the scope for legislative *disagreement* with courts as part of a process of 'dialogue'. One of the distinguishing features of the Canadian model of constitutional rights protection is that s. 33 of the Charter gives express power to the Canadian Parliament and provincial legislatures to pass laws 'notwithstanding' key provisions of the Charter. Section 33, however, does not apply to all rights (it does not, for example, apply to the core democratic and mobility rights in ss. 3–6 of the Charter). There is also a clear history of legislative *non*-use of the power as a means of overriding court decisions in Canada.[46] In the more than thirty years since the Charter was adopted, the Canadian Parliament has never relied on s. 33 to override or modify a decision of the SCC.[47] The power has also been rarely used by provincial legislatures outside Québec.[48]

Almost all constitutional 'dialogue' in Canada has thus occurred through the passage of dialogic 'legislative sequels' – i.e., ordinary legislation that in some way modifies or overrides the effect of a court decision under the Charter. Canadian dialogue scholars also often overstate the scope for truly *successful* legislative dialogue of this kind.[49]

One of the key institutional guarantees of dialogue in Canada, according to almost all Canadian dialogue theorists, is s. 1 of the Charter, which allows legislatures to impose 'reasonable limits' on Charter rights. In applying s. 1, since *R* v. *Oakes* [1986] 1 S.C.R. 103, the SCC has also tended to adopt a quite flexible approach to assessing the reasonableness of legislation. In the United States, in contrast, the notion of 'strict

---

[46] See Kahana, 'Understanding the notwithstanding mechanism'; Janet L. Hiebert, *Charter Conflicts: What Is Parliament's Role?* (McGill-Queen's University Press, 2002); Cameron, 'Collateral thoughts on "dialogue's" legacy'. See also relevant chapters in this volume.

[47] Kahana, 'Understanding the notwithstanding mechanism'; Hiebert, *Charter Conflicts*; Waldron, 'The core of the case against judicial review', 1356–57.

[48] Tsvi Kahana, 'The notwithstanding mechanism and public discussion: Lessons from the ignored practice of section 33 of the Charter' (2001) 44 *Canadian Public Administration*, 255.

[49] See e.g., dialogue critics within Canada such as F. L. Morton, 'Dialogue or monologue' (1999) 20 *Policy Options*, 23. See also Christopher P. Manfredi and James B. Kelly, 'Six degrees of dialogue: A response to Hogg and Bushell' (1999) 37 *Osgoode Hall Law Journal*, 513.

judicial scrutiny' can make it difficult for the Supreme Court to uphold dialogic legislation, consistent with prior precedents.[50] The US Court, however, has also insisted that a test of strict scrutiny is not in fact 'fatal' to the validity of legislation, and has upheld various laws under a test of strict scrutiny.[51] In many ways, the approaches taken by the SCC and the US Supreme Court in this context are thus actually quite similar: in both countries, courts may choose to uphold legislation as valid under the relevant form of proportionality test. And whether they do so, or not, will largely depend on the degree to which they are willing to show *deference* to legislative constitutional judgments.

Consider the history of legislation imposing limits on the voting rights of prisoners in countries such as Canada and South Africa. The right to vote in s. 3 of the Canadian Charter is expressly excluded from the scope of s. 33, so that any limitations on such rights must be upheld by the Supreme Court as reasonable and justifiable under s. 1. In South Africa, the right to vote is also arguably protected by quite stringent require-ments for constitutional amendment, or the more demanding of the two 'tracks' for amendment provided for by s. 74 of the Constitution.[52] For the National Assembly to succeed in imposing limits on such a right, the Constitutional Court of South Africa (CCSA) must thus again be willing to uphold such limitations as reasonably justifiable in terms of s. 36 of the South African Constitution.

In a series of cases, the courts and legislatures in Canada and South Africa also engaged in a clear form of 'dialogue' over the legitimate scope for limiting rights in this context: in both *Sauvé* v. *Canada* [1993] 2 S.C.R. 438 (*Sauvé I*), and *August* v. *Electoral Commission*, 1999 (4) BCLR 363, the SCC and CCSA invalidated legislative and administrative restric-tions on access to the franchise by prisoners, but in doing so expressly left open the possibility that legislators could (re)impose some limitation on voting by prisoners. The Canadian Parliament and South Africa National Assembly also responded by (re)imposing limits on the ability of certain offenders to vote in federal elections.

---

[50] See e.g., *United States* v. *Eichman*, 496 U.S. 310. Compare Rosalind Dixon, 'Weak-form judicial review and American exceptionalism' (2012) 32 *Oxford Journal of Legal Studies*, 487.

[51] See e.g., *Grutter* v. *Bollinger*, 539 U.S. 306 (2003).

[52] Compare Rosalind Dixon and David Landau, 'Tiered constitutional design' (2017) 86 *George Washington Law Review*.

In *Sauvé I*, the SCC struck down a federal law imposing a blanket ban on prisoners voting in federal elections, but in doing so adopted quite narrow, minimalist reasons for its decision. It did not suggest that the government lacked any legitimate purpose in adopting such a law, or that because of the fundamental importance of the right to vote for democracy, and individual human dignity, a law of this kind could never be reasonable and justifiable in a democratic society, or truly proportionate for the purposes of s. 1. Instead, in writing for the Court, Justice Frank Iacobucci simply noted that the law was 'drawn too broadly' and thus 'fail[ed] to meet the proportionality test, particularly the minimal impairment component, as expressed in the section 1 jurisprudence of the Court'.[53] The SCC thus left *explicit* scope for Parliament to re-enact a more narrowly tailored form of prisoner voting disqualification. The Canadian Parliament, in the aftermath of the decision, also responded to this opportunity to adopt a new, more narrowly tailored or proportionate prisoner disqualification regime, by passing new, amended provisions in the federal Elections Act disqualifying all inmates serving sentences of two years or more.

Similarly, in South Africa, in *August* the CCSA took a distinctly narrow or minimalist approach to defining the voting rights of prisoners, or the constitutional flaw in an electoral scheme that did not effectively allow prisoners to register to vote. Unlike the 1993 Constitution, the 1996 South African Constitution makes no express mention of the possibility of prisoner disenfranchisement. Prior to 1999, the National Assembly also took no active steps to address the issue. Thus, when the issue came before the CCSA in *August*, it was effectively the Electoral Commission, not the National Assembly, who were said to have limited the voting rights of prisoners. In upholding this claim, and ordering the Commission to register otherwise eligible prisoners, the CCSA also took a deliberately narrow or minimalist approach, and avoided the question of how far the National Assembly could go in imposing limitations in this context. In writing for the Court, Justice Sachs expressly noted that 'the question whether legislation disqualifying prisoners or categories of prisoners, from voting could be justified under section 36 was not raised in [the] proceedings and need not be dealt with'. He also went on to add that 'the judgment should not be read . . . as suggesting that Parliament is prevented from disenfranchising certain categories of voter'.[54] Several

---

[53] *Sauvé* v. *Canada* [1993] 2 S.C.R. 438, 439–40.
[54] CCT, 8/99 para.[31].

years after the decision, in 2003, the South African National Assembly also passed legislation that *did* explicitly limit the right to vote of certain categories of prisoner – i.e., prisoners serving a sentence of imprisonment without the option of a fine.[55]

Courts in both countries, however, subsequently went on to invalidate this 'dialogic' legislation as an unreasonable limitation of prisoners' rights. Thus, in *Sauvé* v. *Canada*, [2002] 3 S.C.R. 519 (*Sauvé II*), the SCC struck down the legislation passed in response to Sauvé I as insufficiently narrowly tailored or proportionate to any legitimate government objective. In writing for the majority, Chief Justice McLachlin emphasized the fundamental importance of the right to vote as standing 'at the heart of [Canada's] system of constitutional democracy', and as fundamental to individual human dignity and the rule of law and legal legitimacy.[56] She also questioned the rational connection between laws barring prisoners from voting and the stated legislative objective of promoting civic responsibility and the rule of law.[57] Further, she held that the law swept too broadly in 'catching many whose crimes [were] relatively minor and cannot be said to have broken their ties to society',[58] and imposed costs on a core democratic right that were disproportionate to any valid government objective.[59]

Likewise, in South Africa, in *NICRO* in 2004, the CCSA held that 2003 amendments to the Electoral Act disqualifying prisoners serving a sentence without the option of a fine were constitutionally overbroad, and disproportionate. Specifically, the Court emphasised that it could apply to prisoners whose convictions and sentences were under appeal, and who were serving sentences of less than twelve months and who were thus eligible to *run* for election.[60] It also noted that, unlike in Canada, the South African government had failed to advance any compelling purpose for the limitation of rights: the court held in this context that its reliance

---

[55] Electoral Laws Amendment Act 34 of 2003, s. 8(2). See discussion in *Minister of Home Affairs* v. *National Institute for Crime Prevention and the Reintegration of Offenders*, 2004 (5) BCLR 445 (*NICRO*).

[56] [2002] 3 S.C.R. 519, 544–47.

[57] Ibid. 548 (suggesting that '[d]enying citizen lawbreakers the right to vote sends a message that those who commit serious breaches are no longer valued as members of the community, but instead are temporary outcasts from our system of rights and democracy').

[58] Ibid. 553.

[59] Ibid. 555–57.

[60] 2004 (5) BCLR 445 [67], per Chaskalson CJ.

on cost and efficiency considerations was largely unpersuasive; and that it was not entitled to rely on voter perceptions about the need to maintain law and order, or send a message that was 'tough on crime', unless those views had some objective basis. The National Assembly was not, the Court held, entitled to pass laws of this kind simply 'in order to correct a public misconception as to its true attitude to crime and criminals'.[61]

The result, in both cases therefore, was that the attempt by legislators to engage in 'dialogue' with the court failed. Leading Canadian commentators, such as Christopher P. Manfredi, point to this as evidence of the limits to the dialogue metaphor in Canada;[62] whereas Kent Roach suggests that the pattern is more exceptional.[63] Whether this is the case or not, however, will depend on one key question – whether in 'second look cases' of this kind, the SCC tends generally to apply a deferential approach to assessing the justifiability of legislation under s. 1 of the *Charter*.

Deference of this kind can take a variety of forms. In some cases, it may simply involve an ongoing commitment to judicial narrowness, or the non-expansion of prior decisions in the face of apparent democratic disagreement. In other cases, courts may be able to avoid hearing a second-look case, in ways that show *implicit* deference to the constitutional judgments embedded in a legislative sequel. But courts may also face legal or practical obstacles to avoidance of this kind, which makes it necessary for them to address the substantive validity of a legislative sequel. To uphold such a sequel, given true legislative dialogue or disagreement with a prior decision, courts will also have only one real option: they must be willing in second-look cases to show some form of additional *substantive* deference to the constitutional judgments of legislators.

One of the key difficulties with dialogue theory, as I have suggested previously, is also that most of the key proponents of the dialogue metaphor explicitly *reject* the idea of deference of this kind.[64] The SCC has itself adopted a variety of views on this question. In *R* v. *Mills*, the SCC affirmed the idea of a constitutional dialogue between courts and legislatures, noting that 'Courts do not hold a monopoly on the

---

[61] Ibid. [56].
[62] Christopher P. Manfredi, 'The day the dialogue died: A comment on *Sauvé* v. *Canada*' (2007) 45 *Osgoode Hall Law Journal*, 105, 122.
[63] Roach, *The Supreme Court on Trial*, pp. 345–46.
[64] Compare Dixon, 'The Supreme Court of Canada'.

protection and promotion of rights and freedoms; Parliament also plays a role in this regard and is often able to act as a significant ally for vulnerable groups', and that the 'court ha[d] an obligation to consider respectfully Parliament's attempt to respond' to the voices of such groups. This was also in the context of legislation sharply narrowing the effect of the SCC's prior decision in *R* v. *O'Connor* [1995] 4 S.C.R. 411.[65] In *Darrach*, in upholding Parliament's attempt to narrow the effect of the court's prior decision in *R* v. *Seaboyer* [1991] 2 S.C.R. 577, striking down rape shield laws in the criminal code, the court again also cited this reasoning.[66]

In other cases, however, members or the court have explicitly rejected the idea of deference in second-look cases: in *RJR-MacDonald Inc.*, a second-look case on the scope to regulate tobacco advertising under the *Charter*, the court suggested that the second-look nature of a case neither 'militate[d] for or against deference' by the Court.[67] And in *Vriend* and *M* v. *H*, while endorsing the idea of dialogue, Justice Iaccobucci suggested that given its connection to the power in s. 33 of the Charter, it pointed toward less rather than more deference by courts to the constitutional judgments of legislators under s. 1.[68]

Dialogue scholars, however, have tended to argue against, rather than in favour of, deference in second-look cases. Reflecting on their earlier article, ten years on, Hogg and Bushell-Thornton explicately argued (with Wade Wright) that courts should 'not approach the second look cases any differently then they approach first look cases'.[69] In separate work, Hogg also explicitly argued that it would be inappropriate for courts to show any form of additional deference in second-look cases,[70] echoing similar arguments to this effect by the SCC in cases such as *Sauve, Vriend* and *M and H.*[71]

---

[65] *R* v. *Mills* [1999] 3 S.C.R. 668, [58]–[59].

[66] *R* v. *Darrach* [2000] 2 S.C.R. 443.

[67] *RJR-MacDonald Inc.* v. *Canada (A.G.)* [1995] 3 S.C.R. 577.

[68] *Vriend* v. *Alberta* [1998] 1 S.C.R. 493, [136]–[140]; *M* v. *H* [1999] 2 S.C.R. 3, [78]–[79]. See Dixon, 'The Supreme Court of Canada'.

[69] Peter M. Hogg, Allison A. Bushell Thornton and Wade K. Wright, 'Charter dialogue revisited – or much ado about metaphors' (2007) 45 *Osgoode Hall Law Journal*, 1, 47–48. See discussion in Dixon, 'The Supreme Court of Canada', p. 251.

[70] Peter W. Hogg, 'Discovering Dialogue', in Grant Huscroft and Ian Brodie (eds.), *Constitutionalism in the Charter Era* (LexisNexis Canada, 2004), p. 5. See Dixon, 'The Supreme Court of Canada', p. 251.

[71] Dixon, 'The Supreme Court of Canada', pp. 283–84.

Kent Roach has likewise argued against the notion of deference by courts in second-look cases, suggesting that courts should instead simply decide both first and second-look cases according to their own preferred understanding of the Charter.[72] In answer to my own prior arguments in favour of second-look deference, he has suggested that: in general the dialogue metaphor 'should not tilt the scales towards either in validation or upholding any piece of legislation. A strategy of deference and under enforcement would be just as wrong as a strategy of activism in over enforcement.' Even in second-look cases, he argues that 'judges should not be swayed by the fact that it is Parliament's second try or that if the government loses again it might invoke section 33'.[73] The second-look nature of a case, he argues, 'should not undermine a litigant's right to a hearing on the merits'.[74]

III   Deference and Its Limits

Why might dialogue theorists reject the idea of deference of this kind? One answer is linguistic or metaphorical in nature: the idea of dialogue connotes an exchange between equals, and critics of the idea of deference suggest that it is inimical to equality for one party to defer to the other.[75] Dialogue scholars also raise additional concerns about the relationship between judicial deference and constitutional commitments to judicial independence and the rule of law, and undermine courts' role in protecting minority rights. Luc Tremblay, for example, raises concerns about the idea of judicial deference as effectively undermining a court's independent and constitutional role.[76] Kent Roach also suggests that a danger of second-look deference is that it threatens to undermine courts' role in protecting 'discrete and insular minorities' or guarding against majoritarian attacks on unpopular majorities.[77]

What, if any, limits are there to this idea of deference, which may help answer the objections or concerns of those who oppose it as implicit in the notion of constitutional dialogue? Roach, in particular, at times suggests that the idea of judicial deference in second-look cases equates

---

[72] Roach, *The Supreme Court on Trial*, p. 51.
[73] Ibid. pp. 400–01.
[74] Ibid. p. 388.
[75] Compare Morton, 'Dialogue or monologue'.
[76] Luc B. Tremblay, 'The legitimacy of judicial review: The limits of dialogue between courts and legislatures' (2005) 3 *International Journal of Constitutional Law*, 617.
[77] Roach, *The Supreme Court on Trial*.

to the idea of 'an automatic rule of deference to Parliament in second look cases'.[78] The idea of deference by courts in second-look cases, however, need not – indeed should not – be understood as automatic, or unlimited, in this way. This part suggests that there are clear logical limits to the idea of deference, which in large part answer these concerns on the part of critics.

A   Limited Deference

Implicit in the idea of deference in *second-look cases* is that there is no justification for *across-the-board* deference by courts to the democratic judgments of legislators in all cases. Deference by courts in second-look cases could be combined by courts with a commitment to certain forms of deference in first-look cases. In the United Kingdom, for example, British courts have identified a number of factors as pointing toward deference by courts to the judgments of Parliament under the HRA, including: the degree of institutional expertise of legislators compared to judges in a particular area, the nature of the particular Convention right at stake or policy under challenge, and the qualified as opposed to absolute nature of the right at stake.[79] Calibrating deference based on factors of this kind is also entirely consistent with the idea of *additional* deference to democratic constitutional judgments in second-look cases.

One of the assumptions behind a weak model of review, I have argued however, is that ordinary legislative processes are often subject to 'blind spots' or 'burdens of inertia' affecting the protection of individual rights, which courts can overcome if they exercise sufficiently broad powers of review *ex ante*. An important argument for confining deference of this kind to *second-look* cases is also that it allows courts effectively to play this role in countering true legislative blind spots and burdens of inertia.[80] This also implies that, in each case, courts must exercise

---

[78] Ibid. p. 357.

[79] See e.g., discussion in Richard Clayton, 'Principles for judicial deference' (2006) 11 *Judicial Review*, 109; Sadat Sayeed, 'Beyond the language of "deference"' (2005) 10 *Judicial Review*, 111; Richard A. Edwards, 'Judicial deference under the Human Rights Acts' (2002) 65 *Modern Law Review*, 859; Gavin Phillipson, 'Deference, discretion, and democracy in the Human Rights Act era' (2007) 60 *Current Legal Problems*, 40.

[80] Compare Lord Steyn, 'Deference: A tangled story' [2005] *Public Law* 346 (arguing deference in first-look cases can undermine the role of courts in protecting human rights under a weak system of review); Tremblay, 'The legitimacy of judicial review' (arguing that any real form of deference is contrary to judicial independence). In many cases, of

independent judgment as to the ongoing justifiability of legislation in a free and democratic society.

A court could also embrace the idea of deference in second-look cases, and still consider whether legislators had in fact paid attention to a court's reasoning in enacting a given legislative sequel. Properly understood, the idea of weak-form review is not that legislatures can succeed in passing legislation simply through multiple attempts – or the constitutional equivalent of the idea that 'if at first you don't succeed, try, try again'.[81] Rather, it is that courts should defer to (in the sense of *showing respect for*) legislation that reflects reasoned deliberation by legislators, or a serious willingness on their part to engage in deliberation about constitutional questions.[82] Thus, it does not require courts to uphold a legislative sequel that simply overlooks or disregards a court's prior reasoning.

Take a recent example of arguable constitutional dialogue in Australia under the 2006 Victorian Charter of Rights and Responsibilities. Following riots at a juvenile detention centre, the Victorian government took steps to relocate certain juvenile offenders to an adult detention facility. The ostensible purpose of this was to allow for repairs and upgrades to the juvenile facility. But in making the transfer, the minister clearly failed to consider the suitability of the relevant adult facility for children, and the rights, and best interests, of children as detainees.[83] The Supreme Court thus struck down the executive order reclassifying the adult facility, and allowing the transfer, as invalid; and the Victorian Court of Appeal upheld this decision, giving the government forty-eight

---

course, there will clearly be cases in which the distinction between 'first'- and 'second'-look cases is somewhat blurred: a court may have spoken on an issue in a recent case, but not directly addressed the issue before parliament. In enacting relevant legislation, parliament will thus in some sense be passing a legislative sequel, but on another acting on a fresh legal slate. To treat a case of this kind as a first-look case may also be overly formalistic: if there is evidence that parliament has in fact engaged with the reasons of a court in adopting relevant legislation, but shown reasoned and reasonable disagreement with that reasoning, a court truly committed to dialogue would adopt the same form of deference to a reasonable legislative sequel.

[81] *Sauvé v. Canada (Chief Electoral Officer) (Sauvé II)* [2002] 3 S.C.R. 519, 17.

[82] Cass R. Sunstein, *One Case at a Time: Judicial Minimalism on the Supreme Court* (Cambridge, MA: Harvard University Press, 2001), p. 70.

[83] See discussion in *Certain Children by their Litigation Guardian Sister Marie Brigid Arthur v. Minister for Families and Children* [2016] VSC 796; *Minister for Families and Children v. Certain Children by Their Litigation Guardian Sister Marie Brigid Arthur* [2016] VSCA 343.

hours to remove the relevant children into a 'lawful youth detention facility'.[84]

The government, however, responded in a completely non-dialogic way: it did not make enquiries as to possible alternative juvenile detention facilities, or investigate ways of modifying the relevant adult detention facility to make it more suitable for children.[85] Indeed, it did not appear to give any meaningful consideration to the substance of the Victorian courts' reasoning – about the need to consider children's specific needs and vulnerability in the context of detention. Instead, it took less than twenty-four hours to re-gazette – or reclassify – the relevant adult facility as a juvenile detention facility, without making any modification to the terms of detention.

The rationale for second-look deference, therefore, would simply not apply in a case of this kind: because the political branches did not engage seriously with the reasoning of the Victorian courts, there would be no reason for the courts to defer to the constitutional judgments of the political branches in enacting a relevant legislative (or delegated legislative) sequel. Instead, the Victorian Supreme Court could legitimately apply a quite demanding form of proportionality analysis, and find that the new classification regime was itself also invalid. This is also exactly what the Supreme Court did, in *Certain Children* v. *Minister for Families and Children (No 2)* [2017] VSC 25, in finding the second set of transfer orders to be in breach of the rights of the child under the Charter, and thereby invalid.

B   *Reasonable versus Unreasonable Disagreement*

The theoretical basis for weak-form review also suggests potential additional limits to the scope of appropriate judicial deference in second-look cases. The reason for endorsing weak-form review, according to proponents such as Mark Tushnet and Stephen Gardbaum, is that there a range of constitutional questions on which reasonable people could disagree. To give courts the final say in these circumstances would also show inherent disrespect for the equal right of all citizens in a democracy

---

[84] *Minister for Families and Children* v. *Certain Children by Their Litigation Guardian Sister Marie Brigid Arthur* [2016] VSCA 343.

[85] *Wearne* v. *Victoria* [2017] VSC 25, 472–76 (*Certain Children* v. *Minister for Families and Children (No 2)*).

to contribute to resolving these questions.[86] It is thus not a theory that suggests that judicial review should be weak in all cases. Rather, it is a theory that suggests that there should be scope for democratic majorities to override courts where there is *reasonable* disagreement among citizens about what constitutional justice entails.[87]

This normative foundation, in turn, entails two broad preconditions for any deference by courts to legislative constitutional judgments: evidence of actual democratic majority disagreement with a court; and a showing that disagreement of this kind is compatible with the notion of reasoned and rational debate, and a commitment to treating all citizens as worthy of equal respect and dignity in such a debate.[88] This itself also rules out the idea that courts should defer to legislation that reflects animus or hostility toward a particular minority group.[89] Legislation of this kind is inherently unreasonable from the perspective of a commitment to self-government among individuals as free and equal persons. It therefore has no claim to respect on democratic grounds.[90]

This provides an important protection for minorities against the risk of majoritarian abuse. Scholars such as Roach suggest that a danger of second-look deference is that it threatens to undermine courts' role in protecting 'discrete and insular minorities' or guarding against majoritarian attacks on unpopular majorities.[91] But as Sunstein and others have shown, doctrines that limit the scope for majority animus toward

---

[86] Jeremy Waldron, *Law and Disagreement* (Oxford University Press, 1999). See also Adam Tomkins, 'The role of the courts in the political constitution' (2010) 60 *University of Toronto Law Journal*, 1. Compare arguments about equality and non-domination made by republican scholars in this context: see e.g., Geoffrey Sigalet in this volume; Tom Hickey, 'The republican virtues of the "new commonwealth model of constitutionalism"' (2016) 14 *International Journal of Constitutional Law*, 794.

[87] Mark Tushnet, *Weak Courts, Strong Rights: Judicial Review and Social Welfare Rights in Comparative Constitutional Law* (Princeton: Princeton University Press, 2009); Tushnet and Dixon, 'Weak-Form Review and Its Constitutional Relatives'.

[88] See e.g., Waldron, *Law and Disagreement*.

[89] Beyond this, scholars such as Waldron argue that there is no guarantee that courts will do a systematically better job than legislators in protecting minorities, or in deciding what counts as a 'right' or a 'minority' from a truly democratic perspective. Compare Waldron, 'The core of the case against judicial review'; Waldron, *Law and Disagreement*.

[90] See *R v. Director of Public Prosecutions, Ex parte Kebeline* [2000] 2 AC 326, at 380G (Lord Hope): 'in some circumstances it will be appropriate for the courts to recognize that there is an area of judgment within which the judiciary will defer, on democratic grounds, to the considered opinion of the elected body'.

[91] Roach, *The Supreme Court on Trial*.

minorities can play an important role in protecting against the worst forms of majoritarian abuse of this kind.[92]

In cases such as *Sauvé II* and *NICRO*, for instance, there could be an argument that courts in both Canada and South Africa were simply enforcing the boundaries of *reasonable* disagreement in a democracy. The notion of reasonable disagreement depends on the idea of disagreement among free and equal citizens. Legislative measures that reflect a fundamental disrespect for the notion of equal citizenship are thus inherently inconsistent, rather than consistent, with the notion of reasonable disagreement in a democracy.

There is also a plausible argument that most if not all prisoner disenfranchisement laws reflect a form of disrespect – or denial of equal human dignity – of this kind.[93] Laws that impinge on the rights of adult citizens to vote arguably undermine the very basis for a system of weak review: by depriving citizens of an opportunity to express their views via the electoral process, laws of this kind arguably undermine a key part of the argument for respecting the judgments that result from that process.[94] Kent Roach has further argued that, in Canada in particular, laws of this kind reflect a form of animus toward criminal defendants, or a form of 'penal populism' that exploits popular fear to justify imposing unreasonable limits on the rights of those convicted of criminal offences.[95] On this basis, it would also clearly have been justified for the SCC in *Sauvé II* to adopt the approach it took, and strike down the relevant legislative sequel.

The contrary argument, of course, is that most prisoner disenfranchisement laws are exactly the kind of provisions reflecting norms of reasonable disagreement, which weak-form systems of review are designed to protect.[96] Prisoner disenfranchisement laws clearly constitute a serious limitation of the voting and equality rights of prisoners. From a practical perspective, they may also undermine the capacity of the criminal justice system to be used as a vehicle for promoting the rehabilitation or reintegration of offenders: exercising the right to vote, and being given the opportunity to do so on an informed basis, may be a valuable and

---

[92] Sunstein, *One Case at a Time*.

[93] Compare arguments of the kind by Chief Justice McLachlan in *Sauvé II* [2002] 3 S.C.R. 519.

[94] Compare Waldron, 'The core of the case against judicial review'.

[95] See e.g., Roach, *The Supreme Court on Trial*; Roach in this volume.

[96] Compare e.g., Stephen Gardbuam, 'What's so weak about "weak-form review"? A reply to Aileen Kavanagh' (2015) 13 *International Journal of Constitutional Law* 1040, 1043.

important means of encouraging greater civic engagement and responsibility on the part of prisoners.[97] But laws of this kind also serve a range of legitimate purposes: they seek to respond to a proven act of wrongdoing on the part of an individual, by attaching further adverse moral and practical consequences to that act. At a symbolic or expressive level, they send a clear signal of disapproval of or moral disapprobation toward the relevant conduct. And at a practical level, they deprive prisoners of the opportunity to organize collectively to influence the direction of law and policy for their own protection or advantage. Providing this additional penalty is proportionate to the wrong of their actions, it thus arguably respects – rather than disrespects – their dignity and agency as individuals.[98] The premise of a system of weak judicial review is also that it is reasonable for citizens with different comprehensive viewpoints to take differing views as to how to balance these competing arguments.

To be clear, my own view is that laws of this kind are unjustified, and ill-advised, in a constitutional democracy committed to freedom and equality for all citizens. But I also believe that reasonable people could disagree with this conclusion; and that given reasonable disagreement of this kind, legislators rather than courts should have the ultimate authority to decide on the appropriate balance to be struck.[99]

On this basis, I would also argue that cases such as *Sauvé II* and *NICRO* were exactly the kind of case in which deference by courts was required to create true constitutional dialogue, or a truly democratically legitimate form of rights-based constitutional review.[100] Any constitutional scheme necessary involves some trade-off in the protection of different rights: while weak forms of review potentially leave unchecked the unjustified legislative infringement of minority rights in certain cases, stronger forms of judicial review involve a sacrifice in citizens' equal right to participate in the process of self-government.[101] The attraction of the dialogue metaphor is that it promises to make this trade-off in the most rights-protective way possible, but it cannot do so if it fails to support judicial deference to *reasonable* as opposed to *unreasonable* legislative sequels.

---

[97] See e.g., Alec C. Ewald and Brandon Rottonghaus (eds.), *Criminal Disenfranchisement in an International Perspective* (Cambridge: Cambridge University Press, 2009).

[98] Compare reasoning in *S v. Makwanyane*, 1995 (6) BCLR 665 per Chaskalson CJ.

[99] Waldron, 'The core of the case against judicial review'.

[100] Compare discussion in Roach, *The Supreme Court on Trial*.

[101] Compare Waldron, *Law and Disagreement*.

IV Conclusion

'Dialogue' is a metaphor that continues to be endorsed and deployed by constitutional scholars and decision-makers around the world, in ways that give it great promise as a tool for constitutional comparison, and shared comparative constitutional conversation.[102] It also has two clear advantages: it helps highlight the persuasive or communicative dimension to judicial review, and thus one key way in which it can help highlight or overcome blind spots and burdens of inertia in the legislative process. It also helps draw attention to the iterative nature of judicial review, in ways that contribute to a more nuanced debate about its democratic legitimacy.

The chapter, however, also notes to key dangers or downsides to current understandings of the dialogue metaphor: the idea of judicial review as dialogue or 'conversation' has a distinct capacity to downplay the coercive dimension to judicial decision-making, and thus the degree to which weak models of judicial review may be inadequate to deal with blind spots and burdens of inertia. Second, the idea that judicial review is *always* provisional, or penultimate, in nature may overstate the actual scope for substantive dialogue between courts and legislatures in a range of circumstances. This, in turn, may also overstate the claim to democratic legitimacy of judicial review itself.

The argument in this chapter is that for judicial review to be de facto weak in nature, in many cases courts must adopt some form of deference toward reasonable legislative sequels. Deference of this kind in second-look cases need not be unlimited in scope: it is fully consistent with the notion of quite strong and searching judicial review toward laws that reflect animus toward minority groups, or unreasonable or unreasoned forms of disagreement. But without some form of deference of this kind, judicial review will inevitably tend to be de facto strong rather than weak in nature, and thus encounter significant potential democratic objections.

This implies one of two ways forward for 'dialogue' as a metaphor for the relationship between courts and legislatures in the interpretation and enforcement of constitutional rights. Either dialogue must be reinterpreted to include a norm of dialogic deference by courts to reasonable legislative sequels, or it must be abandoned by comparative scholars in

---

[102] Comparing Constitutional Adjudication, An Evolving Interactive Constitutional Scenario in Europe: The Framework of the Research (2016), http://cocoaproject.eu/index .php/co-co-a-research.

favour of a term that more fully captures the idea of the contingency of de facto weak review, and the degree to which its achievement depends on important doctrinal choices by courts, rather than an inevitable interaction between courts and legislatures in a democratic system.

Both Aileen Kavanagh and Eoin Carolan have proposed a number of potential alternatives in this context, including the idea of judicial review as 'cooperative', partnership-based or 'collaborative' in nature.[103] Others have suggested the use of the notion of 'institutional interaction', or an 'iterative' approach to implementation of constitutional norms.[104] While many of these labels seem to have some of the same problems as 'dialogue' (i.e., they downplay both individual coercion and inter-branch conflict in the process of judicial review), some also go further toward capturing the contingency of how judicial–legislative interaction unfolds.[105]

In earlier work I advocated the first path of retaining but refining the dialogue metaphor, to incorporate a stronger emphasis on notions of second-look deference; whereas in more recent work I have suggested that it may be useful to use the concept of de facto weak or 'responsive' judicial review to convey this same idea.[106] New labels, however, may also risk adding greater confusion, rather than clarity, to existing debates over the proper relationship between courts and parliaments in the resolution of rights-based disagreements in a democracy.

Whether this risk – inherent in shifting labels or metaphors – is worth taking may also ultimately depend in part on the contributions, and responses, to this volume: if the scope and meaning of the dialogue metaphor can be clarified, it remains a promising way to describe patterns of de facto weak review. But if current disagreements as to its meaning and scope continue, it may be time to replace it with a new word that more accurately captures the communicative, coercive *and* potentially non-final nature of judicial review in many democracies.

---

[103] Eoin Carolan, 'Dialogue isn't working: The case for collaboration as a model of legislative-judicial relations' (2016) 36 *Legal Studies*, 209; Aileen Kavanagh, 'The lure and the limits of dialogue' (2016) 66 *University of Toronto Law Journal*, 83; Aileen Kavanagh, *Constitutional Review under the UK Human Rights Act* (Cambridge: Cambridge University Press, 2009).

[104] See Leighton McDonald, 'Rights, "dialogue" and democratic objections to judicial review' (2004) 32 *Federal Law Review*, 1; Swati Jhaveri, '"Dialogic" judicial review: Interrogating the metaphor' (Unpublished manuscript, 2017 (on the iterative nature).

[105] Compare Jhaveri, '"Dialogic" judicial review'; Roach, *The Supreme Court on Trial*, p. 389.

[106] Dixon, 'Responsive Judicial Review'; Persily, 'Introduction'.

7

Dialogue, Finality and Legality

JEFF KING*

The metaphor of 'dialogue' suggests a process of iterative exchange between courts and legislatures, in which both help to define the scope of rights and hence specify the political arrangements required to secure them.[1] Beyond this, however, the metaphor is understood in various ways. In an earlier piece, I suggested that we should not be distracted by the metaphor of dialogue and the debates about its accuracy and significance.[2] My thought was that we should dig beneath the termino- logical issue, and absorb whatever insights stem from the rich literature on the subject. In doing so, however, it has become increasingly apparent

---

* An earlier draft of this paper was presented at a Topics in Constitutional Theory seminar hosted by Aileen Kavanagh at the University of Oxford (12 May 2017), and again at the Annual Conference of the International Society of Public Law (ICON-S) in Copenhagen, Denmark, 28 June 2017, on a panel together with Eoin Carolan, Stephen Gardbaum and Gavin Phillipson. I am heavily indebted to Aileen Kavanagh for her comments on the day and written comments afterwards. These improved the piece immensely and saved it from some crude mistakes. I am also grateful to Justice Catherine O'Regan and Justice Robert Sharpe who attended the Oxford seminar and gave helpful critical remarks. I would also like to thank Alison L. Young and Pavlos Eleftheriadis for further comments in Oxford, and Tom Hickey, Colm O'Cinneide and other participants for the discussion in Copen- hagen. Each of the editors of this volume also provided very helpful and constructive substantive comments.
[1] For a recent survey and strong critique of the use of the term, see Aileen Kavanagh, 'The Lure and Limits of Dialogue' (2016) 66 *University of Toronto Law Journal* 83. Kavanagh's important article makes a number of similar criticisms to the ones expressed in this piece, and is the most thorough examination of the provenance and varieties of the metaphor I have read. For a contemporary restatement of the idea, see Alison L. Young, *Democratic Dialogue and the Constitution* (Oxford: Oxford University Press, 2017).
[2] Jeff King, 'Parliament's Role Following Declarations of Incompatibility under the Human Rights Act' in Murray Hunt, Hayley Hooper and Paul Yowell (eds.), *Parliaments and Human Rights: Addressing the Democratic Deficit* (Oxford: Hart Publishing, 2015). For sceptical views about the relevance of the debate and metaphor, see Aileen Kavanagh, *Constitutional Review under the UK Human Rights Act* (Cambridge: Cambridge Univer- sity Press, 2009), pp. 408–411; Stephen Gardbaum, *The New Commonwealth Model of Constitutionalism* (Cambridge: Cambridge University Press, 2013), pp. 15–16 and esp. 111–121.

that the dialogue metaphor is open to such divergent views about the judicial and legislative roles, and is in competition with a set of more well-weathered theories concerning this relationship, that a closer and more critical examination is appropriate.

This chapter hence has three tasks. The first is to clarify different senses of the term 'dialogue'. I will explore whether it implies an egalitarian relationship between institutions, whether it justifies judicial review, who has the last word under the metaphor and how, importantly, it relates to the 'passive virtues' tradition of judicial restraint associated with Alexander Bickel, John Hart Ely and Cass Sunstein. The second task is to point out certain problems with the dialogue metaphor. I argue that the equivocation over who has the last word in rights-disputes puts rights at substantial risk; that the dialogue metaphor pays insufficient attention to the need for finality and authoritative resolutions of law; and that the separation of powers is put in doubt where legislatures are invited to reject the constitutional interpretations of the judicial branch, at least where those interpretations are put forward as interpretations of *law*. Agreeing with these criticisms does not commit one to a robust view of judicial supremacy, one that makes no room for judicial restraint. To the contrary, the passive virtues tradition that it seeks to replace or compete with has fewer of these problems.

I Dialogue: Its Meaning and Evolution (in Canada)

There has been a significant amount written about constitutional or democratic dialogue, notably in Canada,[3] in respect of the UK Human

---

[3] See the (2007) 45 *Osgoode Hall Law Journal* 1 for an issue dedicated entirely to the metaphor of dialogue and reply by the principal authors of the idea in Canadian law to their critics. Kent Roach has expounded and defended the idea in a range of publications: see e.g., 'Dialogic Judicial Review and Its Critics' (2004) 23 *Supreme Court Law Review* 49, and 'Sharpening the Dialogue Debate: The Next Decade of Scholarship' (2007) 45 *Osgoode Hall Law Journal* 169. For a fresh perspective, see Rosalind Dixon, 'The Supreme Court of Canada, Charter Dialogue, and Deference' (2009) 47 *Osgoode Hall Law Journal* 235. For more critical perspectives, see Christopher P. Manfredi and James B. Kelly, 'Six Degrees of Dialogue: A Response to Hogg and Bushell' (1999) 37 *Osgoode Hall Law Journal* 513; Andrew Petter, 'Twenty Years of Charter Justification: From Liberal Legalism to Dubious Dialogue' (2003) 52 *University of Brunswick Law Journal* 187; Christopher P. Manfredi, 'The Day the Dialogue Died: A Comment on *Sauvé v. Canada*' (2007) 45 *Osgoode Hall Law Journal* 105; Grant Huscroft, 'Rationalizing Judicial Power: The Mischief of Dialogue Theory' in James B. Kelly and Christopher P. Manfredi (eds), *Contested Constitutionalism: Reflections on the Canadian Charter of Rights and Freedoms* (Vancouver: University of British Columbia Press, 2009); Andrew Petter, 'Taking Dialogue Theory Much Too

Rights Act 1998,[4] and in at times unfairly neglected earlier work on this theme by Barry Friedman in the United States.[5] The basic idea as outlined in the seminal article by Hogg and Bushell (now Bushell Thornton), is as follows: 'Where a judicial decision is open to legislative reversal, modification, or avoidance, then it is meaningful to regard the relationship between the Court and the competent legislative body as a dialogue.'[6] The authors argue that, where dialogue occurs, 'any concern about the legitimacy of judicial review is greatly diminished'.[7] They later back down from this normative claim, however.[8] Within this version, we see most of the initial promise of the dialogue metaphor. It had two key aspects. The first is the idea that a judicial ruling is not final, in the sense of the court having the *last word*. The legislature could reverse, modify or

Seriously (or Perhaps Charter Dialogue Isn't Such a Good Thing After All)' (2007) 45 *Osgoode Hall Law Journal* 147; Grégoire Webber, 'The Unfulfilled Potential of the Court and Legislature Dialogue' (2009) 43 *Canadian Journal of Political Science* 443.

[4] Tom Hickman, 'Constitutional *Dialogue*, Constitutional Theories and the Human Rights Act 1998' [2005] *Public Law* 306; Alison L. Young, *Parliamentary Sovereignty and the Human Rights Act* (Oxford: Hart Publishing, 2009), esp. ch. 5; Alison L. Young, 'Deference, Dialogue and the Search for Legitimacy' (2010) 30 *Oxford Journal of Legal Studies* 815. Young's views are developed and restated in great depth in her recent book *Democratic Dialogue and the Constitution*. It may be that her version escapes many of the criticisms in this essay. To the extent, however, that it locates dialogue as a 'middle-ground' between legal and political constitutionalism, as stated in Young's introduction and developed in chapter 2, it may well be subject to my skepticism over Gardbaum's similar claims about the new Commonwealth model, above note 2. See Jeff King, 'Rights and the Rule of Law in Third Way Constitutionalism' (2015) 30 *Constitutional Commentary* 101, 113–120. I also agree with Kent Roach's comments in this volume about the tendency of dichotomies such as 'weak-form/strong-form', and categories such as the Commonwealth model, to risk oversimplifying the true position. My review essay of Gardbaum's book seeks to expose some of the relevant differences.

[5] Barry Friedman, 'Dialogue and Judicial Review' (1993) 91 *Michigan Law Review* 577. At 653, for instance, he states: 'The Constitution is not interpreted by aloof judges imposing their will on the people. Rather, constitutional interpretation is an elaborate discussion between judges and the body politic.'

[6] Peter W. Hogg and Allison A. Bushell, 'The Charter Dialogue between Courts and Legislatures (Or Perhaps the Charter of Rights Isn't Such a Bad Thing After All)' (1997) 35 *Osgoode Hall Law Journal* 75, 79. I take this definition as a seminal starting point. The various nuances of the term are best explored in Kavanagh, 'Lure and Limits', and the most developed contemporary conception is in Young, *Democratic Dialogue and the Constitution*, both above note 1.

[7] Ibid. 80.

[8] Peter W. Hogg, Allison A. Bushell Thornton and Wade K. Wright, 'Charter Dialogue Revisited: Or "Much Ado about Metaphors"' (2007) 45 *Osgoode Hall Law Journal* 1, 29: ('Dialogue theory does not provide a justification for judicial review.') See also, Kavanagh, 'Lure and Limits', fn. 49, above note 1.

avoid the decision. That is an empirical claim. It suggests the power of the legislature to disagree with the court, and offers examples of 'legislative sequels' in which it is claimed the Canadian federal parliament did just that. As Justice Gonthier put it in his dissent in the Canadian *Sauvé II* case, 'the heart of the dialogue metaphor is that neither the courts nor Parliament hold a monopoly on the determination of values'.[9] In Justice Gonthier's formulation, however, the idea is not offered as a description. He invokes it as a normative principle of deference. The court spoke in *Sauvé I*, finding that a blanket ban on prisoner voting was unconstitutional. The legislature modified the ban to limit it to prisoners sentenced to more than two years' imprisonment. It came up for consideration in *Sauvé II*. At that point, Justice Gonthier invoked the idea, in dissent, of 'no monopoly' to mean that the court had said its bit earlier and ought now to defer. So, the *not having the last word* claim can be advanced as an empirical description, or a normative prescription about judicial deference to legislative reconsiderations.

The second claim evident in the original statement of dialogue theory is a somewhat mixed message about the normative significance of the metaphor. The original article was clearly offered as a riposte to the counter-majoritarian objection to judicial review. It was received that way by judges, other scholars and critics in Canada and abroad, and developed in that fashion by Kent Roach. Since the authors of the original article sent mixed messages about this, we need to idealize for a moment what the metaphor at first looks to promise. It is this: that there is a relationship of approximate equality between courts and legislatures in the task of defining rights. For that reason, dialogical constitutional judicial review does not result in outright judicial supremacy of the sort familiar in the US *Lochner* era. It at the very least leads to joint authorship of rights determinations, or even a complex determination more reflective of legislative than judicial input. Hence those who decry the counter-majoritarian aspect of judicial review are mistaken in fact about what happens in rights litigation, in the long run. And perhaps that factual mistake means the political, normative critique is also misguided.

So much for the idealized version, the one conveyed in the gist of so many seminars and lectures. Hogg, Bushell Thornton and Wright in fact clarify their initial intentions with the metaphor in a piece published in 2007: 'What "Charter Dialogue" demonstrated was not that judicial

---

[9] *Sauvé v. Canada (Chief Electoral Officer)* [2002] 3 SCR 519 [104]. Cf. the majority judgment of McLachlin CJ at [17].

review was good, but that judicial review under the Charter was weaker than is generally supposed.'[10] Putting aside for a moment the question of whether the concept was meant to justify judicial review, we now can receive the thesis as a straightforward empirical claim about the attenuated impact of judicial review. Hogg and Bushell Thornton, as well as Kent Roach, locate their substantive justification for judicial review elsewhere. Dialogue is a comment on how the practice unfolds.

But this defence of the idea, taken alone, gives rise to further problems. It simply does not appear to be true that the legislature ordinarily reaffirms the original policy. The thesis that the legislature does do so holds true only on the assumption that we define the objective very widely and assume that the means the legislature initially chose were not themselves part of the actual policy choice. Sometimes legislators may be indifferent as to means. Many times they may not be, and the intrusion will appear to interfere with the policy directly rather than its implementation on points of detail. As it happens, judges do rule out certain policies, and legislatures tend on the whole to comply. Advocates of judicial review should squarely confront the challenge here, and justify the role of courts.

Some authors point to the 'second look' cases as examples of where legislatures have reaffirmed the original policy and offered new evidence to support it,[11] all of which ultimately is accepted by the courts on reconsideration. A good example is the 1995 judgment of the Supreme Court of Canada that a ban on virtually all advertising and promotion of tobacco products and requirement to affix unattributed health warning labels on tobacco product packaging would violate a constitutionally recognized corporate freedom of expression.[12] In 2007, it laudably reversed course and accepted that the health case for similar legislation made it Charter compliant.[13] One might celebrate this as a case of

---

[10] Hogg, Bushell Thornton and Wright, 'Charter Dialogue Revisited', 1, 29, above note 8.

[11] Dixon, 'The Supreme Court of Canada, Charter Dialogue, and Deference' (generally but esp. 272), above note 3; Hogg, Bushell Thornton and Wright, 'Charter Dialogue Revisited', 19–25, above note 8.

[12] *RJR-MacDonald Inc. v. Canada (AG)* [1995] 3 S.C.R. 199.

[13] *Canada (Attorney General) v. JTI-Macdonald Corp.*, [2007] 2 S.C.R. 610. Though I describe the second case as a 'reversal', the Court took the view not that the first decision misunderstood the scope of the right, but rather that there was simply more evidence to support the justifiability of the restriction and that the statutory scheme was more modest. My own view is that the first decision was wrong to recognize a corporate freedom of expression for advertising (or any) purposes.

dialogue in action,[14] even though the Court in the later case explicitly rejected any contention that it was ceding to the legislature's voice in the conversation.[15] But even here – perhaps one of the best cases to illustrate a judicial willingness to listen – there are two subtle drawbacks about the episode. The first relates to regulatory uncertainty and delay between the adoption of the first statutory scheme (in 1988) and final decision in the second case (in 2007). To be sure, the law was in force at various points during this period but in other cases the regulatory scheme was invalidated, suspended pending appeal, and one can assume not vigorously enforced where litigation was pending. Second, the second statute was found by the Supreme Court to be 'more restrained and nuanced than its predecessor'.[16] While the first included a comprehensive ban on advertising, the second permitted it for information and brand-preferencing advertising. The difference is not minute. Article 11 of the 2003 WHO Framework Convention on Tobacco Control provides that '[e]ach Party shall, in accordance with its constitution or constitutional principles, undertake a comprehensive ban of all tobacco advertising, promotion and sponsorship'. The Supreme Court of Canada's first judgment impeded the core policy called for by 'one of the most widely embraced treaties in United Nations history'.[17]

At any rate, second-look cases are quite exotic. There have been four in the history of the Canadian Supreme Court, and I have counted over

---

[14] Dixon, 'The Supreme Court of Canada, Charter Dialogue, and Deference', 275, 285, above note 3.

[15] Ibid.; 'None of these developments remove the burden on the Crown to show that limitations on free expression imposed by the legislation are demonstrably justified in a free and democratic society, as required by section 1 of the Charter. The mere fact that the legislation represents Parliament's response to a decision of this Court does not militate for or against deference': Hogg, Bushell Thornton and Wright, 'Charter Dialogue Revisited', 47–48, above note 8. The legal template set out in *Oakes* and *RJR* remains applicable. However, when that template is applied to the evidence adduced by the government in this case more than a decade later, different conclusions may emerge. *RJR* was grounded in a different historical context and based on different findings supported by a different record at a different time. The *Tobacco Act* must be assessed in light of the knowledge, social conditions and regulatory environment revealed by the evidence presented in this case.

[16] *JTI-Macdonald Corp.* above note 12. The court found this to be a dialogical virtue: 'It represented a genuine attempt by Parliament to craft controls on advertising and promotion that would meet its objectives as well as the concerns expressed by the majority of this Court in *RJR*.'

[17] WHO Framework Convention on Tobacco Control, 'Parties to the WHO Framework Convention on Tobacco Control', www.who.int/fctc/cop/en/.

sixty-two federal and provincial statutes struck down on Charter grounds between 2000 and 2012 alone, excluding those struck down by courts in the province of Quebec.[18] There are some nuances to the data, however, which must be taken into account here. In addition to those second-look cases, we must look at examples of legislative sequels that are claimed to modify or narrow the original judicial finding but are not followed by subsequent litigation. Rosalind Dixon has compiled data showing cases where the federal parliament of Canada narrowed a Supreme Court Charter interpretation in its legislative sequel. Dixon identifies twelve such cases, between 1982 and 2005.[19] Four of them led to second-look cases in the Supreme Court, only one of them (*Sauvé II*) not affirming the legislative sequel. The remaining eight were not followed up in litigation. Furthermore, there are the provincial courts' decisions. In that same time period, forty-seven statutes were struck down by such courts, and on Dixon's calculation eight of these were followed by legislative sequels that rejected the judicial interpretation, with six ultimately being upheld in second-look cases. These figures are admittedly very interesting, and belie to some extent the image of outright judicial domination. However, even accepting the classifications as presented, the substantial majority of strike downs are not followed by a contradictory legislative sequel,[20] and it is also not clear how much the legislatures sought to accommodate the court judgments in their legislative sequels. Such accommodation might be described by some as democratic dialogue, and by others as policy distortion. So it is hard to derive any strong conclusion about the merits of institutional dialogue or the protection of the legislative power from this data. In the United Kingdom, furthermore, Parliament has amended the law in response to all but one declarations of incompatibility that called for legislative response, though there is certainly evidence of minimalist compliance in a number of cases.

Such is the experience in these two of the most 'dialogical' systems. Even here, the norm is that after the court rules, the policy is brought into line. If it is not, then further litigation will follow – lawyers aren't stupid.

---

[18] King, 'Parliament's Role Following Declarations of Incompatibility under the Human Rights Act', above note 2. The number offered here is approximate. The original article contains precise details, including in the methodological appendix.

[19] Dixon, 'The Supreme Court of Canada, Charter Dialogue, and Deference', 273, above note 3.

[20] For example, there were seventeen laws struck down by the Supreme Court between 2000 and 2012 alone.

And legislators have good legal advice.[21] If the point of dialogue theory is that this process results in *far less* policy distortion than it would in a non-dialogical system of judicial review, it is hard to see how that answers the counter-majoritarian objection. According to some versions of that objection, any is too much. And there are anyway more than a few cases in which the 'distortion' is more than marginal.

The answer from dialogue theorists, again, is that the theory is not meant to answer the counter-majoritarian objection. Hogg and Bushell Thornton, as well as Roach, believe in strong judicial review at the end of the day. Most of the leading Canadian proponents of the original dialogue metaphor themselves are unequivocal about saying that in second-look cases as well, the courts should have the final word.[22] To critics of that use of the dialogue metaphor, of course, this gives the game away – it is according to them a misleading use of the term 'dialogue'.[23] To be fair, we would do well to consider the comments of Hogg and Bushell Thornton on the equality of input issue in their original piece:

> Is it possible to have a dialogue between two institutions when one is so clearly subordinate to the other? Does dialogue not require a relationship between equals? The answer, we suggest, is this. Where a judicial decision is open to legislative reversal, modification, or avoidance, then it is meaningful to regard the relationship between the Court and the competent legislative body as a dialogue. In that case, the judicial decision causes a public debate in which Charter values play a more prominent role than they would if there had been no judicial decision. The legislative body is in a position to devise a response that is properly respectful of the Charter values that have been identified by the Court, but which accomplishes the social or economic objectives that the judicial decision has impeded.[24]

---

[21] Admittedly Dixon's data points to cases where the legislative sequel is unanswered in further litigation. She helpfully summarises each case at 276–277 of the article. However, in my view these legislative sequels are not examples of legislative pushback – they do not appear to me to depart from the holdings they respond to. In some cases they are minimal compliance at most.

[22] Hogg, Bushell Thornton and Wright, 'Charter Dialogue Revisited', 31, above note 8.

[23] Manfredi, 'The Day the Dialogue Died', 120–123; Manfredi and Kelly, 'Six Degrees of Dialogue', 515–521; Webber, 'The Unfulfilled Potential of the Court and Legislature Dialogue', 457–460, all above note 3. I would thank Aileen Kavanagh for very helpful corrections to the initial formulation of this paragraph. As she clarified, much of the disagreement concerned clashes between conceptions of dialogue rather than whether the concept should be abandoned altogether.

[24] Hogg and Bushell, 'The Charter Dialogue between Courts and Legislatures', 79–80, above note 6. See also Aileen Kavanagh's penetrating analysis of the ambiguities contained in aspects of this passage, above note 1 at 92–93.

In this initial understanding of dialogue, the possibility of legislative power to disagree (*reverse, modify, avoid*) seems intrinsic to the idea. That is incompatible with the idea of courts having the last word in second-look cases. The reasons they offer in their later, 2007 piece, for assigning interpretive finality to courts are in my view sound. Without it, there would be 'interpretive anarchy' and we would need to assign different legal status to different areas of the constitution.[25] But then, what are we to make of the original metaphor?

The dialogue thesis might thus best be understood as an empirical claim that the actual democratic distortion (if one prefers to regard it that way) is less significant in Canada than what was evident in the American experience, and that this might count significantly if one is conducting some sort of cost–benefit analysis in assessing the institutional design implications of adopting a justiciable bill of rights. So understood, the thesis is neither a legitimating device, nor a deep truth about constitutional judicial review. It is an empirical snapshot of a moment in time in Canadian constitutional adjudication, coupled with an admonition to critics not to exaggerate the scope of the counter-majoritarian difficulty. In that sense, perhaps the metaphor can't really say much about whether the Charter of Rights is such a bad thing after all.

This type of attenuated role for dialogue theory might be defended, but it does seem quite out of line with the original ambitions for the idea. Indeed, the court-sceptical critics of dialogue theory were critical for a reason – they thought the expression shored up the legitimacy of judicial review. And it was taught that way in Canadian law schools. If dialogue theorists were to fully decouple the 'dialogue' phenomenon from a substantive theory that justifies judicial review – whether Dworkinian or based on representation reinforcement – then perhaps they too should be critical of the observed phenomenon they call dialogue. If constitutional rights do not impede policy, and their counter-majoritarian (in the beneficial sense) impact is slight, then this metaphor might be seen to legitimize if not indeed call for that.

II   Dialogue Theories and the Passive Virtues

An important unresolved issue is what relationship exists between dialogue theory and what might be called the constitutional theories that

---

[25] Hogg, Bushell Thornton and Wright, 'Charter Dialogue Revisited', 31, above note 8; they borrow the expression 'interpretive anarchy' from Larry Alexander and Frederick Schauer, 'On Extrajudicial Constitutional Interpretation' (1997) 110 *Harvard Law Review* 1359, 1379.

emphasize the 'passive virtues'.[26] The expression 'passive virtues' is drawn from Alexander Bickel's famous book, *The Least Dangerous Branch* (1962), which emphasized a modest but affirmed role for constitutional judicial review in the post-*Lochner* era. John Hart Ely's *Democracy and Distrust* (1981) sought to meet the counter-majoritarian objection by showing that the US Constitution was best understood as reinforcing democratic choices. His representation-reinforcing view meant that the court should ensure channels are open for political action, and that minorities are adequately represented in the process. Cass Sunstein's varieties of civic republicanism and judicial minimalism set out in the 1990s and 2000s offer sophisticated contemporary contributions in the same vein, now emphasizing the connection to political pluralism and reasonable disagreement as well as the epistemic limitations of judging under uncertainty. In the United Kingdom, a range of scholars who embrace constitutional judicial review, myself included, also offer a prominent role for judicial restraint within their recommended approaches.[27]

Hogg and Bushell draw some inspiration from Bickel.[28] Kent Roach originally argued that the 'passive virtues' were misplaced in a properly dialogical system, because 'robust dialogue' would be sensible having regard to the other features of Canadian constitutionalism, namely, section 1 (limitations clause), 33 (notwithstanding clause) and the suspended declaration of invalidity.[29] However, Roach has later 'revised [his] opposition' to these views, after contemplating some of the more recent Canadian experience. My own view is that much of his work on

---

[26] Alexander Bickel, *The Least Dangerous Branch: The Supreme Court at the Bar of Politics* (New Haven: Yale University Press, 1962); John Hart Ely, *Democracy and Distrust: A Theory of Judicial Review* (Cambridge, MA: Harvard University Press, 1981); Cass R. Sunstein, *One Case at a Time: Judicial Minimalism on the Supreme Court* (Cambridge, MA: Harvard University Press, 2001); see also Lawrence G. Sager, *Justice in Plainclothes: A Theory Of American Constitutional Practice* (New Haven: Yale University Press, 2004) and his work on judicial 'underenforcement' of constitutional norms.

[27] This includes the work of Murray Hunt, Aileen Kavanagh, Alison L. Young, Paul Craig, Tom Hickman and Others. I examine a range of these 'institutional approaches' in Jeff A. King 'Institutional Approaches to Judicial Restraint' (2008) 28 *Oxford Journal of Legal Studies* 409.

[28] The debt is suggested in Hogg, Bushell Thornton and Wright, 'Charter Dialogue Revisited', 32, above note 8, but they subscribe in passing to Dworkin's moral case for taking rights seriously at 27; Roach's debt is much clearer in 'Sharpening the Dialogue Debate', 178–179, above note 3.

[29] Kent Roach, *The Supreme Court on Trial: Judicial Activism or Democratic Dialogue?* (Toronto: Irwin Law, 2001), pp. 147–154.

the whole fits congenially within that tradition. The fit depends on the extent of judicial restraint within the given theory, and this can vary widely between the theories that all recognize limitations of the judicial role.

Rosalind Dixon also acknowledges that her approach 'inherits' many of the insights within the 'passive virtues' tradition, when she offers a restatement that she dubs 'new dialogue theory'.[30] More than any other writer on dialogue, she sets out the contrasting implications of the two ideas. For Dixon, there are two options for the judicial response to a constitutional rights claim. One is *ex ante deference,* which she associates with the 'passive virtues' and judicial minimalism tradition.[31] In this model, the judges limit themselves to a 'narrow statement' of the law, in the effort to 'leave things undecided' as Cass Sunstein famously puts it. In new dialogue theory, by contrast, judges show no deference *ex ante,* but do defer *ex post* – that is to say, in a second-look case that returns to them. There is a rationale for this assertiveness in the first instance. In exercising this role, the court can help unblock aspects of the process: it can help legislatures overcome 'blind spots' (inability to see the nefarious consequences of a choice) or 'burdens of inertia' (political difficulties for groups to put their issue on the political agenda). In Dixon's contention, *ex ante* deference does not counteract these pressures sufficiently because it is too circumscribed. New dialogue theory, on the other hand, 'preserves the maximum scope possible for review ex ante – thereby countering blockages in the legislative process – and adopts a more deferential position ex post'.[32] Yet *ex post* deference is quite strong in her approach. Where the legislature has had another go at defining the same law and it returns to court for reconsideration, the court should show strong (presumptive) deference, only rejecting it if the law is not 'reasonable' in a minimal sense. By that she presumably means it must amount to a 'clear mistake' in the tradition of James B. Thayer's classic article advocating

---

[30] Dixon, 'The Supreme Court of Canada, Charter Dialogue, and Deference', 257 (fn. 100), above note 3, considering it an inheritor to Ely's representation reinforcing judicial review. See further along these lines Dixon's 'The Core Case for Weak-Form Judicial Review' (2017) 38 *Cardozo Law Review* 2193, as well as her chapter in the present volume. It is evident that in recent work she has become a bit more ambivalent about the term 'dialogue', though the substance of her proposals for democratically legitimate (weak-form) judicial review remains largely the same.

[31] Dixon, 'The Supreme Court of Canada, Charter Dialogue, and Deference', 261–262, above note 3.

[32] Ibid. 262.

judicial deference to legislative determinations.[33] As she makes clear, her view is that 'a court ... cannot legitimately seek to enforce a wholly freestanding historical or moral conception of Charter rights'.[34] Essentially, it holds out the promise of strong judicial review to get the issue on the agenda, but strong, Thayerian deference after that has occurred.

This type of approach is in all relevant respects also evident in the new commonwealth model of rights review defended in Stephen Gardbaum's leading book, although he is largely sceptical of the uses of the dialogue metaphor in Canada.[35] In Gardbaum's presentation of the new commonwealth model of review, the court offers 'unapologetic' judicial review, but the legislature enjoys the legal and political power to disagree and prevail. In his system, 'cultivating the passive virtues would be structurally misplaced and counterproductive in a system of penultimate judicial review'.[36] Here again, this leading model suggests strong judicial review up front, and strong judicial deference after the legislature has revisited the issue.

I see four problems with this strategy. First, it probably underestimates how many legislative rights determinations were settled in plain understanding of how it would disadvantage a rights claimant. I have elsewhere called this issue 'legislative focus on rights issues'[37] and investigated it in the UK context. I define absence of legislative focus as being either (1) the legislative failure to consider either explicitly or implicitly the key rights-issue that the court identifies or (2) the adoption of the statute at a time when the conception of rights was significantly different than now legally applicable in the country (for example, in a nineteenth-century anti-sodomy statute). In examining twenty-four declarations of incompatibility in the UK experience, I determined roughly that thirty-seven per cent of

---

[33] Ibid.; James B. Thayer, 'The Origin and Scope of the American Doctrine of Constitutional Law' (1893) 7 *Harvard Law Review* 129. In fact, Dixon says it must be 'patently unreasonable' (256) and not be 'reasonable, according to any plausible interpretive theory'. Later in the article she mentions it must be reasonable according to the basic commitment to freedom and democracy, and that it agrees with the court's prior judgments (269). I equate these here with Thayer's idea, since it has fairly wide currency and any more robust an idea of reasonableness might weaken her theory.

[34] Dixon, 'The Supreme Court of Canada, Charter Dialogue, and Deference', 257, above note 3.

[35] Gardbaum, *The New Commonwealth Model of Constitutionalism*, pp. 111–121, above note 2 (a critique of Canadian dialogue theory).

[36] Ibid. 85.

[37] Jeff King, *Judging Social Rights*, (Cambridge: Cambridge University Press, 2012), 164–165.

those eliciting legislative response concerned cases in which legislative focus had not occurred.[38] While that means there is a lot to Dixon's claims about the importance of blockages and blind spots (as I credit to her in my analysis), it also means that in the majority of cases the rights-issue was arguably or definitely in plain view. This is the normal situation in laws concerning antiterrorism, torture, political advertising and campaign finance, cigarette packaging, compulsory health insurance, the restriction of religious symbols and dress, banning political parties, affirmative action, and many other leading issues in constitutional litigation.

The second problem is that the approach gives insufficient weight to the likelihood that a legislature would feel pressure not to be seen to push back against a judicial finding. This means that robust judicial review might translate into legislative deference that the theories of dialogue and of the passive virtues want to reject. This problem or likelihood might explain why there are few second-look cases in Canada. It suggests that courts should consider anticipating this problem and perhaps consider being open to restraint in first-look cases.

A third problem is that the theory seems to assume that the parliament that passed the law is the same parliament that gets to judge whether the judicial decision was correct. But in fact the composition of the legislature changes frequently. Passing legislation requires significant levels of political capital, time and energy. Even if the same party is in power after a court invalidates a law, it might prefer under different leadership to concentrate its energy on a current legislative programme rather than revive the challenged law. One cannot assume that apathy in such cases would mean that the legislature actually endorses the outcome, or that there is no democratic loss occasioned by the episode. At any rate, often a different party or coalition will be in control of some chamber of the legislature. In that case, the ruling party may welcome an adverse judgment on a rival party's older law, because it is a political victory with none of the usual political costs of formal repeal.

The fourth and perhaps most obvious problem is that if the second and perhaps third problems were somehow addressed by affirming and making easier the legislative capacity to disagree, then the substantive protection of minority rights could become significantly weakened.

---

[38] King, 'Parliament's Role Following Declarations of Incompatibility under the Human Rights Act', 177–178, above note 2. A further nineteen per cent could not be judged, and forty-four per cent did involve statutes having legislative focus. However, the overall numbers are low, hence these percentages could easily change over time.

Notably, John Hart Ely's theory fully accepted that the court could intervene with hard remedies to protect minorities and keep open the channels for political change. That's part of the reason why his 'flight from substance must end in substance', in Dworkin's damning verdict.[39] But this is not an option available in Dixon's theory (assuming counterfactually that issues of substance aren't significantly present in the first-look cases). In a second-look case, Dixon's theory becomes Thayerian. Such is also the effect of referring to judicial review as 'penultimate' in Gardbaum's scheme. Whether or not the case for the judicial protection of minority interests is rebutted effectively by critics of judicial review is a matter of debate. But it seems difficult for a dialogue or new commonwealth model theorist to argue that minorities deserve judicial protection from political marginalization but then abandon them when that marginalization is predictably given direct legislative imprimatur.[40]

III   The Problem of Finality, Legal Certainty and the Authority of Law

Dixon's view on the court's role in showing *ex post* deference shares affinities not just with Stephen Gardbaum, but also, in the United Kingdom, with Francesca Klug and Danny Nicol. Each writer believes that courts should be what Gardbaum calls 'unapologetic' about judicial review in the first instance, but defer to the legislature's final view in the resulting exchange.

Each of these theories in my view is vulnerable to that critique, but Gardbaum, Klug and Nicol consider it a peculiar democratic virtue that the legislature can simply disregard the court judgment in this way. For

---

[39] Ronald Dworkin, *A Matter of Principle*, (Oxford: Oxford University Press, 1985), p. 69.
[40] In *Judging Social Rights*, ch. 6 (above note 37), I consider and defend this rationale for judicial review, and in my review of Gardbaum (King, 'Rights and the Rule of Law in Third Way Constitutionalism', above note 4), I point out at 117–120 why I feel Gardbaum's approach admits the problem of minority vulnerability but offers an unsatisfactory solution. In Rosalind Dixon and Brigid McManus, 'Detaining Non-Citizens: Political Competition & Weak v. Strong Judicial Review' (2017) 57(3) *Virginia Journal of International Law* 1, the authors suggest that the attractiveness of weak- vs. strong-form review depends on the extent to which the political parties compete to secure the good-faith protection of rights. They are concerned that weak-form review is not enough to protect rights in some cases. I agree – and for these reasons think a presumption commending deference to 'reasonable' legislative sequels is likely to be inapt. The extent of partisan (and popular) support for rights varies between rights, groups, and across time.

Klug and Nicol it is inherent in the legislative scheme contained in the Human Rights Act 1998.[41] For Gardbaum, it is a deep normative argument about how a 'third way' constitutional theory of weak-form review ought to operate. In his contention, a legislature should decline to follow judicial decisions – as a presumption – provided that members of the legislature abide by two conditions that Gardbaum prescribes. The first is that legislators engage meaningfully with the judgment; the second is that they only decline to follow the judgment if they believe their own disagreement with the court to be reasonable.[42] In a review of Gardbaum's book, I argued that this second requirement is plainly implausible as any form of constraint.[43] No one resolves in real time that her own view is unreasonable, let alone a majority of a chamber of representatives who take the whip and have to face the tabloids in the morning.[44]

A different and more refined legal problem is that it is hard to see on what legal theory the court would exercise authority in the first-look cases to offer judgment. The court's key function is to offer judgment on the law. It is not a parliamentary or specialist committee. Tom Hickman, an active barrister as well as scholar, recognized this problem early on. He calls it the 'principle proposing' version of dialogue and shows how it is

---

[41] Francesca Klug, 'Judicial Deference under the Human Rights Act 1998' (2003) *European Human Rights Law Review* 125, 131: 'there is a widespread, and erroneous, assumption that legislative amendment *must* follow a declaration'; Danny Nicol, 'Law and Politics after the Human Rights Act' [2006] *Public Law* 722, 744 (advocating the 'uninhibited use of declarations of incompatibility' on the proviso that Parliament not feel obliged to agree with the courts).

[42] Gardbaum, above note 2. Gardbaum does not regard this as a dialogue theory, and he is critical of the term for the reasons alluded to earlier. But the form in which I recast it in here, he is arguing along similar lines. His view is broadly similar to Dixon's new dialogue theory in this respect.

[43] King, 'Rights and the Rule of Law in Third Way Constitutionalism', above note 4.

[44] I do not wish to suggest a lack of care or depth in Professor Gardbaum's proposals for legislative reconsideration in *The New Commonwealth Model of Constitutionalism* at 87–94 (above note 2). Furthermore, in the Copenhagen ICON-S conference I refer to in the credits at the outset of this chapter, Gardbaum expressed the view that legislatures in the new Commonwealth model would *presumptively* respect the decisions of the courts. However, there is a different emphasis in the book: 'within the normative framework of the new model, there is no good reason for not permitting a procedurally sound and substantively reasonable legislative view to prevail' (p. 90). I do not doubt, nevertheless, that the norms relating to the use of legislative reconsideration could be adjusted in the direction stated in Copenhagen without prejudice to the theory as a whole. As I claimed in my review of his book, a standard with real bite in my view would be that parliamentarians could disagree with the court if it found the *court's* view to be unreasonable. In mature political systems, that is not a decision taken lightly.

incompatible with the current role for judges in the British and indeed most constitutions.[45] To be clear, the court can find that the law requires a legislature to give formal, due consideration to people's rights when it enacts laws that infringe those rights.[46] But all existing bills of rights promise more than just that. Beyond enforcing such a procedural right, this theory seems committed to a role for the judge as seeking to 'persuade'[47] or impose a 'practical constraint'[48] on the legislature. The theory envisages judges offering, within contentious litigation, a view that is extralegal and non-binding – one to be taken up and pondered at the legislative stage, but nothing more. That would require a significant reconfiguration of our understanding of the judicial role, as well as an odd if not incomprehensible basis for striking down a statute in the first place.[49] It would require developing a separate theory for interpreting rights provisions and other provisions of the constitution. Much of constitutional adjudication concerns issues and provisions of the constitution other than those concerned with constitutional rights. For instance, one of the two chambers of the Federal Constitutional Court of Germany is concerned with disputes between branches of government.

But it seems that Gardbaum, Klug, Nicol and Dixon are bidding for that type of reconfigured understanding. I feel that such a reform would create significant problems for the role of legal authority. First, there is the distinctly legal issue of the real time need for legal certainty – what politicians and jobbing lawyers alike refer to as the need for 'clarity'. Dialogue theorists at times write as though courts and legislatures have the luxury of time in resolving constitutional disputes. But in fact, in many cases claimants and the public at large need resolution fairly quickly, and at any rate clearly and with finality. A statute under constitutional challenge will in all likelihood not be enforced vigorously. A prolonged dialogue in that case means regulatory inaction. From a

---

[45] Tom Hickman, *Public Law after the Human Rights Act*, (New York: Bloomsbury Publishing, 2010), pp. 83–87.

[46] I commend this approach in *Judging Social Rights*, 171–173, above note 37. Yet it is only one aspect of a broader approach.

[47] Dixon, 'The Supreme Court of Canada, Charter Dialogue, and Deference', 262–263, above note 3 (arguing that the rejection of narrow *ex ante* deference offers a 'greater ability to use persuasion as a tool for promoting the enjoyment of rights'.)

[48] Gardbaum, *The New Commonwealth Model of Constitutionalism*, 44, above note 2.

[49] This is less an issue in the United Kingdom model, where the statute remains in force, but the legal incongruence is no less striking: see my review of Gardbaum in King, 'Rights and the Rule of Law in Third Way Constitutionalism', above note 4 at 124–125, for comment.

different perspective, a suspected terrorist or person denied the right to marry her female partner could grow old waiting for the dialogue to run its course. While in both cases there are at times virtues to not deciding the entire issue upon first impression, it is often also the case that cases are preceded by years of discussion, or have the dimension of urgency that does not befit a dialogical approach. The experience in the United Kingdom concerning whether the UK executive branch had the discretionary authority to give notice to the European Union of the United Kingdom's intent to leave, or required an Act of Parliament to authorize it to do so, was a case in point.[50] Such a politically controversial issue at a particularly urgent time could not helpfully be resolved by the political branches, which were committed to an opportunistic view and displayed no sophisticated understanding of the relevant legal materials. A ruling on the law was needed.

The second problem with proactive reconfiguration is that such a practice would undermine the constitutional position of the courts. Without a norm requiring the legislature to not depart from judicial findings lightly, the courts will know that to issue judgments that will be ignored will undermine their credibility and thus institutional integrity.[51] It will ultimately result in an exercise of brinksmanship in which one of the two sides will back down – presumably the courts. Admittedly, whether this happens depends considerably on local political conditions. In some countries, perhaps judges will have no qualms about issuing declarations that are ignored. My sense is that in the long run, either the courts will show restraint in the effort of raising the impact of particular declarations of incompatibility, or the legislature will repeal the instrument as an anomalous form of quasi-legal irritant. In either case it would undermine the very benefits of judicial review in the first place, and make 'unapologetic' judicial review prior to legislative reconsideration, integral in both Dixon and Gardbaum's approaches, rather unlikely in the long run.

A third problem is that the ordinary operation of constitutional government is based in part on some notion of the separation of powers, or of comity between institutions: that each institution accept and work with the determinations of other branches of government. There is

---

[50] The litigation concluded in *R (Miller) v. Secretary of State for Exiting the European Union* [2017] UKSC 5.

[51] Some feared that this would occur in the United Kingdom, since the UK Parliament can not only ignore judicial decisions but must act affirmatively to remedy the incompatibility. It is not clear that this has happened, but the point is arguable.

clearly room for checks and balances, of course. But an important principle of comity is that political bodies do not attack the integrity of the accountability institutions established to monitor them. If local councils rejected ombudsman and auditor reports whenever they reasonably disagreed (according to their own lights), the system would decay rapidly. In the case of judges, the issue is particularly acute. Judges are responsible for maintaining the rule of law throughout the entire political order, including in the interpretation of statutes, regulations, bylaws, as well as applicable international law, and of course the constitution itself. That is a job of the highest political order. To secure it, there are already a range of constitutional conventions that separate judges from politics, and limit the kinds of criticisms of judicial conduct that can be made in Parliament (to take the United Kingdom as an example). For instance, the Supreme Court judges who still sit in the House of Lords are bound by a constitutional convention, not always observed, that they do not express views on controversial political matters in debates. Parliamentarians, for their part, are (subject to some exceptions) not permitted to refer to cases in which proceedings are active in United Kingdom courts in any motion, debate, question or supplementary question: the *sub judice* rule.[52] And furthermore, any statements interpreted as impugning the integrity of a judge of a superior court will be ruled out of order by the Speaker of the House of Commons.[53] The full rule governing criticism of judicial rulings after they are rendered does in fact permit polite disagreement with, and criticism of, judicial findings 'within certain limits'.[54] There is therefore no hard constitutional impediment forbidding critical discussion of judicial rulings in Parliament – nor should there be. However, the collective weight of the tradition of judicial independence and the importance of the rule of law has made the practice or criticizing judgments rather rare in the UK Parliament. In all of the Hansard

---

[52] The rule is stated with the relevant qualifications in Malcolm Jack (ed.), *Erskine May's Treatise on the Law, Privileges, Proceedings and Usage of Parliament* (24th edn, London: Lexis Nexis/Butterworths, 2011), p. 518.

[53] Ibid. p. 443–444.

[54] (1973–1974) HC Deb. Vol. 865, Col. 1092, 1144, 1199: The Speaker: 'Any Act of Parliament which the courts have to operate can be criticised as strongly as hon. or right hon. Members desire. It can be argued that a judge has made a mistake, that he was wrong, and the reasons for those contentions can be given, within certain limits.' The limits are cited to a speech of Lord Atkin as follows: 'provided that members of the public abstain from imputing improper motives to those taking part in the administration of justice, and are genuinely exercising a right of criticism, and not acting in malice or attempting to impair the administration of justice, they are immune.'

I examined for cases following a section 4 declaration of incompatibility under the Human Rights Act 1998, only one involved any heated disagreement with a UK court ruling – the one concerning the possibility for persons on the sex offenders register to obtain a right to appeal their inclusion and make representations for why they should be removed from it.[55] While there is in principle a recognizable dividing line between criticizing a judge personally and impugning the soundness of her or his reasoning, it will arguably become frayed quickly if parliamentarians are invited to directly engage with and reject the reasoning of the courts on a regular basis. The consequences are hard to know, but they are at any rate not likely to be good.

IV   Conclusion: The Comparative Virtues of the Passive Virtues

The aim of this essay is not to deliver any condemnation of the dialogue metaphor. Indeed, the idea has important merits. Important among them is that judges report that in live constitutional litigation, they are well aware that they are taking part in a process of potentially iterative exchange, and that this conditions how they decide cases.[56] Another key contribution is that, whatever the ambiguity of the concept, *any* conception of dialogue rules out the kind of judicial supremacy we associate with some of the early US experience, notably the *Lochner* era.

Nevertheless, the disadvantages of the metaphor are also plain. Part of them relate to a studied lack of clarity about how definitional authority over constitutional rights determinations is and should be distributed. The original dialogue theory implied that it is and should be distributed, but not in a way that detracts from a potent constitutional role for courts. But the empirical claim that dialogue in fact allowed legislatures to modify or reject most Supreme Court decisions seems unsubstantiated.

---

[55] This is the response to the case of *R (Thompson) v. SSHD* [2010] UKSC 17, which I discuss in King, 'Parliament's Role Following Declarations of Incompatibility under the Human Rights Act', above note 2, at 185–186. A similar attitude of non-conflictual cooperation is found in Aruna Sathanapally, *Beyond Disagreement: Open Remedies in Human Rights Adjudication* (Oxford: Oxford University Press, 2012), pp. 172–180. Notably, the heated disagreement that did come to the fore over prisoner voting was occasioned not by a UK court decision but by that of the European Court of Human Rights.

[56] This point was emphasized unequivocally by Justice Robert Sharpe of the Ontario Court of Appeal, and Justice Catherine O'Regan, formerly of the Constitutional Court of South Africa, at the seminar at the University of Oxford indicated in the credits note at the start of the chapter.

What Hogg and Bushell Thornton referred to as 'legislative reversal, modification or avoidance' appears in fact to be very rare in Canada, and is definitely rare in the United Kingdom. If the evidence is rather read as supporting the view that legislative sequels entailing important legislative input are a frequent feature, then that seems borne out by the evidence. But the question then is whether that is the product of legislative pushback or the judicial exercise of the passive virtues the first time around, consistently with Bickel's central recommendation.

This leads naturally to the second ambiguity, which is the question of how judges should respond in both first- and second-look cases. Here we see a split between old and new forms of dialogue theory. The older theories have had less to say about how assertive judges should be in the first-look cases, but clear that in second-look cases they should have final interpretive authority. The newer theories examined earlier suggest that there should be no judicial restraint in first-look cases, but strong, Thayerian deference in second-look cases. This latter proposal chimes with some critics of how the dialogue metaphor has been used in Canada, on the view that strong deference in second-look cases is the only approach that properly respects it.[57] Yet I argued that several constitutional problems followed from this type of approach. It underestimates the actual extent of direct legislative focus on rights-issues; it overestimates the political viability of legislative pushback; it underestimates the importance of different parliamentary composition over time; and it underrates the threat to minority interests if the proposal were taken quite seriously. Above all, I argue that the proposal would undermine the functions of legal authority and generate tensions that would fray the kind of comity between branches that is actually integral to the rule of law.

I close by emphasizing that in my view, the passive virtue theories can acknowledge many of the advantages of dialogue theory without calling for any reconfiguration at all of the judicial role in the contemporary constitution. If the endgame is to secure the right balance of legal oversight, rights protection and democratic legitimacy, then the passive virtues tradition offers an approach that, whether ultimately successful or not, recognizes the merits of the dialogue metaphor with fewer of the problems mentioned in this chapter. These theories recognize that courts

---

[57] Webber, 'Unfulfilled Potential of the Court and Legislature Dialogue', 457–460; Manfredi and Kelly, 'Six Degrees of Dialogue: A Response to Hogg and Bushell', 515–521; Manfredi, 'The Day the Dialogue Died', 120–123, all above note 3.

perform the role of constitutional judicial review, but affirm grounds for pursuing that role with a measure of humility.[58] This is in view of the chequered political history of judicial review, the epistemic limitations of the judicial process and the inflexibility of political reversals of significant political changes. To the extent that Charter dialogue has worked in Canada, and the Human Rights Act 1998 in Britain, my sense is that it is because the judicial temperament in both countries is largely attuned to these facts already. Yet since this approach affirms a cautious but distinctly legal role for the courts, the issues of finality, legal certainty and the rule of law that I draw attention to in the earlier analysis are to a significant extent addressed or manageable.[59] The need for clarity and authoritative ruling, where pressing, can be considered and weighed against the risks arising from epistemic and political uncertainty. This is part of the ordinary craft of judging, including under conditions of uncertainty.

It is possible to conceptualize dialogue theory in a manner that is congenial to all of these observations. Indeed, in reading the contribution of Kent Roach to this volume I found myself agreeing with nearly all of his analysis of the substantive issues he examines. Yet he resists giving the term 'dialogue' a crisp definition in that contribution, and it remains a stubborn fact that proponents have contrasted the idea with the passive virtues tradition. That a new conception may be emerging which is closer to that tradition is almost certain to be welcomed. But if we reach the point when we have to speak of 'conceptions' of metaphors, the rationale for the metaphor is on the ropes.

---

[58] I can add that the emphasis on humility does not suggest a conservative political or even constitutional programme. I believe this approach is consistent with my advocacy of judicially enforceable constitutional social rights as outlined in *Judging Social Rights*, above note 37.

[59] Admittedly, the issue is not so easily dispatched: see Owen M. Fiss. 'The Perils of Minimalism' (2008) 9 *Theoretical Inquiries in Law* 643 for a similar critique of the timidity of minimalism.

PART III

Dialogue and Rights

8

Canada's Notwithstanding Clause, Dialogue, and Constitutional Identities

DWIGHT NEWMAN*

I Introduction

Canada's 1982 Charter of Rights and Freedoms contains the interesting, rather unique, and often-discussed section 33 notwithstanding clause. The text of that clause reads as follows:

33. (1) Parliament or the legislature of a province may expressly declare in an Act of Parliament or of the legislature, as the case may be, that the Act or a provision thereof shall operate notwithstanding a provision included in section 2 or sections 7 to 15 of this Charter.

(2) An Act or a provision of an Act in respect of which a declaration made under this section is in effect shall have such operation as it would have but for the provision of this Charter referred to in the declaration.

(3) A declaration made under subsection (1) shall cease to have effect five years after it comes into force or on such earlier date as may be specified in the declaration.

(4) Parliament or the legislature of a province may re-enact a declaration made under subsection (1).

(5) Subsection (3) applies in respect of a re-enactment made under subsection (4).[1]

The clause, as its text states, permits the federal parliament or a provincial legislature to declare that a particular statute or statutory provision operates notwithstanding its impact on fundamental freedoms, the right to life, liberty, and security of the person, criminal justice rights, and/or

---

* I am grateful for detailed comments on the chapter from Geoffrey Sigalet and Grégoire Webber and for comments from or discussion with Dennis Baker, Sarah Burningham, Grant Huscroft, Aileen Kavanagh, Rainer Knopff, Michael Plaxton, and Kent Roach.
[1] The Constitution Act, 1982 (Canada).

the right to equality.[2] The most common type of reaction to this clause has perhaps been a worry of some legal academics that the clause marks some tragic undermining of the contents of the Charter.[3] That mythology has had a public face as well, perhaps most notably in Canadian Prime Minister Paul Martin's surprise position in a 2006 national party leaders' debate that he would work to remove the clause from the Charter over its allegedly fundamental inconsistency with the spirit of the Charter. But it was present as well in indications by other prime ministers, such as Brian Mulroney, of principled objections to the clause.

The story of Canada's notwithstanding clause, though, has been filled with complex historical ironies. Prime Minister Martin's position was perhaps an especially surprising about-face, given that Martin had been one of only two prime ministers to ever openly contemplate the use of the clause at the national level, when he had indicated in 2003 that he would consider using it to protect religious freedom rights in the context of same-sex marriage.[4] The other, perhaps even more surprisingly, had been Prime Minister Pierre Trudeau. Despite having agreed to the clause with some reluctance, Trudeau was also ready to use the clause in his politicking for the Charter – it emerged later that Trudeau, in private communications with the Catholic Archbishop of Toronto, made a definitive commitment to use the clause to prevent the courts from

---

[2] See generally *Ford* v. *Quebec (Attorney General)*, [1988] 2 SCR 712. See also the chapter on the notwithstanding clause in Guy Régimbald and Dwight Newman, *The Law of the Canadian Constitution*, 2nd edn. (Toronto: LexisNexis, 2017), ch. 21.

[3] For just some examples, Donna Greschner and Ken Norman, 'The Courts and Section 33' (1987) 12 *Queen's Law Journal* 155; John Whyte, 'Sometimes Constitutions Are Made in the Streets: The Future of the Notwithstanding Clause' (2007) 16 *Constitutional Forum* 79. There have, of course, been exceptions, with some academics writing more favourably of the clause: e.g., Peter H. Russell, 'Standing Up for Notwithstanding' (1991) 29 *Alberta Law Review* 293; Tsvi Kahana, 'Understanding the Notwithstanding Mechanism' (2002) 52 *University of Toronto Law Journal* 221. Others write of the clause favourably in theory but seem never to like any use in practice: see e.g., Kent Roach, 'Is Brad Wall Really Defending School Choice with His Use of the Notwithstanding Clause?', *Globe and Mail* (2 May 2017). And others stand in complex relationships to the clause, offering a mixture of positive and negative comments on the clause: see e.g., Janet Hiebert, 'The Notwithstanding Clause: Why Non-Use Does Not Necessarily Equate with Abiding by Judicial Norms', in Peter Oliver, Patrick Macklem, and Nathalie des Rosiers, (eds.) *The Oxford Handbook of the Canadian Constitution* (Oxford: Oxford University Press, 2017), p. 695.

[4] See discussion in Dave Snow, 'Notwithstanding the Override: Path Dependence, Section 33, and the Charter' (2008–2009) 8 *Innovations* 1 at 10.

dictating abortion policy were the courts ever to strike down Canada's abortion law.[5] Neither prime minister ever took such action.

Significant international scholars who might have been more favourable towards Canada's notwithstanding clause have not necessarily themselves spoken well of it. Notably, some of those who might have thought it had a role in sustaining aspects of parliamentary democracy have sometimes gone so far as to suggest that its text limits its usefulness so much that its history of limited use verges on an inevitable outcome. For example, Jeffrey Goldsworthy suggests that the clause is textually limited in that it applies only to certain rights for a maximum of five years and, in any event, does not permit amendment of the Charter.[6] Given these textual limits, he suggests that its rare use was to be expected because any use of it puts legislatures in the awkward position of explicitly overriding rights and of having to renew this override every five years if it is to continue.[7] In one of his key pieces on dialogue theory, Jeremy Waldron largely accepts Goldsworthy's account on these fronts and agrees that a reluctance to use the clause stems from the perception that legislatures using it would be overriding rights themselves rather than enunciating a different interpretation of rights.[8] So, some who might have been potential friends of the notwithstanding clause have at times seemed to help bury it.

The same might be thought of Adrian Vermeule's quick reference to Canada's notwithstanding clause as an example of a constitutional provision fallen into legal desuetude.[9] Here again, someone who favours legislative rather than judicial enforcement of rights comments unfavourably on a clause that potentially constrains judicial power in respect of rights enforcement. No doubt, Vermeule struggles with what to make of his good faith reading of the relatively limited use of the notwithstanding clause. However, that sort of reading from abroad and removed from daily political conversation in Canada is almost bound to miss the degree

---

[5] Nichols, Marjorie (1989) 'Trudeau promise comes back to haunt Liberals' *Ottawa Citizen* (15 April 1989) A3. The Supreme Court of Canada's involvement on abortion commenced only in 1988, several years after the end of Trudeau's time as prime minister.

[6] Jeffrey Goldsworthy, *Parliamentary Sovereignty: Contemporary Debates* (Cambridge: Cambridge University Press, 2010), p. 202.

[7] Ibid. pp. 218–19.

[8] Jeremy Waldron, 'Some Models of Dialogues between Judges and Legislators' (2004) 23(2) *Supreme Court Law Review* 7 at 38.

[9] Adrian Vermeule, 'The Atrophy of Constitutional Powers' (2012) 32 *Oxford Journal of Legal Studies* 421.

to which the notwithstanding clause is very much alive in ongoing discussions in Canada, including (perhaps even especially) at the very real level of debates amongst members of the general public communities. The clause has been used much more commonly at the provincial level than many observers fully appreciate,[10] its use has been mooted regularly and recently,[11] and the province of Saskatchewan introduced legislation to use it in the context of a complex debate about religion and education as recently as 2017.[12]

In this chapter, I re-engage with the philosophical foundations of the notwithstanding clause, and I argue that the clause helps to establish a relatively unique mode of constitutionalism attentive to traditions of parliamentary democracy and respect for distinctive identities within Canada. In that way, it is highly responsive to historical forerunners of modern Canadian constitutionalism, and it offers ongoing space for legitimate expression of parliamentary and legislative views on rights interpretation.

This argument is partly in line with the thinking of Stephen Gardbaum, who sees Canada's notwithstanding clause as an example of a 'new Commonwealth model of constitutionalism' that finds a 'third way' between judicial supremacy and legislative supremacy on rights questions.[13] To some degree, however, I will also suggest that it is important not to forget the nuanced, specific differences between the constitutionalism of different states within this model. Gardbaum himself is alive to these nuances. He indicates that his model covers a 'set' of varying alternatives between the dichotomies of judicial versus legislative supremacy.[14] In respect to Canada, he is also attentive to its leaning

---

[10] For an account of seventeen uses by provincial governments to the time of his article, see Tsvi Kahana, 'The Notwithstanding Mechanism and Public Discussion: Lessons from the Ignored Practice of Section 33 of the Charter' (2001) 44 *Canadian Public Administration* 255.

[11] One would find many suggestions of its possible use over the last decade, including the several recent contexts discussed in the last section of this chapter.

[12] See Saskatchewan Bill No. 89 of 2017: An Act to Amend the Education Act, 1995. In addition to the discussion in the last section of this chapter, for my past explanation and discussion of this, see Dwight Newman, 'Premier Wall's Decision to Override a Messy Court Ruling Is Completely Proper', *National Post* (9 May 2017). For an insightful comment, see also Joanna Baron and Geoffrey Sigalet, 'Saskatchewan's Brad Wall and the Rehabilitation of the Charter', *Policy Options* (19 May 2017).

[13] Stephen Gardbaum, *The New Commonwealth Model of Constitutionalism: Theory and Practice* (Cambridge: Cambridge University Press, 2013).

[14] Ibid. p. 35.

towards a stronger judicial role than in some other states within his model, although with the notwithstanding clause clearly separating it from American-style judicial supremacy and having helped to inspire thinking in other states within this new Commonwealth model.[15] However, the very terminology of a 'model' in the singular tends to lead some more casual readers to miss the texture of constitutions as constitutions of specific places. The notwithstanding clause in Canada is not only an abstract clause within a transnational model of constitutionalism but is part of Canadian constitutionalism specifically. It is an example of a constitutional specificity within a set of constitutionalisms that escape simple dichotomies.

To make the argument, first, I draw on the history of the clause and the broader thought of the premiers who argued for it, notably Saskatchewan's social democratic premier Allan Blakeney and Alberta's conservative premier Peter Lougheed – despite their political differences, they both saw the clause as being rooted in their broader theories of constitutionalism and identity.[16] Second, I will argue that returning to their conception of the clause opens up a different reading of the text of the notwithstanding clause than has been presumed by the likes of Goldsworthy and Waldron, whose commentary on the clause is ultimately decontextualized in problematic ways. I will argue that recontextualizing the clause can escape an overly narrow focus on limits on the clause and open up possibilities of coordinate constitutional interpretation. Third, I will show how the notwithstanding clause actually has a distinctive fit with Canadian circumstances. In considering how parliaments and legislatures can best engage in use of the notwithstanding clause, I will argue that the notwithstanding clause opens the potential not only for dialogue on rights interpretation of the sort one would anticipate in most well-functioning parliamentary democracies, but also for more coordinate approaches to rights interpretation and the colocation of rights with other aspects of national identity in ways necessarily distinctive to Canada. In some respects, I will argue that the clause alters inter-institutional interactions connected to dialogue theory in such a manner

---

[15] Ibid. ch. 5.

[16] For an account focused on the thought of Allan Blakeney in relation to the clause, see Dwight Newman, 'Allan Blakeney and the Dignity of Democratic Debate on Rights', in David McGrane et al., (eds.), *Challenges Facing Canadian Democracy in the 21st Century: Essays in Honour of Allan E. Blakeney* (Regina, Sask.: University of Regina Press, forthcoming 2019).

as to alter the form of dialogue theory that fits Canadian constitutionalism if the notwithstanding clause were understood in this recontextua-
lized and ultimately reinvigorated manner.

II   The Context for Canada's Notwithstanding Clause

One of my major claims in the present account is that the context for the
notwithstanding clause matters and helps to make clear that s. 33 was not
an incoherent compromise and was not a rights override, but was
adopted as a clause permitting legislatures to protect unenumerated
rights and to engage in reasonable disagreements with courts about
rights. The dominant story of the notwithstanding clause is that it was
not based on any theoretical vision and was simply a last-minute concession by Prime Minister Pierre Trudeau to get recalcitrant premiers on
board with the Charter.[17] But this story must change rapidly when
confronted with facts. The introduction of the notwithstanding clause
into Canada's Charter built upon historical antecedents and deep
thought by premiers of varying ideologies concerning the very nature
of parliamentary democracy, with both of these dimensions having
implications for how the proper public understanding of the time bears
on the meaning of the Charter's ultimate text.

The notwithstanding clause, first, was not a spur-of-the-moment
invention during the final round of constitutional negotiations with the
premiers in late 1981. It had been under discussion at the First Ministers'
meeting in February 1979 and under discussion again in mid-1980. These
two preliminary discussions on the concept of a notwithstanding clause
made it, as Barry Strayer puts it, 'available' as an idea during the final
discussions in November 1981.[18] Moreover, the idea of a notwithstanding clause had not simply originated in these discussions with the
premiers but actually tracked text from the Canadian Bill of Rights, a

---

[17] Elements of this account appear even in Hiebert, above n 3, p. 695 (stating that the clause
was 'not the product of any grand normative theory about constitutional design' and was
simply pursued by some premiers as a way of tempering judicial review under the
Charter).

[18] Barry L. Strayer, 'The Evolution of the Charter', in Lois Harder and Steve Patten, (eds.),
Patriation and Its Consequences: Constitution Making in Canada (Vancouver: University
of British Columbia Press, 2015), p. 90.

quasi-constitutional statute enacted by the Diefenbaker government in 1960.[19] Section 2 of that Bill of Rights reads as follows:

> Every law of Canada shall, unless it is expressly declared by an Act of the Parliament of Canada that it shall operate notwithstanding the *Canadian Bill of Rights*, be so construed and applied as not to abrogate, abridge or infringe or to authorize the abrogation, abridgment or infringement of any of the rights or freedoms herein recognized and declared . . . [20]

This clause concerns only federal law, and it provides for construal and application rather than invalidation. However, the same language as in the Charter is present that provides for a statute to operate notwithstanding the textually enumerated rights. As in much of the rest of the Charter, the Charter carried forward concepts (and text) from the Bill of Rights.[21] Rights in Canada did not originate with the Charter – nor with the Bill of Rights, which itself simply applied in a specific statutory form many liberties long known within the English common law.[22] Earlier rights discourse recognized the same point recognized in the Charter's notwithstanding clause – that there must be a reconciliation between rights and the traditions of parliamentary democracy.

That the notwithstanding clause concept contained in s. 2 of the Bill of Rights was adopted in the Charter text responded to this deep-seated need to find a reconciliation between entrenched rights and the Canadian parliamentary system of government. The premiers who most pushed for the inclusion of the notwithstanding clause were two leaders amongst the premiers who came from very different ideological perspectives. The social democrat Allan Blakeney and the conservative Peter Lougheed found common cause in seeking something that fit together the traditions of Canadian parliamentary democracy and the entrenched rights model that Pierre Trudeau drew from a variety of other traditions. Both

---

[19] Ibid., discussing *Canadian Bill of Rights*, S.C. 1960, c. 44. See also its prior presence in provincial bills of rights: *Alberta Bill of Rights*, R.S.A. 1980, c. A-16, s. 2; *Saskatchewan Human Rights Code*, S.S 1979, c. S-24.1, s. 44; *[Quebec] Charter of Human Rights and Freedoms*, R.S.Q., c. C-12, s. 52.

[20] Canadian Bill of Rights, ibid., s. 2.

[21] For discussion of some examples (and the counterexample of property rights, which were excluded due to intellectual currents of the time and chance political factors), see Dwight Newman and Lorelle Binnion, 'The Exclusion of Property Rights from the Charter' (2015) 52 *Alberta Law Review* 543.

[22] The Charter itself, in s. 26, recognized preexisting rights and freedoms beyond those enumerated in the Charter, although this recognition has received scant attention thus far.

Blakeney and Lougheed have written insightfully on the ideas behind the notwithstanding clause, and their expression of these ideas fleshes out the meaning of the Charter text by explaining what such a text connoted at the time of its adoption.

Blakeney discusses aspects of the legal interpretation of the Charter in his memoirs, but there he is principally concerned with discussing the judicial expansion of s. 7 of the Charter carried on rapidly after the Charter was enacted, in judicial defiance of the intention of the drafters.[23] His fuller discussion of the notwithstanding clause itself appears elsewhere. In reply to a 2007 article by one of his 1982 constitutional advisors critiquing the clause, Blakeney maintained his position on the provision and published a 2010 reply in *Constitutional Forum*, in which he offered an account defending the clause.[24]

Blakeney's published argument there implicitly rests on the view that there are moral rights – entitlements that are morally justified, whether or not they appear within the law – that go beyond the legal rights embodied in the Charter's text and that we should be concerned with conflicts between moral rights and with not giving the upper hand to some rights over others simply because they are in the Charter.[25] Blakeney cites the example of a moral right to basic health care and suggests not only that it is not in the text, but that such rights do not belong in the text because their proper enforcement is not through the courts.[26] In other words, the Charter inherently leaves out some rights.

Blakeney's argument is that legislatures and governments need to be able to work out ways of implementing those other rights, without the courts' interpretation of Charter rights interfering with that

---

[23] Hon. Allan E. Blakeney, *An Honourable Calling: Political Memoirs* (Toronto: University of Toronto Press, 2008), pp. 200–02.

[24] Hon. Allan E. Blakeney, 'The Notwithstanding Clause, the Charter, and Canada's Patriated Constitution: What I Thought We Were Doing' (2010) 19 *Constitutional Forum* 1, replying to Whyte, 'Sometimes Constitutions Are Made in the Streets', above n 3.

[25] Ibid. at 4 (Blakeney states: 'In selecting some rights and freedoms for inclusion in the Charter, there was no intention to create a hierarchy of rights in the sense that the rights included in that document were more important than others. Rather, the rights and freedoms chosen for inclusion in the Charter were selected because it was reasonable to give the courts a role in their enforcement. On the other hand, it was felt that the courts were ill equipped to enforce freedoms from fear and want. The enforcement of these rights would remain with the legislative and executive branches of government.')

[26] Ibid. at 5–6. Here, Blakeney of course departs from the view of many social democrats at the time or in later constitutional discussions, with many left-wing commentators having argued for the inclusion of more rights in the Charter.

implementation. In some circumstances, the defence of a basic moral right not contained within the Charter may even require the limitation of a right that is within the Charter, and the limitations clause in the Charter may not be a sufficient means of finding the appropriate reconciliation.[27] Then, Blakeney says, legislatures may need to be able to act despite an interpretation by the courts of what the Charter requires.[28] The means of doing so, when necessary, is the notwithstanding clause.

The published version of Blakeney's article was significantly shorter than the manuscript that he submitted to the journal. The shortening may have been justified on standard editorial and stylistic grounds but arguably had the unfortunate side effect of diminishing the historical record existing on Canadian constitutionalism. Fortunately, the original version that Blakeney submitted still exists.[29] In that version, he includes an extended reflection on the origins of the Canadian system of government, tracing (albeit briefly) the continuation in Canada of ideas from Greek and Roman democracy, the British parliamentary system, and various other aspects of world history on the development of democratic government.[30] Though accepting of the wider recognition in recent decades of the role of rights entrenchment in ensuring the better protection of some rights, Blakeney constantly returns to the theme of the greater complexity of rights than is reflected in enumerated rights that might be enforced by judges and the need, then, for the possible interaction of parliamentary views on rights with the views that might be implemented through judicial interpretation.[31]

Like Blakeney, Peter Lougheed has also written on his reasons behind his advocacy of the notwithstanding clause, notably in a 1991 lecture delivered at the University of Calgary that was preserved for posterity when it was published seven years later by the University of Alberta's Centre for Constitutional Studies.[32] He recounts, in the first instance,

---

[27] Ibid. at 5.

[28] Ibid.

[29] A copy is on file with the author.

[30] These themes are present in Blakeney, above n 24 at 2. The more extended discussion in the original arguably warranted editing, but its significant length reflects the importance that this part of the article had for Blakeney.

[31] This idea similarly is present in Blakeney, ibid. at 4–7, though it receives slightly longer treatment in the original draft.

[32] Hon. Peter Lougheed, 'Why a Notwithstanding Clause?', in *Centre for Constitutional Studies Points of View, No. 6* (Edmonton: University of Alberta Centre for Constitutional Studies, 1998), publishing the Marv Leitch Q. C. Lecture, delivered at the University of Calgary, 20 November 1991.

how Alberta came to include a notwithstanding clause in its own Bill of Rights in the 1970s, before turning to explain how he had helped to advocate for a notwithstanding clause in the Charter during the discussions leading up to its adoption.[33] Through the lecture, he discusses many different aspects of the notwithstanding clause and the more recent debate on it. One key theme of his defence is that it permits a certain responsiveness to interpretations of rights with which there is ultimate democratic disagreement: 'what we have, in fact, chosen as a nation is a constitutionalization of rights, subject to a final political judgment in certain instances, rather than a final judicial determination as to the extent of all rights'.[34]

Indeed, Lougheed refers to the clause as a way of dealing with judicial decisions with which there is disagreement without the need for recourse to some of the more extreme measures that have been used elsewhere, such as court-packing. As he puts the point, 'The drafters of the Canadian Charter foresaw the problem created by judicial supremacy in the United States, and opted to form a system of checks and balances between the judiciary and legislators before judicial supremacy could assert itself. Thus, at least one premise supporting the existence of s. 33 is that it allows effective political action on the part of legislators to curb an errant court.'[35] Here, one of the principal advocates of the clause makes clear that the clause was in pursuit of a distinctive model of constitutionalism.

Blakeney and Lougheed, of course, have different emphases in their accounts. Blakeney emphasizes the need for a check on readings of enumerated rights that exclude unenumerated rights that may be of as much (or more) moral weight, and indeed could even be part of Canada's longer legal tradition as well. He thus tends to emphasize a role for the notwithstanding clause in permitting the protection of unenumerated rights, while suggesting that there will always be important unenumerated rights in respect of which only the legislature has institutional capacity. Lougheed emphasizes the need to contest judicial interpretations of rights in some instances. But such legislative decisions to replace judicial interpretations would presumably be on the basis of moral considerations – rights or other interests – that the legislature saw as being as of equal (or more) moral weight. Lougheed implicitly takes the

---

[33] Ibid. at 2–3.
[34] Ibid. at 14
[35] Ibid. at 13.

view that in some circumstances the institutional limits of courts imply that there needs to be a check from the legislature. Even while there are different emphases in these accounts, there is a profound compatibility between them. When they are taken alongside the historical antecedents of the notwithstanding clause, they would reflect significantly the meaning and purposes that the text of the notwithstanding clause would have been understood to have.

These accounts by the proponents of the notwithstanding clause, grounded in its longer history, warrant more attention in the interpretation of the role of the notwithstanding clause. That said, some textual restrictions on the clause were inserted as a compromise with Prime Minister Pierre Trudeau, who insisted particularly on the time limit and need for re-enactment when agreeing to the insertion of s. 33,[36] and these restrictions have occupied significant attention from those reading the effects of the clause. However, the clause was grounded in constitutional precedent, and its proponents' writing identifies two key purposes the text would properly have been understood to have. First, the notwithstanding clause's text creates a means by which legislatures may act in light of rights beyond those enumerated in the Charter when Charter case law interferes with those rights, as emphasized in Blakeney's discussion. Second, the notwithstanding clause's text creates a means by which legislatures may engage with and disagree with judicial interpretations of rights, as emphasized in Lougheed's account.

III   Coordinate Interpretation: Overcoming Narrow Readings of the Notwithstanding Clause

The notwithstanding clause has received international attention from major constitutional theorists like Jeffrey Goldsworthy and Jeremy Waldron. Particularly given their general views on the role of courts versus legislatures, both of them might have been anticipated to find the clause in line with their democratic and parliamentary theories. However, they have narrowed their readings to try to explain how the clause's wording might have contributed to what could appear to be a record of limited use. But s. 33 is more actively discussed than they realize, and their reading in my view vastly understates the relevant and proper use of the clause.

---

[36] See Howard Leeson, *The Patriation Minutes* (Edmonton: University of Alberta Centre for Constitutional Studies, 2011) p. 70. See also the discussion in Strayer, above n 18, p. 90.

In his comment on the clause, Goldsworthy suggests that any legislatures using the notwithstanding clause are inherently in an awkward position where they are explicitly overriding Charter rights, and he suggests that this fact helps to explain the limited use of the clause.[37] Waldron essentially accepts this view and expresses that any legislatures using the clause end up in a position of overriding Charter rights rather than enunciating a different interpretation of rights.[38]

Given the discussion in the last section, it becomes apparent that these readings of the text are not consistent with the view of those who advocated for the inclusion of the clause in the text, with these proponents having been grounded in a longer historical tradition on the clause. Frankly, the views of those who actually advocated for the main text of the clause, rather than those opposing it, deserve primary attention in an understanding of the clause.

One key consideration in this sort of question would be that any text would need to be legally effective if it were to be meaningful. The Goldsworthy/Waldron perspective that the s. 33 text implies an override of rights rather than an override of an interpretation of rights may seem correct in the abstract. However, with respect, in the realm of practical constitutional drafting, it is not clear that the textual phrasing is anything other than the inevitable phrasing that reflects a textual permission to legislatures to adopt a different interpretation of a right. This point becomes clearest if one considers what other wording the clause could have had that would have met the Goldsworthy/Waldron argument. If the clause were phrased in terms of a law operating 'notwithstanding the judicial interpretation' of ss. 2 and 7 through 15, there would be legal questions as to the effectiveness of the clause against various scenarios. Which judicial interpretation is referenced by such wording, and is there any better wording that makes that point clearer? If legislatures were to make use of the notwithstanding clause, and the courts then slightly altered their interpretation, would the particular use of the clause still be effective? There are practical legal questions of just how Goldsworthy or Waldron would envision a legally effective approach other than via a permission to legislatures that looks like it overrides the rights themselves when it overrides the judicial interpretation of the rights.

This analysis is reinforced by the presence of historical antecedents to the clause. The drafters in 1981 preferred to avoid drafting a new clause

---

[37] Goldsworthy, above n 6, pp. 218–19.
[38] Waldron, above n 8 at 38.

of unpredictable effect, and they followed established wording that would accomplish their aim. The practical realities of textual drafting ought not to lead to dramatic conclusions of constitutional theory that undermine the purposes of a text.

To read s. 33 as involving the inherently necessary legal wording to accomplish the legal purpose at hand is, then, to realize that it may be the constitutional text that embodies the perspective of the proponents of the clause as fully as any other would have. If that is the case, then their perspective arguably remains highly pertinent to the significance of the clause and its effects within Canadian constitutionalism.

The dominant purpose of s. 33, as expressed in the lead features of its text, is to permit a Canadian federal parliament or provincial legislative assembly to have the last word on rights questions by making declarations that ensure the operation of particular statutory enactments. It would be a mistake to call this a 'constitutional override'.[39] The very authority of any such declaration enacted by a parliament or a legislative assembly stems from the Constitution itself, so it is not an override of the Constitution. Rather, it is a constitutionally supported decision to enact a statute, regardless of views that judges might hold as to the conformity of that statute with certain sections of the Charter. The fact that the constitution itself invites ordinary statutes to operate independently of rights that could normally be altered only through the amending formula implies that the notwithstanding clause does not challenge those rights; rather, it relocates who is constitutionally empowered to interpret those rights.

This legal authority of legislatures to have the last word on certain rights questions does not sit easily with the judicial supremacist views held by many legal academics. Many legal academics would prefer that power both to determine rights issues and perhaps in general be held by those arguably most like them, appellate judges. And early assertions of judicial power in Canada's post-Charter era saw judges seeking to ascend to such a role. In the 1980s Charter jurisprudence, judges waxed on about Canada's transition to a system of 'constitutional supremacy' and declared themselves 'guardians of the constitution'.[40]

---

[39] Cf. Régimbald and Newman, above n 2, c. 21. In the context of the dominant description of the clause, we ourselves made this mistake in the first edition of the treatise but have corrected it in the second.

[40] See e.g., *Hunter v. Southam*, [1984] 2 S.C.R. 145 at 155, 169.

Such an assertion effectively excluded parliaments and legislatures from their shared role in constitutional guardianship, and set up an antagonistic relationship between legislatures trying to achieve particular policy aims, supposedly regardless of rights, and judges acting as guardians of fundamental rights continually threatened by legislatures. The 'dialogue theory' as developed in Canadian scholarship arguably simply reinforced this model.[41] As Grant Huscroft has powerfully argued, 'dialogue theory' continued to presume that legislatures would function within interpretive parameters on the constitution as set by judges.[42] In other words, 'dialogue theory' as developed within the prevalent Canadian scholarship plays into a presumption that judges are 'guardians of the constitution'.

That need not be the case. If one sets aside the idea of judicial supremacy, which has no specific foundation in the constitutional text, more possibilities become apparent, and dialogue theory can take on a different tone. In his important work on interpretation, Dennis Baker highlights the fuller possible continuum of interpretive approaches, with dialogue theory falling somewhere in between judicial interpretive supremacy and coordinate interpretation where both courts and legislative bodies have a role in constitutional interpretation.[43] Baker's work on coordinate interpretation thus offers an important account that shows the potential roots for such an approach, with judicial interpretive supremacy being a much newer phenomenon within constitutional thought than often realized.[44]

On the notwithstanding clause specifically, Baker admits that the notwithstanding clause has sometimes been used as part of an argument against coordinate interpretation and then offers an initial challenge to that argument based on arguments much along the lines of the Goldsworthy/Waldron take on the clause.[45] In essence, those judges

---

[41] For the theory, see Peter W. Hogg and Allison Bushell, 'The Charter Dialogue between Courts and Legislatures (Or Perhaps the Charter of Rights Isn't Such a Bad Thing After All)' (1997) 35 *Osgoode Hall Law Journal* 75.

[42] Grant Huscroft, 'Rationalizing Judicial Power: The Mischief of Dialogue Theory', in James B. Kelly and Christopher P. Manfredi, (eds.), *Contested Constitutionalism: Reflections on the Charter of Rights and Freedoms* (Vancouver: University of British Columbia Press, 2009).

[43] Dennis Baker, *Not Quite Supreme: The Courts and Coordinate Interpretation* (Montreal: McGill-Queen's University Press, 2010), p. 3.

[44] Ibid.

[45] Ibid. pp. 44–45.

purporting to be 'guardians of the constitution' have sometimes taken the presence of the notwithstanding clause as an extra reason for judicial interpretive supremacy and as a reason to feel free to engage in interpretation without thought for legislative bodies' approaches to the Constitution.[46] The view of such courts is, in a sense, that the notwithstanding clause exists as an emergency hatch and legislatures can effectively be taken as consenting to judicial interpretations unless they make use of that hatch. Baker's response is that the notwithstanding clause is in practical terms difficult to use, much for the reasons that Goldsworthy and Waldron referenced and because it is difficult to use, courts should not take it as authorization to engage in their own audacious interpretive approaches.[47]

This aspect of Baker's work manifests a certain danger to some degree. In continually describing the difficulties in using the notwithstanding clause, even academics who support the clause risk reifying those constraints. They contribute to a legal and democratic culture in which the use of the clause is portrayed as being a 'last resort' or an 'escape hatch'.[48] Nothing in the text of the clause, however, suggests that its use must be so limited. The text of s. 33 does have a five-year time limit, so as to maintain democratic accountability on uses of the clause, with that five-year limit also corresponding to the maximum term of a parliament or legislative assembly under the Constitution. But that is effectively the sole explicit textual limit on the clause as read within the section itself. Nothing in the Charter text suggests that the clause ought to be a 'last resort'.

Obviously, the use of the notwithstanding clause is not meant to be entirely routine. If it were inserted in every bill that potentially affected ss. 2 or 7 through 15 of the Charter, it would effectively amount to a rejection of the entire course of case law on those sections of the Charter as part of Canada's Constitution. If parliament or a legislature considered that step necessary, it would indicate a profound problem in either the

---

[46] See e.g., *Vriend v. Alberta*, [1998] 1 S.C.R. 493 at para. 137 (the Court invoking the presence of the notwithstanding clause option for legislatures as part of the justification for the Court's vigorous remedy in the Charter case); *Re Application Under s. 83.28 of the Criminal Code*, [2004] 2 S.C.R. 248, 2004 SCC 42 at para. 37 (using the fact that Parliament did not invoke the notwithstanding clause in enacting particular legislation as the reason to read the legislation in terms limited by the Court's approach to constitutional values in interpretation).

[47] Baker, above n 43.

[48] Cf. also Baron and Sigalet, above n 12.

courts, the first and principal vehicle of interpretation, or in the legislature that showed no comity towards the institutional role of the courts.

Quebec's early, principally symbolic usage of the notwithstanding clause in precisely that manner may have achieved certain aims, but it did not enhance the perceived standing of the notwithstanding clause. Apart from even this sort of routine usage, it would not be appropriate to have legislatures excessively involved in second-guessing judicial decisions on an everyday basis. Doing so would effectively subvert a proper institutional division. Parliamentarians are not placed so as to re-adjudicate every (constitutional) case, and if they did so, they would introduce enormous unpredictability for litigants. Although legislatures act by means of statutes, which might seem to reduce unpredictability, the prospect that they are prospectively passing a statue on every constitutional issue would leave litigants in the position of waiting for that statutory determination rather than one of generally being able to rely on indications building upon case law.[49]

All of that said, to conclude from a suggestion that the notwithstanding clause should not be used routinely that it must be used only on a 'last resort' or 'escape hatch' basis – as has commonly been presumed – is to fall into a fallacy of false alternatives. There is a wide middle ground as between re-adjudicating every case and using the clause only as a last possible resort. Selective substitution of parliamentary determinations may be more respectful of the human considerations underlying the constitutional rights system than judicial supremacy. Indeed, that is what Blakeney's argument for the notwithstanding clause implicitly asserted for whole categories of cases. In particular, Blakeney suggested that where rights within the Charter could come into tension with moral rights not receiving legal expression within the Charter, there would be a category of cases in which it was preferable for parliamentarians to have the ability to substitute their approach to reconciling the rights considerations at play.[50] One might add, as well, such contexts as those in which judges are simply ill-equipped to understand the realities of governing so as to lead them to make determinations that simply do not fit with what is constitutionally plausible.[51]

These situations may well not be narrow ones. First, there are many moral rights not contained within any written constitution. In addition to

---

[49] I am indebted to discussion with Aileen Kavanagh on this point.
[50] Blakeney, above n 23.
[51] See also the chapter by Grégoire Webber in this volume.

substantive rights, there is also what Jeremy Waldron has called the 'right of rights'[52] – the right to participate in self-government and for a community to be a self-governing people. Excessive deference to judicial interpretation of rights may well undermine participation in self-government and thus undermine that fundamental right.[53] There are bases to see a role for parliamentary and legislative engagement with rights interpretation in part simply to safeguard this right, along with other moral rights not part of the written constitutional text. Second, situations in which judicial interpretations of rights do not reflect good understandings of the realities of governing will also not be rare, especially in an era when judges may increasingly be drawn from different circles of nominees who have not had practical experience with governing as had been more common in the past.

One might add one further note on Canada's notwithstanding clause that often does not receive explicit notice from those writing from abroad or even from those writing within the beltways of central Canadian power. This is that the clause does not just empower government abstractly, as in debates about rights in general, but empowers both the federal parliament and provincial legislatures. As an exception to the general neglect of this point, Janet L. Hiebert makes in passing the comment that the notwithstanding clause is the 'Charter's most explicit recognition of federalism'.[54] Although she does not explain the point further other than to say that provinces may use the clause to give priority to local or provincial interests, she has implicitly identified the important point that the notwithstanding clause functions to permit the preservation of different identities and provincially different value choices within the Canadian federation. Within their spheres of jurisdiction, the provincial legislatures can use the notwithstanding clause, and they can do so differently from one province to another, just as in the context of any choices protected by federalism. Indeed, considering federalism and the notwithstanding clause together within Canada's constitutional structure, Canada's Constitution actively facilitates different interpretation on rights questions as between different provinces. Dialogue must be understood in a sense consistent with the value of federalism, and that recognition further reaffirms that 'last-resort'

---

[52] Jeremy Waldron, *Law and Disagreement* (Oxford: Oxford University Press, 1999), p. 254.
[53] I develop this argument at more length in Newman, above n 16.
[54] Hiebert, above n 3 p. 695.

accounts of the notwithstanding clause are insufficient to reflect the range of circumstances in which the clause has important roles to play.

Indeed, the fact that the notwithstanding clause has been used by provincial legislatures but not by the federal parliament is perhaps not surprising. By the very nature of a federal state, it is more likely that some provinces' governments will diverge from the political median than that the federal government will, or at least that they will do so more often. A centralized constitutional instrument like the Charter *of Rights* is less likely to cause issues for the federal government than for the provinces and their more diverse identities. The notwithstanding clause has a particular role in facilitating coordinate interpretation within a federal state.

The presence of the notwithstanding clause is challenging for those adhering to theories in which governments must always be constrained. At their extreme, such theories effectively presume that governments will generally act irresponsibly in respect of rights. The notwithstanding clause, not making such a presumption that would implicitly deny the very idea of democratic governance, precisely calls upon governments to make deliberate, responsible choices. In doing so, it challenges them to their best. Parliaments and legislatures contemplating the use of the notwithstanding clause must act in a politically responsible manner. Like many aspects of the Canadian constitutional tradition, their decisions to use the clause will not be justiciable, but their applications of the clause are no less normatively binding for that fact. The political responsibilities of governing mandate that each use of the notwithstanding clause must be carefully contemplated in light of its effects on rights, on the rule of law, and on Canadian constitutionalism generally, all the while considering the salutary effects in terms of rights or other weighty moral considerations of the policy goals pursued through the legislation at issue. In so acting, legislatures enter partly into a coordinate interpretation of the proper scope of Charter rights, along with judges, with legislatures institutionally placed so as to consider unenumerated rights, and other moral considerations bearing on the scope of rights in ways going beyond the judicial role. Rights fulfilment becomes a genuinely shared endeavour.

Within such an endeavour, the usual concept of judicial deference to legislatures remains pertinent but can also be turned on its head. Conceptual questions properly arise of when legislatures should and should not defer to judges. Legislative deference to judges may be more appropriate where judges have decided based on distinctively legal reasoning, and may be less required where judges have decided based on general moral values on which legislatures have as much, or perhaps even more, institutional capacity. It may similarly be less required where judges have decided based on incorrect assumptions on legislative facts, including on how governments function, particularly if legislatures have better institutional capacity on those issues. Implicit in some of these points is that less legislative deference to judges is owed where judges have themselves overstepped their roles and failed to show sufficient deference to legislatures in circumstances mandating their deference – within this account, issues of deference actually take on aspects of mutuality and reciprocity. Legislatures deciding upon a potential use of the notwithstanding clause operate within the grand traditions of constitutionalism and all of the values it protects and within a complex set of institutional relationships that can embrace a larger dialogue than much 'dialogue theory' has contemplated.

IV   Applications to Implementation of the Notwithstanding Clause

The preceding sections would support an argument that the notwithstanding clause opens the door to a constitutionally efficacious dialogue on rights, in which legislative bodies have the authority to substitute their view of a particular rights conflict or rights interpretation for the view at which courts have arrived. Quite simply, that is the legal effect of the text, supported by what it meant at the time it was adopted in light of historical antecedents and articulated explanations by those who proposed the clause that would have been understood in some measure by those adopting it. As discussed in the last section, the clause opens possibilities for coordinate interpretation of rights.

At the same time, deep political and even constitutional responsibilities attach to each potential use of the notwithstanding clause. In light of the considerations discussed in this chapter, it is possible to say something as to some of the recently contemplated applications of the clause and how they fit with these considerations. They illustrate several potential categories of uses building upon the principles identified by Blakeney and Lougheed, and they illustrate the appropriateness of nuanced consideration within any of these categories.

First, in the most general terms, there is the possibility of the use of the clause to reverse a Charter decision or potential Charter application where other moral rights outside the Charter or other moral considerations lead legislatures towards a different interpretation of rights and their appropriate limits. All such uses must be contemplated carefully, as they do involve engagement with questions on which courts will presumably have considered matters carefully in accordance with their distinctive modes of legal reasoning. However, there will nonetheless be instances in which there is good reason for a use of the notwithstanding clause within this category.

Some actual cases will, of course, partake of more than one category of considerations. The recent case that has led to a use of the notwithstanding clause by the province of Saskatchewan is illustrative. The controversy arose after a Saskatchewan trial court declared it constitutionally impermissible for the province to fund non-Catholics to attend Catholic schools.[55] That Catholics can attend publicly funded separate schools is not in dispute, as a specialized constitutional provision exists permitting these schools. However, the court held that there was a violation of religious neutrality and of the equality rights of other religions if non-Catholics were permitted to attend funded Catholic schools.[56] The Court nonetheless ended up rendering a decision with a province-wide effect on thousands of non-Catholic students who are attending Catholic schools for a variety of reasons, although the full number is not known because the province has not traditionally been in the business of applying 'religion tests' to individuals. This decision would have had effect in just over one year's time.

The decision to apply the notwithstanding clause to this case has several elements. In part, it reflects a quasi-procedural decision that only appealing the decision allows for too much chaos in the interim period. So, in the context of a trial decision that might well be in error on standard legal grounds, the province is acting to resolve matters more quickly by using the notwithstanding clause, considering the impact on morally important interests arising from this interim issue. At another level, it reflects a statement about the realities of governing, and a realization that the Court did not have a full record and did not appreciate fully the problems of entering into the business of testing students' religions in considering which publicly funded schools they were permitted to attend.

However, perhaps most importantly for present purposes, it reflects a statement that a different interpretation of rights ought to apply than that

---

[55] *Good Spirit School Division No. 204 v. Christ the Teacher Roman Catholic Separate School Division No. 212,* 2017 SKQB 109.

[56] The issue arose not out of any complaint by any student or parent but out of a funding squabble involving a small rural school division that decided to litigate the point. Because of the way the case went before the court, it went without the full record that would have gone had it been litigated by students themselves. As I have indicated elsewhere, the case also did not see the Court engage with some of the most current case law on some of the constitutional issues at stake. See generally Newman, above n 12.

instantiated by a judicial decision. Interestingly, the case belies suggestions that uses of the notwithstanding clause will be by majorities out to
oppress minorities – it is actually a case that sees the government
protecting the integrity of the (minority) Catholic school system from
threats by the courts and the rights of individual parents and children to
exercise choice in schooling based on complex matters of faith. In my
view, it was a proper instance for the use of the notwithstanding clause.

The Saskatchewan schools case, incidentally, also illustrates the federal
dimensions of the notwithstanding clause. Saskatchewan has made a
different decision on rights interpretation than some other provinces
might be inclined to do. Where some provinces have worked in recent
years to remove specialized constitutional protections for minority religious education,[57] Saskatchewan has worked to support those minority
rights, even to the extent of protecting them as against other Charter rights
by recourse to the notwithstanding clause. There can be different choices
on the reconciliation of various rights in different provinces, and the
notwithstanding clause thus also functions in safeguarding some of the
complex variety of Canadian constitutional identities. Were the recently
developed religious neutrality principles to be turned upon Indigenous
religious or spiritual practices – such as if the Supreme Court of Canada's
prohibition of opening prayers at municipal council meetings were to be
applied in the context of Indigenous governmental institutions – the
notwithstanding clause would similarly provide a means of protecting
some of the diverse identities within Canadian constitutionalism.

Second, there is the possibility of using the clause to express a strong
legislative view on the morally concerning impracticalities of a particular
interpretation of rights. The Supreme Court of Canada's 2016 decision in
Jordan sought to achieve a culture change in terms of trial delays,
imposing new time-delimited ceilings beyond which delay from the
criminal charge to the end of trial is presumed to be in violation of the
Charter.[58] With the possibility of widespread stays of proceedings arising
if governments could not adjust procedures so as to bring criminal cases
to trial faster, there was some discussion in some provinces of the
possibility of using the notwithstanding clause to reverse the Court's
decision. What those advocating such a use desired was, in effect, a
legislative statement that the courts must not grant stays in cases where

---

[57] There have been bilateral constitutional amendments made in Quebec and
Newfoundland.
[58] *R. v. Jordan*, 2016 SCC 27, [2016] 1 S.C.R. 631.

the Court's prescriptions concerning maximum trial delays were exceeded (which would likely need to be via federal legislation) Although there was not ultimately the appetite for such legislation, it could have marked a legislative statement that moral considerations arising from the practical effects of the decision were unacceptable as a means of attempting to shift the culture on the issue, potentially amounting to a legislative statement that the courts should not shut down trials of particular offenders as a means towards an end of reform on trial delay.

However, considering it nonetheless as an example permitting the application of the considerations considered earlier, there could be said to be further reasons why this category of uses is permissible but this particular use might have been unwise. Where courts make decisions that are impractical because of misperceived legislative facts or because they do not understand realities of governing, such considerations can give meaningful support to legislatures in using the notwithstanding clause to alter the courts' rights interpretation. However, in the particular case at issue, an understanding of trial delay would seem to be something meaningfully within the institutional knowledge of judges themselves. A legislative intervention on the point might well not have improved matters. It would need to have involved extremely careful consideration of all of the matters at issue. But the case certainly illustrates the possibility of legislators interpreting rights questions differently.

Third, at a final and more technical level, there is the possibility of a quasi-procedural use of the clause. In early 2016, the newly elected federal government applied to the Supreme Court of Canada for additional time to develop a careful implementation of the Court's 2015 decision on assisted suicide, on which the Court had granted a suspension that did not give enough time in practical terms for parliamentary consideration of the issue in the context of an intervening election campaign. As pointed out by at least one constitutional scholar and by one of the justices of the Court itself, parliament could have used the notwithstanding clause to grant itself an extension. The Court did accommodate the request for more time and Parliament complied with the extended timeline.[59]

---

[59] Sarah Burningham called for the use: 'Use the Notwithstanding Clause, If You Must' *National Post* (21 December 2015). Justice Brown referred to the possibility during the hearing, although the Court's decision on the extension request made no reference to the notwithstanding clause: *Carter v. Canada (Attorney General)*, 2016 SCC 4, [2016] 1 SCR 13. The attorney general requested an extension of six months; the Court awarded Parliament an extension of four months.

In my view, such contemplated uses of the notwithstanding clause ought to be relatively uncontroversial, particularly if tailored to the actual need in the context of governing. Legislatures are more familiar than the Court with realistic times for responding to complex new invalidations of Canadian law, and the standard twelve-month suspended declarations granted in many judicial decisions reflect no particular attention to the considerations applying to any particular case. So a parliamentary use of the notwithstanding clause to secure time for a responsible parliamentary response to a judicial decision would not even involve interference with contemplated legal reasoning. It would mark a practical use of the clause to maintain opportunities for full parliamentary consideration of rights issues. Such a use is derivative of the more general principled case for the clause but still significant in many practical contexts.

V   Conclusions

Canada's notwithstanding clause is a remarkable piece of constitutional statecraft. Though critiqued incessantly by those of certain mindsets, it actually reflects an abiding faith in self-government and ought to reflect a real check against the imposition of guardianship by a judicial elite. That check arguably ought also to be as much in the context of its non-use as in actually compelling legislatures to use it, although they also should not have so much reluctance to use it as seems to have been common. Despite some aspects of what had to be in the legal text, the real meaning of a use of the notwithstanding clause is an expression of a difference on interpretation of rights, which can be developed out into several categories of principled uses of the clause. In these uses, it arguably safeguards rather than undermines the best of our rights traditions.

The notwithstanding clause need not be an 'escape hatch' or 'last resort' but can legitimately be used by legislatures across a range of scenarios, with principled reasoning available that can help to guide their choices on uses of the clause. In that aspect, it is a direct part of dialogue as it functions in Canada and a specifically permitted last word to legislatures from which they should not shy away in appropriate cases, including in respect of cases that concern distinctive parts of complex identity issues within Canada as well as in respect of cases on differing interpretations of fundamental rights and their limits. As referenced at the outset, a closer examination of the notwithstanding clause helps to situate Canada in a fully nuanced way within Gardbaum's set of new Commonwealth constitutions. While Canada has moved a significant distance towards American-style judicial review, the notwithstanding clause is an important check on this, with a fuller understanding of its philosophical foundations supporting a greater readiness to use the clause.

Legislatures should consider in a specific case whether legislative deference is owing to judges on a particular issue; analogously, judges should consider the degree of judicial deference owing to legislatures on a particular issue. Those issues can be worked through in particular instances as part of the fundamental political responsibility of legislatures considering uses of the clause, just as judges ought to work through carefully whether they should exercise powers of judicial review in a particular case.

However, the presence of the notwithstanding clause also has a greater dialogue-related significance. The reasoning in this chapter concerning the nature of the notwithstanding clause also leads to significant implications for judges in the context of dialogue. Taking the notwithstanding clause as I have read it here marks the inclusion of a clause authorizing legislative disagreement with judicial interpretation of rights. The textual features of the clause that some have taken as implying that legislatures may be 'overriding' rights have been given an alternative reading. The text of the clause preserves the ability of legislatures to inject their differing interpretation of rights, including within particularistic identities as opposed to just universalistic rights discourses, as envisioned by those proposing the clause and as rooted in the longer history of the clause. And that means that legislatures are textually recognized as having a legitimate role as part of the interpretation of rights. The result is not that courts should act audaciously and invite legislatures to override them but that courts should respect the interpretive role being shared with legislatures. This should imply an initial respect for legislation where courts go beyond a presumption of constitutionality under which they reinterpret legislation as needed to fit the judges' *prima facie* view of the scope of constitutional rights. Rather, courts should interrogate their initial assumptions in light of a premise that legislatures may be offering a different interpretation of rights, thus effectively taking legislatures as themselves having meaningfully opened the dialogue rather than the opening gambit being for the courts. Where courts nonetheless invalidate statutes, they should do so in light of a full understanding of legislative purposes in terms of legislative understandings of rights, including within the range of identities and values within Canadian federalism, and consider whether there is any way to develop remedies that more fully respect those legislative understandings. There is a shared role in interpretation and the possibility of a more meaningful dialogue than the received account.

If the notwithstanding clause serves to further legitimate the concept of coordinate interpretation, it has implications beyond uses of the clause itself. Though it is still developing at this moment, Canada's recent judicial and legislative action on assisted suicide might serve as an interesting example of the distinctions between the received accounts of dialogue theory and the sort of dialogue that appears more appropriate in the context of the presence of the notwithstanding clause. On dominant approaches, the Supreme Court of Canada would arguably strike down the proposed new legislation. The Supreme Court of Canada's narrow but significant conclusion on assisted suicide in the *Carter* decision was that

's. 241(b) and s. 14 of the *Criminal Code* are void insofar as they prohibit physician-assisted death for a competent adult person who (1) clearly consents to the termination of life; and (2) has a grievous and irremediable medical condition (including an illness, disease or disability) that causes enduring suffering that is intolerable to the individual in the circumstances of his or her condition'.[60]

The federal statute passed in response in 2016 largely tracks the language of the judgment, but it adds a requirement that death be 'reasonably foreseeable' before an individual qualifies for physician-assisted suicide.[61] The dominant constitutional view contested in this chapter would affirm that this requirement qualifies the right to assisted suicide in a manner inconsistent with the Supreme Court judgment. The Court would invalidate this restriction on access to assisted suicide, leaving it open for Parliament to respond by using the notwithstanding clause to trample over rights.

This is not what I would foresee, nor presumably is it what the Government of Canada did in moving forward with its legislative amendments. The new provisions represent a concession to the *Carter* decision, but introduce a new point at which to stand on the slippery slope that otherwise ensues. There will be arguments to extend the regime, and it is not necessarily clear that this standing point works. But the legislative

---

[60] *Carter* v. *Canada (Attorney General)*, 2015 SCC 5, [2015] 1 SCR 331 at para. 127.
[61] *An Act to Amend the Criminal Code and to Make Related Amendments to Other Acts (Medical Assistance in Dying)*, S.C. 2016, c. 3.

pursuit of it marks a different read from the Court's initial read on the impact on the rights of others, notably vulnerable persons, that would ensue from a regime simply instituting the Court's first interpretation. The bill potentially marks an injection of legislative interpretation of rights. My argument on the notwithstanding clause would support the idea that the Court should respect this legislative response, in part because the notwithstanding clause signals a legislative role in coordinate interpretation *even when* the clause is not invoked. The presence of the notwithstanding clause does not imply the Court should be more audacious so as to test if legislatures will use the notwithstanding clause. It emphasizes the constitutional and legal responsibilities on the Court, operating in mutuality and reciprocity with legislatures.

Traditional received accounts of 'dialogue theory' understate the nature of the interplay between courts and legislatures that should apply in the context of the notwithstanding clause. In my view, these accounts of 'dialogue theory' tend to describe a dialogue that has not tended to occur while understating the normative requirements that should actually apply in respect of dialogue. Canada's notwithstanding clause has a larger message than it is usually understood to carry and needs to receive much more sympathetic attention from scholars. Reengaging with the philosophical foundations of the notwithstanding clause can reinvigorate it and allow it to contribute meaningfully to constitutional dialogues and constitutionalism more generally.

9

Intra-Parliamentary Dialogues in New Zealand and the United Kingdom

A Little Less Conversation, a Little More Action Please

JANET L. HIEBERT AND JAMES B. KELLY

I Introduction

In our book *Parliamentary Bills of Rights: The Experiences of New Zealand and the United Kingdom*, we conducted a comprehensive review of all section 7 reports issued by New Zealand's attorney general under the New Zealand Bill of Rights Act (NZBORA) 1990, and ministerial statements required by section 19 of the United Kingdom's Human Rights Act (HRA) 1998. As well, our study provided a detailed investigation of major government bills introduced with compatibility reports that were scrutinized by parliamentary select committees in New Zealand and the Joint Committee on Human Rights (JCHR) in the United Kingdom.[1] This study produced three general conclusions about the parliamentary approach to bills of rights. First, rights-based scrutiny is well institutionalized during the design of legislation, and it is unlikely that government is unaware of whether and how legislation implicates rights when approving bills for introduction to parliament. Second, governments appear willing to promote legislation that is not consistent or compatible with rights-based norms. The third conclusion is that rights-based dialogue occurs infrequently within Parliament once a reporting obligation is dispensed with, and thus bills with compatibility issues generally pass without rights-friendly amendments. In the case of New Zealand, this transpired because of parliamentary indifference to the attorney general's reporting obligation under section 7 of the NZBORA that was demonstrated by the Cabinet, government members on the

---

[1] Janet L. Hiebert and James B. Kelly, *Parliamentary Bills of Rights: The Experiences of New Zealand and the United Kingdom* (Cambridge: Cambridge University Press, 2015), pp. 411–412.

backbenches, and, most surprisingly, most of the opposition parties. In the United Kingdom, rights-based dialogue is thwarted by the Cabinet's insistence that government bills comply with the UK HRA, despite mounting evidence to the contrary, and the inability of the JCHR to generate meaningful dialogic engagement on the part of the Cabinet, backbench members, and the opposition parties regarding public bills. While this has been considered a 'pessimistic assessment' of the dialogue model by leading commentators such as Aileen Kavanagh,[2] these are the conclusions that a systematic testing of the dialogue model in New Zealand and the United Kingdom produced.

We believe that the normative assumptions of the dialogue model, once tested in the parliamentary arena, generate less than optimal outcomes. Perhaps more damaging, it may not result in rights-based dialogue at all. As we concluded, it is simply not enough for the attorney general or the JCHR to be the 'dialogue whisperers' in the parliamentary arena to demonstrate the viability of the 'new Commonwealth model'.[3] What explains the detachment between the optimism of the dialogue model as a theory, and our conclusion of stunted dialogue and limited policy impact? In our study, we argued that dialogue scholarship began with a problematic normative starting point with respect to parliamentary institutions: that a statutory bill of rights will change legislative behaviour and result in a rights-based culture emerging within the parliamentary setting. In this respect, the dialogue model, while it acknowledges that statutory bills of rights are ordinary acts of parliament, strongly believes that these statutory documents will come to function as a higher set of norms that regulate political behaviour. In effect, parliamentary deference to rights assessments and reporting obligations by law officers such as the attorney general can see a statutory bill of rights function as a de facto supreme law document.

As political scientists, we considered this the wrong normative starting point, as it downplayed the interaction between the principles of parliamentary democracy, the reality of parliamentary institutions as executive dominated arenas, the interplay between the Standing Orders that exist in each parliamentary setting, and the new rules introduced by statutory bills of rights. Finally, we considered that the dialogue model overlooked that a

---

[2] Aileen Kavanagh, 'A Hard Look at the Last Word' (2015) 35 *Oxford Journal of Legal Studies* 836–837.

[3] Stephen Gardbaum, *The New Commonwealth Model of Constitutionalism: Theory and Practice* (Cambridge: Cambridge University Press, 2013).

rights-based discourse, while it is initiated by ministerial statements such as the attorney general's section 7 report in New Zealand, competes with other well-established, entrenched, and dominant policy discourses that exist within these respective parliaments. In effect, a rights-based discourse vies for political space within the parliamentary setting, and our study found that it faced a number of barriers inherent in these Westminster parliamentary democracies. Barriers, incidentally, that generally denied dialogue theory voice and space within parliamentary debates. For these reasons, we concluded that the theory of this model did not translate into parliamentary practice, and we questioned whether, in fact, it is a viable alternative to strong-form, constitutional bills of rights.[4]

Thus, we approach the question of the new model from a very different vantage point. Instead of viewing these bills of rights as a set of norms that structure parliamentary behaviour, we contend that parliamentary democracy, as a set of institutions and rules, condition, constrain, and ultimately shape these statutory instruments.[5] They are first and foremost *parliamentary* bills of rights that operate differently in each context because of the distinctive institutional designs of these Westminster systems. For instance, the United Kingdom is a bicameral parliament, whereas New Zealand is a single chamber. The United Kingdom operates under the single member plurality (SMP) electoral system, while New Zealand adopted mixed-member proportional (MMP) in 1996, six years after the adoption of the NZBORA. The United Kingdom has a dedicated parliamentary scrutiny committee to engage the HRA 1998, the JCHR, whereas New Zealand assigns this as a general responsibility to all parliamentary select committees. These differences are not insignificant. And critically, these differences question whether there is a dialogic or new Commonwealth model because of tremendous institutional variation amongst these Westminster parliamentary democracies.[6]

In this chapter, we elaborate on the general conclusions presented in *Parliamentary Bills of Rights*, and the wide-ranging difficulties of a rights-based dialogue emerging within these distinct parliamentary democracies. And we attempt to answer Aileen Kavanagh's provocative question – what's so weak about weak-form review?[7] – by way of

---

[4] Mark Tushnet, *Weak Courts, Strong Rights: Judicial Review and Social Welfare Rights in Comparative Constitutional Law* (Princeton: Princeton University Press, 2008), pp. 43–47.
[5] Hiebert and Kelly, *Parliamentary Bills of Rights*, pp. 9–11.
[6] Ibid. pp. 409–411.
[7] Aileen Kavanagh, 'What's So Weak about "Weak-Form Review"? A Rejoinder to Stephen Gardbaum' (2015) 15 *International Journal of Constitutional Law* 1008–1039.

K. D. Ewing's equally provocative critique of the failings of the UK HRA in an executive-dominated parliamentary setting: 'This is the problem of centralized power and executive dominance, and the ability of governments with the support of the House of Commons to do pretty much what they want.'[8] We agree that weak-form review, as a framework, has focused 'too narrowly on the formal features of the constitutional design, detached from how those features operate in practice'.[9] Indeed, we readily concede – and hypothesized at the beginning of our research project – that the dialogue model may be stronger than its formal elements suggest.[10] However, as we came to learn, this is a conclusion that can only be reached – and was not reached – after examining how the rules, norms, and principles of parliamentary democracy interact with these parliamentary bills of rights.

II   New Zealand Bill of Rights Act 1990

The New Zealand Bill of Rights Act (NZBORA) 1990 is considered a prime example of the dialogic model, or the 'new Commonwealth model of constitutionalism'.[11] For instance, it is a statutory instrument that protects the principle of parliamentary supremacy, as it does not allow the courts, under section 4, to declare acts of parliament invalid or ineffective. In a further concession to parliamentary supremacy, the courts are required, where possible under section 6, to interpret acts of parliament in a manner that is consistent with the NZBORA. Although this creates the possibility that the courts can amend statutes by providing an interpretation that ensures compatibility with the NZBORA, and thus 'read-out' constitutional defects, the courts have only recently created this power, revising an earlier position that a 'declaration of inconsistency' must be created by parliamentary amendment of the NZBORA.[12] Similar

---

[8] K. D. Ewing, *Bonfire of the Liberties: New Labour, Human Rights, and the Rule of Law* (Oxford: Oxford University Press 2010), p. 2.

[9] Kavanagh, 'What's So Weak about "Weak-Form Review"?', 1010.

[10] Janet L. Hiebert, 'Parliament and the Human Rights Act: Can the JCHR Help Facilitate a Culture of Rights?' (2006) 4 *International Journal of Constitutional Law* 1; James B. Kelly, 'Legislative Activism and Parliamentary Bills of Rights: Institutional Lessons for Canada' in James B. Kelly and Christopher P. Manfredi (eds.), *Contested Constitutionalism: Reflections on the Canadian Charter of Rights and Freedoms* (Vancouver: University of British Columbia Press, 2009), pp. 107–125.

[11] Gardbaum, *The New Commonwealth Model of Constitutionalism*, pp. 132–33.

[12] Claudia Geiringer, 'Declarations of inconsistency dodged again' (2009) *New Zealand Law Journal* 232.

to the United Kingdom's HRA 1998, it is best to characterize the NZBORA 1990 as a parliamentary bill of rights because judicial review is weak-form in nature. Indeed, the NZBORA does not provide for judicial declarations of incompatibility, and it was only in 2017 that the Court of Appeal of New Zealand determined that the higher courts have the ability to issue a declaration of inconsistency.[13] This stands in direct contrast to the Supreme Court of Canada, as section 24(1) of the Canadian Charter of Rights and Freedoms authorizes strong-form judicial review that allows the higher courts to declare act of Parliament and the provincial legislatures unconstitutional.

There are several additional justifications for the designation of NZBORA as a *parliamentary* bill of rights. The NZBORA is the statutory responsibility of the attorney general, who is required under section 7 to report to Parliament when bills are considered incompatible with rights and freedoms. The intention of this reporting obligation is to facilitate, within Parliament, a rights-based discourse on bills deemed by the attorney general to be incompatible with the NZBORA. The principle framer of the NZBORA, Geoffrey Palmer, considers section 7 to be the defining and innovative feature of this statutory bill of rights, despite his preference for a higher law, constitutional document.[14] The attorney general's statutory report is the end product of a thorough rights-based scrutiny process that exists within the New Zealand civil service under the direction of the Ministry of Justice and the Crown Law Office. It is a transparent process, as all section 7 reports have been made publicly available since 2003, including 'BORA' vets that conclude proposed bills are compatible with the NZBORA.[15] This process suggests the institutionalization of rights-dialogue within the New Zealand civil service, and, like Andrew Geddis,[16] we have discussed this process elsewhere in some detail.[17]

The New Zealand approach, therefore, exhibits the main principles and institutional mechanisms of 'third wave' or dialogic bills of rights:

---

[13] *Attorney-General* v. *Taylor* [2017] NZCA 2017. See now *Attorney General v Taylor* [2018] NZSC 104.

[14] Geoffrey Palmer, 'Muldoon and the Constitution', in Margaret Clark (ed.), *Muldoon Revisited* (Palmerston North, NZ: Dunmore Press, 2004), pp. 208–210; Interview with Sir Geoffrey Palmer, New Zealand Law Commission, Wellington, New Zealand (6 May 2004).

[15] Since 2003, the attorney general has released all BORA vets and section 7 reports, and they are available on the Ministry of Justice website: www.justice.govt.nz/.

[16] Andrew Geddis, 'Rights Scrutiny in New Zealand's Legislative Processes' (2016) 4 *The Theory and Practice of Legislation* 355–379.

[17] Hiebert and Kelly, *Parliamentary Bills of Rights*, pp. 50–61.

first, judicial review is provided for while the principle of parliamentary supremacy is safeguarded; second, a rights culture has emerged within the legislative processes under the direction of the Ministry and Justice and the Crown Law Office that links policy objectives to the NZBORA; third, political-rights review is prioritized as the attorney general's reporting obligation under section 7; and finally, Parliament retains the final word as it is permitted to pass legislation, without amendment, even if the attorney general reports incompatibilities to the House of Representatives.[18] The only institutional aspect of the dialogue model that is not present in New Zealand is a dedicated parliamentary committee tasked with rights-based scrutiny, such as the JCHR in the United Kingdom, or the Scrutiny of Acts and Regulations Committee in Victoria.[19] This is a general responsibility of all select committees in New Zealand, which, as we found, poses a set of challenges for parliamentary engagement of the attorney general's section 7 report.[20]

The dialogic features of the NZBORA are demonstrated by the large number of section 7 reports issued to Parliament, their transparency, accessibility, and the comprehensive nature of the attorney general's assessments of incompatibility. Unfortunately, however, the impact of these reports tell a different story, as there has been limited engagement of section 7 reports at the select committee stage, and limited evidence that a report of inconsistency has compelled Parliament to seek changes to legislation reported on by the attorney general. Of the thirty-five government bills where the attorney general has reported an inconsistency to Parliament (1990–2014), only two bills have been amended to ensure greater compatibility with the NZBORA. What does the limited engagement of the attorney general's report suggest about dialogic constitutionalism in New Zealand? Does it suggest a robust model because Parliament retains the ability to overlook, ignore, and disregard legislative rights review by the Ministry of Justice and Crown Law Office on behalf of the attorney general? Further, in the case of the attorney general, is dialogue evident when Parliament fails to engage political

---

[18] Claudia Geiringer, 'What's the Story? The instability of the Australasian Bills of Rights' (2016) 14 *International Journal of Constitutional Law* 158–159; Scott Stephenson, *From Dialogue to Disagreement in Comparative Rights Constitutionalism* (Sydney: The Federation Press, 2016), pp. 180–196.

[19] James B. Kelly, 'A Difficult Dialogue: Statements of Compatibility and the *Victorian* Charter of Human Rights and Responsibilities Act' (2011) 46 *Australian Journal of Political Science* 257–278.

[20] Hiebert and Kelly, *Parliamentary Bills of Rights*, pp. 179–185.

rights review when a section 7 report is submitted to Parliament? Indeed, is dialogue a viable model if the main dialogic instruments of the New Zealand model have produced negligible changes in parliamentary behaviour and outcomes?[21]

The dialogue model must be more than a process and, as a precondition for its viability as an alternative model of rights protection, must demonstrate measurable impact. This can manifest as explicit parliamentary disagreement with ministerial reports of rights-based incompatibles; alternatively, parliamentary acceptance of ministerial reports at the select committee stage that produce rights-friendly amendments that may – or may not – be present in the final Act of Parliament. In this respect, we suggest that the impact of ministerial reporting obligations is demonstrated by explicit parliamentary engagement, and not, as has generally occurred in respect the attorney general and section 7 reports in New Zealand, parliamentary indifference to political and legislative rights review.[22]

What explains the limited impact of the attorney general's section 7 report? This is a particularly important query, as dialogic bills of rights are defended as delivering robust parliamentary scrutiny initiated by mechanisms such as section 7 of the NZBORA. We offer the following explanation: as the NZBORA is a statutory instrument, it is simply a set of rules that must coexist with other rules and principles of New Zealand's variant of parliamentary democracy. Instead of the NZBORA changing parliamentary culture and practice, we suggest that older and more established rules within these political systems have exerted greater influence on legislative outcomes. Thus, our analysis of the NZBORA prioritizes the interplay of *parliamentary* rules such as the Standing Orders of the House of Representatives with *statutory* rules such as the NZBORA, the overlooked implications of the mixed-member proportional (MMP) electoral system for the effectiveness of NZBORA, as well as the presence of alternative policy discourses within the parliamentary setting, such as penal populism.[23]

---

[21] Alison L. Young has considered these questions in the context of the United Kingdom's Human Rights Act 1998 – see Alison's chapter in this volume, and also Alison L. Young, *Democratic Dialogue and the Constitution* (Oxford: Oxford University Press, 2017).

[22] Hiebert and Kelly, *Parliamentary Bills of Rights*, pp. 29–30.

[23] Nicola Lacey, 'The Prisoners' Dilemma and Political Systems: The Impact of Proportional Representation on Criminal Justice in New Zealand' (2011) 42 *Victoria University of Wellington Law Review* 617–618.

Given that the NZBORA is a parliamentary bill of rights, we suggest that it has been conditioned by the principles and practices of parliamentary democracy that were altered to accommodate the transition to the MMP electoral system in New Zealand. We now turn to a consideration of several of these to demonstrate that the theory of the new model has not produced the intended outcomes.[24]

III   Mixed-Member Proportional, Parliament, and the NZBORA 1990

According to David Erdos, the Labour Party's acceptance of a bill of rights is explained by 'adversarial constitutionalism' during the Muldoon years that served as the political trigger resulting in the adoption of the NZBORA in 1990.[25] In short, the deficiencies of the SMP electoral system within a unicameral Parliament, an extended period in opposition, and a perception that the Muldoon government had failed to respect the limits on its political authority, saw the Labour Party slowly accept a bill of rights as an essential check on unbridled political power and executive dominance. This occurred because Parliament's unwritten system of checks and balances proved unworkable in the face of long term, single-party majority government. This assessment is consistent with the writings of Geoffrey Palmer, who entered Parliament in 1979 with the position that New Zealand's constitution was in crisis during the Muldoon era.[26] Once elected as Deputy Leader of the Labour Party, and then appointed as attorney general in the fourth Labour government, and finally, as prime minister, Palmer advocated a bill of rights as a necessary addition to New Zealand's parliamentary structure to address adversarial constitutionalism resulting from the rise of prime-ministerial-centred government.

Why is this relevant? It suggests that the political motivation to adopt the NZBORA was a response to the failure of parliamentary rules to adequately constrain the power of the cabinet and, by extension, the prime minister. In this respect, the NZBORA was designed in light of the

---

[24] See for instance the discussion in Orzan O. Varol, 'Constitutional Stickiness' (2015–2016) 49 *UC Davis Law Review* 899–961.

[25] David Erdos, 'Aversive Constitutionalism in the Westminster World: The genesis of the New Zealand Bill of Rights Act 1990', (2007) 5 *International Journal of Constitutional Law* 343–69.

[26] Geoffrey Palmer, *New Zealand's Constitution in Crisis: Reforming Our Political System* (Dunedin, NZ: John McIndoe, 1992), p. 59.

failure of existing parliamentary checks and balances that were exacerbated by the deficiencies of the SMP electoral system, which, throughout the Muldoon years, saw the Labour Party win the plurality of the vote, yet occupy the opposition benches.[27] What this suggests, therefore, is that the interplay between the electoral system and Parliament is a critical component in understanding whether the NZBORA can alter parliamentary behaviour.

What are the implications of New Zealand's jettisoning of the SMP system and the adoption of the MMP electoral system in 1996? As Claudia Geiringer has remarked, this is an important inquiry in regard to the NZBORA that has not been fully considered.[28] Anticipating that the adoption of a form of proportional representation may result in government instability, a series of procedural rule changes to the Standing Orders were adopted. In addition, the parties in Parliament adopted cooperative practices to allow for full parliamentary terms of three years. Changes were made to the Cabinet Manual to ensure that a government's legislative agenda could navigate – and be passed – in a multiparty Parliament where no party controlled a majority of the seats.[29]

The most significant effect of the transition from SMP to MMP is the type of government within Parliament: from SMP's single-party *majority* government, to MMP's multiparty *minority* governing coalitions dependent on smaller parties to secure passage of government bills.[30] MMP has seen multiparty minority coalitions secure working majorities through 'supply and confidence' agreements with minor parties. In exchange for supporting key policy initiatives of minor parties and their passage as Acts of Parliament, single-party minority governments or multiparty coalition governments secure majority backing on issues such as the budget (supply) and any matter deemed critical to the survival of the government (confidence). As an illustration, the former National minority government (2008–2017), negotiated formal agreements with the same 3 minor parties over the life of three parliaments – ACT New Zealand, United Future, and the Maori Party – and each Parliament experienced a full three-year mandate.

---

[27] Geoffrey Palmer and Matthew Palmer, *Bridled Power*, 4th edition (Melbourne: Oxford University Press, 2004), p. 12.

[28] Claudia Geiringer, 'Inaugural Lecture: Mr. Bulwark and the Protection of Human Rights', (2014) 45 *Victoria University of Wellington Law Review* 385.

[29] Jonathon Boston, *Governing under Proportional Representation: Lessons from Europe* (Wellington: Institute of Policy Studies, 1998), pp. 94–112.

[30] Hiebert and Kelly, *Parliamentary Bills of Rights*, pp. 84–87.

While 'supply and confidence' agreements are a direct response to
MMP and the need to construct stable governments, these formalized
arrangements have serious implications for parliamentary engagement of
the attorney general's report under section 7 of the NZBORA. For
instance, they are negotiated immediately after an election and before a
new Parliament is called to session. These agreements bind the parties to
policy commitments – and legislation – that must be pursued to ensure
the support of minor parties throughout the life of a parliament. In the
context of the NZBORA, we found that seventy per cent (18/26) of the
government bills passed under MMP, where the attorney general reported
to Parliament under section 7 that rights-based incompatibilities existed,
were part of 'supply and confidence' agreements with minor parties.[31] Is it
reasonable to expect rights-based dialogue to follow a section 7 report, if,
for instance, the bill in question is tied to a 'supply and confidence'
agreement that is vital for the stability of a multiparty governing coalition?

The answer is further complicated by a significant change to the
Standing Orders adopted in the context of MMP and government stability – the party vote. Under Standing Orders 138 and 140, the designate of
each political party casts a single vote for the entire caucus, unless the
matter has been designated as a conscience vote.[32] This procedure is
particular relevant in regard to bills introduced as part of a 'supply and
confidence' agreement, once a corresponding change to the Cabinet
Manual is factored in. Like the Standing Orders, the New Zealand
Cabinet Manual was revamped in light of MMP to ensure that, once a
government-sponsored bill is introduced into a multiparty setting, it can
progress to Royal Assent. The significance of 'supply and confidence'
agreements is recognized in the Cabinet Manual, as legislation must be
referred to the relevant party caucuses for approval before it is introduced
into Parliament.[33] In the context of section 7 of the NZBORA, the
attorney general reports to parliament *after* two MMP-inspired changes –
support agreements and the party vote – guarantee that a majority of
parliamentarians support the bill in question regardless of a finding of
incompatibility by the attorney general.

[31] Hiebert and Kelly, *Parliamentary Bills of Rights*, pp. 100–109.
[32] Parliament of New Zealand 2011, Standing Orders of the House of Representatives, SO
138 and SO 140.
[33] Cabinet Office (New Zealand) 2008, Department of the Prime Minister and Cabinet,
Cabinet Manual 2008 (Wellington, New Zealand). In particular, see 7.53–7.56 (Reference
to caucus[es]) and 7.57–7.59 (Consultation with non-government parliamentary parties).

Thus, the attorney general as the initiator of rights-based dialogue is placed at a serious disadvantage, given that the bill already has the votes to pass, regardless of the issues raised in a section 7 report. The implications of these MMP-inspired changes are so significant that Jeremy Waldron has concluded that dialogue and deliberation have been compromised within New Zealand's House of Representatives.[34] These measures, which contribute to a 'dialogic deficit', have been criticized by Claire Charters, who concludes that 'MMP has not increased the airing of disagreement in Parliament. The executive does not secure other parties' support for its position within the legislature by utilizing a transparent and inclusive process. Instead, it makes deals away from public input and scrutiny.'[35]

There is a final aspect of the Standing Orders that has direct implications for parliamentary engagement of the attorney general's report at the select committee stage: Standing Order 283, which allows a member introducing a bill to decide which select committee will review the bill before reporting back to the House of Representatives. While it is unclear whether this change occurred in response to MMP, the implications for the NZBORA and rights-based dialogue are profound. Under the Standing Orders, bills are normally sent to the select committee that has the 'subject matter' responsibility. For instance, the Justice and Electoral Select Committee receives bills introduced by the Minister of Justice or the attorney general, as this committee has responsibility for sentencing, justice matters, and criminal law. Further, each select committee is assigned a department to serve as committee advisor, and in this respect, the Justice and Electoral Select Committee is supported by the Ministry of Justice and the Crown Law Office – which are, incidentally, the two government departments that are the lead agencies on the NZBORA and rights-based dialogue within the bureaucracy. As most section 7 reports involve amendments to criminal policy, they are the 'subject-matter' responsibility of the Justice and Electoral Law Select Committee.

In our study, we found that Standing Order 283 has been used, at times, to direct bills to select committees that did not have subject-matter responsibility for them. This will be illustrated later in the chapter, when

---

[34] Jeremy Waldron, *Parliamentary Recklessness: Why We Need to Legislate More Carefully* (Maxim Institute John Graham Lecture, 2008), pp. 24–25.

[35] Claire Charters, 'Responding to Waldron's Defence of Legislatures: Why New Zealand's Parliament Does Not Protect Rights in Hard Cases', (2006) 5 *New Zealand Law Review* 636.

the Sentencing and Parole Reform Act 2010 is discussed. This bill should have been sent to the Justice and Electoral Select Committee but, instead, was sent to the Law and Order Select Committee. Our analysis of this phenomenon is consistent with Claire Charters's finding in the context of the Foreshore and Seabed Act: Standing Order 283 is used in a strategic way to direct bills to select committees where the multiparty government, in collaboration with its 'confidence and supply' partners, control a majority of the seats on the select committee.[36] Indeed, we noted a pattern in the committee membership of the key select committees that received the lion's share of government bills with section 7 reports. Even though Standing Order 103 specifies that committee membership should reflect party standings in Parliament, and thus the membership of select committees should be composed of a majority of the opposition parties, over the course of successive Parliaments under MMP, these key committees have become increasingly composed of a majority of government members, despite there never being a majority government under MMP.[37] This unexplained development under MMP is significant, as the control of key select committees by the government, in combination with the party vote introduced as part of a 'confidence and supply' agreement with a minor party, significantly reduced the possibility of rights-based dialogue, and thus, the very justification of the new Commonwealth model.

The previous discussion is an institutional account of the limited nature of parliamentary engagement of the attorney general's section 7 report, as it focused on the interplay between MMP-inspired rule changes, as well as the significance of 'supply and confidence' agreements reached outside the parliamentary arena. The second explanation for the underdevelopment of intra-parliamentary dialogue centres on the failure of rights-based discourse to become a significant policy narrative when parliamentarians discuss legislation reported on by the attorney general. Indeed, proponents of the dialogue model assume that a rights-based approach to legislation will materialize simply because the attorney general has reported rights-based incompatibilities to Parliament. This assumption overlooks the policy context in which most section 7 reports have been issued – the criminal policy context. Amendments to statutes such as the Misuse of Drugs Act,[38] the Sentencing and Parole Reform

---

[36] Ibid. 640; Hiebert and Kelly, *Parliamentary Bills of Rights*, pp. 90–92.
[37] Hiebert and Kelly, *Parliamentary Bills of Rights*, pp. 118–123.
[38] Ibid. pp. 113–159.

Act,[39] the disenfranchisement of prisoners,[40] and the mandatory collection of DNA samples from the accused,[41] saw the attorney general conclude that the collective efforts of successive New Zealand governments pursuing extreme 'law and order' were excessive and incompatible with the NZBORA.

Why did these section 7 reports fail to generate parliamentary engagement with the attorney general's attempts to facilitate a rights-based discourse by reporting to the House of Representatives? Our explanation suggested that the policy context of many section 7 reports (criminal policy), the affected constituency (individuals convicted or accused of a crime), as well as penal populism as the dominant criminal policy discourse in New Zealand, account for the limited emergence of a bill of rights inspired dialogue. Penal populism emerged as the dominant criminal justice discourse in 1999 after a citizen-initiated referendum saw ninety-two per cent support for a tougher approach to crime and the accused.[42] As a policy framework, penal populism advances a 'tough on crime' narrative that includes a retributive approach to criminal justice policy, marginalizes elements of the bureaucracy that traditionally develop criminal justice policy such as the Ministry of Justice in New Zealand, and relies on populist actors such as single-issue interest groups for policy inspiration and validation.[43]

Nicola Lacey identifies New Zealand as an outlier amongst proportional representation systems in regard to criminal policy, as those systems tend to depoliticize this issue through a reliance on the professional bureaucracy, as well as demonstrating 'moderate penal politics'.[44] Lacey argues that New Zealand is an outlier because smaller parties that have emerged under MMP are not organized around the traditional cleavage of proportional representation systems, which is the socioeconomic divide along a left–right axis. Instead, smaller parties that have emerged under MMP in New Zealand have largely been concerned with

---

[39] Ibid. pp. 216–229.

[40] Ibid. pp. 159–173.

[41] Ibid. pp. 208–216.

[42] The following question was posed during the 1999 Citizen Initiated Referendum: 'Should there be a reform of our justice system placing greater emphasis on the needs of victims, providing restitution and compensation for them and imposing minimum sentences and hard labour for all serious violent offences?'

[43] John Pratt, *Penal Populism* (London: Routledge, 2007), pp. 12–20.

[44] Nicola Lacey, 'Political Systems and Criminal Justice: The Prisoners' Dilemma After the Coalition' (2012) 65 *Current Legal Problems* 217.

specific issues such as crime and the need for a tougher approach to 'law and order'.[45] These smaller 'law and order' parties, such as ACT New Zealand, tend to be heavily influenced by populist pressure groups such as the Sensible Sentencing Trust,[46] and are attractive coalition partners for major parties that need to construct multiparty governing arrangements 'because their specific focus means that a bargain can be struck with them without the larger party having to negotiate across a range of issues'.[47] ACT New Zealand is the natural partner of the National Party when in office.

One of the surprising aspect of New Zealand politics is that a consensus exists on criminal justice policy as all parties, with the exception of the Green party, adopt penal populism as the policy discourse to understand criminal justice amendment, and not, as hoped for by the dialogue model, a rights-based discourse initiated by the attorney general under section 7 of the NZBORA. To demonstrate the institutional barriers to rights-based dialogue in New Zealand, as well as the dominance of penal populism within criminal justice policy, the chapter now considers the Sentencing and Parole Reform Act 2010 that was passed by the National party as a minority government at the urging of ACT New Zealand.

IV   Sentencing and Parole Reform Act 2010

The 2008 election saw the National party win a plurality of seats (58/122), and for the first time under MMP, formed a single-party minority government. To ensure a stable Parliament, the National party negotiated 'confidence and supply' agreements with three parties: ACT New Zealand (five seats), United Future (one seat) and the Maori party (five seats). This provided the minority National government with a working majority, as it now had the guaranteed support of sixty-nine party votes on matters of confidence and supply. The agreement with ACT New Zealand is particularly significant, as it committed both parties to pursing a 'tough on crime' legislative agenda. This agreement committed the National Party to 'introduce legislation to remove the right of the worst repeat violent offenders to be released on parole', and to 'introduce

---

[45] Ibid. 219.

[46] Nicola Lacey, 'The Prisoners' Dilemma and Political Systems: The Impact of Proportional Representation on Criminal Justice in New Zealand' (2011) 42 *Victoria University of Wellington Law Review* 633–634.

[47] Lacey, 'Political Systems and Criminal Justice', 219.

legislation to clamp down on criminal gangs and their drug trade'.[48] Further, it obligated National to 'toughen the bail laws to make it harder for criminals awaiting trial to get bail' and to 'introduce legislation to require DNA testing for every person arrested for an imprisonable offence'. In response to these measures and others introduced as part of National's agreements with ACT after the 2008, 2011, and 2014 elections, the attorney general issued a total of nine section 7 reports.[49] None of these bills were amended to address compatibility issues flagged by the attorney general, and none of the parliamentary debates saw engagement with the section 7 report issued by the attorney general.[50]

The Sentencing and Parole Reform Bill is particularly illustrative of the challenges that MMP-inspired changes have created for rights-based dialogue emerging in New Zealand, once the attorney general submits a section 7 report to Parliament. This bill included a prominent aspect of ACT party policy – the three-strikes sentencing policy modelled after a similar provision in California – that targeted repeat serious offenders by significantly increasing the penal sanction with each new offence as a way to improve confidence in the justice system.[51] The Sentencing Parole Reform Bill provided, in the case of forty offences, for sentences ranging from a minimum of twenty-five years in prison without parole, to life in prison.[52]

The Sentencing and Parole Reform Bill 2009 was accompanied by a section 7 report issued by the attorney general, which was largely ignored by MPs from the governing New Zealand National and their 'confidence and supply' partner ACT New Zealand. The bill was defended by the Corrections Minister within the paradigm of penal populism, and its content was strongly influenced by nontraditional policy advocates such as the Sensible Sentencing Trust. In contrast, the influence of traditional

---

[48] Confidence and Supply Agreement 2008, *Confidence and Supply Agreement*. National and ACT New Zealand (16 November 2008).

[49] The attorney general issued section 7 reports in relation to the following National-ACT 'law and order' commitments: Criminal Investigations (Bodily Samples) Amendment Bill 2009; Sentencing and Parole Reform Bill 2009; Parole (Extended Supervision Orders) Amendment Bill 2009; Misuse of Drugs Amendment Bill 2010; Criminal Procedure (Reform and Modernization) Bill 2010; New Zealand Bill of Rights Section 24(e) Amendment Bill 2010; Electoral (Disqualification of Convicted Persons) Amendment Bill 2010; Alcohol Reform Bill 2010; Land Transport (Admissibility of Evidential Breath Test) Amendment Bill 2012.

[50] Hiebert and Kelly, *Parliamentary Bills of Rights*, chs. 3–5.

[51] Lacey, 'Political Systems and Criminal Justice' 225.

[52] Warren Brookbanks, 'Punishing Recidivist Offenders in New Zealand Using Three Strikes Legislation: Sound Policy or Penal Excess?' (2012) 9 *US-China Law Review* 3–6.

policy actors such the New Zealand Law Society and the New Zealand Human Rights Commission was not evident, despite pointed criticism that the bill was incompatible with the NZBORA. In this respect, the Sentencing and Parole Reform Bill 2009 is an excellent example of the policy context labeled as penal populism by scholars such as Pratt.[53]

Before considering the Sentencing and Parole Reform Bill 2009, it is important to understand key developments that preceding its introduction into Parliament, as well as critical developments that occurred as it progressed to royal assent. The bill was originally assigned to the Minister of Justice, Simon Power, who presided over the cabinet deliberations in December 2008 that approved the introduction of the bill into Parliament on 18 February 2009. As the bill was the responsibility of the Minister of Justice, it was developed by the Ministry of Justice, which acted as the lead departmental advisor from December 2008 until January 2010. At a cabinet meeting in February 2009 that agreed to introduce the bill into Parliament, the Minister of Justice recommended that the bill be referred the Justice and Electoral Committee for consideration.[54] However, at first reading the Minister of Justice instead referred the bill to the Law and Order Committee.[55] The Minister of Justice remained responsible for the bill and the Ministry of Justice served as the lead departmental agency advising the Law and Order Committee until 19 January 2010, at which point responsibility was transferred to the Minister of Police and Minister of Corrections, Judith Collins.

In a letter to the Chair of the Law and Order Committee, Judith Collins informed the committee that Cabinet decided on 17 December 2009 to transfer the bill from the Minister of Justice to the Corrections Minister.[56] In an unusual move, the Corrections Minister requested that the New Zealand Police 'be the lead advisers on this Bill during the remainder of [the Committee's] consideration of it, and that the Department of Corrections is also invited to be an adviser to the Committee'.[57] Both requests were complied with, and the Ministry of Justice ceased to have any responsibility for the bill it had developed on behalf of the

---

[53] John Pratt, 'When Penal Populism Stops: Legitimacy, Scandal and the Power to Punish in New Zealand' (2008) *The Australian and New Zealand Journal of Criminology* 370–371.

[54] Office of the Minister of Justice (New Zealand) 2009. Cabinet. Sentencing and Parole Reform Bill: Final Approval for Introduction (February 12), 6.

[55] Hon. S. Power – National Party (18 February 2009) 652 NZPD 1420.

[56] Office of Hon. Judith Collins 2010. Letter to Sandra Goudie MP, Chair, Law and Order Committee (19 January), 1.

[57] Ibid. 1–2.

Minister of Justice. In this respect, the attorney general's report lost traction once responsibility shifted from the Ministry of Justice to the Department of Corrections.

The Sentencing and Parole Reform Bill demonstrates the challenges that MMP poses for the NZBORA and intra-parliamentary dialogue. Based on the theory of the dialogue model, the attorney general's report should have facilitated parliamentary engagement of the draft bill, resulting in either an informed debate that passed the bill as is, or with amendments to address the attorney general's report to Parliament. This is not what happened when the Sentencing and Parole Reform Bill was submitted to Parliament, nor with any bills that we analyzed in *Parliamentary Bills of Rights*.

What lessons can we draw to explain the limited engagement of the attorney general's section 7 report, as well as the inability of the attorney general to convince the Cabinet to amend problematic bills such as the Sentencing and Parole Reform Bill? The principal lesson involves how the MMP-inspired rule changes designed to ensure the stability of multiparty governing coalitions have proven counterproductive to rights-based parliamentary dialogue. The fact that these bills are tied to agreements with minor parties, as the Sentencing and Parole Reform Bill was, make it rather difficult, if not virtually impossible, for any changes to be made. In effect, the MMP-inspired rule changes ensure agreement and passage before the attorney general reports to Parliament under section 7 of the NZBORA. This parliamentary reality is even more problematic for intra-parliamentary dialogue when the party vote is considered, as government sponsored bills have secured multiparty support *before* the attorney general reports, and the party vote ensures that the bill will pass regardless of the section 7 report issued to Parliament. As we discuss later in the chapter, the inability of the attorney general to influence Parliament, despite a strong rebuke of the Sentencing and Parole Reform Bill in his section 7 report, demonstrates that the theory of the dialogue model does not match the reality of this parliamentary bill of rights.

V   NZBORA Scrutiny and Cabinet Deliberations

The documentation presented to Cabinet by the Minister of Justice demonstrates that the Ministry of Justice had serious reservations about the bill and its compatibility with the NZBORA. For instance, the discussion paper written by the Minister of Justice (5 December 2008) is heavily redacted under the 'Human rights implications' section, but does indicate that the Ministry of Foreign Affairs and Trade (MFAT) considered the bill incompatible with New Zealand's international human rights obligations.[58] At a subsequent meeting, the Minister of Justice reiterated that the bill remained incompatible with the NZBORA and 'directed that further consideration be given to options for addressing New Zealand Bill of Rights Act concerns about the proposals for sentences of life without parole for the worst repeat offenders and those convicted of the worst murders'.[59] The 'three-strikes' sentencing approach was added to the Sentencing and Parole Reform Bill at the Cabinet Domestic Policy Committee meeting (5 February 2009). Opposition to the bill was initially led by the Ministry of Justice, and now joined by the Ministry of Maori Development, as well as the New Zealand Treasury.[60] The document presented to Cabinet seeking final approval to submit the bill to Parliament concluded 'The Bill does not comply with BORA or relevant international obligations'.[61]

As well as disregarding the advice presented by the Minster of Justice, Cabinet recommended that the bill be referred to the Law and Order Committee, despite the subject matter of the bill falling under the mandate of the Justice and Electoral Committee. The section 7 report by the attorney general echoed the assessment provided by the Ministry of Justice, as Christopher Finlayson concluded that the penalty for a third-strike offence 'may raise an inconsistency with the right against disproportionately severe treatment affirmed by section 9 of the Bill of Rights Act'.[62] The attorney general determined that the three-strikes sentencing regime, particularly the third offence sentencing approach, 'may result in gross disproportionality in sentencing',[63] as '[a]bsent manifest injustices, the sentencing court is obliged to impose a sentence on a qualifying offender that may be significantly more severe than that imposed on a more culpable, but non-qualifying, offender'.[64]

---

[58] Office of the Minister of Justice (New Zealand) 2008. Cabinet Business Committee. No parole for worst repeat offenders and worst murder cases (5 December 2008), 9–10.

[59] Office of the Minister of Justice (New Zealand) 2009. Cabinet. Final Approval for Introduction of Sentencing and Parole Reform Bill (29 January 2009), 1.

[60] Office of the Minister of Justice (New Zealand) 2009. Cabinet Domestic Policy Committee. Worst repeat violent offender policy (5 February 2009).

[61] Office of the Minister of Justice (New Zealand) 2009. Cabinet. Sentencing and Parole Reform Bill: Final Approval for Introduction (12 February 2009), 4.

[62] Report of the Attorney General under the New Zealand Bill of Rights Act 1990 on the Sentencing and Parole Reform bill, para. 4.

[63] Report of the Attorney General, para. 16.

[64] Report of the Attorney General, para. 13.3.

VI   The Law and Order Select Committee

The Sentencing and Parole Reform Bill 2009 was sent to the Law and Order Select Committee, after a first reading party vote (64 to 58). In its briefing to the select committee, the Ministry of Justice reiterated the attorney general's concerns that the bill did not comply with New Zealand's human rights obligations, and strongly cautioned against proceeding with the bill.[65] This report represents the last time the Ministry of Justice formally advised the Law and Order Committee, as the responsibility for the bill was transferred to the Minister of Police and Corrections Minister by the Cabinet in December 2009, at the request of the Corrections Minister.

In March 2010, the Law and Order Committee released its report to Parliament on the Sentencing and Parole Reform Bill, which included a minority report by New Zealand Labour. As noted in the minority report, New Zealand National and ACT New Zealand passed resolutions to prevent the Ministry of Justice from continuing as advisors to the Law and Order Committee. Labour's minority report noted that it opposed all of these changes, and in particular, the committee's decision to appoint new departmental advisors at the request of the Corrections Minister:

> New Zealand Police advisors told the committee that this is only the second time Police have been the lead agency on a sentencing bill – the other occasion being the Vehicle Confiscation and Seizure Bill – and further admitted to the committee that the Police would not have the expertise to lead a review of this legislation, should a review by clause be undertaken. They said that the Ministry of Justice would be the more appropriate agency to lead a review. If the Police do not have the expertise to lead a review of the legislation, how can they have the expertise to lead the formation and implementation of the legislation?[66]

For the Labour Party, this was counterproductive as the Ministry of Justice developed the bill and possessed the institutional capacity to properly advise the committee, whereas New Zealand Police admitted that they had rarely served as the principal advisor on a bill, and further, that this agency could not properly advise the committee on sentencing policy.

Given that New Zealand Police admitted a limited capacity to serve as the lead advisor to the Law and Order Committee, why would New

---

[65] Ministry of Justice (New Zealand) 2009. Law and Order Committee. Sentencing and Parole Reform Bill – Initial Briefing (29 April 2009), para. 60.

[66] Parliament of New Zealand 2010. Sentencing and Parole Reform Bill. As reported by the Law and Order Committee (26 March 2010), 12.

Zealand National and ACT New Zealand use its voting power to weaken the effectiveness of this select committee? The answer is clearly revealed during the second reading debate led by the Corrections Minister, as the importance of penal populism is evident.[67] In her closing remarks at second reading, Judith Collins noted that '[t]his bill is tangible evidence that the Government is delivering on its election promise to toughen up on criminals'.[68] However, to do so, New Zealand National had to overcome significant bureaucratic resistance to the Sentencing and Parole Reform Bill, which proved more significant than parliamentary attempts by the opposition parties to block the passage of the bill. Although opposition members made some reference to the attorney general's section 7 report at the Committee of the Whole House, as well as at third reading, the Labour Party focused its criticism on the resolutions passed at the Law and Order Committee that barred the Ministry of Justice from advising the committee. In effect, the substantive concerns in the section 7 report were not raised by opposition members, and did not appear to influence the select committee's considerate of the bill.[69]

The Sentencing and Parole Reform Bill 2009 passed third reading on a party vote of sixty-three to fifty-eight. It passed without amendments to address the NZBORA concerns raised by the Ministry of Justice and the attorney general, as well as the concerns raised by MFAT that it breached New Zealand's international human rights obligations. This bill passed without amendment despite the concerns raised by the Ministry of Maori Development that it would unfairly target Maori, and thus, was discriminatory and would breach the NZBORA. The design and implementation of the Sentencing and Parole Reform Bill 2009 demonstrate the influence of penal populism, and the importance of 'confidence and supply' agreements under MMP that allowed New Zealand National to control the rules and, thereby, marginalize parliamentary and bureaucratic oversight of legislation as it relates to the NZBORA.

VII   The United Kingdom's Human Rights Act 1998

The Human Rights Act came into force in 2000 and incorporates the European Convention of Human Rights into domestic law. A broad intent was to increase the salience of rights in legislative decision-making

---

[67] Hon. Judith Collins – National Party (4 May 2010) 662 NZPD 10674.
[68] Ibid. 10675.
[69] Hiebert and Kelly, *Parliamentary Bills of Rights*, p. 228.

and for how public authorities interpret their powers, while also formally preserving the principle of parliamentary supremacy.

The HRA authorizes two forms of judicial remedies. The first, in section 3, authorizes courts to interpret legislation 'as far as possible' in a manner that ensures conformity with Convention rights. This power enables courts to alter the scope or effects of legislation to impose a rights-compliant interpretation. The second form of remedy in section 4 allows a superior court to issue a 'declaration of incompatibility' where a rights-compliant interpretation is not possible. Some might dispute the characterization of this as a remedy because the immediate effect of a section 4 ruling is not apparent, as it does not alter the legal status of legislation. However, the treaty character upon which the HRA is based provides an important incentive for taking judicial rulings seriously, both when engaging in pre-legislative scrutiny and when determining how to respond to a judicial declaration of incompatibility. In recognition of this latter point, the HRA has a fast-track mechanism for passing remedial measures in response to a negative judicial ruling. A study by Jeff King of Parliament's record on remedial action indicates that although the time-line for legislative responses to a negative judicial ruling is generally longer than in other models where courts have authority to establish a time frame for legislative responses, there is a political convention emerging that parliament responds to these rulings.[70]

Regardless of which form a judicial remedy takes, the HRA formally retains the principle of parliamentary supremacy, ensuring that Parliament has final legal authority over the validity of legislation. Thus, the United Kingdom embraces a more juridical orientation of normative principles than in the past, while also preserving the essence of political constitutionalism, in that Parliament retains the final authority for the legality of legislation.[71]

---

[70] Jeff King, 'Parliament's Role Following Declarations of Incompatibility under the Human Rights Act' in Murray Hunt, Hayley J. Hooper, and Paul Yowell (eds.), *Parliament and Human Rights. Redressing the Democratic Deficit* (Oxford: Hart Publishing, 2015), pp. 165–168.

[71] This interpretation is not intended to suggest that normative values were absent from the UK constitution prior to the adoption of the HRA, or even that these principles did not have a legal dimension. However, the HRA has placed a much stronger emphasis on the juridical dimension of constitutional principles. For an insightful discussion of the evolution of these principles, see Colm O'Cinneide, 'The Human Rights Act and the Slow Transformation of the UK's "Political Constitution"', Institute for Human Rights Working Paper Series, working paper no. 01.

Despite the retention of parliamentary supremacy, proponents of the HRA emphasized that the combined effects of judicial review and a statutory reporting obligation for compatibility would change the culture for governing. Rights would be protected not simply through judicial review but also by encouraging consistency with rights in the various stages through which legislative initiatives are transformed and approved as bills, as well as in their evaluation by Parliament. The institutional incentive for so doing was the inclusion of section 19 in the HRA, requiring that the sponsoring minister of a bill declare that a bill is compatible with protected rights or that, alternatively, he or she is unable to make a positive statement of compatibility. As a former Lord Chancellor said of the HRA, 'we didn't bring in the Human Rights Act to get a litigation culture. We brought it in to get a human rights culture'.[72]

The United Kingdom was well situated to reflect on constitutional innovations elsewhere and to adapt and alter these where considered appropriate. For example, Canada's inclusion of the notwithstanding clause in section 33 of the Canadian Charter of Rights and Freedoms as a way to mitigate the political effects of strong judicial remedial powers was considered insufficient for preserving parliamentary supremacy, principally because of political reluctance to invoke this power, whereas New Zealand's extremely constrained form of judicial review was considered too weak a check on parliamentary judgment. The United Kingdom also adapted the reporting mechanism on legislative consistency with rights, by requiring a compatibility statement for all bills (either a positive affirmation of compatibility or an indication of the inability to report compatibility), decentralizing this responsibility and requiring a statement by any minister introducing a bill, adapting this reporting obligation to the bicameral nature of the UK Parliament, and creating a specialized joint parliamentary committee to scrutinize bills that implicate rights (the JCHR).[73]

VIII   Assessing Whether and How Considerations for Compatibility with Rights Influences Legislation

Our research on the United Kingdom addressed the following two questions. First, what impact is the statutory reporting obligation on

---

[72] Lord Falconer, Speech to the Law Society and Human Rights Lawyers' Association, London, 17 February 2004.

[73] Hiebert and Kelly, *Parliamentary Bills of Rights*, pp. 244–261.

compatibility having on legislative assessments of bills prior to their introduction in Parliament? Second, how is Parliament responding to this new focus on whether bills are compatible with rights? As we argue, to understand whether and how a concern for rights affects legislative decisions it is essential not only to understand the institutional dimension – how constitutional or statutory provisions conceive of judicial interpretive and remedial powers – but also to explore the political dimension – the relationship between processes and incentives for internalizing rights-based norms that reinforce or constrain their use as critical standards when designing, evaluating and approving legislation.

Research on the United Kingdom involved interviewing government lawyers and public officials to learn whether and how the introduction of the HRA and this new reporting obligation on compatibility have altered legislative processes, which criteria are used for evaluating compatibility, how receptive political ministers are to advice that legislative initiatives implicate rights in an adverse manner, and how influential the JCHR is in putting pressure on departments to revise bills or how ministers report on compatibility.[74]

Determinations of compatibility are based on risk-based assessments of the likelihood that legislation will be declared incompatible with Convention rights if subject to litigation. The general criterion used is whether a legislative bill has a greater than fifty per cent chance of being declared incompatible or inconsistent with Convention rights by UK and European courts. Legal advisors inform ministers of the difficulty of reporting that a bill is compatible with rights when there is a stronger than fifty per cent chance that the government would lose if legislation is litigated.[75] Nevertheless, we were advised that ministers and cabinet have on occasion approved a bill where the risk level exceeds this standard.[76]

This willingness to report that a bill is compatible, even when advisors alert ministers of a high level of risk associated with the bill, is consistent with changes to cabinet guidelines since the HRA was adopted. Initially, cabinet guidelines instructed ministers that they were to give primacy to legal advice in their determination of whether a positive or negative compatibility report was appropriate. Ministers were advised they were only to issue an affirmative report of compatibility where this was

---

[74] For a fuller list of questions asked, see Hiebert and Kelly, *Parliamentary Bills of Rights*, pp. 20–23. From here on, 'Interviews'.
[75] Ibid.
[76] Ibid.

supported by 'the balance of [legal] arguments'. They were also instructed that even if they consider a policy objective to be compatible with Convention rights, their reasons are not a 'sufficient basis' to claim compatibility if their legal advisors do not believe that these arguments would 'ultimately succeed before the courts'. However, legal advisors' views on compatibility no longer appear to be as important in these determinations. This change occurred between 2006 and 2007. More recent cabinet guidelines authorize a minister to make a statement reflecting whether in his or her personal view, the bill's provisions are compatible with Convention rights.[77]

IX   Legislative Bills and Assessments of Compatibility

To date, all but two bills introduced have had a positive claim of compatibility, and two more bills have had a negative report (an inability to claim compatibility) after amendments were introduced in the House of Lords.[78] However, the JCHR often contests affirmative claims of compatibility. The JCHR is highly respected for its robust and critical review of legislation in terms of possible rights infringements. The committee regularly identifies contentious claims and assumptions that are relevant for compatibility determinations, engages in correspondence with relevant departments and ministers seeking clarification and explanations, and makes recommendations for departments, ministers and parliamentarians to consider with respect to making the legislative initiative more compliant with rights.

An obvious question is what accounts for the frequency with which the JCHR contests ministerial claims of compatibility? This discrepancy in judgment about compatibility suggests either that government lawyers and/or ministers utilize a different understanding of how compatibility should be interpreted than the JCHR, or they differ in how robustly they conduct their compatibility assessments.

In interviews, public officials were asked explicitly if they incur pressure to alter their advice on compatibility to enable a minister to pursue a high-risk legislative objective without being compelled to acknowledge an inability to claim compatibility. Those we interviewed

---

[77] Cabinet Office. *Guide to Making Legislation*, July 2017, p. 113. www.gov.uk/government/uploads/system/uploads/attachment_data/file/645652/Guide_to_Making_Legislation_Jul_2017.pdf.

[78] Hiebert and Kelly, pp. 278–279.

denied unequivocally this was the case, and insisted that even if the situation were to arise, they would put their professional reputations ahead of good working relationship with senior department officials and ultimately ministers.[79]

We have no reason to doubt the sincerity of public officials' assurances of professionalism in how they evaluate if a proposed bill is compatible with rights. Moreover, it is important to recognize that an essential part of determining whether a legislative initiative is compatible with Convention rights will turn on proportionality assessments that require evaluating the relationship between the importance of the objective and the severity of the impact it might have for rights. This focus inevitably requires policy and public officials to contemplate alternative legislative scenarios, and assess their likely success and consequences for rights. Our point in speaking to the uncertainty and subjective elements of a proportionality assessment is to underscore the strong possibility of contestation around the issue of whether legislation satisfies proportionality considerations. Thus, the mere fact that differences of opinion occur between ministers and the JCHR on the question of whether a bill should be considered compatible with rights does not in of itself demonstrate that in any one situation, one perspective is obviously correct and the other is not.[80]

Yet even given the strong potential for contestation when identifying appropriate and rights-compliant ways of achieving legislative objectives, we identified several reasons for scepticism that affirmative ministerial reports of compatibility should be taken at face value.

One reason for scepticism about the preponderance of affirmative reports of compatibility is the way bureaucratic compatibility assessments are framed, which discourages a sharper focus on whether the final decisions made are compatible with rights. The reason for this is that for some controversial bills, the advice will be structured in a manner that allows ministers to effectively cherry-pick from different options, in which decisions may be shaped by the desire not to have legislative objectives altered or overly constrained by rights-based principles. This became apparent from interviews when public officials confirmed that the advice they provide on compatibility will sometimes be framed as a thought process about the arguments on either side of the issue, and where legal advisors believe the balance lies.[81]

---

[79] Interviews.
[80] Hiebert and Kelly, *Parliamentary Bills of Rights*, pp. 281–282.
[81] Interviews.

A second, and related reason for scepticism that affirmative reports of compatibility should be taken at face value is reliance on a relatively flexible threshold for determining compatibility for statutory reporting purposes. As mentioned earlier, the criterion for advising a minister when not to affirm a bill's compatibility is if the chances are greater than not that government would lose if litigation occurs. Yet, the autonomy ministers have to make their own judgment about compatibility, even if it differs from that of their legal advisers, suggests the threshold for determining compatibility might actually be broader than suggested. Some of those we interviewed confirm that ministers have chosen the position that is more risky than government lawyers believe is appropriate for a subsequent affirmation of compatibility, and by implication, represents a position that tolerates a higher level of risk of judicial censure than is reflected in the criterion legal advisers use.[82]

Our point in raising this is not to suggest that government should only pursue legislation if it is unequivocally confident that it will survive any litigation challenge. Such a risk averse orientation would lead to unambitious legislation and prevent government and Parliament from contributing to broader societal, political and jurisprudential debates about how rights principles appropriately guide and constrain particular legislative objectives.

The problem is not that political judgment occurs about whether a bill is justified in light of its potentially adverse implications for rights. Indeed, it is difficult to imagine how ministerial or cabinet interpretations of compatibility can escape political judgments of some kind because of the subjective nature of predicting the implications of earlier legal cases for new issues, political and ideological differences between political parties on how protected rights implicate the role of the state, and the subjective dimension of ascertaining whether the relationship between policy objectives and the means chosen to achieve these comply with notions of proportionality. The problem is that affirmative reports of compatibility generally shield the often contested nature of these judgments because they are not accompanied by more substantive explanations of the reasons and assumptions the minister and government have relied upon to conclude that a bill should be interpreted as being compatible with rights, even in circumstances where there is a higher level of risk that courts might disagree with this conclusion.

---

[82] Hiebert and Kelly, *Parliamentary Bills of Rights*, pp. 286–288.

A third reason for scepticism flows from the strong presumptive expectation against introducing legislation that would require a negative report of incompatibility.[83] This reluctance is likely due to apprehension that an inability to report on a bill's compatibility could lead to strong pressure from the JCHR and House of Lords to amend the bill. This apprehension can also be attributed to concerns that if legislation is litigated, it will be more difficult for the government to successfully defend it, having already acknowledged an inability to claim compatibility. This preference for affirmative claims of compatibility almost certainly has an impact on policy officials and legal advisors, because it places more pressure on them to come up with arguments to justify legislative choices that implicate rights in an adverse manner. However, a focus primarily on policy justifications does not necessarily pay sufficient attention to whether the legislative initiative warrants a positive affirmation of compatibility, given the nature of the right at issue or severity of the restriction in question. To the extent that a preoccupation with justifying potentially rights-infringing legislation becomes embedded in bureaucratic practices and assumptions, this detracts from a more critical focus on whether the legislative objective should be revisited and reconceived, and also whether less restrictive or more compliant means should be adopted to pursue the goal.

A fourth reason for scepticism about whether ministerial reports of compatibility should necessarily be taken at face value is that when deciding if a minister can report positively that a bill is compatible with rights, public and political officials have chosen to make a sharp distinction between legislation that authorizes rights infringements, from legislation that permits rights-based infringements if not carefully interpreted by public authorities. Thus, if legislation does not include strong safeguards to help ensure public authorities interpret their powers or authority in a rights-compliant manner, this is not interpreted as requiring the minister to acknowledge an inability to claim compatibility. Yet this can lead to legislation that stands a high likelihood of producing rights-offending actions by public authorities, despite not triggering a negative report of compatibility. The rationale for this distinction is that public authorities have a legal obligation to act in a rights-compliant manner. However, the absence of specific safeguards to help ensure that legislation

---

[83] Interviews.

is interpreted in a rights-compliant manner places a high level of faith in public authorities. It is an approach that the JCHR contests.[84]

X Parliament And Compatibility Assessments

The JCHR provides an extremely valuable resource for Parliament, arising from its willingness to conduct evidence-based hearings when not convinced by unsubstantiated government claims for new coercive power; its tenacious pursuit of explanations and clarifications when a bill's provisions appear inconsistent with rights; the transparent account of the committee's queries and replies; its capacity to function in a principled and nonpartisan manner and to act independently from government influence; its determination to report on bills while debate is still ongoing in at least one house of Parliament; its willingness to follow up on ongoing issues; and the messages it frequently provides reminding Parliament of its obligation to take rights seriously in its legislative capacity. In short, JCHR reports provide Parliament with a strong foundation to engage in reasoned judgment about whether legislation should be passed, amended or defeated in terms of its implications for rights.[85] As Stephen Gardbaum appropriately characterizes the JCHR's contributions, it represents a gold standard for emulation by other jurisdictions.[86]

Yet despite bold promises made about the transformative potential of the HRA, government leaders and ministers have been extremely critical of arguments that they should be constrained by rights-based norms, particularly when they introduce legislation they consider to be essential for public security or some other broadly defined public purpose. It is not simply that government leaders are not anxious to alter bills when serious rights-based concerns are identified (most likely by the JCHR and the House of Lords), it is also that they are willing to exploit two fundamental characteristics of the political system – executive dominance of the House of Commons and reliance on party discipline – to minimize the extent to which legislation will be altered because of parliamentary and extra-parliamentary pressure to consider rights-improving reforms.

---

[84] Hiebert and Kelly, *Parliamentary Bills of Rights*, pp. 284–285.
[85] Ibid. pp. 296–300.
[86] Gardbaum, *The New Commonwealth Model of Constitutionalism*, p. 225.

Two particularly strong examples of Parliament's reluctance to hold government to account for bills that raise serious concerns of compatibility, particularly as raised by the JCHR, occurred in the context of national security measures and the issue of whether to revise the ban on prisoner voting after the European Court of Human Rights had ruled the ban was inconsistent with Convention rights.

Both Labour and the Conservative-led Coalition government demonstrated strong reluctance to allow JCHR concerns of compatibility to constrain their ability to pass national security measures. Governments frequently disregarded concerns raised by the JCHR, House of Lords, and independent overseers who recommend greater emphasis on human rights. Moreover, political debate in the House of Commons rarely addressed concerns of compatibility, despite frequent critical JCHR reports that disagreed with ministerial affirmations of compatibility. For example, in contrast to JCHR warnings of serious rights problems and its urging to assess legislation within a human rights framework, Parliament approved of indefinite detention, control orders, and terrorism prevention investigation (TIPMs)[87] with little acknowledgement of JCHR concerns or arguments that questioned the veracity of ministerial affirmations of compatibility. Although concern for whether these measures were consistent with the HRA had considerably more resonance in the House of Lords, rights-inspired amendments in the Lords were frequently defeated in the House of Commons. Even when amendments were successfully introduced, such as extending the pre-charge detention period and forcing government to seek and attain parliamentary approval for prolonged use of indefinite detention and control orders, these amendments did not substantially constrain the government from retaining intact the essential elements of its legislation agenda, which included, at various stages, indefinite detention, control orders, and long periods of detention without charge. It was these measures that critics and the JCHR identified as posing the most problematic features in terms of consistency with protected rights. Moreover, despite the Lords' insistence that indefinite detention and control orders should be subject to parliamentary approval for renewal, the intent of requiring that government demonstrates why the continued use of these coercive powers was

---

[87] These are measures that imposed a broad range of constraints on individuals' choice of residence and on their freedom of association, restrictions on their use of electronic communication devices, and electronic monitoring of their movements, communications and other activities.

warranted, proved little obstacle as the House of Commons passed these without little regard for the JCHR's warnings that their prolonged use would undermine respect for human rights.[88]

XI Prisoner Voting

The long-standing ban on prisoner voting was successfully challenged when the European Court of Human Rights ruled in 2004 that the ban breached its Article 3 of protocol 1. This outcome was confirmed in 2005 by the Grand Chamber, which characterized the ban as a blunt instrument that falls outside any acceptable margin of appreciation. Both Labour and Coalition governments defended the ban and demonstrated strong reluctance to pass remedial measures.

The JCHR strongly criticized inaction and addressed, in no fewer than eight reports, the government's obligation to pass remedial measures. Even after the JCHR characterized the importance of remedial measures as a matter of urgency, the Conservative government refused to introduce remedial legislation. This inaction is explained by philosophical and political disagreements with the idea that convicted criminals should be allowed to vote, as well as cost–benefit assessments of the political and fiscal consequences that might accrue should Parliament refuse to pass remedial legislation.[89]

To the extent that the House of Commons engaged in arguments about constitutional principles, its deliberation did not address the basic rights issue behind the challenge, preferring instead to focus on the idea of parliamentary sovereignty, and why this principle should prevail over compliance with the Strasbourg Court's order. As Danny Nicol argues, parliamentary backbench debate was 'replete with references to parliamentary sovereignty' in which MPs adopted a 'looser, more political conception' of the concept than usually understood by constitutional scholars, and focused principally on the idea 'that the latest expression of Parliament's will should prevail'.[90] In making these arguments, MPs emphasized the idea of the democratic accountability of the legislature as

---

[88] Hiebert and Kelly, *Parliamentary Bills of Rights*, pp. 304–345.
[89] Ibid., pp. 381–388.
[90] Danny Nicol, 'Legitimacy of the Commons Debate on Prisoner Voting' [2011] *Public Law* 681, 681, 683.

an essential justification for Parliament's will prevailing over that of the European court.[91]

Some might interpret this debate about parliamentary sovereignty as echoing what Jeremy Waldron has referred to a debate involving 'the right of rights'[92]; the democratic participation of citizens, as interpreted via the judgment of their elected representatives. However, this debate failed to confront a serious tension between claims that parliamentary supremacy justifies Parliament's will prevailing on this particular issue and the deliberate exclusion of a specific segment of the adult polity from voting for their elected representatives. Waldron had occasion to alert parliamentarians of this tension in evidence given to the JCHR, when he explicitly addressed the implications of denying prisoners the right to vote as the basis for claims that parliamentary sovereignty justifies Parliament's preference for a ban. Waldron advised the JCHR that he believed disenfranchisement to be 'a serious mistake'.[93]

In summary, notwithstanding the HRA's quasi-constitutional status, our research emphasized the important fact that for all the intended focus on whether legislation is compatible with protected rights, the HRA has not displaced the two central characteristics that shape how the United Kingdom's Westminster parliamentary system operates, which are executive dominance of Parliament and cohesive political parties. The HRA also has not displaced a key focus any government has, which is to protect its legislative agenda from potential obstacles and anticipate and manage challenges that could result in the governing party losing outright or incurring a substantially diminished majority in the next election.

The HRA complicates rather than changes how governments conceive and pursue their legislative priorities. Contrary to political claims that the HRA would facilitate a proactive rights culture, our research supports the conclusion that political behaviour under the HRA is better explained by governments' strategic assessments of how to manage the risks and consequences associated with the HRA, and also by the House of Common's weakness and relative indifference to compatibility-based assessments.

---

[91] Ibid. 685–686.
[92] Waldron borrows the phrase 'right of rights' from a much earlier discussion by William Cobbett, *Advice to Young Men* (London, 1829), as referred to by Jeremy Waldron, *Law and Disagreement* (Oxford: Oxford University Press, 1999), p. 232.
[93] Parliament of the United Kingdom, JCHR, Oral Evidence, 15 March 2011, Q 58.

XII   Conclusion

Notwithstanding our findings in *Parliamentary Bills of Rights*, dialogue will continue to be an attractive theory, as, in theory, it decouples judicial review from judicial supremacy. It is an attractive institutional arrangement for the proponents of statutory bills of rights and their position that, rather than generate a cost for parliamentary democracy, these statutory rights instruments elevate parliamentary debates through a rights-based discourse. Our findings agree with parts of this assumption, as we did not detect a cost for parliamentary democracy once these statutory instruments were introduced. Indeed, critical pieces of legislation continue to be introduced in New Zealand and the United Kingdom, the pace of the legislative process does not appear to be affected by rights-based dialogue, and, at the end of the day, legislation is passed without amendment, despite rights-based incompatibilities identified by a section 7 report in New Zealand, or a report issued by the JCHR in the United Kingdom.

Instead of concluding that the dialogue model has been a 'cost-free' success, we demonstrated that parliamentary debate has not been elevated to a new plane of rights consciousness. This is because parliamentarians respond to a host of pressures, norms, and values, that haven't been jettisoned by statutory bills of rights. These include the importance of disciplined parties within executive-dominated parliamentary settings, the imperatives of government survival in a post-SMP political environment in New Zealand, the career aspirations of backbench government members, and, finally, the arithmetic of parliamentary committees and their continued control by the government benches. And what should be the way forward? Perhaps a little less conversation about the dialogue model, and a little more action on those aspects of parliamentary democracy that have allowed the passage of legislation with reported rights incompatibilities.

10

Dialogue in Canada and the Dangers of Simplified Comparative Law and Populism

KENT ROACH

Introduction

Dialogic understandings of judicial review remain deeply embedded in local political and legal cultures. As Aileen Kavanagh has recently observed, the Canadian debate over dialogue has become 'polarized'.[1] As such, it has replicated some of the initial objections that critics on the right and the left had to increased judicial power under the Charter. The Canadian experience provides warnings that dialogue can fail to achieve its aspirations to move beyond tired debates about judicial review.

The recent history of dialogue in Canada also reveals how executive and legislative replies to judicial decisions can be influenced by populist resistance to both court decisions and the rights of the unpopular. Judges should take care not to allow their independence or their commitment to the rule of law to be eroded by concerns about maintaining institutional comity.

The first part of this chapter will argue that reports about the death of dialogue in Canada have been greatly exaggerated. Dialogue offers a good explanation of the centrality of proportionality analysis under ss. 1 and 7 of the Canadian Charter of Rights and Freedoms and the use of suspended declarations of invalidity. Dialogue is also promoted by the traditional ability of majority Canadian governments to legislate quickly in response to judicial decisions. The legislative replies to recent Charter decisions on labour relations, supervised injection sites, sex work and assisted dying have disappointed those who successfully litigated the cases. Nevertheless, they affirm the reality of dialogue and the importance of electoral politics in Canada.

---

* I thank the editors of this volume for helpful suggestions on an earlier draft of this chapter. Remaining errors are my own.
[1] Aileen Kavanagh, 'The Lure and Limits of Dialogue' (2016) 66 *University of Toronto Law Journal* 83 at 96.

The second part of this chapter will argue that applying dialogic insights to comparative law is a difficult enterprise, and there is a danger in applying abstract models of judicial review across different constitutional systems. Even if one concludes that Canada should be classified in Mark Tushnet's category of strong-form review,[2] this hardly means that judicial review in Canada is similar to American judicial review or does not contain distinct dialogic qualities. Likewise, contrary conclusions that Canada has weak-form judicial review, or it fits Commonwealth or parliamentary models, can obscure important differences between judicial review under Canada's constitutional bill of rights and statutory bills of rights in the United Kingdom, New Zealand, or Australia. There are different dialogic elements in many constitutions. It is a mistake to think there is one universal model of dialogue or any other system that seeks alternatives to judicial and legislative supremacy. The Canadian approach to Charter dialogue has been influenced by Canada's history of majority governments, its strict party discipline, its prior experience under a statutory bill of rights, the drafting of the Charter, and Canada's weak system of pre-enactment rights review. The complexities of comparative law defy binary models of judicial review.

The third part of this chapter will be more normative. I will argue that Jeremy Waldron's defence of majoritarian democracy[3] does not pay adequate attention to the problem of persistent minorities. In an age of penal and anti-migrant populism that is prepared to demonize and scapegoat the unpopular, celebrations of majoritarian democracy are misplaced. They can also facilitate populist attacks on judges as 'elites'. This is a general normative argument about the importance of judicial review. Waldron's approach has influenced many Canadian critics of dialogue, especially those who defend co-ordinate construction that allows the legislature (and sometimes even the executive) to reject the way that the court interprets Charter rights. I will argue that rejections of judicial interpretations of rights should be done with the special legislative signals and sober second thoughts of the use of the s. 33 override. The populist turn in politics suggests that the infrequent Canadian use of the override might change in the future.

The populist challenge to judicial review suggests that the most important criticism of dialogue comes from those commentators who argue that it can undermine the strength and integrity of the judiciary

---

[2] Mark Tushnet, *Weak Courts, Strong Rights* (Princeton: Princeton University Press, 2004).

[3] Jeremy Waldron, *Law and Disagreement* (Oxford: Oxford University Press, 1999).

and its commitment to rights protection. In the last part of this chapter, I will argue that dialogue can be saved from such criticisms, but doing so requires at least three refinements. The first is that there should be no automatic judicial deference to legislative replies. Each legislative reply should be judged on the evidence and arguments provided to justify it. Second, courts should not accept symbolic legislative objectives that are not amenable to evidence-based proportionality analysis. Finally, courts should ensure that litigants receive effective remedies even while they provide legislatures and the executive an opportunity to craft systemic remedies for the future.

I   Dialogue in Canada

The Canadian Debate About Dialogue

Ever since Peter Hogg and Allison Bushell published their seminal 1997 article,[4] the Canadian dialogue about dialogue has been fractious. For example, former Alberta Conservative Minister Ted Morton and former British Columbia NDP Minister Andrew Petter have agreed that dialogue between the courts and legislatures under the Charter is the opposite of what it claims to be: it is a monologue based on judicial supremacy.[5]

The disdain that some commentators have for idea that the Charter allows a dialogue between courts and governments is palpable. Jeremy Waldron has suggested that dialogue proponents want courts to play the role 'of a colonial administrator looking for ways to encourage a group of natives in taking its first faltering steps in the practice of deliberation'.[6] Grant Huscroft asserted that dialogue proponents 'would prefer that important decisions be made by the Supreme Court of Canada rather than Canadian legislatures. They cannot bring themselves to admit this essentially elitist position, however, because democracy has a greater hold

---

[4] Peter W. Hogg and Allison A. Bushell, 'The Charter Dialogue between Courts and Legislatures (Or Perhaps the Charter of Rights Isn't Such a Bad Thing After All)' (1997) 35 *Osgoode Hall Law Journal* 75.

[5] F. L. Morton, 'Dialogue or Monologue?' in Paul Howe and Peter Russell, eds., *Judicial Power and Canadian Democracy* (Montreal: McGill-Queen's University Press, 2001) p. 111; Andrew Petter, *The Politics of the Charter* (Toronto: University of Toronto Press, 2010). Similarly, the late Robert Bork asserted that Charter decisions were 'almost immune to legislative revision . . . even with the Canadian notwithstanding clause'. Robert H. Bork, *Coercing Virtue: The Worldwide Rule of Judges* (Toronto: Vintage Canada, 2002), p. 95.

[6] Jeremy Waldron, 'Some Models of Dialogue between Judges and Legislators' (2004) 23(2) *Supreme Court Law Review* 7 at 28.

on the public imagination than judicial review.[7] Such denials of dialogue are best understood as expressions of objections to constitutional bills of rights enforced by courts, as opposed to engagement with the evidence about judicial review under the Charter.

Widespread refusal to accept that elected governments have much room to respond to Charter decisions has also helped keep alive a heated debate about 'judicial activism' that has influenced judicial appointments. Prime Minister Harper's appointments to the Supreme Court all pledged support to a declaratory theory of law that rejects judicial law-making, while Prime Minister Justin Trudeau's first appointment claimed the opposite.[8] This development is unfortunate, especially if one accepts that Canadian governments can limit or override particular Charter decisions without attempting potentially destabilizing changes to the Court or the Constitution.

Hogg and Bushell's empirical claim that dialogue occurs in the form of legislative replies to about two-thirds of Charter decisions invalidating laws[9] has been rebutted by other scholars claiming that the true figure is closer to one-third or one-fifth.[10] This empirical debate has been driven by a normative debate: those who have found lower rates of dialogue believe that dialogue does not occur unless the legislature disagrees with the court in a manner consistent with the American practice of co-ordinate construction or departmentalism.[11]

---

[7] Grant Huscroft, 'Rationalizing Judicial Power: The Mischief of Dialogue Theory' in James B. Kelly and Christopher P. Manfredi, (eds.) *Contested Constitutionalism: Reflections on the Canadian Charter of Rights and Freedoms* (Vancouver: University of British Columbia Press, 2009), p. 61.

[8] On the Harper appointments, see Kent Roach, *The Supreme Court on Trial: Judicial Activism or Democratic Dialogue*, revised edn. (Toronto: Irwin Law, 2016), pp. 422–426. In contrast, Trudeau's first appointment Malcolm Rowe wrote on his application to serve the Court that 'the Supreme Court judges ordinarily make law, rather than simply applying it'. The Honourable Malcolm Rowe Questionnaire' at www.fja-cmf.gc.ca/scc-csc/2016-MalcolmRowe/nominee-candidat-eng.html.

[9] Peter W. Hogg, Allison A. Bushell Thornton, and Wade K. Wright, 'Charter Dialogue Revisited: Or "Much Ado About Metaphors"' (2007) 45 *Osgoode Hall Law Journal* 1 at 51 (sixty-one per cent reply rate by legislatures to Charter decisions).

[10] Christopher P. Manfredi and James B. Kelly, 'Six Degrees of Dialogue: A Response to Hogg and Bushell' (1999) 37 *Osgoode Hall Law Journal* 513; Emmett Macfarlane, 'Dialogue or Compliance? Measuring Legislatures' Policy Responses to Court Rulings on Rights' (2012) 34 *International Political Science Review* 39.

[11] Another normative debate is whether the existence of dialogue justifies judicial review. For my previous arguments, which acknowledge that dialogue needs to be supplemented by a range of rationales for judicial review, including following the text and purpose of the constitution, protecting minorities, and protecting rights, see Kent Roach, 'Dialogic

Even if one accepts that outright compliance is not dialogue, the critics' approach ignores how legislatures can accept some Charter decisions, but can expand the field of the debate in a way that a court cannot. For example, Emmett MacFarlane classifies Quebec's legislative reply to the controversial *Chaoulli*[12] Medicare decision as compliance because Quebec followed the Court in allowing its residents to purchase private health insurance. Nevertheless, such a classification misses that the Supreme Court suspended its declaration of invalidity for a year and Quebec used this time to expand the debate by improving its mechanisms for managing wait times, thus dampening the demand for private insurance.[13] Even if one thinks that *Chaoulli* is as bad as the US *Lochner* decision constitutionalizing free market economics, Quebec was able to craft a democratic response without attempting to change the Court or the Constitution. The idea that dialogue only occurs when the legislature disagrees with the court also accounts for many of the distortions that Aileen Kavanagh attributes to the state of dialogue scholarship.[14]

Much of the Canadian debate about dialogue has been an unfortunate Round II to Canada's original and sophisticated debate about whether the Charter was a good idea in which both conservative defenders of parliamentary supremacy and socialist sceptics about courts played an important and constructive role.[15] The fact that so much of the dialogue debate has taken on elements of old battles about judicial review may be explained in part by the domination of normative debate in academe. There has been relatively less scholarship examining dialogue from more empirical and legal process approaches that attempt better to understand

Judicial Review and its Critics' (2004) 23(2) *Supreme Court Law Review* 49 at 67–75; Roach, *The Supreme Court on Trial* above n 8, ch. 12.

[12] *Chaoulli v. Quebec (Attorney General)*, 2005 SCC 35. Andrew Petter also ignored this legislative reply when essentially blaming dialogue theory for the *Chaoulli* case. Petter, *The Politics of the Charter* above n 5, p. 180. Elsewhere, however, he recognized that dialogue can mitigate some of the less progressive impacts of judicial review. Ibid., at 141.

[13] *An Act to Amend the Act Respecting Health Services and Social Service and Other Legislative Processes*, SQ 2006, c. 43.

[14] These include false assumptions that legislatures must disagree with courts, an undue focus on legislative overrides, the casting of binding decisions in a negative light, and assuming that courts and legislature have equal and not distinct roles. Kavanagh, 'The Lure and Limits of Dialogue' above n 1 at 111–120.

[15] For an account of that original debate and how those who framed the Charter struggled to reconcile judicial power with democracy, see Roach, *The Supreme Court on Trial* above n 8, ch. 4. On the role played by Saskatchewan socialist Premier Alan Blakeney with respect to the s. 33 override, see Dwight Newman in this volume.

legislative, executive, and social responses to court decisions, and how such responses can frame judicial decisions.

There have been some exceptions. In 2007, Christopher P. Manfredi penned an article in the *Osgoode Hall Law Journal* with the arresting title, 'The Day the Dialogue Died: A Comment on *Sauvé* v. *Canada*'.[16] In 2016, he published another article in the same journal resurrecting dialogue, by documenting how Parliament had aggressively responded to the Court's decisions on prostitution and safe drug sites.[17] Professor Manfredi's follow-up piece is admirable in attention to the evidence and its attempt to refine the dialogue debate by drawing distinctions between governments that enact laws and different ones that defend them. It avoids the surprisingly common but glib argument that dialogue is simply a monologue based on undemocratic judicial supremacy.

Qualitative Examples of Dialogue under the Charter

My preferred approach to understanding dialogue is informed by legal process approaches to scholarship and case studies that allow for a contextual examination of a large range of judicial and political variables.[18] Such a contextual approach avoids the simplistic and often binary categories of quantitative studies, or those based on abstract and dichotomous models.

Labour Relations

The Supreme Court has become much more active in striking down laws that prohibit collective bargaining and strikes, but legislatures have also been quite active in asserting their regulatory role. In 2001, the Court struck down a law enacted by the Ontario government that deprived agricultural workers of collective bargaining. Although the law was rationally connected to the legitimate objective of protecting the family farm, it violated the freedom of association of agriculture workers more than was necessary by preventing all forms unionization. The Court

---

[16] (2007) 45 *Osgoode Hall Law Journal* 105.

[17] Christopher P. Manfredi, 'Conservatives, the Supreme Court and the Constitution: Judicial-Government Relations, 2006–15' (2016) 52 *Osgoode Hall Law Journal* 951.

[18] For similar but more detailed studies see Janet L. Hiebert, *Charter Conflicts: What Is Parliament's Role?* (Montreal: McGill Queens Press, 2002), and Janet L. Hiebert and James B. Kelly, *Parliamentary Bills of Rights: The Experiences of New Zealand and the United Kingdom* (Cambridge: Cambridge University Press, 2015).

suspended its declaration of invalidity for eighteen months, noting that the workers were not entitled to any particular legislative regime and that the legislature would play an important role in formulating a less restrictive regime.[19] A decade later, the Court upheld Ontario's reply legislation establishing a separate labour relations regime for agricultural workers, stressing that the Charter did not require any particular statutory regime.[20]

In a more recent case, the Court struck down a Saskatchewan law that restricted the right of public employees to strike. This decision drew a strong dissent that argued that the Court was constitutionalizing 'a political position' and ignoring the rights of employers and the public.[21] Saskatchewan Premier Brad Wall speculated about using s. 33 if necessary to maintain essential services, something that has been done before in Saskatchewan.[22] Saskatchewan did not, however, use the override. It used the time provided by a suspended declaration of invalidity to consult with 135 public sector employers and unions before enacting the Saskatchewan Employment (Essential Services) Amendment Act, 2015.[23] The new law provided a process for bargaining for an essential services agreement, and created an essential services tribunal to resolve any outstanding issues. The legislation did not reject the premises of the Court's controversial decision, but it reached a creative result that was not open to the Court.

In 2015, the Court decided that legislative prohibitions on collective bargaining by Royal Canadian Mounted Police officers was an unjustified violation of freedom of association.[24] The new Justin Trudeau government responded with a bill that precluded collective bargaining on a wide range of issues including harassment, probation, discharge, transfers and demotions, and law enforcement techniques. The bill was passed by the Liberal majority in the House of Commons, but the Senate exercised its new freedom from party discipline to amend it to remove many of the restrictions on collective bargaining. Many, but not all, of these amendments

---

[19] *Dunmore v. Ontario (Attorney General)*, 2001 SCC 94.

[20] *Ontario (Attorney General) v. Fraser*, 2011 SCC 20.

[21] *Saskatchewan Federation of Labour v. Saskatchewan*, 2015 SCC 4 at para. 125.

[22] 'Brad Wall Open to Using "Notwithstanding Clause" over Labour Ruling' CBC News, 4 February 2015.

[23] SS 2015, c. 31. Saskatchewan, Legislative Assembly, *Hansard*, 19 October 2015, 7359–360 (Don Morgan).

[24] *Mounted Police Association of Ontario v. Canada (Attorney General)*, 2015 SCC 1.

were eventually accepted by the government.[25] This episode demonstrates how the increased independence and power of the Senate will affect the dialogic balance between courts and Parliament. Nevertheless, all of the responses described thus far in this section demonstrate how both the federal and provincial legislatures can enact ordinary legislation to limit union rights as interpreted by the Court under the Charter. Dialogue occurs when, as in these cases, ordinary legislation limits rights as interpreted by the courts and places them in a broader regulatory context.

National Security

Dialogue has played an important role in national security matters. In 2007, the Supreme Court invalidated parts of Canada's security certificate regime of administrative detention on the basis that it disproportionately pursued the government's legitimate objective in secrecy by not allowing any adversarial challenge to the sometimes dodgy intelligence used by the government to designate noncitizens a threat to national security.[26] Parliament responded with new legislation that allowed security-cleared special advocates to see and challenge secret material that otherwise would only be seen by government lawyers and the reviewing judge. The Court upheld the constitutionality of the new regime in 2014, but only after carefully evaluating its operation and holding that the gist of the government's case should be disclosed to the detainees so that they can properly defend themselves and inform the security-cleared advocate of their side of the story.[27] This is another example of dialogue between the Supreme Court and Parliament that allowed the government to maintain its (misguided) policy of using immigration law as antiterrorism law.

In 2010, the Supreme Court reversed a lower court's order that the Government of Canada request Omar Khadr's repatriation as a remedy for violating his rights by interrogating him at Guantanamo Bay while he was still a teenager. In recognition of a dynamic situation and the range

---

[25] *An Act to Amend the Public Service Labour Relations Act, the Public Service Labour Relations and Employment Board Act and other Acts and to provide for certain other measures*, S.C. 2017 c.9.

[26] *Charkaoui v. Canada*, 2007 SCC 9.

[27] *Canada (Minister of Citizenship and Immigration)* v. *Harkat*, 2014 SCC 37. This case also resulted in sub-constitutional dialogue in the sense that Parliament reversed the Court's common law decision that the human sources of Canadian's security intelligence agency should not be protected from identification by a class privilege. *Protection of Canada from Terrorists Act* S.C. 2015 c. 9.

of options open to the Canadian executive in its dealings with the American government, the Court simply issued a declaration that Khadr's Charter rights had been violated.[28] The Harper government's initial response to this judicial decision illustrates some of the vices of departmentalism in an age of populism. The minister of foreign affairs, and perhaps more importantly, the prime minister's press secretary, said that the government would do nothing for the son of an unpopular and self-confessed al Qaeda family. A few weeks later, the government relented – albeit in a minimalist way – by asking that the United States not use the fruits of the Canadian interrogation in Khadr's trial before a military commission at Guantanamo. The executive reply was much less transparent than a legislative one, raising concerns about giving executive replies to Charter decisions as much respect as legislative ones, as some Canadian enthusiasts for departmentalism have advocated.[29] Giving the executive the power to substitute its views for those of the Court would undermine rule of law values and often result, as it did in *Khadr*, in successful litigants receiving ineffective remedies.[30]

Supervised Injection Sites

The executive's somewhat cavalier approach to the Court's *Khadr* declaration may help to explain why the Court issued a less deferential, mandatory order to require a reluctant Minister of Health to issue a ministerial exemption from drug laws to allow a supervised injection site to continue to operate on Vancouver's skid row. The celebrated injection site, Insite, served 'some of the poorest and most vulnerable people in Canada', including 4,600 intravenous drug users.[31] Its clients had injected drugs on average for fifteen years, eighty per cent had been incarcerated, thirty-eight per cent were involved in the sex trade, twenty per cent were homeless, eighteen per cent were Indigenous, and seventeen per cent had HIV.[32] These are the type of unpopular groups who are vulnerable in a legislative and executive process inspired by populism.

---

[28] *Canada (Prime Minister) v. Khadr*, 2010 SCC 3.
[29] Dennis Baker, *Not Quite Supreme: The Courts and Coordinate Constitutional Interpretation* (Montreal: McGill-Queen's University Press, 2010), pp. 134–135.
[30] See Kent Roach, '"The Supreme Court at the Bar of Politics": The Afghan Detainee and Omar Khadr Cases' (2010) 28 *National Journal of Constitutional Law* 115 for a fuller account of the Khadr case, including follow-on litigation.
[31] *Canada v. PHS Community Services* 2011 SCC 44 at para. 4.
[32] Ibid. at para. 9.

The Court rejected the government of Canada's rather cruel argument that the addicts who used Insite were simply there as a matter of personal choice and that the government bore no responsibility for the harms they suffered from dirty needles and overdoses. It unanimously concluded that the minister's decision not to grant Insite an exemption was arbitrary and grossly disproportionate given the evidence that the site had achieved health benefits without increasing crime. The Court's decision was remedially aggressive because it made a mandatory order that required Insite to be granted an exemption, but it was also quite narrow because it was limited to the facts of the particular case. The Court underlined that going forward, governments retained the ability to devise health and criminal justice policy and to consider each application for a supervised injection site on its merits.

Once it had achieved a majority in the House of Commons, the Harper government responded to the Insite case by enacting the Respect for Communities Act.[33] This Act placed an astounding array of barriers before those seeking to establish new supervised injection sites.[34] The new law discouraged applications for exemptions and then encouraged the minister of health not to grant them. It was influenced by populism. Dr Kellie Leitch, who would later unsuccessfully run for the Conservative leadership on an 'anti-elite' platform patterned after Trump's successful presidential campaign, accusing a fellow Member of Parliament who opposed the legislation of being 'pro-Heroin'.[35] The legislative response was dialogue with a vengeance.

At the same time, the legislation helped reveal the government's attitudes towards addicts and those who were concerned about their health. By forcing governments opposed to Charter decisions to enact and defend ordinary legislation to limit those decisions, dialogue can help reveal the true colours of our elected governments. The reply legislation was mean legislation, but it was more transparently mean than the attempted executive cancelation of Insite's licence. Both the decision and the reply revealed some of the implications of the Harper government's 'tough on crime' policies. The result was a more democratic dialogue than what would have occurred without the Charter, where

---

[33] SC 2015, c. 22.

[34] Ibid., amending s. 56.1(3) of the *Controlled Drugs and Substances Act*, SC 1996, c. 19. The list of hurdles to obtaining an exemption from drug laws in the reply legislation started at subsection (a) and ended at subsection (z.1).

[35] As quoted in Roach, *The Supreme Court on Trial* above n 8, p. 366.

Insite's exemption would likely have been removed by one government and reinstated by another through the exercise of executive discretion. The defeat of the Harper government shortly after it enacted the mean-spirited legislation also raises doubts about why legislative replies to court decisions should receive special judicial deference, as suggested by some, including Rosalind Dixon in her contribution in this volume.[36]

Sex Work

In 2013, the Supreme Court invalidated a number of Canada's prostitution laws, accepting extensive expert testimony at trial that one of the unintended effects of these laws was to make sex workers less safe. At the same time, the Court suspended its declaration of invalidity for one year in recognition that the regulation of prostitution is 'a complex and delicate matter' and that 'greater latitude in one measure – for example, permitting prostitutes to obtain the assistance of security personnel – might impact on the constitutionality of another measure – for example, forbidding the nuisances associated with keeping a bawdy-house'.[37]

The Harper government responded aggressively to the Court's decision by enacting the Protection of Communities and Exploited Persons Act within the year. Its preamble declared a desire 'to denounce and prohibit the purchase of sexual services because it creates a demand for prostitution', which has 'a disproportionate impact on women and children'. It also referred to 'the exploitation inherent in prostitution' and 'the social harm caused by the objectification of the human body and the commodification of sexual activity'.[38] Much of the Act was premised on a conceptualization of all sex workers as victims and the purchasers of sex as the real criminals. It made the purchase of sex a crime for the first time in Canadian history.[39] The new offence was subject to the government's policy of imposing mandatory minimum penalties, albeit fines of between $500 and $4,000. In their avoidance of imprisonment, these minimum fines recognized the routine nature of the sex trade in most

---

[36] Rosalind Dixon, 'The Supreme Court, Charter Dialogue and Deference' (2009) 47 *Osgoode Hall Law Journal* 235; Scott Stephenson, *From Dialogue to Disagreement in Comparative Rights Constitutionalism* (Sydney: Federation Press, 2016), pp. 178–179, 217–218; Rosalind Dixon, 'Constitutional Dialogue and Deference' in this volume.

[37] *Canada (Attorney General)* v. *Bedford*, 2013 SCC 72 at para. 165.

[38] SC 2014, c. 25.

[39] *Criminal Code*, s. 286.1.

Canadian cities. The government stressed that the exemption of sex providers from the new crime was not intended in any way to condone prostitution, but to recognize sex workers were 'victims' who required protection. This revealed the roots of the new crime in moral disapproval of prostitution.

Opposition parties and expert witnesses in parliamentary committees argued against the new law on the basis that criminalizing customers would force sex workers to take the same type of evasive and risky actions (such as perfunctory screening of customers and street sex) that had led the Supreme Court to hold that the previous offences were unconstitutional. The government ignored these arguments as well as requests that the bill be referred to the Supreme Court. To my mind, this suggests that the arguments about the need for judicial 'comity' and deference towards legislative replies are not sufficiently nuanced[40] and should not determine the result when the new law is challenged again under the Charter.

There should be no rule of thumb in second-look cases. In an age of populism where there are votes to be had in rejecting rights and Court decisions, it should not be surprising if a court committed to the rule of law strikes down a legislative reply to its previous decision. Each case must be judged on the merits and the evidence. Cases such as the supervised injection site and prostitution legislation where Parliament has legislated with disregard for the evidence should not merit undeserved deference even if that pushes a determined legislature to respond to a second round of judicial invalidation with the override.

Both episodes also affirm that a majority government is still able to legislate on Charter issues quickly and vigorously. It also suggests that those seeking Charter-based reforms often have to win both in Court and in Parliament. This is demanding but consistent with the idea of democratic dialogue. It also belies Morton and Knopff's idea that elites aligned with a 'Court Party' can easily impose their policy preferences without engaging with the legislature.[41]

---

[40] See Dixon, 'The Supreme Court, Charter Dialogue and Deference' above n 36.

[41] F. L. Morton and Rainer Knopff, *The Charter Revolution and the Court Party* (Peterborough: Broadview Press, 2000). For arguments that dialogic approaches are compatible with the new emphasis on civil society constitutionalism and constitutional culture, see Roach, *The Supreme Court on Trial* above n 8, pp. 408–410.

Assisted Dying

In 2015, the Supreme Court held that an old Criminal Code offence against all forms of assisted suicide violated the Charter because it was overbroad as applied to competent adults with an irremediable medical condition causing intolerable suffering. The Court stressed that the trial judge had found on the evidence that the vulnerable could be protected from being coerced into a premature death even in the absence of an unqualified prohibition against assisted dying. The Court did not decide issues relating to minors or those who made advance directives. As with the sex work case, the Court refused to issue an immediate remedy and suspended the declaration of invalidity for one year on the basis that '[c]omplex regulatory regimes are better created by Parliament than by the courts'.[42]

The Court's suspended declaration of invalidity was far from toothless. Once the suspension expired, Canada's assisted suicide offence would under s. 52 of the Constitution Act, 1982 be of no force and effect, to the extent that it criminalized medically assisted dying of adults who had made voluntary and competent decisions to end their life. This differed considerably from either the unenforceable declaration of incompatibility, or even softer, less formal advice given by some judges of the UK Supreme Court that an absolute offence against assisted suicide could not be justified as a reasonable or proportionate means to protect the vulnerable.[43] This again illustrates the importance of context and differences between the Canadian and UK systems.

In May 2016, the new Liberal majority government introduced a bill with a preamble stressing concerns that the elderly, ill, or disabled might be coerced into suicide. The Minister of Justice argued that the new bill was not a 'cut and paste' job that simply copied the Supreme Court's Carter decision. Indeed, the bill controversially required that death be 'reasonably foreseeable', that the underlying disease must be 'incurable', and that the person be in 'an advanced state of irreversible decline in capability', all matters not contained in the Supreme Court's decision. The bill followed Quebec and US models of end-of-life legislation and rejected more expansive models used in the Netherlands and Belgium. These features of the bill led those who had successfully litigated the case to oppose the bill and argue that at least one of the applicants in *Carter*

---

[42] *Carter* v. *Canada (Attorney General)*, 2015 SCC 5 at para. 125.
[43] *R. (on the application of Nicklinson)* v. *Ministry of Justice*, [2014] UKSC 38.

would not have qualified under it. The bill also contained a waiting period and deferred questions of mature minors, advance directives, and psychiatric conditions to additional study.

The House of Commons passed the bill, but the Senate exercised its new independence from party discipline to amend it. The government rejected the most important amendment that would have deleted the requirements that a person's death be foreseeable and based on an incurable disease producing an advanced state of irreversible decline. The government argued that these additional requirements were necessary not only to protect the vulnerable, but also to disapprove of suicide and to counter negative perceptions of the quality of life of the disabled, the ill, and the elderly.[44] The unelected Senate avoided a standoff with the government and enacted the bill as amended by the Commons into law.[45]

Not everyone was satisfied with the parliamentary response. A few argued that the Court and Parliament both went too far and that the law should impose even more restrictions and include a specific exemption for those with religious beliefs opposed to assisted dying. Many others argued that the new law was too restrictive and would deny assisted dying to those who qualified under *Carter* and those who most needed relief from intolerable suffering with no end in sight. Indeed, new Charter litigation targeting these aspects of the new law was launched soon after the bill's enactment.[46] In my view, such follow-on litigation should be decided on the merits without any automatic preference for judicial deference. In any event, the episode demonstrates the bipartisan nature of dialogue in Canada as a new Liberal government used the same freedom as the previous Conservative government to legislate aggressively in response to a Charter decision.

Parliament used the limited nature of the Court's decision to punt some issues such as the eligibility of mature minors, those with psychiatric issues, and those who made advance directives to future study. No one judicial or legislative decision is likely to constitute the final word on this difficult subject. Indeed, the focus in many dialogue debates about

---

[44] Department of Justice, Canada *Addendum to Legislative Backgrounder: Medical Assistance in Dying (Bill C-14)* (Ottawa: Minister of Justice, 2016) at www.justice.gc.ca/eng/rp-pr/other-autre/addend/index.html. I will address whether these objectives are important enough to justify limits on Charter rights in Part III of this chapter.

[45] *An Act to Amend the Criminal Code (Medical Assistance in Dying)* SC 2016 c.3.

[46] 'Assisted dying legislation faces new challenge in B.C.' CBC News, 27 June 2016.

which institution will have the last word may not be helpful. Societal debates can be enriched by involving different institutions. The courts will tend to focus on the facts of individual cases while legislatures will focus on regulatory issues and the protection of politically salient vulnerable groups.[47] The performance of each institution may be improved by increased awareness and sensitivity to the issues that the other institution focuses upon. Society's attitudes will continue to evolve with experience and time.

Summary

There is a need for a fair and qualitative assessment of the extent of dialogue after Charter decisions. Such an assessment should not be unfairly loaded by presuming that only legislative or executive rejection of Charter decisions constitute genuine or legitimate dialogue. Such an approach expects governments routinely to reject or ignore Charter decisions in a way that would threaten the rule of law.

The study of dialogue should also not be stunted by binary categorizations of legislative replies as either 'compliance' or 'rejection'. Dialogue should be examined in a qualitative and contextual manner attentive to a broad range of factors that influence the courts, legislatures, and the executive. In my view, it is difficult to contend that the range of institutional interaction documented so far can simply be characterized as a monologue of compliance.

II The Dangers of Simplified Comparative Law

The American Origins of Dialogue

Both Mark Tushnet and Stephen Gardbaum have proposed alternative terms to dialogue in large part because they identify dialogic aspects in the American constitution that they present as a type of anti-model to their 'weak form' and 'Commonwealth' models of judicial review respectively. They are correct to note that there are dialogic elements in the

---

[47] These can include groups protected under s. 15 such as the disabled and the elderly. See Bruce Ackerman 'Beyond Carolene Products' (1985) 98 *Harvard Law Review* 713. My focus on the dangers of executive and legislative populism is mainly concerned with less popular and politically salient groups such as the accused and migrants, and influenced by my primary interest in criminal justice and national security matters.

American constitution. Indeed, I regard Alexander Bickel[48] as the founder of dialogical understandings of judicial review. I have made clear the debts I owe to Bickel and to my former teacher Guido Calabresi, who refined and applied Bickel's views in an underappreciated and brilliant 1991 foreword to the *Harvard Law Review*.[49] A key feature of Bickel's and Calabresi's work, however, is that they both locate dialogue between American courts and legislatures at the sub-constitutional level. A recent example of such sub-constitutional dialogue was the string of cases that culminated in the US Supreme Court's decision that habeas corpus applied to Guantanamo Bay.[50] That said, to the extent that American constitutional law follows proportionality based reasoning, dialogic responses by legislatures are possible, albeit not in the form of explicit limits and overrides of rights as contemplated under ss. 1 and 33 of the Charter.[51]

A finding of dialogic aspects in the American constitution should not discredit dialogue. It also does not mean that there are not important contextual differences between dialogue in Canada and the United States. In Canada, dialogue is achieved by governments in a parliamentary system building a s. 1 file to refine their objectives and justify their means, and by responding to the frequent use of suspended declarations of invalidity. In the United States, dialogue is more often achieved when courts initially avoid constitutional decisions to give Congress more space to respond to their decisions, or when courts minimize the ambit of their constitutional decisions to give both Congress and the executive more policymaking space.[52]

When American legislatures have responded to full-blown constitutional decisions by rejecting *Miranda* warnings, denying same-sex

---

[48] Alexander M. Bickel, *The Least Dangerous Branch*, 2nd edn. (New Haven: Yale University Press, 1985), p. 24.

[49] Guido Calabresi, 'Foreword: Antidiscrimination and Accountability (What the Bork Brennan Debate Avoids)' (1991–1992) 105 *Harvard Law Review* 80.

[50] *Boumediene v. Bush* 553 U.S. 723 (2008).

[51] The US Supreme Court has even at least once experimented with a remedy similar to a suspended declaration of invalidity in *Northern Pipeline Construction v. Marathon Pipe Line Co.* 458 U.S. 50, 87–9 (1985) as discussed in Eric Fish, 'Choosing Constitutional Remedies' (2016) 63 *UCLA Law Review* 322 at 360–62. In another indication of the importance of local context, Congress with its looser party discipline was unable to enact a prompt legislative response.

[52] Cass Sunstein, *One Case at a Time* (Cambridge, MA: Harvard University Press, 1999).

marriage, or criminalizing flag burning, the reply laws have been struck down.[53] Other dialogic responses including attempts to reduce the jurisdiction of federal courts, and to secure commitments from judicial nominees are common in the United States, but less so in Canada. Constitutional amendments are also more frequently proposed in the United States as a form of protest politics. American attempts to engage in dialogue by attempting (often unsuccessfully) to change the Court or the Constitution are arguably corrosive to the rule of law. My point has never been that dialogue does not exist in the United States, but rather that the Canadian approach to dialogue allows ordinary legislation to limit and overrule full-blown constitutional decisions without dangerous and frequently futile attempts to change the Court or the Constitution.

The Danger of Dichotomous Models of Judicial Review

Models can be a helpful way of simplifying details, but they abstract away from political and legal context. Comparative law is increasingly shy about relying on models, especially dichotomous ones. The emphasis is often on how local circumstances shape responses to more universal demands and problems, the migration of constitutional ideas, and how ideas that mean one thing in one context change as they migrate to other contexts.[54] The idea that the world's legal systems may be divided into a few models, let alone two, seems odd. In the contentious field of bill of rights, it risks that the descriptive task of models will be driven by normative arguments for and against judicial review.

Canada has never been a good fit for Tushnet's weak-form model of judicial review because Canadian courts, like American courts, have the power 'to declare statues enacted by a nation's highest legislature unconstitutional'.[55] It is thus not surprising that Tushnet has expressed

---

[53] *Dickerson v. United States* 530 U.S.428 (2000); *Obergefell v. Hodges* 135 S.C. 2584 (2015); *Texas v. Johnson* 491 U.S. 397 (1989); *United States v. Eichman* 496 U.S. 310 (1990).

[54] Pierre Legrand, 'The Impossibility of "Legal Transplants"' (1997) 4 *Maastricht Journal of European & Comparative Law* 111; Sujit Choudhry, ed., *The Migration of Constitutional Ideas* (Cambridge: Cambridge University Press, 2006); Ran Hirshl, *Comparative Matters: The Renaissance of Comparative Constitutional Law* (Oxford: Oxford University Press, 2014).

[55] Tushnet, *Weak Courts, Strong Rights*, above n 2, p. ix.

concerns that the Charter has evolved into strong-form judicial review, primarily because of the lack of use of the s. 33 override.[56]

Both Janet L. Hiebert and Stephen Gardbaum express misgivings about placing Canada into their respective parliamentary and Commonwealth models. Professor Hiebert recognizes that Canada has a stronger form of judicial review than the United Kingdom or New Zealand.[57] Professor Gardbaum reluctantly includes Canada in his Commonwealth model on the basis of pre-legislative rights review and the availability of the s. 33 override. One problem to be discussed in the third part of this chapter is that Canada's system of pre-enactment rights review is weak. Another related problem is that s. 33 is rarely used. Gardbaum sees s. 33 as critical because 'democratic legitimacy requires that the reasonable view of a legislative majority to trump the reasonable view of a judicial majority . . .'[58] His emphasis on the need for legislatures to have the final word does not fit well with s. 33, which requires legislative reconsideration after five years. As suggested above, the focus on the final word may not be helpful.

Professor Gardbaum suggests that legislative replies to Court decisions cannot be a basis for distinguishing the Charter from the American Bill of Rights because they happen in the United States. He does not, however, account for the greater number and prominence of the Canadian replies, or the fact that some American replies have been rejected as defiance of the Court's authority in a way that has not occurred in Canada.[59] He also dismisses what I regard as the key features of democratic dialogue under the Charter: the ability of governments to justify infringements of Charter rights under s. 1, and the ability to respond to suspended declarations of invalidity. Here, Gardbaum's selection of countries may limit his vision. He ignores the use of suspended declarations of invalidity in South Africa, perhaps because he wrongly equates

---

[56] Mark Tushnet, 'The Rise of Weak-Form Judicial Review' in Tom Ginsburg and Rosalind Dixon, (eds.), *Comparative Constitutional Law* (Northampton, MA: Edward Elgar Publishing, 2011), p. 330.

[57] Janet Hiebert, 'Constitutional Experimentation: Rethinking How a Bill of Rights Functions' in Tom Ginsburg and Rosalind Dixon, (eds.), *Comparative Constitutional Law* (Northampton, MA: Edward Elgar Publishing, 2011), p. 313; Janet Hiebert, 'Parliamentary Bills of Rights: An Alternative Model?' (2006) 69 *Modern Law Review* 7.

[58] Stephen Gardbaum, *The New Commonwealth Model of Constitutionalism* (Cambridge: Cambridge University Press, 2013), p. 67.

[59] Kent Roach, 'Dialogue or Defiance? Legislative Reversals of Supreme Court Decisions in Canada and the United States' (2006) 4 *International Journal of Constitutional Law* 347.

'constitutional supremacy' – something that clearly exists in both Canada and South Africa – with 'judicial supremacy'.[60] He also dismisses proportionality analysis as a site for dialogue because it is used under the US Constitution, which he, like Professor Tushnet, presents as a model of strong judicial review.[61]

In the end, these three alternatives to dialogue – weak-form review, parliamentary bills of rights, and the new Commonwealth model – all reluctantly include the Charter. As such, they do not seem to be a good fit for Canada. They also fail to account for the differences between the Charter and the US Bill of Rights even if, in both countries, courts can strike down legislation. It is a crude form of modelling that places an eighteenth-century bill of rights with no explicit limitation or override powers and a congressional system in the same category as a twentieth-century bill of rights with limitation and override powers tied to a centralized parliamentary system. Conversely to the extent that the weak-form, new Commonwealth, or parliamentary bill of rights models include Canada, they miss the importance of the ability of Canadian courts to strike down laws. Reducing legal systems to two competing models neglects important issues of political and legal context.

In my view, the alternative models of weak-form, Commonwealth, or parliamentary bill of rights do not improve on dialogue as a model for Canada. They are, however, helpful (in a way that semantic debates about the metaphor of dialogue are not[62]) because they underline the need for caution when applying the dialogue metaphor[63] or constructing models across countries.[64] The construction of binary models is a simplified approach to comparative law that obscures important legal and political

---

[60] Gardbaum, *The New Commonwealth Model* above n 58, p. 14.

[61] Ibid., p. 115.

[62] Hogg, Bushell Thornton, and Wright, 'Charter Dialogue Revisited' above n 9 at 7. To be sure, the term 'dialogue' is not perfect, especially to the extent that it fails to capture the formality and apparent finality of judicial or legislative decisions. Nevertheless, alternative phrases such as 'partnership' or 'collaboration' seem to be equally problematic. Aileen Kavanagh has suggested to me the more neutral alternative of 'institutional interaction', which does seem to capture the essence of dialogue.

[63] Po Jen Yap has found elements of dialogue in common law Asia, but his sophisticated approach is not to try to transplant a Commonwealth or a Canadian model, but to move the common law in a dialogic direction in a way that is sensitive to the particular law, politics, and history of the region. See Po Jen Yap, *Constitutional Dialogue in Common Law Asia* (Oxford: Oxford University Press, 2015).

[64] I concede that in the first edition of *The Supreme Court on Trial*, I may have overstated the dialogic similarities between the Charter and the UK Human Rights Act and the New Zealand bill of rights.

differences between the countries studied. There should not be one universal model of dialogue even though there may be aspects of dialogue or institutional interaction in many domestic and supranational legal systems.[65] What is common in all forms of dialogue, however, is that judicial decisions on rights are not necessarily final and can be subject to limits and overrides by ordinary legislation.

III   The Importance of Judicial Review and the Dangers of Populism and Co-Ordinate Construction

Waldron and the Dangers of Majoritarian Populism

The dialogue debate is perhaps inevitably shaped by assumptions about the desirability of judicial review. A number of Canadian critics of dialogue have been inspired by the influential work of Jeremy Waldron. A simplified version of Waldron's argument is that we have reasonable disagreements about issues like abortion, same-sex marriage, and assisted dying; judges themselves disagree; they resolve these disagreements by voting. In a healthy democracy with basic commitments to rights and equality of all citizens, such issues should be resolved and revisited by legislators having a vote. This should not produce a tyranny of the majority because some people will find themselves in a minority on some issues, but in a majority on others.[66]

I am increasingly sceptical about Professor Waldron's defence of majoritarian democracy on the 'you win some, you lose some' basis. His emphasis on reasonable disagreements about rights can easily blur into a profound scepticism about rights. For example, Christopher P. Manfredi asserts, 'Charter cases only rarely involve disputes about fundamental rights, and almost never involve disputes about fundamental moral principles' before making the complacent conclusion that courts will do no good, should the legislative process ever become 'a zero-sum game for some groups or individuals'.[67] Professor Manfredi made these comments in 2001, and subsequent history suggests that for

---

[65] For my first exploration of supranational systems in dialogic terms, see Kent Roach, 'Constitutional, Remedial and International Dialogues About Rights' (2005) 40 *Texas International Law Journal* 537.

[66] Jeremy Waldron, 'The Core of the Case against Judicial Review' (2006) 115 *Yale Law Journal* 1346; Jeremy Waldron, *Political Political Theory* (Cambridge: Harvard University Press, 2016), ch 9.

[67] Christopher P. Manfredi, *Judicial Power and the Charter: Canada and the Paradox of Liberal Constitutionalism*, 2nd edn. (Toronto: Oxford University Press, 2001), pp. 195, 198.

the unpopular, such as the accused and migrants, populist politics can resemble a zero-sum game. Waldron's distinction between reasonable disagreement about rights and misgivings or rejections of rights can be difficult to sustain,[68] especially in the age of Trumpian populism.[69]

Penal Populism

Professor Waldron comes closer than many of his Canadian followers[70] to conceding that judicial review might be justified if laws persistently violated the rights of minorities. He recognizes there may be a problem if vulnerable minorities in society consistently overlap with decisional minorities in the legislature. Nevertheless, he seems unconcerned about how punitive criminal justice legislation increasingly dominates the legislative agenda and the reality that there will always be votes to be gained by being tough on crime, sympathetic to victims and hard on offenders.[71]

The gross overrepresentation of Indigenous persons in prisons in New Zealand, Australia, and Canada, and African Americans and Hispanics in American prisons, adds another dimension to penal populism. Yet Waldron pulls back from recognizing the danger of the tyranny of the majority because of his fears that judicial protection of minorities

[68] Aileen Kavanagh, 'Participation and Judicial Review: A Reply to Jeremy Waldron' (2003) 22 *Law and Philosophy* 451.

[69] It may be the case that some of Professor Waldron's assumptions about a community committed to individual and minority rights but engaging in reasonable disagreements no longer hold true given the animus towards the press, Muslims, and other unpopular minorities in the United States after President Trump's election, or in the United Kingdom after the vote to leave the European Union. As of 2016, however, Professor Waldron remained committed to making the case against judicial review and specifically warned against those who argue that his assumptions do not apply 'to American or British society, as they understand it, leading them to ignore the core argument altogether'. Waldron *Political Political Theory* above n 66, p. 203.

[70] See, for example, Huscroft, 'Rationalizing Judicial Power: The Mischief of Dialogue Theory' above n 7, and Baker, *Not Quite Supreme* above n 29, both appealing to Waldron. Christopher P. Manfredi notes the problem of ganging up on minorities, but dismisses it by arguing that the Court has 'blurred the distinction between genuine mistreatment of discrete and insular minorities and the ordinary vicissitudes of democratic politics'. See Manfredi, *Judicial Power and the Charter* above n 67, p. 135. Andrew Petter also pays little attention to the problem of the accused, prisoners, or Indigenous people in *The Politics of the Charter* above n 5.

[71] For a related recognition of blind spots of perspectives, see Dixon, 'The Supreme Court, Charter Dialogue and Deference' above n 36 at 258. See also Kavanagh, 'Participation and Judicial Review' above n 68 at 471–472, noting that majorities may support tough-on-crime measures with little concern for the rights of suspects and offenders.

will be a 'Trojan horse'[72] for more expansive forms of judicial review.[73] In my view, Waldron does not pay enough attention to the dangers that some unpopular groups – especially the accused, prisoners, and migrants – may consistently come out on the short end of the legislative stick. Elected politicians, especially in fearful and populist times, will have an incentive to minimize and reject rights claims by the truly unpopular.

The problem of penal populism is not trivial once it is recognized that much human rights litigation occurs in the criminal process and penal populism is a political phenomenon across parties and countries.[74] Given the importance of the rights of the accused, migrants and other unpopular minorities such as Muslims to the judicial and legislative agendas of most democracies, this undermines the 'win some, lose some' assumptions behind Waldron's core case against judicial review.

The current populist reality of legislating against rights claims by the unpopular is much harsher than the 1960s debates about abortion that feature in Professor Waldron's arguments that the legislative process can be relied upon to consider rights claims seriously and respectfully.[75] For example, in Canada between 2006 and 2015, the Harper government enacted over sixty pieces of crime legislation. Their titles tell a story: the Tougher Penalties for Child Predators Act,[76] Protections of Communities and Exploited Persons Act,[77] Increasing Offenders' Accountability for Victims Act, Eliminating Entitlements for Prisoners Act,[78] Faster Removal of Foreign Criminals Act,[79] and the Zero Tolerance for Barbaric Cultural Practices Act.[80] The fact that such populist laws ignored rights as interpreted by the courts was a political virtue. Harper's former chief of staff revealed how the opposition from defence lawyers, civil

---

[72] Waldron, 'The Core of the Case Against Judicial Review' above n 66 at 1404–406.

[73] Ibid., 1395–1401.

[74] Hiebert and Kelly, 'Parliamentary Bills of Rights' above n 18, pp. 411, 186, 220. See also their chapter in this volume.

[75] Waldron, *Political Political Theory* above n 66, pp. 196, 224. Waldron's continued use of the abortion example as an example of how legislatures will fairly consider rights is telling, given arguments that abortion may not even involve the rights of minorities. See John Hart Ely, *Democracy and Distrust: A Theory of Judicial Review* (Cambridge, MA: Harvard University Press, 1980).

[76] S.C. 2015 c.23.

[77] S.C. 2014 c.25.

[78] S.C 2010 c. 22.

[79] S.C. 2013 c.16.

[80] S.C. 2015 c. 29.

libertarians, and academics to this type of legislation increased support for it.[81] Penal populism is a particular problem for Waldron and his many followers. It has been and will likely continue to be a site for populist attacks on both criminals and the judges who defend their rights.

Prisoner disenfranchisement has been a particularly lightning rod for penal populism. In the United States, 2.2 million African Americans are disenfranchised as a result of a criminal conviction accounting for an estimated 7.7 per cent of black adults as compared to 1.7 per cent of non-black adults who are disenfranchised.[82] In the United Kingdom, prisoners were denied the vote in the face of domestic and European Court of Human Rights decisions that the disenfranchisement of all prisoners cannot be justified.[83]

Celebrations of representative democracy and the ability of legislatures to reject judicial interpretations of rights are singularly unsuited to an era of populist scapegoat politics and aversive constitutionalism where there are votes to be gained by depicting judges as the enemy of the people and by objecting to the notion that unpopular and feared people such as offenders and migrants have rights. All of this, to my mind, confirms the importance and wisdom of the Supreme Court's statement in the *Sauvé* case when it struck down restrictions on prisoner voting that would have disproportionately affected Indigenous and other racialized groups that 'a simple majoritarian political preference for abolishing a right altogether would not be a constitutionally valid objective'.[84]

---

[81] Ian Brodie argued that 'we never really had to engage in the question of what the evidence actually shows about various approaches to crime' because the 'sociologists, criminologists and defence lawyers' who opposed it were all 'held in lower repute than Conservative politicians': John Geddes, 'Ian Brodie offers a candid case study on politics and policy' *Macleans*, 27 March 2009, at www.macleans.ca/politics/ottawa/ian-brodie-offers-a-candid-case-study-in-politics-and-policy/.

[82] The Sentencing Project, *Felony Disenfranchisement Laws in the United States*, 28 April 2014 at www.sentencingproject.org/publications/felony-disenfranchisement-laws-in-the-united-states/.

[83] For my arguments that the UK response has been fuelled by Prime Minister Cameron's sense of disgust at prisoners voting, as witnessed by his famous remarks that the thought of prisoners voting made him 'sick in the stomach', see Kent Roach, 'The Varied Role of Courts and Legislatures in Rights Protection' in Murray Hunt, Hayley Hooper , and Paul Yowell, (eds.), *Parliaments and Human Rights: Redressing the Democratic Deficit* (Oxford: Hart Publishing, 2015), pp. 413–416.

[84] *Sauvé* v. *Canada (Chief Electoral Officer)*, 2002 SCC 68 at para. 20.

The False Dichotomy of Legal and Political Constitutionalism

A dialogic approach to constitutionalism continues in the tradition of common law constitutionalism where courts articulated their ideal bill of rights, but legislatures could displace judicial decisions protecting rights with clear legislation.[85] Most civil society groups live this duality, engaging with both courts and governments as well as with the media[86] This lived experience suggests that the choice that many theorists pose between relying on court-based legal constitutionalism or legislative-based political constitutionalism is a false choice.

Dialogue draws on the virtues of both political and legal constitutionalism.[87] It respects the virtues of all three branches of government while trying to compensate for each branch's weaknesses. The weak spots of majoritarian democracy can be strengthened by judicial reminders about the rights of unpopular minorities, and of fundamental values that both the legislature and the executive may cast overboard in response to real or perceived emergencies. Judicial mistakes can be corrected by legislation that broadens the policy debate, refines legislative objectives, and educates the court about the practical trade-offs and difficulties in achieving legislative objectives. Judicial remands to the legislature and the executive recognize their often superior capacities and knowledge. Dialogue is built on the foundations of legal process thought that is preoccupied with the respective strengths and weaknesses of each branch of government and how they interact.

Dialogue and Proportionality

Another site for courts and legislatures to interact and build on their strengths and counteract their weaknesses is proportionality analysis. Such analysis looms large in modern human rights law and plays an important role under both ss. 1 and 7 of the Charter.

---

[85] On the connections between dialogue under the common law and under the Charter see Kent Roach, 'Common Law and Constitutional Dialogues About Rights' (2001) 80 *Canadian Bar Review* 481.

[86] David Cole, *Engines of Liberty: The Power of Activist Citizens to Make Constitutional Law* (New York: Basic Books, 2016); Marian Botsford Fraser, *Acting for Freedom: Fifty Years of Civil Liberties in Canada* (Toronto: Second City, 2014).

[87] Jeff King, 'Rights and the Rule of Law in Third Way Constitutionalism' (2014) 30 *Constitutional Commentary* 101 at 116. Gardbaum also sees his Commonwealth model as a 'hybrid' of legal and political constitutionalism: see Gardbaum, *The New Commonwealth Model*, above n 58, p. 45.

Some dialogue critics are concerned that dialogic understandings of constitutionalism are rigged against the legislature. They argue that the courts maintain 'a monopoly on correct interpretation'[88] in s. 1 determinations. This very phrase, however, misunderstands proportionality analysis that is based on judicial testing of the arguments and evidence presented by the government to justify limits on Charter rights rather than abstract and static questions of interpretation.

Critics love to point to the Supreme Court's 1995 case striking down restrictions on tobacco advertising case, but they rarely point to the fact that the majority struck down absolute bans on tobacco advertising in large part because it concluded that the government had not revealed its own studies about whether less restrictive approaches could achieve its important objectives in discouraging people from smoking.[89] Governments have many instruments that can contribute to and enrich proportionality analysis. They include the collection and commissioning of evidence, the use of legislative preambles to explain legislative objectives and why less rights invasive means were not selected and the ability to expand the policy debate beyond the specific points in issue in judicial decisions.

To be sure, there are critics of proportionality analysis[90] and a full discussion of its strengths and weaknesses is beyond the scope of this chapter. Nevertheless, proportionality analysis remains central to the Charter and its main engine of dialogue. As Mattias Kumm has argued,[91] proportionality analysis invites judges to ask governments tough Socratic-like questions to determine if governmental action can be justified. Judicial intervention and questioning can make the legislature and

---

[88] Manfredi, *Judicial Power and the Charter* above n 67, p. 179. See also his argument that 'the major weakness of the intended internal check contained in the 'reasonable limits' clause of s. 1 is that its meaning and application is determined by the Court itself' (ibid. at 22).

[89] *RJR Macdonald v. Canada* [1995] 3 SCR 199 at paras 165, 191. Reply legislation was enacted and upheld from Charter challenge in *Canada v. JTI Macdonald Corp.* 2007 SCC 30.

[90] Grégoire Webber, *The Negotiable Constitution: On the Limitation of Rights* (Cambridge: Cambridge University Press, 2009).

[91] Mattias Kumm, 'Institutionalizing Socratic Contestation' (2007) 1 *European Journal of Legal Studies* 143; Roach, 'Dialogic Judicial Review and its Critics' above n 11 at 95–97. The Socratic metaphor is not perfect because judges, unlike Socrates, must ultimately decide whether the government has justified the limits on rights. Roach, *Supreme Court on Trial* above n 8, pp. 393–394.

the executive more careful and evidence-based when implementing policies that affect rights, especially the rights of the unpopular.

I agree with Professor Webber that the potential for dialogue 'lies in the prospect that legislature and court may learn from each other'.[92] In my view, however, such learning should primarily take place within proportionality analysis. Legislators should remind judges of the practical problems, trade-offs and alternatives considered as they try to achieve important legislative objectives, while judges should remind legislators about the importance of the rights of the unpopular and about less convenient but less rights invasive alternative policy options. Viewed through a legal process framework, such as approach, capitalizes on the advantages of both elected legislatures and independent courts. Moreover, it forces democracy by requiring clear legislative authorization when the executive infringes rights. Proportionality analysis can mitigate zero-sum contests about whether the Court's or the Parliament's view of the constitution should prevail, which seem to be implicit in many debates about co-ordinate construction.

The Dangers of Co-Ordinate Construction

Some Canadian critics of dialogue contend that democratic dialogue has become a fraudulent monologue of judicial supremacy because genuine dialogue requires Parliament to interpret the Charter differently from the courts and act on that interpretation. Co-ordinate construction has been rescued from the rough corners of American constitutionalism and recently defended by Mark Tushnet and Larry Kramer.[93] As Rosalind

---

[92] Grégoire Webber, 'The Unfulfilled Potential of the Court and Legislative Dialogue' (2009) 42 *Canadian Journal of Political Science* 443 at 456.

[93] These American scholars give co-ordinate construction a progressive orientation by focusing on serious judicial mistakes, such as *Scott v. Sandford*, 60 U.S. 393 (1857) and *Lochner v. New York*, 198 U.S. 45 (1904), as well as decisions confining Congress's ability to enact remedial legislation to enforce equality. They downplay its less noble sides, such as Andrew Jackson's refusal to act on Supreme Court decisions recognizing Indigenous rights and the South's use of co-ordinate construction based on states rights to oppose *Brown v. Board of Education of Topeka*, 347 U.S. 483 (1954), or overbroad presidential claims of unfettered war powers. See Mark Tushnet, *Taking the Constitution Away from the Courts* (Princeton: Princeton University Press, 1999), p. 14, and Larry Kramer, *The People Themselves: Popular Constitutionalism and Judicial Review* (Oxford: Oxford University Press, 2004), pp. 182–183. Canadian defenders of co-ordinate construction such as Christopher P. Manfredi, Grant Huscroft, and Dennis Baker generally invoke it to express disagreement with the Court's more expansive approach to rights.

Dixon has suggested, however, it remains somewhat odd in the Canadian setting. It has a firmer foundation in American constitutional history and under statutory bills of rights that contemplate that legislatures can disregard judicial findings of incompatibility.[94]

Christopher P. Manfredi and Dennis Baker have provided the most extended Canadian defences of co-ordinate construction. They both rely heavily on American concepts of 'case and controversy' requirements and limited government based on checks and balances[95] that are not part of the Canadian tradition. Professor Manfredi argues that it is a mistake for any branch of government to have unlimited powers and concludes that judicial supremacy will follow from a judicial monopoly on the correct interpretation of the Charter. His approach, however, elides distinctions between judicial interpretations of Charter rights that can be final, but not supreme if legislatures can justify reasonable and proportionate limits on such rights.[96]

Professor Baker relies on Waldron, but without paying as much attention as Waldron to the potential for persistent unpopular minorities. He also seems to grant the executive the same democratic legitimacy as the legislature when engaged in co-ordinate construction. There is support for this approach in American approaches to departmentalism, but it is in tension with Waldron's theory that rightly prefers the 'dignity of legislation'[97] to the less transparent and deliberative executive action.

---

[94] Dixon, 'The Supreme Court, Charter Dialogue and Deference' above n 36 at 264–65. I will suggest later in the chapter that the Canadian place for co-ordinate construction is the s. 33 override. The co-ordinate construction discussed here is limited to legislative responses to judicial interpretations of rights. In cases where governments act in areas of genuine legal uncertainty, they may have to interpret the constitution to determine if proposed legislation or executive action is consistent with the relative norm. As suggested at notes 103–105, I favour robust, transparent forms of pre-enactment rights vetting by executive or legislative bodies that enjoy some independence from the government of the day.

[95] Baker, *Not Quite Supreme* above n 29 at 40–41; Manfredi, *Judicial Power and the Charter* above n 67, pp. 179–181.

[96] One concern is that the Canadian court has not been willing to accept reasonable limits on the due process protections in s. 7 of the Charter. One response is that s. 7 is itself increasingly influenced by the proportionality concepts discussed earlier. For my own arguments that the court has not justified the preferred position of s. 7 under s. 1, see Kent Roach 'Mind the Gap: Canada's Different Criminal and Constitutional Standards of Fault' (2011) 61 *University of Toronto Law Journal* 545.

[97] Jeremy Waldron, *The Dignity of Legislation* (Cambridge: Cambridge University Press, 1999).

Co-ordinate construction tends to focus on the interpretation and the existence of rights. It seems designed to allow the legislature to reject, or at least express reservations about, rights as interpreted by the courts. It is not a good fit with the proportionality analysis that lies at the heart of s. 1 and, increasingly, s. 7 of the Charter.

The Override

My own position is that when Canadian governments wish to engage in co-ordinate construction that rejects or disagrees with rights as interpreted by the Court, they should only do so with the special signals of the s. 33 override and the sober second thoughts of requiring legislative renewals every five years.[98] Such safeguards and signals are warranted when a majoritarian institution such as the legislature departs from how the independent courts interpret rights designed to protect minorities. In other words, co-ordinate construction best fits the Charter when used to inform legislative uses of the override and it should not be used to allow the executive to reject court decisions.

Reports of the death of the override may be premature. The override could be revived, especially if, as Ted Morton has advocated[99], it is tied to the use of populist referenda. Such referenda would likely target the accused, migrants, prisoners and other unpopular groups. Waldron has complained that the s. 33 override forces the legislature to say it is overriding rights, whereas, in his view, it is only expressing reasonable disagreement with the views of perhaps five Supreme Court Justices about rights. In a book published in 2016, however, he has suggested that even if the language of s. 33 were changed to avoid the appearance that the legislature was rejecting rights, it might not matter, because 'as a matter of practical politics, the legislature is always somewhat at the mercy of the court's public declaration about the meaning of the society's Bill or Charter of Rights'.[100] Andrew Petter has similarly argued that

---

[98] Roach, *The Supreme Court on Trial* above n 8 ch. 13. Professor Baker ignores this when he asserts that I am a judicial supremacist who 'excludes all non-judicial participation in the interpretative process'. Baker, *Not Quite Supreme* above n 29, p. 37.

[99] F. L. Morton 'Can Judicial Supremacy Be Stopped?' (2003) *Policy Options* at 29, appealing to Waldron and arguing that judicial decisions on prisoner voting rights and gay marriage constitute 'de facto constitutional amendments' by judges drawn from 'the elite lawyering class', whereas 'constitutional rules should command a substantial degree of public consensus and support before being adopted'.

[100] Waldron, *Political Political Theory* above n 66, p. 354 n. 30.

'those who speak in the language of justice and rights have a huge rhetorical and political advantage over those who speak in the language of policy and interests'.[101]

Waldron and Petter can point to the fact that the federal Parliament has never used the override as support for their views. Waldron is correct that it is not easy to justify the override, but if it is used in response to a court decision, the informed public should understand that the legislature is rejecting a specific judicial decision as opposed to the right in general,[102] Petter may be correct that right claims are more rhetorically compelling than interest claims, but his own position is that there are competing right claims implicit in most Charter issues. Perhaps, as he acknowledges, politicians need to raise their game. The unwillingness of politicians to use s. 33 with its increased burden of public justification may be related to the widely felt malaise in politics that alas may be cured by the global tide of populism.

Rights Vetting and the Override

Another reason why the override has not been used is Canada's weak system of pre-legislative rights vetting. This makes it possible for legislatures to enact legislation overriding Charter rights without being called on it by a report that such bills are inconsistent with the Charter. The federal Minister of Justice has never made such a report. In the past, the Minister of Justice has taken the view that no such report is required if any credible Charter argument can be made in support of a legislative proposal.[103] Such a weak approach to rights vetting has been defended by Scott Stephenson on the basis that it allows harms to the rule of law that could be caused by

---

[101] Andrew Petter, 'Legalize This: The Chartering of Canadian Politics' in James B. Kelly and Christopher P. Manfredi, (eds.), *Contested Constitutionalism: Reflections on the Canadian Charter of Rights and Freedoms* (Vancouver: University of British Columbia Press, 2009), p. 33.

[102] The Quebec public accepted the most famous use of the override in response to *Ford v. Quebec* [1988] 2 SCR 712 not as a statement that their government did not accept freedom of expression but that it disagreed with the Supreme Court's judgment that the French language could be protected by only requiring the predominant as opposed to the exclusive use of French in public signs. Quebec did, however, allow the override reinstating the exclusive use of French to expire after five years and in response to international criticism. See generally Kent Roach 'Constitutional, Remedial and International Dialogues About Rights' (2005) 40 *Texas International Law Journal* 537 at 556–558.

[103] *Schmidt v. Canada (Attorney General)*, 2016 FC 269 aff'd 2018 FCA 55.

both the use of the override and continued disagreement between the courts and governments to be finessed without the use of the override.[104] But this presumes that disagreements among the courts and governments will be reasonable and should be settled or fudged for reasons of institutional comity. Like Waldron, this assumes a 'win some, lose some' approach that discounts the danger that in an era of populism, unpopular groups like the accused, prisoners and migrants can be perpetual losers in the legislative arena and that courts may have duties to defend the rights of the unpopular even if that results in the eventual use of the override.

In my view, an executive official or legislative body with some independence from the government of the day should take a robust approach to pre-enactment rights vetting. Examples of such rights vetting mechanisms include New Zealand's attorney general and the UK's Joint Committee on Human Rights. Both bodies have concluded that governmental legislative proposals have violated rights. They seem less inclined than the Canadian Minister of Justice to minimize rights and maximize the government's self-interest at the pre-enactment stage. In the Canadian context, a more independent and robust rights vetting process could make clear that populist legislative proposals that simply reject rights as interpreted by the Court and that cannot be justified as reasonable limits on such rights should only be enacted with the special signals and safeguards of the override.[105] Such an approach could result in the legal rights of accused, offenders, and migrants being overridden as well as the expressive and equality rights of unpopular minorities. The critical

---

[104] Stephenson, *From Dialogue to Disagreement in Comparative Rights Constitutionalism* above n 36, pp. 168–169, 175–179. For support of non-reporting, see Grant Huscroft, 'Reconciling Duty and Discretion: The Attorney General in the Charter Era' (2009) 34 *Queen's Law Journal* 773 at 794.

[105] See Kent Roach, 'Not Just the Government's Lawyer: The Attorney General as Defender of the Rule of Law' (2006) 31 *Queen's Law Journal* 598 for arguments that the Minister of Justice drawing on the independence that she as attorney general has from government should not hesitate in an appropriate case to conclude that the only way that a government proposal would respect the Charter would be through the use of the override. New legislation in Canada formalizes a new practice of the Minister of Justice issuing Charter statements about the effects of government bills on Charter rights. *Bill C-51: An Act to Amend the Criminal Code and the Department of Justice Act* 42nd Parliament 1st Session First Reading, 6 June 2017, s. 73. There is a danger that the proposed requirement does not apply to private member bills, which are sometimes enacted and can be a source of populist politics, and that it does not require that the Minister conclude whether a government's legislative proposal that infringes the Charter can be justified under s. 1. The new and vague reference to "impacts" on Charter rights seems influenced by the Waldronite idea of reasonable disagreement about rights.

difference, however, is that the public and the international community would be alerted, and the government would have to win re-election before renewing the use of the override five years after it was first used.

Dialogue does not guarantee that societies will be just. This is why it is a democratic dialogue. This is why elections still matter regardless of whether democracies have a bill of rights or not. Nevertheless, dialogue does provide a structured means that allows all branches of government to struggle in a candid and clear manner about how rights will be reconciled with social objectives. A commitment to democratic dialogue in a populist age means learning to live with results that one finds very disagreeable and perhaps increased derogation from rights. Derogation can make clear what is at stake. It may galvanize democratic opposition to harsh measures.

IV   The Most Worrying Objection to Dialogue: Can It Erode the Role of Courts?

As is apparent from the discussion in this chapter, I do not believe that those who deny dialogue, or who restrict dialogue to cases where governments disagree with rights as interpreted by the courts, have been particularly persuasive or helpful in advancing our understanding of dialogue. The dialogue debate in Canada has regrettably become another battlefield to fight political and cultural wars over the role of the judiciary. This is troubling because dialogue had the potential[106] to move us beyond tired and polarized debates between legislative and judicial supremacy.

That said, some of the Canadian opponents of dialogue are not sceptics or opponents of judicial review. They have argued that the dialogue metaphor undercuts judicial review by failing to capture the fact that judges make enforceable decisions and do not simply engage in casual conversations.[107] For me, these critics offer the most worrying criticism of dialogue. My worries only increase as the world moves towards harsh forms of populism.

---

[106] Kavanagh acknowledges that dialogue expanded the range of institutions and data studied, and 'provided a counter-balance to the lamentable tendency to romanticize one's favoured institution', in 'The Lure and Limits of Dialogue' above n 1 at 107.

[107] Luc B. Tremblay, 'The Legitimacy of Judicial Review: The Limits of Dialogue between Courts and Legislatures' (2005) 3 *International Journal of Constitutional Law* 617; Tom Hickman, 'Constitutional Dialogue, Constitutional Rights and the Human Rights Act 1998' [2005] *Public Law* 306; Kavanagh, 'The Lure and Limits of Dialogue' above n 1.

Canadian Critics of Dialogue Who Fear It Will Weaken Judicial Review

As early as 2003, Jean Leclair warned that the dialogue metaphor could undermine judicial independence and the separation of powers.[108] Carissima Mathen has argued that the metaphor of dialogue suggests 'co-operation, exchange and most importantly the possibility of mutual moderation', which she suggests does not easily fit with the strong role of courts in enforcing the Charter.[109] Jamie Cameron has expressed concerns that dialogue may undermine the judicial role especially with respect to second-look cases.[110] All of these critiques express concern that dialogue does not take judicial rulings or, indeed, rights seriously enough. They give me pause, especially in an age of populism and aversive constitutionalism.

Luc Tremblay outlines two possible understandings of dialogue: dialogue as conversation and dialogue as deliberation. Professor Tremblay seems to accept that dialogue as conversation captures much of the back and forth between courts and legislatures under the Charter, but he fears that such an approach does not account for the fact that judicial decisions are authoritative interpretations of the relevant text that are meant to resolve disputes, not provisional conversational parries.[111]

I would not draw the distinction between dialogue as conversation and as deliberation quite as sharply as Professor Tremblay. Dialogue can be both deliberative in the sense of recognizing that both the judiciary and the legislatures have thought through and debated the issues in their different ways before reaching what they conclude is the best and final decision, while also being conversational in the sense that the two institutions can engage with and learn from each other, especially in the context of proportionality analysis. In this way, dialogue can respect the integrity and strengths of both legislation and adjudication.

Professor Tremblay's worry that dialogue can undermine the judicial role should be taken seriously. Similar concerns have been expressed outside of Canada. Aileen Kavanagh argues that the idea of dialogue

---

[108] Jean Leclair, 'Réflexions critiques au sujet de la métaphore du dialogue en droit constitutionnel canadien' (2003) Revue du Barreau 379.

[109] Carissima R. Mathen, 'Dialogue Theory, Judicial Review and Judicial Supremacy' (2007) 45 Osgoode Hall Law Journal 125 at 128.

[110] Jamie Cameron 'Dialogue and Hierarchy in Charter Interpretation' (2001) 38 Alberta Law Review 1051; Jamie Cameron 'Collateral Thoughts on Dialogue's Legacy as Metaphor and Theory: A Favourite from Canada' (2016) 35 University of Queensland Law Review 157.

[111] Tremblay, 'The Legitimacy of Judicial Review' above n 107.

'evokes an image of an equal rather than hierarchical relationship', which is implicit in judicial review.[112] Tom Hickman shares this worry and argues that dialogue that simply proposes principles to Parliament on a take-it-or-leave-it basis could undermine basic rule of law values.[113] Writing in the UK context, Hickman fears that declarations of incompatibility can reduce judicial contributions to dialogue to a form of judicial lobbying. The Australian High Court similarly concluded that such unenforceable declarations were not a judicial function and made its views about dialogue clear by referring to it in scare quotes.[114] But not all judges are so sceptical about dialogue. As Aharon Barak wrote when he was president of Israel's Supreme Court: 'there is a constant dialogue between the judiciary and the legislature. The dialogue does not take place in meetings between judges and legislators; it takes place when each branch carries out its constitutional role.'[115]

Dialogue is not something that judges do in either first- or second-look cases. Dialogue is something that happens in a democracy where strong courts and strong legislatures discharge their roles with vigour and integrity. The courts will discharge their legitimate role when they defend the rights of the unpopular and consider the evidence that the government presents about why limits on rights are proportionate. The legislature will discharge its legitimate role when it engages in a responsive manner with proportionality concerns articulated by the courts and when it takes responsibility for derogating from rights.

The criticisms that understanding judicial review in dialogical terms can weaken the judicial review are significant, especially given the rise of populist movements that are willing to run against unpopular groups and the courts. In the remainder of this chapter, I will outline three areas where refinements to some understandings of dialogue could better equip courts to withstand populist challenges.

Refining Dialogue: Second-Look Cases

Some critics of dialogue will rightly be concerned by arguments made by some dialogue proponents that courts should generally defer to legislative

---

[112] Kavanagh, 'The Lure and Limits of Dialogue' above n 1 at 85.

[113] Tom Hickman, 'Constitutional Dialogue, Constitutional Theories and the Human Rights Act 1998' above n 107.

[114] *Momcilovic v. The Queen*, [2011] HCA 34.

[115] Aharon Barak, *The Judge in a Democracy* (Princeton: Princeton University Press, 2006), p. 236.

replies to judicial decisions.[116] For what it is worth, both Peter W. Hogg and myself have separately argued against such a rule of deference.[117] More importantly, the Court made clear in 2007 that 'the mere fact that the legislation represents Parliament's response to a decision of the Court does not militate for or against deference'.[118]

Invalidation in Canadian second-look cases is not so exceptional.[119] It may become more prevalent when the Court considers legislative replies to its recent supervised injection, sex work, and assisted-dying cases. If the Court upholds legislative replies, this should be the result not of any *ex ante* posture of judicial deference, but rather because the legislature has successfully engaged with proportionality issues by clarifying its legitimate objective and why less rights-restrictive alternatives will not work. Such an approach can also counter populist replies where the legislatures do not really engage with the evidence or the concerns that the courts have raised about specific laws. To be sure, rejections of reply legislature could inspire the use of the override, but that is an option that is open to legislatures under the Charter and one that wisely requires special signals and second thoughts.

As suggested in the first part of this chapter, Parliament ignored much of the evidence that criminalization makes sex work riskier than it needs to be when it responded to the Supreme Court's decision in *Bedford* by criminalizing the purchase but not the sale of sex. Similarly, Parliament's response to the *Insite* decision neglected evidence that supervised injection sites can save lives without necessarily increasing crime. It is difficult to see why courts should approach populist legislative rejection of such decisions and the rights of the unpopular with an *ex ante* posture towards judicial restraint or the maintenance of institutional comity.

Refining Dialogue: Are All Legislative Objectives Legitimate?

Another area that needs refinement is how courts should conduct proportionality reasoning in a 'post-factual' age of populism and symbolism.

---

[116] Gardbaum, *The New Commonwealth Model* above n 58.

[117] Hogg, Bushell Thornton, and Wright, 'Charter Dialogue Revisited' above n 9 at 48; Kent Roach, 'Sharpening the Dialogue Debate' (2007) 45 *Osgoode Hall Law Journal* 169 at 174–176.

[118] *Canada (Attorney General) v. JTI-Macdonald Corp.*, 2007 SCC 30 at para. 11.

[119] For invalidation or partial invalidation of laws in second-look cases, see *Sauvé v. Canada* [2002] 3 SCR 519; *R. v. Demers*, 2004 SCC 46; *R. v. Hall* 2002 SCC 64.

Legislatures influenced by populism may increasingly claim that legislation that limits the rights of foreign or domestic enemies is necessary to defend countries, families, victims, and traditional ways of life and to express disapproval and enmity towards unpopular groups. Expressive and symbolic objectives are often achieved by the mere passage of legislation regardless of its impact or success in achieving such lofty goals. They are not easily amenable to evidence-based proportionality analysis that focuses on the relation between means and ends and the overall costs and benefits of legislation.

I have argued elsewhere that the Supreme Court's *Sauvé* voting right case striking down prison disenfranchisement is best defended not on the basis that depriving prisoners serving sentences of two years or more was disproportionate compared to other somewhat arbitrary cut-offs, but on the basis that Parliament's vague and symbolic objectives of affirming the rule of law and imposing additional punishment on prisoners were symbolic expressions of brute majoritarian preferences that were not important enough to limit Charter rights because they amount to little more than an expression of disgust of offenders.[120] The expression of disgust has, of course, has been defended by Lord Devlin and other legal moralists[121] as a legitimate aim of the criminal law. Nevertheless, as Chief Justice McLachlin stated in *Sauvé*:

> 'the rhetorical nature of the government's objectives advanced in this case renders them suspect ... Vague and symbolic objectives such as these almost guarantee a positive answer to this question. Who can argue that respect for the law is not pressing? Who can argue that proper sentences are not important? ... vague and symbolic objectives make the justification analysis more difficult ... The broader and more abstract the objective, the more susceptible it is to different meanings in different contexts, and hence to distortion and manipulation.'[122]

---

[120] Roach, 'The Varied Role of Courts and Legislatures in Rights Protection' above n 83, pp. 412–416; Roach, *The Supreme Court on Trial* above n 8, pp. 339–346.

[121] For severe criticisms of the majority's decision in *Sauvé*, and criticism of prisoner voting as 'decadent', see John Finnis 'Judicial Law-Making and the "Living" Instrumentalisation of the ECHR' in N. W. Barber, Richard Ekins, and Paul Yowell, eds., *Lord Sumption and the Limits of the Law* (Oxford: Hart Publishing, 2016), p. 101. See also Finnis, 'Prisoners' Voting Rights and Judges' Powers' in this volume.

[122] [2002] 3 SCR 519 at paras. 22 and 24. I disclose that I represented Aboriginal Legal Services of Toronto in its intervention in this case, which argued that Parliament's objectives in promoting the rule of law and punishing prisoners were not important enough to limit Charter rights.

One of the more troubling aspects of Parliament's recent reply legislation to the assisted dying case was that the Justin Trudeau government responded to criticism of the bill by releasing a legal statement that offered up new symbolic objectives of disapproving of suicide and affirming the values of the lives of the disabled as legitimate objectives for limiting Charter rights. These objectives, like the rule of law and punishment objectives in *Sauvé*, are so vague that they are difficult to contest. They confirm that populist and symbolic objectives can come from governments on the left as well as on the right. Symbolic and expressive objectives such as disapproving of suicide and affirming the value of the life of the disabled have a self-fulfilling and all-or-nothing quality that makes it difficult to apply proportionality analysis with its focus on less restrictive means and overall balance.

In an age of populism, there will be an increasing need to distinguish between rhetorical and expressive objectives for rights-infringing laws and instrumental objectives that, by addressing concrete as opposed to symbolic problems, are amenable to evidence-based proportionality analysis. Judicial rejection of populist and symbolic legislative objectives, however, could lead to increased conflict between courts and legislatures including over judicial rejection of legislative replies to Charter decisions. They could also lead to increased use of the override, perhaps supported by the use of referenda.

Refining Dialogue: The Need for Effective and Two-Track Remedies

Remedies are the final area where dialogic understandings may have to be refined in take into account populist challenges to rights and courts. The assumption that Canadian courts frequently make that Canadian governments will respond voluntarily and in good faith to their decisions may in some contexts need to be rethought.

Bruce Ryder and Robert Leckey have both raised objections to the Court's increased use of suspended declarations of invalidity on the basis that they could leave litigants without effective remedies and that governments could abuse their powers during a period of suspension.[123] I agree that courts should often exempt successful litigants from a suspended declaration of invalidity to ensure that they receive effective remedies. I also agree that more should be done to limit the harms caused by suspensions including perhaps creating guidelines about how

---

[123] Bruce Ryder, 'Suspending the Charter' (2003) 21(2) *Supreme Court Law Review* 267; Robert Leckey, 'The Harms of Remedial Discretion' (2016) 14 *International Journal of Constitutional Law* 584.

unconstitutional laws will be administered during the suspension.[124] Nevertheless, I cannot agree that Canadian suspended declarations of invalidity are similar to unenforceable declarations of incompatibility.[125] The dialogic features of these remedies should not obscure the significant legal differences discussed in the second part of this chapter between the Canadian Charter and bills of rights that explicitly deprive courts of the power to strike down legislation.

The Court in the *Carter*-assisted dying case was able to avoid confronting its responsibility for providing effective remedies because the two lead plaintiffs in the case, Lee Carter and Gloria Taylor, had already passed away by the time of the Court's first decision, the former having made a difficult trip to Switzerland to receive medical assistance in ending her life. Individual litigants should not be made to suffer for the sake of dialogue or giving the legislature an opportunity to respond to a Charter decision. Fortunately, a 5:4 majority of the Supreme Court recognized the need for individual remedies a year later when it extended the original twelve-month suspension for another four months because of parliamentary time lost during the 2015 general election campaign. At that time, the majority of the Court indicated that qualified adults could seek court-ordered exemptions during the continued period of suspension and that Quebec's new law could also operate to the extent it applied to qualified people seeking physician assistance in dying.[126]

In my view, courts should pursue a two-track approach to remedies such as those employed in the second *Carter*-assisted[127] dying case.

---

[124] Leckey, 'The Harms of Remedial Discretion' above n 123 at 602. My only reservation would be that courts should be careful to indicate that such guidelines are not necessarily a blueprint for legislative replies, and the legislatures retain their ability to broaden the policy debate and devise and justify creative legislative responses that were not thought of by, nor perhaps open to, the courts.

[125] Robert Leckey, 'Enforcing Laws that Infringe Human Rights' [2016] *Public Law* 206.

[126] *Carter* v. *Canada (Attorney General)*, 2016 SCC 4.

[127] Ibid. For further explanation and defence of two-track remedial approaches, which draw on the strengths of courts in providing effective remedies for past and present violations of the rights of litigants and the strength of legislatures and the executive in formulating systemic approaches to govern the future, see Kent Roach 'Remedies for Laws that Violate Human Rights' in John Bell, Mark Elliott, Jason N. E. Varuhas, and Philip Murray, (eds.), *Public Law Adjudication in Common Law Systems: Process and Substance* (Oxford: Hart Publishing, 2016); Grégoire Webber also draws distinctions between judicial primacy in responding to the past and legislative primacy in shaping the future in his 'Past, Present, and Justice in the Exercise of Judicial Responsibility' in this volume. In contrast and in building on his strong- and weak-form judicial review models, Mark Tushnet has drawn a dichotomy between strong remedies such as injunctions and

A two-track approach will build on judicial strengths in providing successful litigants with a tangible remedy for past and ongoing rights violations while also recognizing the important roles that legislatures and the executive can play in formulating systemic remedies for the future. A two-track approach would require courts to take the lead in granting remedies for individual litigants while being more flexible or deferential to the executive and the legislature about the proper systemic response going forward.

Another remedial practice that may need to be refined is the assumption that governments will respond promptly and in good faith to all judicial declarations. The Supreme Court has frequently relied on declarations in order to give the executive flexibility in implementing a range of rights. Controversial executive responses to declarations in minority language school cases[128] and the *Little Sisters* gay pornography case[129] suggest that courts should in such cases be willing to retain jurisdiction to ensure that the litigant receives an effective remedy. As discussed in the first part of this chapter, this process may already have started as the Supreme Court used a mandatory remedy in the *Insite*-supervised[130]

---

individuals' remedies and weak remedies such as declarations. See Tushnet, *Weak Courts, Strong Rights* above n 2, pp. 247–264. For my own arguments that a two-track approach can profitably combine strong individual remedies even at the risk of queue-jumping with a more judicially deferential approach to systemic remedies, see Kent Roach, 'Dialogic Remedies' *International Journal of Constitutional Law* (forthcoming):
    Two-track remedies, like other transnational applications of the dialogue concept, should be attentive to institutional and legal context. For arguments that a two-track approach in the context of the Human Rights Act 1998 and the European Convention of Human Rights would involve a legislative remand to Parliament on the systemic issue of prisoner voting, but individual remedies such as damages for prisoners who continue to be denied the right to a vote, see Jacqueline Hodgson and Kent Roach, 'Disenfranchisement as Punishment: European Court of Human Rights, UK and Canadian Responses to Prisoner Voting' [2017] *Public Law* 450 at 454–455. It appears that the May government may allow 'fewer than 100' UK prisoners on short sentences to vote without amending the law found by the courts to be incompatible with rights. 'Up to 100 prisoners on short sentences to be given the right to vote', *The Guardian* 2 November 2017. Such a response demonstrates the dangers of token compliance and executive construction or minimization of the relevant norms inspired by the unpopularity of prisoners and judges.

[128] For a case where the Court in a 5:4 decision upheld judicial retention of jurisdiction after Nova Scotia had delayed responding to previous declarations about rights to minority language rights and facilities, see *Doucet-Boudreau v. Nova Scotia* [2003] 3 SCR 3.

[129] [2000] 2 SCR 1120. Problems in customs administration continued, but the small bookstore was forced to abandon a subsequent Charter challenge after being denied advance costs. *Little Sisters v. Canada* [2007] 2 SCR 28.

[130] *Canada v. PHS Community Services* [2011] 3 SCR 134

injection site case a year after the government's lacklustre response to the use of a declaration in the *Omar Khadr*[131] case. One of the dialogic challenges going forward will be for the courts to ensure effective remedies without being overly prescriptive and usurping roles best left to the legislature or the executive. As with dialogue in general, the courts may have particular expertise in crafting a fair and transparent process that will facilitate participation by both the government and affected parties about the optimal systemic remedies.[132]

In the end, judicial deference to the legitimate legislative and executive roles in formulating systemic remedies should not be absolute, especially in an age of populist resistance to court decisions. Courts may have to be interventionist if a legislature or executive fails to use the freedom given to them by dialogue in a good faith manner. As Alexander Bickel recognized, remedial remands to legislatures and the executive can reconcile 'authoritarian judicialism and the practice of democracy' and allow courts 'to engage in a continual colloquy with the political institutions, leaving it to them to tell the Court what expedients of accommodation and compromise they deemed necessary'. Nevertheless, Bickel's warning that courts must reject dialogic responses when 'a suggested expedient amounted to the abandonment of principle'[133] holds as true in today's populist era as it did with respect to Southern resistance to *Brown* v. *Board of Education.*[134]

Conclusion

Dialogue as a theory that seeks to provide an alternative to judicial and legislative supremacy is not perfect and more work should be done on refining it. Nevertheless, it is real and it persists. Dialogue has been offered in good faith as a new and helpful understanding of judicial

---

[131] *Canada (Prime Minister)* v. *Khadr* [2010] 1 SCR 44.

[132] An alternative to the present dichotomy between a simple declaration and a prescriptive mandatory order is a 'declaration plus' in which courts leave room for the executive to fashion its response to the declaration while also retaining jurisdiction to require the executive to publicize its response and to allow the parties, if necessary, to challenge the executive's response. See Kent Roach, 'Polycentricity and Queue Jumping in Public Law Remedies: A Two Track Approach' (2016) 66 *University of Toronto Law Journal* 3 at 27–35.

[133] Bickel, *The Least Dangerous Branch* above n 48, pp. 244, 250. Bickel's reference to judicial rejection was to *Cooper* v. *Aaron* 358 U.S. 1 (1958) where the entire Court reversed a trial judge who had ordered a two-and-a-half-year delay in the desegregation of Central High because of Arkansas's rejection of *Brown*.

[134] 347 U.S. 483 (1954).

review. It does not deserve the glib denial, scare quotes, and vituperative criticism it has received. Claims that dialogue is really a fraudulent monologue or that dialogue only occurs if the legislature rejects the Court's Charter decisions have not advanced our understanding of dialogue. They have resulted in a debate not so much about dialogue and interaction between courts, legislatures, the executive, and society, but about the desirability of giving judges increased power of judicial review under the Charter.

Comparative law is complex. It should not be reduced to abstract and dichotomous models, especially on matters as politically charged as judicial review. If the ability of courts to strike down legislation is the definition of strong-form judicial review, then the Charter is a strong form of judicial review, but that hardly means it has the same effects as the US Bill of Rights. Similarly, the (opposite) conclusion that the Charter promotes weak-form or a Commonwealth model of judicial review obscures important contextual differences between judicial review in Canada and even in similar countries such as the United Kingdom and New Zealand. It would be wrong to posit one model of dialogue across constitutional different systems. Dialogue as a process that allows legislative limits and overrides on judicial interpretations of rights may occur in many different systems but in distinct ways.

The many Canadian academic supporters of majoritarian democracy and co-ordinate construction as defended by Waldron and Tushnet might wish to rethink their position in the age of populism, where disagreement will not always be reasonable and co-ordinate construction that assigns the legislature and the executive the power to reject judicial interpretation of rights can allow the legislature and the executive to deny that the unpopular – especially the accused, prisoners, and migrants – have rights. There is a place for legislative rejection of judicial interpretation of rights under the Charter, but that place is with the special signals and second thoughts that should accompany the use of the override.

An acceptance of the exclusive role of the independent judiciary as the interpreter of rights designed to protect the vulnerable remains the best means of ensuring that legislatures and executives have to own up to and take responsibility for the limits and derogations they place on rights. To be sure, in an age of populism, democratic dialogue presents risks that the rights of the unpopular will not prevail. The answer to these risks, however, cannot be to retreat to formulaic recantations of either judicial or legislative supremacy. Those who care about the rights of the unpopular must engage both judicially and politically.

Care should be taken that understanding judicial review in dialogic terms does not undermine the independent role of the courts and the rule of law. In particular, dialogue should not place judicial deference and institutional comity above principled decision-making on the evidence in second-look cases. Similarly, courts need to ensure that legislative objectives are amenable to proportionality analysis and not simply all-or-nothing symbolic articulations of disgust, anxiety, national solidarity, animus, or other strong and hostile emotions.

Finally, the independent courts will have to struggle to ensure that their remedies are effective in an age of populist resistance to rights and courts. Courts should honour as far as possible the need for litigants to receive an effective remedy while also recognizing that legislatures and the executive can play a role in devising and refining systemic remedies. These are dangerous and dark times, but they affirm the importance of examining not only how courts make their decisions but also the way that the executive, the legislature and society respond to such decisions.

11

Bills of Rights with Strings Attached

Protecting Death Penalty, Slavery, Discriminatory Religious Practices, and the Past from Judicial Review

RIVKA WEILL*

I Introduction

We customarily think that we need a constitution with a big C, or a supreme constitution, to prevail over future laws, but we take for granted the fact that constitutions prevail over statutes that preceded them.[1] The regular maxim of interpretation is that the later statute prevails over the earlier one to the extent of the inconsistency unless the earlier enactment is more specific in nature. Thus, even without a supreme constitution, when two norms share the same normative basis, the later one prevails. This maxim reflects the nature of democracy: the later will of the legislature should prevail over its earlier will. It is also supported by logic: the later enactment is preferred because it incorporates the most up-to-date information on the subject.[2]

Scholars are aware that a few constitutions deviate from this expectation. They do not prevail over the past. This is usually done through a "savings clause" or a "preservation of laws" mechanism that is *explicitly* included in the constitution. The typical savings clause states that preexisting laws – that is laws existing at the time of establishing the

* I thank Daniel Abebe, Rosalind Dixon, Tom Ginsburg, James Gathii, Geoffrey Stone, Mark Tushnet, and Grégoire Webber. This article benefited from comments of participants at the conference on "Sacred/Secular Space" organized by the Emory University School of Law and Harry Radzyner Law School (IDC Herzliya) in 2017; Yale Law School Jewish Law Students' Association Public Talk in 2018; The Xth World Congress of the International Association of Constitutional Law in 2018 (Seoul); the I*CON-S Annual International Conference on Identity, Security, Democracy: Challenges for Public Law in 2018 (University of Hong Kong).

[1] *Marbury v. Madison*, 5 U.S. (1 Cranch) 137, 176–77 (1803).
[2] Antonin Scalia and Bryan A. Garner, *Reading Law: The Interpretation of Legal Texts* (West, 2012).

constitution – are "valid" even if inconsistent with the constitution. This declaration is necessary not only because the constitution is the later enactment, but also to avoid invalidation by the courts through judicial review.

These clauses may be *general* in nature, protecting all laws existing at the time of the constitution's adoption,[3] or *specific* or *partial*, protecting only certain specified laws.[4] Furthermore, the courts may *implicitly* read savings clauses into the constitution, as discussed in this chapter.[5] These savings clauses may be *temporary*, lapsing after a few years, or form part of the *permanent* features of the constitution.[6] The law protected from constitutional review may be written enactments or more broadly all law, including the common law.[7]

While scholars are aware of this phenomenon of "savings clauses," they believe it is esoteric, even exotic, appearing in Caribbean or African countries alone.[8] They provide an analysis of it on a regional or even country-specific basis, typically in connection with the death penalty or, in recent years, in connection with the preservation of criminal penalties for homosexual relationships.[9] However, this chapter argues that this phenomenon is quite widespread, covering both civil law and common law countries. Savings clauses appear in over forty percent of the constitutions of the world. They are not just African or Caribbean in nature, but appear in constitutions widely considered to be archetypes of

---

[3] See e.g., *Barbados Constitution*, §26; *Trinidad and Tobago Constitution*, §6; *Guyana Constitution*, §152.

[4] See e.g., *Botswana Constitution*, §19(2)(3) (protecting the disciplinary law of the disciplined forces from invalidation).

[5] See this chapter Part II.A.

[6] See this chapter Part III.

[7] Thus, for example, the Barbados and Guyana Constitutions save only existing "written law." *Barbados Constitution*, §26; *Guyana Constitution*, §152. In contrast, the Trinidad and Tobago Constitution saves all existing law, including the common law: *Trinidad and Tobago Constitution*, §6.

[8] See e.g., Andrew Novak, 'Constitutional Reform and the Abolition of the Mandatory Death Penalty in Kenya,' (2011–2012) 45 *Suffolk University Law Review* 285; Margaret A. Burnham, 'Indigenous Constitutionalism and the Death Penalty: The Case of the Commonwealth Caribbean,' (2005) 4 *International Journal of Constitutional Law* 582; Margaret DeMerieux, *Fundamental Rights in Commonwealth Caribbean Constitutions* (University of the West Indies, 1992) pp. 53–71; Margaret DeMerieux, 'Existing Law and the Implementation of a Bill of Rights: A Caribbean Perspective,' (1986) 19 *Law and Politics in Africa, Asia and Latin America* 5.

[9] See Human Rights Watch, 'This Alien Legacy: The Origins of "Sodomy" Laws in British Colonialism' (2008); Simeon C. R. McIntosh, 'Homosexuality and the Constitution', *The Trinidad Guardian Newspaper*, January 1, 2012.

constitutionalism. Savings clauses appear in the United States, the United Kingdom, Canada, India, and Israel, to name but a few examples. They should lead us to rethink our most basic conceptions of constitutionalism. As evidenced in the historical development of these and other nations, we typically tell constitutional stories involving a notorious break with the past. However, savings clauses suggest that constitutionalism is more evolutionary in nature than is often acknowledged. Savings clauses are about preserving continuity, even during and after constitutional adoption.

Scholars also typically suggest that a country's motive for adopting a savings clause is to preserve problematic, maybe even unconstitutional statutes, from judicial review.[10] But while this is one of the motives for adoption of a savings clause, it is not the only one. Rather, this chapter argues that there are three types of savings clauses categorized according to the motivations of the constitution-makers for including such a clause – motivations explicitly discussed during the constitution-drafting period. Moreover, I argue that the type of savings clause affects the nature of the dialogue between the branches of government over interpretation of the constitution and existing laws. At times, the same country may adopt several types of savings clauses depending on the topic at stake.

The first category of savings clause is associated with constitutional founders who glorify the past and are proud of it. These constitution-makers include a savings clause to make sure that all political actors share their view that the past should be revered and respected. They adopt a savings clause to guarantee that not only will past laws be treated as valid but that past laws will define the scope of rights included in the constitution. Rather than have the constitution affect the interpretation of past laws, they want past laws to affect the interpretation of the constitution. This type of constitutional interpretation is typically associated with originalism in the United States or the "frozen concepts" idea in Canada.[11]

The second type of savings clauses is a stabilizing mechanism. These clauses reflect a neutral attitude by constitution-makers about the nation's history; they are neither proud of the past nor ashamed of it. They may not know what their position is or should be with regard to

---

[10] See e.g., Aharon Barak, 'Preservation of Laws' in Aharon Barak, *Selected Essays – Constitutional Inquiries* (vol. 3, 2017) (Hebrew), p. 247 (dealing with the Israeli Basic Laws alone). See also Novak, above n 8; DeMerieux, both above n 8.
[11] See this chapter, Part II.

past laws. At the time of adoption of the constitution, they do not have the resources, especially the time, to make up their mind with regard to past laws. They adopt a savings clause as a stabilizing mechanism, to guarantee that the adoption of the constitution does not have unanticipated effects on the current legal status quo, until they have time to revisit the issue. In such cases, we may more often find a temporary sunset savings mechanism rather than a savings clause that serves as a permanent feature of constitutionalism. Because this type of savings clause is not about glorifying the past, liberal courts feel more comfortable to minimize the effects of the savings clause when it leads to the preservation of anachronistic undesired constitutional practices. In such cases, courts may come to interpret the savings clause narrowly and the rest of the constitution in a purposive, broad way to develop a more coherent constitutional identity despite the savings clause.[12]

The third type of a savings clause is a compromise mechanism. Such mechanisms are necessary to enable the adoption of the constitution and are useful when constitution-makers are aware that savings clauses will preserve problematic, even unconstitutional, laws. Typically, there will be factions within society that are reluctant to adopt a supreme constitution or bill of rights. They may fear the effects of these new governing documents on legislative sovereignty and the legal status quo more generally. To appease the fears of these factions, the constitutional founders may include a savings clause that guarantees that the adoption of the constitution will be primarily future-looking, not designed to destabilize current arrangements.

Sometimes the savings clause is motivated by the desire of the founders to engage in a major redistribution of wealth within society during the founding moment. They may want to do so without paying full or even partial compensation for such a major reform by preventing the judiciary from invalidating the reform. The savings clause may serve as the means to shelter such redistribution of wealth.

Since the protected preexisting law is not incorporated into the text of the constitution, it enjoys protection from constitutional attack but does not enjoy the status of a supreme constitutional provision. The legislature may amend past laws without the need to resort to the constitutional amendment process. This technique also enables the constitutional founders to reap the benefits of constitutional adoption while hiding

---

[12] See this chapter, Part III.

some of the embarrassing implications of the savings clauses by making them less salient. This type of savings clause may lead the courts, if they are liberal, to narrow their interpretation of the savings clauses as well, treating them as shelters for unconstitutional practices.[13]

The following discussion will tackle each of the three types of savings clauses in turn and their effect on the constitutional dialogue between the branches of government. While all types of savings clauses are about constitutional continuity to some extent, the motivations for adopting them are different and apparent in the constitutional debates leading to the adoption of the constitution. These savings clauses protect some of the more problematic aspects of democratic societies, such as the death penalty, slavery, and discriminatory religious and cultural practices. The chapter will conclude by suggesting that savings clauses might postpone conflict rather than resolve it. It will enumerate cases in which overcoming the savings clauses' effect on society led to major constitutional transformations.

II   Glorifying the Past Savings Clauses

One type of savings clauses is utilized when the constitutional founders are proud of the past and intend the constitution to codify the past, rather than break from it. They want to ensure that all branches of government treat past laws as valid. They even want past laws to dictate the scope of constitutional rights, rather than have the constitution affect the interpretation of past laws.

These constitutions often declare that they are about the recognition of existing rights rather than the creation of new rights. To examine what rights the people "already" enjoy, courts examine laws existing at the time of formation of the constitution. These existing laws become the benchmark for interpreting the scope of rights within the constitution. Since existing laws define the scope of constitutional rights, by implication they cannot themselves be treated as unconstitutional. The courts may imply the existence of a savings clause in this type of constitution (an "implied savings clause"), or the constitution may include an explicit savings clause to this effect.

Why would the founders downplay their contribution to society? The explanation is twofold and includes a historical as well as a theoretical

---

[13] See this chapter Part IV.

explanation. Historically, the idea that rights preexist and are embedded in the people rather than granted to them appears at least as early as the Magna Carta in 1215. The Magna Carta speaks in the language of "grant" of rights on the one hand and "confirmation" of preexisting rights on the other.[14] John Locke's influence on American and French constitutional development consists of the idea that people have natural rights that they do not relinquish.[15] These ideas have fundamentally influenced the constitutional development of various countries, leading some to acknowledge that even positive law includes what would otherwise be recognized as mere natural rights.

Theoretically, founders of constitutions believed that, if they down-played their constitutional contribution and portrayed rights as preexist-ing, this would enhance the protection of rights. If they are not the granters of rights, neither could they nor potentially others take these rights away. It is thus ironic that this attempt to strengthen the protection of rights by declaring that they preceded the constitutional enterprise led to the opposite result of downgrading the protection of rights. This portrayal of constitutional rights as predating the formal constitutional document led to the adoption of explicit or implied savings clauses in various countries. I will provide three examples of these dynamics from Canada, Trinidad and Tobago, and the United States.

A   Canada

The Canadian Bill of Rights Act 1960 (CBORA) is considered a pioneer of the commonwealth model of constitutionalism.[16] It is a parliamentary bill of rights, not entrenched and easily amended but nonetheless the courts recognized their power to exercise judicial review over primary

---

[14] 'We have granted to God, and by this our present Charter have confirmed . . . Reserving to all Archbishops, Bishops, Abbots, Priors, Templars, Hospitallers, Earls, Barons, and all Persons, as well Spiritual as Temporal, all their free Liberties and free Customs, which they have had in time passed.' *Magna Carta*, 1297, retrieved from www.constituteproject.org.

[15] Peter Laslett, ed., *Locke: Two Treatises of Government*, 3rd ed. (Cambridge: Cambridge University Press, 1988). Jefferson thus led the US Declaration of Independence to state: "We hold these truths to be self-evident, that all men are created equal, that they are endowed by their Creator with certain unalienable Rights, that among these are Life, Liberty, and the pursuit of Happiness."

[16] Stephen Gardbaum, *The New Commonwealth Model of Constitutionalism: Theory and Practice* (Cambridge: Cambridge University Press, 2013).

legislation based on the CBORA.[17] It is a quasi-constitutional document. The courts repeatedly emphasized that the CBORA did not affect interpretation alone.[18]

The CBORA includes an explicit savings clause that declares that the CBORA does not intend to derogate from rights already existing to the people. It clarifies that the Bill should not be construed "to abrogate or abridge any human right or fundamental freedom not enumerated therein that may have existed in Canada at the commencement of this Act."[19] In fact, this type of savings clause is common in international treaties that clarify that the new treaty does not intend to derogate from rights already provided for in international law.[20]

This, however, is not the savings clause I am interested in.[21] Rather, I want to focus on the first two clauses of the CBORA that declare that the enumeration of rights in the CBORA is not about the creation of new rights but about the recognition of rights that preexist to the people. Section 1 reads: "It is hereby recognized and declared that in Canada there have existed and shall continue to exist ... the following human rights and fundamental freedoms."[22] Section 2 likewise suggests that the CBORA merely "recognized and declared" the existence of fundamental rights.[23] This declaration, even if fictional,[24] led the courts to recognize the existence of an *implied* savings clause. Not only will past laws be

---

[17] *Regina v. Drybones*, (1969) 9 D.L.R. 3d 473.

[18] Ibid. See also *Miller and Cockriell v. The Queen*, (1977) 2 SCR 680, 690.

[19] Canadian Bill of Rights S.C. 1960, c.44, §5(1).

[20] Thus, for example, Article 15 of the European Convention on Human Rights, article 4 of the International Covenant on Civil and Political Rights, and article 27 of the American Convention on Human Rights, all allow derogation from rights provided within them but only when such derogations are not inconsistent with other obligations under international law. These are general savings mechanisms of international obligations of member states. See Christoph Schreuer, 'Derogation of Human Rights in Situations of Public Emergency: The Experience of the European Convention on Human Rights,' (1982) 9 *Yale Journal of International Law* 113, 129–130.

[21] A similar clause appears in the Canadian Charter of Rights and Freedoms, § 26: 'The guarantee in this Charter of certain rights and freedoms shall not be construed as denying the existence of any other rights or freedoms that exist in Canada.'

[22] Canadian Bill of Rights S.C. 1960, c.44, at §1.

[23] Ibid. at §2.

[24] This portrayal of the rights enumerated in the Bill of Rights as already preexisting in Canada does not match the historical reality. Canadians did not enjoy the general legal right to be free from discrimination prior to the CBORA. The Bill of Rights further provided for other "new" rights, such as the right to counsel when a person is compelled to give evidence and a right to an interpreter in judicial or quasi-judicial proceedings.

treated as valid (with one exception),[25] but they will serve as the benchmark to define the scope of rights within the constitution. Justice Ritchie in the 1963 *Robertson and Rosetanni* case held that "the Canadian Bill of Rights is not concerned with 'the human rights and fundamental freedoms' in any abstract sense, but rather with such 'rights and freedoms' as they existed in Canada immediately before the statute was enacted."[26] Similarly, in 1972, he repeated: "[T]he meaning to be given to the language employed in the Bill of Rights is the meaning which it bore in Canada at the time when the Bill was enacted."[27] This is a variant of originalism; the public understanding of the people at the time of adoption of the CBORA defines the scope of rights. In Canada, this type of originalism is titled the "frozen concepts" theory. What was constitutionally acceptable during the adoption of the CBORA is frozen and incorporated into it.[28]

Thus, for example, when the question arose whether death penalty (before its abolition by the legislature) rises to the level of cruel and unusual punishment forbidden under the CBORA, the Court decided that it did not because it existed during the founding of the CBORA. As the CBORA intended to codify preexisting rights and "did not create new rights,"[29] the cruel and unusual punishment must be interpreted to allow for the death penalty.[30] Another example is the law requiring, under criminal penalty, Jews and Muslims to close their stores on a Sunday as the official Sabbath in Canada. The Court decided that this cannot be an infringement of the right to religious freedom, because at the time the CBORA was adopted this Sunday law was an accepted practice. "It is therefore the 'religious freedom' then existing in this country that is safeguarded."[31]

---

[25] The Court held that the Indian Act's criminal provision that 'Indian' people may not be intoxicated off of a reserve was discriminatory, as no such provision applied to non-"Indian" persons, and against section 1(b) of the CBORA. *Regina v. Drybones*, (1969) 9 D.L.R. 3d 473.

[26] *Robertson and Rosetanni v. The Queen*, (1963) 41 D.L.R. 2d. 485, 491.

[27] *Curr v. The Queen*, (1972) 26 D.L.R. 3d 603, 607.

[28] Walter S. Tarnopolsky, 'The Historical and Constitutional Context of the Proposed Canadian Charter of Rights and Freedoms,' (1981) 44 *Law & Contemporary Problems* 169.

[29] *Miller and Cockriell v. The Queen*, (1977) 2 SCR 680, 704.

[30] Ibid.

[31] *Robertson and Rosetanni v. The Queen*, (1963) 41 D.L.R. 2d. at para. 6 of Ritchie J.'s majority opinion.

B Trinidad and Tobago

Scholars typically cobble together the Caribbean constitutions as though they are made of one cloth. But, while Caribbean constitutions were typically modeled after the European Convention of Human Rights, the Trinidad and Tobago Constitution was modeled after the CBORA.[32] It, too, tries to convey a perception of continuity with the past and declare that the rights enumerated in it predated the Constitution. "It is hereby recognized and declared that in Trinidad and Tobago there have existed and shall continue to exist ... the following fundamental human rights and freedoms."[33]

However, in contrast to Canada, where this perception of rights led to a judicially implied savings clause, the Trinidad and Tobago Constitution included an explicit savings clause preserving preexisting laws. Section 6(1)(a) of the Trinidad and Tobago Constitution states that "[n]othing in sections 4 and 5 shall invalidate an existing law." Section 6(3) further defines "existing law" as "a law that had effect as part of the law of Trinidad and Tobago immediately before the commencement of this Constitution."[34]

It, too, led to an originalist interpretation of constitutional rights. Thus, for example, when the courts were confronted with the question whether the right to strike is part of the explicit enumerated constitutional right of association, they answered negatively. Because the English common law that predated the adoption of the Constitution did not recognize the right to strike as part of the right of association, and because the Constitution preserved preexisting law, the explicit right to association included in the Constitution was interpreted as excluding the right to strike.[35]

C United States

The US Constitution is considered an archetype of constitutionalism. During the founding moment there was a great debate between federalists and antifederalists about the need to adopt a bill of rights. The antifederalists wanted one, but the federalists argued that there was no need because the people already enjoyed rights that the government may

---

[32] *Roodal v. The State,* [2003] UKHL 78, paras. 59, 61–68.
[33] *Trinidad and Tobago Constitution,* §4.
[34] *Trinidad and Tobago Constitution,* §6.
[35] *Collymore v. Attorney General of Trinidad and Tobago,* [1967] 12 W.I.R. 5 (C.A.) [1970] A.C. 538.

not take away unless explicitly granted the power to do so, and the Constitution made sure no such powers were granted. Ultimately, the Bill of Rights was adopted a few years after the initial adoption of the Constitution. The perception of rights as preexisting influenced the Supreme Court's interpretation of certain constitutional rights. When the Court treats rights as preexisting, it often tends to adopt an originalist interpretation of the meaning of those rights. Preexisting laws are not only valid, but they dictate constitutional interpretation.

Thus, for example, the Supreme Court found it difficult to treat the death penalty per se as amounting to cruel and unusual punishment prohibited by the US Constitution because it existed at the time of adoption of the Constitution. The prohibition of cruel and unusual punishment dates to the British Bill of Rights Act of the seventeenth century, and it was adopted at a time when the death penalty was considered an acceptable practice.[36] Similarly, the right to bear arms is not just about the individual or even collective right to be part of the militia; it is also about the personal right to self-defense, based on laws existing at the time of the adoption of the Constitution that permitted individuals to bear arms for purposes of self-defense. Therefore, the Constitution is understood to have codified rather than invented this constitutional right. In the words of Justice Antonin Scalia, who wrote the majority opinion, in *Heller*:

> Putting all of these textual elements together, we find that they guarantee the individual right to possess and carry weapons in case of confrontation. This meaning is strongly confirmed by the historical background of the Second Amendment. We look to this because it has always been widely understood that the Second Amendment . . . codified a pre-existing right. The very text of the Second Amendment implicitly recognizes the pre-existence of the right and declares only that it "shall not be infringed." As we said in *United States v. Cruikshank*, 92 U.S. 542, 553 (1876), "[t]his is not a right granted by the Constitution. Neither is it in any manner dependent upon that instrument for its existence. The Second amendment declares that it shall not be infringed . . . [37]

Another example relates to incorporation of the Bill of Rights to the states through the 14th Amendment. Here, too, preexisting rights became the benchmark for what is incorporated vis-à-vis the states.[38]

---

[36] *Furman v. Georgia*, 408 US 238 (1972).
[37] *District of Columbia v. Heller*, 554 US 570, 592 (2008).
[38] *McDonald v. City of Chicago*, 561 US 742 (2010).

To summarize, this type of savings clause – whether explicit or implicit – entails a nation's belief that it is proud of its past and wants its past laws to govern current constitutional affairs. This type of savings clause suggests that constitutional adoption is not aimed at transforming national identity or self-understanding, but rather at ensuring their preservation. The mechanism to accomplish this is the guarantee that preexisting laws are valid and saved. This often leads to originalist interpretations of the constitution under which preexisting laws affect constitutional interpretation, rather than the constitution affecting the interpretation of past laws. Of course, one can envision a different constitutional development that rejects originalism even in the face of savings clauses that intend to glorify and codify the past. But one cannot ignore comparative constitutional development suggesting that various countries chose to link savings clauses that glorify the past with originalist interpretations of the constitution, whatever the exact variant of originalism was adopted. Moreover, American scholars often assume that their system is unique in adopting originalism for interpretation of some constitutional provisions, but savings clauses suggest that originalism exists in other countries as well.[39]

III   Stabilizing Savings Clauses

Another type of savings clause is one that does not glorify the past, nor reluctantly or shamefully protects it. Rather, it protects past laws as a stabilizing device to ensure that the constitutional adoption does not affect the legal status quo in unanticipated ways. This device, by its nature, is intended to be temporary. It allows time for society to revisit its legal system and determine which laws it desires to preserve, which to discard, and which to amend considering constitutional adoption. Some of this type of savings clauses are explicitly temporary by embodying a sunset provision.

Countries that at one time or another have been ruled by the United Kingdom have often adopted such savings clauses. When gaining their independence, these states had to address what laws will govern the country from day one. They did not want to suffer the chaos of

---

[39] See e.g., Jamal Greene, 'On the Origins of Originalism,' (2009) 88 *Texas Law Review* 1; Jack Balkin, 'Why Are Americans Originalist?' in Richard Nobles and David Schiff, (eds.), *Law, Society and Community: Socio-Legal Essays in Honour of Roger Cotterrell* (Ashgate, 2014) p. 349.

lawlessness, yet they could not adopt a whole new corpus of law at once. When these countries declared independence, they adopted a savings clause in regular law that incorporated preexisting laws, while declaring that this incorporation is subject to the "necessary alterations" resulting from the establishment of a new state with a new constitutional identity.

This category of savings clauses is common in British colonies and dominions because British law was considered satisfactory as an interim arrangement, especially since it allowed for cultural and religious variations in personal law, particularly marriage and divorce law.[40] Also, the savings clause was a familiar mechanism in the UK legal system, and the nation began using it on an extensive basis in the nineteenth century in consolidation statutes that unified different statutes addressing the same issue. Consolidation statutes streamlined disparate and duplicative laws, revoked statutes that were no longer enforced, and established better mechanisms to coordinate the legal subjects' expectations. In this technical process, lawmakers worried about unintended material changes, so they included savings clauses.[41]

Colonies and dominions not only included a savings clause in regular statutes during independence, but they also included such clauses in their constitution. These states did not have the resources or will to canvass through preexisting laws to determine which did or did not align with new constitutional norms. From their perspective, adopting carte blanche savings clauses in the constitution was easier and secured the validity of preexisting laws, despite the adoption of the new constitution.

While the United Kingdom never adopted a full-fledged constitution, this did not prevent it from encouraging its colonies and dominions to adopt a formal constitution and embody in it a savings clause. Such savings clauses served British as well as local interests. From the UK's perspective, the savings clauses assured it that the locals would protect rights at least as much as the United Kingdom did. Preexisting laws, including common law, would become the minimum benchmark for the protection of rights. Savings clauses soothed United Kingdom fears by promising that minority rights, especially, white minority rights, would be protected. They further

---

[40] See e.g., Francis Alexis, 'When is "An Existing Law" Saved?,' [1976] *Public Law* 256; Peter M. McDermott, 'Imperial Statutes in Australia and New Zealand,' (1990) 2 *Bond Law Review* 162.

[41] Jonathan Teasdale, 'Statute Law Revision: Repeal, Consolidation or Something More?,' (2009) 11 *European Journal of Law Reform* 157; Peter M. McDermott, 'Statute Law Revision Statutes – Westbury Savings,' (1998) *Statute Law Review* 139.

offered protections for British and foreigners' property and investment rights.[42] From the locals' perspective, such savings clauses served as a signaling device that they will be part of the Western bloc, rather than the Soviet bloc.[43] With that international recognition, they advanced their desire to attract foreign investment in them.

Somewhat ironically, these savings clauses led at times to the protection of anachronistic, problematic laws, long abandoned in the United Kingdom. One prominent example is the United Kingdom's abolition of the death penalty. In contrast, many Caribbean and African countries were founded with specific or general savings clauses in their constitutions that shielded archaic criminal penalties from judicial review, thus preserving the death penalty.[44] At other times, the anachronistic statutes were not of British import but rather emerged from customary law that the savings clause protected. The savings of customary law as part of preexisting law proved a major obstacle to gender equality.[45]

When savings clauses are matters of stability, the drafters may choose to limit their duration. The founders may require the legislature to revise existing laws within a certain period, typically of two to five years, and align them with the new constitutional order before the savings clause lapses. The Israeli Basic Law: Freedom of Occupation may serve as an example. It had a general savings clause designed to lapse after two years. But the Israeli legislature extended its protection three times, until it finally lapsed ten years after its original adoption.[46] Moreover, the Israeli legislature time and again extended the protection of the savings clause in Basic Law: Freedom of Occupation after it lapsed, thus effectively retroactively validating preexisting laws.[47] Letting the general savings clause

---

[42] Novak, above n 8, at 272, 330; William Dale, 'The Making and Remaking of Commonwealth Constitutions,' (1993) 42 *The International and Comparative Law Quarterly* 67; McDermott, above n 41.

[43] Burnham, above n 8, at 592.

[44] Andrew Novak, 'The Abolition of the Mandatory Death Penalty in Africa: A Comparative Constitutional Analysis,' (2012) 22 *Indiana International & Comparative Law Review* 267, 272–273. See e.g., *Bangladesh Constitution*, §35(6) ('Nothing in clause (3) or clause (5) shall affect the operation of any existing law which prescribes any punishment or procedure for trial.')

[45] See e.g., Celestine I. Nyamu, 'How Should Human Rights and Development Respond to Cultural Legitimization of Gender Hierarchy in Developing Countries' (2000) 41 *Harvard International Law Journal* 381.

[46] Basic Law: Freedom of Occupation, 5754, SH No. 1454 p. 90 (Isr.)

[47] The Knesset enacted Basic Law: Freedom of Occupation for the first time on March 3, 1992. Basic Law: Freedom of Occupation, S.H. 1387 p. 114. It included a savings clause preserving preexisting laws for two years. On March 10, 1994, ten days after the savings

regarding the single right of Freedom of Occupation to lapse was less challenging than eliminating the general savings clause in the more comprehensive and broadly construed Basic Law: Human Dignity and Liberty. Thus, the latter's savings clause is permanent.

Similarly, Belize was the only Caribbean state to include a transitory rather than permanent savings clause, which stated, "Nothing contained in any law in force immediately before Independence Day nor anything done under the authority of any such law shall, for a period of five years after Independence Day, be held to be inconsistent with or done in contravention of any of the provisions of this Part."[48] Belize was the last Caribbean state to gain Independence and adopt a constitution and, by the time it had done so in 1981, the problematic effects of the savings clauses on the democratization of the legal system were known to all. Thus, Belize opted for a temporary savings provision.[49]

Since these savings clauses were not about the idea of glorifying the past but rather stabilizing the present, liberal courts – and especially the Privy Council sitting as a Court of Appeals over Caribbean courts before the Caribbean Court of Justice was established as a constitutional review court – interpreted them narrowly when they determined that these clauses shielded problematic and dubious constitutional practices. Savings clauses could be interpreted narrowly, even as other parts of the constitution were interpreted in a broad, purposive and even majestic ways. Judges legitimized this approach by portraying narrow interpretations as a way to minimize the grip of the past over contemporary constitutional rights and thus foster the development of a coherent identity around compatible social values.

---

clause's protection expired, the Knesset amended the Basic Law and reenacted the savings clause, preserving again preexisting laws for two more years. Basic Law: Freedom of Occupation, S.H. 1454 p. 90. Only on November 7, 1996, almost eight months after the expiration of the savings clause's protection, did the Knesset amend the Basic Law to provide that the savings clause was valid for four years instead of two. Basic Law: Freedom of Occupation (Amendment), S.H. 1602 p. 4. Again, nine days late, the Knesset extended the protection for the last time until March 14, 2002. Basic Law: Freedom of Occupation (Amendment No. 2), S.H. 1662 p. 178. This technique of retroactive revalidation of statutes was evident also during the founding era with regard to statutes overriding the Basic Laws. See Rivka Weill, 'Reconciling Parliamentary Sovereignty and Judicial Review: On the Theoretical and Historical Origins of the Israeli Legislative Override Power,' (2012) 39 *Hastings Constitutional Law Quarterly* 457.

[48] *Belize Constitution*, §21.

[49] Novak, above n 8, at 298.

The courts also justified narrow applications when a savings clause was itself narrow in nature, protecting some rather than the entire past legal corpus. Thus, for example, when the savings clauses preserved only criminal penalties, not all past laws, the courts interpreted them as preserving death penalty per se, but not the accompanying attributes of the death penalty machinery. Specifically, courts decided that the death penalty was preserved, but not the death row syndrome, which arose when a prisoner had to wait many years to be executed. Even if the prisoner contributed to his waiting period by appealing his verdict and petitioning for mercy and pardon, nonetheless the lengthy waiting period was cruel and unusual, and the prisoner therefore could not be executed.[50] Or, even if the death penalty per se was preserved, the system could not impose a *mandatory* death penalty. Requiring courts to issue death penalties for murder amounted to a cruel and unusual punishment[51] or an undue infringement of the right to life or an unconstitutional infringement of separation of powers, or it even amounted to an unconstitutional denial of access to the courts.[52] This was so because the requirement prevented courts from fulfilling their discretionary functions of taking mitigating circumstances into account. The courts emphasized that the savings clauses should be read narrowly and in a way compatible with constitutional rights as far as possible.

The examples in this section have all dealt with situations in which the savings clauses were specific rather than general. They were phrased to protect certain specified preexisting laws rather than all law. This enabled the courts to "interpret between the lines" and argue that the savings clauses did not extend to unwanted features of the statute under examination. In contrast, when savings clauses were worded in general terms, to cover all preexisting law, courts have found it more difficult to appeal to narrow interpretations. Thus, the Privy Council ruled in majority opinions that these general savings clauses prevented it from holding that mandatory death sentences were inoperative,[53] whereas it felt free to reach the opposite conclusion when only specific savings clauses were in place. The courts found that a narrow interpretation of the general

---

[50] See e.g., *Pratt and Morgan v. AG for Jamaica*, [1994] 2 A.C. 1 (P.C. 1993) (appeal from Jamaica).
[51] See e.g., *R. v. Hughes*, [2002] 2 A.C. 259 (P.C.) (appeal from St. Lucia); *Fox v. R.*, [2002] 2 A.C. 284 (P.C.) (appeal from St. Christopher & Nevis).
[52] Novak, above n 8; Novak, above n 44.
[53] *Boyce v. The Queen*, [2004] 3 W.L.R. 786 (P.C.) (appeal from Barbados); *Matthew v. The State*, [2004] 3 W.L.R. 812 (appeal from Trinidad & Tobago).

savings clauses was impossible and they would grudgingly uphold the death machinery as a whole.

IV Shielding Unconstitutional Laws Savings Clauses

Savings clauses that are intended to shield problematic and even unconstitutional past laws are often compromise mechanisms needed to enable the adoption of the constitution. There may be factions within society that oppose the adoption of the constitution or bill of rights. They might want to preserve legislative supremacy or protect the current legal scheme with discriminatory practices. They might also want to prevent a situation in which the court is extensively engaged with a review of past legislation to the degree that it becomes a full-time backward-looking "negative legislator," in Kelsian terms.[54] The way forward in these societies might entail the adoption of a savings clause that protects unconstitutional arrangements from judicial invalidation, but at least provides for future law that will align with constitutional rights.

Sometimes the founders of the constitution may want to engage in redistribution of wealth at the founding moment without bearing the economic costs of such a social enterprise. They may adopt a savings clause to protect such redistribution from constitutional challenge. I will bring three examples of such a motive for the adoption of a savings clause from India, Israel, and the United States protecting in turn redistribution of wealth, discriminatory religious practices, and even slavery. When the courts in these societies recognize these savings clauses as protecting otherwise unconstitutional laws, they may come to interpret the savings clauses narrowly and the rest of the constitution broadly and purposively, to minimize the grip of such savings clauses on society.

A India

The founding fathers of the Indian Constitution had to deal with major inequalities within society, particularly in the distribution of land rights. The state had already fixed in perpetuity the dues owed on land in the eighteenth century. The problem was that there were landowners, "*zamindars*" in Persian, who served as intermediaries between the peasants

---

[54] Hans Kelsen, *General Theory of Law and State* (Anders Wedberg trans., 1945), p. 268. See also Hans Kelsen, 'Judicial Review of Legislation: A Comparative Study of the Austrian and the American Constitution,' (1942) 4 *The Journal of Politics* 183.

cultivating the land and the state. While the zamindars and their equivalents paid fixed dues to the state, they kept raising the dues owed to them from the peasants, reaping a substantial profit from a population that was already struggling economically. R. S. Gae, the then-Permanent Secretary to the Ministry of Law and Justice in India, wrote in 1973: "In political parlance the term 'zaminder' came to mean a large landowner holding thousands of acres of land and scores of villages and thereby conveyed the image of a rich absentee landlord or oppressive local boss extracting exorbitant rents from those who toiled the soil."[55]

The inequalities were unbearable, and the adoption of the constitution was to address these inequalities by enabling a major redistribution of land. The founders of India wanted to remove the middlemen between the peasants and the state by abolishing the zamindari system (and its equivalents), and by granting ownership over the land to those cultivating it. Large segments of the public, as well as representatives of the states in need of major agrarian reform, feared that the constitutional right to property provided for in the draft constitution would prevent such a revolutionary redistribution of wealth or require market-value compensation for such reforms, which the public was unable to pay.[56] They inserted savings clauses into the Indian Constitution to prevent the invalidation of agrarian reform based on inadequate compensation.

The prime minister, Pandit Jawaharlal Nehru, who led the movement for the adoption of these clauses, explained the rationale for them: "[T]he equity does not apply only to the individual, but to the community."[57] He further suggested that Indian society cannot withstand protracted litigation over redistribution schemes, nor could it pay full compensation for such redistribution. "Obviously you cannot leave that piece of legislation to long, widespread and continuous litigation in the courts of law. Otherwise the future of millions of people may be affected, otherwise the whole structure of the State may be shaken to its foundations."[58]

The founders did not want to adopt a broad, sweeping savings clause that would weaken the influence of the constitutional adoption upon constitutional rights. Instead, they tailored the savings clause to protect

---

[55] R. S. Gae, 'Land Law in India: With Special Reference to the Constitution,' (1973) 22 *The International and Comparative Law Quarterly* 312, 314.

[56] B. Shiva Rao, *The Framing of India's Constitution* (Indian Institution of Public Administration, 1968), pp. 289–293.

[57] Ibid., p. 291.

[58] Ibid.

against the most expected form of attack against redistribution of wealth – an attack based on property rights. Article 31(4) originally read as follows:

> If any Bill pending at the commencement of this Constitution in the legislature of a State, has after it has been passed by such legislature, been reserved for the consideration of the President and has received his assent, then notwithstanding anything in this constitution, the law so assented to shall not be called in question in any court on the ground that it contravenes the provisions of clause (2) [requiring compensation for compulsory takings of property].[59]

This savings clause is unique in that it protected *bills* underway in different states rather than just existing *laws*.

Article 31(6) further originally provided:

> Any law of the State enacted not more than 18 months before the commencement of this Constitution may within 3 months from such commencement be submitted to the President for his certification; and thereupon, if the President by public notification so certifies, it shall not be called in question in any court on the ground that it contravenes the provisions of clause (2) of this article or has contravened the provisions of sub-section 299 of the Government of India Act 1935 [that also required compensation for takings].[60]

This additional savings mechanism was intended to shield certain existing laws from judicial review. Although the clause's general language covered all existing laws enacted within the eighteen months preceding the adoption of the Constitution, in essence it was intended to protect specific statutes that abolished the zamindari system.

The Indian drafters' belief that it would be enough to protect land redistribution provisions from constitutional challenge under the property clause proved mistaken. They left these provisions vulnerable to constitutional challenges based on other clauses of the Constitution. The courts would interpret the savings clauses narrowly, protecting redistribution against attack based on property rights alone, but they found a way to intervene under equality and other constitutional provisions. This was not anticipated by the Indian constitution-makers because the land reforms infringed primarily on property. While the

---

[59] John Murphy, 'Insulating Land Reform from Constitutional Impugnment: An Indian Case Study,' (1992) 25(2) *Comparative and International Law Journal of Southern Africa* 129, 145 at n. 52.
[60] Ibid.

land reforms infringed on other constitutional rights, those were secondary and incidental to the main infringement on property rights. Thus
they believed that, if the savings clauses prevented challenge under the
property clause, the land reforms would be immune from challenge in
the courts.

In the 1960s and 1970s, these clauses led to a major struggle between
the courts and the representative bodies over redistribution schemes.
Already in the first seventeen months after the adoption of the Constitution, the legislature amended it in response to judicial decisions to
include article 31B and the Ninth Schedule, in which the legislature may
enumerate a list of statutes that may be immune from invalidation by the
courts. The Ninth Schedule was originally intended to primarily protect
land reform.[61] This power struggle between the courts and the representative bodies culminated in the triumph of the courts in instating the
doctrine of an "unconstitutional constitutional amendment," which
empowers the courts to protect the "essential features" of the constitution
from change.[62] While the traditional story hails the courts as champions
of constitutional rights and denounces the representative bodies as over-
stepping their authority, the courts were frustrating the constitutional
compromise of the founding moment, and preventing greater equalization within society.

B   Israel

Israel planned to adopt a full-fledged constitution during its founding
period. Its Declaration of Independence expressed this commitment and
set a timetable for its achievement. But, this plan was never acted upon
due to the breakout of the War of Independence. Instead, the Israeli
legislature, the Knesset, adopted the Harrari Resolution, which stated
that the Knesset would adopt the constitution in stages by enacting

---

[61] See Rivka Weill, 'The New Commonwealth Model of Constitutionalism Notwithstanding:
     On Judicial Review and Constitution-Making,' (2014) 62 *American Journal of Compara-
     tive Law* 127; Baldev Singh, 'Ninth Schedule to Constitution of India: A Study,' (1995) 37
     The Indian Law Institute 457; Sandipto Dasgupta, *Legalizing the Revolution: Indian
     Constitution and Constitutionalism in the Twentieth Century* (Cambridge: Cambridge
     University Press, forthcoming 2019); Chintan Chandrachud, 'Nehru, Non-Judicial
     Review, & Constitutional Supremacy,' (2018) 2 *Indian Journal of Constitutional &
     Administrative Law* 45.
[62] David G. Morgan, 'The Indian – Essential Features Case,' (1981) 30 *The International
     and Comparative Law Quarterly* 307.

"Basic Laws," and they would be consolidated into one document to serve as Israel's constitution. As typical of compromise resolutions, each member of the Knesset understood this resolution differently. It was left unclear whether the Basic Laws would enjoy supreme status once enacted or only when consolidated into one document. Over the years, Israel adopted various Basic Laws dealing with the structure of government and separation of powers issues. But no bill of rights was adopted, though various proposals were tabled to adopt one. There was no consensus on the desirability of its adoption or its content.

In 1992 there was a breakthrough with the adoption of two Basic Laws dealing with individual rights – Basic Law: Human Dignity and Liberty and Basic Law: Freedom of Occupation. They included an explicit enumeration of rights that amount to a partial Bill of Rights. Excluded were some of the most important rights one would want to find in a constitution including equality, freedom of religion, and freedom of speech. This omission did not prevent the Supreme Court from seizing the opportunity and declaring that the adoption of this partial bill of rights amounted to a constitutional revolution. The courts now have the power of judicial review over primary legislation. The Court later read the omitted rights as implicitly encompassed in the right to human dignity explicitly included in Basic Law: Human Dignity and Liberty.[63]

How was the adoption of this partial bill of rights made possible? The answer is that those supporting the bill of rights were willing to compromise and adopt a less than ideal version of a bill of rights. They further explicitly recognized the Jewish as well as democratic nature of the state, which is supported by the overwhelming majority of the Jewish population and is a foundational principle of the Israeli state, as recognized in its Declaration of Independence. They further included savings clauses preserving preexisting laws, thus soothing the fears that the bill of rights would upset security or religious legal arrangements that may be constitutionally problematic.[64]

The motives for adopting the savings clause in each of the two 1992 Basic Laws were different. Basic Law: Freedom of Occupation embodied a general savings clause as a stabilizing mechanism. The Knesset was not sure which laws and regulations would be threatened by the adoption of this Basic Law. It wanted to give the government time to examine

---

[63] Weill, above n 47.
[64] Judith Karp, 'Basic Law: Human Dignity and Liberty: A Biography of Power Struggles,' (1993) 1 *Law & Gov't* 323 (Hebrew).

economic laws and determine which should be preserved and amended to suit the new constitutionally recognized right, and which should be discarded. Originally, this Basic Law included a two years' sunset provision that would have led to the lapse of the general savings clause. But this two years' period proved too short. The Knesset time and again renewed the general savings clause until it lapsed ten years after its original adoption.

There was no real thought or work put in the interval between the original adoption of the general savings clause and its ultimate lapse. The Knesset did not stand up to its task to study economic legislation in light of the new Basic Law. Rather, many unconstitutional past laws are part of Israeli law without enjoying the protection of the general savings clause. No one truly challenges these problematic arrangements. They are taken as part of the constitutional status quo. A possible explanation for the lack of persistent constitutional challenge to outdated economic legislation is the fear of the industrial and economic interests in Israel from being publicly perceived as too greedy or as promoting self- rather than public-related interests.

The general savings clause that forms part of Basic Law: Human Dignity and Liberty is permanent. Section 10 of this Basic Law reads: "This Basic Law shall not affect the validity of any law (*din*) in force prior to the commencement of the Basic Law."[65] This Basic Law is the major constitutional engine through which legislation in Israel is attacked. As the famous Jewish story regarding Hillel the elder that summarized Jewish commands into "love your neighbor as yourself," the Court treats human dignity as encompassing rights not explicitly enumerated in the 1992 Basic Laws.

Members of the Israeli legislature had numerous justifications for using a savings clause in the Basic Law: Human Dignity and Liberty. They wanted to preserve from constitutional challenge both the Jewish identity of the state and its Law of Return, granting preference to Jewish people and their relatives in immigration to Israel.[66] Despite its

---

[65] Basic Law: Human Dignity and Liberty, 5752, SH No. 1391 p. 150, § 10 (Isr.)

[66] The Law of Return, 5710–1950, SH No. 51 p. 159 (Isr.). The Court later clarified that it does not treat the Law of Return as an abridgement of constitutional rights but rather as a foundational principle of Israeli constitutionalism. The Court stated that Israel must equally treat those within its borders but may grant preference to Jews in immigration to Israel. HCJ 6698/95 *Ka'adan v. Israel Lands Administration*, 54(1) P.D. 258 (2000) (Isr.). Thus, under the Court's approach, there was no need for a savings clause to protect the Law of Return from unconstitutionality.

abridgement of the most basic rights to equality and dignity, they wanted to protect the Jewish Orthodox religious monopoly over marriage and divorce, treating it as one of the essential components of a Jewish state.[67] Also, they believed that they needed to shield Israel's national security and military legislation from review, including some of the harsh measures incorporated into Israeli law from the British mandate. These include laws enabling preventive detention, demolition of houses, curfew, and the like.[68] Rather than tailoring a savings clause to each of these areas of law, the legislature preferred a holistic savings clause, shielding all preexisting law to avoid leaving some laws vulnerable. Legislators also worried that were they to list particular legislation shielded from judicial review, they would create an unjustified inference that the statutes enumerated in the list enjoy a unique preferred status in Israeli law.[69]

Despite the fact that equality is recognized as an implied right found in the explicit right to human dignity, Israel's laws allow for harsh gender discrimination against women in matters of marriage and divorce that are dictated by religious laws. While Israeli law recognizes civil law marriages conducted abroad in interfaith marriage cases, as well as homosexual marriage, those cannot be legally conducted in Israel. Israeli law also recognizes common law marriage in all those cases.[70] This discriminatory reality is not the result of any conservative constitutional interpretation of the right to equality. Neither is it the result of a narrow constitutional interpretation of the right to freedom of religion, which is recognized as part of human dignity as well. Rather, this reality is made possible as a result of the savings clause. Many of the problematic security measures undertaken by Israel as part of an emergency regime were also preserved under the savings clause. In fact, Israel, like many other countries with a savings clause of preexisting laws, may have a dual system: anachronistic with regard to laws that predated constitutional adoption, and liberal with regard to post-constitutional adoption statutes.

The Israeli Supreme Court has attempted to interpret this savings clause narrowly to minimize its anachronistic effects on society. It instructed the courts to reinterpret protected laws in a way that aligns

---

[67] Jurisdiction of Rabbinical Courts (Marriage and Divorce) Law, 5713–1953, SH No. 134 p. 165 (Isr.).

[68] Karp, above n 60.

[69] Matan Goldblatt, 'Preservation of Laws Clause: Its Application and Influence on Criminal Offenses' (MA Thesis, Haifa U., 2010) (Hebrew); Barak, above n 10.

[70] Rivka Weill, 'The Power of Understatement in Judicial Decisions,' (2014) XXX Annuaire International de Justice Constitutionnelle 125.

with constitutional rights as much as possible.[71] Rather than treat protected laws as a benchmark for interpreting the constitution, as has happened in countries with savings clauses that glorify the past, the constitution became the benchmark for interpreting protected statutes because the savings clause was treated as a problematic, undesired, but necessary compromise tool. There is a limit, however, to what the Court may do via interpretation when faced with a broad all-encompassing savings clause in Basic Law: Human Dignity and Liberty, preserving all preexisting law from constitutional attack.

C   United States

At the time it adopted its Constitution, the United States adopted a savings clause that protected slavery for twenty years' time. But the phrasing of this savings clause is different than that typically found in constitutions. Rather than state that preexisting laws are saved, this savings clause states that Congress "shall not" enact laws that will prevent the trade in slaves until 1808. In the words of the US Constitution, "The Migration or Importation of such Persons as any of the States now existing shall think proper to admit shall not be prohibited by the Congress prior to the Year one thousand eight hundred and eight, but a Tax or duty may be imposed on such Importation, not exceeding ten dollars for each Person."[72] The reason for this phrasing is that during this period the fear was mainly of congressional action rather than invalidation by the courts. This was not a time in which judicial review loomed as a substantial potent threat to legislation.[73]

Slavery was a central issue of contention at the Constitutional Convention and ratification debates. Abolitionists portrayed this partial savings clause as progress because, under the Articles of Confederation, Congress lacked the power to regulate interstate trade and thus could not abolish slavery. Under the trade clause, Congress might had been able to abolish the trade in slaves, if it had mastered the required majorities in twenty years' time, after the adoption of the Constitution.[74] James

---

[71] DCR 537/95 *Genimat v. State of Israel,* 49 (3) PD 355 (1995) (Isr.).

[72] *US Constitution,* §1(9).

[73] This is not to argue that judicial review did not exist during the founding era in the United States. See William Michael Treanor, 'The Case of the Prisoners and the Origins of Judicial Review,' (1994) 143 *University of Pennsylvania Law Review* 491.

[74] James Oakes, '"The Compromising Expedient": Justifying a Proslavery Constitution,' (1995–1996) 17 *Cardozo Law Review* 2023.

Madison explained that the slave trade was a great evil but the "dismemberment of the Union would be worse."[75] He further suggested that the divide between free and slave states was more significant than the division between big and small states.[76]

Retentionists treated the clause as a major victory. General Charles Cotesworth Pinckney explained to the South Carolina House of Representatives that, "considering all circumstances, we have made the best terms for the security of this species of property it was in our power to make."[77] The Southerners stood on firm grounds in boasting about their victory of preserving slavery in the Constitution. The Constitution provided in its three-fifths clause that Representatives "shall be apportioned among the several States … according to their respective Numbers, which shall be determined by adding to the whole Number of free Persons … three fifths of all other Persons."[78] "All other persons" meant slaves. With the continued trade in slavery for an additional twenty years and the translation of ownership of slaves into more voting powers to the Southern states, as well as the slave owners' right to regain ownership of a fugitive slave,[79] Southern political power was expected to increase over those years. It would require a civil war, and not just the expiration of the partial savings clause, to abolish slavery in the United States.

In contrast to India and Israel, where the courts tried to interpret the savings clause narrowly, understanding that it preserved unconstitutional laws, the US courts overwhelmingly did not treat slavery as constitutionally problematic. They held that the protection of slavery was about the defense of property rights, not the grave denial of the most basic human right to liberty.[80]

This type of savings clause, which affirms in the constitution that preexisting laws are valid even though they would have otherwise been found unconstitutional, enables countries to conceal some of the embarrassing practices of society. The founding fathers may make their

---

[75] Ibid. at 2025.

[76] Ibid. at 2032.

[77] John P. Kaminski, ed., *A Necessary Evil?: Slavery and the Debate Over the Constitution* (Rowman & Littlefield, 1995), p. 170.

[78] *US Constitution*, § 1(2)(3).

[79] 'No Person held to Service or Labour in one State, under the Laws thereof, escaping into another, shall, in Consequence of any Law or Regulation therein, be discharged from such Service or Labour, but shall be delivered up on Claim of the Party to whom such Service or Labour may be due.' *US Constitution*, § 4(2)(3).

[80] *Dred Scott v. Sanford*, 60 U.S. 393 (1857).

protection of rights salient and reap the internal as well as international benefits associated with constitutional adoption, even as they allow discriminatory practices to continue through the hidden language of savings. To study what laws are valid despite the adoption of the constitution, one must be familiar with the legal corpus that is not enumerated in the constitution. Even when a savings clause is tailored to protect specific embarrassing practices, it often uses an opaque language that does not disclose the true nature of the arrangement at stake. The US Constitution did not use the word slaves but "other people" when it protected the slavery institution until 1808. The Israeli Basic Law: Freedom of Occupation did not disclose that it was protecting the prohibition against importation of nonkosher meat to Israel even when it violates the right to freedom of occupation, but rather included an opaque permanent specific savings clause to this effect.[81]

V Conclusion

We typically treat constitutional adoption as a revolutionary story of a break with the past. But the prevalence of savings clauses in the world suggests that constitutional adoption may be more of an evolutionary story than acknowledged. The story of savings clauses suggest that we misperceived this phenomenon in fundamental ways. We thought they were unique and uncommon while they are widespread. We thought they were an issue for Caribbean or African countries alone while the world at large embodies them. We thought they meant that the constitution was only future-looking in those cases while savings clauses shape the nature of the constitutional dialogue rather than preclude it. Even if savings clauses prevent the invalidation of past statutes, they may enable interpretation of past laws in light of constitutional law. We assumed there was a single one-size-fits-all type of savings clause intended to preserve unconstitutional law, when in fact there are three types of savings clauses: those glorifying the past, those stabilizing the system, and those sheltering unconstitutional law. Moreover, the motive for adopting savings

---

[81] It stated: 'The provision regarding the expiration of validity, as stated in clause (a), shall not apply to a law adopted before the end of a year from the inception date of this Basic Law.' Basic Law: Freedom of Occupation; § 8(b). For the full story, see Rivka Weill, 'Juxtaposing Constitution-Making and Constitutional Infringement Mechanisms in Israel and Canada: On the Interplay between Common law Override and Sunset Override,' (2016) 49 *Israel Law Review* 103.

clauses affect the nature of the constitutional dialogue between the branches of government.

But the story of savings clauses is more than all of that. It suggests that savings clauses may postpone rather than resolve conflicts. In three of the countries examined – Canada, India, and the United States – the savings clause ultimately required a restart of the system and a new beginning. Canada could not develop a robust protection of rights under the "frozen concepts" burden of the implied savings clause. It needed to restart the system through the adoption of the Charter while facing the opposition of Quebec.[82] India's savings clauses did not shelter redistribution as expected by the founders. Rather, a major political power struggle between the courts and the representative bodies ultimately led to a new constitutional regime, which incorporated the "unconstitutional constitutional amendment" doctrine. And, in the United States, the savings clause did not resolve the conflict nor ease the burden of slavery. Rather, the United States would have to face its ghosts in a bloody civil war costing the lives of two percent of its population. Even today, the shadow of slavery haunts US political and civic life. While savings clauses were largely ignored in the literature, analyzing them deepens our understanding of constitutionalism.

---

[82] In contrast to the CBORA, the Charter did not portray the constitutional rights embodied in it as preexisting. It took the necessary steps to prevent another implied savings clause.

PART IV

Case Studies of Dialogue

12

Prisoners' Voting and Judges' Powers

JOHN FINNIS

I From *Hirst* to *Scoppola*: Judicial Power Misused

On the day of the 2010 general election in the United Kingdom, voters reading *The Times* found themselves addressed by Lord David Pannick QC, arguably England's and Oxford University's most prominent and successful barrister, in his fortnightly opinion column. He told voters they were participating in a democratic process of dubious legitimacy, because 'in a close contest, when the result in many seats may depend on a small number of votes, the unlawful exclusion of 85,000 prisoners from the right to vote is a constitutional disgrace that undermines the legitimacy of the democratic process'. His claim that the exclusion was unlawful was in substance erroneous, though of course not simply and absolutely so. More interesting is his conclusion: 'there could not be a clearer demonstration of why this country needs a proper Bill of Rights'.[1]

There could. Indeed, the judicial decisions on which Pannick was relying, like (as we will see) the parallel decisions in Canada, South Africa, New Zealand and Australia, suggest, powerfully, the opposite conclusion: Britain might well be better off without even the constitutionally watered-down Bill of Rights it has (the Human Rights Act 1998).

The grain of truth in Pannick's claim that British prisoners were (and are) being disenfranchised *unlawfully* and unconstitutionally was this: in October 2005, in *Hirst* v. *United Kingdom (No. 2)* the Grand Chamber of seventeen judges of the European Court of Human Rights in Strasbourg ruled, 12:5, that the United Kingdom was violating Article 3 of the First Protocol to the European Convention on Human Rights by disenfranchising all persons in prison after criminal conviction,[2] and no steps had

---

[1] David Pannick, 'Prisoners may be unpopular but they should still vote' *The Times* (6 May 2010).

[2] *Hirst* v. *United Kingdom (No. 2)* (2005) (74025/01), 6 October 2005 (GC). Representation of the People Act 1983, s. 3: '(1) A convicted person during the time that he is detained in a penal institution in pursuance of his sentence ... is legally incapable of voting at any

been taken by the British Parliament to amend the franchise to comply
with this judgment – none have been taken to this day. The substantial
gap between Pannick's statement and the truth is that the European
Convention is a treaty, and treaties have no effect in British law except
to the extent that they are incorporated into it by Act of Parliament; and
while the Human Rights Act 1998 does import European Convention
rights into UK law, it gives them legal effect only to the extent that they
are not overridden by incompatible present or future Acts of Parliament
(such as the Representation of the People Act 1983). Nor are judgments
of the Court established by the Convention enforceable in Britain. (Until
Hirst, the United Kingdom, a principal author of the Convention in 1950,
has faithfully complied with the judgments and doctrine of the European
Court of Human Rights [ECtHR].) There was nothing constitutionally
disgraceful about the 2010 general election, nor even about the United
Kingdom's non-compliance with the Strasbourg court.

It was the judgment of the Strasbourg Court in *Hirst* that was rather
disgraceful. Consider first the juridical background. Article 3 of the First
Protocol to the European Convention on Human Rights (ECHR),
adopted in 1951, reads:

> Right to Free Elections. The High Contracting Parties undertake to hold
> free elections at reasonable intervals by secret ballot, under conditions
> which will ensure the free expression of the opinion of the people in the
> choice of the legislature.

Not until 1987 did the Strasbourg Court hold that this Article, despite the
interstate colouring of its wording, creates or recognizes rights and
freedoms 'directly secured to' individuals within the states party to the
Convention, just like the other Convention rights. In this holding,
Mathieu-Mohin and Clerfayt v. *Belgium*,[3] the Court referred appropriately to some aspects of the wording of the Convention's preamble, and
made use of the Protocol's *travaux préparatoires* and drafting history,
indeed, correct use. The Strasbourg Court further held – again with
reference to the *travaux préparatoires* – that the implied rights to vote
and to stand for election are subject to implied limitations and conditions. Each state has 'a wide margin of appreciation' in determining these

---

parliamentary or local election.' The disqualification does not apply to persons imprisoned
for contempt of court (section 3(2)(a) or to those imprisoned only for default in, for
example, paying a fine (section 3(2)(c)). Throughout this essay, 'convicted prisoner' refers
to this class of persons detained pursuant to sentence.

[3] *Mathieu-Mohin and Clerfayt* v. *Belgium* (1987) (9267/81), 2 March 1987 (GC).

conditions for its own elections, provided 'that the conditions do not curtail the rights in question to such an extent as to impair their very essence and deprive them [the rights] of their effectiveness; that they [the conditions] are imposed in pursuit of a legitimate aim; and that the means employed are not disproportionate ... In particular, such conditions must not thwart "the free expression of the opinion of the people in the choice of the legislature"'.[4] So far, so good.

Mathieu-Mohin and Clerfayt v. *Belgium* concerned constitutional and electoral arrangements adopted in 1970 and 1980 as part of Belgium's ongoing struggle to maintain itself as a state; it is a country weighed down by the extensive burdens, irritations and grievances of multicultural existence. The Commission that in those days was the quasi-judicial first tier of litigation under the Convention upheld by 10:1 the French-speaking applicants' complaints against their de facto lack of representation in one of the regional councils; but the plenary ECtHR rejected them by 13:5, finding the electoral/constitutional arrangements to be within the margin of appreciation left to each state under the Protocol. Again, so far, so good.

But the court's judgment in *Mathieu-Mohin* has a flaw at its centre. At a crucial stage in its own argumentation towards the conclusion that Article 3 creates legal rights in individuals, the judgment recounts without criticism the Commission's practice, initiated in the 1960s, of basing that conclusion on the premise that Article 3 requires universal suffrage. And that premise is completely contrary to the Protocol's *travaux préparatoires* and drafting history. Early drafts of Article 3 contained a clause *substantially* identical to the final form of Article 3 with this sole significant difference: the final version speaks of 'free elections at reasonable intervals by secret ballot', whereas the versions prior to August 1950 said 'free elections at reasonable intervals with universal suffrage and secret ballot'. So: all reference to universal suffrage was deliberately omitted from Article 3, and omitted not because it was replaced by some other phrasing intended to have the same meaning, such as 'under conditions which will ensure the free expression of the opinion of the people' – for that phrase or its substantial equivalent had coexisted in draft with 'universal suffrage'. No, it was omitted because of objections to it by the United Kingdom, objections to which I shall return.[5] Suffice it to

---

[4] *Mathieu-Mohin and Clerfayt* v. *Belgium*, para. 52.
[5] See fn. 39–41.

say now that the Court's references to the Protocol's *travaux préparatoires* and drafting history, correct so far as they went, were defective in what they omitted. The omission allowed the Grand Chamber in deciding *Hirst* in 2007 to say with bland complacency (and a spice of equivocation between reporting and endorsing and adopting as a premise): 'Universal suffrage has become the basic principle (see *Mathieu-Mohin and Clerfayt* at para. 51 citing [a Commission decision of 1967]).'[6] When *Hirst* was reaffirmed (against the United Kingdom) in *Scoppola* v. *Italy* in 2012, the equivocation fell away, the ratcheting was completed, and the past and its promises and reliances were openly left behind: 'In the twenty-first century, the presumption in a democratic State must be in favour of inclusion and universal suffrage has become the basic principle (see *Mathieu-Mohin and Clerfayt*, § 51, and *Hirst (No. 2)* [GC], § 59)'.[7]

Now we can get to grips with the *Hirst* case in its own right. Shortly before the fiftieth anniversary of the Protocol's adoption, John Hirst,

---

[6] *Hirst (No. 2)*, para. 59:

> As pointed out by the applicant, the right to vote is not a privilege. In the twenty-first century, the presumption in a democratic State must be in favour of inclusion, as may be illustrated, for example, by the parliamentary history of the United Kingdom and other countries where the franchise was gradually extended over the centuries from select individuals, elite groupings or sections of the population approved of by those in power. Universal suffrage has become the basic principle (see *Mathieu-Mohin and Clerfayt*, cited above, p. 23, § 51, citing *X* v. *Germany*, no. 2728/66, Commission decision of 6 October 1967, Collection 25, pp. 38–41).

[7] *Scoppola* v. *Italy (No. 3)* (2012) (126/05), 22 May 2012 (GC), para. 82; see also para. 84:

> 84. However, it is for the Court to determine in the last resort whether the requirements of Article 3 of Protocol No. 1 have been complied with; it has to satisfy itself that the conditions do not curtail the rights in question to such an extent as to impair their very essence and deprive them of their effectiveness; that they are imposed in pursuit of a legitimate aim; and that the means employed are not disproportionate (see *Mathieu-Mohin and Clerfayt*, cited above, § 52). In particular, any conditions imposed must not thwart the free expression of the people in the choice of the legislature – in other words, they must reflect, or not run counter to, the concern to maintain the integrity and effectiveness of an electoral procedure aimed at identifying the will of the people through universal suffrage. Any departure from the principle of universal suffrage risks undermining the democratic validity of the legislature thus elected and the laws it promulgates. Exclusion of any groups or categories of the general population must accordingly be reconcilable with the underlying purposes of Article 3 of Protocol No. 1 (see *Hirst (No. 2)* [GC] . . .).

born in 1950 (the year that Article 3 reached its final form among the drafters), applied to the English courts for a declaration that the 1983 statute disqualifying him from voting violated Article 3. Hirst had been imprisoned since 1980 after conviction on indictment for murder; he had pleaded guilty to manslaughter on grounds of diminished responsibility and his plea had been accepted 'on the basis of medical evidence that he was a man with a severe personality disorder to such a degree that he was amoral'.[8] On that basis he had been sentenced to discretionary life imprisonment, and since mid-1994 he was being detained under that sentence, on grounds of risk and dangerousness. The English High Court in April 2001 rejected his application; it reviewed the then-existing case law in the United States, Canada, South Africa and, of course, under the ECHR, and found that the statutory provision disenfranchising Hirst while he remained in prison pursuant to his sentence was fully compatible with Article 3, having legitimate aims and using criteria that fell within the range of 'proportionate means' of pursuing those aims.[9] After his applications for leave to appeal were refused as hopeless, Hirst applied to the ECtHR, of which a seven-judge Section Chamber in March 2004 unanimously held that Britain's statute violates Article 3.[10] The seventeen-judge Grand Chamber in Strasbourg upheld his application by 12:5 in October 2005. The judgment of the majority, which included the English judge, is long but very weak, and flawed in at least three substantial ways.

First, its review of proportionality lacks competence and care. The judgment *said* that it accepted the United Kingdom's case that disenfranchisement has two legitimate **aims**: (1) to promote civic responsibility by giving expression to the *link* between the exercise of social rights (such as voting) and the acceptance of social duties such as respect for the lawful rights of other citizens – acceptance and respect plainly violated by the commission of an offence serious enough and/or an offender cumulatively culpable enough to be met by imprisonment; and (2) to enhance the essential retributive rationale of punishment by accompanying the punitive deprivation of liberty of movement with pro rata punitive deprivation of the right to have a say (as elector) in the making of rules

---

[8] *Hirst (No. 2)*, para. 12.
[9] *Hirst v. HM Attorney General* (2001) [2001] EWHC Admin 239.
[10] *Hirst v. United Kingdom (No. 2)* (74025/01) (30 March 2004) (Fourth Section).

of the kind breached by the convicted prisoner.[11] But when purporting to
assess the proportionality of disenfranchisement as a **means** to these two
ends, the Court paid the ends (these aims) no attention whatever, and in
effect substituted its own end or aim, stated a little earlier in the judgment: 'the protection of democratic society against activities intended to
destroy the rights or freedoms set forth in the Convention ... [protec-
tions by] ... restrictions on electoral rights ... imposed on an individual
who has, for example, seriously *abused a public position* or whose
conduct threatened to *undermine the rule of law or democratic foundations*'.[12] Having (in effect) made this substitution, the majority judgment
had, of course, no difficulty in holding that disenfranchisement of
imprisoned burglars, muggers, rapists and non-terrorist murderers is
quite disproportionate to the end the Court dreamed up for the measure
in place of its actual ends – ends that the Court pretended (but only
pretended) to accept.

Second, the judgment is viciously circular, helping itself to the conclusion by treating it as a premise. For it takes as an axiom that a sentence of

---

[11] *Hirst (No. 2)* [GC], e.g., at para. 37 (emphasis added):

> The minority opinion given by Gonthier J [in *Sauvé (No. 2)*] found that the
> objectives of the measure were pressing and substantial and based upon a
> reasonable and rational social or political philosophy. The **first objective**,
> that of enhancing civic responsibility and respect for the rule of law, related
> to the promotion of good citizenship. The social rejection of serious crime
> reflected a moral line which safeguarded the social contract and the rule of
> law and bolstered the importance of the nexus between individuals and the
> community. The 'promotion of civic responsibility' might be abstract or
> symbolic, but symbolic or abstract purposes could be valid of their own
> accord and should not be downplayed simply for being symbolic. As
> regards the **second objective**, that of enhancing the general purposes of
> the criminal sanction, the measure clearly had a punitive aspect with a
> retributive function. It was a valid objective for Parliament to develop
> appropriate sanctions and punishments for serious crime. The disenfran-
> chisement was a civil disability arising from the criminal conviction. It was
> also proportionate, as the measure was rationally connected to the object-
> ives and carefully tailored to apply to perpetrators of serious crimes. The
> disenfranchisement of serious criminal offenders served to deliver a mes-
> sage to both the community and the offenders themselves that serious
> criminal activity would not be tolerated by the community. Society, on this
> view, could choose to curtail temporarily the availability of the vote to
> serious criminals to insist that civic responsibility and respect for the rule
> of law, as goals worthy of pursuit, were prerequisites to democratic
> participation.

[12] *Hirst (No. 2)*, para. 71, emphasis added.

imprisonment involves the forfeiture of no other right save the right to liberty (plus such other exercises of rights as would prejudice prison security).[13] But English law, like the laws of most states, has long defined the consequences of such a sentence as including the forfeiture not only of personal liberty but also of the legal capacity and right to vote.

Third, the Court's ruling that disenfranchisement of all convicted prisoners during their imprisonment is arbitrary and disproportionate was itself arbitrary. It did nothing more than restate the content of the British disenfranchisement rule in opprobrious terms: 'general, automatic and indiscriminate'.[14] The fact that sentences to prison in Britain are never indiscriminate, and that in England only eight per cent of convictions for crime result in such a sentence,[15] is simply ignored. The British disenfranchisement was no more a 'blanket ban' (to use the Court's phrase) than a rule disenfranchising all persons serving a sentence of (say) ten years or more. The *link* between the exercise of social rights (such as voting) and the acceptance of social duties such as respect for the lawful rights of other citizens is properly *expressed* by the straightforward and very moderate rule that, of convicted violators of the rights of others, those eight per cent or so whose violations are so serious that they are in prison for it cannot exercise the right to vote. This 'link' can readily be understood to be simply an expression of the reciprocity that leading liberal thinkers such as H. L. A. Hart[16] and John Rawls[17] made the foundation of their account of the obligation to obey the law: those who have benefited from others' compliance with the law should accept the same burden of compliance when the law applies to their own choices: reciprocity of benefits and burdens.[18]

---

[13] *Hirst (No. 2)*, paras. 69–70.

[14] *Hirst (No. 2)*, para. 82.

[15] See *R (Chester)* v. *Secretary of State for Justice* [2013] UKSC 63 at para. 129.

[16] H. L. A. Hart, 'Are there any natural rights?' (1955) 64 *Philosophical Review* 175, 185.

[17] John Rawls, *A Theory of Justice* (Cambridge, MA: Harvard University Press, 1971) p. 112.

[18] The UK government had formulated the objectives or grounds of convict prisoner disenfranchisement, at the outset of the English proceedings in *Hirst*, in these not entirely syntactical terms, quoted in para. 16 of the Strasbourg judgment:

> 'By committing offences which by themselves or taken with any aggravating circumstances including the offender's character and previous criminal record require a custodial sentence, such prisoners have forfeited the right to have a say in the way the country is governed for that period. There is more than one element to punishment than forcible detention. Removal from society means removal from the privileges of society, amongst which is the right to vote for one's representative.'

So the Grand Chamber's judgment, under its literate and lawyerly surface, was much inferior in quality to the sort of reasoning on display in some legislative discussions of such matters. The arbitrariness of its ruling that the disenfranchisement was disproportionate because it was 'blanket'-like in its ban on eight per cent of all convicted offenders was surely noticed and understood, albeit tacitly, by the ECtHR Section Chamber that in April 2010 ruled against Austria's disenfranchisement of prisoners serving sentences of one year or more for an offence involving criminal *intent*. This seven-judge court pulled together some stray elements in the disorderly *Hirst* judgment, to come up with a coherent basis for a finding of disproportionality: all disenfranchisement is disproportionate *unless* it is imposed case-by-case by a judge, and for an offence linked to 'issues relating to elections and democratic insti-tutions'.[19] Applauding the *Frodl* decision a month later in *The Times* article, Lord Pannick noted that it would enfranchise all but a tiny number of Britain's prisoners. He praised it for this heart-warming result, not for restoring some integrity to the ECtHR's doctrine, as it did.

But this gain in integrity did not last. Confronted with Italy's law (and with the United Kingdom's seven-year-long defiance), the Grand Chamber in *Scoppola* in 2012 ignominiously (but of course entirely tacitly) abandoned the two requirements that the *Frodl* judges had extracted from *Hirst*. Italy's main disenfranchising provisions were *legislative* 'blanket bans' on voting by any prisoner serving a sentence of three years or more, and a (revocable) lifetime ban on those sen-tenced to five years or more. Despite the much greater severity of the latter ban, the *Scoppola* Grand Chamber judgment upheld all of Italy's voting bans. Unlike Britain's bans, which the Court again explicitly condemned, Italy's were declared to be not 'general, automatic and indiscriminate'.

There is no reason to see in this reference to privilege any denial of that voting is a matter of right, such that any law restricting it must have substantial justification; rather the reference is a compressed reminder that voting is not like living or speaking or associating or worshipping, but is a social construct, the existence let alone the worth of which depends on favourable social conditions of a kind attacked directly by 'enemies of the state' [see n 51 in this chapter] and indirectly by all serious criminal violation of the rights of others.

[19] *Frodl* v. *Austria*, (20201/04), 8 April 2010 (First Section).

In 2013, with great moderation, two Justices of the UK Supreme Court described the ECtHR's position as 'very curious':

> the Strasbourg Court has arrived at a very curious position. It has held that it is open to a Convention state to fix a minimum threshold of gravity which warrants the disenfranchisement of a convicted person. It has held that the threshold beyond which he will be disenfranchised may be fixed by law by reference to the nature of the sentence. It has held that disenfranchisement may be automatic, once a sentence above that threshold has been imposed. But it has also held that even with the wide margin of appreciation allowed to Convention states in this area, it is not permissible for the threshold for disenfranchisement to correspond with the threshold for imprisonment. Wherever the threshold for imprisonment is placed, it seems to have been their view that there must always be some offences which are serious enough to warrant imprisonment but not serious enough to warrant disenfranchisement. Yet the basis of this view is nowhere articulated.[20]

II 'Your Vote Has Been Nullified by Some Convict's'

My concern is more with judges' power and its abuse than with prisoners' votes. But it is worth saying a bit more about the latter, so far as may shed a little more light on the former. The Grand Chamber judgments in both *Hirst* and *Scoppola* include surveys of case law from

---

[20] *R (Chester)* v. *Secretary of State for Justice* [2013] UKSC 63, [135], Lord Sumption (with Lord Hughes), concurring. Subsequent ECtHR judgments remain blankly unresponsive to rational argumentation such as this: e.g., *Kulinski and Sabev* v. *Bulgaria* (63849/09) (21 July 2016) (Fifth Section). The sophistry of the Grand Chamber judgment in *Hirst (No. 2)* and all its offspring is well exposed by para. 6 of the dissenting judgment of Judge Wojtyczek in *Firth* v. *UK* [2014] ECHR 874 (12 August 2014); the first of the six arguments set out elegantly in that very long paragraph includes this:

> in the UK legislation there is no 'blanket' restriction imposed on all convicted persons. The UK legislation carefully differentiates between those detained in a penal institution and other convicted persons. At the same time, if we take as the reference group those sentenced to a prison term of at least three years, then the Italian legislation should be regarded as imposing a 'blanket' restriction imposed on this category of persons. The notion of a 'blanket' restriction seems to be useless as a tool for identifying 'suspicious' restrictions on rights because of its relativity. If the Court means that the personal scope of a restriction was too broad, then it should say so clearly and explain why.

The whole paragraph and the whole dissenting judgment deserve to be read by everyone interested in prisoners' votes – or indeed in the Convention and its proper application – and ought to be adopted and followed by the Grand Chamber.

non-Convention states such as the United States, Canada and South Africa. The surveys are far from even-handed. Some pride of place, even typographically, is given, in each of these two judgments, to a dictum of the Supreme Court of post-Apartheid South Africa, in 1999:

> The universality of the franchise is important not only for nationhood and democracy. The vote of each and every citizen is a badge of dignity and personhood. Quite literally, it says that everybody counts.[21]

Well, yes. And the badge when worn by a convicted prisoner 'says' to every law-abiding citizen that your vote is liable to be cancelled out, and nullified in its effect, by the contrary vote of someone who is currently removed from society, and under the forcible control of government, on account of his demonstrated contempt for the dignity and rights of fellow citizens – someone whose conditions of life may well be substantially more comfortable than those of law-abiding poor or unwell people, and whose opportunities for informing himself and others about the issues of national self-determination at stake in the election are entirely subject to government control. In other words, enfranchising convicted prisoners during their imprisonment carries a message of radical devaluation of the votes of all, and actually nullifies the votes of the scores of thousands (or, in the United States, many millions) of law-abiding voters who each have the misfortune to cast a vote contrary to the vote of some convicted criminal voting in prison under government control.[22]

The political philosophising in this South African dictum needs much amplification if it is not to be mere sophistry. For *having the vote* is neither a necessary nor a sufficient condition for *counting* as a citizen and a person with human dignity and rights. It is not **sufficient**, for many reasons: to mention only one, having the vote is insufficient to establish that one counts when the only candidates for whom one can vote hold one's views and interests in contempt, and have a plan perhaps literally to deprive you of the vote in future or to deprive you of your property, or to swamp the nation with new voters culturally inclined to favour the marginalising or suppression of your religion or the corrupting of the rule of law, and so forth. And having the vote is not **necessary** either, as

---

[21] *August* v. *Electoral Commission* [1999] 3 SA 1.

[22] On the significance of the control of imprisoned voters for the wider and deeper meaning of the right to participate in government, see Peter Ramsay, *Faking Democracy with Prisoners' Voting Rights* (2013), LSE Law, Society and Economy Working Paper No. 7/2013.

the established lawful status and constitutionally guaranteed rights of all underage citizens and of all lawfully resident non-citizens demonstrate. These matters were more accurately understood by the Justices of the Supreme Court of the United States who in 1959, after years of insisting on 14th Amendment equality and of overriding Southern devices, electoral and otherwise, for frustrating interracial equality, nonetheless unanimously held, the liberal Justice Douglas writing for all, that states can include among the qualifications of voters not only age, residency status and previous criminal record, but also, to promote intelligent use of the ballot, a racially and in other ways non-discriminatory *literacy* test.[23] Such talk of intelligent use of the ballot goes some way towards bringing issues about enfranchisement back to their true foundations: the common good in which every member of the community is entitled, and in a basic way equally entitled, to share – that is to say, the good in which everyone counts and towards which everyone's good counts, especially the honouring of their rights.

The Grand Chamber in *Hirst*, and again in *Scoppola*, cited the South African dictum without the qualifications that were made later in the judgment, allowing the justice and presumptive constitutionality of some disenfranchisement of criminals. In any event, the South African legislature in 2003 adopted a rule like the United Kingdom's: no votes for convicted prisoners. In proceedings conducted rather hugger-mugger just before the 2004 general election, this rule was invalidated by 9:2 in the Constitutional Court of South Africa in *Minister for Home Affairs v. NICRO*.[24] The two dissenting judgments reach the issues of principle – aims and proportionality – and persuasively, and without response from the majority, argue that (as Madala J put it):

> the temporary removal of the vote and its restoration upon the release of the prisoner is salutary to the development and inculcation of a caring and responsible society. Even if the prisoner loses the chance to vote by a day, that will cause him or her to remember the day he or she could not exercise his or her right because of being on the wrong side of the law.[25]

Or as Ngcobo J put it:

> This limited limitation of the right to vote sends an unmistakable message to the prisoner. ... a reminder that the duties and responsibilities of a

[23] *Lassiter v. Northampton County Board of Elections*, 360 US 45 at 51–2 (1959).
[24] [2004] ZACC 10.
[25] Ibid., para. 116.

citizen also include an obligation to respect the rights of others and comply with the law. The convicted prisoners break the law in breach of their constitutional duty not to do so.[26]

Ngcobo J adopted a passage from the judgment of the Canadian Federal Court of Appeal in 2000 in *Sauvé (No. 2)* – a judgment that had been quoted as highly persuasive, in detail after detail, by the English court in *Hirst*, but was simply ignored by the Grand Chamber on the inadequate ground that, as we shall see, the Supreme Court of Canada had reversed it (by 5:4). The passage in the Canadian Federal Court of Appeal judgment adopted by Ngcobo J points to 'salutary effects of this legislation as well as valid objectives which were identified to the Court'.[27] I interject to say that the Canadian legislation in question disenfranchised convicted prisoners only where sentenced to two years or more, and had been enacted because in 1991 the Supreme Court of Canada had, in a one-sentence oral judgment, annulled the rule in place in Canada since 1898 disenfranchising *all* convicted prisoners. The Federal Court of Appeal majority judgment goes on:

> The legislation dramatically expresses the sense of societal values of the community in relation to serious criminal behaviour and the right to vote in our society. It is not merely symbolic. This legislation sends a message signalling Canadian values, to the effect that those people who are found guilty of the most serious crimes will, while separated from society, lose access to one of the levers of electoral power. This is an extremely important message, one which is not sent by incarceration alone. Incarceration is essentially separation from the community. Incarceration alone signals a denunciation of the offender's anti-societal behaviour and indicates society's hope for rehabilitation through separation from the community. Incarceration by itself, however, leaves those convicted of serious crimes free to exercise all the levers of electoral power open to all law-abiding citizens. This maintains a political parity between those convicted of society's worst crimes and their victims. Disqualification from voting, however, signals a denunciation of the criminal's anti-societal behaviour and sends the message that those people convicted of causing the worst forms of indignity to others will be deprived of one aspect of the political equality of citizens[:] the right to vote.[28]

---

[26] Ibid., para. 147.

[27] *Sauvé* v. *Canada*, [2000] 2 F.C. 117, para. 136, cited by Ngcobo J in *Minister for Home Affairs* v. *NICRO* at para. 150.

[28] *Sauvé* (Federal Court of Appeal), para. 137.

Among the passages quoted by the English court in *Hirst*: in the course of an examination that the Strasbourg Grand Chamber would later, unreasonably, say omitted to make a proportionality assessment – is the following remark of the Canadian Federal Court of Appeal:

> Where someone, by committing a serious crime, evinces contempt for our basic societal values, their right to vote may be properly suspended. Indeed, *not* to do so undermines our democratic values.[29]

That undermining may take the cause-and-effect character – of course mainly speculative or common sense, rather than provable or disprovable – that Ngcobo and Madala JJ were pointing to. But I think it also pertains to the entailments I pointed out in commenting upon 'it says that everybody counts'. *Allowing* serious criminals to vote during incarceration under sentence says to the law-abiding that *their* vote does not count very much, and says to the criminal that his own vivid defiance *of the communal project of self-government* (so far as that project called upon him to respect his victim) leaves his right to continued participation *in that project* unimpaired, *entirely* unimpaired. It says to him that he can defy the rules, even grossly or repeatedly, and treat his victim(s) and his fellow citizens as unequals, but go on claiming equality with them in rights of participation in communal self-government, without even temporary interruption. The Grand Chamber's unwillingness even to envisage this conception of reciprocity – one could also call it proportionality – I regard as rationally inexplicable, and as a manifestation both of a deep-going political decadence, and of indefensible judicial indifference to the separation of powers inherent in entrusting self-government primarily to an elected legislature. With lofty complacency, even contempt, this neglect to consider the idea of forfeiture – an idea that everyone uses in other contexts of association – is an oversight or refusal that – it too – tellingly *says* to all electors, especially the law-abiding, *you do not count for very much*. It gives the political philosophy and preferences of unelected, unaccountable and philosophically not too skilful or careful judges a reach and sway that have a quite inadequate support in the justice, law and constitution entrusted to their administration.

The judicial disarray in Strasbourg, the unprincipled to-ing and fro-ing between the pre-*Hirst* ECHR (Commission) jurisprudence, then *Hirst*, then *Frodl* and then *Scoppola*, is a manifestation of this plain degeneration of adjudication into legislation by judges. Such paradigmatically

---

[29] *Sauvé* FCA [139]; *Hirst* v. *Attorney-General* [37].

legislative action as drawing a line between disenfranchising eight per cent of convicted criminals – unlawful! – and disenfranchising (say) five per cent of them – lawful! – or between the whole class of one-year sentences and the whole class of three-year sentences, is the kind of exercise that ought to be repudiated in principle by our judges. There is hereabouts no constitutional problem of the kind that has sometimes made plausible certain line-drawing judicial interventions, such as the problem of apportioning electoral boundaries by a legislature presumptively motivated by self-interest to leave them malapportioned – the 'democracy and distrust' or democratic process theory elaborated by John Hart Ely.[30] Nor is there in Britain or Europe or South Africa or Canada any suggestion that either the electoral or the criminal justice system is biased or manipulated against racial or other discrete and insular minorities in need of protection from legislative or popular majorities.

III 'Irreversibility' and Extremism

Let me summarise the episodes from Canada, South Africa, New Zealand and Australia. First Canada. The Charter of Rights imported into the Constitution in 1982 affirms by its s. 3 that every citizen of Canada has the right to vote, and by s. 1 that such rights are 'subject only to such reasonable limits ... as can be demonstrably justified in a free and democratic society'. In 1992, as I mentioned, the Supreme Court summarily declared that disenfranchising all convicted prisoners was not a reasonable delimitation of the right to vote. By the date of that judgment the law had already been amended, to provide for disenfranchisement only of prisoners serving a 'sentence of two years or more'. That new provision, having been (as I mentioned) upheld by majority in the Federal Court of Appeal in 2000, came before the Supreme Court in 2002, and was invalidated 5:4. The judgments of McLachlin CJ for the majority and Gonthier J for the minority remain by far the most elaborate judgments on the issue anywhere, so far as I know, and are cited in all the other cases in my lineup. Though the *Sauvé* majority judgment is cited with favour in both *Hirst* and *Scoppola*, its extremist reasoning about proportionality denies, in substance, that there is or can in modern democracies be any legitimate disenfranchising of criminals, and is in

[30] John Hart Ely, *Democracy and Distrust: A Theory of Judicial Review* (Cambridge, MA: Harvard University Press, 1981).

fact reasoning manifestly incompatible with *Scoppola*, and with *Hirst* itself unless *Hirst* is interpreted in the manner adopted in *Frodl* and repudiated in *Scoppola*. I will quote the core of this reasoning in a moment.

To continue meanwhile with the sequence: South Africa's Constitutional Court in 2004, as I mentioned, invalidated a disenfranchisement very much like Britain's. The minority judges point appreciatively to the minority judgment in *Sauvé*. But while the South African majority point to the majority judgment in the Canadian case, they do not adopt its reasoning. Instead they rest their decision on the obvious inadequacy of the Government's evasive and minimalist explanation of the legislative ban; they complained that there was no information about the sort of offences concerned, the sort of persons likely to be affected and the number of persons who might lose their vote for a minor offence. Obviously, they envisaged their Court trying – some time in the future, when equipped by others with the appropriate information – to make the sort of fine-tuned line-drawing that, I am suggesting, has nothing to do with legal learning or the application of legal rules or practice-standards (as in the assessment of damages or costs) but is paradigmatically a task for responsible legislative policy choice.

Now to New Zealand, where a 2010 reform to electoral laws banning prisoner voting reduced the threshold for the ban from sentences of three years or more to imprisonment (by sentence after conviction) of any duration. In 2015, the High Court concluded against the measure's conformity with the New Zealand Bill of Rights Act 1990 by simply endorsing the Attorney General's Bill of Rights compliance report to the House of Representatives mandated by s. 7 of the 1990 Act. That report's reasoning, as approvingly recounted by the High Court, repeats the Strasbourg error of calling the 2010 reform a 'blanket ban'. It refused to consider the reform's objective by the simple device of 'assum[ing]' that it was (tautologously) to have 'serious offenders' forfeit the right to vote. With that objectiveless objective in place, the Attorney General had no difficulty in concluding, with the High Court's subsequent effortless endorsement, that the measures lacked rational basis: 'the blanket ban . . . is both under and over inclusive':

> It is under inclusive because a prisoner convicted of a serious violent offence who serves a two and a half year sentence in prison between general elections will be able to vote. It is over inclusive because someone convicted and given a one-week sentence that coincided with a general

election would be unable to vote. The provision does not impair the right
to vote as minimally as reasonably possible as it disenfranchises in an
irrational and irregular manner.[31]

The High Court does not explain how any of this is irrational or irregular. On appeal before the New Zealand Court of Appeal, the Attorney
General declined to dispute the claim that the 2010 reform imposed an
'unjustified limitation', thus relieving that Court of the responsibility of
explaining to legislators (and citizens) just what was 'irrational and
irregular' or (in the Court of Appeal's word of choice) 'undiscriminat-
ing'[32] in a measure that to so many has seemed, and continues to seem,
reasonable, proportionate, regular and discriminate, for reasons that
they – unlike these courts – are willing to articulate rationally.

Finally, then, to Australia, where of course there is no national bill or
charter of rights, though many academics and (rather fewer) politicians
and judges would love to have one, and some powerful judges, sometimes
in a majority, take what steps they can to 'find' some rights 'implied' in
the interstices or resonances of constitutional language or structure. In
2007, in *Roach* v. *Electoral Commissioner*,[33] the High Court of Australia
(the country's highest court) held by majority of 4:2 that disenfranchisement of all convicted prisoners was disproportionate to the idea of
representative government implicit in the only directly relevant words
of the Constitution: 'elected by the people'. But the majority then immediately proceeded to hold that the previous statutory rule disenfranchising all prisoners serving sentences of *three* years or more was valid, being
proportionate. This slicing between *all convicted prisoners* and *three-year
convicted prisoners* – a kind of foreshadowing of *Scoppola* – was made
with a scant couple of rushed sentences by the joint judgment of three of
the majority Justices (Gummow, Kirby and Crennan JJ), and with some
adoption of the *Sauvé* minority position by the fourth (Gleeson CJ).
A reading of these judgments leaves one able to conclude that a disenfranchisement of prisoners under (say) six months' or certainly of one
year's imprisonment would pass all the majority's tests, other these

---

[31] *Taylor* v. *Attorney-General* [2015] NZHC 1706, para. 29 and paras. 33–34
[32] *Attorney-General* v. *Taylor* [2017] NZCA 215, para. 185. The Court of Appeal noted
(para. 180) that the Attorney General's lack of argument was 'an unusual stance in
litigation of this kind', which was 'worth emphasising because it may distinguish this
case from others to come'.
[33] [2007] HCA 43.

judges' captivation by the symmetry, surely in substance irrelevant, between a three-year threshold and the so-called three-year cycle of elections. The two dissenting (Oxford alumni) judges, Justices Hayne and Heydon, pointed to the full compatibility of prisoner disenfranchisement with electoral provisions in force before and after the instituting of the federal Constitution of Australia in 1900, provisions then judged consistent with the only relevant ruling idea articulated in the Constitution: that the legislative Houses be 'directly chosen by the people'. No theory of representative government, or of penological, political-philosophical or other appropriate grounds for disenfranchisement, was adopted by the Constitution; no such theory, therefore, should be imposed by judges. Justices Hayne and Heydon rejected in particular the thesis that there could constitutionally be no 'winding-back' of the right to vote, such as the Parliament had made in 2006 when reducing the threshold for disenfranchisement from three years imprisonment to any term of imprisonment. Indeed, the dissenting Justices robustly imply that, however undesirable and unlikely a return to franchise limitations like those of 1900, such a winding-back would not be *unconstitutional.*

The contrary, normative, bootstrapping theory that politically 'irreversible' legislative innovations are somehow constitutionally protected from winding back is an important and express part of relevant Canadian decisions from 1990 on, and is detectable in less absolutist form in the ECtHR's repeated statements that 'in the twenty-first century, the presumption in a democratic state must be in favour of inclusion and universal suffrage has become the basic principle'.[34] What the ECtHR calls a presumption is treated by the majority in *Sauvé* v. *Canada* in a manner I have called extremist.[35] The five-justice majority, having granted for the sake of argument (or 'prudence') that the Canadian legislation's two-year threshold disenfranchisement of prisoners had legitimate aims – of encouraging civic responsibility and punishing crime – swept aside all possible defences of proportionality with the following:

---

[34] *Anchugov and Gladkov* v. *Russia*, 4 July 2013 (ECtHR, First Section), para. 103, following *Scoppola.*

[35] Michael Plaxton and Heather Lardy, 'Prisoner Disenfranchisement: Four Judicial Approaches' (2010) 28 *Berkeley Journal of International Law* 101–141. Though they favour the results, Plaxton and Lardy find it hard to defend the reasoning of McLachlin CJ, and remain puzzled about the non-enfranchisement of aliens (resident, in the first instance – but the puzzlement and implied argument go through to any alien affected by the policies of the country in question, perhaps every adult in the world).

> In a democracy such as ours ... delegation from voters to legislators gives
> the law its legitimacy or force. Correlatively, the obligation to obey the law
> flows from the fact that the law is made by and on behalf of the citizens. In
> sum, the legitimacy of the law and the obligation to obey the law flow
> directly from the right of every citizen to vote.[36]

Does anyone know a more indefensible general proposition in any law
report in any English-speaking country during the last one hundred
years?

> As a practical matter, we require all within our country's boundaries to
> obey its laws, whether or not they vote.[37]

And indeed, they would have the obligation – unjust laws aside – to obey
whether or not we 'required it' of them.

> But this does not negate the vital symbolic, theoretical and practical
> connection between having a voice in making the law and being obliged
> to obey it. This connection, inherited from social contract theory and
> enshrined in the *Charter*, stands at the heart of our system of consti-
> tutional democracy. ... The 'educative message' that the government
> purports to send by disenfranchising inmates is both anti-democratic
> and internally self-contradictory. Denying a citizen the right to vote
> denies the basis of democratic legitimacy. It says that delegates elected
> by the citizens can then bar those very citizens, or a portion of them, from
> participating in future elections. ... the history of democracy is the
> history of progressive enfranchisement. The universal franchise has
> become, at this point in time, an essential part of democracy. From the
> notion that only a few meritorious people could vote (expressed in terms
> like class, property and gender), there gradually evolved the modern
> precept that all citizens are entitled to vote as members of a self-governing
> citizenry. ... As Arbour J. A. observed in *Sauvé No. 1*: '... the slow
> movement toward universal suffrage in Western democracies took an
> irreversible step forward in Canada in 1982 by the enactment of s. 3 of
> the *Charter*'. The disenfranchisement of inmates takes us backwards in
> time and retrenches our democratic entitlements.[38]

Thus a proportionality analysis purporting to measure rational connection between aims and means not only denied the very possibility of
legitimately disenfranchising criminals or any criminal however gross or
treasonable or subversive of elections, but also employed premises from a
homemade grand political-philosophical theory well beyond the mandate

---

[36] *Sauvé (No. 2)*, para. 31.
[37] *Sauvé (No. 2)*, para. 31.
[38] *Sauvé (No. 2)*, paras. 31–33.

of the courts and the philosophical competence of these judges. Their theory that your obligation to obey the law depends on your having the right to vote cannot be rationally defended, as they half recognise when half conceding that 'as a practical matter' noncitizens have the obligation to obey the law. The only relevant proposition that could be defended is this: your obligation to comply with the law is impaired (though still not by any means dissolved) if your participation in government is *unjustly* denied – a proposition of no use to the majority, since what they are here trying to *show* is that *this* denial is unjust (is contrary to acknowledged rights). For a court to pronounce, as this Canadian majority pronounces, that convicted prisoners lawfully disenfranchised in mature democracies such as the United Kingdom or Italy or Australia have no obligation to comply with the law is, once again, beyond reasonable defence. And the rhetoric about it being self-contradictory for 'delegate' legislators to disenfranchise any of those who participated in their election is, again, logically false and, furthermore, is absurdly in contradiction with the Court's pretence that it accepted the legitimacy of the *aims* of the disenfranchisement and was only assessing proportionality of *means*. The reliance, finally, on 'social contract theory', a theory quite implausibly asserted to have been adopted into the Canadian constitutional order, ignores the oft-demonstrated disqualifying weaknesses of every such theory, save in those versions that limit themselves to observing the justice of reciprocity, of relating benefits to burdens and of regulating many present rights by reference *inter alia* to past performance of related obligations – those versions, in other words, that lend *support* to the disenfranchisement of criminals. These were judges far out of their depth, needlessly swimming out to sea.

IV   A Lesson from Experience: Established Legal Meanings or Judicial Unreason?

So, what lesson emerges from this series of incompetent decisions by courts of supreme jurisdiction? The one that interests me here is this. Original public meaning is the primary guide to and constraint upon appropriately judicial exercise of the judicial power and duty to apply the law of the constitution. Neglect of that meaning delivers the law into the hands of judges to change it without the merit of frankness in doing so, to change it with, again and again, astonishing ineptitude in argumentation, and to insult the elected lawmakers without the slightest benefit to the rule of law, democracy or any other constitutional value.

A constitution is like a treaty or international convention in that it represents a series of agreements between parties, often representative of vulnerable groups which undertake a risk in conferring authority on new organs and institutions. These parties and groups are betrayed, to a greater or less degree, if an understanding on faith of which they entered into or ratified the package is set aside without compelling reason of the kind that they would have accepted as fair in kind if it had come under discussion (as a future possibility) at the time of the agreement. This being so, what would or would not be betrayal is in these matters established by the **original public meaning** – that is (to stipulate what I mean), the set of propositions that are and were public because they were ascertainable by reasonable participants in and observers of the formative deliberations about the document (whether as proponents or opponents of it or of any statement in it) who sought or could then seek to ascertain from the public record *what propositions* the makers of the document *meant (intended) – and took – their document to bring into force as propositions of law*; and also what reasonably ascertainable propositions those makers certainly intended and meant it *not* to be bringing into law. ('Living tree' or 'living instrument' construction, wherever it runs contrary to original public meaning, is as a matter of strong presumption unjustified and, where that original public meaning gave expression to *reliance* by a vulnerable party or group, any such novel construction should be strongly presumed to implicate the judicial administration of justice in injustice savouring of ambush or at best cynicism – 'You or your forebears acting for you should have tried harder to exclude what we're now imposing.') And then the very same concern with original public meaning (as I have just stipulatively defined it) should be the primary guide to interpretation and constraint upon judicial decision in respect of provisions that did *not* have the character of risk-taking bargains, compromises and settlements between groups; there is, in general, no case for having judges adopt varying methods of interpretation depending on their investigation and assessment of the political background to different parts of the document.

At the Experts' Committee meeting in Strasbourg on 2 February 1950, the UK representative objected to draft Article 3, especially its then reference to 'universal suffrage':

> It is probable that the suffrage is as wide in the United Kingdom as in any other country; yet even in the United Kingdom as in any other country it is inaccurate to speak of the suffrage as 'universal'. In no State is the right to vote enjoyed even by citizens without qualifications. The qualifications

required differ from State to State . . . And it is our view that the variety of circumstances to be considered may justify the imposition of a variety of qualifications, as a condition of the exercise of suffrage.[39]

The response of the other experts is given in the Committee's report on 9 or 10 March 1950:

> The other Committee members, however, were of the opinion [1] that the term 'universal suffrage' had a sufficiently clear and precise meaning for the European countries and [2] did not exclude the usual restriction[s][40] on the right to vote.[41]

But the proposition that I have here labeled [1] was not the view that prevailed. By late August 1950, the article had taken (via other organs of the drafting and negotiating process) the form it now has, essentially identical to that objected to by the United Kingdom in February and March *but now omitting reference to universal suffrage* and warmly welcomed by the United Kingdom representatives. Thus, both the omission of the phrase and concept and the assurances given (and reasonably given) as proposition [2] (in the preceding quotation) when it was still in the draft combine to show that making universal suffrage the very principle of the article is an act of legislation and thus of usurpation by the Strasbourg Court.[42] The obligation assumed by the parties to the

---

[39] European Court of Human Rights, 'Preparatory Work on Article 3 of Protocol No. 1 to the European Convention on Human Rights' (1986), p. 8. www.echr.coe.int/LibraryDocs/Travaux/ECHRTravaux-P1-3-Cour(86)36-BIL1221606.pdf.

[40] The singular in the typescript English is a typographical error: the French is '*les restrictions* de droit de vote qui y sont d'usage'.

[41] ECtHR, above n 39, p. 11.

[42] This is true even if one does not accept without qualification the proposition of Judge Gerald Fitzmaurice (dissenting as to Article 6) in *Golder v. UK* [1975] 1 EHHR 524 (4451/70) 21 February 1975, para. 45: 'In the technique of treaty interpretation there can never be a better demonstration of an intention not to provide for something than first including, and then dropping it.' Note that Judge Fitzmaurice, an international law expert on treaty interpretation, gave a whole series of dissenting judgments elaborating the objection that the Court was departing both in particular and in principle from its obligation to respect the intentions of the states party and the object of the Convention (an object that could not reasonably be detached, as if *in abstracto*, from those intentions): *Golder* (reading in a right of access to the courts, obviously intentionally omitted); *National Union of Belgian Police v. Belgium* [1975] 1 EHHR 578 (extending Article 14 anti-discrimination provisions to rights not provided for in the Convention, against the terms of Article 14); *Ireland v. UK* [1978] 2 EHHR 25; *Tyrer v. UK* [1978] ECHR 2 (treating as degrading treatment a mode of punishment of juveniles accepted in a self-governing part of the British Isles in 1950); *Marckx v. Belgium* [1979] 2 EHHR 330 (treating the right to family life as outlawing Belgium's historic law about legitimacy).

ECHR was 'to secure to everyone within their jurisdiction the rights and
freedoms *defined* ... *in the Convention*' (Article 1(1), emphasis added),
and no right such as is denoted by 'universal suffrage' was so defined or,
therefore, included, still less a right whose definition could distinguish
between disqualification of all and disqualification of three-year prisoners. Original public meaning, as I said, is what would be judged to be the
meaning by reasonable, well-informed and legally competent or well
advised observers in and of the circumstances of the time; those circumstances include the reference to universal suffrage in the Universal
Declaration of Human Rights 1948, and in the first version of the
Convention's Article 3 publicly adopted by the Consultative Assembly
of the Council of Europe in 1949, and in drafting history such as I have
referred to, but then, after objections to its breadth, eliminated from the
wording.

Such considerations of original public meaning and intention are
brushed aside in the Strasbourg Court by appeal to the theory, to
which the Court first publicly subscribed in 1978, that the Convention is a 'living instrument which ... must be interpreted in the light
of present-day conditions'.[43] That bland statement sugars its poison;
no one could object to its literal sense,[44] but its real and intended
meaning is that the instrument can and should be applied in the

---

[43] *Tyrer* v. *UK* [1978] ECHR 2, (5856/72), 25 April 1978, para. 31.

[44] As Bradley Miller says, in relation to 'changing circumstances, such as unanticipated
technological changes like the telephone and atomic energy, as well as social changes such
as the full participation of women in the workforce', the sort of 'progressive interpretation' that is 'a matter of specification, or gap-filling, of the *eiusdem generis* variety' is
'equally supported by originalist and non-originalist interpreters': Bradley W. Miller,
'Origin Myth: The Persons Case, the Living Tree, and the New Originalism' in Grant
Huscroft and Bradley W. Miller (eds.), *The Challenge of Originalism: Theories of Constitutional Interpretation* (Cambridge: Cambridge University Press, 2011), pp. 120–146, esp.
pp. 136–137. With this illuminating essay I disagree only on one point: I am confident
that what the Lord Chancellor meant by the 'living tree' he spoke of in the Persons Case
(*Edwards* v. *Attorney-General Canada* [1930] AC 124) – as something 'planted' in North
America by the British North America Act and 'capable of growth and expansion within
its natural limits' – was not what Miller calls 'the Canadian Constitution in its entirety –
written and unwritten, convention and law'; rather, the living tree intended and spoken of
was *the Dominion itself*, as (what the Lord Chancellor called one page earlier) one of the
'communities included within the Britannic system ... and undergoing a continuous
process of evolution', and referred to again on the judgment's last page as 'a responsible
and developing State'. So Canadian 'living tree constitutionalism', so far as it has appealed
to the Lord Chancellor's dictum, is even more confused and myth-ridden than Miller
contends.

light of present-day conditions *and opinions about better political or social arrangements*, be applied in ways not included in, or even contrary to, its original public meaning (intent). But what was agreed by those who drafted the Protocol is true of the rest of the Convention too:

> No one expected that the minority would modify their legal systems in order to bring them into line with a Protocol acceptable to the majority. It was thus the task of the experts to find texts ... which represented the minimum standards obtaining in Western Europe as a whole.[45]

Such was the project, and such the agreement, and yet now it is regularly demanded that the minority or even a majority of states modify their legal systems to bring them into line not with a majority of equal partners in negotiation, but of judges attending only to the cramped and, as we have seen, so often sophistical rhetoric of textual phrases and scattered precedents.

Clearer examples of the point I am suggesting about original public meaning are afforded by the Australian position I have mentioned, in particular the position of the dissenters in the High Court of Australia in

---

[45] A. W. Brian Simpson, *Human Rights and the End of Empire: Britain and the Genesis of the European Convention* (Oxford: Oxford University Press, 2004), p. 791, quoting a formal and, it seems, universally well received British statement to the meeting of Ministers and Advisers, 30 April to 1 May 1951. Simpson comments that this corresponds to the position taken more generally by the Juridical Section (committee) that launched the drafting of the Convention itself in 1949, and that said of its proposals:

> It is applicable to States possessing different constitutional systems, and which do not have precisely the same criteria in the matter of rights and liberties. In addition, this provisional solution appears as readily acceptable to governments, since *it does not require any modification of the constitutional laws of their countries* [emphasis added].

Ibid. 661 (commentary by the Juridical Section on its draft Convention, 12 July 1949). Again, the motion proposed by the chairman of that Section and forty-four others, and acted upon if not adopted in August 1949 by the Consultative Assembly, was for a Convention:

> to maintain intact the human rights and fundamental freedoms assured by the constitutions, laws, and administrative practices *actually existing in the respective countries at the date of the signature of the convention* [emphasis added].

Ibid. 671.

Roach:[46] that the meaning of vague general words, 'chosen by the people', does not operate to invalidate electoral or enfranchisement provisions of a kind that the Constitution itself, in or by reference in directly related

---

[46] Similarly, the majority of the US Supreme Court in *Richardson* v. *Ramirez* 418 US 24 (1974). The 14th Amendment (July 1868) by s. 1 forbids any State to 'deny to any person within its jurisdiction the equal protection of the laws'. In the 1960s the US Supreme Court held, and applied in many contexts, that this creates a constitutional right to participate in elections on an equal basis with other citizens, such that disenfranchisement of any person or class of persons is lawful only if necessary to achieve a legitimate and substantial state interest, if the classification is drawn with precision, and if there are no other reasonable ways to achieve the legitimate goal with a lesser burden on the constitutionally protected interest in voting. In *Richardson* v. *Ramirez* the dissenting minority held that this invalidated the California law that disenfranchised, permanently, anyone convicted of felony; this minority (Marshall and Brennan JJ) stressed that the disenfranchisement extended to felons who had 'paid their debt to society' by serving out their sentence and parole; these justices thereby implied that a law disenfranchising felons still serving their sentences would be compatible with the 14th Amendment. But the majority held that the whole matter was settled by s. 2 of the 14th Amendment, considered as a guide to the meaning of s. 1. For s. 2 provides that a state's representation in Congress is to be reduced to the extent that the state's law has disenfranchised male adult citizen inhabitants of the state, except where such disenfranchisement is 'for participation in rebellion, or other crime'. As the majority justices put it, those upholding the California disenfranchisement of felons argue:

> that those who framed and adopted the Fourteenth Amendment could not have intended to prohibit outright in § 1 of that Amendment that which was expressly exempted from the lesser sanction of reduced representation imposed by § 2 of the Amendment. This argument seems to us a persuasive one unless it can be shown that the language of § 2, 'except for participation in rebellion, or other crime', was intended to have a different meaning than would appear from its face.

After musing on the difficulty of interpreting 'the "intention" of a constitutional provision', the majority held that 'what legislative history there is indicates that this language was intended by Congress to mean what it says' (418 US 43). 'The exclusion of felons from the vote has an affirmative sanction in § 2 of the Fourteenth Amendment, a sanction which was not present in the case of the other restrictions on the franchise which were invalidated' by the Supreme Court in the late 1960s and early 1970s:

> We hold that the understanding of those who adopted the Fourteenth Amendment, as reflected in the express language of § 2 and in the historical and judicial interpretation of the Amendment's applicability to state laws disenfranchising felons, is of controlling significance in distinguishing such laws from those other state limitations on the franchise which have been held invalid under the Equal Protection Clause by this Court. ... § 1, in dealing with voting rights as it does, could not have been meant to bar outright a form of disenfranchisement which was expressly exempted from the less drastic sanction of reduced representation which § 2 imposed for other forms of disenfranchisement (418 US 54–55).

clauses of its text, treated as compatible, as a class, with the requirement of popular election or equality of voting rights respectively. The casualness with which the Supreme Court of Canada, in the decade after 1982, deployed comparably vague, or even vaguer Charter wording to strike down pre-Charter national legislation both of uncontroversial long standing (such as the disenfranchisement of convicted prisoners) and of recent enactment by substantially the same legislators as secured the enactment of the Charter (such as the regulation of termination of pregnancy),[47] was I believe an affront to the rule of law, one that would be widely and fiercely commented upon in legal-academic circles were it not that the results are so pleasing to most legal academics – prisoners' voting rights at least as much as abortion.

And the judges who speak of every voter counting are, it seems, the same sort of judges as those who in the United States, without attention to evidence or concern for factual support, declare vast numbers of voters, majorities indeed, to be bigots – motivated in their voting and legislating by animus, animosity, malice, a 'bare desire to harm' and demean, and a purpose to injure[48] – whose votes and laws and referendum-approved constitutional amendments can therefore be simply set aside as nullities. Such declarations, as in the homosexual rights cases of *Romer* v. *Evans* (1996) and *US* v. *Windsor* (2013), mistake (or misrepresent) these voters' reasonable fear for their children's and their fellow-citizens' wellbeing and for their country as animus against persons. The declarations' remote direct origins in slavery, scalawags and black Republican governments and the reaction to the memory or legend of them among newly enfranchised white voters, and much else, need to be remembered; but equally or more worthy of investigation and reflection are their more proximate possible origins in such biases of modern liberalisms as Ronald Dworkin's refusal[49] to investigate the reasons relied on by majority voters. In any event, it is generally an unreasonable and

---

[47] *R* v. *Morgentaler* [1988] 1 SCR 30.

[48] *Romer* v. *Evans* 517 US 620 (1996) at 632, 634–635; *US* v. *Windsor* 570 US 744 (2013), Opinion of the Court (Kennedy J), part IV. In *Obergefell* v. *Hodges* 576 US ___ (2015), the judicial rhetoric of the judicial majority is smoothed out so as to make only implicit the allegation of bad intent, but their talk (slip opinion p. 19) of demeaning, disparaging and stigmatizing *persons* is rightly identified by the Chief Justice in dissent as an allegation of voters' and legislators' bigotry – and is not mere talk: it is an essential premise.

[49] See John Finnis, *Philosophy of Law: Collected Essays: Volume IV* (Oxford: Oxford University Press, 2011), pp. 24–26 (1985) and p. 271 (2009); John Finnis, *Intention and Identity: Collected Essays: Volume II* (Oxford: Oxford University Press, 2011), pp. 110–111.

sinister argument, systematically confusing side effect with objective or purpose, and refusing to attend sincerely to public reasons. It is an extremist version of the disdain shown also, in a low-keyed way, by courts nullifying prisoner disenfranchisement when they speak of all historical restrictions on the franchise, all fallings short of universal suffrage, as having been motivated merely by the self-interest or prejudice of elites[50] – as if the most deep-thinking and well-informed philosophers had never argued, dispassionately, for restricting the franchise for the sake of the *common* good, the good of each and every one, unless and until and *while* the conditions are stably and sustainably in place to make likely a responsible and just use of the vote.[51]

The founders and drafters of the Constitution of the Commonwealth of Australia took a great interest in the Bill of Rights provisions of the US Constitution, and while establishing a High Court that they knew and intended would have great power of oversight of the federal division of powers, they nonetheless with deliberation and firmness rejected the

---

[50] *Hirst* [59]: 'the franchise was gradually extended over the centuries from select individuals, elite groupings or sections of the population approved of by those in power'. *Sauvé (No. 2)* [33]: 'From the notion that only a few meritorious people could vote (expressed in terms like class, property and gender), there gradually evolved the modern precept that all citizens are entitled to vote as members of a self-governing citizenry.'

[51] In *Sauvé (No. 2)* the majority go all the way to making constitutionally irreversible the legislative gamble (admittedly given the appearance of ratification by s. 3 of the Charter) they describe in these terms (at para. 34):

> The right of all citizens to vote, *regardless of virtue or mental ability or other distinguishing features*, underpins the legitimacy of Canadian democracy and Parliament's claim to power. A government that restricts the franchise to a select portion of citizens is a government that weakens its ability to function as the legitimate representative of the excluded citizens, jeopardizes its claim to representative democracy, and erodes the basis of its right to convict and punish law-breakers [emphasis added].

In para. 32 they quote with approval Arbour J's dictum in *Sauvé (No. 1)*:

> By the time the *Charter* was enacted, exclusions from the franchise were so few in this country that it is fair to assume that we had abandoned the notion that the electorate should be restricted to a 'decent and responsible citizenry', previously defined by attributes such as ownership of land or gender, in favour of *a pluralistic electorate which could well include domestic enemies of the state* [emphasis added].

As an argument for invalidating the exclusion of convicted prisoners from the franchise, these passages are of course viciously circular, but the present point concerns these judges' *attitude* to what previous generations, with philosophical support, judged to be prudence and justice.

transfer of power away from elected legislatures into the hands of a few judges, the transfer that would inevitably result from adoption of a Bill of Rights in the Commonwealth Constitution. The judicial hubris and incompetence on display in the Strasbourg and Canadian prisoners votes cases, and determining their outcomes, are significant items on the long list of cases that I believe help vindicate that choice of the founders of the Australian Constitution.

V   The Moral for Voters in and for Our Legislatures

All public authorities – indeed, all citizens and others – have the duty to accord to others the rights they in truth have. The particular mandate of the courts is to uphold *our law* about what human rights people in truth have.

That law, in the United Kingdom today, includes prior judgments of the superior courts (including Strasbourg) and Acts of Parliament, all presumptively made on the basis of (or at least presupposing) an understanding of (i.e., an opinion about) what human rights people in truth have. Each or any of these judgments, understandings or opinions may be in error. So too, the countervailing judgments, understandings or opinions pressed upon the court by advocates of a 'living instrument' interpretation of the existing law – interpretation that both in intention and effect is amendment or abrogation – may be in error about what human rights people truly have. To the extent that the judicial precedents themselves are founded upon a living instrument interpretation of the Convention, they may rightly be discounted and, for the future, overridden by the appropriate institution constitutionally authorised to rectify our law.

13

'All's Well That Ends Well?'

Same-Sex Marriage and Constitutional Dialogue

STEPHEN MACEDO

"Today ... the Court takes the extraordinary step of ordering every State to license and recognize same-sex marriage. ... [F]or those who believe in a government of laws, not of men, the majority's approach is deeply disheartening. Supporters of same-sex marriage have achieved considerable success persuading their fellow citizens – through the democratic process – to adopt their view. That ends today. Five lawyers have closed the debate and enacted their own vision of marriage as a matter of constitutional law. Stealing this issue from the people will for many cast a cloud over same-sex marriage, making a dramatic social change that much more difficult to accept."

- Chief Justice John Roberts, dissenting in *Obergefell*

I Introduction

Conservative opposition to same-sex marriage has been linked with charges that courts overstep their bounds in recognizing gay rights. Some liberals join in arguing that rights protections accomplished by judicial review bear a taint of democratic illegitimacy. One purported advantage of the legislative route is a fuller and fairer airing of the merits of the issue: the greater opportunity for "meaningful and fruitful dialogue," as Jeremy Waldron puts it, in which "representatives of the people in all their diversity ... might fruitfully converse on issues of rights." What we should hope for, says Waldron, is a "*dialogue* ... from which either party might learn and in the course of which either party might be expected to modify positions that it reached on its own in light of what the other party has said."[1]

That sort of dialogue on important political issues is certainly a thing to be hoped for and welcomed. In our current polarized political climate in the United States, at least, it is all too rarely to be expected.

---

[1] See Jeremy Waldron, 'Some Models of Dialogue Between Judges and Legislators' (2004) 23 *Supreme Court Law Review*, 7, 7.

Yet how telling is the idea of dialogue when offered as a supposed alternative to the strong form of judicial review that is exercised by the US Supreme Court? With respect to marriage equality in the United States, the Court's decision in *Obergefell* was certainly a landmark exercise of strong judicial review. Yet we can and should properly see it as the culmination of a decades-long political process involving citizens and public officials at all levels. Gay rights have been realized in America, not completely but impressively from the perspective of even a decade ago, because of a constitutional and political debate and deliberation at all levels of politics and society, including but not especially in courtrooms. Admittedly, the relevant "dialogues" have often had more the character of a pitched political battle rather than a philosophy seminar, but the important point is that arguments have been aired, responded to, revised, and aired again, over decades and in a way that has frequently engaged the public. The contest over gay rights in America has been as much a contest over public opinion as it has been a struggle to define the meanings of liberty and equality under the Constitution.

Indeed, one important difference between abortion and gay rights in the United States is the fact that decades of intense political mobilization and contestation preceded the culminating decision of *Obergefell*: the modern gay rights movement can be traced back fifty years or more, depending on how one wants to look at it.[2] We might say that in *Obergefell* the Supreme Court synthesized and brought to culmination a long democratic dialogue.[3] The Court's part in the American dialogue about gay rights differs in this respect from the role it played, in *Roe v. Wade*, in the abortion controversy: in which it catalyzed the subsequent and ongoing debate.[4] In the gay rights dialogue that culminated in *Obergefell*, courts at different levels of government played recurring roles, but only as one set of political actors among many others. Indeed, for over forty years the political right – especially the "moral majority," the Christian right, and social conservatives – have been intensely mobilized over the issues of abortion and gay rights. The arguments on both sides had time to develop fully, not simply in political arenas but in the mustiest halls of the academy. As an example, scholars associated with

---

[2] A point made to me by Keith Whittington.

[3] I owe this to Geoffrey Sigalet, and am indebted to him and Grégoire Webber for many improvements.

[4] For a characterization of *Roe* as a 'catalyst' for the abortion debate, see Barry Friedman, 'Dialogue and Judicial Review' (1993) 91 *Michigan Law Review* 577, 660.

the "New Natural Law" school of legal and political philosophy, who
typically defend positions on ethical issues such as abortion and marriage
that parallel the teachings of the Roman Catholic Church, developed an
account of a new basic good of marriage in the 1980s and 1990s in response
to the controversy over same-sex marriage.[5] Indeed, our decades-long
national conversation about gay rights involved every department of public
and private life, including popular media and entertainment.

Against this background, which I will briefly describe, the right to gay
marriage has secured both moral and sociological legitimacy. By the time
of *Obergefell*, the case for same-sex marriage was much stronger than the
case against. Moreover, the right is more secure thanks to its broad and
growing acceptance in the public mind. I will say more about this later in
the chapter.

At the most basic level of principle, I argue against Jeremy Waldron,
Mark Tushnet, and others who cast American-style judicial review as
democratically illegitimate. It is, *in principle*, not only fully compatible
with democracy, but democracy-enhancing. Strong judicial review[6] as
practiced in America, moreover, often provides far more opportunity for
extended democratic contestation of important constitutional questions
than is often recognized, and the case of same-sex marriage illustrates
that. *In practice*, judicial review in the United States has a mixed record,
as does every other political institution and practice. I do not argue that
American constitutional arrangements, including judicial review, are
optimal. I do not know of anyone who argues that.[7]

---

[5] Compare John M. Finnis, *Natural Law and Natural Rights* (Oxford: Oxford University
Press, 1980), with his first (so far as I know) foray into these issues, 'Personal Integrity,
Sexual Morality, and Responsible Personhood' (1985) *I Anthropos: Rivista di Studi sulla
Persona e La Famiglia* (now *Anthroptes*), 43, 45–46; and later, 'Law, Morality, and Sexual
Orientation' (1994) 69 *Notre Dame Law Review* 1049. The arguments were most fully
developed, further from the margins of public law, in Germain Grisez, *The Way of the
Lord Jesus, Volume 2: Living a Christian Life* (St. Paul's, 1993) p. 662. For a wider
discussion and critique, see Stephen Macedo, *Just Married: Same-Sex Couples, Monog-
amy, and the Future of Marriage* (Princeton: Princeton University Press, 2015).

[6] Both Waldron and Tushnet distinguish between 'strong' and 'weak' forms of judicial
review, with the former including the power of courts to invalidate acts of legislation, and
the latter involving only the judicial power to require or facilitate legislative reconsideration of legislation. See Jeremy Waldron, 'The Core of the Case Against Judicial Review'
(2006) 115 *Yale Law Journal* 1346; and see Mark Tushnet, *Weak Courts, Strong Rights:
Judicial Review and Social Welfare Rights in Comparative Constitutional Law* (Princeton:
Princeton University Press, 2009).

[7] Ronald Dworkin, among the warmest defenders of judicial review, for example, advocated term limits for US Supreme Court justices; see his *Justice for Hedgehogs*

I sympathize *in some cases* with some criticisms of US-style strong-form judicial review. If abortion seems a weak case for the US model, due to the broad sweep and peremptoriness of *Roe* v. *Wade*, the gay rights issues seem much stronger, as I argue below. Waldron says, "I cannot think of any case in the United States where the judges have made, so to speak, an original contribution on the merits on some issue of rights that had not already been raised in the legislature (and voted on)."[8] This strikes me as a strange claim and not really to the point. There are many legislators and judges, and other political actors, all of variable quality. In the context of gay rights, judges contributed notably, along with many others including legislators. One of the best statements in the entire record is the opinion of Federal Appeals Court Judge Richard Posner in *Baskin* v. *Bogan*, decided not long before *Obergefell* reached the Supreme Court. Chief Justice Margaret Marshall's opinion in *Goodridge*, for the Supreme Judicial Court of Massachusetts, is widely admired and for good reason. And Justice Anthony M. Kennedy's opinion in *Obergefell*, while flawed, has since been quoted by many thousands of officiants at weddings, gay and straight, often along with the Court's opinion in the case striking down state bans on interracial marriage, *Loving* v. *Virginia*. I have written about all of these matters elsewhere[9], and here focus on the protracted complexity of the interactions of legislatures, executives, courts, and many other political actors.

There is no doubt, finally, that these matters will look differently from the standpoint of *different constitutional traditions*. At the most abstract level, democracy and judicial review are fully compatible, but judicial review is not one thing but several – it is organized differently *vis à vis* the legislative process in different countries. Indeed, state courts and legislatures interact more easily than federal courts and Congress.[10] There is no

---

(Cambridge, MA: Harvard University Press, 2011), p. 399. I am far less convinced than others that US constitutional institutions are so dysfunctional as to justify a resort to the very burdensome and distracting amendment process or a convention; see for example Sanford Levinson *Our Undemocratic Constitution: Where the Constitution Goes Wrong (And How We the People Can Correct It)* (Oxford: Oxford University Press, 2006), to which I have written a partial reply: Stephen Macedo, 'Our Imperfect Democratic Constitution: The Critics Examined' (2009) 609 *Boston University Law* 89; part of the symposium issue: 'Toward a More Democratic Congress?'.

[8] Waldron, 'Some Models of Dialogue Between Judges and Legislators' above n 1, 26.
[9] See Macedo, above n 5.
[10] See for example Douglas S. Read, *On Equal Terms: The Constitutional Politics of Educational Opportunity* (Princeton: Princeton University Press, 2003); also, Douglas S. Read, 'Court-Ordered School Finance Equalization: Judicial Activism and Democratic

question that ultimately rights and principles of justice are secured politically and not by courts alone. The concern with premature judicial settlement, and judicial peremptoriness with respect to political processes, is legitimate. Even then, we should not exaggerate what is sometimes called "judicial finality" or "judicial supremacy." I use the term "judicial supremacy" to describe strong forms of judicial review where the judicial exercise of this formal power is often helpfully reinforced and supported by democratic dialogues in which executive and legislature share in the interpretation of constitutional rights.

II Same-Sex Marriage and Democratic Legitimacy

The recognition of a national right to same-sex marriage was the result of a decades' long process that involved countless citizens, county clerks, mayors, governors, state courts and legislatures, presidents, justice department officials, leaders of the Armed Forces, members of both houses of Congress, the federal courts at all levels, business leaders, celebrities, clergy, educators, students, and many others. This complicates and ultimately decisively defeats any simple story about an undemocratic Supreme Court foisting the issue on an unready public. In fact, by May 2015, a month before the Supreme Court decision, sixty percent of the American public told Gallup pollsters that same-sex marriage should be legal, with only thirty-seven percent opposed.[11] Plurality support for same-sex marriage was reached in 2011, and growing majorities have supported it in Gallup polls ever since. Other polls preceding *Obergefell* showed closer results, but no one would have denied that by June 2015, at least a clear plurality of Americans favored legal recognition of same-sex marriage. The *Obergefell* decision seems to have caused a slight and temporary downturn in the percentage of those expressing support, but by late June 2017, polls indicated that it was sixty-two percent in favor and thirty-two percent opposed.[12]

*****

Opposition' in William J. Fowler (ed.), *Developments in School Finance* (US Department of Education Office of Educational Research and Improvement, 1996).

[11] Gallup, 'In Depth: Topics A–Z, Marriage', www.gallup.com/poll/117328/marriage.aspx.

[12] Sarah McCammon, 'Same-Sex Marriage Support At All-Time High, Even Among Groups That Opposed It', *National Public Radio*, June 26, 2017, www.npr.org/2017/06/26/534443 494/same-sex-marriage-support-at-all-time-high-even-among-groups-that-opposed-it.

How far back should we trace the political and constitutional roots of marriage equality? One candidate for an origins story can be found in the reaction against Cold War McCarthyism, and its lingering effects on the United States Civil Service and federal employment.[13]

In 1953, President Dwight Eisenhower signed an executive order declaring that "the interests of national security require" the exclusion from federal employment of those found to have engaged in "any criminal, infamous, dishonest, immoral, or notoriously disgraceful conduct, habitual use of intoxicants to excess, drug addiction, sexual perversion."[14] The order was understood to include homosexuals. Defense contractors and all corporations with federal contracts were required to seek out and discharge homosexual employees, and many private employers with no federal contracts followed suit, as did state and local governments.[15] Indeed, a broader police crackdown on gays and suspected gays was encouraged.

Consider the case of Dr. Franklin Kameny, a veteran of World War II, who was fired from his job with the Army Map Service in 1957 because he was gay. At the time, same-sex sexual relations were criminalized in all fifty states, and "even the American Civil Liberties Union declared it had no interest in challenging laws 'aimed at the suppression or elimination of homosexuals'."[16] Yet, Kameny, calling his treatment "an affront to human dignity," joined with others and began to organize. He helped found a Washington, DC chapter of the Mattachine Society, and in 1961, he prepared his own appeal petition to the Supreme Court, the first for a violation of civil rights based on sexual orientation.[17] A remarkably forward-looking document, the petition invoked America's founding principles:

---

[13] The paragraphs that follow draw heavily from James E. Fleming, Sotirios A. Barber, Stephen Macedo, and Linda C. McClain, *Gay Rights and the Constitution* (Foundation Press, 2016), ch. 1, drafted by Stephen Macedo.

[14] Executive Order 10450 – Security Requirements for Government Employment. Source: The provisions of Executive Order 10450 of April 27, 1953, appear at 18 FR 2489, 3 CFR, 1949–1953 Comp., p. 936, unless otherwise noted. Sec. 8, (a)1(iii). www.archives.gov/federal-register/codification/executive-order/10450.html.

[15] David K. Johnson, '"Homosexual Citizens": Washington's Gay Community Confronts the Civil Service' (Fall/Winter 1994–95) 6 *Washington History* 45–63.

[16] Dale Carpenter, 'How the Law Accepted Gays' *New York Times*, April 28, 2011.

[17] Associated Press, 'Library of Congress Exhibits Gay Rights History' *Washington Post*, May 9, 2011. www.washingtonpost.com/blogs/the-buzz/post/library-of-congress-exhibits-gay-rights-history/2011/05/09/AFklNtYG_blog.html.

Not only are the government's present policies on homosexuality irrational in themselves, but they are unreasonable in that they are grossly inconsistent with the fundamental precepts upon which this government is based. ... [W]e may commence with the Declaration of Independence, and its affirmation, as an "inalienable right," that of the "pursuit of happiness." Surely a most fundamental, unobjectionable, and unexceptionable element in human happiness is the right to bestow affection upon and to receive affection from whom one wishes. Yet, upon pain of severe penalty, the government itself would abridge this right for the homosexual.[18]

In 1965, after the Supreme Court refused to take his case, Kameny and a handful of others protested the federal government's exclusion of gays from employment by picketing the White House and the Pentagon.

The "gay rights" agenda in the 1970's involved seeking basic protections from harassment by the police, decriminalization of gay sex, hate crimes legislation, and antidiscrimination rights in employment and housing. Marriage was rarely discussed, but it was pushed to the fore briefly by a few activists emboldened by the revolutionary advances of the civil rights movement and the women's movement of the 1960s and 1970s.[19]

Jack Baker and Michael McConnell fell in love soon after meeting at a party in 1966. The men applied for a marriage license in Hennepin County, Minnesota, in 1970, after noticing that Minnesota law did not explicitly prohibit same-sex marriage. The clerk asked, "Who's going to be the wife?" "We don't play those kinds of roles," Baker and McConnell replied.[20] Other gay rights activists in Minnesota reportedly regarded the two as "lunatics" for pressing the marriage issue at the time, and some opposed monogamous marriage as "a trap."[21]

The Minnesota Supreme Court eventually ruled, "The institution of marriage as a union of man and woman, uniquely involving the

---

[18] Kameny's petition for a writ of certiorari to the United States Supreme Court, January, 1961 in Charles Francis, '50th Anniversary of a Legal Revolution' *Huffington Post*, March 25, 2011. www.huffingtonpost.com/charles-francis/frank-karmeny-supreme-court_b_840659 .html; See also William N. Eskridge, *Gaylaw: Challenging the Apartheid of the Closet* (Cambridge, MA: Harvard University Press, 2002), pp. 97, 125–26.

[19] Eskridge, above n 18; Dudley Clendinen and Adam Nagourney, *Out for Good: The Struggle to Build a Gay Rights Movement in America* (Simon and Schuster, 2001).

[20] Kay Tobin and Randy Wicker, *The Gay Crusaders* (Paperback Library, 1972), p. 145 (quoted in Mary Anne Case, 'Marriage Licenses' (2005) 89 *Minnesota Law Review* 1758, 1784.

[21] Thomas Kraemer, 'Jack Baker and Michael McConnell: Lunatics or Geniuses' *GayToday. com*, June 21, 2004.

procreation and rearing of children within a family, is as old as the Book of Genesis."[22] The US Supreme Court's precedents establishing the fundamental right to marry simply did not apply, said the Minnesota court, because such cases involved marriage between husband and wife. Further, the court interpreted the Supreme Court's famous *Loving* decision as confined solely to "patent racial discrimination," and reasoned that "in common sense and in a constitutional sense, there is a clear distinction between a marital distinction based merely upon race and one based on the fundamental difference of sex."[23] In 1972, the US Supreme Court declined to hear arguments in *Baker* v. *Nelson*, "for want of a substantial federal question."[24]

A few county clerks in Colorado and elsewhere noticed – as had Baker and McConnell – that the law was silent on the question of whether a same-sex couple could file for a marriage license, and they issued such licenses to gay and lesbian couples on their own discretion. These short-lived forays led state legislatures to reaffirm "traditional" marriage.

Baker and McConnell, incidentally, remain together after forty-five years of marriage. A Methodist minister performed a marriage ceremony for them in 1971.[25]

The Stonewall riots in New York City gave gay rights activists a boost, but then and for decades after, most saw marriage equality as an unimaginably distant goal, and some regarded it with profound ambivalence. Radicals considered marriage the enemy, a patriarchal bastion of male supremacy and sexual repression.[26] An early gay tract denounced the "rotten, oppressive institution" of traditional marriage. "Marriage is a great institution," quipped Paula Ettelbrick (riffing on Mae West), "if you like living in institutions." Marriage rights "would force our assimilation into the mainstream" and sap efforts to transform society

---

[22] *Baker* v. *Nelson*, 191 N.W.2d 185, 186 (Minn. 1971).

[23] Ibid. 187.

[24] 410 U.S. 810 (1972). See Patrick Condon, 'Baker and McConnell, Couple in 1971 Minnesota Gay Marriage Case, Still United' *Associated Press*, December 10, 2012; *Huffington Post*. www.huffingtonpost.com/2012/12/10/jack-baker-michael-mcconnell-minnesota-gay-marriage-_n_22715573.html.

[25] Indeed, after being turned down in Hennepin County, they traveled to Minnesota's Blue Earth County, 'where they obtained a marriage license on which Baker was listed with an altered, gender-neutral name.' Though challenged in court, says Baker, the license was never actually invalidated by a judge. Condon, 'Baker and McConnell'.

[26] William N. Eskridge, *Equality Practice: Civil Unions and the Future of Gay Rights*, (Routledge, 2013), p. 4.

more radically.[27] Nonetheless, some feminist theorists within the LGBT movement contended that same-sex marriage had the potential to further erode gendered marriage by denaturalizing and calling into question the "spousal roles of husband and wife."[28]

*****

Gay rights first captured the national headlines in a sustained way in 1977 as a consequence of a vote by the Miami-Dade County Metro Commission to proceed with consideration of an ordinance to extend civil rights protection in order to bar discrimination in housing, employment, and public accommodations based on "affectional or sexual preference."[29] The ordinance was taken up by the Commission as a result of the leadership of the local chapter of the National Organization of Women and some local gay rights groups. Fierce opposition was quickly mounted by religious leaders and conservative groups, who gathered petitions to place the matter before the voters. They also secured the leadership of Anita Bryant, a Sunday school teacher and singer, who had entertained the troops in Vietnam with Bob Hope, performed at both the Democratic and Republican national conventions in 1968, and became famous nationally as TV spokesperson for the Florida Citrus Commission. To oppose gay rights, Bryant founded the group Save Our Children, Inc., dedicated to protecting "God's moral codes as stated in the Holy Scriptures."[30]

When Dade County voters went to the polls, nearly seventy percent supported Bryant. "We will now carry our fight against similar laws throughout the nation," she declared, to oppose laws, "that attempt to legitimize a lifestyle that is both perverse and dangerous to the sanctity of the family, dangerous to our children ... dangerous to our survival as a nation."[31]

---

[27] Ibid. 208–09; Michael J. Klarman, *From the Closet to the Altar: Courts, Backlash, and the Struggle for Same-Sex Marriage* (Oxford: Oxford University Press, 2012), pp. 48–49. For the classic debate on this issue, compare Paula L. Ettelbrick, 'Since When Is Marriage A Path to Liberation?' in Suzanne Sherman (ed.), *Lesbian and Gay Marriage* (Temple University Press, 1992), p. 20, with Thomas B. Stoddard, 'Why Gay People Should Seek the Right to Marry' in Suzanne Sherman (ed.), *Lesbian and Gay Marriage* (Temple University Press, 1992), p. 13.

[28] Nan Hunter, 'Marriage, Law, and Gender: A Feminist Inquiry' (1991) 1 *Law & Sexuality* 9; Klarman, ibid. p. 49; see generally Eskridge, above n 26, pp. 206–29.

[29] Clendenin and Nagourney, *Out for Good*, above n 19, p. 295.

[30] Ibid. p. 296, and see ch. 22 generally.

[31] Ibid. p. 309.

For the next thirty-five years at least, gay rights – and increasingly gay marriage – joined abortion as the two great mobilizers of social conservatives and the Christian right in American politics.

*****

Beginning in the 1980s, some municipalities created new legal statuses, such as domestic partnerships, that accorded some recognition to non-marital (including same-sex) adult relationships. In 1984, Berkeley, California "became the first city in the United States to enact domestic partnerships"; in the late 1980s, West Hollywood and Madison, Wisconsin followed, as did San Francisco and New York in 1990 and 1993, by which time around twenty-five cities had enacted partnership laws, though they remained unpopular with most Americans.[32] Such ordinances sought to advance a governmental interest in "strengthening and supporting all caring, committed, and responsible family forms."[33] In 1992, the first American universities – Iowa, Stanford, and the University of Chicago – provided partnership benefits to same-sex employees.[34]

Many gay and lesbian baby boomers wanted the right to become parents. "The control of gays and lesbians over their own children remained vulnerable to the discretion of judges, as illustrated by the Sharon Bottoms case from Virginia in 1993. Bottoms lost custody of her son to her mother when a judge decided that it was not in the child's best interests to be raised by an open lesbian."[35] At that time, Virginia, like many other states, viewed homosexuality as evidence of immorality and, therefore, of parental unfitness. However, a growing number of states began to move away from such an approach, requiring instead that a parent's sexual orientation had a concrete harmful impact on a child. Since many gay men and lesbians of an earlier era had married straight partners, had children, and had divorced, this move away from an assumption of parental unfitness was critically important.

Adoption became another important pathway to parenthood for tens of thousands of gay and lesbian couples. And, as Michael Klarman puts it, "once same-sex couples were permitted to adopt children, explaining why those couples should not be permitted to marry became much harder."[36]

---

[32] Klarman, *From the Closet to the Altar*, above n 27, p. 45.
[33] Ann Arbor Code ch. 110, Sect. 9:86 (2015).
[34] Klarman, *From the Closet to the Altar*, above n 27, pp. 46, 59, 77.
[35] Klarman, *From the Closet to the Altar*, above n 27, p. 51.
[36] Ibid.

States were hard-pressed to justify excluding same-sex couples from marriage – lauded as a child-protective institution – when other state laws facilitated such couples becoming parents. Such considerations resonated powerfully decades later with Justice Kennedy of the US Supreme Court.[37]

* * *

In the 1980s, Americans confronted AIDS and also witnessed the rise of the religious right and the moral majority. Opposition to gay rights increased. From the late 1970s to the late 1980s, the percentage of Americans who thought that homosexual relations were always wrong rose from around seventy percent to nearly eighty percent. And whereas forty percent of Americans "opposed legalization of consensual sodomy" in 1982, it was fifty-five percent in 1986 (the year the Court decided *Bowers*).[38] In a Kansas telephone survey in the late 1980s, it took 1,650 calls – or "55 hours of random dialing – before pollsters found the first person willing to admit being lesbian or gay."[39] Progress toward anti-discrimination laws was halted or reversed.

Fear of contagion with AIDS by gay men using the same water fountain or public telephone or toilet seat led some to call for the quarantine of AIDS carriers. Republican Congressman William Dannemeyer, running for a California Senate seat, charged that, "AIDS carriers emitted deadly spores and that they might be engaged in 'blood terrorism'."[40] *National Review* editor William F. Buckley, Jr., proposed that, "Everyone detected with AIDS should be tattooed in the upper forearm, to protect common-needle users, and on the buttocks, to prevent the victimization of other homosexuals."[41]

---

[37] See *Obergefell v. Hodges*, 135 S.Ct. 2584, 2600 (2015).

[38] Klarman, *From the Closet to the Altar*, above n 27, pp. 35–41 (explaining that the wording of the question changed).

[39] David L. Chambers, 'What If? The Legal Consequences of Marriage and the Legal Needs of Lesbian and Gay Male Couples' (1996) 95(2) *Michigan Law Review* 447, 449, n. 3 (citing Larry Hatfield, 'Methods of Polling' *San Francisco Examiner*, June 5, 1989, at A20).

[40] See Klarman, *From the Closet to the Altar*, above n 27, p. 34; Eskridge, *Equality Practice*, above n 26, p. 66.

[41] William F. Buckley, Jr., 'Crucial Steps in Combating the Aids Epidemic; Identify All the Carriers' *New York Times* op-ed, March 18, 1986. www.nytimes.com/books/00/07/16/specials/buckley-aids.html.

A more lasting consequence of AIDS, however, was that it encouraged many gays to come out of the closet, and forced out others. Coming out spread beyond the hard core of urban activists, and openly gay people came to include a wider cross section of society. The percentage of Americans who reported knowing someone gay doubled between 1985 and 1992. Moreover, the example of gay men caring for each other and forming various types of family ties and support networks in the face of crisis also likely helped counteract some of the stigmas associated with the disease.[42] The Americans with Disabilities Act, which took effect in 1992, was interpreted by courts to require employers to accommodate those with AIDS and to bar discrimination against those who were HIV-positive, unless they posed a clear risk to others.[43]

It was in the inauspicious climate of the mid-1980s that the gay rights organization Lambda Legal sought to overturn existing state anti-sodomy laws. In 1986, the Supreme Court granted review in *Bowers* v. *Hardwick*. A Georgia police officer saw Hardwick engaging in consensual sodomy with another man in the bedroom of his home. After being charged with violating Georgia's law criminalizing sodomy, Hardwick challenged the law's constitutionality, eventually losing by a close 5:4 vote in the Supreme Court.[44]

Bowers was a stinging defeat, yet many reacted against it. A Gallup poll conducted "a week after the decision found that more people disapproved it than approved it."[45] The language and reasoning employed by the conservative majority was condemned by major newspapers. Justice Byron White's opinion for the Court termed the idea of a "fundamental [constitutional] right to engage in homosexual sodomy" as "at best, facetious." Chief Justice Warren Burger referred to "millennia of moral teaching" that homosexuality was wrong, and quoted antique authorities such as William Blackstone's judgment that homosexual sodomy was a crime of "deeper malignity" than rape.[46] *Bowers* energized gay rights activists and produced a mini-backlash in public opinion.

Opinion polls in the early 1990s showed support for gay marriage between eleven and twenty-three percent. Same-sex marriage was *not on the agenda of any of the major gay rights organizations*, and the gay

[42] Klarman, *From the Closet to the Altar*, above n 27, pp. 39–40.
[43] Ibid. p. 40.
[44] Ibid. p. 37; Eskridge, *Gaylaw*, above n 18, pp. 150, 166–67.
[45] Klarman, *From the Closet to the Altar*, above n 27, p. 37.
[46] *Bowers*, 478 U.S. at 197.

community itself "remained deeply divided over whether to pursue gay marriage." Polls showed that gay Americans were much more interested in "securing equal rights in employment, housing, and health care," not to mention AIDS research, sodomy law reform, and hate crimes legislation. Opinion polls showed, however, that younger gays were much more supportive of gay marriage than their elders.[47]

Though generally unpopular, same-sex marriage was thrust onto the national agenda in the early 1990s, not by national gay rights activists or activist judges, but by three couples in Hawaii who challenged their exclusion from marriage in state court. Lambda Legal, as well as the ACLU, declined to support the litigation on the grounds that it was premature.[48] Litigators limited their claims to state law in order to keep the case out of federal court. The Hawaii trial court dismissed the claims but, on appeal in 1993, the Hawaii Supreme Court deemed the denial of the right of a lesbian to marry her female partner a matter of sex discrimination in violation of the state constitution's Equal Rights Amendment.[49] The case was sent back to the trial judge with the admonition that marriage could be limited to opposite sex couples only if the state could produce a "compelling state interest" for so doing.[50] The state argued that marriage should be limited to opposite sex couples to promote and recognize the optimal setting for raising children. In December 1996, the trial court ruled these arguments insufficient.

The state appealed and, in 1997, the Hawaii state legislature passed a proposed constitutional amendment that would, subject to voter approval, overturn the Hawaii courts' decisions. The voters approved the amendment by sixty-nine to thirty-one percent. The state legislature meanwhile extended to same-sex couples domestic partnerships containing most of the benefits associated with marriage under state law. A similar scenario played out in Alaska.[51]

---

[47] 'One opinion poll showed that 18-year-old gays were 31 percentage points more likely to support gay marriage than were 65-year-old gays.' Klarman, *From the Closet to the Altar*, above n 27, pp. 45, 48, 50–51, and see his discussion of the debate within the gay community over pressing for marriage equality at that time, 5–55; *see also* Eskridge, *Equality Practice*, above n 26, pp. 15–17.

[48] See David Cole, *Engines of Liberty: The Power of Citizen Activists to Make Constitutional Law* (Basic Books, 2016), p. 26.

[49] *Baehr* v. *Lewin*, 74 Haw. 645, 852 P.2d 44 (1993). See more at: http://family.findlaw.com/marriage/1993-the-hawaii-case-of-baehr-v-lewin.html#sthash.DbY0yEUX.dpuf

[50] Ibid. 27–28.

[51] Ibid. 28–29.

Before the denouement of same-sex marriage in Hawaii, a panic gripped much of the country: it was feared that the US Constitution's "full faith and credit" clause would force other states to recognize Hawaiian gay marriages.[52] Overwhelming majorities in the US House of Representatives and Senate passed the federal Defense of Marriage Act (DOMA), which President Bill Clinton signed in 1996. DOMA declared that states would not have to recognize same-sex marriages performed in other states and that, for purposes of all federal laws, marriage was a union of one man and one woman.[53] In support of DOMA, lawmakers and witnesses invoked Judeo-Christian morality, the procreative functions of the human body, and the need to stop judges in Hawaii from promoting "the newly-coined institution of homosexual 'marriage'."[54] By 2001, thirty-five states had also passed "mini-DOMAs," defining marriage in state law as the relation of one man and one woman.[55]

The intense backlash – federal and state – precipitated by the temporary gains for marriage equality in Hawaii had, in retrospect, a silver lining. That short-lived victory made marriage rights seem like an actual possibility to ordinary gay men and lesbians across the country.

California established the first statewide domestic partnership registry in 1999. Just one year later, California voters approved a "defense of marriage act," limiting marriage to the union of one man and one woman, but the legislature worked around that law to expand the domestic partnership law to afford domestic partners more of the rights, protections, and duties of married couples. Some other states followed suit.

In Vermont, as in Hawaii, the initiative to litigate same-sex couples' exclusion from marriage percolated up from below. A lesbian couple managed to obtain a marriage license from a Vermont town clerk, in error, in 1994. The clerk rescinded the license. Having heard about the Hawaii legislation, they wanted to sue. But their attorneys, Susan Murray and Beth Robinson, convinced them that in light of the reversals in

---

[52] Article IV, Section 1: 'Full faith and credit shall be given in each state to the public acts, records, and judicial proceedings of every other state. And the Congress may by general laws prescribe the manner in which such acts, records, and proceedings shall be proved, and the effect thereof.'
[53] Defense of Marriage Act of 1996, 28 U.S.C. Section 1738C (1996).
[54] H. R. Rep. No. 104–664 (1996).
[55] Eskridge, *Equality Practice*, above n 26, pp. 17–85 and passim; and see Klarman's excellent account in *From the Closet to the Altar*, above n 27, ch. 3.

Hawaii, it would be necessary to build political support first, so that any gains achieved in court would not be reversed.[56]

The Vermont Coalition for Gay and Lesbian Rights – the only state-wide organization in Vermont – staged annual "queer town meetings" beginning in 1993. In the first meeting, only a handful of people even showed up and, after hearing a debate between Paula Ettelbrick and University of Michigan Law Professor David Chambers, the audience was split. The result was the same in 1994: local gays themselves shared no consensus on the value or timeliness of pressing for marriage rights. In 1995, a state legislator proposed barring gay and lesbian second partner adoptions, and that mobilized gay and lesbian Vermonters. They organized a letter-writing campaign and testified at numerous public hearings. The original sponsor publicly changed his mind and, in 1996, the law preserved gay and lesbian adoption rights. This also turned the tide on marriage equality within the gay and lesbian community in Vermont: it was needed for self-protection.[57]

On December 20, 1999, the Vermont Supreme Court decided by unanimous vote, in Baker v. State, that same-sex couples are entitled to "the same benefits and protections afforded by Vermont law to married opposite-sex couples," but it gave the legislature an option. It could extend full marriage rights, or create a new status with the same legal benefits under state law.[58] The Vermont Supreme Court in fact quoted Cass Sunstein, an advocate of judicial minimalism, to the effect that "Courts do best by proceeding in a way that is catalytic rather than preclusive, and that is closely attuned to the fact that courts are partici-pants in a system of democratic deliberation."[59] Proponents of judicial dialogue should take note.

In response to Baker, the Vermont legislature created same-sex civil unions in 1999. At the next election, many supporters of the bill lost their seats in the state legislature,[60] but the backlash was contained, and opponents of civil unions failed to secure a reversal through the polit-ical process.

---

[56] Cole, Engines of Liberty, above n 48, pp. 33–34. My discussion throughout has benefitted tremendously from Cole's important book.

[57] Ibid. pp. 34–37.

[58] Ibid. pp. 34–35, 38–39.

[59] Quoted in ibid. p. 39.

[60] Baker v. State, 744 A.2d 864 (Vt. 1999); Klarman, From the Closet to the Altar, above n 27, pp. 82, 78–83.

In Massachusetts, local activists again took care to lay political ground-work. In 1989, Massachusetts had added sexual orientation to its non-discrimination law, and in 1991 added it to the state hate crimes law. In 1993, the Supreme Judicial Court granted the right of a lesbian partner to joint adoption and Republican governor William Weld extended same-sex domestic partnership benefits to state employees.[61]

The Massachusetts Supreme Judicial Court 2003 ruling in *Goodridge v. Mass. Dept. of Public Health* made Massachusetts the first state to require the recognition of same-sex marriage under its constitution. Nationwide media coverage ensued, along with considerable but not overwhelming opposition within the state. Governor Mitt Romney called for a constitutional amendment to reverse the decision and the state legislature sat as a constitutional convention to consider such proposals in 2004, 2005, and 2007. A bare majority of legislators voted to approve an amendment in 2004, but on a required second vote by a new legisla-ture in 2005, the proposed amendment was defeated by 157 to 39. Opponents pursued a second constitutional track: a citizens' initiative, needing only twenty-five percent of the votes in two successive state legislatures to get a reversal question on the state ballot. They got the necessary signatures and secured about thirty percent legislative support on the first legislative vote, but fell short of twenty-five percent in 2007. By that time, polls showed that fifty-six percent of those responding to a state poll favored same-sex marriage, and political efforts to reverse the Supreme Judicial Court died.[62]

Goodridge may have tipped the 2004 presidential election to George W. Bush over John Kerry, a US Senator from Massachusetts. Although Democratic presidential candidates opposed a federal *constitutional* amendment barring same sex marriage, which was supported by Bush and many Republicans, they also declined to support same-sex marriage. This was also true of many leading Democrats including Al Gore in 2004, and Barack Obama in 2008: they expressed support for same-sex civil unions and letting states decide.[63] It was only in 2012 that the

---

[61] Cole, *Engines of Liberty*, above n 48, pp. 44–45.

[62] Ibid. pp. 48–49.

[63] Ibid. pp. 111–12, 126 and passim; Gerald N. Rosenberg, *The Hollow Hope: Can Courts Bring About Social Change?* (2nd ed., University of Chicago Press, 2008), part IV.

Democratic Party and President Obama embraced marriage equality as
part of their platform and declared support for such marriage.[64]

All of these controversies and others we have not mentioned – such as
President Clinton's "Don't Ask, Don't Tell" policy for gay and lesbian
service members – kept gay rights in the headlines for a generation. All
the while, more and more Americans came out of the closet, media
depictions of gay people became ever more common, and countless
conversations took place at kitchen tables, office water coolers, town
meetings, churches, and elsewhere.

*****

How did gay marriage finally make its way to the US Supreme Court?
This is another long story involving a myriad of actors. I will highlight
two aspects indicative of the prominent role of politics outside the courts.

In 2003, the California legislature passed a comprehensive domestic
partnerships law that gave same-sex couples the same benefits and
obligations under state law as opposite-sex couples. That same year,
Lambda Legal's Jon Davidson warned a meeting at the UCLA School of
Law's Williams Institute that the time was *not ripe* for a push for same-
sex marriage in California: it would be too difficult to defeat a subsequent
anti-gay-marriage initiative.[65]

Gavin Newsom was not at that meeting. Newly elected as Mayor of
San Francisco, he did attend George W. Bush's State of the Union
Address in January 2004. Newsom was enraged by Bush's condemnation
of *Goodridge*. Without consulting anyone in the gay rights community,
he ordered City Hall to issue same-sex marriage licenses, beginning on
February 12, 2004. Four thousand couples were married in the first
month. In March, the state Supreme Court ordered him to cease, pending
a ruling on the legality of his actions, and in doing so invited a constitutional challenge to current state law. The Mayor immediately accepted,
once again without consulting gay rights groups. Newsom filed a lawsuit
challenging the constitutionality of denying same-sex couples' right to
marry. Months later, the California State Supreme Court held that the
Mayor lacked the authority to override state law. Four years later,

---

[64] For an account of this evolution on marriage, see Linda C. McClain, 'Federal Family
Policy and Family Values from Clinton to Obama, 1992–2012 and Beyond' (2013)
Michigan State Law Review 1621, 1653–68, 1709–15.

[65] This draws on Cole, *Engines of Liberty*, above n 48.

however, in 2008, the State Supreme Court held that Mayor Newsom was right, in effect, and required full marriage equality.[66]

The response to the California Supreme Court came quickly. Proposition 8 sought to overturn marriage equality via a state referendum to amend the California Constitution; it attracted nationwide attention and support, including from the Mormon and Catholic Churches, and the Princeton, New Jersey-based National Organization for Marriage. In the end, Californians approved Proposition 8 and voted against same-sex marriage by fifty-two to forty-eight percent.

National gay rights groups strongly opposed as premature any immediate challenge to Proposition 8 under the US Constitution. Only four states recognized same-sex marriage and over forty explicitly banned it.[67] This time it was Hollywood director and liberal activist Rob Reiner who grabbed the reins, mounting a federal constitutional challenge to Prop 8 and enlisting Ted Olson, a well-known Republican litigator and former Bush administration solicitor general, and David Boies, who led the Democratic legal team against Olson in the contest over the Florida presidential vote count. As they pressed forward, California Governor Arnold Schwarzenegger, a moderate Republican, and Attorney General Jerry Brown both *declined to defend Proposition 8 in federal court*, a step that would also be taken by President Obama and US Attorney General Eric Holder years later when the federal Defense of Marriage Act was challenged before the US Supreme Court. The decisions by Schwarzenegger and Brown were crucial. Proponents of Proposition 8, led by State Senator Dennis Hollingsworth, mounted a feeble legal defense. The few expert witnesses called to defend Prop 8 wilted under questioning. Prop 8 was declared unconstitutional in a Federal District Court.[68]

A Federal Appeals Court issued a clever opinion that limited application of the District Court's ruling *to California*, where marriage rights had existed for a time only to be taken away. When *Hollingsworth v. Perry* went to the Supreme Court, the justices avoided deciding the case on the merits by holding that State Senator Hollingsworth and other Prop 8 proponents lacked standing to bring their appeal.[69] Thus, the effects of the protracted political and legal contests in California

---

[66] This is drawn from Cole, *Engines of Liberty*, above n 48.
[67] As of May 2009.
[68] See David Boies and Theodore B. Olson, *Redeeming the Dream: The Case for Marriage Equality* (Penguin Books, 2004).
[69] I draw here as above on Cole, *Engines of Liberty*, above n 48, pp. 61–62.

were contained within California, leaving the rest of the country to decide on its own.

More politics and litigation followed, as advocates of marriage equality learned from their many losses and few, but gathering, successes. All the while, public opinion shifted steadily in favor of marriage equality. Maine voters reversed an earlier refusal to recognize same-sex marriage, and New York State enacted marriage equality by a vote of the state legislature after electing a new Democratic Governor, Andrew Cuomo.[70]

In the end, a series of federal court opinions played a crucial and culminating role, but only after decades of complex interactions – and dialogue – among political actors at all levels and branches of government, voters, litigants, and state and federal courts. Rarely, if ever, has a constitutional and moral revolution occurred so quickly. Yet it was no judicial coup orchestrated from on high, but rather the culmination of a complex series of political, moral, religious, and familial debates that took place in every corner of American life.

III   Constitutional Democracy

Criticisms and defenses of judicial review take place against the backdrop of differing conceptions of democracy. Simplistic conceptions of democracy locate its essential core in majority rule voting and direct electoral accountability. So, Samuel Issacharoff says, in an (otherwise) excellent article, that, "Constitutionalism exists in inherent tension with the democratic commitment to majority rule."[71] But this seems to me clearly wrong: there is no democracy without constitutionalism. Democracy requires constitutional rules specifying, at a minimum, the eligibility of voters and other electoral rules, and the terms and powers of various offices. And these rules must limit the power of majorities if the system is to be regarded as democratic: at the very least, majorities must be prevented from disenfranchising minorities, harassing opposition candidates and parties, and restricting press freedoms. The current wave of populist authoritarianism dramatizes the close connections between

---

[70] See the excellent account of the New York State debates in James E. Fleming and Linda C. McClain, *Ordered Liberty: Rights, Responsibilities, and Virtues* (Cambridge, MA: Harvard University Press, 2013), ch. 8.

[71] Samuel Issacharoff, 'Constitutionalizing Democracy in Fractured Societies' (2004) 82 *Texas Law Review* 1861.

democracy and many liberal rights.[72] So the issue is not whether democracy needs constitutionalism but rather *which constitutional arrangements best serve democracy?*

On the constitutional conception of democracy, all power originates from the people, is directly or indirectly accountable to the people, and is to be exercised on behalf of the people as a whole. Mass elections help insure that legislators and executives are held accountable to the people, and that is an important aspect of democracy. Yet unchecked majority rule is majority tyranny (or the tyranny of a powerful plurality), not democracy, and so in constitutional democracies a wide variety of constraints, some authorized by supermajority requirements, are designed to check what simple majorities can do. Government becomes more rather than less democratic, when we insure that minority interests are fairly attended to and the equal rights of minorities – their basic interests – are protected. Democracy requires that the powerful are held in check by the prospect that abuses of power will be detected and publicized, which implies public access to information and rights to criticize the government. Competing public institutions, and a system of checks and balances including legislative bicameralism, politically independent courts, and administrative agencies with specialized expertise, can help insure that elected representatives and other public officials must defend their policy choices publicly against robust criticism, and that errors are identified and corrected. It is an enhancement of collective self-rule *as such* when deliberation is thorough because that helps insure that the public can *live with and own* political choices over time.

The constitutional conception of democracy stands for the proposition that constitutional institutions and mechanisms can enhance the ability of the people as a whole to govern itself, on due reflection, over the long run, and on the basis of the political equality of all citizens.[73] Such a conception is more complex than simpler majoritarian accounts, but it is clearly normatively superior.

*****

Jeremy Waldron argues that "final decisions" about political questions – including individual rights and political processes themselves – should be

---

[72] See Jan-Werner Müller, *What is Populism?* (University of Pennsylvania Press, 2016).
[73] This sentence and the previous paragraph are drawn from Robert O. Keohane, Stephen Macedo, and Andrew Moravcsik, 'Democracy-Enhancing Multilateralism' (2009) 63(1) *International Organizations* 1.

made by majoritarian procedures.[74] Majoritarianism respects our political and moral equality (it appears) by submitting political questions to a procedure in which everyone has an equal say; no one has a greater say than anyone else. Majoritarianism instantiates one straightforward understanding of the principle of political equality: equal votes for equal people and let the greatest number win.[75]

But majority rule is merely a voting rule. Ronald Dworkin refers to it – deflatingly but appropriately – as the "head counting principle."[76] It has strengths that operate under restrictive conditions: it is a decisive voting rule when there are only two options. When there are more than two options, then there can be cycling of preferences such that there will be no majority winner.[77] Majority rule cannot get us to the point at which majority decision making is possible, so it cannot be all there is to democracy.

More basically, the fundamental moral principle of democracy it is not majority rule but the deeper principle of the political equality of individuals.[78] Even on Waldron's account, majority rule gains its attraction as an *interpretation and application of the principle of political equality*, and majority rule is only one of many possible decision procedures that are consistent with the underlying principle of political equality. Other decision rules may be fairer and more inclusive. Different procedures yield different accounts of what "the people" prefer, *but no one procedure is clearly superior on the basis of fundamental normative principles*, nor on the axioms of social choice theory.[79]

---

[74] Jeremy Waldron, 'The Constitutional Conception of Democracy' in David Estlund (ed.), *Democracy* (Blackwell Publishing, 2002) p. 68. Democracy is founded on the premise of political equality: individuals are equally rights holders, and that includes an equal right to participate in making majority decisions (the right to participate is, he says, the 'right of rights').

[75] These paragraphs draw on a draft paper coauthored with Christopher L. Karpowitz and Evan Oxman, 'Two Conceptions of Democracy' (Unpublished ms. on file with author). And see also, Stephen Macedo, 'Against Majoritarianism: Democratic Values and Institutional Design' (2010) *Boston University Law Review* 1029.

[76] In Ronald Dworkin, *Justice for Hedgehogs*, above n 7.

[77] Add a third alternative and the possibility of intransitive preferences and the familiar Arrow-type cycling problems (varying the order in which several pair-wise alternatives come up for a vote) make it impossible to say that any particular results are preferred by a majority.

[78] Normal adult individuals who satisfy residency or other such requirements.

[79] See Mathias Risse, 'Arguing for Majority Rule' (2004) 12(1) *Journal of Political Philosophy* 41–64; and see Charles R. Beitz, *Political Equality: An Essay in Democratic Theory*

Perhaps most importantly, alternatives to majority rule might do a better job of assuring minorities that their interests will be taken into account. And indeed supermajorities might – and in the real world often do – *prefer systems of collective self-rule in which minority interests gain special protection*: we *all* might prefer that given the possibility of finding ourselves in the minority. So proponents of majoritarianism such as Waldron are simply wrong to argue that majoritarianism is, in practice, the best we can do to realize democratic values. In reality we can *and do* better: few, if any, of the newer constitutional democracies embrace simple systems of unicameral parliamentary supremacy (which Waldron's principles might seem to argue for).[80]

Part of the apparent appeal of majority rule is its fairness (everyone counts for one). But under realistic conditions the choice of majority rule procedures would seem both imprudent and *unfair* from the point of view of political minorities. If majority factions develop (clusters of voters or linkages across issues) the minority may *never* get its way via majority rule, and its fundamental interests – or rights – may be ignored.[81]

(Princeton: Princeton University Press, 1989); Waldron, 'The Core of the Case Against Judicial Review' above n 6, cites Kenneth O. May, 'A Set of Independent Necessary and Sufficient Conditions for Simple Majority Decision' (1952) 20(4) *Econometrica*, 680–684. Under a stringent set of conditions, majority rule does indeed have some uniquely equality-preserving properties (including features designated as "neutrality" and "anonymity"). However, the specified conditions (which include strictly pair-wise alternatives), strictly individualistic preferences (no factions or coalitions), no linkages across decisions, no accounting for intensity of preferences, no asymmetry of gains and losses (no preference for avoiding "bads" over achieving "goods") do not hold under real-world conditions, particularly in the presence of known majority and minority factions, see Douglas W. Rae, 'Decision-Rules and Individual Values in Constitutional Choice' (1969) 63(1) *American Political Science Review* 40. If we depart from these conditions (by allowing for the existence of factions, by including non-individualistic preferences, etc.), majority rule loses its appeal.

[80] Though, oddly, he argues that New Zealand's unicameral parliamentary system exacerbates various legislative pathologies, including adequate attention to minority interests, that might be better dealt with in bicameral (and therefore supermajority) systems; see, Jeremy Waldron, 'Compared to What? Judicial Activism and the New Zealand Parliament' (2005) 1 *New Zealand Law Journal* 441; and James Allan and Andrew Geddis, 'Waldron and Opposing Judicial Review – Except, Sort Of, in New Zealand' (2006) 2 *New Zealand Law Journal* 94. Although Waldron has recently developed his defense of bicameralism, and the separation of powers in *Political Political Theory* (Cambridge, MA: Harvard University Press, 2016), pp. 72–92.

[81] See Beitz, *Political Equality*, above n 80; Douglas W. Rae, 'Decision Rules and Individual Values in Constitutional Choice' (1969) 63(1) *American Political Science Review* 40.

Majoritarianism is not a uniquely authoritative decision rule in conditions of disagreement among political equals. It has the virtue of simplicity, and it is decisive when there are two options. Majoritarianism as an ideology is a simplistic solution to the problem of collective self-rule amidst the great diversity and disagreement of modern mass societies. It is not a very promising way of taking seriously the principle of fair treatment that we should also want our politics to represent. It does not secure the equal standing of citizens. It is a distracting fetish, and more than that: it can all too easily furnish a rationalization for populist authoritarianism.

The idea of government by the people on the constitutional conception answers to several principles. One bedrock principle is the political equality of individuals.[82] Another is *inclusiveness*.[83] Critics of judicial review like Waldron and Tushnet accept these principles.[84] Constitutional democracies employ various means to promote inclusive collective self-rule, including the reservation of individual rights enforced by politically independent courts.[85]

Another democratic desideratum at which constitutional institutions aim is *the value of deliberation*. If minority views are aired, they stand a better chance of being heard and incorporated into political decision-making. Deliberation can also help canvass all relevant information; it can help gather and pool expertise so as to improve the quality of decisions.

---

[82] See Ronald Dworkin, *Freedom's Law: The Moral Reading of the American Constitution* (Cambridge, MA: Harvard University Press, 1997), ch. 1; Beitz, *Political Equality*, above n 80.

[83] As Mill argued: 'The pure idea of democracy, according to its definition, is the government of the whole people by the whole people, equally represented. Democracy as commonly conceived and hitherto practiced is the government of the whole people by a mere majority of the people, exclusively represented. The former is synonymous with the equality of all citizens; the latter, strangely confounded with it, is a government of privilege, in favor of the numerical majority, who alone possess practically any voice in the State.' John Stuart Mill, *Representative Government*. http://philosophy.eserver.org/mill-representative-govt.txt, ch. 7, section 1.

[84] See Waldron, 'The Core of the Case Against Judicial Review', above n 6.

[85] They may do so procedurally and substantively, by insuring that channels for political discussion and change remain open (see John Hart Ely, *Democracy and Distrust* (Cambridge, MA: Harvard University Press, 1980), but also by insuring that particular substantive individual interests are protected against encroachment. The process/substance distinction is superficial, because substantive values underlie fair process, and because "substantive" rights often correct for process-based flaws, including "nosey preferences" and prejudices: they protect individuals and minorities against preferences that ought not to operate in an egalitarian political system (preferences at odds with the premise of political equality on which democracy is based).

So, on the constitutional conception, we have at least three basic values that we want to realize in practice, and that we can understand as regulative principles of democracy: political equality, inclusiveness (including rights protection and faction control), and deliberateness.[86] *Political equality* is an abstract principle: it does not require majority rule and it may be furthered by constitutional institutions.[87] *Inclusiveness*: everyone's basic interests should be respected and the law should take into account the interests of all; in practice this stands for institutional mechanisms designed to protect minority rights and control factions. Reflectiveness or *deliberateness*: reasons should accompany power, reasons that have been articulated and tested in public debate and by high standards of expert scrutiny.

IV   Constitutional Democracy, Judicial Review, and Gay Rights

I agree with Dworkin, Christopher L. Eisgruber, and others that the Supreme Court can itself be seen as a representative institution. The small size and consequent high visibility of the high court and the justices' need to justify their decisions in reasoned opinions help to concentrate their responsibility for reasoned judgment. The secure tenure of Supreme Court justices, their independence from periodic electoral accountability, and the fact that justices are at the summit of their profession and do not need to worry about earning a living when out of office, can all help promote the justices' impartiality.[88] Institutional design thus helps make the justices well placed to reflect on principles of justice on behalf of the American people.

Judicial review most clearly supports constitutional democracy when it is conceived as playing the sort of "representation-reinforcing" function that John Hart Ely assigned to the institution.[89] In addition, however, I agree with James E. Fleming and Corey Brettschneider (among others), who argue that we should understand the Court equally importantly as protector of the autonomy of citizens to make

---

[86] These are not exhaustive – responsiveness and decisiveness would be other principles or values that we would want a political system to answer to, and there are others.

[87] It rules out Mill's proposals for extra votes for the better educated (plural voting). Beitz holds that the "foundational requirement" of egalitarianism is that "fair terms of participation should be reasonably acceptable to everyone," *Political Equality*, above n 80, p. 24.

[88] Dworkin, *Freedom's Law*, above n 83; Christopher L. Eisgruber, *Constitutional Self-Government* (Cambridge, MA: Harvard University Press, 2009).

[89] See above n 86.

important personal decisions, in addition to protecting their political liberties and equal civic standing.[90]

*****

Judicial review is not to be confused with judicial supremacy or finality. Elected officials at all levels and citizens also interpret the constitution and *act on their interpretations in appropriate ways*, whatever the Supreme Court might have said. This is obvious in the account of the progress of gay rights and same-sex marriage in the United States that I've set out. I agree with those who would promote the interpretive capacities of citizens and elected officials, but there is no good reason to think that that agenda requires (or will be advanced by) curbing the interpretive role of the courts.[91] Dworkin emphasizes the potential for courts to infuse principled considerations into ordinary politics.[92] Against Dworkin, I would emphasize that while the courts can and often do enhance democratic decision making, we should not exaggerate their role at the expense of political mobilization of voters and other institutions.

With respect to gay rights politics and litigation in America, courts played a significant and ultimately decisive role, but only after and with the support of intense, sustained, and widespread political mobilization. Obviously, this has not always happened – the abortion decision, *Roe* v. *Wade*, would seem to be a contrast case – but it often does happen.

What has seemed clear for two decades or more is the relative weakness of arguments for denying equal basic rights and eventually marriage rights to same-sex couples. And under the US Constitution, citizens are entitled to believe that if the best arguments are clearly on their side they in fact *have the constitutional right they claim* and they are entitled to seek to have their rights vindicated in a court of law. As Dworkin put it nearly forty years ago, "I insist that the [judicial] process, even in hard cases, can sensibly be said to be aimed at discovering, rather than inventing, the rights of the parties concerned, and that the political

---

[90] See James E. Fleming, *Securing Constitutional Democracy: The Case of Autonomy* (Chicago: University of Chicago Press, 2006); Corey Brettschneider, *Democratic Rights: The Substance of Self-Government* (Princeton: Princeton University Press, 2010).

[91] A point well made in Fleming, ibid.

[92] See Ronald Dworkin, 'The Forum of Principle' in *A Matter of Principle* (Cambridge, MA: Harvard University Press, 1986).

justification of the process depends upon the soundness of that characterization."[93] It is, indeed, one of the most striking features of Dworkin's account of rights and judicial review that he makes *citizens* interpreters of our fundamental law, thus embracing what Sanford Levinson once called a "protestant" theory of the law: "Our legal system [invites] citizens to decide the strengths and weaknesses of legal arguments for themselves, or through their own counsel, and to act on these judgments, although that permission is qualified by the limited threat that they may suffer if the courts do not agree."[94] The leveling of judicial authority demanded by the rights thesis implies an ideal of citizenship in which the judiciary is not simply brought "down," but the office of citizenship itself is elevated.

The progress of gay rights litigation and legislation nicely illustrates Dworkin's vision of citizen litigants taking the Constitution into their own hands and demanding that their rights be vindicated. However, participants in the process I surveyed above also often recognized that rights cannot be secured by courts alone. Though the Supreme Court occasionally played an important role, as in *Bowers*, in a negative way, and in *Romer v. Evans*, *Lawrence*, *Windsor*, and *Obergefell*, more positively, it also acted prudently, in *Hollingsworth*, by not rushing to a decision on the merits, as Alexander Bickel would have recommended.[95]

Overall, the strategy involved a good deal of patience, hard work in many venues, and incremental progress, along with the constant building and widening of political support.

V Democracy-Enhancing Judicial Review: From Theory to Practice

There are a variety of ways of structuring the interactions among courts and legislatures, and there may be arrangements that are better than the American national model when it comes to promoting considerations of constitutional principles throughout our politics, including in legislatures.

Regarded from the standpoints of either democracy or justice, the record of judicial review in America is mixed. I agree with Mark Tushnet's assessment of many of the court's mistakes (that money is a

---

[93] Ronald Dworkin, *Taking Rights Seriously* (Harvard University Press, 1978), p. 280.
[94] Ibid. p. 217.
[95] See Alexander M. Bickel, *The Least Dangerous Branch: The Supreme Court at the Bar of Politics* (Yale University Press, 1986), especially the chapter "The Passive Virtues".

form of constitutionally protected speech, for example).[96] And certainly the court has sometimes failed to adequately defer to reasonable disagreement.

But the "backlash" arguments that have been directed against judicial recognition of gay rights, especially in *Baehr* (Hawaii) and *Goodridge* (Massachusetts), now seem overstated. I admire the scholarship of Gerald Rosenberger and Michael Klarman, but the question of whether litigation strategies make sense for social movements seeking more equal treatment or other reforms – civil rights, abortion rights, gay rights – seems to me hard to answer.[97] Counterfactual history is almost all guesswork. With respect to *Brown* v. *Board of Education*, Michael Klarman argues that the decision did more to mobilize Southern white opposition than it did to encourage civil rights protest, and that it was the resulting violence that led to civil rights legislation in the 1960s.[98] The causal claims here are difficult to assess; there is no doubt, in any event, that constitutional change is complex and political mobilization is crucial.

In the case of gay rights, the litigation that did take place was often the result of decentralized decisions rather than coordinated national movements. Individuals and local groups made their own decisions in our highly decentralized system. Initiatives often percolated up from below.

It is also be important here to consider the arguments advanced by Mark Graber, Keith Whittington, and others, arguing that some cases that are widely regarded as counter-majoritarian and mistaken – such as *Dred Scott* – might more accurately be seen as reflections of the dominant party coalition of the time.[99] More broadly, Whittington has argued that the relationship between the courts and other political actors is complex, and executives and legislatures often have reasons for supporting judicial action ("Courts can build authority by specializing in the type of issues that complement the agenda of other political actors"[100]). This likely has often been true with gay rights.

---

[96] Mark Tushnet, *Taking the Constitution Away from the Courts* (Princeton: Princeton University Press, 2000)

[97] See above n 63.

[98] See Michael J. Klarman, *Brown v. Board of Education and the Civil Rights Movement* (Oxford: Oxford University Press, 2007).

[99] Mark Graber, *Dred Scott and the Problem of Constitutional Evil* (Cambridge: Cambridge University Press, 2006).

[100] Keith E. Whittington, *Political Foundations of Judicial Supremacy: The Presidency, the Supreme Court, and Constitutional Leadership in U.S. History* (Princeton: Princeton University Press, 2009), p. 122.

VI   Better Models of Constitutional Dialogue?

Mark Tushnet argues that the peculiar features of US-style judicial review may not be optimal for democratic deliberation and interbranch dialogue. That is altogether plausible: "optimal" is a high standard!

Under US "strong form" judicial review, it can be very difficult to reverse an erroneous Supreme Court decision, notwithstanding the fact that sitting justices do sometimes change their minds, and they do get replaced. Tushnet defends "weak form" judicial review, according to which the executive or legislative branch can respond to and reject exercises of constitutional rulings by the judiciary, as long as they do so publicly.[101] But in a volume dedicated to the issue of *constitutional dialogue* we should not forget that even if reversal of Supreme Court decisions is hard, citizens, political candidates, and public officials at all levels frequently disagree with and contest Court decisions that they disagree with: they argue, protest, campaign for reversal, and they can also limit their effects via various forms of resistance. Federal and state legislators can repass laws to challenge or test the edges of announced constitutional limits. The effects of Court decisions can often be limited by legislative or executive action, at the federal or state level, or by lower court resistance.

The US Supreme Court announced a sweeping constitutional right to abortion in the early stages of a pregnancy in *Roe v. Wade*. That decision has not been reversed, but it has been narrowed and contested. Moreover, no opponent's voice was stilled: many have been mobilized to speak and act in opposition to the Court. Public opinion on this issue has not shifted massively, as in the case of gay rights. Opposition to abortion rights in many parts of the country remains intense, and the subsequent actions of hospitals, doctors, state legislatures, governors, and other officials mean that in much of the country it is *very difficult for women to get access to abortion services*. In the first half of 2016 alone, the *Washington Post* reports that, "antiabortion advocates passed some 30 laws in 14 states to make it harder for people to get abortion."[102]

So I accept that in the case of abortion, the Supreme Court operated in too peremptory and sweeping a manner. Greater modesty and

---

[101] Tushnet, *Weak Courts, Strong Rights*, above n 6.
[102] Amber Phillips, '14 states have passed laws making it harder to get an abortion already this year' *Washington Post*, June 1, 2016. www.washingtonpost.com/news/the-fix/wp/2016/06/01/14-states-have-passed-laws-making-it-harder-to-get-an-abortion-already-this-year/.

incrementalism would have been more consistent with the understanding of constitutional democracy I have advocated in this chapter. But even in the case of abortion we should not overstate the effects of the Supreme Court's decision on public discussion.

Keith Whittington has characterized "judicial supremacy" as the view that "the Constitution is what judges say it is ... because there is no alternative interpretive authority beyond the Court." Judicial supremacy, he says, obliges coordinate officials "to follow its [the Court's] reasoning in future deliberations." Indeed, the opinions of the Court have the capacity to mark some political contestants and their positions as distinctly un-American and beyond the pale of legitimate American political discourse."[103]

Yet Whittington also points out that "The American judiciary has been able to win the authority to independently interpret the Constitution because recognizing such an authority has been politically beneficial to others."[104] That is, it suits political actors very often, for their own reasons, to defer to the courts' interpretive role. *But when it doesn't, they often won't.* Please note that judicial "supremacy" thus characterized is qualified and conditional; indeed, I would not myself call it "supremacy" except in a restrictive sense. It is a "supremacy" that depends in practice on many other forms of political decision-making.

*****

In the United Kingdom, Canada, and elsewhere, there are institutional mechanisms that allow exercises of judicial review to be confronted and in turn overridden by legislative action. It is certainly possible that some of these models do a better job of promoting the democratic virtues of political equality, inclusiveness (including rights protection and faction control), and deliberateness.

My argument here is not that the American form of judicial review is perfect. It is rather that it is in principle fully compatible with democracy properly understood: indeed, it is designed to be democracy enhancing. In practice, its record is flawed but on balance defensible.

In addition, I would say that the American system has worked well in the context of the gay rights cases examined here: courts have played a

---

[103] Keith E. Whittington, *Political Foundations of Judicial Supremacy* (Princeton: Princeton University Press, 2009), pp. 6–8.
[104] Ibid. p. 27.

significant but not the dominant role. The process overall has been highly political and also highly deliberative, though not in every particular phase. Debate has been sustained over decades, and as the argument developed public opinion has shifted seemingly inexorably – one can now say – in one direction, and that direction has been consistent with what most correctly see as the underlying merits: toward greater justice and a fuller realization of our central American ideals of equal liberty for all.

VII   But Would There Have Been a Better Way?

In the end, I judge the triumph of marriage equality in America to be fully politically legitimate and more than that: it serves as an admirable example of widespread political engagement at all levels of society and government. Significant social changes require this. Would it have been better still for more states to have embraced same-sex marriage in the way New York State did: pursuant to legislative debate and with the governor's signature? Perhaps. Legislative enactment may often signal the presence of broader public support, and rights are more secure when they have broad public support and the support of public officials. But minority factions can veto legislation supported by the majority, and there is also a very significant cost in telling couples and their children that their well-founded rights claims must await legislative endorsement. How long would it have taken Alabama to recognize these basic rights?

I agree with those who worry about premature judicial resolutions of constitutional questions that have not been sufficiently debated and discussed. Judges should often seek ways of progressively recognizing well-supported rights claims without foreclosing ongoing deliberation in other departments of government. When the public mind is unsettled or, as in the case of gay rights in the 1980s, generally opposed, incrementalism is often the best path, allowing for feedback and ongoing debate and deliberation.

These issues can play out in a remarkable diversity of ways. In Ireland the process was one that many democrats will probably regard as a kind of "gold standard": the national electorate voted, in May 2015, on whether to approve a simply worded amendment to the Irish Constitution: "Marriage may be contracted in accordance with law by two persons without distinction as to their sex." After a spirited and engaged campaign, sixty-one percent of the eligible voters turned out and sixty-two percent of voters approved (with thirty-eight percent opposed).

Well and good: three cheers for the Irish! Yet it would be absurd to conclude as a general matter that countries are well advised to adopt systems of popular referenda for deciding constitutional questions. Witness the ill-informed and utterly unnecessary vote on Brexit in the United Kingdom. The record on referenda at the state level in the United States is mixed, to say the least.[105] I certainly would not advocate any move toward national referenda in the United States, which would be deeply at odds with its constitutional tradition.

In Costa Rica, an anti-gay-marriage presidential candidate was defeated after running his campaign principally on this issue. The Costa Rican government had previously asked the Inter-American Court of Human Rights for an opinion on whether it was obliged, as a consequence of its having signed the American Convention on Human Rights, to extend rights to same-sex couples. The Court ruled that it did, on January 9, 2018, teeing the issue up for contestation in the presidential campaign and late March election. The election result is seen as a vindication of the legitimacy of the Inter-American Court, as well as acceptance of the Court's decision on same-sex marriage.

In Canada there was "intricate maneuvering" over same-sex marriage among the judicial and political branches, including provincial courts and the national legislature and the executive. In 2002 and 2003, provincial courts in Quebec, British Columbia, and Ontario found the common law restriction of marriage rights to opposite-sex couples an "unjustified limitation" on section 15(1) of the Canadian Charter of Rights and Freedoms, which guarantees "equal protection and equal benefits of the law without discrimination." Owing to the fact that the federal Department of Justice and the House of Commons Standing Committee on Justice and Human Rights were already considering some form of recognition of same-sex relationships, the BC Court of Appeal suspended its declaration, but only so as to give provincial and federal "governments time to review and revise legislation to bring it in accord" with its decision.[106] The Quebec Court did likewise, while also seeming to grant Parliament a wider scope for action in response. The Ontario court, on the other hand, refused to suspend its judgment and so it took immediate

---

[105] See David Broder, *Democracy Derailed: Initiative Campaigns and the Power of Money* (Harcourt, 2000).

[106] I am following Graham Gee and Grégoire Webber, 'Same-Sex Marriage in Canada: Contributions from the Courts, the Executive and Parliament' (2005) 16(1) *The Kings College Law Journal* 132, 133–34.

effect. Eventually, most but not all of the provincial courts found the right to same-sex marriage to be guaranteed by the Charter.

Subsequently, the federal executive under Prime Minister Jean Chrétien proposed a bill extending marriage rights to same-sex couples, and also reaffirming that this should not affect the freedom of religious officials to refuse to perform such marriages (something that New York State legislators also made clear). The prime minister also sought a reference opinion from the Supreme Court on whether the proposed bill was in the exclusive legislative authority of the federal Parliament, whether the extension of marriage to same-sex couples was consistent with the Charter, and concerning freedom of religion. After a change in leadership within the federal government, the new prime minister, Paul Martin, added a fourth reference question concerning whether the opposite-sex definition of marriage in common law was consistent with the Charter.

The Supreme Court of Canada, in answer to the reference, did not rule on whether the common law (man–woman) conception of marriage was in violation of the Canadian Charter of Rights, but it did rule that Parliament could alter the definition of marriage to include same-sex unions. The Liberal government then enacted a statute legalizing same-sex marriage. Alberta's Progressive Conservative government protested, but in Canada the federal Parliament has exclusive jurisdiction over the capacity to marry. Attitudes were changing, and same-sex marriage gradually gained acceptance.

I will not here recount the further details, but note only that Graham Gee and Grégoire Webber argue that the reference questions were an attempt on the part of the executive "to pre-empt Parliament's discussion of the bill's merits." They applaud "the Supreme Court's decisional minimum," and argue that it honors both marriage equality and the "more general value of civil and constitutional participation."[107]

I generally agree. In the parallel litigation in the United States, an important moment occurred in February 2012, when a three-judge panel of the Federal Appeals Court for the Ninth Circuit limited to California the effect of a ruling recognizing the right of same-sex couples to marry.[108] The wide-ranging debates concerning gay rights and

---

[107] Ibid. 142–43.
[108] See Adam Nagourney, 'Court Strikes Down Ban on Gay Marriage in California' *New York Times*, February 7, 2012. www.nytimes.com/2012/02/08/us/marriage-ban-violates-constitution-court-rules.html.

same-sex marriage, described in this chapter, exhibit judicial and political incrementalism. A wide variety of actors, including some judges but also very many others, have taken their turns moving gay rights forward, sometimes provoking backlash, often contributing to what we can now see as steady if unsmooth progress. This protracted political contest over same-sex rights in the United States honored the values of "civil and constitutional participation," while achieving marriage justice.

In closing, let us acknowledge that incrementalism has a cost: people are denied recognition of rights that are in fact well supported. Still, and especially given the real dangers of backlash and reversal, this would seem a price that must sometimes be paid to really secure the enjoyment of rights.

14

A Feature, Not a Bug

A Coordinate Moment in Canadian Constitutionalism

DENNIS BAKER

The 'Canadian case' in comparative constitutionalism has always been an awkward one to theorize. This is due, at least in part, to its peculiar combination of diverse institutional features (as a Westminster federation with an entrenched bill of rights), but is also reflective of an apparent disconnect between its constitutional principles and their implementation. Stephen Gardbaum includes it as one of his 'new Commonwealth models', but, as an 'early adopter', Canada is, in Gardbaum's assessment, 'currently operating in a way that is too close to judicial supremacy for it to be the most distinct or successful version of the new model'.[1] In his strong-form/weak-form categorization, Mark Tushnet sees for Canada 'the possibility that, as implemented, these apparently weak forms of judicial review will actually be somewhat, perhaps even a great deal, stronger than one might think simply by reading their descriptions'.[2] Regarding 'constitutional dialogue', the Supreme Court of Canada was briefly (1997–2002) enthusiastic in explicitly adopting Hogg and Bushell's 'dialogue' metaphor[3] for its own self-understanding of its role, but dropped the label when it might have meant sharing some interpretive authority.[4] The metaphor may have lost its appeal for the judiciary, but interpretive disputes between the Supreme Court and

---

[1] Stephen Gardbaum, *New Commonwealth Model of Constitutionalism: Theory and Practice* (Cambridge: Cambridge University Press, 2013), p. 128.

[2] Mark Tushnet, *Weak Courts, Strong Rights: Judicial Review and Social Welfare Rights in Comparative Constitutional Law* (Princeton: Princeton University Press, 2008), p. 33.

[3] Peter W. Hogg and Allison Bushell, 'The Charter Dialogue Between Courts and Legislatures (Or Perhaps the Charter of Rights Isn't Such A Bad Thing After All)' (1997) 33 *Osgoode Hall Law Journal* 75.

[4] Christopher P. Manfredi, 'The Day the Dialogue Died: A Commentary on Sauvé v. Canada' (2007) 45(1) *Osgoode Hall Law Journal* 105. This may also have reflected some disagreement on the Court regarding the nature of the metaphor (see Justice Frank Iacobucci's claim in *R. v. Hall* [2002] 3 S.C.R. 309 that the Chief Justice had 'transformed dialogue into abdication' at para 127). See also Rosalind Dixon, 'The Supreme Court of

Parliament still occur[5] regardless of whether they are identified as such. The Canadian scholarly debate over dialogue has been characterized recently as reflecting a schism between 'Charter lovers' and 'Charter haters'.[6] While those labels might be overly reductive at best, there is a real division among Canadian scholars who perceive 'dialogue' as simply an acknowledgment that subsequent legislation would be enacted to implement the Court's constitutional commands, and those of us who desire a form of 'dialogue' that would allow Parliament to participate in the development of constitutional rights. Added to this mix is perennial confusion about whether Canada has a true 'separation of powers', or if that is simply a notion that has been smuggled across its southern border.[7] In short, Canada's constitutionalism resists simple models and easy characterizations.

Such slipperiness might be less of a sign of constitutional incoherence and more a consequence of a complex constitutional order that allows for informal flexibility within formal boundaries. As such, and as a unique variant of Westminster constitutionalism, the Canadian model offers much for the international understanding of 'constitutional dialogue' and separation of powers theory. To appreciate its subtleties, however, one requires a clear understanding of the relationship between informal and formal power in the context of its separation of powers. Properly understood, the Canadian model combines a regular, ordinary mode of constitutional politics, where informal power normally dictates outcomes, but also allows for exceptional moments where formal power is advanced and accepted. Since this feature of the model is relational between institutions, it is often difficult to discern in discrete cases; it is

Canada, Charter Dialogue and Deference' (2009) 47 *Osgoode Hall Law Review* 235. For more on the Canadian experience with 'dialogue theory', see Peter W. Hogg, Allison A. Bushell Thornton, and Wade K. Wright, 'Charter Dialogue Revisited: Or "Much Ado About Metaphors"' (2007) 45(1) *Osgoode Hall Law Journal* 1; F. L. Morton, 'Dialogue or Monologue?' (1999) *Policy Options* 23; Kent Roach, *Supreme Court on Trial: Judicial Activism or Democratic Dialogue* (Toronto: Irwin Law, 2001); Grégoire Webber, 'The Unfulfilled Potential of the Court and Legislature Dialogue' (2009) 42(2) *Canadian Journal of Political Science* 443.

[5] Rainer Knopff, Rhonda Evans, Dennis Baker, and Dave Snow, 'Dialogue: Clarified and Reconsidered' (2017) 54(2) *Osgoode Hall Law Journal* 609.

[6] Aileen Kavanagh, 'The Lure and Limits of Dialogue' (2016) 66(1) *University of Toronto Law Journal* 96.

[7] James B. Kelly, *Governing with the Charter: Legislative and Judicial Activism and Framers' Intent* (Vancouver: University of British Columbia Press, 2005); David Schneiderman, *Red, White, and Kind of Blue?: The Conservatives and the Americanization of Canadian Constitutional Culture* (Toronto: University of Toronto Press, 2015).

best observed in 'sequences', where iterations of judicial and legislative responses occur (a typical sequence: a judicial decision provokes a 'legislative sequel' that is subsequently reviewed by the Court in a 'second look' case).[8] This complexity of formal and informal power – and some of the confusion it generates – is evident in the politics of the federal government's response to the Supreme Court of Canada's decision in the assisted suicide case of *Carter*.[9] In that sequence, we see a judicial decision offering a broad policy prescription, ostensibly as an extension of its formal settlement of a particular case, met with a rare exercise of Parliament's formal power to craft a response at odds with the more pre-emptive elements of the decision. As it continues to unfold, the stresses of inter-institutional disagreement in the *Carter* sequence brings the relationship between formal and informal legislative, executive, and adjudicative powers of Canadian constitutionalism into a sharper relief than more benign political interactions between the branches. Viewed this way, rather than simply as an oddity in unidimensional frames of constitutional power, the complex Canadian system has more to contribute to the comparative study of inter-institutional law and politics.

More specifically, the *Carter* sequence informs our understanding of how the separation of powers in a Westminster system may play out in the context of an entrenched, largely written constitution. My aim in this chapter will be limited to demonstrating that the Westminster variant of the separation of powers can be compatible with the constitutional supremacy that typifies an entrenched constitution; moreover, the combination can better allow for political disagreement – even over matters subject to 'constitutional interpretation' – to be expressed and managed through institutional forms. What might otherwise be seen as a 'bug' – and some Canadian commentators considered the *Carter* response a waste of resources (at best) or an unconstitutional act (at worst) – is really a desirable 'feature' of what might otherwise be a dysfunctional constitutional order. Here, the Canadian case is simply one possible constitutional alignment of this type, but its existence and continuing operation may itself be instructive for other

---

[8] Dixon, 'The Supreme Court of Canada, Charter Dialogue and Deference', 235.

[9] *An Act to amend the Criminal Code and to make related amendments to other Acts (medical assistance in dying)* (2016) S.C. c.3 (Bill C-14, 1st Session, 42nd Parliament, 2015–2016); *Carter* v. *Canada (Attorney General)* [2015] 1 S.C.R. 331; *Carter* v. *Canada (Attorney General)* [2016] 1 S.C.R. 13.

Westminster systems, and perhaps as part of a broader continuum that includes non-Westminster systems.

I   Deviating from a Judicial Pronouncement: Responding to *Carter* v. *Canada*

Aiding or abetting suicide has been a criminal offence in Canada at least since the enactment of the first Criminal Code of Canada in 1892.[10] With the increasing acceptance of medically assisted dying, the provision has been subjected to constitutional scrutiny. In the 1993 decision of *Rodriguez* v. *British Columbia*,[11] a majority of the Supreme Court of Canada upheld the provision against a constitutional challenge using section 7 of the Charter of Rights and Freedoms, which guarantees 'life, liberty and security of the person' and to not be 'deprived thereof except in accordance with the principles of fundamental justice'.[12] In the aftermath of the *Rodriquez* decision, various private member's bills attempted to repeal or modify the provision with no success.[13] Despite its 1993 precedent, the Supreme Court reversed itself and found Canada's criminal prohibition against assisted suicide to be constitutionally deficient in the February 2015 decision of *Carter* v. *Canada (Attorney General)*.[14] The Court did so even though neither the Criminal Code provisions nor the text of the Charter right (the section 7 guarantee of liberty) had changed in the twenty-two years since its earlier decision, relying instead on the Court's own evolving jurisprudence.[15] This chapter takes no position on the underlying substantial issue of medical assistance in dying, other than to suggest that the Supreme Court of Canada's own shift in position proves UK Lord Steyn's appraisal in *Pretty* v. *Director of Public Prosecutions* that these are 'ancient questions on which millions in the past have taken diametrically opposite views and still do'.[16] With considerably less

---

[10] *Criminal Code*, SC 1892, s. 237. At the time of *Carter*, the provision read 'Every one who ... (b) aides or abets a person to commit suicide, whether suicide ensues or not, is guilty of an indictable offence and is liable to imprisonment for a term not exceeding fourteen years', *Criminal Code* (R.S.C., 1985, c. C-46), s. 241.

[11] *Rodriguez* v. *British Columbia (Attorney General)*, [1993] 3 S.C.R. 519.

[12] Ibid.

[13] Bill C-215, *An Act to Amend the Criminal Code (Aiding Suicide)*, 1st Session, 35th Parliament, 1994.

[14] *Carter* v. *Canada (Attorney General)* [2015] 1 S.C.R. 331.

[15] *Canada (Attorney General)* v. *Bedford*, [2013] 3 S.C.R. 1101. See especially Hamish Stewart, 'Bedford and the Structure of Section 7' (2015) 60(3) *McGill Law Journal* 575.

[16] *Pretty* v. *Director of Public Prosecutions*, [2001] UKHL 61, para. 54 (Lord Steyn).

humility, the Supreme Court of Canada in 2015 declared the criminal provisions void 'insofar as they prohibit physician-assisted death for a competent adult person who (1) clearly consents to the termination of life; and (2) has a grievous and irremediable medical condition (including an illness, disease or disability) that causes enduring suffering that is intolerable to the individual in the circumstances of his or her condition'.[17] The Court noted that '[t]he scope of this declaration is intended to respond to the factual circumstances in this case' and, while 'to the extent that the impugned laws deny the s.7 rights of people like Ms. Taylor they are void', it also made it clear the Court was making 'no pronouncement on other situations where physician-assisted dying may be sought'.[18]

By delaying its declaration of invalidity for twelve months, the Court was anticipating a legislative response but warned '[i]t is for Parliament and the provincial legislatures to respond, should they choose, by enacting legislation *consistent with the constitutional parameters set out in these reasons*' (emphasis added).[19] Other than establishing two expert panels to provide advice, Stephen Harper's Conservative government was seemingly content to ignore the issue in the lead-up to the 2015 election, leaving Justin Trudeau's new Liberal government to address the impending deadline after Parliament resumed on 3 December 2015. With only a few months to develop the new legislation (and coordinate with the provinces with respect to the healthcare aspects), the Government successfully applied to the Court for an extension and was awarded a further delay of four months.[20] As the Government drew closer to introducing legislation, several reports were delivered offering policy alternatives that either favoured an enactment of the Supreme Court's remedy[21] or an even more

---

[17] *Carter* v. *Canada (Attorney General)* [2015] 1 S.C.R. 331, para. 127.

[18] Ibid.

[19] Ibid. para. 126.

[20] *Carter* v. *Canada (Attorney General)* [2016] 1 S.C.R. 13; On this motion for an extension of the suspension of the declaration, the Court's unanimity in the earlier case broke with Justices Abella, Karakatsanis, Wagner, Gascon, and Côte, granting the motion but also exempting the province of Quebec and several individuals from that extension; the Chief Justice and Justices Cromwell, Moldaver, and Brown dissented on the issue of the exemptions to the extension. While this is explicitly a disagreement over the remedial actions to be taken, it may also suggest that the Court's cohesion on the first decision was more fragile than initially thought.

[21] External Panel on Options of a Legislative Response to *Carter* v. *Canada*, 'Consultations on Physician-Assisted Dying: Summary of Results and Key Findings', 15 December 2015 (which was 'sympathetic to the adoption of a permissive policy regime for assisted dying',

liberalized approach.[22] Instead, the Government chose to limit the impact of the Court's ruling in its Bill C-14 by restricting access to assisted suicide with additional requirements that the Court did not find necessary, namely that the patient's 'natural death has become reasonably foreseeable, taking into account all of their medical circumstances' and that the patient be 'in an advanced state of irreversible decline in capability'.[23] While the legislation presents these additional requirements as elements of the Court's 'grievous and irremediable medical condition', they restrict the pool of people who might potentially use the criminal law exemption and that group is smaller than the *Carter* Court likely had in mind.

The government's failure to codify the broadest interpretation of *Carter* was criticized by political and legal commentators. Peter W. Hogg testified to Parliament that the law was 'not consistent with the constitutional parameters set out in the *Carter* reasons', since it amounted to 'taking away a right that had just been deliberately granted by the Supreme Court'.[24] University of Ottawa Professor Amir Attaran had 'no doubts' that 'Bill C-14 is unconstitutional by the bucketful'.[25] The Barreau du Quebec[26] and the Canadian Civil Liberties Association[27]

---

as described by Dave Snow & Kate Puddister, 'Closing a Door but Opening a Policy Window: Legislating Assisted Dying in Canada' in Emmett Macfarlane, (ed.), *Policy Change, Courts, and the Canadian Constitution* (Toronto: University of Toronto Press, 2018), p. 57.

[22] The Special Joint Committee on Physician-Assisted Dying suggested that 'individuals not be excluded from eligibility for medical assistance in dying based on the fact that they have a psychiatric condition', and also recommended 'a second stage of legislation' that might open the procedure up to 'mature minors'.

[23] Bill C-14, above n 9.

[24] Peter W. Hogg, 'Presentation to the Standing Senate Committee on Legal and Constitutional Affairs, Bill C-14 (medical assistance in dying)', 6 June 2016. Hogg notes that the Court would 'have no reason to object to the *widening* of the entitled class' as opposed to the '*taking away*' of a right, as Bill C-14 does in his view.

[25] The Standing Senate Committee on Legal and Constitutional Affairs Evidence, 1st Session, 42nd Parliament, 6 June 2016. https://sencanada.ca/en/Content/Sen/committee/421/lcjc/52666-e.

[26] Barreau du Québec, 'Mémoire du Barreau du Québec: Project de loi C-14'. www.barreau.qc.ca/pdf/medias/positions/2016/20160502-memoire-pl-c14.pdf.

[27] Canadian Civil Liberties Association, 'Submission to the Standing Committee on Justice and Human Rights, Bill C-14: medical assistance in dying', May 2016. www.ourcommons.ca/Content/Committee/421/JUST/Brief/BR8300051/br-external/CanadianCivilLibertiesAssociation-e.pdf. The CCLA argues that the provision requiring a 'reasonably foreseeable' natural death is 'unduly vague, contrary to the Supreme Court's decision in *Carter*, and will lead to further violations of Charter rights and avoidable litigation' at p. 2.

made similar critiques. Senator Serge Joyal assessed the Bill as constitutionally defective ('the parameters have been defined by the Supreme
Court of Canada, like it or not') and introduced an 'essential amendment
... to make sure [Bill C-14] will not be challenged on the very next day
by the very people that Parliament will have excluded'.[28] Joyal's amendment failed and Bill C-14 was enacted, but its constitutionality continues
to be questioned, both on its merits and as simply delaying the inevitable
restoration of the Supreme Court's position. Was it constitutional for
Parliament to pass such legislation when it was clearly in tension with the
Court's supposedly definitive ruling? Far from being an example of
constitutional disobedience, Bill C-14 illustrates how Parliament might
creatively exercise its formal legislative powers in answer to the Court's
informal legislative guidance.

II Separating Constitutional Powers

One can understand the *Carter* dialogue as a reflection of the separation
of powers and, in particular, the fundamental difference between legislating and adjudicating. Even though the two can be closely intertwined
at times, there remains an important formal difference between them
that continues to shape the institutional dynamics of constitutional
politics. Understanding the inter-institutional dimensions of the *Carter*
controversy invites a broader examination of the constitutional principle
of separated powers, as well as the question of the principle's very
existence in Westminster systems. To address every prospective concern
and objections on this matter would require a book-length treatment,
but, for the purposes of this chapter, I offer a rough sketch of my account
of the Canadian separation from its roots in Anglo-American constitutional first principles to its specific implementation in Canada's institutional design.

Constitutionalism is best understood as a limitation on power.[29] In
one common articulation, we might understand the constitution
as delineating the boundaries between the state and the citizenry

---

[28] Bill to Amend – Third Reading – Debate Adjourned. 8 June 2016. https://sencanada.ca/
en/speeches/speech-by-senator-serge-joyal-during-the-third-reading-of-bill-c-14-medical-
assistance-in-dying-amendment-joyal/.

[29] Constitutions may be empowering, such that the assignment of power clearly legitimates
its use. When they do so, however, the assignment is typically to one institutional actor
and thus implicitly a restraint on the others.

(the familiar conception implicit in 'rights' documents). As James Madison perceptively notes, these rights are likely to be mere 'parchment barriers' without also embedding a separation *within* the state to utilize the conflict of political elites and allowing 'ambition to counteract ambition'.[30] In this respect, Madison was following Montesquieu, who understood that 'constant experience shows us that every man invested with power is apt to abuse it, and to carry his authority as far as it will go . . . [t]o prevent this abuse, it is necessary from the very nature of things that power should be a check to power'.[31] The fact that this is Montesquieu, writing in praise of the English constitution, and not an invention of Madison's, should indicate that the roots of this idea run deeper than the American Constitution, as some commentators suggest.

The American stamp on the separation of powers doctrine has led many to downplay its influence over British constitutionalism and its progeny. As Colin Munro put it, most twentieth-century theorists of British constitutionalism 'speak almost with one voice in denying that the separation of powers is a feature of the constitution'.[32] Similarly, in the Canadian context, James B. Kelly worries that 'too much of the works of James Madison and Alexander Hamilton has been used in the Canadian debate' and sees 'the absence of a separation of powers theory' as an element of Canada's 'distinct political culture'.[33] When Canadian authors accept that there must be some institutional separation – as they must, given that the Constitution Act, 1867 explicitly identifies executive,[34] legislative,[35] and judicial powers[36] – they undermine its centrality by referring to it as a 'veneer of separation'[37] and 'largely a fiction'.[38] There is often much to these objections that can help better understand constitutional nuances – there are, for example, real differences between what theorists meant by 'mixed', 'balanced', and

---

[30] James Madison, The Federalist *no. 48, no. 51* (New York: Modern Library, 2001).

[31] Montesquieu, *The Spirit of the Laws* (New York: Prometheus Books, 2002), p. 150.

[32] Colin Munro, *Studies in Constitutional Law* (Cambridge: Butterworths, 1987), p. 193, cited in Adam Tomkins, 'Of Constitutional Spectres' [1999] *Public Law* 525 at 531.

[33] James B. Kelly, *Governing with the Charter: Legislative and Judicial Activism and Framers' Intent* (Vancouver: University of British Columbia Press, 2005), pp. 12, 81.

[34] *The Constitution Act, 1867* (United Kingdom), 30 & 31 Victoria, C 3. ss. 9–16.

[35] Ibid. ss. 17–57.

[36] Ibid. ss. 96–101.

[37] Schneiderman, Red, White, and Kind of Blue?, p. 119.

[38] Ibid. p. 118.

'separated' doctrines[39] – but the broader argument seem to suggest that these dissimilarities are enough to abandon or obscure the principle that animated them all. It has become somewhat commonplace in the separation of powers literature to focus narrowly on different implementations to find some constitutions meeting the standard of being labelled a true 'separation of powers' arrangement while finding others falling short.

By contrast, economist Scott Gordon identifies a useful 'countervailance doctrine', that encompasses a very wide range of constitutional arrangements that includes the Anglo-American constitutions of the United Kingdom, United States, Canada, Australia, and New Zealand.[40] Gordon recognizes that there is considerable variance in how this doctrine is put into operation, but points to a broad familial relationship with a shared understanding that state authority is to be divided among governing institutions who may choose to compete or cooperate. Legal theorist Eric Barendt envisions something like Gordon's countervailing doctrine when he argues that the British separation of powers is not a 'strict distribution' but 'a network of rules and principles which ensure that power is not concentrated in one branch'.[41] Barendt's description is neutral about which institution may present the problem that the principle solves: 'In practice the danger now is that the executive has

---

[39] American theorist Martin Diamond, for example, deemed the 'mixed' and 'separated powers' regimes as 'about as unlike and unrelated as any two political arrangements can be expected to be' (Martin Diamond, *As Far as Republican Principles Will Admit*, ed., William A. Schambra (Washington, DC: AEI Press, 1992), p. 64; cited in Schneiderman, *Red, White and Kind of Blue?*, p. 123. This exaggeration does point to differences in the changing mode of politics (the mixed regime '[presupposing] politics as a high and all-embracing art . . . requiring high, ultimately aristocratic deliberation and statesmanship'), but it is an unconvincing rebuttal to the countervailing notion described in this chapter. Diamond himself concedes that the mixed regime, even though it provides each institution with the 'whole' governing power, institutions would have to interact with each other: 'By virtue of the necessity that the community could act only when the two agree, each had an absolute veto over the other' (Diamond, *As Far as Republican Principles Will Admit*, p. 60). For more on the mixed regime and the separation of powers, particularly as it applies to Canada, see Philip Resnick, 'Montesquieu Revisited, or the Mixed Constitution and the Separation of Powers in Canada' (1987) 20(1)*Canadian Journal of Political Science* 97; and Janet Ajzenstat, 'Comment: The Separation of Powers in 1867' (1987) 20(1) *Canadian Journal of Political Science* 117.

[40] Scott Gordon sees it applying even further afield, as evidenced by his title: *Controlling the State: Constitutionalism from Ancient Athens to Today* (Cambridge, MA: Harvard University Press, 1999).

[41] Eric Barendt, 'Separation of Powers and Constitutional Government' [1995] *Public Law* 599, 608–609.

too much power, though it is worth remembering that at other times there was more anxiety about self-aggrandizement of the legislature.'[42] Commenting on Barendt's work, Nicholas Barber writes that '[t]he purpose of the doctrine ... is not, primarily to identify the best, or natural, holder of a particular power ... [t]he precise delineation of this division is not of great significance; all that separation of powers requires is that *some* division of power be decided upon and adhered to'.[43] This baseline – admittedly a low one – is not without normative content and implications for institutional design. In the Westminster context, for example, it unfolds itself in the form of responsible government (where one institution holds another responsible) and, potentially, with the notion of 'constitutional dialogue' (where countervailing institutions might participate in the enforcement of the constitution).

What does this most basic articulation of the separation require? While the relative power of the governing institutions, their distinct functions, and their comparative advantages are all left open to particularization in a specific constitution, there are two elements that must be present if the countervailance doctrine is to be meaningful: each institution must have an inviolable constitutional status and each institution must interact with the others in the process of governing. While there can be institutions that dominate others (thus, *equal* powers are not necessary), no institution can be so dominant that it can formally sideline the others. This is a very modest requirement, but, as we shall see, it has important consequences for the assignment of the interpretive power. For now, it is sufficient to note that this requirement still allows for a wide inclusion of models, including those with supposedly 'strong' executives, legislatures, or judiciaries. The question for the limited model of the separation of powers is not the question of which institution may dominate in every day political controversies, but one of formal constitutional status: can one branch effectively prohibit another from fulfilling its constitutional role. If any institution is able to entirely exclude another from participating in the exercise of power then the countervailing doctrine collapses; if it is to be maintained, separated institutions must possess a modicum of formal constitutional authority to ensure they stay relevant to the exercise of power.

---

[42] Ibid. 609.
[43] Nicholas Barber, 'Prelude to the Separation of Powers' (2001) 60(1) *Cambridge Law Journal* 59 at 61.

What legal scholar Aileen Kavanagh calls the 'desderatum of inter-action' is actually a necessity.[44] While some strong forms of American 'departmentalism' may allow for institutions to go on frolics of their own,[45] a more sensible approach to the separation of powers requires *interaction* among the branches. Gordon finds this notion well estab-lished in Montesquiuean thinking: 'Obviously his concept of "separation" is not meant to denote a complex of *completely independent* institutions; he plainly states that the preservation of liberty requires that the execu-tive and legislative organs of the state be dependent on each other ... [i]t is not the separation in itself that protects liberty, but the arrangement of the separated powers in a system of mutual control.'[46] It should be noted that, as Gordon puts it, '[t]he idea that the different functions of the state should be performed by different institutional organs is not, in itself, a countervailance doctrine' because '[i]f each of the separate institutions were endowed with absolute authority in its own specific domain, they could not limit the powers of each other within those jurisdictional boundaries'.[47] For this reason, we should be wary of doctrines that purport to assign unanswerable powers to a single institution; for this reason, more extreme notions of absolute executive power[48] and absolute Parliamentary sovereignty[49] deserve some scepticism. Conversely, a judi-cial reluctance to answer 'political questions' is only permissible because it is self-imposed, and it would be another matter entirely if the repre-sentative branches were to deem their actions 'political questions'

---

[44] Aileen Kavanagh, 'The Constitutional Separation of Powers' in David Dyzenhaus and Malcolm Thorburn (eds.), *Philosophical Foundations of Constitutional Law* (Oxford: Oxford University Press, 2016), pp. 221–239.

[45] Kevin C. Walsh 'Judicial Departmentalism: An Introduction' (2016) 58(5) *William & Mary Law Review* 1713. There are variations in 'departmentalism' that make it difficult to fairly assess, in passing, in a chapter of this sort. In addition, for good reasons, Rosalind Dixon cautions against taking the Commonwealth–US constitutional differences for granted in making these sorts of comparisons ('Weak-Form Judicial Review and Ameri-can Exceptionalism' (2012) 32(3) *Oxford Journal of Legal Studies* 487). My comments here are aimed primarily at those who would completely immunize the actions of one branch from any review of the other (including the most rudimentary and deferential inquiries).

[46] Gordon, Controlling the State, p. 282.

[47] Ibid. p. 281.

[48] John Yoo, *Crisis and Command: A History of Executive Power from George Washington to George W. Bush* (New York: Kaplan Publishing, 2010); Kevin C. Walsh 'Judicial Depart-mentalism: An Introduction' (2016) 58(5) *William & Mary Law Review* 1713.

[49] Jeffrey Goldsworthy, *The Sovereignty of Parliament: History and Philosophy* (Oxford: Oxford University Press, 1999).

immune from legal scrutiny. It is the *interaction* that is key and it simply (but significantly) requires institutions that can maintain the capacity for an intervention. With this standard for a 'separation of powers' regime set so low, all the Anglo-American constitutions would qualify even though they vary considerably in their institutional design beyond this minimum bar.

Of course, the 'separation of powers' is usually taken to mean something more robust than simply institutions interacting with each other. For most, it implies some sort of logic for the assignment of power, which usually takes the form of a 'functional' design: legislatures to make laws, executives to apply those laws, and a judiciary to adjudicate disputes. But it is at this stage of the argument that the separation of powers comes under fire for its failure to accord with the reality of institutional behaviour. Kavanagh argues that '[c]learly the strict "one branch–one function" view cannot be sustained as a descriptive matter, because all three branches exercise all three functions to some degree'.[50] It is an 'open secret', legal academic Victoria Nourse tells us, that 'the departments all perform the functions of other departments'.[51] Similarly, in an oft-cited American article, law scholar Elizabeth Magill calls it the 'embarrassing secret' of the separation of powers: 'there is no principled way to distinguish between the relevant powers ... government authority cannot be parceled neatly into three categories, and government actors cannot be solely understood as members of a branch of government'.[52] The notion that legislatures legislate, executives execute, and judges adjudicate may not be just an oversimplification, but perhaps fatal to the entire idea of a separation of powers. After all, if judges and bureaucrats often create rules that appear indistinguishable from legislation, then what is the point of using such labels at all? The executive in Westminster systems is so deeply implicated in the drafting of laws that it appears to effectively wield legislative power, much more so than the legislature, which is often regarded by political scientists as playing more of an 'accountability' role.[53] If there ever was a formal separation of powers, this argument

---

[50] Kavanagh, 'The Constitutional Separation of Powers', p. 226.
[51] Ibid. p. 227.
[52] Elizabeth Magill, 'Beyond Powers and Branches in Separation of Powers Law' (2001) 150 (2) *University of Pennsylvania Law Review* 604, 606.
[53] Even Barendt, an otherwise stalwart defender of the separation, hedged on this point: 'The truth is that there is no effective separation of powers between legislature and executive in the United Kingdom in the sense of a system of "checks and balances" ... Except on the rare occasions when there is a significant party split, the government

runs, perhaps it has been subsumed by the flexible and fluid nature of modern governing institutions.

While the interplay of institutional power is undeniable, it is less clear that this makes the separation of powers unworkable. Blurred lines were anticipated even by early proponents of the idea. Madison, for example, concedes that '[e]xperience has instructed us that no skill in the science of government has been able to discriminate and define, with sufficient certainty, its three great provinces – the legislative, executive and judiciary'.[54] But this did not mean jettisoning the functional separation. For Barendt's Westminster separation, Barber notes, '... it does not matter whether powers are always allocated to the most appropriate institution ... [a] rough, perhaps intuitive, division will suffice'.[55] This 'rough' and 'intuitive' account can be aided by acknowledging the distinction between formal and informal power. Madison offered an account of the separation of these provinces of governmental power, which permitted branches 'partial agency' in the exercise of another branch's power. Interplay was subject to an important qualification, however: such interference or assumption of power must always be 'partial' and thereby preserve the constitutional status of the infringed branch and allow for continuing countervailance.

As I argue at length in *Not Quite Supreme*, Harvey C. Mansfield's conceptualization of executive power as both formal and informal provides a useful means of understanding how Madisonian inter-branch agency works.[56] Mansfield describes the 'ambivalent' interplay of formal and informal powers: legislative, executive, and judicial powers may not be *wholly* assumed by institutions to which they are not formally allocated, but that still allows wide scope for informal and partial assumptions of power to be wielded. This informal, non-assigned power may be permissible so long as the formally assigned institution retains the opportunity to modify or reject the informal exercise, even if we would not expect such formal responses in the usual course of events. Mansfield

---

effectively controls the legislature' ('Separation of Powers and Constitutional Government', 614). Barendt later stresses that this does not mean there is no formal separation: 'government may control the legislature (and certainly there is overlapping membership), but it must legislate through Acts of Parliament' (615).

[54] Madison, *The Federalist* #37.

[55] Nicholas Barber, 'Prelude to the Separation of Powers' (2001) 60(1) *Cambridge Law Journal* 59, 62.

[56] Dennis Baker, *Not Quite Supreme* (McGill-Queen's University Press, 2007), pp. 69–77, 83–92.

notes that even the strong executive – i.e., even one that effectively wields informal legislative power (say, influence over the shape of legislation) and informal judicial power (say, through the management and control of the administrative state) – is limited by the weakness inherent in the very definition of the 'executive' role. Formally, the executive 'remains an agent' that 'executes' on behalf of someone or something else.[57] While 'the executive is informally much stronger than that because [the] job is not as easy as its harmless title promises',[58] its agential role makes it vulnerable to a formal response – an executive decision can be rebutted by a clear statutory change, for example. Formal responses of this type provide ample scope for the exercise of informal power, but limit such informal exercises by providing for the possibility of countervailing formal power. This basic framework accommodates a wide variety of potential arrangements, including those where the constitutional formalities will only rarely be invoked. Like many Westminster systems, and perhaps more so than most, the Canadian institutional arrangement relies heavily on informal power, which is only subject to formal responses on very rare occasions. Both elements remain important: those infrequent formal checks mean that the informal assumption of another institution's assigned power can only go so far. At the same time, the informal exercises – operating with the formal limits – allows for the 'efficiency' in Westminster governance that commentators like Walter Bagehot have long praised.

The distinction between formal and informal power complements other attempts to defend the separation of powers from the functionalist critique. Jeremy Waldron's conception of the 'articulated' separation of powers suggests a subtler appreciation of functionalism rooted in the recognition that judging is different from legislating and both are distinguishable from executing the law.[59] Like Mansfield's formal power, Waldron relies upon the widespread acknowledgment that underpins functionalism and, more importantly, makes 'transparent' assumptions of power by another branch untenable. With respect to judicial power, Waldron concedes that '[c]ourts make and change the law all the time'

---

[57] Harvey C. Mansfield, Jr. *The Taming of the Prince: The Ambivalence of Modern Executive Power* (Portland: Free Press, 1989), p. xxiii.

[58] Ibid. p. xxiii.

[59] Jeremy Waldron, *Political Political Theory: Essays on Institutions* (Cambridge, MA: Harvard University Press, 2016), pp. 44–71.

but 'they do not do so transparently'.[60] They cannot do so because '[there] are institutions publicly dedicated to lawmaking . . . [b]y contrast, the official line in the case of judges is that this is not one of their tasks at all; indeed, this is a task they are supposed to be prohibited from performing; and they are most reluctant to talk about it'.[61] Understanding judicial power this way is hardly alien: common law judges have long made rules that could amount to 'judicial legislation' but those 'laws' yield to a direct and explicit statutory enactment, the formal legislative response to the informal judicial exercise of legislative authority. This approach is complicated in the context of an entrenched constitutional text, but, as the discussion of the Canadian enactments later in the chapter make clear, the logic of such 'partial agency' remains compelling.

Waldron sees this ordering reflected in textual rules about institutional powers, but also engrained as a 'separation of thought', where a single actor may play multiple roles – legislating and executing, for example – by consciously shifting from one role to the other.[62] Can human beings, with all their frailty of judgment, maintain such compartmentalization and commitment to constitutional forms? While there is reason to be sceptical, we should recognize that this technique is frequently employed throughout government and politics. In fact, proponents of judicial power routinely accept that judges can separate their policy preferences from their assessment of what the law demands. While that notion has been treated sceptically by some, the literature on judicial role perception does indicate that judges take the difference between judging and legislating seriously.[63] Similarly, with respect to prosecutions in some jurisdictions, a single individual may perform the duties of both the attorney general and the minister of justice where it is expected that different

---

[60] Ibid. p. 127.

[61] Ibid.; Mansfield notes that 'what is said in private may often be more interesting, but what can and cannot be said in public is more important: the latter is the best indicator of who rules'. *The Taming of the Prince*, p. 30.

[62] Ibid. ch. 3.

[63] Cornell W. Clayton and Howard Gillman, 'Beyond Judicial Attitudes: Institutional Approaches to Supreme Court Decision-Making' in Cornell W. Clayton and Howard Gillman, (eds.), *Supreme Court Decision-Making: New Institutionalist Approaches* (Chicago: University of Chicago Press, 1999), pp. 4–5. Some form of role perception plays a role in many social science modes of judicial decision-making: see James L. Gibson, 'Judges' Role Orientations, Attitudes and Decisions: An Interactive Model' (1978) 72(3) *American Political Science Review* 911; Michael A. Bailey and Forrest Maltzman, *The Constrained Court: Law, Politics and the Decisions Justices Make* (Princeton: Princeton University Press, 2011).

considerations be taken with the adoption of each role.[64] The connection
between the individual and the institutional role is not unproblematic but
it is an expected demand of many political officials. The primary protection we have from its abuse is the correlative expectation that the actors
publicly justify their decisions in terms of their role: judges must offer
justifications based on precedents; executives identify the statutory
authority for their actions; legislators justifying the enactment of bills
as contributing to good public policy.

Drawing attention to institutional roles is especially important for
Westminster systems, since it defeats the specious claim that the executive and legislative actors have been 'fused'. Since Westminster systems
require the executive to be drawn from the legislature (thus some of the
same people that sit as legislative representatives are given an additional
role as members of Cabinet), it has become commonplace to suggest that
such systems cannot be understood as having a separation of powers, or
that they have a 'defective' or less-than-'strict' separation. While no one
would deny that Westminster systems are characterized by a close and
intimate connection between the executive and the legislature, it must
always be a *'near* fusion', as Bagehot was initially careful to label it,[65] and
the incompleteness is as significant as the overlap. The formality of the
institutional separation can be seen in the (admittedly infrequent)
instances when the legislature rebuffs the executive's legislative initiatives,[66] but it is obvious in situations of minority government, where the
political party of the executive does not have its co-partisans as a majority
of the legislature. In that context, the 'fusion' of the institutions, even
with respect to the most strikingly 'executive-dominated legislatures', is
regularly proven false. Such 'fusion' is even more doubtful when bicameralism is present and where, as in the United Kingdom, the government
cannot count on a majority in the House of Lords, and in Canada, where
the new appointment process promises only non-affiliated senators.
In sum, the Westminster executive–legislative relationship is best

---

[64] In some jurisdictions, the single actor/dual role has been replaced by the introduction of
an independent prosecutor to guard against inappropriate political considerations
seeping into the prosecutorial role. This 'reform' is not without costs in terms of political
accountability and it has not been adopted everywhere. Moreover, even where an independent director of public prosecutors has been established, the attorney general continues to play a non-partisan role in providing legal advice to cabinet and when directing
civil litigation.

[65] Dennis Baker, *Not Quite Supreme*, p. 66.

[66] Ibid. pp. 74–77.

characterized as a form of 'partial agency': we would expect the informally powerful executive to be able to effectively wield legislative power on a regular basis, but only within formal limits – the acquiescence of the legislators – that may only infrequently be denied but dominates when invoked. The formal limits – always lurking in the background – may also temper and caution the informal power, but this is more difficult to observe and prove.

When it comes to 'roles', we must also recognize that the formal separation of powers only creates *opportunities* for checks and balances. Unless actors are willing to invoke their formal powers, informality reigns supreme. In this respect, constitutional principles are heavily contextualized by political reality. Actors who have little political capital – whether because they are unpopular, unknown, or untrusted – will fare poorly in what is ultimately and unavoidably a political contest. We might be ultimately disappointed by the separation of powers, since political actors may enable abuses instead of checking them. In ensuring political moderation, the separation of powers is better understood as a necessary but not sufficient constitutional mechanism, in need of additional supports from engaged and responsible actors. Where actors *are* behaving responsibly, however, scholars should highlight the features of the system working properly; the Canadian assisted-suicide dialogue is just such an illustration of institutional actors playing their proper roles.

I present one final note about the separation of powers generally, before turning to that specific Canadian example. It is important to be careful not to strictly align an institution's formal role with either majoritarian or minoritarian interests. No institution is immune from either the scare-quoted 'tyranny' of the majority or minority, even if some institutional features may help curb some tendencies. Kent Roach, for example, highlights cases where the minority interest should prevail through judicial intervention. In comparing legislative and executive actions with judicial rulings in the case of minority language rights in Manitoba, he persuasively argues that the judiciary protected minority rights in the face of executive and legislative intransigence.[67] But this is not the only possible alignment – with respect to Canadian labour rights, for example, legislatures have historically been the active and progressive

---

[67] Kent Roach, 'The Judicial, Legislative and Executive Roles in Enforcing the Constitution: Three Manitoba Stories' in Richard Albert and David R. Cameron, (eds.), *Canada in the World: Comparative Perspectives on the Canadian Constitution* (Cambridge: Cambridge University Press, 2017). See also the discussion in Baker, *Not Quite Supreme*, p. 49.

actors in the face of judicial resistance until very recently.[68] In this volume, Roach also offers an account of 'penal populism' that poses a stark contrast between the rights of the vulnerable accused against a citizenry riled up for vengeance. While such cases can and do arise, it does not easily capture the dynamic in more complex cases, like those where the rights of the accused may need to be balanced against other legitimate societal interests – as in the cases regarding the admissibility of therapeutic records of sexual assault, where the Court's accused-friendly constitutional ruling was modified by legislation more sensitive to the societal interest in encouraging victims to report crimes against them.[69] Roach sees such balancing as part and parcel of the Charter's section 1 limitations test, but that continues to leave the judiciary as the sole authority over rights.[70] Moreover, the equation of rights-bearing minorities with vulnerable groups is also problematic: politically strong interest groups, like the tobacco lobby, can also use constitutional rights to thwart what might otherwise be sound public policy.[71] In these instances, the judicial vindication of rights might undermine the protection of vulnerable interests (the public health, the environment, etc.). It is therefore difficult to label any institution as the exclusive protector of vulnerable minorities. Politics is far too complex for such easy connections.

III   Canada's Separation of Powers in Action

Canada's institutional design implements the separation of powers principle in the context of a federated[72] Westminster system with an entrenched constitution. Section 52 of the Constitution Act, 1982 establishes the Constitution of Canada as 'the supreme law of Canada' and declares 'any law that is inconsistent with the provisions of the

---

[68] Paul C. Weiler, *In the Last Resort: A Critical Study of the Supreme Court of Canada* (Toronto: Carswell, 1974), ch. 5.

[69] Dennis Baker, *Not Quite Supreme*, pp. 22–24.

[70] The Supreme Court of Canada has made it clear that any invitation to Parliament to rebalance their legislation is subject to an invalidation if the resulting legislation does not comply with the Court's view of the Constitution. This is illustrated most clearly in the prisoner voting cases, where the Court initially suggested a more proportional restriction could be valid (*Sauvé v. Canada [Attorney General]*, [1993] 2 S.C.R. 438), only to later declare that no restriction would be permissible (*Sauvé v. Canada [Chief Electoral Officer]*, [2002] 2 S.C.R. 519). Any such section 1 'freedom to legislate' discussion might be seen as rhetorical, especially with a future invalidation looming.

[71] *RJR-MacDonald Inc. v. Canada (Attorney General)* [1995] 3 S.C.R. 199.

[72] Federalism can be considered another reflection of the countervailance principle.

Constitution is, to the extent of the inconsistency, of no force or effect'. While this section clearly secures *constitutional* supremacy, does it require a concomitant *judicial* supremacy? Peter W. Hogg argues that the connection is 'ineluctable', and mainstream legal opinion in Canada has followed his lead in effectively reading the section as empowering only the courts to find laws inconsistent and deny their effect. Two considerations should temper this 'ineluctable' move towards judicial supremacy: (1) the drafters of section 52 must have been aware of the then-decades-long interpretive questions haunting American constitutionalism, so it is surprising that, if they sought to establish judicial supremacy, they would not have explicitly identified the Supreme Court as its exclusive and authoritative interpreter; (2) section 24(1) of the same Constitution Act explicitly identifies a judicial role but construes it entirely as a power to be exercised in the context of an individual case brought by particular litigants ('Anyone whose rights or freedoms, as guaranteed by this Charter, have been infringed or denied may apply to a court of competent jurisdiction to obtain such remedy as the court considers appropriate and just in the circumstances'). Instead of treating them both as empowering only the judiciary, and essentially reading 'the judiciary' into section 52 to correct the 'bug' of its supposed omission, we might understand the distinction as a 'feature' of Canadian constitutionalism. By *not* identifying a single institution as supreme, the ambiguity of section 52 suggests inter-institutional responsibility to determine which laws are inconsistent with the Constitution, which in turn suggests inter-institutional participation in interpreting the Constitution. In short, the judiciary has a clear formal power to authoritatively settle the disputes before it, but, when it comes to broader questions of constitutional application, all three branches might participate legitimately.

The assignment of the power of constitutional interpretation is crucial for a well-functioning separation of powers regime. If – as some judicial supremacist might have it – section 52 enshrines an exclusive and authoritative judicial power to interpret the constitution, then the Canadian model runs afoul of the most minimal requirement of the separation of powers, the 'countervailance doctrine'. It would allow the Court to entirely shape institutional dynamics and sideline any of its competitor institutions upon its own interpretive whim. It would also make the interpretation of the constitution superior to the constitution itself. As Bishop Benjamin Hoadley put it, 'whoever hath an absolute interpretive authority to interpret any written or spoken laws, it is he who is truly the lawgiver, to all intents and purposes'.[73] To preserve the potential for countervailing institutions, it is necessary to read section 52 as it is, and not as if it identified a solely judicial power. While other Westminster constitutions reflect this interpretive compromise in different ways (as in the United Kingdom, by making judicial findings of inconsistency between legislation and Convention right solely declaratory and dependent on subsequent Parliamentary action), the Canadian model allows the judiciary to find constitutionally invalid legislation inapplicable to the dispute directly before the courts, but establishes space for multi-institutional input on the more general legislative scheme to follow.

This coordinate reading of sections 52 and 24 is consistent with the Trudeau government's response to *Carter*. In the Parliamentary debates over Bill C-14, Justice Minister Jody Wilson-Raybould argued that the eligibility criteria, including the requirement that 'natural death be reasonably foreseeable', is consistent with the 'circumstances of the plaintiffs in the *Carter* case, including Gloria Taylor, who was suffering from fatal ALS, and Kay Carter, who was also in a state of irreversible decline and nearing the end of her life'.[74] In this way, Bill C-14, defers not only to Court's direct settlement for the litigants personally but also to others similarly situated. That said, the Government did not accept the broadest interpretation of the Court's ruling, and instead chose to limit the Court's proposed general policy for assisted suicide in Canada. The justice minister relied upon this functional separation when she stated that, while 'Parliament must respect the court's ruling, so too must the court respect Parliament's determination of how to craft a statutory scheme in response'.[75] This legislative response is, in her words, 'never as simple as simply cutting and pasting the words from a court's judgement into a

---

[73] Benjamin Hoadley, bishop of Bangor, sermon before the King of England (31 March 1717), in Gary Wills, *Explaining America: The Federalist* (New York: Penguin Books Ltd., 2001), p. 130. Clinton notes that this comment was 'often recalled' by the American founders in Robert Clinton, *Marbury v. Madison and Judicial Review* (Lawrence, KS: University of Kansas Press, 1989), p. 7.

[74] Hon. Jody Wilson-Raybould (Minister of Justice and Attorney General of Canada), House of Commons Debates, 22 April 2016, Bill C-14, Second Reading, 148(45) *Hansard* (1st Session, 42nd Parliament), 1020. Peter W. Hogg argues, to the contrary, that Lee Carter would have been ineligible: 'Carter herself would not have satisfied the conditions in the bill' (Ian MacLeod, 'Assisted-dying in legal twilight zone while battle to pass Bill C-14 rages', *National Post*, 6 June 2016).

[75] Hon. Jody Wilson-Raybould, House of Commons Debates, 31 May 2016, Bill C-14, Third Reading, 148(62) *Hansard* (1st Session, 42nd Parliament), 1015.

new law',[76] but instead requires Parliament 'to listen to diverse voices and decide what the public interest demands'.[77] In this respect, as the Department of Justice 'backgrounder' defending Bill C-14 puts it, 'the question is not whether the Bill "complies with *Carter*" but rather, whether it complies with the Charter'.[78] Rather than 'a simple comparison of the Bill to the *Carter* decision', the legislation should be assessed 'in light of its new and distinct purposes, as compared to the purposes of the total prohibition, and the legislative record'.[79] In what might be the starkest assertion of a coordinate power of interpretation by a Canadian justice minister,[80] Wilson-Raybould rejected the claim of an exclusively judicial hold on the Constitution by emphasizing that 'the key takeaway is that nobody has a monopoly on interpreting the Charter'.[81] Just as 'only Nixon could go to China', perhaps only a government led by the Prime Minister who is the son of the 'Father of the Charter' could assert such a coordinate power and not be subject to vociferous condemnation from the legal community.[82] The Trudeau factor is an undeniable reminder that, despite the Charter's elevation of judges in Canada's political order, the Charter remains a product representative governments and its interpretation need not be entirely in the Court's hands.

But it is not entirely in Parliamentary hands either. As I have argued elsewhere, the notion of an institutional 'final word' on constitutionality is misguided. In a well-functioning separation of powers system, institutional rebuttals and modifications should be possible so long as they are politically feasible.[83] It is hardly surprising that Bill C-14 was quickly

---

[76] Hon. Jody Wilson-Raybould, House of Commons Debates, 22 April 2016, Bill C-14, Second Reading, 148(45) *Hansard* (1st Session, 42nd Parliament), 1016.

[77] Ibid. at 1016.

[78] Department of Justice, 'Legislative Background: Medical Assistance in Dying (Bill C-14) – Addendum', 15 June 2016. www.justice.gc.ca/eng/rp-pr/other-autre/addend/index.html#archived.

[79] Ibid.

[80] Eleni Nicolaides and Matthew Hennigar, 'Carter Conflicts: The Supreme Court of Canada's Impact on Medical Assistance in Dying Policy' in Emmett Macfarlane, (ed.), *Policy Change, Courts, and the Canadian Constitution* (Toronto: University of Toronto Press, 2018), pp. 326–27.

[81] Hon. Jody Wilson-Raybould, House of Commons Debates, 13 May 2016, Bill C-14, Second Reading, 148(55) *Hansard* (1st Session, 42nd Parliament) at 1040.

[82] Geoffrey Sigalet and Joanna Baron, 'The "Charter Party's" new dance with the judiciary' *Policy Options* (8 September 2016). http://policyoptions.irpp.org/magazines/september-2016/the-charter-partys-new-dance-with-the-judiciary/

[83] Which is to say they will not be endless, given the scarcity of resources. In this respect, the Court, which is often regarded as constrained by the 'costs of litigation', etc., is arguably

subjected to constitutional challenge in the (ongoing) follow-up case of *Lamb v. Canada*.[84] In his submissions to the Senate on Bill C-14, Hogg concluded that the bill was inconsistent with *Carter* and asked rhetorically '[w]hat judge would not strike down the end-of-life provisions?'[85] It is true that lower court judges may find it difficult to not follow a Supreme Court decision that they are likely to construe in its strongest and fullest sense,[86] and therefore may find Bill C-14 of no force or effect on the litigation before them. That said, Canadian jurisprudence has seen the Supreme Court of Canada itself endorse legislative responses that strayed from its earlier rulings.[87] Like Bill C-14, those legislative responses were initially presumed to be unconstitutional, and their ultimate acceptance by the Supreme Court is usually shrugged off by constitutional theorists who find it hard to account for them. If constitutional dialogue is to be meaningful, however, those statutes should not be perceived as anomalies to be summarily dismissed, but celebrated as illuminating an important feature of Canadian constitutionalism.

With Bill C-14, Hogg is perhaps right that the Court will continue to insist upon the preference it expressed in *Carter* in subsequent cases, but this is hardly a certainty and Parliament need not limit itself solely on a prediction of what the courts might do. From a separation of powers perspective, we should be wary of attempts to short-circuit inter-institutional dialogue (and this would apply with equal force to the usage of the notwithstanding clause, section 33, which might have been used to immunize C-14 from judicial Charter scrutiny).[88] A better course of events, and one that might lead to optimal policy outcomes and

---

advantaged over a Parliament that finds its time precious and the burden of the legislative process heavy. Applying a clear precedent in a 'second-look' case seems to me much less burdensome than passing entirely new legislation, even in a majority Parliament.

[84] *Lamb v. Canada (Attorney General)*, 2017 BCSC 1802.

[85] Peter W. Hogg, 'Presentation to the Standing Senate Committee on Legal and Constitutional Affairs, Bill C-14 (medical assistance in dying)', 6 June 2016.

[86] In recent years, however, Canadian lower courts have pre-emptively overturned the Supreme Court ruling regarding prostitution (*Bedford*) and, of course, the lower court decisions in *Carter* did not yield to the Supreme Court's earlier decision in *Rodriguez*.

[87] *R. v. Mills* [1999] 3 S.C.R. 668 (upholding the response to *R. v. O'Connor* [1995] 4 S.C.R. 411); *R. v. Hall* [2002] 3 S.C.R. 309 (upholding the response to *R. v. Morales* [1992] 3 S.C.R. 711); *R. v. Bouchard-Lebrun* [2011] 3 S.C.R. 575 (effectively upholding the response to *R. v. Daviault* [1994] 3 S.C.R. 63).

[88] There may be conceptions of the notwithstanding clause that can be accommodated within the framework of 'partial agency', but the popular notion that it is an 'override' makes it problematic. A better approach to the clause can be found in Dwight Newman's contribution to this volume.

enduring constitutional principles, is to permit the interplay of formal and informal power through multiple iterations of inter-institutional exchanges. Under this approach, the Trudeau government was well within its power to advance formal legislation to replace the Court's informal exercise of the legislative power. The formal legislation is under review again and the formal power of adjudication may render it ineffective for the new litigants. If so, Canada's coordinate moment on assisted suicide will quickly pass. Regardless, the extended process of the inter-institutional 'dialogue' is merited in this case,[89] where the stakes are literally life and death.

From an institutional standpoint, the Canadian separation of powers and its infrequent-but-revealing coordinate moments suggest that proponents of constitutional dialogue should pay more attention to the formal and informal dynamics at play in the exercise of power. This is not an easy subject for comparative analysis, since it requires not only an appreciation of a formal constitutional design but also an understanding of the subtle ways routine exercises of informal power may complement it.[90] Recognizing this difficulty, I have not strayed far from the Canadian system in this chapter, but it is not difficult to see potential applications of the formal/informal approach to other separation of powers regimes, especially Westminster systems. Too often in those Westminster arrangements the underlying principle of separated powers is easily dismissed and yet that separated design – at least in the limited sense defended here – is baked into them all, with their responsible executives accountable to legislative bodies and all institutions operating within the rule of law as patrolled by independent courts. The insights generated by an informal/formal approach to these systems may also help us better understand 'cohesive' elements in this constitutional order. Political parties, for example, are often informally strong in Westminster systems but traditionally insignificant in a formal, legal sense. It is therefore

---

[89] A drawback, of course, is the 'waste' of judicial resources and the human suffering that persists during this period. While these are important considerations, they are no less important as the case ascends the judicial hierarchy. We are willing to tolerate these factors during the lengthy judicial process of appeals in the hopes of 'getting it right'. The same arguments might be made in favour of a Parliamentary opportunity to revisit the issue and, indeed, it would seem odd to highlight these regrettable costs only after the courts have finished their process.

[90] As Rosalind Dixon notes, '[t]o be tractable, most forms of constitutional comparison require some simplification in how they treat foreign constitutional practices'. Dixon, 'Weak-Form Judicial Review and American Exceptionalism', 503.

intriguing that Stephen Gardbaum is now investigating how the 'separation of parties' thesis[91] might add a contextual element to his 'new Commonwealth model'.[92] Constitutional conventions also play an intriguing role in bridging the distance between constitutional formality and actual political practice. Recent scholarship, for example, has suggested that we should emphasize *constitutional* conventions to 'avoid specifying whether they are legal or conventional in nature', and such avoidance may help distinguish informal political practices from formal constitutional rules.[93] Expounding on these elements is a task for the future, but further exploration in this direction may yield a more satisfying understanding of constitutional dialogue as it pertains to the separation of powers.

---

[91] Daryl Levinson and Richard Pildes, 'Separation of Parties, Not Powers', (2006) 119 *Harvard Law Review* 2312.

[92] Stephen Gardbaum, 'Political Parties, Voting Systems, and the Separation of Powers', (2017) 65(2) *The American Journal of Comparative Law* 229.

[93] Nicholas Aroney, 'Law and Convention' in *Constitutional Conventions in Westminster Systems: Controversies, Changes and Challenges* (Cambridge: Cambridge University Press, 2015), p. 45.

PART V

International and Transnational Dialogues

15

Dialogue and Its Discontents

FREDERICK SCHAUER

I Introduction

The idea of dialogue looms large in contemporary constitutional thought. But although the terminology is widespread, it remains important to distinguish two different contexts in which the term "dialogue," and the idea that the term designates, occur. In one, "dialogue" serves as ubiquitous label for an approach to constitutional adjudication and judicial review in which the decisions of courts, even apex courts, are subject to further modification, override, or nullification by legislative bodies.[1] In Canada, for example, the national parliament and the provincial legislatures may, by an express declaration that an act should become law notwithstanding a judicial determination that the Charter of Rights and Freedoms has been violated, re-enact the same legislation that has been found by the courts to be unconstitutional, and the re-enactment has the effect of making the legislation valid law for a renewable period of five years.[2] And in the United Kingdom, judicial pronouncements of a

---

[1] See, initially, Peter W. Hogg and Allison A. Bushell, 'The Charter Dialogue between Courts and Legislatures (Or Perhaps the Charter of Rights Isn't Such a Bad Thing After All)' (1997) 35 *Osgoode Hall Law Journal* 75. And see also, and subsequently, Christine Bateup, 'The Dialogic Promise' (2006) 71 *Brooklyn Law Review* 1109; Jamie Cameron, 'Dialogue and Hierarchy in Charter Interpretation: A Comment on *R v. Mills*' (2001) 38 *Alberta Law Review* 1051; Rosalind Dixon, 'Creating Dialogue about Socioeconomic Rights: Strong-Form versus Weak-Form Judicial Review Revisited' (2007) 5 *International Journal of Constitutional Law* 391; Stephen Gardbaum, 'The New Commonwealth Model of Constitutionalism' (2001) 49 *American Journal of Comparative Law* 707; Anne Meuwese and Marnix Snel, 'Constitutional Dialogue: An Overview' (2013) 9 *Utrecht Law Review* 123; Mark Tushnet, 'Dialogic Judicial Review' (2008) 61 *Arkansas Law Review* 205.

[2] Canadian Charter of Rights and Freedoms (Canada Act, 1982), §33. Importantly, the "notwithstanding" power of the national and provincial legislatures does not apply to the "democratic rights" of democratic procedure contained in sections 3, 4, and 5 of the Charter, nor to the "mobility rights" in section 6. For discussion of the

statute's inconsistency with the quasi-constitutional Human Rights Act are no more than declarations of incompatibility, leaving Parliament and its subordinate enforcement and administrative bodies free to consider the statute as binding law despite its inconsistency with the Human Rights Act.[3] And much the same procedure and status of judicial rulings exists in New Zealand under its Bill of Rights Act, although somewhat less explicitly so.[4]

The term "dialogue" has often been used to refer to this form of judicial review because it is often thought that the process of formal legislative reaction to judicial action can be understood as one step in an iterative dialogue between the legislative and judicial branches of government. The legislature enacts a law, and if the judiciary invalidates it, or issues a declaration of incompatibility, then the legislature can subsequently consider the merits of the judicial action and thereafter choose to persist with the same law, or accept the judiciary's action, or modify the statute. In the last of these options, especially, the judiciary can then consider the modified statute and issue another ruling, which the legislature can then take into account in determining what actions to take thereafter. And so on. The process, so it is said, is one in which the courts and the legislature are engaged in a continuous dialogue about the meaning and effect of the constitution or of the quasi-constitutional rights-protecting document.

In a somewhat different context, however, the language and idea of dialogue has also been employed to refer to a transnational process in which constitutional courts (and commentators) take account of the constitutional provisions and decisions in other nations.[5] This process of mutual learning, although the subject of considerable controversy in the United States,[6]

---

notwithstanding clause, see Dwight Newman, 'Canada's Notwithstanding Clause, Dialogue, and Constitutional Identities' in this volume.

[3] Human Rights Act 1998, §4. Declarations of incompatibility may be made not only by the Supreme Court, but also by the High Court, the Court of Appeal, and several other courts.

[4] New Zealand Bill of Rights Act 1990, §4. The power to issue a declaration of inconsistency was recently judicially developed: *Attorney-General v. Taylor* [2018] NZCA 104.

[5] See Vicki C. Jackson, *Constitutional Engagement in a Transnational Era* (New York: Oxford University Press, 2013); Vicki C. Jackson, 'Constitutional Dialogue and Human Dignity: States and Transnational Constitutional Discourse' (2004) 65 *Montana Law Review* 1.

[6] See, for example, Jeremy Waldron, *"Partly Laws Common to All Mankind": Foreign Law in American Courts* (New Haven, CT: Yale University Press, 2012); Robert J. Delahunty and John Yoo, 'Against Foreign Law' (2005) 29 *Harvard Journal of Law & Public Policy* 291; Norman Dorsen, 'The Relevance of Foreign Legal Materials in U.S. Constitutional Cases: A Conversation between Justice Antonin Scalia and Justice Stephen Breyer' (2005) 3

and increasingly discussed elsewhere,[7] tends to be celebrated by constitutional and international lawyers, again under the rubric of dialogue, and again in the belief that this transnational dialogic process will, broadly speaking, result in better outcomes than would be produced absent the transnational consultation and the consequent (and alleged) transnational influence.

My goal in this chapter is to examine the claims for dialogue with a less celebratory focus than is common in the existing literature.[8] I will start with the question of transnational constitutional dialogue, and then look into whether what we might learn about transnational constitutional dialogue can have something to teach us about the separate topic of national constitutional dialogue between courts and legislatures.

II Constitutional Conversations across National Boundaries

In 1996, the Republic of South Africa adopted its first post-apartheid Constitution,[9] and among its many noteworthy provisions is section 39 (1)(c), which provides that the Constitutional Court, in interpreting the Bill of Rights contained in the Constitution, "may consider foreign law."[10] This provision was adopted in the midst of an era of worldwide constitutional transformation, some of that transformation being the

---

International Journal of Constitutional Law 519; Daniel A. Farber, 'The Supreme Court, The Law of Nations, and Citations of Foreign Law: The Lessons of History' (2007) 95 *California Law Review* 1335; Jenny S. Martinez, 'Who's Afraid of International and Foreign Law?' (2016) 104 *California Law Review* 1579; Vlad F. Perju, 'The Puzzling Parameters of the Foreign Law Debate' (2007) *Utah Law Review* 167; Ganesh Sitaramam, 'The Use and Abuse of Foreign Law in Constitutional Interpretation' (2009) 32 *Harvard Journal of Law & Public Policy* 653; Ernest A. Young, 'Foreign Law and the Denominator Problem' (2005) 119 *Harvard Law Review* 148.

[7] See, for example, Tania Groppi and Marie-Claire Ponthoreau (eds.), *The Use of Foreign Precedents by Constitutional Judges* (Oxford: Hart Publishing, 2013); Elaine Mak, *Judicial Decision-Making in a Globalised World: A Comparative Analysis of the Changing Practices of Western Highest Courts* (Oxford: Hart Publishing, 2013); Jacob Foster, 'The Use of Foreign Law in Constitutional Interpretation: Lessons from South Africa' (2010) 45 *University of San Francisco Law Review* 79.

[8] I do not claim that I am the first or the only skeptical voice. See, for example, David S. Law and Wen-Chen Chang, 'The Limits of Transnational Judicial Dialogue' (2011) 86 *Washington Law Review*.

[9] The final South African Constitution, which closely tracks the interim constitution of 1993, was approved by the Constitutional Assembly in 1995, approved by the Constitutional Court in 1996, and took effect in February 1997.

[10] The "may" is important, because the same section makes reliance on international law mandatory and not optional.

remnants of a period of postcolonial constitution-making that had started decades earlier, but most of it the product of a spate of post-1990 constitution-making in Eastern Europe and in the republics of the former Soviet Union.

A noteworthy feature of this era of constitutional transformation was (and to some extent remains) the presence[11] of numerous non-national advisors and commentators during the process of constitution-making. Although the actual influence of these (often self-appointed) advisors and commentators was almost certainly far less than the advisors and commentators themselves claimed, the presence of these individuals, frequently from the United States, Canada, and Germany, plainly built on an increase in knowledge of and interest in foreign constitutional regimes, as exemplified in the explicit reference to foreign law in the South African Constitution.

Just as American, Canadian, and German constitutionalists were ubiquitous in constitutional transformations outside of their home countries, so too, and more or less simultaneously, were lawyers, judges, and academics in these and other older constitutional systems increasingly interested in the constitutional decisions and approaches of other nations. Such interest became most controversial in the United States, where a series of Supreme Court decisions dealing with the death penalty[12] and sexual privacy and sexual orientation[13] included favorable mentions of the decisions in other jurisdictions, and over the vehement objection of Justice Antonin Scalia, most prominently, and to the annoyance of other Justices and judges as well.[14] The judicial debates about the relevance and authority of foreign law attracted considerable academic commentary, most but by no means all of it sympathetic with the use of foreign law in American courts.[15]

---

[11] I use the word "presence," and not "influence," advisedly. See David S. Law and Mila Versteeg, 'The Declining Influence of the United States Constitution' (2012) 87 *New York University Law Review* 762. See also Rosalind Dixon and Vicki C. Jackson, 'Constitutions Inside Out: Outsider Interventions in Domestic Constitutional Contests' (2013) 48 *Wake Forest Law Review* 149. I do not deny the existence of some influence, but the influence may be less than is claimed by those who most frequently attempt to exercise it.

[12] See *Roper* v. *Simmons*, 543 U.S. 551 (2005); *Atkins* v. *Virginia*, 536 U.S. 304 (2002).

[13] *Lawrence* v. *Texas*, 539 U.S. 558 (2003).

[14] See Richard Posner, 'No Thanks, We Already Have Our Own Laws' *Legal Affairs*, July/August 2004.

[15] See references above n 7. See also Vicki C. Jackson, 'Constitutional Comparisons: Convergence, Resistance, Engagement' (2005) 119 *Harvard Law Review* 109; John O.

The confluence of all of these developments generated a widespread discussion of what was often described as transnational constitutional dialogue.[16] Connecting in interesting ways with arguments about the desirability and effects of transnational legal dialogue more generally,[17] celebrants of this cross-border dialogue offered two different forms of arguments for its desirability and thus for its continuing growth and promotion.

Some of the claims in support of transnational legal dialogue have been explicitly or implicitly epistemic, by which I mean the claim that dialogue is a desirable method for distinguishing sound (or true) ideas from unsound (or false) ones, where soundness or unsoundness or truth and falsity are defined independently of the process that might be used to locate the independently defined soundness or truth. Assuming that some legal and constitutional ideas are better than others – superior in substance and thus superior independent of the process that has produced them – it was argued that transnational dialogue about these ideas would cause the better ideas to be more widely accepted and adopted, and the weaker ones to have their weaknesses more widely exposed, recognized, and consequently rejected.[18] Tracking traditional ideas about the unregulated marketplace of ideas as a valuable and comparatively reliable mechanism for the growth of knowledge and thus as the foundation for a regime of freedom of expression,[19] the epistemic arguments for

McGinnis, 'Foreign to Our Constitution' (2006) 100 *Northwestern University Law Review* 303.

[16] See, for example, Brun-Otto Bryde, 'North and South in Comparative Constitutional Law – From Colonial Imposition towards a Transnational Constitutionalist Dialogue' in Wolfgang Benedek, Hubert Isak, and Renate Kicker (eds.), *Development and Developing International and European Law: Essays in Honour of Konrad Ginther on the Occasion of his 65th Birthday* (Frankfurt: Peter Lang, 1999), p. 697; Mario Mendez, 'The Legal Effect of Community Agreements: Maximalist Treaty Enforcement and Judicial Avoidance Techniques' (2010) 21 *European Journal of International Law* 83.

[17] See Michael Kirby, 'Transnational Judicial Dialogue, Internationalisation of Law and Australian Judges' (2008) 9 *Melbourne Journal of International Law* 171; Anne-Marie Slaughter, 'Judicial Globalization' (1999) 40 *Virginia Journal of International Law* 1103; Melissa A. Waters, 'Mediating Norms and Identity: The Role of Transnational Judicial Dialog in Creating and Enforcing International Law' (2004) 93 *Georgetown Law Journal* 487.

[18] See Vicki C. Jackson, 'Constitutional Comparisons: Convergence, Resistance, Engagement' (2005) 119 *Harvard Law Review* 109; Jeremy Waldron, '"The Experience and Good Thinking Foreign Sources May Convey": Justice Ginsburg and the Use of Foreign Law' (2012) 63 *Hastings Law Journal* 1243.

[19] The arguments have been around at least since John Milton, who in the *Areopagitica* (1644) asked, rhetorically, "[W]ho even knew Truth put to the worse, in a free and open

transnational constitutional dialogue appeared from the beginning to embody similar claims about the ability of sound constitutional ideas to prevail over unsound ones, at least in the long run, when both the sound and the unsound ideas are offered and become the subject of discussion and criticism.

The epistemic argument just described should not, of course, be understood as the claim that better constitutional ideas will necessarily or always prevail over worse ones, even in the long run. That argument would be implausible, and no one makes it. Even the most enthusiastic proponents of the marketplace of ideas acknowledge that bad ideas sometimes survive, and that good ideas are sometimes permanently extinguished in the process of public discussion. Rather, the more plausible and more common version of the "argument from truth" is that the soundness of an idea, constitutional or otherwise, has considerable explanatory power in determining which ideas will be accepted – which will prevail – even as other factors also play a role, and sometimes a determinative one. The most plausible version of the claim is therefore that the soundness of an idea or the truth of a proposition has a significant causal effect on its acceptance for some group of potential acceptors or rejecters. Even as so qualified, however, the argument is still an important one, maintaining that dialogue's epistemic value will generate more sound ideas over time, all other things being more or less equal, than will an environment in which there is less or no dialogue.

To be distinguished from these epistemic arguments for transnational constitutional and legal dialogue are those arguments that treat transnational dialogue as either facilitative or constitutive of transnational cooperation or even something close to transnational unity.[20]

---

encounter?". Subsequent prominent articulations of the same theme dominate chapter 2 ("On the Liberty of Thought and Discussion") of John Stuart Mill's *On Liberty* (1859), and Justice Oliver Wendell Holmes's famous dissenting opinion in *Abrams* v. *United States*, 250 U.S. 616 (1919), where he asserted that the "best test of truth" was the power of an idea "to get itself accepted in the competition of the market." On the general ideas, see Frederick Schauer, *Free Speech: A Philosophical Enquiry* (Cambridge: Cambridge University Press, 1982), ch. 2; Vincent Blasi, 'Holmes and the Marketplace of Ideas' (2004) *Supreme Court Review* 1; Daniel E. Ho and Frederick Schauer, 'Testing the Marketplace of Ideas' (2015) 90 *New York University Law Review* 1160; Eugene Volokh, 'In Praise of the Marketplace of Ideas/Search for Truth as a Theory of Free Speech Protection' (2011) 97 *Virginia Law Review* 595; Christopher T. Wonnell, 'Truth and the Marketplace of Ideas' (1986) 19 *University of California at Davis Law Review* 669.

[20] Most of the existing arguments for constitutional dialogue (see above n 1) do not distinguish sharply between what I am characterizing as the epistemic and constitutive

Understood instrumentally, the argument is that transnational constitutional dialogue is the vehicle for increased transnational cooperation, and that such cooperation is a good in itself, independent of the soundness of the knowledge, ideas, or policies that may emerge from that cooperation. And understood constitutively and not instrumentally, the idea of dialogue becomes more of a metaphor, such that dialogue is now seen as the word used to describe the cooperation itself – cooperation that, again, is often thought to be a good in itself, and cooperation that may or may not rely heavily on the actual speaking or writing that the word "dialogue," understood literally, most often brings to mind.

III   Market Failure in the Marketplace of Constitutional Ideas

Although the distinction I have just drawn between epistemic and constitutive arguments for constitutional dialogue is a useful clarifying preliminary, I want to focus on the epistemic claims, and thus to start with the assumption that some constitutional ideas are better than others, independent of their provenance. That is, I want to assume, for example, that a constitutional regime and a constitutional culture with, say, freedom of political communication or freedom from racial discrimination is better than one with no such freedoms or practices, and that this would be true even if the constitutional protections for freedom of political communication and against racial discrimination were imposed by a dictator, accepted merely for historical reasons, or adopted for any of a number of other reasons whose procedural bona fides might be suspect.[21] The

arguments for constitutional dialogue, but the distinction is nonetheless important in clarifying the issues and evaluating the claims. And the distinction I draw here parallels that in the theory of democracy, where the argument that democratic decision-making inclines towards sounder results and better policies – the epistemic argument – is often distinguished from the argument that democratic decision-making is justified by its moral or political rightness independent of whether it often, usually, or even ever produces better results or sounder policies. See William N. Nelson, *On Justifying Democracy* (London: Routledge & Kegan Paul, 1980).

[21] Indeed, given the extent to which substance-independent political, sociological, psychological, cultural, and economic considerations influence constitutional borrowing and transplantation, the notion that constitutional ideas are typically selected for their substantive merit alone by the "home" country seems fanciful, or at the very least unduly optimistic. For a discussion of the various considerations other than the perceived merit of a constitutional idea that would lead a nation to select one constitutional idea rather than another, see Vlad F. Perju, 'Constitutional Transplants, Borrowings, and Migrations' in Michel Rosenfeld and András Sajó (eds.), *Oxford Handbook of Comparative Constitutional Law* (Oxford: Oxford University Press, 2012), p. 304; Frederick Schauer,

basic point, therefore, is that there are good procedures for constitutional development, and there are good substantive constitutional norms, and the existence of the latter is logically independent of, and not defined by, the former.

With this assumption in place, we can then ask the constitutional dialogue question in a different way: what is the explanatory power of the soundness of a constitutional idea in determining which constitutional ideas will be accepted and which not? Or, to put the same question in a different way, to what extent, if at all, does the soundness of a constitutional idea causally contribute to the possibility that the idea will be accepted and opposing ideas be rejected?

As is often the case, it is important to supplement questions of this variety with the "Compared to what?" question. And here two different comparisons are relevant. One is the comparison with other factors that might explain the acceptance or rejection of constitutional ideas. So, for example, we might think that, in addition to (or instead of) the soundness of a constitutional idea, its acceptance would be a function of the frequency with which an idea is offered, the incentives supporting acceptance or rejection of an idea, the rhetorical or related power with which the idea is articulated, the authority or reputation or charisma of the individuals or institutions offering the idea, the reputational effects to receiver of an idea of accepting or rejecting that idea, the prior beliefs and prejudices of the acceptor or rejecter of an idea, the value to an accepting (or rejecting) community of accepting or rejecting the idea, the costs (in the broadest sense of costs) of identifying the soundness of an idea, and much, much more. We might think of these potential factors, and others like them, as soundness-independent considerations for why some nation or regime might choose to accept one constitutional idea rather than another.

The other important comparison is with non-dialogic approaches to constitutional design and constitutional decision-making. And thus a constitutional decision-maker – possibly a court, possibly a political body, and possibly the individuals and institutions charged with constitutional design – could make a decision without consulting or listening to any of some number of non-national voices. Insofar as dialogue implies

'The Migration of Constitutional Ideas' (2005) 37 *Connecticut Law Review* 904; Frederick Schauer, 'The Politics and Incentives of Legal Transplantation' in Joseph S. Nye, Jr. and John Donahue (eds.), *Governance in a Globalizing World* (Washington, DC: Brookings Institution Press, 2000).

consultation, an alternative would thus be constitutional creation or transformation with no (or, more plausibly, little) consultation of other models or other sources. The question, then, is whether decisions made in such a more unilateral – monologic, if you will – way will be systematically better or worse in some institutional context than those that are made in a more collaborative, cooperative, or dialogic manner.

It is, of course, impossible to offer conclusive or even persuasive answers to any of these questions. Nevertheless, what we do know from other settings and from serious empirical social science research does not provide very much cause for optimism. We know, for example, that the degree of confidence with which a proposition is asserted has a causal effect on the likelihood of its acceptance, even controlling for other attributes of the proposition's assertion, and so too with the attractiveness (along many dimensions) of the offeror of the proposition, the medium in which the proposition is asserted, the recipient's stake in the outcome, the recipient's prior beliefs, and the various different group dynamics that so commonly lead people to accept a proposition simply because others have accepted it.[22]

Plainly some of these factors, which for the most part have been researched and identified in individual social rather than in institutional contexts, are more applicable to cross-national institutional contexts than others. Nevertheless, the existing empirical research does provide some basis for wondering whether the soundness of an idea, even in institutional context, has as much epistemic power as seems often to be asserted. Indeed, there may be some reason to believe that some of the factors just listed may have even greater importance in cross-national institutional settings than they do in individual social ones. For one thing, and even sticking with the assumption that some constitutional ideas are indeed sounder than others, many issues of constitutional design and constitutional substance are normative or prescriptive rather

---

[22] An accessible entry into the research on the various content-independent factors that influence acceptance or rejection of a proposition or idea is Chip Heath and Dan Heath, *Made to Stick: Why Some Ideas Survive and Others Die* (New York: Random House, 2007). For additional references to the primary research on the various factors other than truth or soundness that lead some ideas to be accepted and others rejected, see Ho and Schauer, above n 19. See also William D. Crano and Radmila Prislin (eds.), *Attitudes and Attitude Change* (New York: Taylor & Francis, 2010); Sharon R. Lundgren and Radmila Prislin, 'Motivated Cognitive Processing and Attitude Change' (1998) 24 *Personality & Social Psychology Bulletin* 715.

than factual,[23] and thus not easily susceptible to verifiably correct answers. We may know that Elvis is dead, that the Earth is round and not flat, that astrology and phrenology are false, and that the attack on Pearl Harbor was not a communist plot, but when the questions turn to restrictions on hate speech, or the permissibility of same-sex marriage, or the constitutionality of governmental support for religious education, or the desirability of race-based affirmative action, opinions are divided, and the answers, even if they exist, are more elusive. Indeed, much the same division exists even within the domain of the normative. Most people agree that genocide is morally wrong, but when it comes to what counts as a genocide, or what is subsequently owed to the surviving relatives of its victims, opinions are again much more divided. And against this background, factors other than soundness may play a greater role in selecting ideas when there are substantial societal disagreements or when there are no underlying verifiable facts. We know, for example, that nations often select their legal models for content-independent reasons of national pride, international reputation, regional affiliations, and advantageous trade partnerships,[24] and there is no reason to believe that such factors are wholly absent from the constitutional realm. And to the extent that this is so, then there may be little basis for very much confidence that a process of transnational constitutional dialogue will systematically incline towards soundness, as opposed simply to replicating or even reinforcing the entire range of discourse-independent factors that influence international relations and interactions more generally.

Much the same might apply as well to the non-epistemic claims for transnational constitutional dialogue. There is much talk these days about international or transnational constitutional law,[25] and although much of that talk is about the question whether international law does or should have the attributes of domestic constitutional law, some of it is about whether there is emerging something of an international

---

[23] On the distinction drawn in the text, see Frederick Schauer, 'Facts and the First Amendment' (2010) 57 *UCLA Law Review* 897.

[24] See above n 19.

[25] See, for example, Philip Allott, 'The Emerging Universal Legal System' (2001) 3 *International Legal Forum* 12; Erica de Wet, 'The International Constitutional Order' (2006) 55 *International and Comparative Law Quarterly* 51; Jeffrey L. Dunoff, 'Constitutional Conceits: The WTO's 'Constitution' and the Discipline of International Law' (2006) 17 *European Journal of International Law* 647; Frederick Schauer, 'On the Relationship between International Law and International Constitutionalism' (2017) 11 *Vienna Journal of International Constitutional Law* 1.

constitutional order, complete with its own rules of recognition, its own ultimate rule of recognition[26] (or Grundnorm, for the Kelsenians[27]), and so on. But insofar as this alleged international constitutional order is facilitated by discourse among nations, the question remains whether the order is one that simply replicates existing international power structures, or whether instead it is something more than that, or better than that. And if instead we think of an international constitutional order as simply a degree of interaction and cooperation among nations – dialogue in the metaphorical and not the literal or instrumental sense – then it is not plain just what the idea of dialogue adds to what we otherwise might know and think about the advantages and disadvantages of international cooperation, cooperation that inevitably will have both winners and losers.

IV The Dialogic Model of Constitutional Design

As noted briefly earlier, the idea of dialogue, in a metaphorical sense,[28] is often used nowadays to refer to a model of constitutional decision-making in which the decisions of constitutional courts, whether specialized courts as in Austria, Germany, and South Africa or courts of general jurisdiction as in the United States and Canada, are subject to some sort of further legislative action and are thus in important ways nonfinal. Because the decisions of courts are thus subject to legislative override or other action, and because the decisions of legislatures are themselves also subject to judicial review, "dialogue" has emerged as the metaphor to describe this serially nonfinal approach to constitutional design and constitutional adjudication.

Although the idea of dialogue here is metaphorical and not usefully accurate, many of the same considerations that apply to literal dialogue appear to be applicable here as well. When a court and a legislature are engaged in a dialogue, even a metaphorical one, there is no reason to believe that the dynamics of power and institutional design that are otherwise applicable to the two institutions would be less

---

[26] The well-known terminology is from H. L. A. Hart, *The Concept of Law* (Oxford: Oxford University Press, 3rd ed., 2012).

[27] Hans Kelsen, *The Pure Theory of Law*, Max Knight (trans.) (Berkeley: University of California Press, 1967).

[28] On dialogue as a metaphor, I am indebted to the valuable (and also skeptical) analysis of the dialogue metaphor in the context of inter-branch interaction in Aileen Kavanagh, 'The Lure and the Limits of Dialogue' (2016) 66 *University of Toronto Law Journal* 83.

applicable here.[29] It is of course possible that a dialogue between two differently constituted and differently accountable institutions will produce results superior to those that would be produced by either institution acting on its own, but confidence in such a process is quite similar to confidence in the marketplace of ideas to produce epistemically better outcomes. In both cases the question is whether the process of talking, literally or metaphorically, will more likely cause bad ideas to give way to good ones than to cause good ideas to give way to bad ones. And once again, there appears scant reason to believe that this is systematically true.

This is not to say, however, that the process described metaphorically as constitutional dialogue is not more representative and thus in some way more democratic. And thus it is worth emphasizing that dialogue may serve various purposes, including but not limited to a conception of democracy, that are independent of the effort to identify better social or policy ideas. But we err if we fail to distinguish clearly between arguments that dialogue locates better social or policy outcomes from arguments that the very process of dialogue has outcome-independent processual virtues.

If dialogue is valued because of its embodiment of democratic values rather than on account of its epistemic virtues, the argument then turns into one about the legitimacy of democracy itself. And although there are epistemic arguments for democracy,[30] the issues are again complex. As an epistemic matter, or as a matter of selecting the best policies, democracy may have the advantage of making bad outcomes more difficult, even as it makes good ones more difficult as well. And thus evaluating even the epistemic arguments needs to engage in a more rigorous process of decision-making under uncertainty, where we weigh the expected harm of a mistaken identification of truth against the expected harm of a mistaken non-identification of truth. But even apart from the epistemic considerations, it may be that representative government in some form or another is simply more legitimate, and thus more morally desirable, independent of the substantive value of the outcomes it generates. This may well be so, but our progression to that conclusion does not appear to have been assisted by the idea of dialogue, and may even have been impeded by it.

---

[29] On institutional design and its relationship to dialogue, see Grégoire Webber, 'Past, Present, and Justice in the Exercise of Judicial Responsibility' in this volume.

[30] See Nelson, *On Justifying Democracy*, above n 20.

V   Conclusion

"Dialogue" – or, sometimes, "discourse," or, sometimes "deliberation" – is a widely touted approach to political decision-making these days. But if the methods of dialogue or its approximate synonyms are to be taken literally, that is, if they are understood to refer to people or institutions or branches of government actually talking to each other, then the question remains about whether talking, in large-scale political settings, is a comparatively reliable approach to decision-making. And if instead the methods described in terms of dialogue and discourse are simply metaphors for various forms of multi-institutional decision-making, then either the same pathologies that apply to talking may apply here as well, or the question reduces to assessing the moral and political considerations relevant to the legitimacy of various forms of governmental decision-making. These last are serious questions, perhaps the most serious there are, but it is not clear that translating them into the language of dialogue and discourse gets us very much closer to answering them.

16

Constitutional Conversations in Britain (in Europe)

RICHARD EKINS

I Introduction

One cannot govern well without deliberation. Whoever rules should reason about how to secure the common good and should choose reasonable means to this complex end. Self-government is impossible without public deliberation, for we only govern ourselves if we reason together and choose jointly how we should live.[1] It follows that law-making should be carried out in a way that makes it possible for us jointly to deliberate and decide. The exercise of other public powers, including the choice of general policies and the direction of public resources, should be framed and limited by such laws and overseen and evaluated by a democratic public and its representatives. The object of deliberation is decision, and we converse with one another in a political community – the members of whom are participants in this shared conversation and joint action – about how best to decide.

Representative institutions make joint deliberation and reasoned decision possible. Public deliberation takes place within and between such institutions, as well as amongst the public at large, that is apart from (and about) these institutions. The conversation amongst a self-governing people is complex. Some arrangements amongst institutions will help support reasonable public deliberation that is likely to result in good government. Other arrangements will frustrate or otherwise distort this deliberation, perhaps by obscuring its objects or by discouraging citizens from sharing in it.

In the Westminster tradition, Parliament stands at the centre of a public conversation about what is to be done. The courts have not been parties to this conversation, but have upheld settled law, which forms part of the framework within which deliberation takes place and is itself

---

[1] Richard Ekins, 'How to Be a Free People' (2013) 58 *American Journal of Jurisprudence* 163.

the object of public deliberation and decision. In the United Kingdom, this arrangement has been unbalanced by a changing understanding of the judicial role and by the reach of international obligations that subject the United Kingdom to the jurisdiction of international courts. In this way, new conversations have been introduced to the British constitution, including exchanges between domestic and European courts, the main significance of which has been to compromise parliamentary democracy. The United Kingdom's decision to leave the EU follows in part from the alienation of citizens from European lawmaking and action and from a corresponding concern to restore self-government. In reaching and implementing that decision to leave, one sees the capacity of parliamentary democracy to enable the political community to reason and act together, but also the risks posed by wayward domestic judicial action.

II The Dynamics of Westminster Parliamentary Democracy

The origins of Parliament lie in the king's need to secure the agreement of his subjects, especially the great men of the realm, to taxation and high policy. The gathering of persons capable of giving the consent of the realm readily formed a group well-placed to converse, both about the king's proposals as well as about other problems and grievances. This was a forum for deliberation and decision. Its early success, in England, was to help support the royal will, such that it became the forum in which the king acted with the advice and consent of the assembled realm, both in making decisions that were to bind all and in uniting the realm in action against others (in the Tudor period, against Rome).[2] The kings required the support of their parliaments, which came increasingly to demand and at times to be able to insist upon a greater share in decision about the government of the realm. The tragic impasse of the Stuart period was resolved thereafter in favour of the Houses of Parliament, leading in time to the Crown itself acting only on the direction of responsible ministers, drawn from and accountable to Parliament rather than truly servants of the king.

Parliament remains the centre of a public conversation about what should be done, in a form that is capable of reaching and communicating authoritative decisions. The government is drawn from and answerable to the Houses of Parliament and the function of Parliament is to form

---

[2] Jeffrey Goldsworthy, *Parliamentary Sovereignty* (Oxford: Oxford University Press, 1999).

and sustain a government, entrusting confidence in a set of ministers who are to direct the great offices of state and voting to fund the administration they lead. Discussion within Parliament will consider what it is that we should jointly do, attending either to some general problem or to some particular proposal for legislation or policy for executive action. This discussion will naturally run into a wider conversation about the record in office of the government, in the sense both of the leading ministers and the majority support party.

The opposition presents itself as a government in waiting, aiming to fracture the unity of the majority party and to establish itself as a credible alternative in the coming election.[3] The duty of the opposition is to outline an alternative, but especially to constantly scrutinise the government, to give voice to objections or overlooked points or problems. But this is not exclusively the function of the opposition. Members of the majority party also monitor the actions of ministers in part to determine whether they continue to warrant support, which turns on their competence and manner in office: ministers who disdain parliamentary accountability rapidly find their position becomes untenable.

The conversations in Parliament about social problems, government policy, and proposed legislation intersect with, and contribute to, wider public conversation. Likewise, deliberation within Parliament has different dimensions, varying sharply in tone and form from Prime Minister's Questions to second reading stage to committee hearings. The action of ministers outside Parliament forms the focus for much discussion within Parliament, with ministerial action and communication (with journalists and the public) both tracking, pre-empting, and driving parliamentary discussion. The large numbers of MPs, their selection in elections across the country, the division into parties united around different principles and interests, and the complex structure of the institution all make considerable space – by design – for a very wide range of perspectives and arguments to be brought to bear.[4] This helps make better policy and lawmaking, but crucially it makes it plausible to take Parliament to represent the whole, to be the nation engaged in conversation, even if much public deliberation rightly and inevitably takes place entirely outside it.[5]

---

[3] Grégoire Webber, 'Loyal Opposition and the Political Constitution' (2017) 37 *Oxford Journal of Legal Studies* 357.

[4] Richard Ekins, *The Nature of Legislative Intent* (Oxford: Oxford University Press, 2012), ch. 6.

[5] The devolution settlements in relation to Northern Ireland, Scotland, and Wales complicate but do not displace this analysis. They introduce a new set of representative

One sees in the key relationships that constitute parliamentary democracy a series of nested conversations, the structure and drivers of which warrant closer attention. The government engages with the Commons about the merits of its policies and with a view to securing support for proposed legislation. Why? Without the ongoing support of the Commons there is no government. The traditional lever of withholding supply is never used, but confidence remains essential, not only because of the convention but also because ministers require political support to succeed in advancing policy and in contesting the next election. In any case, ministers are already members of Parliament, and will remain so if they cease to be ministers: they address the House as leading members, not as interlopers. And they share with other members, and the wider public, the view that every government *should* answer to Parliament, should explain itself to the Houses and thence to the public, and should have to defend its legislative proposals or executive policies in this forum.[6]

The relationship of the government to the Lords is similar but different. The Lords lacks the power or legitimacy of the Commons, but can make life difficult by delaying or vetoing proposed primary or secondary legislation. The Lords have a weak but real entitlement to participate in the legislative process and in scrutiny of the executive. Failure to engage with the Lords would be politically damning, not least since it would surrender to one's opponents a prominent forum in which to develop criticism of the government. There are other reasons for engagement too. The difference in tone between Commons and Lords, and the lesser political salience of the latter, makes it less risky for the government to agree to changes in legislation in the latter.[7] Interestingly, these changes were often first broached in the Commons and may be picked up by the Lords on advice from the other House. The Commons and Lords must cooperate if legislation is to be enacted in orderly fashion. The Commons concede that the Lords have a contribution to make to the process, at

---

institutions into public life, and call forth a new set of conversations between these institutions and their Westminster counterparts, echoing the relationships that obtained for a time between the Imperial Parliament and representative legislatures in settled colonies. The important difference is that all in the United Kingdom are represented in Westminster and in a sense form a single democratic public. This chapter does not otherwise consider devolution (but see the discussion at n 69).

[6] Timothy Endicott, *Parliament and the Prerogative: From the Case of Proclamations to Miller* (Policy Exchange, 2017).

[7] Susanna Kalitowski, 'Rubber Stamp or Cockpit? The Impact of Parliament on Government Legislation' (2008) 61 *Parliamentary Affairs* 694.

least for now. The Lords defer to the Commons on financial matters and in relation to manifesto commitments, partly by way of long-standing convention and partly by recognition of political reality and moral principle. The Lords are conscious of their weak position and of the risk that they will overstep the mark and provoke abolition. And the Parliament Acts 1911 and 1949 may break the deadlock.[8]

The structure of the Houses of Parliament makes provision for extensive, far-reaching public deliberation, both within and between each House.[9] The government is that subset of leading parliamentarians that enjoys the confidence of others and is active in and in relation to both Houses, and is the bridge between Parliament and the vast machinery of state by which that machinery is subject to public scrutiny and decision. In the mutual dependency between government and majority party in the Commons, the cooperative contestation between opposition and government in both Houses, and the support provided by the weakened Lords to the Commons, one finds a series of relationships that jointly constitute a framework for public deliberation capable of culminating in reasonable action. These lines of conversation enrich the public conversation without obscuring the location of responsibility. There is much that can and does go wrong, but taken as a whole this is a remarkably effective way of making provision for reasoned self-government.

III   Ordinary Judging and Constitutional Dialogue

Parliament has long been the centre for public deliberation and choice in the British constitution. Notwithstanding that the highest appellate court was for a time a committee of one chamber of the legislature, the courts have been separate from the political authorities and have not been a main forum for public deliberation or choice. The duty of the courts has been to adjudicate disputes in accordance with settled law and, incidentally, thereby to clarify and perhaps develop existing legal propositions. The courts have not obviously stood to Parliament or executive as participants in a conversation about what should be done. Their duty has instead been to adjudicate disputes, including disputes with the

---

[8] The Acts make provision for bills to become Acts of Parliament notwithstanding the Lords do not assent, provided certain conditions are satisfied. See further, Richard Ekins, 'Acts of Parliament and the Parliament Acts' (2007) 123 *Law Quarterly Review* 91.

[9] Ekins, *The Nature of Legislative Intent*, chs. 6 and 8.

executive, in accordance with the law of the land, including law that Parliament has made.[10]

The traditional judicial role has not involved dialogue with executive or Parliament, save in the attenuated sense that the Crown addresses the courts in the course of litigation at the conclusion of which the courts may declare authoritatively the Crown's legal duty, and may also quash actions of servants of the Crown that are in excess of power or are otherwise unlawful. True, the way in which the courts understand Parliament's enactments or the way in which the courts develop or declare the common law are of interest to executive and Parliament and novel or important decisions on point may attract a response. But this is just to say that there may be feedback between adjudication, including especially adjudication that seems (perhaps in retrospect) to break new legal ground, and the future development of policy and/or the revision of the statute book, including to reform the common law. In some cases, judges refuse counsel's invitation to develop the common law, reasoning that any such change must be left to the legislature, which is better placed to undertake it (with reference to capacity to devise sound policy and to introduce it in a way that is consistent with the rule of law).[11] This refusal contemplates, and often expressly invites, subsequent legislative action, but this too is only dialogue in a limited sense. The court's act is still to adjudicate in accordance with settled law, hoping that the injustice or inaptness of that law will later be revised.

Is there any more explicit – self-conscious and institutionally grounded – mode of exchange between court and government – or legislature – in the Westminster constitution? Judicial review of executive action often involves the courts requiring some decision to be made afresh, taking into account some consideration or extending a hearing to some person. This exchange involves the courts addressing the executive as to the bounds within which it is free to act. Within those bounds the executive remains free to choose, but of course it may be that the judicial specification rules out some options entirely. In many cases, the judicial action informs, without taking over, the subsequent executive deliberation and action. Having said this, the executive is not free to reject the terms on which the court stipulates that any subsequent

---

[10] For further information, see Grégoire Webber's chapter in this volume.

[11] John Finnis, 'Judicial Lawmaking and the "Living" Instrumentalisation of the ECHR' in Nicholas Barber, Richard Ekins, and Paul Yowell (eds.), *Lord Sumption and the Limits of the Law* (Hart Publishing, 2016).

deliberation and action is to proceed: the judicial contribution is by way of a decision that binds, not by way of a defeasible proposal.

The courts have enjoyed no equivalent capacity to oversee the actions of the sovereign Parliament or even the Houses of Parliament, which each guard their privileges jealously. But the judicial evaluation of the relationship between Parliament and executive has informed how the courts approach review of the latter. For some judges, the late twentieth century confirmed that the executive dominated Parliament, such that the government's accountability to Parliament was more nominal than real.[12] This perception drove an expansion of the scope and intensity of judicial review, with judges aiming to fill the void. Is this dialogue? Not strictly, but it is related, for the court reorders its own function by aiming to supplement or bypass what it perceives to be the dysfunctional dialogue between executive and legislature. One of the fruits of this reordering has been increasing judicial interference with the exercise of legislative mechanisms that are designed to facilitate parliamentary accountability. Take two examples. First, the extension of judicial review to the substance of the government's response to ombudsman reports, where the ombudsman is a parliamentary office that reports to a committee, and which can table reports in Parliament criticising that very government response.[13] This judicial action takes for granted, wrongly as it happens, that parliamentary accountability in such cases is weak, and, worse, derails the relationship that should hold between government and Parliament.[14]

The second example is more complex. The Freedom of Information Act empowers ministers to veto decisions of the Information Commissioner or Tribunal (a judicial body hearing appeals from the Commissioner) ordering disclosure of information on the grounds that the balance of public interest requires as much.[15] The minister in question is then accountable to Parliament for this decision and the Commissioner may table a report before Parliament commenting on the exercise of this power if he or she so chooses. The Supreme Court in *Evans* viewed this

---

[12] For (critical) discussion, see Timothy Endicott, *Administrative Law* (3rd ed., Oxford: Oxford University Press, 2015), ch. 2.

[13] *R (Bradley)* v. *Secretary of State for Work and Pensions* [2008] EWCA Civ 36; [2008] 3 All ER 1116; *R (Equitable Members Action Group)* v. *HM Treasury* [2009] EWHC (Admin) 2495.

[14] Jason Varuhas, *Judicial Capture of Political Accountability* (Policy Exchange, 2016).

[15] Freedom of Information Act 2000, s. 53.

power with suspicion and, by majority, quashed its effective exercise.[16] The (dubious) major premise has been that making provision for ministerial override in this way is to flout the rule of law. The minor premise has been that the political accountability of ministers, which the Act aims to enable, is no substitute for judicial action.

Judicial disdain for political accountability has serious consequences, including, as I say, the improper and problematic extension of judicial review of executive action. It also supports – or is at least related to – another unfortunate course of action, viz. rationalisation of an unsound mode of statutory interpretation. The principle of legality is an odd name for the sensible idea that one should be slow to conclude that Parliament has intended to legislate in ways that are inconsistent with the existing constitutional order, including the framework of individual rights and liberties.[17] Still, the interpreter's task is to infer what Parliament decided in enacting this or that statute and the presumption of continuity is thus defeasible. In his powerful articulation of the principle in the late 1990s, Lord Hoffmann argued that its virtue was in part that it required any breach of fundamental rights to be squarely faced by Parliament rather than to be adopted by a side-wind.[18] Parliament should, I say, consider the consequences of its actions with care, and ought to take particular care to make only the changes to the law that it truly intends. This truth, which should inform the reasoning of any reasonable legislator, helps support the interpretive disposition Lord Hoffmann outlines, for one should expect Parliament to introduce major changes directly and clearly. The risk in this approach is that it slips from a sound presumption to an imposition, which licenses judges refusing to do what Parliament clearly intended.

One sees this risk in action in my second example from this section, in Lord Neuberger's lead judgment,[19] which sought to impose an admittedly weak interpretation on the statute, such that the ministerial veto was almost never open to use. The judges rationalised this interpretation by insisting that it was consistent with the principle of legality and by reasoning that Parliament would remain free to legislate more clearly if it chose to do so. Thus, the judges excused themselves from the charge of

---

[16] *Evans v. Attorney General* [2015] UKSC 21; [2015] AC 787.
[17] Phillip Sales, 'A Comparison of the Principle of Legality with Section 3 of the Human Rights Act 1998' (2009) 125 *Law Quarterly Review* 598.
[18] *R v. Secretary of State for the Home Department, Ex Parte Simms* [2000] 2 AC 115, 131.
[19] *Evans v. Attorney General* [2015] UKSC 21.

flouting parliamentary sovereignty by taking the court to be in a dialogue with Parliament, a dialogue in which Parliament speaks first in legislating, the court speaks next in interpreting, and Parliament may speak again in legislating in response – which the court would then have to interpret and so forth. Some academic commentators have stressed this feature of the judgment,[20] and indeed have made it more explicit than did the judges, and have reasoned further that the government's apparent decision now not to propose legislation in response is a tacit affirmation of the court.[21]

The judicial duty to obey the law is not conditional in this way, such that one is free to flout the law once, provided that one then falls into line if Parliament later responds (not that all commentators would accept the latter condition in any case).[22] The failure of Parliament to respond does not launder the earlier judicial malpractice – no subsequent parliamentary action, not even deeming legislation, can make it the case that the court was right at the time of adjudication to act thus. It is confused to think that Parliament's failure to respond means that it approves of the judicial misinterpretation. The dialogic theory here just presumes (a) that the judicial action will always come to the attention of the political authorities and (b) that parliamentary time will or should always be made available to address it. But neither of these presuppositions is well made, and even legislators fully committed to the rule of law and the separation of powers will often not be able to justify the time required to put right the judicial misinterpretation. The assertion that the court and legislature here participate in a dialogue is unsound and wrongly takes the possibility of legislative response to entail the courts are free to depart from what Parliament likely intended in order to force Parliament to be clearer still.

The duty of the court is to adjudicate disputes in accordance with settled law. This adjudication often limits the executive's freedom of action, requiring it to act within the bounds of the law. There is a standing risk that such review may overreach, especially if the court aims

---

[20] Mark Elliott, 'A Tangled Constitutional Web: The Black Spider Memos and the British Constitution's Relational Architecture' [2015] *Public Law* 539.

[21] Mark Elliott, 'A Postscript on the *Evans* Case: The Report of the Freedom of Information Commission and the Government's Response', *Public Law For Everyone*, 2 March 2016. https://publiclawforeveryone.com/2016/03/02/a-postscript-on-the-evans-case-the-report-of-the-independent-commission-on-freedom-of-information-and-the-governments-response/.

[22] Phillip A. Joseph, 'Parliament, the Courts, and the Collaborative Enterprise' (2004) 15 *King's College Law Journal* 321.

to compensate for the perceived deficiencies of the conversation between ministers and other parliamentarians. Judicial action may, and often should, spur legislative action in response, reforming problematic common law, correcting a statutory scheme, or even putting right the misinterpretation of some scheme. But the prospect of such a response should not empower courts: it is a discipline, not a permission. It is unsound to think of statutory interpretation as dialogue, and doing so invites judges to exploit the dynamics of legislative feedback, in which scarcities of parliamentary time and the changing politics of the legislature provide opportunities for courts to impose novel meanings without fear of response. The rule of law condemns such exploitation, which loose talk of dialogue is likely to encourage.

IV Rights Adjudication and Public Deliberation

The decision in *Evans* did not involve the Human Rights Act 1998 (HRA) or the European Convention on Human Rights (ECHR). But it is fair to speculate that without the changes in judicial culture ushered in by the enactment of the HRA the judges would not have been likely to misinterpret the statute or to review intensely the exercise of the power.[23] How does the HRA bear on constitutional dialogue? The Act partly incorporates the ECHR, giving these 'convention rights' domestic legal force (they are attached as a schedule to the Act): the rights limit the scope of lawful public action and are directly actionable in court, save to the extent that another statute requires or permits another course of action. In the event of possible conflicts between convention rights and another statute, s. 3 of the HRA requires one to strive to read the other statute consistently with convention rights. When this is not possible, the superior courts have a statutory discretion under s. 4 to declare the statute in question incompatible with convention rights. This declaration does not change the legal rights and duties of the parties (but does trigger a Henry VIII power, authorising ministers to amend the statute).[24]

Many scholars have taken the HRA to be a measure intended to create a new constitutional dialogue about rights between court and Parliament.[25]

---

[23] See further, Richard Ekins and Christopher Forsyth, *Judging the Public Interest: The rule of law vs. the rule of courts* (Policy Exchange, 2015).

[24] HRA, s. 10.

[25] Alison L. Young, *Parliamentary Sovereignty and the Human Rights Act* (Hart Publishing, 2008). See also Alison Young's chapter in this volume.

However, the point of the Act seems to me to have been to minimise the number of cases in which the United Kingdom is held by the European Court of Human Rights (ECtHR) to be in breach of its obligations under the ECHR, which bind the United Kingdom as a matter of international law.[26] The HRA introduces convention rights into British law with this aim in mind, not, I suggest, intending to foster a dialogue between domestic courts and Parliament about human rights. The Act does bear on parliamentary deliberation quite directly, by requiring ministers to speak to the rights-compatibility of bills they introduce to the Houses of Parliament.[27] For the courts, the task is either to interpret legislation consistently with convention rights, such that no opportunity for dialogue arises (save perhaps in the attenuated way outlined in the previous section), or to consider whether to declare the legislation inconsistent with convention rights. The latter certainly looks as if it might involve a contribution to a constitutional dialogue, articulating for Parliament a view as to the merits of the statute but leaving responsibility for change to Parliament. But, importantly, the Act may require the courts effectively to relay the conclusion about how the ECtHR would likely understand the statute. That is, the domestic courts are not so much developing their own views about convention rights as articulating the likely position as a matter of international law, per the statutory vehicle for partial incorporation.

The HRA aims to square an increased judicial role in rights protection with the United Kingdom's long-standing commitment to parliamentary sovereignty. Sections 3 and 4 are fundamental to the scheme of the Act. The interplay between them is significant, for s. 4 only comes into view when it is not possible, in the terms of s. 3, to interpret the statute consistently with convention rights. In the early years of the HRA, the courts often seemed anxious to avoid recourse to s. 4, reasoning that Parliament had taken for granted that most statutes would be consistent with convention rights and that a s. 4 declaration would be an exceptional event.[28] Many judges took a s. 4 declaration to be a failure of the Act, for it would leave the applicant without just satisfaction and the United Kingdom exposed before Strasbourg. Strictly, this must be a

---

[26] Phillip Sales and Richard Ekins, 'Rights-Consistent Interpretation and the Human Rights Act 1998' (2011) 127 *Law Quarterly Report* 217.

[27] HRA, s. 19.

[28] See further Aileen Kavanagh, *Constitutional Review under the UK Human Rights Act 1998* (Cambridge: Cambridge University Press, 2009).

confused reading of the Act, for s. 4 is part and parcel of the statutory scheme and it is no failure at all when s. 3 does not license reinterpretation of a statute. But it confirms the extent to which many judges were committed to avoiding s. 4. The advantage of s. 3 was thus that it was thought to provide a much better remedy and to avoid risk of an adverse Strasbourg finding. Further, unlike s. 4, it avoided any judicial confrontation with Parliament. True, Parliament might respond but, as I noted in the previous section, this may happen only rarely.

The misuse of s. 3 to avoid confrontation (or conversation) with Parliament is in evidence in R v. A (No 2),[29] in which the court relied on s. 3 to undermine the United Kingdom's new rape shield legislation (enacted after the HRA but before the HRA came into force). The statute ruled out cross-examination of complainants about their sexual history, save in one of three specified circumstances. The court held, first, that the scheme would breach the accused's right to a fair trial unless he could cross-examine the complainant in a fourth circumstance, and second, that the scheme should therefore be interpreted to permit cross-examination whenever a fair trial requires as much. This interpretation effectively destroys the statute. The court's action is explicable partly because it was concerned about the justice of this trial, which a declaration of incompatibility would not have addressed. But it turns also on unwillingness so early in the HRA's life to challenge publicly a recently enacted statute, especially one that involves a clash between the lawyerly status quo and feminist critique thereof. Much better to reinstate that status quo quietly, not least since there is no guarantee that Parliament would have agreed with the judicial declaration. Entering into dialogue at this point and on those terms, the court may have reasoned, would have placed judges in a vulnerable position and risked damage to the HRA and their institutional heft.

There have not been very many s. 4 declarations, all things considered. And most such have prompted, eventually, legislation to change the law.[30] Quite arguably this is the HRA working as it should, bringing to Parliament's attention legislation that would likely be found in breach before Strasbourg and inviting Parliament to remedy the situation. The courts have interpreted s. 3 to authorise very radical reinterpretation

---

[29] R v. A (No 2) [2002] 1 AC 45.
[30] Jeff King, 'Parliament's Role following Declarations of Incompatibility under the Human Rights Act' in Murray Hunt, Hayley Hooper, and Paul Yowell (eds.), Parliaments and Human Rights (Hart Publishing, 2015).

indeed, the limits on which have had less to do with Parliament's intentions and more to do with perceived limits on the institutional capacity of the court.[31] Hence, courts have sometimes declared legislation incompatible precisely in order to leave to Parliament the question of quite how to replace some problematic scheme with another workable scheme.[32] For a time, scholars speculated that a convention was emerging that Parliament would (should) always legislate in conformity with the judicial declaration.[33] This convention would have made the exchange even less dialogic. But the alleged convention was overstated as Parliament's flat refusal to license prisoner voting has demonstrated.[34] (One might add that the alleged convention fits awkwardly with the scheme of the Act and with the larger governing principles of parliamentary sovereignty and responsible government.) This unsteady development rather confirms that the HRA has introduced an uncertain relationship between courts and Parliament, which involves a mix of collaboration, confrontation, and diversion.

One sees confrontation in the most famous HRA case of all: *A v. Home Secretary*.[35] The Appellate Committee of the House of Lords quashed the government's derogation from the ECHR and declared the legislation authorising detention of non-British suspected terrorists to be incompatible with the ECHR, most notably with the right to liberty. The declaration succeeded in the sense that it politically crushed the government's policy and prompted legislative change. The case is regularly hailed as a victory for the HRA, vindicating its potential to give voice to marginalised persons, in this case to non-British terror suspects. But there are reasons to temper enthusiasm for the judgment. The statutory regime authorised detention *pending deportation*, which makes the focus on non-British suspect rather less arbitrary and discriminatory than the court suggests. Moreover, the court fails to consider whether the scheme can be read consistently with the right to liberty. The statute should have been read to authorise continuing detention for so long as a genuine intention to deport was in place, together with activity to remove the obstacles to deportation. The court did not attempt any such reading and

---

[31] *Ghaidan v. Godin-Mendoza* [2004] 2 AC 557; see further, Kavanagh, *Constitutional Review under the UK Human Rights Act*, above n 28.

[32] *Bellinger v. Bellinger* [2003] UKHL 21; [2003] 2 AC 467.

[33] Jeff King, 'Rights and the Rule of Law in Third Way Constitutionalism' (2014) 30 *Constitutional Commentary* 101.

[34] See also John Finnis's chapter in this volume concerning prisoner voting.

[35] [2005] 2 AC 68.

indeed, extraordinarily, did not even mention s. 3 of the HRA at all. The court was intent, it seems clear, on crushing the legislative policy, on condemning it as arbitrary and discriminatory and as a regime for indefinite detention rather than a regime for ongoing detention while efforts to deport were in progress.

These features of the case have been little noted.[36] They confirm that the interplay between ss. 3 and 4 can be used either to avoid confrontation, as in *R* v. *A (No 2)*, or to engineer it. This is not a healthy dialogue in which judicial action aids citizens and their representatives in better determining what justice requires. The context of the Act, in which the international dimension looms large, tends to undercut the potential for such dialogue in any case, for it supports the framing of each declaration as a legal conclusion about what rights require – not a conclusion about the fundamental law of the United Kingdom, it is true, but about the relevant body of human rights law, with the implication (effective, for a time, in the political realm at least) being that Parliament acts unlawfully if it fails to conform.

My argument about the significance of the international dimension of the HRA risks overstatement and in any case may have been overtaken by events. The domestic courts for many years aimed to follow settled Strasbourg jurisprudence and to interpret convention rights neither more nor less generously than that jurisprudence requires.[37] This consensus began to fracture about ten years ago, and the fractures have widened since. I consider with more care in the following section some dimensions of the British courts' engagement with the ECtHR. For now the point is that domestic courts are increasingly willing to aim to secure by interpretation or declaration understandings of convention rights that go beyond what Strasbourg insists upon, viz. to take as rights-incompatible legislation to which the ECtHR would not object.[38] This is a transformation of the HRA and one that perhaps oddly presages its possible repeal and replacement with a British Bill of Rights.

One sees the willingness to go beyond Strasbourg in the important recent case of *Nicklinson*,[39] which concerned a challenge to England's

---

[36] But see John Finnis, 'Nationality, Alienage and Constitutional Principle' (2007) 123 *Law Quarterly Review* 417.

[37] The so-called mirror principle, per *R (Ullah)* v. *Special Adjudicator* [2004] UKHL 26; [2004] 2 AC 323.

[38] *In re G (Adoption: Unmarried Couple)* [2008] UKHL 38; [2009] 1 AC 173.

[39] *R (Nicklinson)* v. *Ministry of Justice* [2014] UKSC 38; [2014] 3 WLR 200.

ban on assisted suicide. The Supreme Court divided on the question of whether to declare the Suicide Act 1961 rights-incompatible. Five of nine judges were willing in principle so to do, but only two were willing to do so here and now (the other three thought more argument was required and that Parliament should have the chance first to amend the law). This is striking because Strasbourg has ruled, in a number of cases,[40] that a ban on assisted suicide does not breach the ECHR. If the Supreme Court had made a declaration, as it contemplated doing and will shortly be invited again to do (the judgment practically invited such a further action in the event that Parliament failed to change the law), it would have been misleading had it failed to make clear that unlike other declarations under the Act this declaration would entail no prediction of likely adverse finding before Strasbourg. Thus, Parliament could reject – or ignore – the declaration safe that in so doing it would not be letting slide a breach of international law.

The case has been misunderstood, with some arguing that a majority of the court did hold the Act incompatible but had declined to exercise the discretionary power to make a declaration.[41] Not so. Of the three judges who thought a declaration could in principle be made but were not willing yet to conclude the Suicide Act was incompatible, two were rather clearly inclined to think the Act was incompatible (the third was less clear). These judges intended to pressure Parliament to change the law, with the threat of a subsequent declaration looming in the air, but without having to pay the cost of making a declaration and perhaps starting a confrontation. Alternatively, they aimed to achieve the same outcome as if a declaration had been made – creating political pressure on Parliament to change the law – notwithstanding that a declaration could not properly be made because the matter had not been fully argued. Either way, these judges attempted to make a declaration without making a declaration. It is perhaps fitting then that in the debate in the Commons that followed, considering the merits of a bill to loosen the ban on assisted suicide, the judgment was given short shrift by most legislators.

The Commons rejected, by a strong margin, the bill in question. Unsurprisingly, shortly thereafter new litigation was initiated, seeking a declaration that the Suicide Act flouts convention rights. After a hotly contested permission stage, the Divisional Court and Court of Appeal

---

[40] Most notably in *Pretty* v. *UK* [2002] ECHR 423 (29 April 2002).
[41] Sir Stephen Sedley, 'The Right to Die' *London Review of Books*, 27 August 2015.

rejected the application. While the Supreme Court has recently refused permission to appeal, it will at some point, when the inevitable next attempt to secure a declaration reaches the Supreme Court, have to decide whether to follow through on its implicit threat (although by then the court will have quite a different composition).[42] Would a declaration have been a helpful contribution to public deliberation? It would not have been giving voice to a marginal or overlooked group of citizens: the British public is divided on the merits of the ban on assisted suicide and much (most) elite opinion opposes the ban. Pace Lord Neuberger's retrospective gloss on *Nicklinson*,[43] this is not an issue that the political process has failed to consider which the court can help Parliament to grasp. Rather, Parliament has repeatedly considered the question and has again and again decided that the ban should remain, not least because it protects the rights of the vulnerable. In making a declaration, the courts would thus be applying a thumb to the scales of this ongoing deliberation, taking advantage of the machinery of the HRA (with its focus on ECHR compatibility) to assert that human rights require permission to assist suicide. Many citizens, including vulnerable persons and their families, reasonably see Parliament's continuing resistance to the campaign for law reform as a victory for human rights. This is a victory secured by public deliberation and decision in Parliament, a decision that judicial action threatens unfairly to unsettle and a deliberation it would distort.

V   Dialogue between Strasbourg and the Supreme Court

I noted earlier the drift over time in the understanding of 'convention rights' and their relationship to the ECHR as authoritatively interpreted by the ECtHR. Domestic courts are increasingly willing, as *Nicklinson* confirms, to go beyond Strasbourg and thus to develop a domestic rights jurisprudence under the banner of the HRA.[44] This development should be seen alongside the increasing tendency of courts to invite arguments about right to be couched in terms of the common law itself.[45] The rationale for replacing the HRA with a British Bill of Rights has been said

---

[42] *R (Conway)* v. *Secretary of State for Justice* [2017] EWHC 2447 and [2018] EWCA Civ. 1431.

[43] See for example Lord Neuberger, "'Judge Not, That Ye Be Not Judged': Judging Judicial Decision-Making', F. A. Mann Lecture 2015.

[44] See *R (Tigere)* v. *Secretary of State for Business, Innovation and Skills* [2015] UKSC 57.

[45] *R (Osborn)* v. *Parole Board* [2013] UKSC 61; [2014] AC 1115; *Kennedy* v. *Information Commissioner* [2014] UKSC 20; [2014] 2 WLR 808.

to be partly to enable domestic courts to develop rights jurisprudence in ways more consistent with the common law tradition, without being required to follow Strasbourg in lockstep. Opponents of change have argued that this is the status quo in any case, per s. 2 of the HRA, which requires courts to take ECtHR rulings into account but does not, in terms, make them authoritative. Still, the 'mirror principle' was for many years good law,[46] and even now it is not quite the case that domestic courts are willing to flout settled Strasbourg rulings they think unsound. This section considers some features of the relationship – the dialogue – between the ECtHR and the domestic courts.

The convention rights introduced to British law by the HRA are at a minimum heavily determined by Strasbourg jurisprudence. Argument before the courts very often turns on what to make of some line of Strasbourg cases, including cases where the United Kingdom was not strictly a party. The reason for this is obvious: it seems wholly consistent with the structure and point of the HRA, and the alternative is that judges inadvertently place the United Kingdom in breach of its international obligations.[47] Other European states incorporate the ECHR less directly, having their own homegrown constitutional rights adjudication, which may make reference to or be informed by Strasbourg, but which does not rely on it so clearly. Arguably, this exposes Britain more directly to the vagaries of Strasbourg jurisprudence than is the case for other European states, where a local rights discourse serves as a filter and a shield.[48] One argument for a British Bill of Rights is precisely that it will sever the direct link and help the UK qua state articulate credibly alternatives to ECtHR rulings.

Persons cannot apply to the ECtHR before exhausting domestic remedies, which, since the HRA, means litigation before the courts about convention rights. Thus, now when a case comes to Strasbourg there are domestic judgments on point, which the United Kingdom may rely upon or aim to support in its representations before the ECtHR. There is thus dialogue between the courts in the minimal sense that the domestic courts frame their judgments with an eye to their reception in Strasbourg. In one sense, Strasbourg is a higher court for it is by treaty the

---

[46] R (Ullah) v. Special Adjudicator [2004] UKHL 26; [2004] 2 AC 323.

[47] Phillip Sales, 'Strasbourg Jurisprudence and the Human Rights Act: A Response to Lord Irvine' [2012] Public Law 253.

[48] Guglielmo Verdirame, 'Why Britain Should Scrap the Human Rights Act' Spectator, 3 October 2014.

authoritative adjudicator of disputes concerning the ECHR. But of course it is not strictly in the judicial hierarchy: it does not stand to the Supreme Court as higher in that sense. Whatever the ECtHR decides does not itself directly change legal obligations within Britain; rather the UK qua state comes under an obligation in international law. But the structure of the HRA is such that these judgments do indirectly change domestic law, at the least by providing material that domestic courts must (per s. 2 of the HRA, if nothing else) consider. The Supreme Court reserves to itself the authority to decide how or if to vary its past decisions in light of new Strasbourg rulings. Thus, the Divisional Court or Court of Appeal are bound by past House of Lords or Supreme Court judgments even if it is quite clear that they have been rejected by Strasbourg and will duly be abandoned by the Supreme Court.[49] Why this reservation? Partly to stop the undisciplined fracturing of precedent, such that there is unified control over how or if some Strasbourg ruling requires change. For it is not always clear whether an ECtHR decision, perhaps involving some state other than the United Kingdom, requires revision of how British courts understand convention rights.

The ECtHR engages with British judgments partly because they are the decisions that form part of the legal materials now before it for decision (and on which the United Kingdom often relies in argument before the court). But it also engages with them because the British courts enjoy a very strong reputation, such that Strasbourg judges think there is something of value to be found in their reasoning and because judicial comity requires as much: that is, engaging with the Supreme Court (or earlier the House of Lords) strengthens the reputation of the ECtHR, especially if the Supreme Court takes Strasbourg seriously. The subsequent effect of Strasbourg rulings turns in part on how domestic courts receive them, to which the reputation of the former is highly relevant. Thus, there are good reasons for Strasbourg and the Supreme Court to attend closely to one another. The membership of the former court is changing and patchy (each of the forty-seven member states has a judge on the court, notwithstanding rather large differences in population size and legal culture) and I share the parochial common law view that Strasbourg tends to benefit from engagement with British judgments. Still, the peculiar institutional features of the ECtHR, which do have something to do with the quality of some of its judgments, make it a difficult

---

[49] *Kay v. Lambeth London Borough Council* [2006] 2 AC 465.

conversant at times. Its successive judgments are often very hard to construe coherently together.[50]

The likelihood that Strasbourg will concur with judgments of the Supreme Court has been increased by two related developments. The first is the domestic judicial assertion that while the Supreme Court will usually conform to ECtHR rulings, it will not always do so. In *Horncastle*,[51] the Court refused so to do, reasoning that Strasbourg had fundamentally misunderstood the English law of hearsay. This defiant rebuke was made palatable, and squared with the international law imperative, by way of the judicial speculation that of course Strasbourg would change its mind when it better perceived the English legal position. This duly took place and is now a standing possibility, viz. a temporary departure from Strasbourg, rationalised on the grounds that the ECtHR has overlooked something. More radical, if as yet underdeveloped, is the claim in *Pham* that if an international court misconstrues its jurisdiction, domestic courts will not necessarily follow its decisions.[52] In view of the extent to which the ECtHR departs from the intended meaning of the ECHR,[53] this dictum would justify significant judicial resistance to Strasbourg rulings.[54] The second development is the rise of British political criticism of the Strasbourg court and indeed of the ECHR system.[55] The prisoner voting decision has been a main spur.[56] The force of this criticism and threat of United Kingdom exit from the ECHR has had some impact on the Strasbourg court, which is politically aware, even if not always institutionally capable of self-discipline.

This is an important dialogue, if of a peculiar kind. The Supreme Court and the ECtHR engage with one another's judgments. The latter has an effective superiority, but the former's high reputation and

---

[50] See, for example, *In re McCaughey* [2011] UKSC 20; [2012] 1 AC 725, where the Supreme Court noted the lack of clarity in the ECtHR's rulings about the temporal reach of the Article 2 duty to investigate deaths.

[51] *R v. Horncastle* [2009] UKSC 14; [2010] 2 AC 373.

[52] *Pham v. Secretary of State for the Home Department* [2015] UKSC 19 at [90], per Lord Mance.

[53] See Nicholas Barber, Richard Ekins, and Paul Yowell (eds.), *Lord Sumption and the Limits of the Law* (Hart Publishing, 2016), chs. 2, 5, and 6 (essays by Lord Sumption, Lord Hoffmann, and John Finnis).

[54] Richard Ekins and Guglielmo Verdirame, 'Judicial Power and Military Action' (2016) 132 *Law Quarterly Review* 206.

[55] See for example Lord Sumption, 'Limits of the Law' in Nicholas Barber, Richard Ekins, and Paul Yowell (eds.), *Lord Sumption and the Limits of the Law* (Hart Publishing, 2016).

[56] *Hirst v. United Kingdom (No 2)* [2005] ECHR 681; (2005) 19 BHRC 546.

newfound assertiveness, amplified by the broader British political scepticism of the ECHR, changes the dynamic. For the United Kingdom, there are good reasons to value the Supreme Court's voice herein, although it comes at the cost of aggrandising the court in the domestic realm. It is plausible to think that one court can speak to another in ways that other institutions cannot address a court.[57] It may be then that if the United Kingdom is to remain in the ECHR, and hence subject to the jurisdiction of the ECtHR, that it will fare better if the Supreme Court remains engaged with Strasbourg jurisprudence.

Rights adjudication led by domestic judges, as opposed to foreign judges, is less likely to be perceived as domination, for the former are members of the same political community and are subject to at least some control – even if awfully thin – in terms of appointment and removal from office.[58] The Strasbourg court is a foreign court over whose members and parameters the United Kingdom has next to no authority. It follows that, even more so than with a national court, the open lawmaking choices made by such a court (in contrast to past commitments qua international law) will encroach on, rather than contribute to, our self-government. But with distance may come, if not perspective, then at least recognition of distance, such that an international court *should* be less confident and should limit itself to correcting only glaring missteps. The history of the ECtHR is not really one of restraint and humility – although of course it could always be worse – but there are reasons to think, in contrasting Strasbourg and the Supreme Court on assisted suicide, say, that the former's distance does limit its reach. And to this self-limitation, fleeting and fickle as it may be, one may add the further point that binding force in international law is much less significant than binding force in constitutional law. An international court's limitation to the former makes its judgments much easier to resist, introducing a kind of dialogue where the judicial ruling is taken into account and defiance has a political cost, but remains possible.

---

[57] Carol Harlow, 'The Human Rights Act and "Coordinate Construction": Towards a "Parliament Square" Axis for Human Rights?' in Nicholas Barber, Richard Ekins, and Paul Yowell (eds.), *Lord Sumption and the Limits of the Law* (Hart Publishing, 2016); Erin Delaney, 'Judiciary Rising: Constitutional Change in the United Kingdom' (2014) 108 *Northwestern University Law Review* 543.

[58] Lord Hoffmann, 'Judges, Interpretation and Self-Government', in Nicholas Barber, Richard Ekins, and Paul Yowell (eds.), *Lord Sumption and the Limits of the Law* (Hart Publishing, 2016).

In short, an international court's detachment from the particular polity over which it exercises an adjudicative function makes it much harder for its judgments to be received as contributions to domestic deliberation and choice. For the polity to engage productively with this court, for its traditions and concerns and conditions to receive proper attention, it may be that dialogue with a leading domestic court has its place. But placing domestic courts in the front line of policy development in this way strongly risks wrongly elevating their place within the public deliberation that makes self-government possible. And the dubious entitlement of an international court to contribute to such self-government, as well as the sheer incapacity that distance imposes, may serve as a powerful restraint on it. There may be worse things than subjection to rights adjudication by an international court, provided that its judgments are not equated with hard, domestic legal obligations. The relative weaknesses of an international court are essential for dialogue to be possible, and unless its judgments are received in this way, no robust polity should tolerate its oversight.

VI   European Integration and the Limits of Conversation

The ECHR is the less important of the two bodies of European law to which the United Kingdom is committed. Much more significant is EU law, which is an intricate legal system in which member states, including Britain, have long been entangled. The EU has many of the institutional trappings of a state – an executive, legislature, and judiciary – but lacks a *demos* capable of deliberating and acting as one.[59] This is a novel form of political arrangement, involving member states adopting far-reaching commitments to each other and to the institutions they thereby create, which institutions have their own self-understanding and agenda for ever deeper integration. The decisions reached by these institutions change how citizens live – change the character of their political communities even – and yet are awfully distant from public deliberation. At best, there is deliberation amongst elites, especially heads of state or governments in each member state, who jointly form the European Council, and officials in the EU institutions, especially the European

[59] Andreas Follesdal and Simon Hix, 'Why There Is a Democratic Deficit in the EU: A Response to Majone and Moravcsik' (2006) 44 *Journal of Common Market Studies* 533; Peter Mair, *Ruling the Void: The Hollowing of Western Democracy* (Verso, 2013), ch. 4.

Commission (the permanent executive of the EU) and the Court of Justice of the European Union (CJEU).

This elite conversation is highly significant and obviously problematic: the EU suffers from a very serious democratic deficit. The attempted remedy has been to ape the institutional form of the nation state, especially by vesting more authority in the European Parliament. But in the absence of any plausible European public there is no joint deliberation and hence as yet no prospect for the kind of close joint action one finds in nation states. The European project is framed by its origins as an executive-led, treaty-based arrangement, which can enable commitments quite apart from any shared political community. Anxiety about the pace and depth of European integration is a common phenomenon in many member states, but has been especially pronounced in the United Kingdom, as its decision to leave confirms.

Parliament enacted the European Union Act 2011 to address public concern about the pace of integration. The Act forbids ministers from committing the United Kingdom to any further EU treaty commitments without first securing approval in a referendum on point. This was an intelligible legislative response to the serious problem that the Crown's capacity freely to enter treaties could be used to expand the powers of an overarching form of government that was and is not answerable to the public – neither the British nor a pan-European public. Lawmaking by treaty upends the balance of power between Parliament and government and alienates the people from continuing involvement in their own government. The structure of European decision-making, in which agreement is reached amongst heads of government in the Council, serves further to diminish responsibility.

The dependence of this new form of supranational government on executive action is bad enough. It is made worse by the further dynamic that European law adopted by the Union's lawmaking institutions or enshrined in the Treaties of the Union falls to be authoritatively construed by the CJEU. This is a problem because the Luxembourg Court has a centralising agenda and is ready to play fast and loose with legal materials.[60] The effective content of EU law, which binds member states in international law but more importantly within EU law itself (which

---

[60] Gunnar Beck, *The Legal Reasoning of the Court of Justice of the EU* (Hart Publishing, 2013); Derrick Wyatt, 'Does the European Court of Justice Need a New Judicial Approach for the 21st Century?', lecture to the Bingham Centre for the Rule of Law, 2 November 2015.

has a complex enforcement system complete with provision for eye-watering daily fines on national governments), is settled by the CJEU. The Court's political agenda and lack of restraint compound the constitutional defects of the European project, distancing still further the law from a conversation in which citizens may participate

Like other member states, the United Kingdom faced the question of how to limit the CJEU. One related question was how to *converse* with the CJEU, such that the United Kingdom's concerns and traditions are taken seriously in the Court's deliberation and decision. In 2014 and 2015, the UK Supreme Court set out to engineer such a conversation, aiming to force the CJEU to attend to the Supreme Court's understanding of how to interpret European law and that law's impact on the United Kingdom, and especially on the common law tradition. The problem was that the Luxembourg Court had no particular need to listen to British courts: it has long been established in the EU legal system that EU law is superior to domestic law and that the CJEU is its authoritative interpreter, such that the British like others are to fall in line.[61] Several member states, however, hold that features of their constitutional order are superior to – or more fundamental than – EU law. In particular, the German Constitutional Court has maintained that the validity or efficacy of EU law in Germany is subject to fundamental rights in the Basic Law; moreover, it reserves the right to determine that acts of EU institutions are ultra vires European law.[62] The Court has largely refrained from finding clashes, but the significance of the jurisprudence has been that for a time the CJEU sought to avoid conflict with it, apparently aiming to accommodate German concerns.

Why did the CJEU (or European Court of Justice as it then was) accommodate the German court? The political and economic centrality of Germany to the EU is one reason of course, but so too is the fact that the German Constitution is in part unchangeable, such that it was very difficult for the Constitutional Court to do otherwise. Recognising this political reality, and aiming to avoid a damaging confrontation, the ECJ sought accommodation. Parliamentary sovereignty makes it possible for EU law to be incorporated with relative ease: an 'ordinary' statute, the European Communities Act 1972, introduces all European law into British law and makes the ECJ its authoritative interpreter. True, it is impossible for Parliament lawfully to adopt the CJEU's understanding of

---

[61] Case C-6/64 *Flaminio Costa v. ENEL* [1964] ECR I-585.
[62] *Solange I* [1974] CMLR 57; *Brunner v. European Union Treaty* [1994] CMLR 57.

the supremacy of EU law, for the effect that such law has in Britain is and barring a revolution always will be conditional on a contingent Act of Parliament (as s. 18 of the European Union Act 2011 reiterates). But in practice, Parliament may avoid the United Kingdom being found in breach of EU law: enacting the 1972 Act and thereafter intending not to legislate inconsistently with European law suffice to achieve this end. Thus one could not say that the United Kingdom was unable, as arguably Germany was, to give full effect to EU law.

What the Supreme Court did in two recent cases is to reflect more closely on the terms by which Parliament chose to incorporate EU law in 1972. In the first case, HS2,[63] the Court brought the principle of legality to bear on the 1972 Act, reasoning that it should not be taken to justify departure from earlier constitutional statutes or principles. The relevant norm in the case was Article 9 of the Bill of Rights 1689, which protects parliamentary proceedings from judicial interference. Arguably, European law required such interference and it is this possibility that the Supreme Court considered in the case. This reading of the European Communities Act is arguable if not watertight. It leaves open the prospect that some future norm of European law or decision of the CJEU will be inconsistent with the fundamentals of British constitutional law and practice, and hence will not be covered by the 1972 Act and given effect in British law. The Supreme Court did not spell out what this would entail, viz. a confrontation with the CJEU that might well escalate into a major diplomatic crisis, which Parliament might resolve by legislating to conform to European law or which might be resolved in other ways. Whatever its merits as a reading of the 1972 Act, the point of the jurisprudence was to establish a deterrent, to spur the CJEU to take the Supreme Court seriously and avoid undercutting long-standing British constitutional arrangements.

The second case, Pham,[64] outlined another arguable limit on the 1972 Act's incorporation of EU law. The limit was to assert that the jurisdiction of the CJEU is not unlimited, but tracks the treaties that establish it, such that actions of the CJEU, or other EU institutions, that are *ultra vires* the treaties are not incorporated by way of the 1972 Act. This limit is a little harder to square with the Act, s. 3 of which affirms the jurisdiction of the CJEU in strong terms. However, the strength of the limit, in contrast perhaps to the HS2 equivalent, is that it stresses the

---

[63] R (HS2 Action Alliance Ltd) v. Secretary of State for Transport [2014] UKSC 3.

[64] Pham v. Secretary of State for the Home Department [2015] UKSC 19.

terms of what was agreed by member states, and thus impugns the legitimacy of the Luxembourg Court's actions as a court. The objection is thus not to the merits of the EU action in question, but to its very legality. This seemed to me to be a strong, principled basis on which the Supreme Court might resist the CJEU and, importantly, on which the UK government might choose to support the Court in this resistance. And the CJEU would have known this. Hence it may have taken care to avoid triggering the deterrent.

This whole line of reasoning presupposed that the CJEU would be minded to avoid confrontation and this would only have been true in certain political circumstances. It was very likely true in the run-up to 23 June 2016, when the British public voted to end continuing membership of the EU. It is an open question whether the Supreme Court's implicit threats will have any force now that the United Kingdom is on its way out *or* whether they would have worked if there had been a remain vote. The European project is in crisis, and it may be that a prudent political court like the CJEU would have preferred to avoid unnecessary risks. Or, alternatively, it may have thought it imperative to crush the Supreme Court's partial rebellion, provided that it was able to choose the time and place for such engagement.

The Supreme Court's innovation was an attempt to widen the European constitutional conversation, forcing the CJEU to attend to the concerns of British courts by threatening defiance and impugning the Court's legitimacy. This might have limited some of the excesses of the CJEU and other EU organs. However, it could not address the fundamental problem that the EU centres on an elite conversation amongst heads of government, which is detached from ordinary citizens and wider parliamentary processes. Membership of the EU embroiled the United Kingdom in an arrangement that was inconsistent with its constitutional tradition, with the balance of responsibilities between government and Parliament and with the maintenance of a public conversation that would shape how institutions acted. It was always open to the United Kingdom to defy the decisions of EU institutions, but this was a costly freedom to exercise; in any case continuing participation in the EU was plausibly thought to be antithetical to robust self-government.

VII   How to Decide to Leave the European Union

The decision to leave the EU is a significant change and reveals much about the character and future of the British constitution. This section briefly considers the shape of the constitutional conversations that resulted in the decision and that have followed in relation to its implementation. There had long been a mismatch between popular and elite views – widespread public disquiet about EU membership but no major political party proposing withdrawal. The Conservative Party committed itself to holding a referendum on withdrawal, partly as a compromise within the party, partly to shore up support from Euro-sceptical voters, and partly with a view to putting the question to rest. After the 2015 election, the government honoured the commitment by proposing legislation to enable an in–out referendum. The government could not have failed to honour that commitment – its support in the Commons and the country would have collapsed – but it did aim to persuade the public to vote remain. However, after a robust public campaign, the electorate voted to leave.

Holding the referendum was an exercise – not an abdication – of parliamentary democracy. Parliament voted overwhelmingly to enact the European Union Referendum Act 2015, reasoning that the right way to settle whether the United Kingdom should remain committed to an arrangement like the EU was to put the question directly to the electorate. This was a responsible recognition of the limits of representative institutions in fairly and stably settling a question of this kind, which goes to the constitutional character of the polity. The referendum was the sharp end of a long-standing and wide-ranging public conversation about the merits of EU membership and the costs of withdrawal. The conversation was led by elected politicians, notwithstanding majority elite support for a remain vote, but involved an extraordinarily broad array of other groups and individuals. The referendum was overseen by depoliticised electoral institutions, and made provision for a clear public decision.

The outcome of the vote may have been decisive, but its consequences were contested. The 2015 Act did not specify the legal consequence of a vote to leave or remain. Within days of the referendum, various public figures contended that Parliament should ignore the result (which they thought unwise or unjust) or should require a second referendum, once an exit arrangement with the EU had been negotiated. However, the government intended to honour the outcome of the referendum by triggering Article 50 of the Lisbon Treaty, which sets in motion the withdrawal of the member state from the EU. Its authority so to do was disputed. Some said that it was for the government to make or unmake treaties. Others argued that leaving the EU Treaties would change domestic law, which required primary legislation. The matter was brought before the courts, with the Supreme Court eventually holding that triggering Article 50 would work too significant a change in the constitution for it to be open to ministers alone.[65] For the referendum to be implemented, Parliament must legislate.

The Supreme Court mistook the law, wrongly limiting the government's authority to make and unmake treaties.[66] The Court's mistake, I argue elsewhere,[67] was to distort constitutional law in order to secure what it thought was sound constitutional practice, viz. to require express parliamentary support for withdrawal from the EU Treaties. This was an improper action on the part of the Court. It is for Parliament to hold the government to account. Judicial intervention was unwarranted and strongly risked being thought to be a stratagem to arm MPs and peers to thwart the referendum result. The government had announced its intentions in advance, and it was always open to the Commons to unseat the government if it chose. In any case, the Commons had clearly signalled their support for Article 50 to be triggered by way of a resolution of the House (on the third day of the Supreme Court hearing). The main significance of the Court's judgment was to force the government to introduce legislation to the Houses and thus to empower the Lords to oppose withdrawal altogether or to propose various (wrecking) conditions thereon.

The government proposed a very narrow bill, effectively restoring the legal status quo ante. This was supported by the Commons, with MPs reasoning that, having put the question to the electorate by way of the 2015 Act, they should honour the decision reached. The Lords proposed various amendments, which the Commons refused to accept. At this point the Lords relented and accepted the original bill, which passed without amendment. The Lords could have stood their ground and forced the Commons to invoke the Parliament Acts 1911 and 1949. This would have meant at least a year's delay and would have been intensely controversial. Anxious to avoid such, and/or conscious of the supremacy

---

[65] *R (Miller and Dos Santos)* v. *Secretary of State for Exiting the European Union* [2017] UKSC 5; [2017] 2 WLR 583.

[66] John Finnis, *Brexit and the Balance of Our Constitution* (Policy Exchange, 2016); Mark Elliott, 'The Supreme Court's Judgment in *Miller*: In Search of Constitutional Principle' (2017) 76 *Cambridge Law Journal* 257.

[67] Richard Ekins, 'Constitutional Practice and Principle in the Article 50 Litigation' (2017) 133 *Law Quarterly Review* 347.

of the Commons and the political temper of the country, the Lords wisely passed the bill.[68]

The judicial intervention unjustifiably forced the triggering of Article 50 to wait on formal parliamentary support by way of a new Act of Parliament. Still, the relations between Parliament and government and Commons and Lords worked effectively. It bears noting that the Supreme Court had avoided a much more dangerous possibility, which would have been to rule that constitutional convention required Parliament not to legislate to authorise the triggering of Article 50 without the consent of the devolved legislatures. This would have been an extraordinary intervention into the public conversation and one that the Court, reasoning soundly about the relevant legal materials,[69] refused to undertake. The protracted public discussion about triggering Article 50 thus illuminates the character of the constitution, rightly centring on relationships within Parliament, in conversation with the wider public, subject to misconceived judicial interference.

VIII   Conclusion

Parliamentary democracy in Britain centres on the twin principles of parliamentary sovereignty and responsible government, which ground public deliberation that culminates in authoritative decisions about what should be done. These decisions remain contestable and may be unwound by subsequent Parliaments, which makes decisive the ongoing conversation amongst citizens and their representatives over time. The courts have traditionally had little involvement in this public deliberation, but uphold the decisions to which it gives rise. The institutional arrangements that constitute parliamentary conversation and contestation involve the mutual dependency and entanglement of different bodies which form parts of a larger whole: Commons and government, Lords and Commons, Parliament and the electorate. The adoption of norms requiring these bodies to take the other seriously, as well as the existence of levers to compel attention, helps encourage deliberation. However, the developments traced in this chapter – the expanded judicial role and increasing reach of international obligations – have served to undermine this parliamentary conversation and contestation. Their effect has been and is to distance citizens from decisions about

---

[68] European Union (Notification of Withdrawal) Act 2017.
[69] Section 2 of the Scotland Act 2016, which recognises the Sewel Convention.

what should be done, limiting the capacity of representative institutions to act decisively for all.

Quite apart from the HRA, some judges conceive of themselves as in dialogue with the political authorities, the assumed inadequacies of which those judges aim to compensate. This new judicial role undercuts the conclusions of the parliamentary process and is grounded on a dubious theory about how courts do and should stand to Parliament. The HRA clearly changes the judicial role in important ways and its judicial reception has armed domestic judges to confront or subvert Parliament on grounds of their choosing. The Supreme Court has succeeded, to some extent, in engaging in conversation with Strasbourg, aided by the wider tide of British political scepticism about the ECHR and subjection to a foreign court. Still, the ECtHR remains legally free to decide as it chooses and cannot effectively be held to account. For membership of the ECHR to support conversation rather than submission, the United Kingdom may need to resist wayward judgments of the ECtHR, to loosen its willingness to take each to be strictly binding. Replacing the HRA with a British Bill of Rights might help develop this disposition, but arguably might change little save to risk further expansion of domestic judicial power, which poses wider dangers to self-government.

The United Kingdom's relationship to the EU posed a related series of problems. The EU's structure privileges an elite conversation amongst heads of government, which is unavoidably detached from ordinary citizens and wider parliamentary processes. And the resulting institutional form is not clearly responsible to anyone, pursuing a centralising agenda that is arguably not supported by any (or very few) member states. The position of the CJEU is particularly important and its willingness to depart from legal commitments compounds the undemocratic nature of supranational government made by way of international agreements. The Supreme Court's attempts to converse with the CJEU confirmed the problem and were an intelligible response to that problem, but are now largely moot. The United Kingdom's decision to leave the EU follows in large part from alienation from EU decision-making and recognition of its incompatibility with parliamentary democracy.

There are good reasons why self-government in Britain has been grounded in a series of relationships that centre on a sovereign, representative Parliament. This institutional arrangement is well-placed to lead and respond to public deliberation about what should be done and to make decisions that are the joint action of citizens. The capacities of this structure are clear even in the strained circumstances of decision about withdrawal from the EU. Not without controversy, political authorities succeeded in making provision for the question of membership to be fairly decided and then given effect. The courts exceeded their authority in superintending Parliament's dealings with the government, but the commitment of the Commons to restore and defend the government's authority drew the sting from the intervention. The process of withdrawal from the EU thus illustrates the far-ranging, ongoing national conversation that should be at the heart of parliamentary democracy. That withdrawal is itself an important – but incomplete – contribution to the project of restoring and maintaining the constitutional framework that makes self-government possible.

INDEX